PROCEED WITH CARE

V O L **2** U M E

PROCEED WITH CARE

FINAL REPORT
OF THE
ROYAL COMMISSION ON
NEW REPRODUCTIVE TECHNOLOGIES

V   O   L **2** U   M   E

This Report is available in both official languages as a set or as individual volumes.

Available in Canada through your local bookseller
or by mail from
Canada Communications Group — Publishing
Ottawa, Canada K1A 0S9

CANADIAN CATALOGUING IN PUBLICATION DATA

Canada. Royal Commission on New Reproductive Technologies

Proceed with Care: Final Report of the Royal Commission on New Reproductive
Technologies

Issued also in French under title: Un virage à prendre en douceur.
Complete work consists of 2 v.
ISBN 0-660-15359-9 (set)
ISBN 0-660-15365-3 (v.1); 0-660-15366-1 (v.2)
Cat. no. Z1-1989/3E (set);
Z1-1989/3-1E (v.1); Z1-1989/3-2E (v.2)

1. Human reproductive technologies — Canada. 2. Infertility — Treatment —
Canada. 3. Human reproductive technologies — Canada — Moral and ethical
aspects. 4. Infertility — Treatment — Canada — Moral and ethical
aspects. 5. Embryology, Human — Canada. I. Title. II. Title: Final report of the
Royal Commission on New Reproductive Technologies.

RG133.5C2 1993   618.1'78   C94-980002-3

The Royal Commission on New Reproductive Technologies and the publishers wish to
acknowledge with gratitude the following:

*   Translation Services, Government Services Canada, for their contribution to the
    translation of this report and related studies. Special thanks are due to the Privy
    Council Translation Service, the Scientific Translation Service and the Montreal Health
    and Criminology Translation Service. We also gratefully acknowledge the contribution
    of the Parliamentary Documents Translation Service to the revision and preparation of
    the French version of this report.
*   Canada Communications Group, Printing Services
*   Biomedical Communications at the University of British Columbia

Consistent with the Commission's commitment to full
equality between men and women, care has been
taken throughout this text to use gender-neutral
language wherever possible.

Royal Commission on
New Reproductive Technologies

Commission royale sur les
nouvelles techniques de reproduction

TO HIS EXCELLENCY
THE GOVERNOR GENERAL IN COUNCIL

MAY IT PLEASE YOUR EXCELLENCY

By Order in Council dated October 25, 1989, we were requested to inquire into and report upon current and potential medical and scientific developments related to new reproductive technologies, considering in particular their social, ethical, health, research, legal and economic implications and the public interest, recommending what policies and safeguards should be applied.

We have been honoured to have the responsibility of working to fulfil this mandate, and beg to submit our Final Report in each official language.

Respectfully submitted,

Patricia Baird, Chairperson

Grace Jantzen

Bartha Maria Knoppers

Susan E.M. McCutcheon

Suzanne Rozell Scorsone

November 15, 1993
Ottawa, Canada

P.O. Box/C.P. 1566, Station/Succursale "B", Ottawa, Canada K1P 5R5, (613) 954-9999 Fax: (613) 954-9998

Biographical Notes on Commissioners

Dr. Patricia A. Baird is a paediatrician, professor in medical genetics at the University of British Columbia, and a member of the Population Health Program of the Canadian Institute for Advanced Research.

Grace M. Jantzen is currently a Reader in Philosophy of Religion, Department of Theology and Religious Studies, King's College, University of London, England.

Bartha Maria Knoppers is an Associate Professor, Faculty of Law, at the University of Montreal, and a Senior Researcher with the Centre de Recherche en Droit public de l'Université de Montréal.

Susan E.M. McCutcheon began her career as a teacher, and was active in the business community. She currently takes part in several community organizations, and holds several corporate directorships.

Suzanne Rozell Scorsone is spokesperson for the Archdiocese of Toronto on family and women's issues, and is the Director, Office of Catholic Family Life. Dr. Scorsone is an anthropologist.

Contents

Volume 1

Part One: New Reproductive Technologies and Canadian Society

1 A Comprehensive Response to Issues of National Importance

2 Social Values and Attitudes Toward Technology and New Reproductive Technologies

Part Two: New Reproductive Technologies: Examination of Conditions, Technologies, and Practices

⟨6⟩ Developing a Comprehensive Picture of Technologies and Practices

⟨19⟩ Infertility Treatments: Assisted Insemination   425

21   Handling of Eggs and Embryos   581

22   Embryo Research   607

Volume 2

23 ◇ Preconception Arrangements   661

24 Commercial Interests and New Reproductive Technologies

25 Prenatal Diagnosis and Genetic Technologies: Introduction and Social Context

26 Prenatal Diagnosis for Congenital Anomalies and Genetic Disease 745

30 ◇ Judicial Intervention in Pregnancy and Birth   949

31 ◇ Uses of Fetal Tissue   967

Part Three: Overview of Recommendations

Part Four: Annex, Glossary, and Appendices

◇ Annex: Suzanne Rozell Scorsone

◇ Glossary

◇ **Appendices**

Tables

Figures

Preconception Arrangements

♦

Preconception arrangements (often referred to as surrogacy or contract motherhood) provoked considerable debate in testimony and submissions before the Commission. For some, prohibiting the practice raised issues of personal liberty and reproductive freedom. Others saw it as a practice that reduces the human experience of reproduction to a commercial transaction, evoking unsavoury images of "wombs for rent" and children as products or commodities. In particular, Canadians told us that they oppose the involvement of brokers and others with a commercial motive in such arrangements. Still others opposed the practice as degrading to women, relegating them to a status in society based solely on their reproductive capacity.

The Commission gathered information to assess the practice of preconception arrangements in several ways. We spoke with people who have participated in preconception arrangements. We investigated the practices surrounding preconception arrangements and the involvement of the various parties. We examined the ethical and legal issues raised by preconception arrangements, considered the psychosocial effects of preconception arrangements on the children and on the participants, and deliberated on the implications of the practice for society at large. We also surveyed Canadians' views on these arrangements. Finally, we investigated how other jurisdictions have dealt with preconception arrangements and their reasons for doing so. (See the research volume, *Social Values and Attitudes Surrounding New Reproductive Technologies*, for the results of these investigations.) Our conclusions and recommendations with respect to preconception arrangements are based on consideration of all these aspects.

Preconception Arrangements: What They Are

Various terms have been used to describe arrangements whereby a woman undertakes to conceive and bear a child with the understanding it will be raised by someone else (the "commissioning" man, or couple). These terms include surrogacy, surrogate motherhood, contract motherhood, and intrauterine adoption. The Commission uses the term "preconception arrangements" to describe all such situations, referring to the fact that, unlike adoption, agreement to transfer custody and parental rights is reached before the child is conceived.

Types of Preconception Arrangements

Genetic-gestational arrangement: The gestational mother is impregnated with the sperm of the man from the commissioning couple through assisted insemination; the resulting child is the genetic child of the gestational mother and the commissioning man. The commissioning woman becomes the child's social mother.

Gestational arrangement: An embryo created from the egg and sperm of the commissioning couple is implanted in the gestational woman, who becomes pregnant and gives birth. The child is the genetic child of the commissioning couple and is not related genetically to the woman carrying the fetus and giving birth.

Commercial arrangement: The commissioning couple pays fees to the woman and/or to a broker to cover the cost of facilitating the agreement and the expenses of the gestational woman; a written contract between the couple and the woman is usually involved.

Non-commercial arrangement: No broker or fees are involved, although a contract may be involved and the commissioning couple may agree to cover expenses; such arrangements usually occur between family members or close friends.

Such a practice — couples who are infertile seeking a woman to assist them in having a child to raise — is far from new, dating back at least as far as the earliest biblical times; the difference today is that procedures such as assisted insemination and *in vitro* fertilization remove the need for sexual intercourse.

The circumstances under which a commissioning couple seeks a preconception agreement vary considerably. The commissioning woman might have been treated unsuccessfully for infertility, or might have had difficulty carrying a fetus to term. Alternatively, the woman might be at risk of passing on a genetic disease to her child or might have a medical condition that makes pregnancy inadvisable. Preconception arrangements enable the couple to have a child that is genetically related to the commissioning man or, more rarely, to both members of the couple.

However, the practice is not limited to couples who are infertile or childless. The literature contains instances, for example, of preconception arrangements being used when the commissioning woman's infertility was the result of voluntary sterilization or menopause, when the couple already had a child or children, and when one or both members of the couple already had adopted or biological children in a previous relationship. As well, there are examples of single men and unmarried couples receiving children through preconception arrangements.

Though difficult to document, these arrangements appear to be growing in number; in some jurisdictions there are now professionals (lawyers, physicians, and others) whose practice concentrates solely on facilitating such arrangements. In the United States, preconception arrangements resulted in the birth of an estimated 4 500 children between 1975 and 1990 and have led to the development of a range of profit-making organizations devoted to this activity. From what little evidence is available, it appears that commercial brokers do not operate in Canada.

Categories of Preconception Arrangements

Preconception arrangements usually fall into one of two categories, depending on the source of the egg and the techniques used. Genetic-gestational arrangements are the most common type. Assisted insemination is used to inseminate the gestational mother with the commissioning man's sperm. A physician usually performs the procedure, although self-insemination is also possible.

Gestational arrangements are where the gestational woman is not the source of the egg, and they require the involvement of a physician because of the technical nature of the procedure. The commissioning woman undergoes an egg retrieval cycle (see Chapter 20), and the eggs are fertilized *in vitro* using her partner's sperm. The resulting zygotes are then transferred to the gestational woman for implantation. This usually requires that both women take fertility drugs — to produce eggs in the commissioning woman, and to ensure that the two women's cycles are coordinated, maximizing chances of implantation. Less commonly, sperm from a donor could be used, or the egg could be donated by a third woman, thus totally separating the genetic, gestational, and social aspects of "parenthood."

Although they are less common than the genetic-gestational type, the number of solely gestational arrangements is rising. In the United States, such arrangements account for a large proportion of some clinics' business. To take one example, in 1990 more than 50 percent of clients at the Center for Surrogate Parenting in Beverly Hills, California, were participating in gestational arrangements. At present this is not being done in Canadian infertility clinics, although there have been reports that two are considering it.

Preconception arrangements also differ according to whether the gestational mother is paid for her participation and whether the parties have known each other before undertaking the arrangement.

In commercial preconception arrangements, the gestational mother receives payment in the form of fees and expenses. Commercial arrangements can be facilitated by a third party, called a broker, or they may take the form of a private agreement between the commissioning couple or man and the gestational woman. The fee can be paid to the broker, who passes on a portion of it to the gestational woman, or directly to the gestational woman.

Non-commercial arrangements occur between a commissioning couple and another woman, often a family member or close friend. Because these arrangements are private, involve fewer people, and may not become public knowledge unless they lead to litigation, relatively less is known about the nature and extent of non-commercial arrangements. The gestational woman may receive payment to cover her personal or other expenses during or related to the pregnancy.

Current Practices

The Commission found little empirical research on preconception arrangements in Canada and elsewhere. Documenting the practice is difficult because of the private nature of these arrangements; much of what we know about them comes from anecdotal accounts. Such information as is available pertains mainly to commercial arrangements; there is little published evidence about non-commercial arrangements. One of the Commission's goals was therefore to determine the extent to which preconception arrangements are occurring in Canada.

The most common type, genetic-gestational arrangements, does not require the involvement of medical professionals; however, when there is such involvement, it can take place in a physician's office and be recorded in a way that preserves secrecy. Arrangements involving a relative or friend as the gestational mother are generally kept private because of the legal uncertainties, as well as apprehension about the reaction of others to the arrangement.

The only effort to date to gauge the prevalence of preconception arrangements in Canada was a 1988 study for the Law Reform Commission of Canada. The study estimated (conservatively, in the authors' view) that there had been at least 118 cases of preconception arrangements involving one or more Canadian participants. Details about these arrangements are scarce, however, as the cases were generally reported by someone not involved directly in the arrangement.

The Commission surveyed programs and services being offered by the 27 fertility clinics across Canada. From our data there was no evidence that any Canadian fertility clinics are currently involved in preconception arrangements. The practice may be occurring in physicians' offices outside clinics, but we have only anecdotal accounts of this. The Commission found, however, that one Toronto clinic plans to offer gestational preconception arrangements. The clinic's consent forms are being given final legal review, and the procedure is being reviewed by various hospital and university committees. One other program outside Ontario also reported considering preconception arrangements involving *in vitro* fertilization.

A survey undertaken for the Commission demonstrated that patients undergoing treatment at fertility clinics would consider a variety of approaches in trying to have a child, including preconception arrangements. Six percent of *in vitro* fertilization patients and 5 percent of people undergoing assisted insemination (using partner's sperm) would consider preconception arrangements in the future, although none of the respondents who had had assisted insemination using donor sperm would contemplate a preconception arrangement. Three percent of patients receiving other fertility treatment would consider preconception arrangements in the future.

Commercial Arrangements

Commercial agreements are difficult to document, because they, too, are not usually public knowledge. The 1988 study for the Law Reform Commission of Canada found that of the 118 cases of preconception arrangements examined, 42 took place in Canada and 76 involved U.S. agencies. In 13 of the cases involving U.S. agencies, Canadians were serving as gestational women; in 62 cases, the Canadians were commissioning couples; and, in one case, a Canadian single man had received a child.

Non-Commercial Arrangements

Information about how non-commercial preconception arrangements are handled is extremely limited. The Commission heard directly from several people who had participated in non-commercial arrangements. Anecdotal accounts suggest that the typical case would involve a relative (often a sister) or close friend of a woman who is infertile being inseminated with her partner's sperm, usually without medical involvement. The gestational mother may have pregnancy care and deliver the child in hospital under the commissioning woman's name and health insurance number, register the birth using the commissioning woman's name (the father does not have to be named on the birth certificate), and relinquish the child to the commissioning couple upon leaving the hospital.

Ways of Dealing with Preconception Arrangements

To date, Quebec is the only Canadian jurisdiction to have enacted specific legislation regarding preconception arrangements; no other provincial statutes deal explicitly with preconception arrangements. Section 541 of Quebec's revised *Civil Code* provides that all agreements for procreation or gestation for payment are null and void.

Apart from these provisions, preconception arrangements remain in a legal void in Canada. In the absence of specific legislation, existing law in several fields, including family law, adoption law, and contract law, may apply to preconception arrangements. The extent to which these laws apply is not clear, however, as there are no official reports of litigation concerning preconception arrangements in any Canadian jurisdiction.

Family Law

The provisions of existing family law could affect preconception arrangements in two ways: (1) the legal status of the agreement and (2) the determination of the legal parentage of a child born as a result of a preconception arrangement. There is certainly a body of legal opinion that states that legitimizing preconception arrangements would be inconsistent with existing family law principles. This is because a contract that provides in advance for handing over a child at birth would be at odds with fundamental principles of family law — that custody must be determined according to the best interests of the child and that parental authority and obligations cannot legally be "contracted away" in anticipation. Adults cannot simply transfer custody of a child at their whim; the child's best interests must guide decisions and actions in this respect.

In Ontario, for instance, family law would appear to make preconception arrangements void because the law gives the courts ultimate power to decide the custody of a child, even where parents have made an agreement in that regard. Since custody is determined in the best interests of the child, a preconception agreement made before the child's birth would be void, because it could only have been made in the interests of the adult participants — the best interests of the child could not have been known. Further, any attempt to transfer maternal rights is subject to adoption law, which forbids payment for adoption and requires a seven-day waiting period before the birth mother can give consent to adoption. Finally, Ontario law makes it illegal for a third party to receive payment for negotiations or arrangements with a view to a child's adoption.

Other provinces have similar provisions in their family law acts. In no province or territory have these provisions been tested in the context of

preconception arrangements, however, so the degree to which the courts would apply them to preconception arrangements is unknown.

The second major impact of family law is in the determination of legal parentage. Despite family law provisions that would appear to make preconception arrangements illegal, the fact remains that children are being born through such arrangements. Establishing their legal parentage is vital both for them and for the other participants in the process, as it affects the rights and obligations of the parties with respect to custody, access, support, and inheritance. Unfortunately, current family law in most jurisdictions in Canada does not always provide clear guidance on the question of legal parentage. By contrast, Quebec, Newfoundland, and the Yukon have specified the legal parentage of children born as a result of assisted conception techniques in the revised *Civil Code*, the *Children's Law Act, 1988* and the *Children's Act, 1986*, respectively. These provisions would presumably apply to children born through assisted conception in the context of preconception arrangements.

Contract Law

The freedom to contract is not unrestricted; the courts may refuse to enforce a contract on the basis of such legal concepts as misrepresentation, inequality of bargaining power, and incapacity of an individual to enter into legal relations for such reason as mental incompetency, and on the basis of public policy considerations. The Commission's research indicates that the courts would probably find preconception contracts contrary to public policy and therefore null and void under existing law. In particular, these arrangements contravene public policies reflected in provincial/territorial legislation across Canada prohibiting for-profit exchanges involving children, requiring proof of parental unfitness before parental rights are terminated, and requiring the surrender of children in such situations to appropriate child welfare authorities.

For these reasons, preconception contracts would likely be deemed unenforceable by the courts, regardless of whether payment was involved, although this interpretation is by no means certain. In the *Baby M* case in the United States, for example, a trial judge ruled that preconception agreements were not contrary to public policy, but this finding was later reversed on appeal. To establish legal certainty, all provinces and territories (except Quebec, which will do so as of January 1, 1994) would have to pass laws clarifying the legal status of these arrangements. If contracts are deemed unenforceable, however, the principles of family law again come into play. The parties' parental status would be determined under provincial family law independently of the contract and perhaps in a manner different from what was intended by the parties to the contract. Most significantly, the best interests of the child test would prevail.

Proposals for Change

Given the considerable uncertainty about the legal status of preconception arrangements in Canada, there have been several proposals for law reform in this area. The Ontario Law Reform Commission's *Report on Human Artificial Reproduction and Related Matters*, released in 1985, is one of the few reports in the world to endorse the practice of preconception contracts, and it generated considerable controversy in this regard. The report's authors believed that the practice would carry on regardless of the state of the law and that its potential dangers would increase if it were driven underground by making it illegal. They therefore proposed a regulatory scheme to govern such agreements. The Ontario government has not implemented the recommendations.

The Canadian Bar Association, on the other hand, recommended in its brief to the Commission that preconception arrangements be handled, as far as possible, under existing adoption law. Under this proposal, preconception contracts would not be illegal, but they would be enforceable only if the birth mother wanted to relinquish the child. As in adoption, she would have a period of time after the birth in which to make the decision. The Canadian Bar Association recommended further that if the gestational mother decided not to relinquish the child, the commissioning couple should not have any visitation or access rights. The Canadian Bar Association submission does not make any distinction between the different types of preconception arrangements (genetic-gestational, gestational, commercial, or non-commercial) in its recommendations.

In its working paper on medically assisted procreation (1992), the Law Reform Commission of Canada recommended that preconception contracts be null and void and that acting as a paid intermediary in such arrangements be a criminal offence.

The Uniform Law Conference of Canada proposed in 1991 that all provinces deem the woman who gives birth, not the woman who produced the egg, to be the mother. This would clarify the identity of the legal mother of children (their "maternal filiation") born through preconception arrangements. It is also important for the well-being of the child, however, that the identity of the man who has legal responsibility as father be clarified; the Uniform Law Conference of Canada report did not recommend a means to do that.

International Experience

Preconception arrangements have been of concern in many countries, and several have enacted legislation or policies to deal with the practice. The Commission examined the response of the United Kingdom, Australia, the United States, and France to see what lessons, if any, might be relevant to the Canadian context.

The Commission's review showed that the trend internationally has been to discourage and even criminalize commercial preconception arrangements. Outright legislative bans on preconception agreements are rare, but most jurisdictions that have taken a position do prohibit commercial arrangements, primarily by making it illegal to advertise for a gestational woman, to act as a broker or intermediary (even if no commercial motive is involved), or to pay for or accept compensation in any form in connection with a preconception arrangement. Most jurisdictions have taken pains, however, not to institute measures penalizing the gestational woman.

The other measure proposed or adopted most frequently to discourage preconception arrangements is to make the contract between the gestational mother and the commissioning man or couple legally unenforceable; in other words, the gestational woman could not be forced by a court to give up the child if she changed her mind about fulfilling the terms of the contract. The element of uncertainty this introduces for commissioning couples and brokers is thought to be an effective means of discouraging such arrangements.

Views on Preconception Arrangements

The Commission's review of the debate on preconception arrangements is based on several sources: the range of views expressed by Canadians in our public hearings, in submissions to the Commission, and in surveys conducted for the Commission; other research we commissioned on the topic; and the published reports of other organizations and jurisdictions that have examined the issue.

We found that opinions on this issue are diverse and difficult to catalogue, ranging from outright opposition to the practice, whatever form it might take, to acceptance and even encouragement of the practice by public policies to regulate it, to enforce contracts, and to provide medical services in support of it. Ranged between these positions are those who oppose commercial arrangements but would tolerate non-commercial arrangements, particularly in cases where the commissioning woman's health was the reason for seeking a preconception arrangement; those who would find commercial arrangements acceptable if certain safeguards or regulations were in place; and those who would not encourage or participate in a (non-commercial) preconception arrangement themselves but would not prohibit others from doing so. We examine this range of positions in the next three sections.

An Unacceptable Practice: The Arguments Against Commercial Preconception Arrangements

Those who hold that commercial preconception arrangements should be prohibited believe that they are inherently exploitive; that they treat children as commodities; that they are dehumanizing and degrading to women and their reproductive capacity; that they are harmful to the participants and to children born as a result of these arrangements; that they foster harmful social attitudes about the role and value of women, children, and families; and that they reinforce and perpetuate sexual inequality in our society. They also point out that such arrangements have significant implications for the gestational woman, who agrees on signing the contract to restrict her behaviour in certain ways (for example, with respect to smoking and drinking) and to abide by the commissioning couple's requirements for her pregnancy care (for example, to undergo tests such as amniocentesis). These arguments are examined in the next few pages.

> Criminalizing the decision of a woman to serve as a so-called "surrogate mother" ... would in fact focus all of the enforcement efforts on the woman. And as enforcement efforts in other areas of law have demonstrated, women are easily made vulnerable by that in ways that other parties are not.
>
> *K. Lahey, Ontario Advisory Council on Women's Issues, Public Hearings Transcripts, Toronto, Ontario, October 29, 1990.*

Potential for Exploitation

Concerns about the exploitive nature of commercial preconception arrangements stem from several sources, in particular the social and economic disparities between gestational women and commissioning couples and the disproportionate assumption of risks and obligations by the parties to a preconception contract. These inequalities in power and resources, it is argued, make gestational women vulnerable to exploitation, no matter how willing they might be to participate, because they can never negotiate on an equal footing with the other parties.

A recurring concern we heard was that women willing to undertake gestational arrangements for others would be those who are economically vulnerable — that a woman who was well off financially would be most unlikely to agree to be a gestational mother. That this is often the case was borne out by our research, which revealed significant socioeconomic differences between commissioning women and gestational women. Although reliable data on participants are scarce, the information available shows that gestational women are younger, less well educated, and of lower income than commissioning couples. The study for the Law Reform

Commission, for example, which examined data on 32 commissioning couples, found that their overall age is much older than that of the gestational women; the youngest commissioning man, at age 35, and the youngest commissioning woman, at age 34, were both older than the oldest gestational woman, who was 33.

Commercial Preconception Contracts

The Commission examined preconception agreements drafted by U.S. commercial agencies. They contained some or all of the following provisions:

1. The gestational woman agrees to become pregnant using the commissioning man's sperm, to carry the fetus to term, and then to relinquish her parental rights and transfer custody of the child to the commissioning couple.
2. The gestational woman and her husband (if she has one) promise to take all steps necessary to have the commissioning man's name entered on the child's birth certificate as the father, and the gestational woman's husband agrees to renounce any legal presumption that he is the child's father.
3. The commissioning couple promises to pay the gestational woman a specified sum (usually U.S.$10 000) when her maternal rights are terminated by a court order and provided he has custody of the child.
4. The parties agree that the specified fee can be reduced significantly if the woman miscarries or gives birth to a stillborn child. In the *Baby M* arrangement, for example, the gestational woman was to receive no payment if miscarriage occurred in the fourth month or earlier, and $1 000 if the fetus miscarried after the fourth month or was born dead.
5. The gestational woman promises that she will undergo amniocentesis.
6. The gestational woman agrees that she will not abort the fetus but that, if the commissioning couple decides on the basis of the amniocentesis results that they do not want the child to be born, she will have an abortion.
7. The gestational woman promises not to form a parent-child bond with the fetus.
8. The gestational woman agrees not to drink alcohol or to take any non-prescription, prescription, or illicit drugs without the permission of a physician specified in the agreement and otherwise to adhere to all medical instructions of the attending physician.
9. Should custody of the child be awarded to anyone not related to the commissioning couple (such as, for example, the gestational woman), the gestational woman and her husband promise to reimburse the commissioning couple for all sums they are ordered to pay in child support.
10. Should the commissioning man die before the child's birth, the gestational mother agrees to renounce her parental rights and to transfer custody of the child to his wife, if any. Should he not be married or should his wife also die before the child's birth, the gestational woman agrees to transfer custody to the person the commissioning couple has named in the arrangement.
11. The commissioning couple agrees to pay specified expenses incurred by the gestational woman, such as medical, hospitalization, laboratory and therapy expenses, travel, accommodation, and child care costs.

As a group, commissioning couples had a higher level of education than the gestational women; 88 percent of commissioning men and 79 percent of commissioning women had post-secondary degrees, compared to only 17 percent of gestational women. This was reflected in occupations, with commissioning couples more likely to be professionals and to have higher incomes. Given the fees involved ($20 000 or more where fees to a broker and the gestational woman are involved), only the affluent can afford a preconception arrangement, so they are a highly select group and not typical of the general population.

Research in this area is of limited reliability in several respects; sample sizes were small, and the Law Reform Commission of Canada study was conducted in 1988. It showed nevertheless that most of the gestational women surveyed were married, usually to someone in a blue-collar occupation, most were of Protestant background, and almost all were Caucasian. Most of the women had not finished high school or had only high school education, and many did not work outside the home. The anecdotal accounts the Commission heard support this description of the situation of gestational mothers and their partners, suggesting that they tend to be of a lower socioeconomic status than commissioning couples and that payment is a major factor in their decision to participate.

> Commercial surrogacy contracts constitute a form of baby-selling; if the mother were merely providing the service of gestation, the mother and father would have equal rights to the child once the gestation was over and the child was born. The fact that many contracts stipulate that a reduced fee be paid to the mother if the product [her child] is "defective" makes it clear that gestation is merely a means to the end of a healthy baby.
>
> *Brief to the Commission from the Canadian Research Institute for the Advancement of Women, September 20, 1990.*

Indeed, this contention is borne out by the experience of one broker in the United States. Only one woman a year came forward to be a gestational mother when arrangements were made on a volunteer basis. Once the broker began to offer payment, the number rose to 20 women per year within two years. Without the financial incentive, then, it can safely be assumed that there would be far fewer willing gestational women.

The inequalities between the gestational woman and the commissioning couple are reinforced by the involvement of brokers. Despite the neutrality of the term "broker," implying an intermediary between the parties, in fact commercial brokers usually represent the interests of the commissioning couple, who pay the broker's fee of U.S.$10 000 to $16 000. The inequality of the parties is then confirmed by the terms of the standard contract, in which the gestational woman agrees to accept all the risks of assisted conception and pregnancy — up to and including her own death — while abiding by behavioural and other rules established by the contract — including the requirement to submit to medical diagnosis and treatment at the commissioning couple's discretion.

The commissioning couple, by contrast, is obliged only to complete payment on delivery of the child and relinquishment of the gestational woman's maternal rights and transfer of custody. They can refuse to accept the child if it proves not to be the genetic offspring of the commissioning man, and there have even been reported cases of commissioning couples refusing to accept the child because it was of the "wrong" sex or had a congenital anomaly or disability.

> One of the most severe results these technologies can have for women is the emergence of a class of professional female breeders, causing women, especially the unemployed, economically stressed, less educated, immigrant, and visible minority women, to be exploited and abused. It is these women who will be manipulated to benefit white upper middle class Canadian women. You ... must insure that these women are protected and respected under the law.
>
> *B. Lee, National Organization of Immigrant and Visible Minority Women of Canada, Public Hearings Transcripts, Moncton, New Brunswick, October 19, 1990.*

Preconception contracts were of particular concern to many of the groups representing minority women who appeared before the Commission. They told us that they fear increased exploitation of lower-income women, a disproportionate number of whom are members of minority groups. The advent of purely gestational arrangements, moreover, raises the possibility of minority women being used by white couples to gestate their children, both here in Canada and in developing countries. This concern was raised, for example, by Immigrant and Visible Minority Women of British Columbia:

> The idea that women would be so poor as not to have any other options than making their living by producing babies is, of course, repugnant ... [S]teps must be taken to ensure that surrogate motherhood is not undertaken for profit and that the legal and ethical issues are seriously addressed.
>
> *D. Ellis, Canadian Federation of Business and Professional Women's Clubs, Public Hearings Transcripts, Toronto, Ontario, October 29, 1990.*

> With the rise of commercial surrogacy, and on the basis of current experience, we foresee devastating consequences for all poor women and for women of colour who are disproportionately represented among the poor ... We recommend that this Commission call for a ban on surrogacy. The costs in the increased potential for exploitation of women

of colour by far outweigh any benefits that might accrue to affluent couples. *(S. Thobani, Immigrant and Visible Minority Women of British Columbia, Public Hearings Transcripts, Vancouver, British Columbia, November 26, 1990.)*

These concerns were given substance by reports that at least one U.S. broker is bringing women to the United States from overseas to act as gestational women; these women are not paid beyond their travel and living expenses, resulting in much lower costs for the commissioning couple. The same broker is also exploring the possibility of initiating the pregnancies overseas and bringing only the resulting children to the United States.

Non-financial forms of exploitation are also a danger, as many groups appearing before the Commission emphasized.

Dehumanizing and Degrading to Women

Apart from the question of whether commercial preconception arrangements are inherently exploitive, witnesses asked the Commission to consider the dehumanizing and degrading aspects of such agreements for the individual women who participate and for women generally:

> In the standard surrogacy arrangement the woman who ovulates, conceives, gestates, labours, and delivers a baby is not called "the mother." She is a mere "surrogate." The presumption is that the real mother is the wife/partner in the infertile couple. We feel this is very degrading to the woman involved. *(J. Lewicky, Alberta Federation of Women United for Families, Public Hearings Transcripts, Calgary, Alberta, September 14, 1990.)*

These aspects are certainly apparent in the contracts gestational mothers are asked to sign, which require them to waive their right to refuse medical treatment — a right guaranteed under the provisions of the *Canadian Charter of Rights and Freedoms* that protect every individual's "life, liberty and security of the person." Moreover, other values inherent in the Charter, such as women's right to autonomy and dignity (implied in section 7) and equality (section 15), would be offended by state legitimation or enforcement of preconception contracts:

> To ensure that the mother provides an appropriate environment for her "product," strict regulations are often placed on her diet, exercise, and intercourse with the male partner. The contracted mother may also be required to undergo medical treatment, including ultrasound, amniocentesis, and abortion, regardless of her wishes. Her right to refuse medical treatment is thus denied by the contract. If surrogacy contracts are made legally enforceable, a dangerous precedent will be set for the rights of all pregnant women. *(Brief to the Commission from the Canadian Research Institute for the Advancement of Women, September 20, 1990.)*

Harm to Participants and Children

Proponents of preconception arrangements downplay the concept of harm to the gestational mothers, arguing that they are free to decide whether to participate. Other witnesses, however, questioned this premise, pointing out that the circumstances surrounding such arrangements have the potential to lead to pressure or even coercion of women by husbands or partners in the interests of adding to the household income. Even without direct coercion, they felt that, given the disparities in the income and social status of gestational women and commissioning couples, the choice, in practice, is not "free." Family pressures in non-commercial situations may also undermine a woman's ability to decide freely whether to participate.

There may also be significant psychological implications for gestational mothers even if they have participated willingly. Pregnancy produces physical and hormonal changes in a woman's body that can affect her emotions and therefore have the capacity to alter her relationships with her partner and any other children she has. These changes may also affect her own thoughts and feelings about what she is doing and the fetus she is carrying. These effects cannot be predicted precisely before pregnancy begins; yet preconception contracts often require gestational mothers to certify in advance that they will not form a maternal bond with the fetus during the nine-month gestation period and will relinquish all ties to the child soon after birth.

> Surrogacy contracts are not really a procedure — we cannot really say that they are a new reproductive technology, but we have to look into them just the same because they are becoming very prevalent in our society. We of course feel that they must be prohibited. Surrogacy contracts are another way of further partitioning the maternity experience, and another way of trading with women's bodies. We consider this a totally exploitive practice and we recommend that it be banned. [Translation]
>
> C. Coderre, Fédération des femmes du Québec, Public Hearings Transcripts, Montreal, Quebec, November 21, 1990.

Some who have investigated the practice contend that many gestational mothers seriously underestimate the emotional and psychological costs of giving up the child. In fact, there is a substantial body of medical, gynaecological, and psychological literature to support the view that the bonding that takes place during gestation should not be underestimated and that any forced separation between mother and child may result in lasting harm to the mother.

Some U.S. brokers have reported that gestational women tend to deny that the child they are carrying is their own and to see it as "belonging" to the commissioning couple. There is anecdotal evidence, however, that women who relinquish a child with little distress at the time can later suffer from the experience. The long-term effects of relinquishment simply are not known, although an analogy can be drawn to studies focussing on adoption. The evidence suggests that the effects of relinquishment, including long-lasting grief, may be common to both practices.

If, on the other hand, the gestational mother decides not to relinquish the child, she may then have to cope with guilt or other feelings evoked by denying the commissioning couple the child they had anticipated. She could also face a court case over custody. Even if her attempt to keep the child is successful — whether because the commis-sioning couple does not challenge it or because she wins the custody case — she then faces the prospect of raising the child of another man with her husband or partner — or alone — with all the potential for strain on family relationships and finances that would entail.

> Commercial preconception arrangements diminish women's status as equal members of society by giving credence to a perception of women as being of value for a reproductive capacity that can be bought and sold.

For commissioning women, the benefits of such arrangements are not unambiguous. Society attaches great importance to the genetic link between fathers and children, and the woman may perceive this as pressure to agree to the man's desire to have a genetically related child. She may believe, for example, that this is something she "owes" her husband because of her feelings of inadequacy at not being able to carry his child herself. Several commissioning women have also reported difficulty dealing with what many would consider a fundamentally unacceptable situation — in essence, their husband having a child with another woman. In short, the voluntary participation of commissioning women, like that of gestational mothers, may be in doubt. Commissioning women too risk being coerced, even if the pressures are subtle, into agreeing to a preconception arrangement.

Other sources of strain can arise as the couple raises the child. Although with arrangements involving zygote transfer to a gestational woman both members of the couple would be related to the child, in most instances this is not the procedure used. As in donor insemination for male infertility, just one member of the couple is genetically related to the child born as a result of a genetic-gestational arrangement. With donor insemination, it is the woman who is related to the child; with preconception arrangements using assisted insemination, however, it is the man. As discussed in Chapter 19 on the use of donor gametes, this may result in the perception that the couple's relationships with the child are unequal. The child may also become a symbol and constant reminder of the woman's infertility.

Although they are not participants in the arrangement, the resulting children can also be affected profoundly by it. First, they have been created not as ends in themselves but to serve the needs of others and, at least in part, to fulfil the financial goals of the broker and possibly those of the gestational woman and her partner as well. Second, there is the issue of multiple parenthood when genetic, gestational, and social roles are separated as a result of a preconception arrangement — a situation that we know, based on experience with adoption, can have a significant impact on a child's personal and emotional development and sense of identity.

> A sign of the deeply personal aspect of procreation can be seen in the cruelly painful, tangled relationships brought about by surrogate motherhood cases ... The law must not attempt to replace this base of family relationship with its own arbitrary structure.
>
> *L. Moreau, Office of Marriage and Family Formation, Archdiocese of Vancouver, Public Hearings Transcripts, Vancouver, British Columbia, November 27, 1990.*

Commercial preconception arrangements are too recent a practice for there to be adults who began their lives under these circumstances. There are, however, several potentially harmful psychosocial implications for the children. Although the child may be very much wanted and loved, he or she has nonetheless been "bought at a price," which could make the child feel like a commodity that can be bought and sold, and create pressure for him or her to live up to his or her "purchase price."

Brokers have a service-oriented approach — their client is the commissioning couple, and the child is seen as a "product," as evidenced by the fact that the couple can opt out of the contract if the "product" is "defective." Also consistent with this approach is the fact that brokers generally do not screen prospective parents to ensure that the children will be going to suitable homes; ability to pay is the only prerequisite.

> The experience of maternal-fetal bonding during pregnancy and childbirth is unpredictable for the gestational mother. Where such bonding occurs, no woman should be expected to surrender custody of her child.
>
> *Brief to the Commission from the Canadian Advisory Council on the Status of Women, March 1991.*

Finally, we have to consider the potential for conflict within families — for example, as a result of disapproval of the arrangement on the part of non-participating family members — and the effects this may have on children who feel, rightly or wrongly, that their existence is the source of the conflict.

The family of the gestational mother is also affected by her pregnancy. If she has other children, they see the child being given away and reportedly wonder whether they too could be relinquished by their parents. Her partner, if she has one, must make allowances for the physical and psychological changes of pregnancy, at the same time perhaps feeling resentful or jealous that his wife is carrying another man's child. Finally, the gestational mother's parents may be affected by the loss of a child that they see as their grandchild.

Social Harms

Beyond the impact on those directly concerned, commercial preconception arrangements have an impact on society and on social perceptions of the role and value of women, families, and children. Many witnesses told the Commission, for example, that they fear that these arrangements will reinforce a social definition of women in terms of their ability to bear children and the perception of their bodies as vessels or tools designed to serve the interests of others.

We heard many concerns that preconception arrangements will alter society's understanding of parenthood, family, and parental responsibilities, reducing parenthood to a transaction — a deal depending solely on the will of the adults who make it — with the child as the product of the deal. This is clearly contrary to any notion of children as ends in themselves, as human beings with their own dignity and identity. Society's view of children could be altered irrevocably as a result, with children being seen as a product, a commodity that can be bought and sold. By contrast, the trend in human rights over the past two decades has been toward increasing recognition of children as persons in their own right, not as parental property.

> Surrogate motherhood ... does nothing to enhance the view that women are equal to men, to being persons in their own right, but, rather, demoralizes and dehumanizes women. Children become assembly line commodities, "factory-built" and exploited.
>
> R. Murray, Prairie Prolife of Portage la Prairie, Public Hearings Transcripts, Winnipeg, Manitoba, October 24, 1990.

Sexual Inequality

Finally, we heard from Canadians that preconception arrangements perpetuate inequalities between men and women in our society, because they reinforce the idea that women's value is defined by serving men's needs and that men have a right to control women's bodies.

We live in a society that has been based, historically, on the idea that women's primary role is motherhood and that men have legal rights over women's bodies. Many of those who oppose commercial preconception arrangements do so on the grounds that they perpetuate the assumption that women's role and value in society are defined by their sexual and reproductive functions and reinforce the notion that men have a right to control these functions.

The principle of equality means that every member of the community is entitled to equal concern and respect. Commercial preconception arrangements diminish women's status as equal members of society by giving credence to a perception of women as being of value for a reproductive capacity that can be bought and sold.

> The production of children for sale logically extends a particular condition of women that is historically longstanding: the commodification of their bodies. Pornography provides a useful analogy for understanding the meaning of "surrogate" motherhood. The commodification of women is at the core of both pornography and prostitution, in which women put their bodies, or, more precisely, body parts, up for sale as market objects.
>
> *C. Boodram, Edmonton Branch, Canadian Federation of University Women, Public Hearings Transcripts, Edmonton, Alberta, September 13, 1990.*

An Acceptable Practice: The Arguments for Commercial Preconception Arrangements

Those who believe that preconception agreements are an acceptable practice and warrant public policy support tend to argue from one of two general perspectives: the perspective of personal autonomy and rights or the perspective of medical necessity.

Personal Autonomy

The essence of the first argument is that a right to participate in a preconception arrangement is inherent in the right of couples to be free from state interference in their right to reproduce by sexual intercourse, which is protected by principles such as marital privacy and liberty. Proponents of this argument thus assert that there is a right to procreate, that those who cannot do so through sexual intercourse are entitled to use any other means at their disposal, and that people are entitled to the assistance of the state in exercising this right.

A second element of this perspective is the argument that a woman has a right to control her own body. Provided she is making a fully informed and free choice, it is argued, the state should not interfere in a woman's decision about whether to become a gestational woman:

We strongly believe that a woman has the right to make the decision if she chooses to be a surrogate. *(E. Mertick, Alberta Advisory Council on Women's Issues, Public Hearings Transcripts, Edmonton, Alberta, September 13, 1990.)*

Medical Necessity

Several physicians' organizations and other groups appearing before the Commission saw assisted insemination and *in vitro* fertilization in support of preconception arrangements as acceptable and medically justifiable responses to certain types of infertility (such as an absent or malformed uterus) or medical conditions in the commissioning woman (severe hypertension, diabetes, or heart condition):

> We are not necessarily recommending surrogacy. We are simply pointing out that under the right conditions, it may be that a woman with a disability would be assisted through a surrogacy arrangement.
>
> *Y. Peters, Canadian Disability Rights Council, Public Hearings Transcripts, Vancouver, British Columbia, November 28, 1990.*

We are in support of surrogacy in medically valid circumstances, that is a woman who has her uterus removed for some condition, who is not able to carry a child, who may have some condition that she would pass on to her child that would be life threatening to the child ... We neither support surrogacy for non-medical indications, nor do we support the commercialization of surrogacy agreements where valid medical indications may exist. *(R. Reid, Society of Obstetricians and Gynaecologists of Canada and Canadian Fertility and Andrology Society, Public Hearings Transcripts, Montreal, Quebec, November 22, 1990.)*

[We are not suggesting] that surrogacy is either right or wrong ... [The question is] whether or not a true need exists for this technology. Many women find themselves incapable of reproducing due to loss of uterine function as a result of surgical intervention for malignant disease, especially carcinoma of the cervix, which affects women in the child-bearing ages. These women are frequently in the prime of child-bearing age and are suddenly deprived of uterine function but not of ovarian function. Such women are ideal candidates for surrogacy in order to achieve their own genetic offspring. *(A. Yuzpe, Department of Obstetrics and Gynaecology, University of Western Ontario, Public Hearings Transcripts, London, Ontario, November 2, 1990.)*

Commercial Arrangements Unacceptable, Non-Commercial May Be Acceptable

The Commission also heard testimony from Canadians who find the commercial aspects of preconception arrangements abhorrent but take a different approach to private, non-commercial arrangements.   Several witnesses drew this kind of distinction between commercial and non-commercial arrangements:

> It has been an occasional practice cross-culturally and since time immemorial for women to bear children for other women known to them personally. These latter arrangements do not involve payment and often provide for continued interaction of all parties. [We do] not believe these arrangements pose problems for public values or the status of women. However, these non-commercial arrangements should be distinguished from the socially novel practice of commercial preconception contracts involving third-party mediation between a woman and other parties desiring children. *(Brief to the Commission from the Canadian Advisory Council on the Status of Women, March 28, 1991.)*

Other witnesses who made this distinction pointed to two factors: the danger of driving a practice underground by making it illegal, and reluctance to deprive people of an option that might permit them to form a family.

The second factor reflects the view of significant numbers of Canadians, according to surveys conducted for the Commission. The surveys revealed that opinion about preconception arrangements varies considerably with the type of arrangement involved (commercial or non-commercial) and the circumstances that lead people to seek a preconception arrangement.   There was, however, no consensus on whether and what types of preconception arrangements should be permitted.

> If I have made at all clear what it has been like to be in my shoes lately, I do hope that you won't recommend an end to what my sister and I have done. Surrogacy, when done without exploitation of anyone, has, I believe, a place in this society.
>
> *Private citizen, Public Hearings Transcripts, Vancouver, British Columbia, November 26, 1990.*

One survey, for example, asked respondents whether a couple should consider a preconception arrangement if the woman had a medical condition that would be life-threatening if she became pregnant. Half the respondents (49 percent) disagreed with a preconception arrangement as the solution, 31 percent agreed, and 19 percent were neutral on the issue. In another survey, 58 percent of respondents disapproved and 23 percent approved of a preconception arrangement in the situation where the woman was infertile and the man's sperm was used to impregnate another woman.

The surveys showed that many Canadians do not wish to close the door on preconception arrangements, even if they would not participate themselves or would not advise others to do so. For example, 46 percent of respondents answering a general question (the situation of the couple was not described) said that a person who is infertile should be able to consider the use of a preconception arrangement; 30 percent said this is something the person should not consider, and 24 percent remained neutral on the issue.

Finally, the surveys showed that a majority of respondents (61 percent) do not believe that preconception arrangements are likely to have a significant impact on society, largely because they will not be used very often. This no doubt reflects the fact that a large majority of respondents said that they would not participate in a preconception arrangement; 90 percent of women surveyed said that it was unlikely they would become a gestational mother in such an arrangement, giving such reasons as "I couldn't give away a baby I gave birth to" and "I wouldn't undergo pregnancy and birth unless it was my child."

Recognition that it would be virtually impossible to enforce a law prohibiting private, non-commercial preconception arrangements is reflected in this and similar testimony:

> It should be emphasized that the Council does not endorse surrogacy as a means of obtaining a child. It does recognize, however, that surrogacy does exist and feels that any effort to ban it would merely send the practice underground ... [I]f it goes underground and is something over which there is no control whatsoever, the children and the women will be victims ... we don't see this as an ideal situation. *(L. Newson, National Council of Women of Canada, Public Hearings Transcripts, Saskatoon, Saskatchewan, October 25, 1990.)*

Given this situation, some witnesses argued, the best approach is to try to reduce the opportunities for abuse or exploitation and to provide for the interests of any children that are born:

> Our attitude is that surrogacy per se is not something that should be specifically encouraged, but also it should not be banned altogether. Therefore the general conclusion we reached ... is that non-commercial, non-binding arrangements that of necessity must be based on generous, sincere motives should not be criminalized or otherwise banned ... We would acknowledge, therefore, the evidence of the existence of this practice and provide an appropriate legal response. *(J. Dillon, Canadian Bar Association, Public Hearings Transcripts, Vancouver, British Columbia, November 27, 1990.)*

Still others saw dangers in tolerating even non-commercial arrangements between close family members:

> No, we do not accept surrogacy between sisters. We consider that the commodification of the human body is absolutely to be condemned. This is a basic ethical principle, but we believe that even in the case of sisters, it opens the door to other things. [Translation] *(L. Fortin, Les Cercles de Fermières du Québec, Public Hearings Transcripts, Montreal, Quebec, November 22, 1990.)*

The Commission's Assessment

As the preceding sections make clear, preconception arrangements raise ethical and legal issues that are neither straightforward nor easy to deal with. As Commissioners listened to the continuing debate about this practice, one conclusion became evident: proponents and opponents are not likely to change each other's minds about the ethical and social dimensions of preconception arrangements. Views on preconception arrangements are based on fundamentally different convictions about human nature and about how the world works or ought to work; therefore, assessments of the actual or potential implications of preconception arrangements for women, for children, for couples, and for our evolution as a society also differ.

Commercial Arrangements

Using our ethical framework and standards, the Commission finds commercial preconception arrangements offensive on several grounds.

First, they offend human dignity by commodifying women's reproductive capacities and commodifying children; they contradict the principle that human reproduction should not be commercialized in any way. Second, we see actual and potential harms for families, for individual women and children, and for specific groups within society. Finally, we believe that public policy that condones or supports the establishment of adversarial relationships is fundamentally flawed; public policy should seek instead to support and encourage humane, non-conflictual family and social relationships. Any attempt to legitimize or support commercial preconception arrangements through public policy would represent the antithesis of this goal.

Commodification of Children and Reproduction

The fundamentally repugnant aspect of preconception arrangements is that they instrumentalize human beings through the deliberate act of creating a child for the express purpose of giving it up, usually in exchange for money. The premise of commercial preconception contracts is that a child is a product that can be bought and sold on the market. The moral point of view requires that people be treated as ends in themselves, not as a means to the ends of others. We must therefore uphold the value of children in and of themselves. Children are not a commodity, nor are they instruments to be used to serve the purposes of others. The commodification of children entailed by preconception arrangements ignores these essential values.

Moreover, commercial preconception arrangements commodify women's reproductive functions and place women in the situation of alienating aspects of themselves that should be inherently inalienable. A preconception contract obliges the gestational mother to sell an intimate aspect of her human functioning to provide someone else with a genetically related child; the capacity to become pregnant and bear a child is reduced to a marketable service. We do not allow people to give up their freedom and become slaves, even if they make a choice to do so, because of our collective conviction that this would negate the value we attach to human dignity and the inalienability of the person. Similarly, assigning a commercial value to the human function of reproduction would result eventually in a new and, in our view, undesirable social understanding of the value and dignity of women, their reproductive capacity, and their bodily integrity.

Commercial preconception contracts by their nature — the exchange of money for a child — contradict one of the fundamental tenets of the Commission's ethical framework. On these grounds alone, we could recommend prohibition of such arrangements, since we believe that all public policy in this field should be based on the principle of non-commercialization of reproduction.

> A preconception contract obliges the gestational mother to sell an intimate aspect of her human functioning to provide someone else with a genetically related child; the capacity to become pregnant and bear a child is reduced to a marketable service.

The evidence is clear that in commercial preconception contracts the principal motivation of both the broker and the gestational woman is money. Far from being the idyllic situation portrayed by brokers — gestational woman as "altruistic angel" giving the gift of a child to a couple who is happy but infertile — commercial preconception contracts are business transactions. The child is a product being sold by one party and bought by the other.

Harms to Individuals

The Commission heard strong arguments that preconception arrangements are detrimental to the autonomy of gestational mothers. We concur. Far from enhancing the gestational woman's autonomy, as some have argued, the practice circumscribes and dictates the gestational woman's behaviour by specifying contractual obligations, including the obligation to be treated by medical personnel selected by the commissioning couple, to have an abortion if the commissioning couple so decides, and to renounce her maternal feelings and rights even before conception. Again, we believe there is clear evidence of the potential for coercion and exploitation of gestational women because of the disparities in power and resources between gestational women and commissioning couples.

A commissioning couple uses a woman as a vehicle to serve their own ends. As the New York State Task Force on Life and the Law observed, they seek the birth components of gestation from the gestational woman while denying the personal, emotional, and psychological dimensions of her experiences and self. If she succeeds in denying her emotional responses during this profound experience, she is dehumanized in the process. If she fails, her attachment to the child produces a conflict that cannot be resolved without anguish for all involved.

Children are not a commodity, nor are they instruments to be used to serve the purposes of others. The commodification of children entailed by preconception arrangements ignores these essential values. Moreover, commercial preconception arrangements commodify women's reproductive functions and place women in the situation of alienating aspects of themselves that should be inherently inalienable.

Moreover, informed choice is a necessary component of autonomy. As we have seen, however, brokers arranging preconception arrangements are not neutral intermediaries; they act in the interests of the commissioning couple. If the gestational mother has her own lawyer, it is often one recommended by the broker. Furthermore, since so little is known about the psychosocial effects of these arrangements on the participants and the resulting child, the woman's decision cannot be made in light of all the information that might influence it. All these factors undoubtedly undermine her capacity to exercise informed choice in deciding to enter a preconception arrangement.

We also conclude that concerns about negative psychosocial consequences for the gestational mother are well founded, particularly because it is impossible for her to predict, at the time she signs the contract, how she will feel about fulfilling its terms after the child has been born.

Even if fully informed choice were possible, society has established certain limits on what people are free to make choices about. Such situations are rare but central to our definition of the kind of society we want to live in. Thus, in a caring society, personal autonomy is not a value that trumps all others, and society may see fit to place limits on the exercise of free choice when the choice concerns an activity that society regards as fundamentally incompatible with values such as respect for human dignity and the inalienability of the person.

We heard the view that preconception arrangements enhance women's autonomy by giving substance to their right to control their own bodies — by allowing them to decide for themselves the meaning and social implications of their ability to bear children. We reject this argument. Although they are strongly held values, freedom and autonomy do not include the right to engage in activities that will result in harms to others, particularly, as in this case, to the child that is eventually born; the limits of autonomy become apparent when its exercise will harm others, as the commodification of children most certainly does.

Harm to children born as a result of these arrangements cannot be ignored. Commissioners reject the argument that these harms could be outweighed by the opportunity for life, as this argument assumes the very factor under deliberation — the child's conception and birth. We concur with the assessment of the New York State Task Force on Life and the Law: "The assessment for public policy occurs prior to conception when the ... arrangements are made. The issue then is not whether a particular child should be denied life, but whether children should be conceived in circumstances that would place them at risk." Nor do we see any practical way of protecting the interests of the child that will eventually be born or even of ensuring that they are taken into account in negotiating and concluding a preconception arrangement.

> In a caring society, personal autonomy is not a value that trumps all others, and society may see fit to place limits on the exercise of free choice when the choice concerns an activity that society regards as fundamentally incompatible with values such as respect for human dignity and the inalienability of the person.

Commercial preconception arrangements do produce benefits — but the benefits are to brokers and commissioning couples at the expense of the interests of vulnerable women and of children who had no part in the arrangement.

Harms to Society

We agree with those who argued that commercial preconception arrangements have potentially negative consequences not only for individuals but also for women collectively and for other groups in society. These arrangements reinforce social attitudes about motherhood as the role that defines women's status and value in society. Furthermore, preconception arrangements could create broad social harms by diminishing the dignity of reproduction and undermining society's commitment to the inherent value of children.

Even if the number of commercial preconception arrangements to date has been relatively small, over time such arrangements would be bound to have a detrimental effect on the way society perceives women, children, and reproduction generally.

In short, we reject the notion that public policy can be based on a description of procreation in terms of a market production model — which is, essentially, that such arrangements should be permissible and legally enforceable because commissioning couples are willing to pay and gestational women are free to sell their labour. Second, we do not accept that the freedom to procreate automatically assumes a right to state support — whether in the form of enforceable contracts or publicly supported medical services — for the exercise of that right. Finally, we reject the arguments of proponents because they are premised on incomplete or inaccurate depictions of preconception arrangements, making them an inappropriate basis for public policy, which must take into account not only the interests of the participants, but also the other interests affected, including those of the resulting child, as well as the potential for individual and/or social harm.

We reject the notion that public policy can be based on a description of procreation in terms of a market production model — which is, essentially, that such arrangements should be permissible and legally enforceable because commissioning couples are willing to pay and gestational women are free to sell their labour.

We also reject the argument of medical necessity. We find it unacceptable that one party — the gestational woman — should be called upon to bear all the medical risks of pregnancy and birth, and possibly those of *in vitro* fertilization and zygote transfer, while all benefits accrue to the commissioning couple. In no other circumstances does society accept that a healthy person be placed at medical risk for the benefit of someone else for money, even when that condition is life-threatening. In this case, the commissioning woman's infertility is *not* life-threatening.

The commonly understood motivation for commissioning couples to enter into a preconception arrangement is because the commissioning woman is unable to conceive and/or carry a fetus to term. This makes preconception arrangements appear as a last resort when infertility is untreatable or treatment has been unsuccessful. As we have seen, however, this is not always the case; not everyone who seeks a preconception arrangement is involuntarily infertile, a member of a couple, or even of childbearing age. But even in cases where it is true, preconception arrangements are not an acceptable remedy.

Goals of Public Policy

As we have argued elsewhere in this report, one goal of public policy in the field of new reproductive technologies should be to seek to prevent conflict — or, at the very least, to avoid knowingly setting up situations where conflict is bound to result. Instead, we would seek to foster healthy family and social relationships through such means, for example, as promoting greater social acceptance of family ties based on other than a genetic component.

The Commission recognizes the value of public policy that supports people's attempts to establish families, and we uphold women's right to autonomy. We believe, nevertheless, that preconception arrangements can cause damage to children, families, and society as a whole and can actually limit, rather than enhance, women's autonomy. We recognize the genuine and legitimate desire of couples who are infertile to have children; but this should not take precedence over the best interests of children, which lie in not being the object of a contract, agreement, or paid transaction.

We believe further that preconception arrangements contradict the ethic of care, as they result — inevitably and intentionally — in the breaking of parental bonds and in strain on family relationships. They can also result in long, acrimonious conflict, in court and in the media, between the gestational woman and the commissioning couple; far from preventing conflict, preconception arrangements actually make conflict more likely.

In reaching our conclusions, we also took into account the Commission's public hearings, consultations, and surveys, which illustrated the ambivalence of Canadians' attitudes toward commercial arrangements. Canadians have seen what has happened in the United States, where several cases have come to public attention through bitter custody disputes, and do not want to see these events repeated here. At the same time, as we saw in our survey of people across the country, Canadians attach great value to having children and appear reluctant to deny others the opportunity to have a child, even if it means permitting a practice they do not condone or would not engage in themselves. It is not clear, however, that public opinion about preconception arrangements is based on a full understanding of their nature and implications, because much of the public information about them comes from brokers or others with an interest in portraying the practice in a positive light.

In some circumstances a preconception arrangement may seem a reasonable response to a particular situation. For example, where a woman has a serious health problem that prevents her from carrying a pregnancy, she might seek a gestational woman to carry a fetus conceived using the commissioning woman's eggs and her partner's sperm. Given the broader social harms we have described, however, we do not believe that using another woman's reproductive capacity is justifiable even in this situation, as difficult as it might be for the individuals involved to accept their inability to have a genetically related child.

> Even if a regulatory system could be designed to overcome these obstacles, the deepest and most serious harms of preconception arrangements would remain. No regulatory system could remedy the basic affront to human dignity occasioned by the commodification of children and the commercialization of reproduction.

We do not deny that a public response in the form of regulation could help to control some of the pressures and abuses identified with respect to preconception arrangements — for example, by requiring the provision of independent legal advice for gestational women or by making counselling mandatory for all parties to an arrangement. We are sceptical, however, that any regulatory scheme could ensure that all parties were able to make free and informed choices. Moreover, a regulatory approach by its nature would invite disputes and conflict.

Even if a regulatory system could be designed to overcome these obstacles, the deepest and most serious harms of preconception arrangements would remain. No regulatory system could remedy the basic affront to human dignity occasioned by the commodification of children and the commercialization of reproduction.

Non-Commercial Arrangements

The Commission's conclusions with respect to non-commercial preconception arrangements between family members or close friends are similar. We do not believe such arrangements should be undertaken, sanctioned, or encouraged. The motivation might be sincere and generous, but the arrangement still results in the commodification of a child and the reproductive process. Even if no money is involved, no one should have the right to make a "gift" of another human being; this is offensive to the human dignity of the child.

Non-commercial arrangements present the potential for coercion in the form of family pressure to participate. They also give rise to the possibility of damage to family relationships before or after the child is born, as well as even greater potential for confusion on the part of the child, because of continuing contact between the birth mother and the commissioning couple. Moreover, the arrangement still results in a healthy woman being placed at medical risk for the benefit of someone else.

At the same time, we recognize that the practice may continue to some degree and so demands a public policy response, particularly because of the uncertainties surrounding the legal status of a child born as a result of such an arrangement and the need to ensure that the child's best interests are served. We wish to make it clear, however, that our recommendations in this latter regard are not intended to sanction the practice, but simply to recognize that it is probably going to occur and that, in the absence of public policy, significant harm to children could result.

Recommendations

Commissioners are strongly of the view that preconception arrangements are unacceptable and do not warrant state support in any form that would signal acceptance or encouragement of them. We do not advise sanctions with respect to gestational mothers, however, as this would simply compound their vulnerability. While we recognize the vulnerability of couples who are infertile and their emotional needs, we believe that making payment for such arrangements should be prohibited. We also believe it is essential, in particular, to prohibit others from assisting in such arrangements — for example, brokers and physicians — by criminalizing the knowing provision of assistance. With these principles in mind, the Commission reviewed the options available and came to the following recommendations to prohibit commercial preconception arrangements.

Our first goal is to ensure that the status of this practice is uniform across the country, to discourage people from travelling to parts of the country where it is permitted. Evidence before the Commission shows that arrangements can take place across provincial/territorial borders. Thus, prohibition only at the provincial level would not be effective with respect to such arrangements. Hence, we sought a comprehensive, uniform, and effective approach to preconception arrangements across the country. This can be achieved by prohibiting certain activities aimed at facilitating such arrangements for gain. Accordingly, the Commission recommends that

> **199. The federal government legislate to prohibit advertising for or acting as an intermediary to bring about a preconception arrangement; and to prohibit receiving payment or any financial or commercial benefit for acting as an intermediary, under threat of criminal sanction. It should also legislate to prohibit making payment for a preconception arrangement, under threat of criminal sanction.**

This proposed criminal prohibition will serve as an effective deterrent to commercial preconception arrangements. Given our recommendations with respect to donor insemination and *in vitro* fertilization (donor insemination restricted to anonymously donated sperm collected by a licensed facility, *in vitro* fertilization restricted to licensed facilities and offered only for diagnosed fallopian tube blockage), physicians too would be barred from participating in any such arrangement.

Second, statutory provisions making preconception contracts unenforceable would operate as a strong deterrent to the practice, because they would generate uncertainty for the commissioning couple, whether or not a broker has been involved. Such provisions would ensure that the gestational woman could not be compelled by a court to give up custody of a child born as a result of a preconception agreement. The Commission therefore recommends that

> **200. Provinces/territories amend their family law legislation to specify that all preconception agreements, whether or not they involve payment, are unenforceable against the gestational woman.**

Commissioners do not wish to leave the impression that we consider non-commercial arrangements acceptable or to imply that non-commercial arrangements have no potential to harm individual women, the status of women generally, children and families, or society at large. However, we believe that the most effective way to deter non-commercial arrangements is to provide for penalties for third parties who facilitate preconception arrangements. The Commission recommends that

> **201. Self-regulating professional bodies, such as provincial colleges of physicians and surgeons and provincial law societies, adopt strict codes of conduct, disciplinary measures, and severe penalties, including loss of licence to practise, against members involved in brokering or performing assisted insemination, *in vitro* fertilization, or zygote/embryo transfer to facilitate a preconception arrangement.**

and that

> **202. Any facility knowingly providing assisted conception procedures in support of a preconception arrangement lose its licence to provide assisted conception services.**

It is important to ensure that the interests of any resulting children are protected. In particular, establishing their legal parentage is vital for the children and for the other participants, as it affects the rights and obligations of the parties with respect to custody, access, support, and inheritance. Without clarification of legal parentage, children could be deprived of the support they are owed and become subject to the trauma of protracted litigation. For these reasons the Commission recommends that

> **203. All provinces/territories that have not already done so amend their family law legislation to ensure that a woman who gives birth to a child is considered the legal mother of the child, regardless of the source of the egg.**

> **204. As in the case of adoption, the birth mother be allowed to relinquish her maternal rights only after a minimum waiting period following the birth of the child.**

and that

> **205. In any dispute over custody arising from a preconception arrangement, the best interests of the child prevail over the interests of the adults involved.**

Finally, in support of our international obligations, Commissioners believe that Canada should demonstrate leadership by supporting policies aimed at achieving an international ban on preconception arrangements. Given that Canadians could go to other countries, particularly the United States, to seek arrangements not permitted in this country, we believe that such a step is needed on the part of the international community to prevent the exploitation of women and the commodification of children. Adopting a domestic policy would be the first step toward this goal; encouraging other countries to adopt similar measures would reinforce and extend it.

The extent to which Commissioners deplore the practice of preconception arrangements is evident in our determination to recommend strong measures to discourage these arrangements and to penalize those who would seek to benefit financially from them. Our goal is to halt commercial practices entirely and to discourage others from participating in these arrangements. We recognize the value Canadians attach to having a genetically related child. In our view, however, this value cannot be upheld in the face of the other values that would have to be sacrificed. A caring society has an obligation to ensure that individual actions — even those intended to benefit others — do not generate greater social harms, and that public policy works to support and foster healthy family and social connections, not to undermine them or set them up to fail.

Preconception arrangements illustrate the ethical dilemmas posed by situations where both benefits and harms can result from a practice. In this case, however, the benefits to a few individuals are far outweighed by the harms to others and to society that are likely to result. This is why we have adopted such a strong stand against preconception arrangements. Taken together, Commissioners believe, the measures we propose will have a strong deterrent effect on preconception arrangements and, in particular, on third-party activities in this area, but without compounding the vulnerability of participants.

General Sources

Decima Research. "Social Values and Attitudes of Canadians Toward New Reproductive Technologies." In Research Volumes of the Royal Commission on New Reproductive Technologies, 1993.

de Groh, M. "Reproductive Technologies, Adoption, and Issues on the Cost of Health Care: Summary of Canada Health Monitor Results." In Research Volumes of the Royal Commission on New Reproductive Technologies, 1993.

Eichler, M., and P. Poole. *The Incidence of Preconception Contracts for the Production of Children Among Canadians*. Report prepared for the Law Reform Commission of Canada. Toronto: Ontario Institute for Studies in Education, 1988.

Guichon, J.R. "'Surrogate Motherhood': Legal and Ethical Analysis." In Research Volumes of the Royal Commission on New Reproductive Technologies, 1993.

Law Reform Commission of Canada. *Medically Assisted Procreation*. Working Paper 65. Ottawa: Minister of Supply and Services Canada, 1992.

New York State Task Force on Life and the Law. *Surrogate Parenting: Analysis and Recommendations for Public Policy*. New York: The Task Force, 1988.

Ontario Law Reform Commission. *Report on Human Artificial Reproduction and Related Matters*. Toronto: Ontario Ministry of the Attorney General, 1985.

SPR Associates Inc. "An Evaluation of Canadian Fertility Clinics: The Patient's Perspective." In Research Volumes of the Royal Commission on New Reproductive Technologies, 1993.

Stephens, T., and J. McLean. "Survey of Canadian Fertility Programs." In Research Volumes of the Royal Commission on New Reproductive Technologies, 1993.

Uniform Law Conference of Canada. *Proceedings of the Seventy-Third Annual Meeting, Regina, 1991*. Toronto: ULCC, 1991.

Williams, L.S. "Legislation, Inquiries, and Guidelines on Infertility Treatment and Surrogacy/Preconception Contracts: A Review of Policies in Seven Countries." In Research Volumes of the Royal Commission on New Reproductive Technologies, 1993.

Commercial Interests and New Reproductive Technologies

The purpose of this chapter is to examine the role of commercial interests in providing and developing new reproductive technologies and to outline our general position in this regard; this position, amplified in preceding chapters, will be further discussed in detailed recommendations in subsequent chapters. Commissioners believe that the development and dissemination of reproductive technologies cannot be left to market forces and corporate goals; rather, the ethical principles we have described should guide any use. These guiding principles, together with the ethic of care, require that our recommendations ensure that any use of the technologies does not commodify human beings or commercialize reproduction.

The crucial principle to be taken into account with regard to the activities of commercial interests is protection of the vulnerable. Clearly, the interests of commercial firms and the interests of those to whom they sell are not identical (for example, one wants to increase price, one to decrease it), but in an open market it is assumed that buyers can protect their own interests. The situation is different when health care is involved — commercial firms can protect their own interests, but individuals cannot, and therefore they require protection through society's rules and regulations. Given that there are vulnerable interests to be protected, the question is not whether there should be regulation of commercial interests but rather what form it should take. Recognition of this need to protect interests that are not able to protect themselves in open market exchanges is at the heart of all professional and health care regulation — acknowledging that regulation is needed. But not only individuals have vulnerable interests that need protection from commercial interests; the wider Canadian community also embodies vulnerable interests in two ways:

- We all have an interest in the nature of the community in which we live — for example, that our society not be one in which people are treated as commodities. This is one reason why societies such as ours choose to regulate what is permitted and prohibited through laws such as those limiting the types of contracts people can enter into.

- The community is also vulnerable to spillover costs from nominally "private" transactions — if the wider community has to bear costs resulting from these transactions, the community also has an interest that it needs to protect.

Obviously, conflicts of interest are inherent in most commercial transactions, but conflicts arising in the medical context are different, in that the individuals' interests are vulnerable because they are at a disadvantage in terms of medical knowledge and its application. Regulation is therefore needed for commercial activities in the health care field. The existence of conflicts of interest is not the problem in itself; it is how such conflicts are resolved that may be a problem. Commercial organizations are designed, both in objectives and in their management, to promote a single interest (profit); they are not designed to balance conflicting interests. Patients do not have the means or knowledge to defend their vulnerable interests, and these interests will therefore be sacrificed when they conflict with profit — hence the need for regulatory protection and the role of government as the guardian of the vulnerable interests.

> The existence of conflicts of interest is not the problem in itself; it is how such conflicts are resolved that may be a problem. Commercial organizations are designed, in both objectives and in their management, to promote a single interest (profit); they are not designed to balance conflicting interests. Patients do not have the means or knowledge to defend their vulnerable interests and these interests will therefore be sacrificed when they conflict with profit. Hence the need for regulatory protection and the role of government as the guardian of the vulnerable interests.

The idea of vulnerable interests that must be protected against commercial interests captures the concerns we heard from many Canadians with respect to the role of commercial interests in reproductive technologies. Many groups and individuals who appeared at the public hearings or made submissions to the Commission expressed concern that commercial motives may be driving the development and provision of reproductive technologies inappropriately. People were worried that the private sector's pursuit of profit may promote high-tech approaches to the treatment of infertility to the detriment of other alternatives and that industry funds research into drugs and treatments for infertility rather than its prevention. We also heard the concern that there are inadequate provisions for ethical review and monitoring in industry-based research involving human subjects and that corporations may avoid Canadian research guidelines by conducting research and product testing in countries with less stringent regulations regarding safety and informed consent. Canadians also told us of their concerns about pricing and marketing practices for reproductive products and services — for example, that companies may be promoting ineffective or unsafe products and services. We also heard the view that the activities of private clinics impose costs on the public health care system,

> It does appear that there exists some legislation governing the breeding of cattle. Are humans less important? As soon as some scientist or researcher finds a commercial application for some of what is happening today we will be away and running and, as stated before, it will then be too late to do anything about it.
>
> *Brief to the Commission from the Provincial Council of Women of British Columbia, July 1990.*

that physician ownership of clinics and laboratories represents a conflict of interest that may not be resolved to the benefit of the patient, and that the existence of private clinics unfairly restricts access to these services. Finally, Canadians told us they were concerned there was potential for commodifying human reproductive tissues and functions through the involvement of commercial interests and that inappropriate technology transfer — for example, from techniques developed by animal breeders — could also be an undesirable consequence of this involvement.

Canadians hold differing views about the appropriate role for commercial involvement in the development, marketing, and provision of products and services related to new reproductive technologies. However, many think that commercial interests have a useful though limited role and that relying solely on governments to

> It is very clear that Canadians believe commercial activity should occur only in the context of a regulatory framework that ensures the profit motive is not the deciding factor behind the provision of reproductive technologies.

fund the development of new reproductive technologies is unrealistic. Nevertheless, it is very clear that Canadians believe commercial activity should occur only in the context of a regulatory framework that ensures the profit motive is not the deciding factor behind the provision of reproductive technologies.

Much of the public debate has centred on the role of the pharmaceutical industry in developing and marketing fertility drugs. However, the range of commercial companies potentially involved in new reproductive technologies extends far beyond the pharmaceutical industry. These companies fall into two broad categories — products and services.

The first consists of companies that manufacture new reproductive technology-related products, such as fertility drugs, medical devices used in assisted conception techniques, and gene probes used in prenatal diagnosis. The second category involves the commercial provision of services, such as medical laboratories, sperm banks, and private clinics offering *in vitro* fertilization or sex preselection.

We have already stated (in Chapter 3) the Commission's position on the commercialization of reproduction. By commercialization we mean activities involving the exchange of money or goods and that are intended to generate a profit or benefit for those engaging in this exchange. Commissioners believe strongly that the ethic of care and the principle of protecting vulnerable interests mean that the development and dissemination of reproductive technologies cannot be left to market forces and corporate goals. We believe that the impact of market forces in the area of human reproduction could, if not properly regulated, undermine important social values and ethical principles and harm people by leading to inappropriate, unethical, or unsafe use of technology.

Within a framework of regulation, however, commercial companies can play a legitimate role in specific areas of research and development related to new reproductive technologies, as they can in other areas of medical care. Many women and couples who are infertile who might otherwise have been unable to have children have benefited from using fertility drugs. Diagnostic tools such as ultrasound and

> The public and private funding of IVF clinics leads to a conflict of interest for physicians involved and a two-tier system of health care with respect to this "treatment" for infertility ... Canadians do not have access to this technology on an equal basis and physicians whose research and training [have] been supported by public money can maximize their profits at private clinics.
>
> *Brief to the Commission from the Canadian Association for Women in Science, January 15, 1991.*

> It appears this new field has competing interests and availability is not ensured unless you are able to pay for it. IVF is being considered and utilized by many as a potential gold mine and not being seen as the complex mine field that it truly is. There are many hazards, known and unknown, associated with IVF and there is real danger in making these technologies a new commercial product. When used they must be used for the benefit of all infertile women and not for the benefit of doctors and commerce. Their accessibility should be ensured for all not just a few.
>
> *Brief to the Commission from S. Andrews, private citizen, April 26, 1991.*

specialized medical devices play an important and useful role in the diagnosis of congenital disorders and the treatment of infertility. Since companies that develop, produce, and market these products exist to make a profit, opposing all forms of commerce or commercialization would jeopardize Canadians' access to beneficial products and services. However, we believe that the provision of these products and activities in research and development in the area of human reproduction must occur under strictly regulated conditions.

Our specific proposals for how to limit and regulate commercial forces are discussed throughout Part Two of our report, as this issue arises in virtually every aspect of our mandate. We make recommendations regarding the appropriate role of commercial interests in the chapters on fertility drugs, assisted insemination, assisted conception, adoption, preconception arrangements, prenatal diagnosis, embryo research, and the use of fetal tissue. Indeed, the need to protect vulnerable interests by limiting or regulating commercial interests is part of the fabric of all the chapters and is woven into our deliberations and recommendations throughout the report.

> The impact of market forces in the area of human reproduction could, if not properly regulated, undermine important social values and ethical principles and harm people by leading to inappropriate, unethical, or unsafe use of technology.

The purpose of this chapter is to give the reader a general picture of the role of commercial interests in reproductive technologies in Canada today. We begin with a brief overview of the extent of commercial interests in the various areas of our mandate, then we go on to consider some of the general issues and concerns raised by the presence of commercial interests and present our stance on the appropriate role and regulation of these interests. We conclude the chapter with a brief discussion of the role of patenting in the field of new reproductive technologies.

The Extent of New Reproductive Technology-Related Commercial Interests in Canada

To assess the extent and nature of industry involvement in reproductive technologies, the Commission undertook a review of private sector activity in the field. We commissioned studies to evaluate the social and economic forces influencing the development of assisted reproductive techniques and to determine the extent of private sector involvement in the provision of fertility drugs, medical devices used for reproductive technologies, and commercial laboratory services. We also conducted surveys of pharmaceutical and biotechnology companies to determine the extent of their involvement in the development of specific products used in reproductive technologies and commissioned research to examine the extent to which IVF clinics, sperm banks, and other services are privately run on a commercial basis. This section contains a brief outline of our findings regarding commercial involvement in products and services related to new reproductive technologies. (Detailed discussion is available in our research volume entitled *New Reproductive Technologies and the Science, Industry, Education, and Social Welfare Systems in Canada.*)

Commercial Involvement in New Reproductive Technology-Related Products

Commercial interests involved in the manufacture of new reproductive technology-related products can be divided into three groups — pharmaceutical companies, which manufacture fertility drugs; biotechnology firms, which produce genetic probes and test kits; and the medical devices industry.

Pharmaceutical Companies and Fertility Drugs

During our public hearings, many people suggested that the pharmaceutical industry has targeted fertility drugs as a major growth area and has engaged in extensive research and marketing in this area. Our evidence suggests that this is not the case. We found that the market for fertility drugs in Canada is small at present, accounting for about four-tenths of 1 percent of the total $4.2 billion pharmaceutical market in this country, or about $16 million annually.

Of the approximately 3 000 drugs listed in the 1991 *Compendium of Pharmaceuticals and Specialties*, approximately a dozen are used in the treatment of infertility. These fertility drugs are produced by just a few companies. A single company, Serono Canada Inc., currently accounts for approximately three-quarters of all fertility drug sales in Canada. Serono Canada Inc. is part of The Ares-Serono Group, based in Geneva, Switzerland, which is the major world producer of fertility drugs. Other companies that market fertility drugs in Canada are Merrill Dow, Ayerst, and Sandoz.

A survey of the members of the Pharmaceutical Manufacturers Association of Canada (conducted for the Commission in November 1991) showed that relatively few pharmaceutical companies are currently marketing drugs to treat infertility and that few have plans to move into this market. Information was also collected separately from Serono Canada Inc., which is not a member of the Pharmaceutical Manufacturers Association of Canada and so did not participate in the survey.

Most companies regard the infertility market as relatively unimportant because the potential users of fertility drugs (primarily women of childbearing age who are infertile) represent only a small fraction of the total population. By contrast, the potential market for fertility control and post-menopausal products is much larger; products in these areas are therefore likely to generate a better return on investment. Also of interest is the fact that generic manufacturers have not moved into the infertility market, even though most fertility drugs are not patented; this is another reflection of the industry's perception that fertility drugs do not have significant volume and profit potential.

Because of the small market, even those companies that do produce fertility drugs often do not advertise or promote their fertility drugs in Canada, but instead put their promotional efforts behind products with greater profit potential. The major exception is The Ares-Serono Group, which specializes in fertility drugs and actively promotes its products in Canada and elsewhere.

Even if the market for fertility drugs is small in relative terms, and even if few firms are involved at present, Commissioners consider it important nevertheless to ensure that regulations are in place to protect vulnerable interests with regard to the activities of commercial companies. We have the opportunity to establish such protections in Canada now, and Commissioners believe Canada should seize this opportunity while it exists.

Biotechnology Companies

In Canada, the biotechnology "industry" consists of between 300 and 400 companies loosely identified as belonging in this category by their use of biological methods in research and manufacturing. These companies are found in many industrial sectors, from mining and aquaculture to waste management and health care. According to Industry and Science Canada, biotechnology is best seen as a technology used in many industries, not as an industry in itself.

Among the Canadian biotechnology firms active in the field of health care, some are the research arms of conventional pharmaceutical companies, demonstrating that the distinction between biotechnology firms and pharmaceutical companies is not a sharp one. Of the almost 300 Canadian companies and research institutes listed in the *Canadian Biotechnology Directory*, about 90 are listed as being active in the area of health care. Seven of these are involved in areas relevant to reproductive health, manufacturing and/or developing reproductive health care products such as diagnostic and therapeutic products for sexually transmitted diseases, pregnancy detection and assessment products, and hormone testing products (including fertility test kits).[1] One of these companies owns the rights to the gene probe technology used in paternity tests, and another is involved in trying to license the probe for the cystic fibrosis gene. In addition, certain biotechnology companies are developing and producing recombinant versions of existing fertility drugs (see Chapter 18).

A common impression that biotechnology companies are widely involved in new reproductive technology-related research may stem from the fact that some of these companies, particularly in the United States, are involved in research related to genetic testing. Like many large pharmaceutical firms, some biotechnology companies on this continent are involved in research aimed at discovering the molecular genetic components of common multifactorial diseases such as auto-immune disorders, neurological disorders, blood diseases, and cancer. The driving force behind this research is the prospect of developing new and potentially profitable treatments (mainly drugs), based on a better understanding of the underlying disease processes.

It is important to distinguish the various categories of use of genetic testing, as the largest potential use is not related to reproduction per se. The first category is genetic testing in the population at large to identify individuals who have a single-gene disorder and who may benefit from treatment for that disease — for example, in Canada, newborn screening for phenylketonuria. Such disorders are uncommon, but there are more common diseases that are not single gene but do have a genetic component — multifactorial disorders — the second category of genetic testing (see Chapter 27).

It is in this category (multifactorial disorders) that some U.S. biotechnology companies see a potential for development, as it could involve a very large testing market. Given the private health insurance system in the United

> First, we strongly believe that neither bodies, nor gametes, nor human embryos, nor any part of our reproductive potential, should be considered fungible or marketable commodities. Permitting the exploitation, conditioning and distribution of the seeds of life, human embryos and infants, in accordance with market forces, ignores the principles of human dignity and individuality.
>
> We demand that the principle of no charge for services that has always guided Canadian law and policy on blood and organ donations be upheld, and we recommend that marketing of gamete and embryo transfers be prohibited. [Translation]
>
> G. Létourneau, Commission de réforme du droit du Canada, Public Hearings Transcripts, Montreal, Quebec, November 21, 1990.

States, there is a large potential market in that country for techniques to identify risk status, especially if health insurance costs continue to be borne by employers. This is not the situation in Canada, where everyone is covered in the publicly supported system. A third category of genetic tests is those used to identify adults who do not and will not themselves have a genetic disease but who are carriers, meaning that they are at higher risk that their children will have a genetic disease. A fourth use of genetic testing is to identify the presence of a genetic disease in a zygote or fetus through preimplantation or prenatal diagnosis.

Biotechnology companies in other countries, particularly the United States, are involved in developing gene probes and tests. Their main motivation is to find large and profitable markets such as that provided by multifactorial disease. Gene testing could theoretically be used or applied in one of the four ways just described. However, the Canadian biotechnology industry is not involved in any significant way in such development or research, although one company, the Hospital for Sick Children Research and Development Limited Partnership, is involved in licensing the probe for the cystic fibrosis gene (which may have uses in the reproductive context for prenatal diagnosis). To date this has not proved profitable. If and when the hospital does start receiving royalties, it expects only modest returns.

There are many reasons for limited commercial involvement in developing genetic tests to apply to prenatal diagnosis (or other uses) in Canada. Ethical issues, for instance, are a major concern with respect to whether it is appropriate to engage in prenatal diagnosis for the most common (and therefore potentially most profitable) genetic conditions, such as susceptibility genes or late-onset genetic diseases, which may not manifest themselves until adulthood. Moreover, the demand for prenatal testing for treatable or adult-onset genetic diseases is less than some people originally expected, and the testing itself has proven to be more complicated than anticipated. Possibly the biggest obstacle to private sector involvement in Canada is the question of who will pay for costly testing and counselling in an era of health spending constraints. Provincial health insurance plans have not funded prenatal genetic testing except for conditions that cause serious congenital disabilities, and this makes it less likely that commercial activities in this area will be profitable. However, the possibility that inexpensive, over-the-counter test kits (even if they prove unreliable and open to misinterpretation) could be developed and marketed to large numbers of people may be motivating some U.S. companies to pursue research. What effect this might have, if such products are then marketed in Canada as well, is unknown.

In summary, it appears that very few Canadian biotechnology companies are engaged in research that is directly relevant to new reproductive technologies. In Canada, the vast majority of such research is being done in universities and funded by government granting agencies or private foundations. Nor are any biotechnology companies in Canada involved in gene therapy (see Chapter 29).

> Any future application of such genetic tests to the area of reproduction should be monitored by the National Reproductive Technologies Commission, and governments should put measures in place to protect vulnerable interests.

Medical Devices Companies

Medical devices are health care products that are not drugs or medicines but are used for diagnostic or therapeutic purposes. According to the industry association, Medical Devices Canada (MEDEC), medical devices generally fall into one of several subgroups: diagnostics; medical imaging and therapy; medical/surgical supply; hospital equipment; implants; and assistive devices.

Some 600 companies sell medical devices in Canada; many are divisions of large multinationals or subsidiaries of major pharmaceutical firms. They supply the $2.5 billion market in Canada with products in 6 500 categories (see research volume, *New Reproductive Technologies and the Science, Industry, Education, and Social Welfare Systems in Canada*). Items range from bedpans to CAT scanners and medical information computer systems. Eighty percent of the medical devices sold in Canada are imported (mainly from the United States).

The medical devices that are most relevant to new reproductive technologies are diagnostics (used in laboratory testing to measure hormone levels); ultrasound equipment; and specialized equipment for use in IVF and other forms of assisted conception. According to industry experts, it is not possible from available data to assess how much of the medical devices industry is devoted specifically to new reproductive technologies, but it is considered very small indeed.

The diagnostics subsector of the industry manufactures test materials (often called "reagents") consumed in the process of laboratory testing, as well as sophisticated equipment and auto-analyzers used to process test samples. The total size of the "consumables" portion of the Canadian market is estimated at $350 million. Despite a major marketing thrust during the 1980s by some companies to promote fertility hormone test lines (seen then as a potential growth area), sales of reagents used in testing fertility hormones today account for only about 2 percent ($7 million) of the annual consumables market. For the diagnostics industry, fertility testing is seen as a very small specialized market, though for certain niche companies it may be an important one.

A second subsector of the medical devices market with relevance to new reproductive technologies is ultrasound. This form of imaging is now used widely in medicine generally. Ultrasound scanning in the field of women's reproductive health is most widely used in the assessment of pregnancy. Ultrasound technology is also used in investigation of infertility (to examine the uterus and fallopian tubes, for instance) and to monitor daily the development of eggs in the ovaries during IVF cycles.

In Canada, the ultrasound equipment market for all medical uses has recently been estimated at approximately $50 million annually — $32 million in hospital sales and the rest in sales to government laboratories, university research centres, and doctors' offices. Ultrasound is used widely in many specialties of medicine and surgery for diagnosis, but no figures are available on what proportion of this use is relevant to reproductive problems.

A third relevant subsector involves specialized devices developed and manufactured specifically for use in IVF, assisted insemination, and related procedures. These items include aspiration needles used during egg retrieval, zygote transfer catheters (tubes), and various other catheters for use in assisted insemination or assisted conception. The total Canadian market for such items has been estimated at approximately $250 000 and is so small that it is not captured in industry data.

In summary, it appears that the market for new reproductive technology-related products in Canada is quite small and constitutes only a fraction of the total market for pharmaceutical, biotechnology, and medical devices companies. Of course, the fact that these markets are small does not mean that the profit motive is absent or that these companies manufacture new reproductive technology-related products out of compassion. On the contrary, like any other industry, the objective for these companies is to make a return on investment. Clearly, the profit motive must be the main driving force behind all research, development, and marketing decisions that companies make about their products — the underlying goal is to make money by making saleable products. This applies to the market for fertility drugs, which has been consistently profitable,[2] as well as to the market for genetic tests and medical devices.

Moreover, Canadian pharmaceutical, biotechnology, and medical devices manufacturers must be situated within the larger global economy. Most of these companies are subsidiaries of foreign-owned companies based in the United States or Europe. In the case of fertility drugs, the global market is estimated to be worth approximately half a billion dollars,[3] so the $16 million Canadian market represents 3.2 percent of the total world market. This means that product development and marketing decisions made in Canada are influenced or made by corporations with headquarters elsewhere. It also means that most research, development, and testing of new drugs or devices take place outside Canada, with only the marketing carried out here. Multinational companies conduct their research where the research facilities exist and where it is most profitable to do so; The Ares-Serono Group, for example, spends less than 1 percent of its research budget in Canada. As we discuss later in this chapter, this international dimension of the manufacture of new reproductive technology-related products raises important issues.

Commercial Involvement in New Reproductive Technology-Related Services

The second major category of commercial interests involves the provision of new reproductive technology-related services on a for-profit basis. This includes commercial laboratories, commercial sperm banks, private (commercial) IVF and sex preselection clinics, and commercial preconception (surrogacy) agencies.

Commercial Medical Laboratory Testing

Medical laboratories provide a range of diagnostic testing services such as routine blood and urine tests, as well as more specialized tests. These laboratories may be associated with hospitals or public health departments, operating on a non-profit basis, or they may be commercial companies, operating for profit. Commercial laboratories conduct medical tests on the written request of a physician and are reimbursed by provincial health plans.

The overall market for commercial laboratory medical testing in Canada has been estimated at approximately $700 million annually. The bulk of commercial testing occurs in Ontario, and indeed some other provinces have no commercial laboratories. Our evidence suggests that commercial laboratories provide very few new reproductive technology-related services. In principle, commercial laboratories could provide two important new reproductive technology-related services: genetic testing and infertility testing. However, no commercial laboratories are used for genetic testing in Canada at this time; all molecular genetic testing is done by universities, teaching hospitals, or government-funded genetics centres. In the United States, by contrast, commercial genetic testing is a $150 million a year industry and growing.

There is some use of commercial laboratories for tests related to fertility assessment and assisted conception, but this constitutes a very small percentage of the overall commercial laboratory market in Canada. One estimate puts the figure for infertility testing in commercial laboratories at $7.5 million annually, or approximately 1 percent of the total. For Canada's largest commercial laboratory company (MDS Laboratories), fertility testing represents 1 to 2 percent of its revenues. The volume of fertility testing by commercial laboratories increased during the 1980s but has now levelled off. This may be partly because some physicians involved in private IVF clinics have set up their own laboratories as part of clinic services.

Commercial Clinics Providing Assisted Conception Services

Commercial laboratories have become a well-established part of the health care system in some provinces, and their services are covered by the provincial health plans. Most other commercial new reproductive technology-related services, however, operate on the margins of the health care system, billing patients directly for uninsured services on a for-profit basis. These include commercial IVF and sex preselection clinics and commercial sperm banks.

Commercial In Vitro Fertilization Clinics: The distinction between commercial and non-commercial clinics is not clear or easy to make in practice.   Three categories of activity in health care that can be distinguished are for-profit (drug companies), not-for-profit (hospitals), and not-only-for-profit (physicians' own practices or clinics). However, this last category includes clinics where (1) the physician is on salary (from a hospital or university); (2) physician income comes only from reimbursements by the provincial medical insurance plan for services rendered; or (3) the patient pays a fee that not only covers costs but provides income for the physician.

For purposes of our analysis, the Commission defines a commercial clinic as any clinic that charges patients fees, unless these are charged simply to recover the clinic's costs of services and the physicians involved derive no additional income from these fees. A Commission survey showed that 4 of the 17 clinics providing IVF in Canada are commercial clinics according to this definition (see Chapter 20). The remaining IVF clinics operate on a non-profit basis, in affiliation with a university or teaching hospital. The four commercial clinics are the Toronto Fertility Sterility Institute; C.A.R.E. Centre (Mississauga, Ontario); IVF Canada (Scarborough, Ontario); and the Institut de Médecine de la Reproduction de Montréal (IMRM) Inc.

The first three are owned and operated by physicians. The fourth is funded in part by local business interests. These clinics charge a fee to their patients, as do most IVF clinics in Canada, since IVF is an insured service only in Ontario. However, at these four clinics, the patient's fee is designed not only to recover the costs of the procedure, but also to provide a profit to the clinic, so that a proportion provides income to the physician or provides a return on investment to the clinic's owners. These four clinics treated about one-quarter (640 of 2 494) of all IVF patients treated in Canada in 1991.

Commercial Sperm Banks: Our survey showed that there are some 15 sperm banks in Canada, of which 4 operate on a for-profit basis. The rest are affiliated with hospitals or teaching hospitals/universities. Donors are paid $75 per sample on average.   This is usually described as compensation for the donor's time and inconvenience, not payment for the sperm itself.   After processing, one donated sample is divided into "insemination units" — 8 to 10 is not an unusual number of units. These units are then sold to physicians involved in infertility treatment. One Toronto sperm bank charges doctors between $100 and $150 per insemination unit.[4] Thus, a $75 sample might yield $1 000 for the sperm bank.

The difference between the payment to the sperm donor and the price charged by the sperm bank for insemination units is not pure profit. Costs for testing the sperm, freezing and thawing, record keeping, and distribution must be taken into account. However, commercial sperm banks do make a profit on the sale of sperm to doctors. Some doctors, in turn, may also mark up the price of the insemination unit charged to the patient, to help cover clinic overhead costs. The cost to the recipient varies greatly but averages $300 to $400 per cycle, which includes two or three inseminations.

There is little published information on sperm banking in this country, and the total value of the Canadian commercial trade in human sperm is not known. Some clinics in Canada use sperm from commercial banks in the United States. In the United States, assisted insemination is estimated to be a $164-million-a-year industry, according to a 1987 Office of Technology Assessment survey,[5] which included both sperm bank earnings and those of doctors providing AI. One U.S. commercial sperm bank, California Cryobank in Los Angeles, stores 100 000 frozen samples and ships 2 300 vials each month. In the United States, there is so little regulation of the industry that no one — not professional groups or governments at any level — knows how many commercial sperm banks exist. Approximately 45 sperm banks are members of the American Association of Tissue Banks, but only 12 are accredited by the association. This kind of activity in the United States shows what could happen in Canada without regulation.

Commercial Sex Preselection Clinics: In 1973, an American researcher, Ronald Ericsson, discovered a technique for separating sperm aimed at yielding samples that are richer in either Y-bearing sperm (which leads to boys) or X-bearing sperm (which leads to girls). He claims that women desiring a boy (or a girl) who are inseminated with sperm treated by his technique increase their chances of having a child of the desired sex to 69 percent for a girl, and 71 to 76 percent for a boy, although these claims have not been independently verified.

This sperm treatment technique has been patented and franchised to 57 clinics in the United States that specialize in this service, often called "sex preselection clinics." There is less interest in such clinics in Canada. However, one clinic using the technique opened in 1987, and a second one opened recently, both in Toronto. The procedure is not covered by the provincial medical insurance plans, and the charge is about $500 per insemination.

Other Commercial Services

In the United States, at least two other types of new reproductive technology-related commercial services exist. Fetal sexing clinics use ultrasound to provide prenatal diagnosis of the sex of the fetus for couples who might choose to abort a fetus of the undesired sex. In fact, an American physician has patented a technique for determining fetal sex at about 12 to 14 weeks' gestation and has opened several clinics offering this service — including one across the border from Vancouver, which he hopes will attract Canadians. There are no fetal sexing clinics in Canada, and the physician in question does not have a licence to practise medicine in British Columbia.

Commercial surrogacy agencies arrange preconception agreements for couples who wish to hire a woman to conceive, bear, and then relinquish a child. An agency's fee for arranging such an agreement may run into the tens of thousands of dollars. There are no such agencies in Canada, and such activities would probably be deemed illegal under provincial adoption laws (see Chapter 23).

The Appropriate Role and Regulation of Commercial Interests

The preceding overview shows that new reproductive technology-related products constitute a small fraction of the pharmaceutical, biotechnology, and medical devices markets and are not seen as priority areas for research and development by most companies in these industries. Similarly, most new reproductive technology-related services are provided through the publicly supported health care system. In Canada, there are four commercial sperm banks, four commercial IVF clinics, two sex preselection clinics, and no commercial surrogacy agencies or fetal sexing clinics. Nevertheless, there is no guarantee that this situation will not change, and even limited commercial interests can have a significant impact on the way new reproductive technologies are developed and disseminated. Moreover, these interests could become much more prevalent, as they are in the United States — technological developments elsewhere could be imported into Canada, and new reproductive technology-related products and services could potentially provide a source of profit in this country. These areas are open to exploitation by business unless safeguards and regulations are put in place. As a society, we must think carefully about the appropriate role for commercial interests and about the best mechanisms for ensuring that they are kept within the desired boundaries and that regulations are in place to provide oversight and protect vulnerable interests. We have a window of opportunity to act, and we should not fail to use it.

> As a society, we must think carefully about the appropriate role for commercial interests and about the best mechanisms for ensuring that they are kept within the desired boundaries and that regulations are in place to provide oversight and protect vulnerable interests. We have a window of opportunity to act, and we should not fail to use it.

Commissioners see nine important aspects that must be addressed in assessing the role of commercial interests. We took these into account in considering the options for regulation and in formulating our recommendations throughout Part Two of our report. The nine aspects are as follows: research priorities; ethical review of research; conflicts of interest; testing of products and services; marketing; access; public subsidy of private clinics; commodification; and technology transfer. We outline these in the following pages, and our specific recommendations on these issues are discussed in subsequent chapters, in the context of the particular technologies or procedures to which they are relevant.

Research Priorities

When making research decisions, those with commercial interests invest in a line of research only if they think it will lead to some product or service that can be sold for a profit. For example, pharmaceutical companies fund research into infertility only if it is likely to lead to the development of a new patentable fertility drug or other potentially lucrative new reproductive technology-related product.

Many forms of research that would be beneficial to Canadians are not likely to lead to profitable products or services. For example, much research into the causes and prevention of infertility is unlikely to lead to the development of a saleable drug, device, or commercial service. Yet, as we have shown in our discussion of the ethic of care, preventing a disease, where possible, is generally preferable to treating it through drugs or surgery after it has already caused harm.

Thus, the kinds of research that are most valuable to commercial interests may not always be the kind that are most valuable to the Canadian public. If commercial interests were able to determine priorities for medical research in Canada, the resulting priorities could be distorted. The possibility of private capture of the public research process is something to which society should be alert and against which society should seek to guard itself. A consequence of the new federal patent legislation means that substantial funds have to be spent by pharmaceutical companies on research in Canada. If this money is channelled into the Medical Research Council and universities, especially in the context of static or declining public research resources, there is a danger the decision-making process regarding research priorities in those institutions will be skewed. The availability of money from pharmaceutical companies carries with it an in-built temptation to frame research questions in a way that might lead to potential applications that could be of benefit to that industry. It is incumbent upon universities and publicly funded research agencies to make this conflict overt; awareness of it should be incorporated into the thinking and approach of decision makers in these settings.

At the heart of this concern is how perceptions of the causes and treatment of disease could be distorted by research that is driven solely by commercial motives. The determinants of disease are in fact extremely complex, highly inter-related, and embedded in a social context, as we discussed in Chapter 4. To tease out only one strand of this web — the one that may be amenable to pharmaceutical treatment — contributes to a simplistic and inappropriate view of health and disease.

It is therefore important that acceptance of money with strings attached by universities and public funding agencies be viewed with great caution. In its discussions with the Commission, the Pharmaceutical Manufacturers Association of Canada argued that the current tax law requires that the money they give to agencies to support research must meet certain criteria of relevance to their commercial activities. This situation should be reviewed and the law amended if necessary so that money given to certain major public research funding agencies, without conditions, is still eligible for tax credits.

As well as the potential to influence research activities, the significant financial resources available in the pharmaceutical industry for research and development of new drugs, compared to the more limited public funds for basic research on human reproduction, may lead to an emphasis on treatment approaches and the relative neglect of research into preventive measures. The distinction between research into causes/ prevention and that geared to developing new patentable drugs is not completely clear. Some pharmaceutical products, notably vaccines, are used specifically in prevention, while others are used to inhibit the progression of disease (for example, antibiotics), thereby preventing more serious health problems. For example, a vaccine against chlamydia (see Chapter 10) would be both profitable and of great benefit. Some drug research is focussed on gaining a better understanding of underlying disease processes, and this knowledge, while it may result in development of a new drug, also adds to the body of scientific knowledge that may lead eventually to prevention methods or ways to minimize the condition without drugs.

The kinds of research that are most valuable to commercial interests may not always be the kind that are most valuable to the Canadian public. The possibility of private capture of the public research process is something to which society should be alert and against which society should seek to guard itself. It is incumbent upon universities and publicly funded research agencies to make this conflict overt; awareness of it should be incorporated into the thinking and approach of decision makers in these settings.

Currently, the private sector provides a relatively small proportion of funding for biomedical research carried out at universities and university-affiliated hospitals in Canada. In 1989-90, $577 million was spent on all biomedical research conducted by Canadian faculties of medicine.[6] The private sector funded 8.3 percent (about $48 million), and just over 70 percent was funded by federal and provincial governments and not-for-profit foundations. (The private sector also conducts a certain amount of in-house research, estimated at $237 million for research in the medical and pharmaceutical fields in 1990.[7]) The federally funded Medical Research Council of Canada alone supports 30 percent of biomedical research carried out at universities in Canada. These public agencies help ensure that the health needs of Canadians, not commercial profit, remain the primary determinant of medical research priorities in universities in Canada.

The current economic situation has curtailed growth in government funding of research, and there is an increasing danger that commercial imperatives will have a greater influence on medical research in the future. This issue arises throughout our report, and we have made recommendations directed to ensuring that the public interest is respected in the determination of medical research priorities. We also discuss ways of improving the use of public research funds, to target areas of medical research that are neglected by commercial interests. We recommend in some cases that commercial interests be encouraged or required to contribute resources to public research funds.

We believe that commercial funding can play a legitimate role in medical research in Canada but that active steps are needed to ensure that this participation does not skew research priorities and activities in universities and publicly funded agencies. We discuss research funding and priorities and make recommendations regarding it throughout Part Two, in the context of infertility prevention, assisted conception, prenatal diagnosis, human zygote/embryo research, and research involving the use of fetal tissue.

> We believe that commercial funding can play a legitimate role in medical research in Canada but that active steps are needed to ensure that this participation does not skew research priorities and activities in universities and publicly funded agencies.

Ethical Review of Research

Most medical research in Canada that involves human subjects is approved by a local research ethics board. Research ethics boards evaluate the scientific aspects of proposed research and consider ethical issues such as whether the procedure for gaining informed consent from research participants is appropriate. Research ethics board approval provides a valuable check to ensure that the interests of research subjects, and of the wider society, are respected in medical research.

Research ethics board approval is required for any publicly funded medical research involving human subjects. Universities and hospitals also require that research within their institutions have research ethics board approval. However, research ethics board review is not legally required, and some important forms of medical research may not be adequately reviewed. This is particularly true of commercially funded research that takes place outside hospitals or universities. For example, commercially funded research conducted by private physicians in their offices, or conducted in-house by commercial firms, may not be reviewed by a research ethics board.

We believe strongly that commercially funded research involving human subjects should receive the same ethical review as publicly funded research. Indeed, the presence of a profit motive means that commercially funded research is particularly in need of independent research ethics board approval.

> The presence of a profit motive means that commercially funded research is particularly in need of independent research ethics board approval.

We have therefore made recommendations, throughout Part Two, to ensure that commercially funded medical research is also subject to research ethics board approval. This applies not only to research involving human subjects, but also to research involving human zygotes and the use of fetal tissue.

As we noted earlier, much of the research conducted on new reproductive technology-related products takes place outside Canada. In some countries, research ethics boards do not exist, raising the possibility that companies may seek to avoid ethical guidelines in developed countries by testing drugs or devices in developing countries, where standards of safety and informed consent are not as rigorous.

It is generally accepted that abuses did occur in the past with drugs such as contraceptives, but the industry denies that they still occur. We were unable to find evidence or documentation regarding such practices. It would, of course, be unacceptable if the burden of experimentation were to fall on women in the developing world, while the benefits accrued to the relatively privileged citizens of Western nations. To help pre-

> We believe strongly that commercially funded research involving human subjects should receive the same ethical review as publicly funded research.

vent such a situation, Canada has a moral responsibility to ensure that fertility drugs, and new reproductive technologies generally, are developed and used in a responsible way both in Canada and abroad. Our recommendations concerning Canada's international role in preventing the abuse of new reproductive technologies are presented later in this part of our report.

Conflicts of Interest in Particular Situations

As explained at the beginning of this chapter, the existence of commercial interests in the provision of new reproductive technologies creates conflicts of interest; vulnerable interests need protection if appropriate resolution of those conflicts is to occur. If pharmaceutical companies become involved in the provision of services related to reproductive technologies, a conflict arises in which vulnerable interests may not be protected. A profit-seeking organization that establishes or purchases an infertility treatment clinic, for example, enabling it to set clinical policy, is not subject to professional controls and monitoring or guided by social and personal expectations (as physicians are expected to be) that it will seek patients' interests first. A similar conflict of interest could arise, with no means to protect vulnerable interests, if pharmaceutical companies set up or directly fund data bases or registries to keep track of the outcomes of fertility drugs used — hence the need for an intervening arm's-length mechanism through which to channel such funding.

Similarly, when commercial IVF clinics own laboratories that provide fertility testing, or when physicians who own laboratories can refer patients to those laboratories for tests, a conflict of interest arises in which protection, in the form of regulation of commercial activities, is needed to ensure the conflict is resolved appropriately.

Commissioners believe that allowing these conflicts of interest to persist without regulatory oversight is not to the benefit of Canadians. It is unrealistic to expect for-profit enterprises to regulate themselves in ways inimical to profits. We have therefore made recommendations regarding the ownership and management of clinics, data bases on treatment, and laboratories with this in mind.

Testing of Products and Services

The issue of product and service testing for safety and efficacy provides a cogent illustration of a conflict of interest in the development and use of medical technologies; the interests of commercial firms and of people seeking treatment do not coincide exactly.

For commercial firms, in the absence of legal requirements, the profit motive determines what products to research and how extensively to test for safety and efficacy. Although it is often in the interests of companies to conduct a certain amount of testing and follow-up apart from that legally required, companies cannot be expected voluntarily to do the research and long-term follow-up needed to ensure that new drugs, devices, or services are safe and effective when used by large numbers of people over a significant length of time. It is in the interests of patients, however, that such testing be stringent and ongoing.

Companies that market unsafe or ineffective products and services may find themselves subject to lawsuits, and sales may be hurt by a poor reputation, so they have a certain interest in product testing.   By themselves, however, these motivations are not sufficient to protect the health of Canadians. The federal government must also require adequate testing and follow-up of new reproductive technology-related products and services to protect the interests of patients.

At present, regulations regarding the testing of medical products and services vary greatly. For example, pharmaceutical products, including fertility drugs, must be approved by the federal government before they go on the market. Pharmaceutical companies must provide evidence of a drug's safety and efficacy before this approval is granted (see Chapter 18). Long-term follow-up on the outcomes of drug use is seriously lacking, however. Nor are all medical devices and diagnostic tests closely regulated. The regulations require submission of test results and pre-marketing approval for only a small fraction of the medical devices and diagnostic tests on the market today. There is no requirement that new services, such as assisted conception techniques, be tested and approved before being provided by commercial clinics if they are provided by physicians.

We believe that appropriate testing and follow-up are essential for all new reproductive technology-related products and services, and we make recommendations throughout Part Two to ensure this. For example, we recommend ways of improving the drug approval process. We also propose a regulatory system for the provision of assisted conception and prenatal diagnosis services; the proposed National Reproductive Technologies Commission would be responsible for approving new procedures and services before they are introduced at licensed clinics. We also recommend a system of record keeping and data linkage, which would allow for improved long-term follow-up.

Marketing of Products and Services

Once a product has been developed or a commercial clinic established, companies use marketing strategies they have found effective to recoup their investment and maximize profits.

Questions have been raised about whether companies are providing the objective information that doctors and patients need as the basis for informed choice; questions have also been raised about the accuracy and comprehensiveness of information provided by pharmaceutical companies to doctors and pharmacists. Similarly, concerns have been expressed that commercial IVF and sex preselection clinics do not provide prospective patients with sufficient objective information and non-directive counselling to ensure that they can exercise informed consent.

Complete, accurate, and objective information is a precondition of informed choice, and doctors and patients must have access to such information.   We make recommendations to this effect, including the standardization of written information materials and consent forms, the monitoring of promotional literature, the need for non-directive counselling, and the provision of independent information by the National Reproductive Technologies Commission and the federal government.

Equal Access

Patients must pay for services provided at commercial clinics; those who are unable to afford the fee will not have access to the service. This creates a two-tier system, in which access to services depends on ability to pay.

The Commission strongly opposes the development of a two-tier health care system. We believe that medical services that are safe, effective, and ethically appropriate should, wherever possible, be included in provincial health plans. Some of the services currently provided are not safe or ethically appropriate, and these should not be provided at all. Others are unproven and should not be provided as treatment unless and until their safety and efficacy have been demon-strated. But we believe, based on our review of the evidence and our ethical assessment, that some reproductive technologies should be included in the publicly funded health care system. Commissioners saw the evidence that having children is an important part of people's lives. The ability to have children is not a luxury or a frill, so that effective assisted conception services for people who are infertile are as or more important than many other services already provided in the health care system. We therefore conclude that if effective and safe procedures exist and can be provided at a reasonable cost, they should be provided through the health care system. In addition, equal access to legitimate medical services is a basic principle of Canada's health care system, and we have structured our recommendations regarding the funding of services and the licensing of clinics with this in mind.

Public Subsidy of Private Clinics

Commercial clinics are seen by some as operating parallel to and complementing the publicly supported health care system. In this view, whereas the publicly supported health care system provides medically necessary services to all on the basis of medical need, commercial clinics provide what are considered optional services to those who are willing to pay. Commercial clinics are perceived as not affecting the public health care system, but simply providing additional services that the public system is unwilling to provide.

Commissioners are strongly opposed to such a view. There are compelling reasons for approved procedures to be carried out only in licensed, publicly supported clinics; principal among them is the strong evidence that commercial clinics impose many hidden costs on the public health care system. For example, although *in vitro* fertilization and embryo transfer are not an insured health service in most provinces, the cost of laboratory tests associated with the procedure is borne by the health care system. Similarly, the public health care system must cover the costs associated with the multiple births that often result from the use of fertility drugs administered at private IVF clinics. Moreover, public resources would be needed to monitor these clinics and ensure their compliance with standards of safety and informed consent, and public resources are used to train their medical and nursing personnel.

There are very strong reasons to resist private medical services or direct commercial offer of genetic testing or reproductive technology to the public. These services need to be developed within a social framework, and quality control and monitoring of service delivery are essential to protect those using the services. For example, counselling is expensive because it takes professional time, and this is likely to be minimized in private commercial services doing genetic

> The predominant force driving the pharmaceutical industry is identical to the driving force behind any other business or commercial venture — the need to make a profit on investment ... That raises the question of whether some NRTs should be provided through the private market. There are private chains of clinics in the United States, and the public/private balance could be shifted in this area. If it were to be, then we have to contemplate not only a private, profit-driven pharmaceutical industry, but a private profit-driven industry which is actually using the products of the pharmaceutical industry.
>
> Under those circumstances, it seems to me that the problems of surveillance and of appropriate utilization become even more acute. At present we are dealing with physicians whose professional motivations are to try to serve patients best, and whose limitations are simply the time and effort and the information that they have available to them. Physicians, to some extent, have interests that are at variance with those of the drug companies.
>
> *R.G. Evans, reviewer, research volumes of the Commission, September 28, 1992.*

testing. Governments have a responsibility to ensure that ad hoc private provision of these kinds of services does not occur.

Given that public funds are currently subsidizing the profit-making activities of commercial clinics providing uninsured services in many ways, we believe that this is an inappropriate use of public resources, which should be used only to provide medical services that are found effective, safe, and ethically acceptable for all Canadians. Our recommendations throughout the report reflect this conviction.

Commodification

The profit motive, taken to its extreme, would lead to a global market in reproductive materials and services. It would be possible to make a profit from the buying and selling of eggs, sperm, zygotes, embryos, and fetuses, as well as from preconception arrangements involving the hiring of "surrogate mothers." Indeed, commercial interests in other countries have already explored some of these possibilities.

As we have discussed, we believe that certain aspects of the human experience must never be commercialized. Among the activities that we see as ethically unacceptable on the basis of the principle of non-commercialization are the buying and selling of gametes, zygotes, embryos, or fetuses, and the use of financial incentives in preconception or adoption arrangements. To allow commercial exchanges of this type would undermine respect for human life and dignity and lead to the commodification of women and children. We recommend stringent· prohibitions on these forms of commercialization throughout Part Two, in the context of assisted insemination, assisted conception, prenatal diagnosis, and research involving human zygotes/embryos and fetal tissue.

> We believe that certain aspects of the human experience must never be commercialized. Among the activities that we see as ethically unacceptable on the basis of the principle of non-commercialization are the buying and selling of gametes, zygotes, embryos, or fetuses, and the use of financial incentives in preconception or adoption arrangements. To allow commercial exchanges of this type would undermine respect for human life and dignity and lead to the commodification of women and children.

Technology Transfer from Animals to Humans

Many of the new reproductive technologies used in assisted conception — such as *in vitro* fertilization, assisted insemination, and embryo freezing — are also used in animal breeding. Indeed, many of these techniques were developed initially to improve the commercial value of livestock (just as some techniques developed originally for use in human beings have been transferred to animals). For example, the genetic alteration of animal embryos is used to create new breeds of animals with commercially valuable properties.

Transfer of technology from agribusiness to human medicine is worrisome to many people who think that the transfer of technology will carry with it a transfer of values. The goals of new reproductive technology use in animals are quite different, however, from the goals of new reproductive technology use in people. New reproductive technologies are used in animals to increase the number and commercial value of the offspring, not to treat infertility. If a given technology is adapted for use in human beings, however, the concern is that it may be used for purposes similar to those motivating its use in animals, leading to the commodification of women and children.

We do not believe that technologies developed originally for commercial animal breeding purposes will be used in similar way with human beings. The values of Canadians (including both potential patients and physicians) are such that use in this way is highly unlikely. To guard against the possibility that technologies developed in animals could be transferred for inappropriate uses for human beings, and to protect the vulnerable interests involved, we make recommendations in several chapters to prohibit various uses that we consider unethical and therefore unacceptable. In addition, many of our recommendations regarding the licensing of facilities that provide new reproductive technology-related services will ensure that they are used only for non-commercial therapeutic purposes within the health care system. Finally, we have recommended the establishment of boundaries by criminalizing some uses of technology in human beings. (We discuss the transfer of technology issue in more depth in Chapter 25.)

> Technical aspects of reproductive manipulation may be similar for humans and domestic animals, but the objectives are quite different. With humans the purpose of reproduction manipulation is to benefit the individual, whereas artificial insemination (AI) and embryo transfer (ET) in domestic animals are done to improve production, which benefits farmers and, ultimately, consumers.
>
> *K. Betteridge and D. Rieger, "Embryo Transfer and Related Technologies in Domestic Animals: Their History, Current Status, and Future Direction, with Special Reference to Implications for Human Medicine," in Research Volumes of the Commission, 1993.*

In summary, commercial interests raise significant issues and concerns. There is an inherent difference of interests in any commercial transaction between seller and buyer. In the area of new reproductive technologies (as in all areas of medical care), there are vulnerable interests to be protected — interests of both individuals and the wider community.

If it remains unregulated, commercial activity in new reproductive technologies has the potential to undermine basic ethical principles and social values. In particular, active federal regulation is required to ensure that unethical uses of technology are prohibited; that Canadians' health priorities are respected; that commercial research is subject to ethical review; that the safety and efficacy of commercial products and services are properly tested; that accurate information is available to patients and physicians regarding these products and services; that conflicts of interest are managed with protection of vulnerable interests; that equitable access to services is protected; that public resources do not subsidize private profit; and that commodification is prevented.

With these boundaries and guidelines in place to protect vulnerable interests, however, we believe that commercial interests can play a legitimate role in developing and providing products and services that might not otherwise be available and that can be of benefit to many Canadians.

Patenting

Our mandate directed us to examine the role of patenting in relation to new reproductive technologies. A patent gives the inventor of a new product or process the right to prevent others from copying, using, or selling the invention for a specified number of years (typically 17 to 20 years) unless the inventor licenses someone else to make use of the product or process. In Canada, patenting is governed by the federal *Patent Act.*

One function of patent law is to encourage commercial investment in the development of useful innovations. Since we have argued that commercial interests can play a valuable (if circumscribed) role in developing new reproductive technology-related products and services, it might seem appropriate to provide a (limited) form of patent protection for some kinds of developments.

As we pursued this question, however, we discovered that very little is known about the implications of patent protection in this area. Indeed, there is some uncertainty about the extent to which the existing patent law already applies. There is no current catalogue of materials, instruments, or processes related to new reproductive technologies that have already been patented, for example, largely because not all inventions that could be used for new reproductive technologies are described in such specific terms in patent documents — to do so would potentially limit the application of the invention, which inventors understandably may not want to do.

The basic principles of patent law, formalized more than 200 years ago, were not designed to deal with some of the issues raised by modern technology, and the law is therefore in a state of flux. The very idea of patenting has become unclear, as various "hybrid" forms of intellectual property rights have evolved to meet the issues raised by new technology. For example, in Canada, a distinct patent regime has evolved for plant breeders, and pharmaceutical manufacturers also face different requirements that place greater constraints on how patent holders can use their discoveries and place more emphasis on the larger interests of society. For example, the prices of patented drugs must be reviewed by the Patented Medicine Prices Review Board to protect the public interest.

Insofar as patenting is appropriate for new reproductive technology-related discoveries, it should perhaps take the form of a "hybrid" regime. However, we believe that this entire topic needs further study. It would not be helpful for this Commission to say that patent protection should or should not be extended to new reproductive technology-related discoveries. Given the diversity of new reproductive technology-related discoveries (from medical devices such as aspiration needles to genetically altered cell lines) and the shifting nature of patent law, such a statement would inevitably be simplistic and misleading. It is more helpful, we believe, to discuss the basic issues that need to be considered when assessing patenting policy in this area and to outline the principles that should guide such a policy and the boundaries within which it should operate.

To begin with, we believe that two clear boundaries must be set on patenting — patenting should not extend to medical treatments or to human eggs, sperm, zygotes, embryos, or fetuses.

Medical Treatments

A significant part of the first boundary is already in place. Innovative medical treatments performed on the human body are not subject to patent protection in Canada. There are several public policy reasons for this, including the need for unimpeded access to medical treatments, the need for impartial evaluation of their success, and the avoidance of conflict of interest for physicians. So an innovative treatment for infertility performed on the body would not be patentable, just as a new technique for treating cancer could not be patented.

However, innovative diagnostic tests and medical devices used in medical treatments can be patented in Canada. It is not entirely clear why medical tests and devices are patentable, while medical treatments are not. This distinction seems to have worked in the past in other areas of health care, but it would be necessary to ensure that the patenting of new reproductive technology-related gene probes and medical devices did not preclude adequate testing of their safety and efficacy and did not create conflicts of interest for new reproductive technology service providers or impede access to treatment.

Zygotes, Embryos, and Fetuses

Commissioners believe strongly that human zygotes, embryos, and fetuses are inappropriate subject matter for intellectual property protection. (Zygotes, embryos, and fetuses would not normally be classified as "innovations," but if they have been the subject of genetic alteration or other research, some may attempt to classify them in this way.) Inherent in the moral point of view and respect for human life is abhorrence of any recognition of property interests of one human being in another; as entities that may have the potential for human life, zygotes, embryos, and fetuses should not be patentable.

Intellectual property rights have not been recognized historically in relation to human fetuses and embryos. Although the *Patent Act* does not expressly forbid the patenting of higher life forms, to date none has been patented in Canada, nor have the courts addressed the issue of whether higher life forms are patentable. In the only case to date in this area, the 1989 *Pioneer Hi-Bred Limited* case, a patent was refused for a new type of soybean plant, but the case did not answer the question of whether a higher life form is patentable, because it was decided on other grounds.

However, the Patent Office does allow the patenting of innovative "microbial life forms." In addition to lower organisms, such as altered viruses, yeasts, and algae, the term "microbial life forms" also refers to cell lines derived from higher organisms, including human beings. Generally speaking, then, human cell lines are patentable if they meet the standards laid out in the *Patent Act*. Patentable inventions must be a novel creation or innovation, not just the discovery of a pre-existing naturally occurring phenomenon, they must be reproducible, and they must have some useful function. However, if researchers find a way to make human cells reproduce indefinitely (a process called immortalizing the cell line) and find a use for them, these cell lines can be patented, even though they already "exist" in nature, if they meet the act's criteria. Similarly, the processes associated with handling, preserving, altering, and using these cell lines can also be patented.

Human cell lines are derived from various tissues of the body, including fetal and embryonic tissue. Although embryos and fetuses cannot be patented, processes, techniques, and cell lines, not only using adult human tissue, but also using tissue from embryos and fetuses, may be entitled to such protection if they meet the act's criteria. For example, pancreatic cell lines used to make insulin are patented, as is the process for making insulin, and human cells that were used to make artificial skin have also been patented. Developing and perfecting such techniques and keeping such cell lines could require a sizable financial investment, beyond what public agencies may be willing or able to provide. Pharmaceutical or biotechnology firms might provide the investment if they have a reasonable expectation of profit, which in turn may depend on the type and extent of patent protection.

Thus, it is possible that the current patent protection for human cell lines will have beneficial consequences for Canadians; at the same time, however, concerns have been raised about the patenting of human cell lines. Some people view this as the first step toward commodifying human life. Will patenting of cell lines derived from human tissue encourage forms of research that may be unethical or socially undesirable? For example, cell lines derived from human tissue could be useful not only in improving transplantation therapy but also in developing cosmetic products. How can limits be set to encourage research into appropriate but not inappropriate uses?

These are some of the issues that need to be addressed by any proposal regarding new patent protection or alterations to existing patent protection in this area. It may be possible to shape a patent regime that promotes desirable research while avoiding these problems of commodification and unethical research. Although clearly zygotes, embryos, fetuses, eggs, and sperm should not be patentable, the problems of commodification and unethical research have more to do with the larger regulatory system within which the patent regime operates than with patenting per se.

We have recommended stringent legislation against the buying and selling of gametes, zygotes, embryos, and fetal tissue. This legislative prohibition would set the boundaries within which any patenting of microbial life forms would operate. Provided such a prohibition is in place, patent protection for cell lines may not, by itself, lead to the commodification of human life. However, if a law prohibiting the sale of gametes, zygotes, embryos, and fetal tissue were not in place, withdrawing patent protection from cell lines would not by itself eliminate the problem of commodifying human life. Patents are not the only reason why people might buy and sell gametes or fetal tissue.

We have also recommended establishment of a licensing system to regulate the use of zygotes and fetal tissue in research, including a requirement for research ethics board approval of all such research (see Chapters 22 and 31). If such a licensing scheme is put in place, patent protection for cell lines will not promote or allow the use of fetal tissue in cosmetics, or other socially undesirable research. Again, if this regulatory regime is not established, then withdrawing patent protection would not solve the problem, since patents are not the only reason why people might engage in unethical research.

In other words, although patenting human cell lines raises certain concerns, we need to distinguish those problems that are intrinsic to patenting from those that result from the lack of adequate safeguards elsewhere in the regulatory system. Moreover, it is important to remember that traditional intellectual property regimes are no longer clear-cut legal categories. Many different kinds of intellectual property regimes are possible, and governments can create "hybrid" regimes. Moreover, governments can require additional approvals that modify the rights of the patent holder in order to protect the public interest. For example, the government could establish a rigorous approval process for certain new reproductive technology-related products, just as pharmaceutical companies must receive federal approval before marketing their patented drugs.

Clearly, this topic deserves further study. The possible forms of regimes are too many, and the existing literature too sparse, for us to generate a specific proposal for how patent legislation should be drafted. Instead, we have outlined the principles that we believe should inform public policy in this area. We believe it is important to encourage research that can potentially benefit human health, and that patenting can play a role in encouraging private investment in such research. However, any patent policy must operate within clear boundaries that preclude the patenting of medical treatments, and of human zygotes, embryos, fetuses, eggs, and sperm. Moreover, patenting in the fields of medical care, health, and reproductive technologies must be situated within a larger regulatory system that deals with issues of commodification, access to treatment, conflicts of interest, quality control, the ethical review of research, and other related matters.

We believe that the best body to engage in this further study of patenting is the National Reproductive Technologies Commission, given the access it will have to information regarding the development and provision of new reproductive technology-related products and services and its representative nature. We therefore recommend that

> **206. The National Reproductive Technologies Commission, in collaboration with Industry and Science Canada (Canadian Intellectual Property Office), undertake further study of the issue of intellectual property protection in the area of new reproductive technologies with a view to making recommendations to the federal government for any necessary amendments to the *Patent Act*.**

Conclusion

In this chapter we have provided an overview of the extent of commercial interests in the development and marketing of new reproductive technologies in Canada. We have also discussed our view about the appropriate role of these interests and the need to provide limits and regulation so as to protect vulnerable individual and societal interests.

We found that new reproductive technologies are not a large part of the pharmaceutical, biotechnological, medical devices, or commercial medical services sectors in Canada; nonetheless, the experience in the United States shows that commercial interests may drive the development and provision of new reproductive technology-related services and technologies if they remain unregulated

It is essential, therefore, that the federal government, as the guardian of the public interest, strictly regulate the research, testing, and marketing activities of commercial interests ... The current window of opportunity will not remain open indefinitely, and we believe it is therefore incumbent upon the federal government to act while it is still possible to do so in this rapidly evolving field.

and may lead to the development and provision of unsafe, inappropriate, or unethical services. It is essential, therefore, that the federal government, as the guardian of the public interest, strictly regulate the research, testing, and marketing activities of commercial interests. Vulnerable interests must be protected, including those of patients, research subjects, and the broader community. We believe that the federal government has full constitutional authority to exercise this role, both under its power to regulate trade and commerce and intellectual property, and under the peace, order, and good government clause. The role of government is to protect the public interest; the current window of opportunity will not remain open indefinitely, and we believe it is therefore incumbent upon the federal government to act while it is still possible to do so in this rapidly evolving field. The implementation of our strong recommendation for a National Reproductive Technologies Commission would be the major instrument in ensuring this needed regulation.

Our specific recommendations on how best to limit or regulate commercial interests so that vulnerable interests are protected (to be carried out by policies of the NRTC sub-committees) are discussed in chapters dealing with specific technologies, procedures, and services. These recommendations include prohibiting the inappropriate commercialization of technologies and services; strengthening the procedures governing the testing of new products and services and their approval for use; monitoring the promotional and marketing activities of commercial interests; ensuring ethical review of industry-funded research; and licensing service provision to ensure quality control and provision of objective information to prospective patients. Adoption of these recommendations would ensure that the commercial impetus is contained and regulated so that the vulnerable interests of individuals and society are protected.

General Sources

Achilles, R. "Donor Insemination: An Overview." In Research Volumes of the Royal Commission on New Reproductive Technologies, 1993.

Chaloner-Larsson, G., F. Haynes, and C. Merritt. "The Role of the Biotechnology Industry in the Development of Clinical Diagnostic Materials for Prenatal Diagnosis." In Research Volumes of the Royal Commission on New Reproductive Technologies, 1993.

Cherniawsky, K.M., and P.J.M. Lown. "New Reproductive Technologies: Commercial Protection." In Research Volumes of the Royal Commission on New Reproductive Technologies, 1993.

Dickens, B.M. "Legal Issues in Embryo and Fetal Tissue Research and Therapy." In Research Volumes of the Royal Commission on New Reproductive Technologies, 1993.

Evans, R.G. *Strained Mercy: The Economics of Canadian Health Care.* Toronto: Butterworths, 1984.

Industrial Biotechnology Association of Canada. *Canadian Biotechnology Directory 1990-91.* Ottawa: Winter House Scientific Publications, 1990.

Litman, M.M., and G.B. Robertson. "Reproductive Technology: Is a Property Law Regime Appropriate?" In Research Volumes of the Royal Commission on New Reproductive Technologies, 1993.

Martin, M., et al. "The Limits of Freedom of Contract: The Commercialization of Reproductive Materials and Services." In Research Volumes of the Royal Commission on New Reproductive Technologies, 1993.

Rochon Ford, A. "An Overview of Select Social and Economic Forces Influencing the Development of *In Vitro* Fertilization and Related Assisted Reproductive Techniques." In Research Volumes of the Royal Commission on New Reproductive Technologies, 1993.

SPR Associates Inc. "Report on a Survey of Members of the Pharmaceutical Manufacturers Association of Canada and Biotechnology Companies." In Research Volumes of the Royal Commission on New Reproductive Technologies, 1993.

Specific References

1. Rowlands, J., N. Saby, and J. Smith. "Commercial Involvement in New Reproductive Technologies: An Overview." In Research Volumes of the Royal Commission on New Reproductive Technologies, 1993. A similar conclusion was reached by a 1989 Science Council of Canada survey of Canadian biotechnology companies to determine their involvement in technology development and/or service delivery related to genetic diseases. See Science Council of Canada.

Genetics in Canadian Health Care. Report 42. Ottawa: Minister of Supply and Services Canada, 1991, p. 95.

2. The size of the market for fertility drugs in Canada is approximately $16 million, or about four-tenths of 1 percent of the total $4.2 billion Canadian pharmaceutical market. Rowlands et al., "Commercial Involvement in New Reproductive Technologies."

3. The Ares-Serono Group. *Annual Report 1990.* Geneva: Ares-Serono Group, 1990, p. 22.

4. Ubelacter, S. "Sperm Donors: Only the Best Make the Grade." *The Montreal Gazette,* January 23, 1992.

5. United States. Congress. Office of Technology Assessment. *Artificial Insemination: Practice in the United States, Summary of a 1987 Survey, Background Paper.* Washington: U.S. Government Printing Office, 1988.

6. Ryten, E. "The Funding of Research Conducted by Canadian Faculties of Medicine." *ACMC Forum* XXIV (3)(1991): 1-6.

7. Canada. Statistics Canada. "Science Statistics." *Service Bulletin* (Cat. No. 88-001) 16 (2)(June 1992), p. 3.

25

Prenatal Diagnosis and Genetic Technologies: Introduction and Social Context

◆

For many Canadians, genetic research and the application of genetic technology embody a basic human conflict — the drive to expand the boundaries of knowledge and apply it for the benefit of humankind, contrasted with the equally real feeling that some mysteries of life should not be tampered with. This perceived conflict is often heightened by the fact that the field is evolving rapidly, often without the social debate necessary to develop a public understanding and response to its implications, and without reliable information available for the public upon which to base such a debate.

Although many areas of study relate to genetics, the Commission's mandate was to examine in particular those aspects of genetic knowledge and technology that apply to human reproduction. Myriad other endeavours are related to genetics — the mapping of human genes currently taking place as part of the international Human Genome Project (see box), for example, or the genetic manipulation of livestock and plants. These issues were outside the Commission's mandate and indeed constitute a vast field of study on their own. Although the Commission's work was necessarily limited to genetics as it relates to new reproductive technologies, it was clear during our work that many of the broader issues involving genetics are troubling for Canadians and should continue to be addressed by other bodies as they evolve.

The Commission identified four applications of genetic knowledge and practice that relate to reproduction. Although each uses genetic knowledge and technology to identify genetic make-up before birth, the application of technology is very different in each case, as are the issues raised by its use.

The first application — prenatal diagnosis for genetic diseases and anomalies — employs techniques such as amniocentesis for identification of fetal anomalies. It has become a well-known part of pregnancy care for women who are at higher risk. Canada's approach to introducing and regulating some PND techniques such as amniocentesis has served as a model internationally. Canadians see PND for those at risk of having an affected fetus as a valuable health care service, yet there were aspects of PND delivery that warranted the Commission's attention. The challenge facing Commissioners was to determine whether PND is offered in the best interests of women and society, to assess the effect of PND use on societal attitudes toward disability and people with disabilities, and to recommend how best to manage the system, ensuring that Canada is prepared to deal with emerging issues and developments in this field.

The Human Genome Project

The Human Genome Project is an international effort, spearheaded and coordinated by the United States, to determine the structure and location of the estimated 100 000 human genes. First conceived in 1986, the project involves research teams around the world working to sequence the DNA, which is contained within human cells. It is hoped that the information gained will lead to the eventual cure of many genetic diseases. To date, about 5 percent of the genes have been identified and mapped, and researchers expect to complete the project by the year 2005. Countries involved include Japan, France, Britain, Germany, Denmark, and Italy, and Canada joined the project in 1992. The Commission did not examine the Human Genome Project per se, as our mandate asked us to examine genetic research and technology as they relate to human reproduction, and reproductive technology in particular.

A second use of PND technology is prenatal testing for late-onset disorders (diseases or conditions that can be identified before birth but do not manifest themselves until adulthood) and susceptibility genes (genes shown to increase an individual's susceptibility to certain conditions that may or may not develop later in life, such as cancers or heart disease). This technology is not in general use at present, and the Commission therefore had the opportunity to research and deliberate on its implications before development goes further. We found, for example, that this technology raises issues with respect to informed consent and confidentiality, as well as concerns about appropriate counselling for those contemplating or receiving testing, and whether it is an appropriate use of medical resources.

Ethical and social issues are also raised by a third use of PND technology — sex selection for non-medical reasons. Genetic technology can reliably identify the sex of a fetus prenatally; this capacity can be used to identify fetuses at risk of genetic diseases linked to one sex or the other. The Commission had to evaluate whether using genetic technology to identify fetal sex is appropriate or acceptable when the presence or absence of genetic diseases is not at issue.

The fourth area of interest to the Commission, gene therapy, is the newest and most complex. This use of technology not only identifies genetic diseases and anomalies, but seeks to cure these conditions by introducing normal genes either pre- or post-natally. Although gene therapy is an emerging technology and has not been attempted in human beings in Canada, it is an expanding field. It is one that raises concerns for many Canadians if the technology were to be used to change the genetic make-up of human beings for reasons other than severe disease. The Commission had a rare opportunity to examine and evaluate a technology, and to analyze its social, ethical, and generational implications, before it becomes a reality in this country. There is an opportunity to recommend policy to set parameters around further development in light of these implications.

The Commission examined these four areas of application of genetic knowledge using the same approach as we did with the other reproductive technologies. Current practices, as well as potential implications for society and for future generations of Canadians, were investigated through wide-ranging research projects in fields such as ethics, sociology, law, and other disciplines, as well as through field studies at clinics across the country. Our findings are detailed in our research volumes entitled *Prenatal Diagnosis: Background and Impact on Individuals*; *Current Practice of Prenatal Diagnosis in Canada*; and *Prenatal Diagnosis: New and Future Developments*. We reached our conclusions and recommendations in light of our ethical principles and also using the approach of evidence-based medicine, which we discussed in Part One of this report. The wide ethical and social implications of technology use were evaluated with the help of commissioned studies, data gathering, and analyses.

> As the public becomes more and more involved in the debate over new reproductive technologies, PND in particular, professionals are being called upon to explain their role in modern medicine and to justify the development of controversial technologies. Increasingly, scientists and health care professionals have to pay close attention not only to professional interests but also to their societal responsibilities. These challenges help to promulgate informed and expert information and opinion on complex and challenging issues.
>
> *I. MacKay and F.C. Fraser, "The History and Evolution of Prenatal Diagnosis," in Research Volumes of the Commission, 1993.*

The Commission investigation revealed interesting and, in some cases, worrisome data. We found, for instance, that researchers and practitioners in these fields overall have not managed to convey adequate information to the public about what genetic services in Canada do. There was little public awareness and much misunderstanding of the technologies. We found that the counselling and information needs of some women undergoing PND were not met. Variation in beliefs and attitudes toward the prenatal diagnostic procedures by physicians referring patients for genetic testing in particular alerted us to troubling implications for patient care and access.

The gaps in public information are not solely the responsibility of researchers and practitioners. Despite the complexity of the issues surrounding these technologies, sensational and oversimplified articles continue to appear in the science, business, and popular press. Although most of these technologies have very limited application and in fact affect only a small proportion of the population, there is a perception that genetic testing has become a large industry, with widespread use of the technologies. Misinformation has contributed to the formation of public knowledge and attitudes in this area.

Another theme that emerged from our investigation of PND and applied genetics was the importance of assessing technology before it is introduced into wide practice. For instance, Canada has been a leader in the field of clinical testing of invasive prenatal diagnosis technologies used at specialized genetics centres, such as amniocentesis and chorionic villus sampling; but non-invasive screening technologies in use in the wider medical community, such as prenatal ultrasound scanning, have not followed the same careful path of technology assessment. Ultrasound use has proliferated to a point where today at least 80 percent of pregnant women in Canada are screened, at enormous cost to the health care system, while there is still debate about whether this procedure is of benefit. These and many other issues are examined in the next four chapters.

From a public policy perspective, addressing the issues raised by PND and genetic technologies involves questions of how to ensure effective and ethical management of the introduction and use of the technologies; it is important to put in place mechanisms to ensure the provision of accountable, effective, and safe health care for women and their children.

The Commission's investigation confirmed the view that these powerful technologies have the potential for rapid development. As existing technology is improved and new technologies are introduced, decisions in this area will become more complex and difficult. The Commission concludes that coordinated national and provincial efforts are called for, to reflect a societal commitment to monitor developments and to set in place systems to ensure adherence to standards of research and practice. The following chapters show how this conclusion flows from the evidence before the Commission.

Our conclusion reflects Commissioners' commitment to an ethic of care, to weighing of individual and collective interests, and to protection of vulnerable interests. The implications of applications of genetic knowledge and technologies vary according to the use proposed and the interests involved; the policy responses must take this into account. The goal of our recommendations is to achieve an integrated system of services and standards and to provide a policy framework that allows for responsiveness as technology evolves, but within a framework that always takes social and ethical aspects into account.

Research and practices in genetic reproductive technologies occur within the framework of the health care system, but the issues they raise have implications for society as a whole. The remainder of this introductory chapter examines the values and attitudes of Canadians with respect to this field and the common themes raised by Canadians about the use of the technologies.

The Views of Canadians

The use of genetic knowledge and technology as relevant to human reproduction was an area of concern for participants in public hearings, private sessions, roundtables, panel discussions, and written submissions. Many individuals and groups presented their views. The Commission heard many concerns about specific technologies — addressed in each of the following chapters — but we also heard opinions about genetics in general. The Commission's national surveys revealed aspects of the overall social context in which PND and genetic technologies are developed and used; some of these concerns were discussed in a general sense in Part One. Some of the issues seemed to produce general agreement among Canadians. There was significant support evident for the use of PND to detect genetic disease, for example, with 84 percent of Canadians overall in favour of its use. An even stronger consensus emerged on the issue of sex selection — 92 percent of Canadians are strongly opposed to the abortion of a fetus when the sex was not the one the parents hoped for.

The public dialogue on the applications of genetics to human reproduction led Commissioners to appreciate the range of views apparent among Canadians — an appreciation that informed our investigations. Some groups representing those carrying or affected by a genetic disorder, for example, argued for the need for genetic research with the goal of effective treatment or cure; others expressed concern about the implications of such research and advocated a moratorium. Several themes in the area of genetics and new reproductive technologies emerged and seemed to define many Canadians' views about new reproductive technologies in general.

"The Future Is Here"

Growing public awareness of and concern about the power of genetics were evident in public consultations with the Commission. Many Canadians expressed fears about what the rapidly increasing capacity to detect genetic make-up would mean for their work opportunities, how they live, and, particularly, the health care they receive and their options with respect to reproduction. Others called for a social policy debate on the emerging role of genetics in Canadian society.

For some, discoveries in the world of genetics are moving at a rate that is simply too fast for society to comprehend, let alone manage. In our national survey, for instance, 35 percent of respondents agreed with the statement that medical science is moving too fast for society to keep up. Many feel that the future is upon us without the chance of proper evaluation and assessment by members of society other than scientists and doctors.

Some felt that genetic technology was market-driven — that commercial interests, not the interests of society, have determined the nature and direction of developments. Some advocated a moratorium in the research, to give governments and the public time to assess the social, ethical, and legal implications before science moves further, but there was little testimony on how this could be implemented in practice.

In the meanwhile it appears that every week new so-called advances are being made in the fields of human reproductive technologies and recombinant DNA research ... We have reached a stage in a technological development where the unthinkable is already being done and the ability to impose total genetic control seems just beyond our reach.

F. Bazos, private citizen, Public Hearings Transcripts, Toronto, Ontario, November 20, 1990.

Some responded on a personal level, showing concern about whether women are being pressured or compelled to use genetic diagnostic technology simply because it exists, not because they wish to do so. Concerns were raised that the proliferation of such technologies compels women to feel that using the technology is "the responsible thing to do," despite the fact that some intervenors felt not enough societal debate had taken place on the usefulness or impact of the technologies.

The potential for the dehumanization and depersonalization of humankind is very real and very frightening. Scientists who practise genetic manipulation, a term considered by many to be offensive, are in fact tampering with nature.

C. Johnson, Federated Women's Institutes of Canada, Public Hearings Transcripts, Winnipeg, Manitoba, October 23, 1990.

The Commission examined current practices, existing guidelines, and research in these fields in Canada. We developed recommendations that, if implemented, will protect the vulnerable interests of individuals and of society and promote greater public information and accountability. Our recommendations will also allow a well-informed public debate about the implications of the use of genetic technology. Our commitment to evidence-based medicine and our guiding principles, including the appropriate use of health care resources, helped us map out a strong framework within which ethical and accountable research and development in these areas can occur. The details of our recommendations with respect to particular technologies, and how their implementation would ensure ethical and responsible development in this area, are explained in the chapters that follow.

Hope for Treatment and Cure

Along with concerns about the need for social control over the development and use of genetic technology, Commissioners heard from Canadians who were personally affected by genetic disease. Many told their stories to the Commission and emphasized that PND had offered them a chance to have a healthy child, while genetic research offered the hope of treatment or cure.

We heard throughout our consultations that it may not be the technologies themselves but rather how technologies are applied that causes concerns for Canadians. In the case of gene therapy, for example, the Commission heard that research into the identification and treatment of specific genetic diseases and anomalies is acceptable and in fact should be encouraged; but the application of the same kind of technology to identify and alter non-medical characteristics would be unacceptable even if it became possible. We heard from people opposed to the use of PND for various reasons, but we also heard from couples who had had a child die of a severe genetic disease and who felt that PND had given them their only chance of having a healthy child; without it, they would have felt unable to have children.

> Gene therapy must be encouraged to help people with diseases have hope for a treatment in their lifetime. In the next decade, the window on our genetic blueprint is going to open wider and wider, and it is important that we develop the kinds of programs that make this knowledge useful and applicable, so people like myself won't just get the news that they are likely to die of a disease or their children will likely have a disease but will have some options: options for treatments, options for predictive testing and options for family planning.
>
> *T. Jung, private citizen, Public Hearings Transcripts, Vancouver, British Columbia, November 27, 1990.*

The Potential for Discrimination

People with Disabilities

Some Canadians fear that the application of genetic knowledge to identify fetuses with anomalies could lead to social discrimination against specific groups of people or segments of society. Those representing people with disabilities were concerned that the use of PND might devalue these groups in Canadian society or perpetuate discriminatory attitudes. We also attempted to find out how different sectors of society see these issues — for instance, ethnocultural or Aboriginal communities. We learned, for example, that the issues may have particular significance to some people in Aboriginal communities, where some feel that people with disabilities are thought to have a special relationship with the Creator.

> Just as society is beginning to open the door to people with disabilities, who have been shut out for so long, NRTs are creating new ways of devaluing the disabled by attempting the creation of the perfect child.
>
> *J. Rebick, National Action Committee on the Status of Women, Public Hearings Transcripts, Toronto, Ontario, October 29, 1990.*

We heard two overall concerns about the use of genetic technologies from people with disabilities. They saw the use of PND to identify fetuses with genetic diseases and anomalies as being aimed largely at eliminating such conditions, and they were concerned it would lead to social devaluation of people with disabilities. They felt that the uncritical existence and acceptance of these technologies reflect and reinforce discriminatory attitudes toward people with disabilities. The second concern was that public resources used in the research, development, and delivery of PND and genetic technologies would detract from the already limited resources available for programs and supports for people with disabilities and their families.

> With the tremendous advances being made in recombinant DNA technology, the capability exists to detect a greater number of disease-related genes, often in presymptomatic individuals. Who should have access to this information? What right has the patient to confidentiality? How might this affect the relationship between industry, employer, and potential employee?
>
> *J. Jung, Regional Medical Genetics Centre, Fetal Development Clinic, and Reproductive Endocrinology Committee of the University of Western Ontario, Public Hearings Transcripts, London, Ontario, November 2, 1990.*

Women

Groups representing women told the Commission that prenatal diagnosis used to detect the sex of the fetus could be used in discriminatory ways. Many women told the Commission that any acceptance of non-medical sex selection would devalue women in society.

Many intervenors were also concerned about the impact of the technologies on the pregnant women who use them. Women's groups asked whether all women have equal access to the technologies, whether they are subject to pressure or coercion to use the technologies or to abort a pregnancy if a genetic disease or anomaly is found, and whether patients receive appropriate counselling and support to help them make personally appropriate choices about testing, treatment, and care.

We heard clearly that Canadians do not condone the use of reproductive technologies in discriminatory ways. We investigated the potential effects of the use of genetic knowledge applied to prenatal diagnosis in such ways at great length. The Commission's recommendations reflect our ethic of care, and we strongly reject the non-medical use of PND or genetic technologies, or their use in discriminatory ways that devalue being female.

Individuals Identified as Being at Genetic Risk

The Commission also heard concerns that genetic screening technologies could be used in the population at large, and that individuals identified as being at risk of genetic disease or susceptibility could be discriminated against. The use of genetic identification outside the context of reproduction is outside our mandate — this is one of the broader issues raised by genetic knowledge alluded to at the beginning of this chapter. However, the concern raises issues that are relevant to our mandate with regard to the confidentiality of information gained through prenatal testing. We make recommendations with regard to protection of information gained from prenatal genetic testing so that it is not misused, and so that individuals with particular genotypes are not discriminated against in employment or insurance coverage.

Concerns About Future Developments and Technology Transfer from Animals

During the Commission's public hearings, some intervenors raised concerns about the similarities between technologies used in domestic animal breeding and those used to assist conception in human beings. Among the concerns raised were that women and reproduction could be exploited and commodified if techniques perfected in the agriculture industry were transferred to the human situation without regard to social and ethical values.

As we discussed in Chapter 24, the transfer of technology between animals and human beings is common in medicine and in fact is generally considered desirable. Indeed, the Medical Research Council's research guidelines require that the safety and efficacy of techniques to be used in people be researched first using animals, if possible. Animal models are also used widely where possible in research intended to benefit human beings. This approach is also part of the international standards set under the Helsinki Declaration. Research involving laboratory animals has permitted the evaluation of new surgical techniques, immunization, new drugs, transplantation, and other strategies. Such research is a widely accepted part of medicine, if carried out in an ethical and regulated way with protections for the animals involved.

> I personally feel that the manipulation or engineering of the human genome is an unacceptable form of public health management.
>
> *D. Tkachuk, private citizen, Public Hearings Transcripts, Vancouver, British Columbia, November 26, 1990.*

The concern about technology transfer with respect to the manipulation of zygotes is not that they were tested originally on animals, but rather that they were developed to increase the profitability of livestock breeding and that, if they were applied in a similar way in human beings, it would be detrimental to the best interests of women and of society. Commercial interests and the interests of women and society are not identical. Some intervenors feared that technology transfer from commercial livestock breeding to human medicine could bring with it commercial values and goals.

> Canadians are deeply concerned about what technological development has done to nature. I don't think we can assume that they are or should be less concerned about what technology can do to themselves, to human nature.
>
> *C. Cassidy, Citizens for Public Justice, Public Hearings Transcripts, Toronto, Ontario, October 29, 1990.*

This is an important issue, and one that should be examined to see whether measures are needed to limit or regulate any such transfer. In the view of Commissioners, transfer of technologies from use in animals to use in human beings is detrimental only if inappropriate technologies, or inappropriate uses of a technology, are transferred. It is important that the goals are not transferred along with transfer of knowledge and technology. Research with animals, where possible, is an ethical prerequisite to research with humans. Applying knowledge about reproductive technologies gained through research involving animals is desirable, then, provided such applications occur in an ethically acceptable way and in a way that results in benefits for women and society.

Animal Research and Assisted Human Conception

Successful zygote transfer occurred up to 44 years earlier in domestic animal species than in human beings (sheep, 1934; pig and cow, 1951; horse, 1974). However, the source of zygotes was either surgery or uterine flushing, not *in vitro* fertilization of eggs. IVF was not used on domestic animals because animal zygotes would not develop *in vitro* past the two- to eight-cell stage, and zygotes at that early stage of development failed to implant in the uterus. Since animal zygotes had to be at a more developed (morula or blastocyst) stage before they implanted, animal breeders relied on uterine flushing or surgery, not IVF, as their source of zygotes.

When scientists started researching IVF techniques in human beings in the 1960s, therefore, they were not applying a technology that was already in use in animal breeding. On the contrary, research on human IVF led to the first birth of a child conceived *in vitro* in 1978, whereas subsequent work in cattle resulted in the birth of the first IVF cow in 1982. So the use of IVF in human medical research predated its use in animal breeding.

The use of endoscopy and ultrasonography during IVF procedures in human beings has stimulated their analogous use in animals, and the recent discovery that growth hormones used in conjunction with ovarian stimulation in human beings enhances the maturation of eggs for retrieval has led to the use of similar procedures in pigs, sheep, and cattle.

Conversely, knowledge gained from efforts to enhance livestock production has greatly improved techniques to alleviate infertility in human beings. Many aspects of human IVF procedures regarding the handling of zygotes were derived from studies on animals. For example, the first successes with frozen human zygotes were owed entirely to processes developed in animals.

The recent discovery that adding somatic cells to the *in vitro* culture medium may improve the maturation of human zygotes was also based on research related to livestock breeding. The development of techniques to support the maturation of animal zygotes to the morula or blastocyst stage has been the focus of a great deal of research because, as noted earlier, animal zygotes can be transferred successfully only at those later stages. The "co-culturing" technique using somatic cells has proved the most successful of these techniques and is now being applied to human zygotes; if successful, IVF practitioners may decide in future to transfer human zygotes at the blastocyst stage (four to seven days) instead of at the two- to eight-cell stage (two to three days). This would enable better identification of developmentally compromised zygotes; if only healthy zygotes were transferred, a better chance of live birth is thought to be likely.

The Commission investigated the history of assisted reproduction in livestock and its relationship to human assisted reproduction. The research clearly confirmed the interdependence between technologies developed for use in livestock and those used in human beings; a glance at the dates of milestones in assisted reproduction shows that the migration of knowledge and procedures has been two-way (see box). This two-way process of technology transfer is likely to continue. Some of the areas for potential transfer of technology developed in work on animal breeding to the human situation include the following:

- the evaluation of zygote viability before transfer, based on metabolic activity;

- the improvement of techniques of freezing and thawing, particularly of eggs; and

- genetic diagnosis by molecular techniques.

As we have made clear, however, only some technologies and only some uses of these technologies are acceptable for technology transfer. Any use of technology in humans should be in the service of ethically appropriate goals. With this in mind, in the remainder of this introduction to prenatal diagnosis we briefly review some specialized and experimental techniques of zygote manipulation in animals and their possible future relevance to human IVF research.

Micromanipulation of Zygotes and Embryos

Micromanipulation is a rapidly advancing technique whereby early animal zygotes or gametes can be altered structurally and functionally using minute, specialized instruments while looking through a microscope.

Broadly speaking, zygotes can be divided or combined at various developmental stages up to and including the blastocyst stage. The simplest application is "embryo splitting" to produce limited numbers of genetically identical animals. This has been used commercially to a limited extent for several years. Most recently, this technique has been extended to produce zygotes and calves from separated cells (blastomeres) from 4- to 16-cell cattle zygotes. This has been referred to, inaccurately, as "cloning" (see below).

Parts of different zygotes of the same or even different animal species can also be combined. This procedure is potentially significant in the preservation of endangered species because it may allow the embryos thus created to be gestated in the uterus of another closely related species. The cells of the "combined" zygote that invade the uterine wall come from the host species, while the inner cell mass giving rise to the embryo comes from the related endangered species.

In October 1993, researchers from the United States reported the first successful splitting of human zygotes into component cells, permitting a zygote with the same genetic information to develop from each one of the cells. It has been said that this technique may be of use in future to assist infertile couples by making more zygotes available.

However, this technique of zygote splitting and manipulation has no foreseeable ethically acceptable application to the human situation, and points to the need in Canada for a system of appropriate limits, accountability, and regulation with regard to new reproductive technologies. Its use in human zygotes offends respect for human life and dignity and provides no benefit that cannot be achieved in other, ethically acceptable ways. For example, if the goal were to enable a couple to have two children using IVF techniques, zygotes not needed for a first attempt could be frozen for later use, or a second egg retrieval procedure could be done.

Cloning (Nuclear Substitution)

Forty years ago, researchers discovered that tadpoles could develop from embryos produced by substituting the nucleus from a frog embryo cell for that of an egg that had had its nucleus removed. Since then, embryos have been produced by similar techniques in other species — amphibians, fish, mice, rabbits, sheep, pigs, and cattle.

The nucleus of a cell is taken from a zygote and placed in the cytoplasm of an egg. The resultant embryo is thus composed of the nuclear genetic material of the embryonic animal and the cytoplasmic structures and contents of the egg. The significance of the procedure in some species (it does not work in mice, for example) is that each of the cells from a particular zygote can be used to produce another zygote when put into an egg. This process may produce several embryos with exactly the same nuclear genotype as the one original zygote. Moreover, after each resulting zygote has gone through several cell divisions, the process could be repeated. In animals, breeding is directed, so that valuable zygotes can be identified. In theory, there may be no limit to the number of copies of a commercially valuable zygote that might be produced in this way. An important difference in humans is that the qualities of the zygote that could give rise to these multiple "copies" cannot be known in advance.

This technique is in commercial use, and patent rights are currently under legal dispute. Recent reports from these operations have shown increased spontaneous abortion rates, excessive birth weights, congenital anomalies, and perinatal death in calves arising from "cloned" zygotes. These problems will have to be rectified before this technique could become commercially useful. Even if it were possible in human beings, this technique would have no foreseeable ethical application.

Sex-Selective Zygote Transfer

An ability to select the sex of offspring would be of substantial benefit to livestock producers in a variety of situations. For example, commercial dairy farming requires a continual supply of heifers, but bull calves are of less commercial value. In contrast, in beef operations, bull calves are considered more desirable because of their higher rates of weight gain, though heifer calves may be required for some types of specialized beef production. For a variety of reasons, animal researchers are seeking to develop non-invasive methods of sexing at the zygote stage. For example, it may be possible to distinguish between male and female zygotes *in vitro* on the basis of quantitative differences in metabolic activity. Such a discovery, if transferable to human beings, might have advantages over the biopsy method currently used to test for sex-linked genetic disorders. Any such transfer of knowledge should be evaluated in light of the values it supports or promotes. Our recommendations on this subject are set out in Chapter 28, where we recommend that sex selection for non-medical reasons be prohibited.

Genetic Alteration of Zygotes

Genetic alteration of animal zygotes is of interest in two ways at present: the production of livestock with higher rates of growth and the possibility of transferring genes into animals so they produce novel proteins, particularly pharmaceutical compounds of significance to human medicine. Particular human genes could be transferred to cattle, for example, in order to produce pharmaceutically important proteins in milk, which could then be concentrated and purified to provide a supply of these compounds for treatment of diseases. In the popular press, this has become known as "genepharming."

In 1982, researchers found that injecting the rat growth hormone gene into one-cell mouse zygotes sometimes produced mice that had greater-than-normal growth after birth. This report was of immense significance to all areas of the life sciences; to animal scientists it was of interest because increased growth rates may be a highly desirable trait for purposes of livestock production. Major efforts were therefore directed to achieving a similar result in domestic animals. These studies led to the successful transfer, incorporation, and expression of human and bovine growth hormone genes in pigs and sheep. These "transgenic" animals transmit these traits to their offspring, so that potentially valuable strains of animals showing increased growth and reduced fat, both desirable features, can be produced.

Although many therapeutically important proteins such as human insulin and growth hormone can be produced by animals developed from zygotes that have had a foreign gene inserted, there are limitations. Gene transfer must take place at the zygote stage and has a high failure rate; in addition, breeding of the resulting animals must be highly controlled, and host animals may not be able to produce many of the desired complex proteins because they lack the appropriate metabolic pathways and mechanisms. Gene transfer into zygotes has also led to various health problems in animals in these strains, from lethargy and infertility to diabetes. It is speculated that the cause of these problems may be inappropriate promoters used in conjunction with the genes that were transferred, which may have caused excess amounts of other gene product to be produced; research is currently under way to find more appropriate promoters.

The use of gene transfer to produce animals with new characteristics is still under investigation, but it potentially has major implications for food production and human medicine. For example, production of dairy cattle that produce lactose-free milk could provide a new source of this important food for people who are lactose-intolerant. The transfer of genes associated with resistance to specific disease could significantly reduce both production losses and the need for antibiotics in animal production. The transfer of genes coding for human cell-surface proteins could even, theoretically, provide donor organs (kidneys, livers) of animal origin that would escape rejection by the human host's immune system.

Although these uses of technology are outside our mandate, many ethical and other questions are raised by such uses of animals.

There is no foreseeable application of gene transfers of the types just described in human zygotes. As we discuss in Chapter 29, even if a zygote could be diagnosed, for example, as lacking the normal gene for growth hormone, it could simply not be transferred to the uterus; one of the couple's other zygotes would be transferred instead.

Ectogenesis

Ectogenesis refers to the idea of supporting the development of a zygote into an embryo and fetus outside a uterus until it is "born" or able to exist independently. Biologists develop techniques for culturing animal embryos in order to observe and learn about the intricate process of development. But no embryologist has succeeded in culturing animal embryos continuously through the whole period of gestation. In the first 10 or 11 days of development in the mouse or rat (which are similar in some respects to the first six to seven weeks of human development),

> The idea that human zygotes could develop and grow into infants in an artificial womb is seen as quite inappropriate by most Canadians. Such research, if pursued, would dehumanize motherhood; some have even envisaged it as opening the way to "baby farms" and femicide. Commissioners regard such research as ethically reprehensible, and we have recommended that it be prohibited.

it is possible to maintain a zygote in culture and watch it develop for several days. By doing this for overlapping three-day periods, it is possible to cover the whole period — but not with the same zygote. No one has succeeded in culturing an early animal embryo through the period of implantation to or beyond the period when the placenta normally becomes its major life support (10 or 11 days after fertilization in the case of the mouse). In a larger zygote with a longer gestation period, such as that of human beings, the problem would be still more intractable.

This technology has no foreseeable ethical application to human beings in any case. The idea that human zygotes could develop and grow into infants in an artificial womb is seen as quite inappropriate by most Canadians. Such research, if pursued, would dehumanize motherhood; some have even envisaged it as opening the way to "baby farms" and femicide. Commissioners regard such research as ethically reprehensible, and we have recommended that it be prohibited.

The concerns raised by Canadians about the use of PND and genetic technologies formed an important part of the backdrop for the Commission's inquiry. These concerns show the importance of examining and evaluating each technology and its current and potential uses to determine whether and under what circumstances society should accept its use, and what conditions society should put in place to govern uses found to be ethically acceptable and socially desirable. In the remaining chapters in this section we present the results of our investigation of the four applications of genetic technology in reproduction — prenatal diagnosis for genetic disease and congenital anomalies; prenatal diagnosis for late-onset disorders and susceptibility genes; sex selection for non-medical reasons; and genetic alteration, including gene therapy. We outline the issues involved in each and conclude with the Commission's recommendations for action.

General Sources

Angus Reid Group Inc. "Reproductive Technologies — Qualitative Research: Summary of Observations." In Research Volumes of the Royal Commission on New Reproductive Technologies, 1993.

Betteridge, K.J., and D. Rieger. "Embryo Transfer and Related Technologies in Domestic Animals: Their History, Current Status, and Future Direction, with Special Reference to Implications for Human Medicine." In Research Volumes of the Royal Commission on New Reproductive Technologies, 1993.

Decima Research. "Social Values and Attitudes of Canadians Toward New Reproductive Technologies." In Research Volumes of the Royal Commission on New Reproductive Technologies, 1993.

Fraser, F.C. "Preimplantation Diagnosis." In Research Volumes of the Royal Commission on New Reproductive Technologies, 1993.

Prenatal Diagnosis for Congenital Anomalies and Genetic Disease

◆

Prenatal diagnosis is increasingly familiar to Canadians. Various diagnostic tests, including amniocentesis, chorionic villus sampling, ultrasound scanning, and others, have become part of the experience of pregnancy for many women. PND has provided hope and assurance to many individual women and couples at risk of having children affected by genetic disease or congenital anomalies.

On the other hand, the use of these powerful technologies raises issues, dilemmas, and challenges that are complex and difficult. From a public policy perspective, addressing these issues involves questions of how to ensure clear and enlightened management of the introduction and use of technologies found to be ethically acceptable, and how to ensure the provision of effective and safe services based on these technologies for people across this country. In all these areas, there are vulnerable interests to be protected, and all the technologies are developing rapidly. This makes it important to put in place structures and processes to set boundaries for technology use and to ensure that any use of technologies within those boundaries occurs in safe and beneficial ways.

Before turning to current practice and to the views of Canadians on prenatal diagnosis, it is essential to know something of the nature and incidence of the congenital anomalies and genetic diseases that these techniques are designed to detect. Basic information on the disorders is therefore provided in Appendix 1, while the chances of these occurring and the tests used to detect them are described below.

The Risk of Congenital Anomalies and Genetic Disease

The risk that a child could be born with a congenital anomaly or genetic disease is inherent in the human condition.   This risk is unavoidable, and every couple must face it.   Some couples, however, are at much greater risk than others; if they are aware of the risk, this can be a source of considerable anxiety to prospective parents, who naturally want their children to be healthy.   Prenatal diagnosis is intended to help individuals and couples at increased risk to manage a pregnancy in light of knowledge about the fetus.

Congenital disorder: a disorder that is present at birth.

Genetic disorder: a disorder that is inherited from one or both parents.

Multifactorial disorder: a disorder that is attributable to a complex interaction of genetic and environmental factors.

Teratogenic disorder: a disorder that arises as a result of the embryo or fetus being exposed to harmful agents or substances *in utero*.

The various disorders that fall into the category of congenital anomalies or genetic disease differ in two important respects.   First, they differ in their cause.   Some disorders have a wholly genetic basis — that is, the disorder results from an anomaly in the genetic material inherited from the parents, either at the chromosomal level or in the sequence of DNA within the genes that compose the chromosome.   Other disorders are clearly the result of environmental factors that interfere with the normal development of the fetus, such as the pregnant woman's exposure to radiation or to a viral illness.   Many disorders are attributable to a complex interaction of genetic and environmental factors.   These are called "multifactorial diseases."   Finally, many disorders are of unknown or unidentified cause.

Second, these disorders differ in their time of onset.   If a disorder resulting from a genetic anomaly is present at birth, it is considered a "congenital" genetic disease; if it develops during adulthood, it is called "late-onset."   For some genetic diseases, the genetic anomaly, though present at birth, may not interfere with the person's development or functioning until months after birth (Tay-Sachs disease) or even until adulthood (Huntington disease).

In short, and as shown in Figure 26.1, not all genetic diseases are congenital (since the disorder may develop only in childhood or adulthood), and not all congenital anomalies are genetic in origin (since they may result from exposure to toxic agents *in utero*); indeed, most studies conclude that the largest category of congenital anomalies is of unknown cause (Table 26.1).

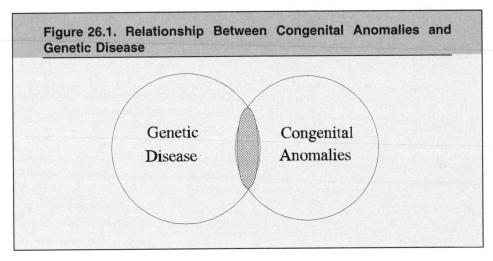

Figure 26.1. Relationship Between Congenital Anomalies and Genetic Disease

The risk of having a child affected by either a congenital anomaly or a genetic disease is not insignificant. Recent studies have concluded that somewhere between 3 and 8 percent of infants are born with either a serious congenital anomaly or a genetic disease that will cause medical problems before adulthood (Tables 26.2 and 26.3). It is difficult to give more precise statistics on the incidence of these disorders for a variety of reasons: researchers use different methods of identifying the disorders, some more intensive than others, and the definition of a "serious" congenital anomaly may differ somewhat from study to study. The figures given in Tables 26.1, 26.2, and 26.3 reflect the particular methodology used; other reputable studies arrive at slightly different numbers. Nevertheless, these figures give a general indication of the incidence of different kinds of disorders.

We explain the different kinds of disorders, explore who is at greatest risk of having a fetus affected by a disorder, and discuss how PND can help people at increased risk to make reproductive decisions in Appendix 1 to this chapter. As explained there, all women and couples face some risk of having children with a congenital anomaly or genetic disease. No one is exempt. As we have noted, the estimated incidence of these disorders in the general population varies from study to study, but data on newborns show that people in the general population (that is, those not known to be at higher risk because of a factor such as family history) face about a 4 percent chance of having a child with a genetic disease or congenital anomaly. This approximate risk does not vary much between cultures or over time where comparable data are available, suggesting that these background risks are inherent in the human condition.

Nevertheless, some women and couples have different kinds and levels of risk for a congenital anomaly or genetic disease in addition to the general background level of risk. For example, some are at higher risk of having a child with particular sorts of disorders — women over the age of 35, known carriers of a genetic disorder, those with a family history of multifactorial disorders, people who have been exposed to a known teratogen, and so on. This is where the use of prenatal diagnosis may be valuable.

Table 26.1. The Causes of Congenital Anomalies

Cause	% of infants with congenital anomaly
Chromosomal	10.1
Single-gene	17.6
Multifactorial	23.0
Unknown	43.2
Teratogens	3.2
Uterine factors	2.5
Twinning	0.4

Source: Nelson, K., and L.B. Holmes. "Malformations Due to Presumed Spontaneous Mutations in Newborn Infants." *New England Journal of Medicine* 320 (1)(January 5, 1989): 19-23.

Table 26.2. The Incidence of Genetic Diseases (Onset by Age 25)

Category	% of total births
Single-gene	0.36
Autosomal dominant	0.14
Autosomal recessive	0.17
X-linked recessive	0.05
Chromosomal	0.18*
Multifactorial	4.64
Genetic unknown	0.12
Total	5.32

* Under-ascertainment likely for this category due to methodology.

Source: Baird, P.A., et al. "Genetic Disorders in Children and Young Adults: A Population Study." *American Journal of Human Genetics* 42 (1988): 677-93.

Table 26.3. The Incidence of Congenital Anomalies

Category	% of total births
Anomalies with a known genetic component	2.66
Anomalies with no known genetic component	2.62
Total	5.28

Source: Baird, P.A., et al. "Genetic Disorders in Children and Young Adults: A Population Study." *American Journal of Human Genetics* 42 (1988): 677-93.

The Role of Prenatal Diagnosis

Before the introduction into the clinical setting of amniocentesis in the 1970s and CVS and obstetrical ultrasound in the 1980s, there was no way to diagnose accurately whether a fetus had a congenital anomaly or genetic disorder. Since then, however, there has been a tremendous increase in the capacity of medical technology to determine through PND testing whether fetuses in higher-risk pregnancies are in fact affected. It is also increasingly possible, through carrier screening and screening of pregnant women, to identify adults in the population who are at increased risk of having an affected fetus. These techniques give couples information on which to base reproductive decisions.

Diagnostic Testing

Some techniques, known as "diagnostic" tests, are intended to determine whether the fetus has a congenital anomaly or genetic disease. These techniques include amniocentesis, CVS, and specialized or "targeted" ultrasound. The first two techniques involve taking fluid or tissue samples containing fetal cells in order to carry out chromosome, biochemical, or DNA analysis. Targeted ultrasound is an imaging technique that involves intensive, prolonged visualization of the fetus using sound waves to look for anatomical or structural anomalies. (It is important to distinguish this targeted ultrasound from routine ultrasound, discussed below.)

Because amniocentesis and CVS are invasive and expensive and carry risks for both the fetus and the pregnant woman, they are offered only to women who have higher-risk pregnancies. The same is true for targeted ultrasound, which requires highly specialized equipment and personnel. In Canada, these tests are provided only to women who have been referred to a specialized centre, usually by their family doctor or obstetrician, because of a specific factor that puts them at higher risk.

Common Diagnostic Tests

Amniocentesis: Amniocentesis is the most common invasive prenatal diagnostic procedure in Canada. It is normally carried out between 15 and 17 weeks of pregnancy. Fluid is removed from the uterus using a needle inserted through the abdominal and uterine walls under ultrasound guidance. The fluid taken out contains fetal cells that are grown in culture and examined in different ways, depending on whether the couple is at higher risk for chromosomal disorders, genetic metabolic disorder, or a neural tube defect. Results usually take two to four weeks.

Chorionic villus sampling (CVS): The chorionic villi are fronds that extend from the fetal membranes into the uterine wall as the placenta forms. A sample of these fronds can be taken by suction through a tube inserted into the uterus through the vagina or through the abdominal wall. CVS can be done several weeks earlier in pregnancy than amniocentesis, and the tissue can be cultured or examined directly without culture, which means test results are available more quickly. However, CVS is more difficult to interpret than amniocentesis and cannot diagnose some disorders — for example, neural tube defects.

Ultrasound: Ultrasound examination involves the transmission of high-frequency sound waves through tissue and the display on a screen of the echoes produced by these waves. In the context of PND, it can be used as both a *screening* test and, when used in a more focussed way for a lengthier examination, a *diagnostic* test. Most pregnant women in Canada now have ultrasound *screening*, usually at about the eighteenth week of pregnancy, to estimate gestational age, to see whether there is more than one fetus, and to look for placental abnormalities and conditions that may require medical attention. This is variously described as "Level I" ultrasound or "routine" ultrasound. In the process, ultrasound screening may produce images that raise the suspicion of a congenital anomaly. If so, the woman is normally referred for further testing to provide a definitive diagnosis, sometimes by a more intensive *diagnostic* ultrasound examination (also known as Level II and III ultrasound or "targeted" ultrasound). Since Level I ultrasound is simply a screening test, it is not a reliable way to diagnose fetal anomalies. Level II and III ultrasound involves a detailed examination of the fetus, section by section, lasting up to an hour, and can accurately diagnose many congenital anomalies. Ultrasound is also used in PND as an adjunct to amniocentesis and CVS, to help guide the needle or tube.

This, in turn, has led to increased efforts to improve identification of higher-risk pregnancies. In the past, high-risk pregnancies were identified almost entirely on the basis of either family history or the pregnant woman's age. However, several "screening" techniques have recently been developed to help identify more accurately those in the general population who are at higher risk. These include carrier screening tests and prenatal screening tests.

Carrier Screening

Carrier screening involves testing men and women in population groups known to be more likely to carry particular genetic disorders to identify which individuals carry the gene. For example, carrier screening is available to identify the carriers of Tay-Sachs disease among Ashkenazi Jews. If both members of a couple are identified as carriers of this disease, they are at higher risk of having an affected fetus, and so they would be offered PND in any pregnancies they were to have subsequently.

Prenatal Screening

Unlike carrier screening, which aims to test prospective parents before conception, prenatal screening tests are designed to be offered to all pregnant women. Their aim is to identify particular women likely to be carrying an affected fetus so that they can be offered more definitive prenatal tests. The techniques include routine ultrasound and the testing of a pregnant woman's blood for levels of fetal proteins (see box). An abnormal result in one of these tests suggests that the fetus has an increased likelihood of having a congenital anomaly; in these cases, the woman would be offered a diagnostic test to confirm or dispel that suspicion. (In the case of routine ultrasound screening, the scan may sometimes incidentally identify a major structural anomaly, such as anencephaly.)

In most cases, the result of prenatal diagnostic testing is reassuring. According to a Commission survey of genetics centres in Canada, approximately 5 percent of the diagnostic tests carried out show that the fetus has a serious congenital anomaly or genetic disease; in cases where a serious congenital anomaly or genetic disease is found, about 80 percent of women and couples choose to terminate the pregnancy.

Prenatal diagnosis cannot and does not identify all disorders or eliminate all reproductive risks. PND is most useful for identifying chromosomal disorders, and, theoretically, all chromosomal disorders could be detected by examination of the chromosomes of the fetus. Although PND can be used currently to detect only several hundred of the several thousand known single-gene disorders, recent scientific and technological developments in genetics make it likely that the ability to test prenatally for single-gene disorders will increase rapidly in coming years.

These chromosomal and single-gene disorders account for a relatively small percentage of congenital anomalies. They are far less common than multifactorial disorders and disorders of unknown cause — and most disorders in these categories cannot be detected at present and will not be detectable in the foreseeable future. For example, many disorders of function (such as blindness, deafness, and muscle paralysis) are not detectable by either analysis of fetal cells or targeted ultrasound examination. The most common type of multifactorial disorder that can be detected is neural tube defects, such as spina bifida and anencephaly.

Screening Tests

These are tests designed to be offered, where available, to all pregnant women, not just those at higher risk. If an abnormal result is revealed in one of these screening tests, the woman is at higher risk of having an affected fetus and so would be offered a diagnostic test to provide a definitive diagnosis of the condition of the fetus.

Blood tests: Several tests can be done on a pregnant woman's blood to provide information about the likely condition of the fetus. These include maternal serum alpha-fetoprotein (MSAFP) testing, triple testing, and, perhaps in future, the testing of fetal cells from the pregnant woman's blood.

Maternal serum alpha-fetoprotein: This test relies on the detection of alpha-fetoprotein (AFP) in maternal blood. AFP is produced by the fetus; a higher than normal level of AFP in the pregnant woman's blood suggests the possibility of an abnormal fetal opening, such as a neural tube defect (anencephaly, spina bifida), allowing the concentration of this protein to become higher in the amniotic fluid and the pregnant woman's bloodstream. Concentrations of AFP rise in some other fetal conditions as well. Thus, a pregnant woman's blood can be screened to detect an increased likelihood of anomalies in the fetus.

Triple testing: As the name suggests, this test relies on a combination of three different indicators in the pregnant woman's blood sample, including AFP. A high risk of a chromosomal disorder is indicated by variations in the extent to which AFP, human chorionic gonadotropin hormones, and estriol hormone are present. For example, triple testing can be used to detect an increased risk of Down syndrome.

Ultrasound scanning: Ultrasound scanning can be used as a diagnostic test or as a screening test. (See "Ultrasound" in previous box.)

Carrier screening: Whereas other screening tests involve testing pregnant women after conception has occurred, carrier screening involves testing both men and women *before* conception to determine who is a carrier of a particular genetic disease. Carrier screening programs try to identify carriers within a particular ethnic group that is at risk for a specific single-gene disorder. For example, Mediterranean populations are screened to identify carriers of thalassaemia. Identified carriers would be offered diagnostic tests on all subsequent pregnancies, as the fetus would be at risk of inheriting the genetic disorder.

Diagnostic testing is offered only to those who are at identified higher risk. Here again, we know more about who is at higher risk from chromosomal disorders and single-gene diseases, since these have relatively clear and predictable patterns of incidence. Even for recessive disorders, however, the risk is usually identified because the couple has a child who is affected — thus showing that they have a one in four risk in any future pregnancy. Little is known about who is at higher risk of multifactorial disorders and disorders of unknown cause.

The higher the identified risk and the easier it is to detect a disorder, the more likely it is that a woman will be referred to a genetics centre for diagnostic testing. For example, although chromosomal disorders associated with pregnancies later in a woman's childbearing years account for approximately 10 percent of congenital anomalies in liveborn individuals, 78 percent of women tested at genetics centres in Canada are referred because of their age. Conversely, although multifactorial disorders and disorders of unknown cause account for more than 66 percent of congenital anomalies, fewer than 10 percent of women are referred in order to be tested for such disorders.

In short, testing for chromosomal disorders accounts for the largest proportion of PND, because there is a test to detect these disorders and because it is possible to identify people at higher risk for them. Multifactorial disorders, though much more common than chromosomal disorders, are less commonly tested for, because it is more difficult to know who is at higher risk, and for most there is no way to detect such disorders in the fetus. We have no reason to think that this will change markedly in the foreseeable future.

The usual background risk of a congenital anomaly or genetic disorder being present at birth (which is about 4 percent for any couple in the general population) is always present for high-risk couples, as well as for those not offered diagnostic testing. By having diagnostic testing, a couple is simply identifying whether the condition for which they are at higher risk — over and above the background risk — has occurred. Essentially, these couples are trying to establish for themselves the same level of risk that is part of every pregnancy. A normal test result puts high-risk couples back into the same risk group as everyone else. If a disorder is found, the couples can make decisions about treatment (if available), care, or termination.

> Using PND cannot be expected to eliminate or greatly reduce disabling conditions in the population at large. Most of these result from prematurity, viral or bacterial diseases, accidents or violence, and aging.

Prenatal diagnosis does not provide all the answers about the health of the fetus, but there is a strong desire for the answers it can provide on the part of women and couples who are at higher risk. Using PND cannot be expected to eliminate or greatly reduce disabling conditions in the population at large. Most of these result from prematurity, viral or bacterial diseases, accidents or violence, and aging. Thus, there will always be a risk of having a child with a congenital anomaly or genetic disease. Human development is too complex to allow easy or simplistic answers, and the application of PND cannot be expected to provide them. Thus, much of what will be stated in the rest of this chapter turns on the recognition that risk entails probabilities, not certainties, and that managing reproductive risks and making decisions with respect to PND will never be easy or straightforward, no matter how powerful the technology.

Issues Raised by Prenatal Diagnosis

As noted in Part One of this report, few previous inquiries into new reproductive technologies, either in Canada or internationally, have included PND in their research or recommendations. However, we believe that the impact of PND technology on reproductive health care, and on society generally, is as great as that of any other reproductive technology. PND raises many of the issues discussed in Part One with respect to new reproductive technologies as a whole. It involves many of our most basic beliefs and values as individuals and as a society; challenges our capacity as a society to manage rapidly changing technology and scientific knowledge with wisdom and humanity; and constitutes a key component of Canada's health care system.

> Many people now fear that the development of new reproductive technologies will exert great pressure on couples, and particularly on women, to use one technology or another. And prenatal diagnosis is often cited as an example in this regard. Our methods of assessing technology, or our methods of technological assessment, must therefore be reviewed from new perspectives if we are to protect the freedom of communities effectively. [Translation]
>
> *H. Doucet, Faculté de Théologie, Université Saint-Paul, Public Hearings Transcripts, Ottawa, Ontario, September 18, 1990.*

With the increasing power of PND technologies come dilemmas and implications for individuals and society alike. Decisions that are intensely personal and painful (for example, a decision about whether to abort a fetus found to be severely affected) have important implications for society. These must be addressed if PND is to be used in a way that is both beneficial for individuals and socially responsible.

In the small proportion of cases where a serious disorder is identified, the majority of couples decide to abort. This raises important questions about the impact of PND on society's view of abortion and whether, as some people fear, it will lessen society's respect for human life. There is also the concern that the use of PND to identify and terminate affected pregnancies will lead to or reinforce prejudice or discrimination against people with disabilities and to intolerance of diversity and "imperfections" in society. Moreover, the extent to which women's decisions regarding PND and abortion are subject to social pressure or legal coercion will affect the status of women in society and the equality of the sexes. These and other issues are discussed later in this chapter.

The rapid development of prenatal diagnostic technologies also raises the issue of technology proliferation. We found evidence that some screening technologies are being widely disseminated before they have been adequately assessed and without adequate support in place, such as the availability of genetics counselling and follow-up diagnostic facilities for those with abnormal test results. These issues provide specific examples of the need to provide only evidence-based health care throughout the system — care that has been assessed for benefits and risks. We return to this question later in the chapter as well.

The introduction and use of prenatal diagnostic technologies cannot be allowed to be a function of either technological imperative or policy drift. A conscious and coordinated approach is needed to ensure that PND is provided in an ethical, safe, and beneficial manner in Canada, now and in the future.

> The social status and realities of those with congenital disabilities, and societal attitudes toward them, warrant serious consideration in the face of advancing PND technologies. There is a need for public discussion about the selection aspect in particular, with a focus on society's fear of disability and the reasons why some disabilities are viewed as socially tolerable, while others are not. As well, society's past and current treatment of those with disabilities, the fears that persist around disability and persons with disabilities, and the question of public policies regarding social and economic support for those with special needs, including women in the caregiving role, deserve closer study. This broader view will allow medicine and society to more adequately address the choices generated by PND.
>
> J. Milner, "A Review of Views Critical of Prenatal Diagnosis and Its Impact on Attitudes Toward Persons with Disabilities," in Research Volumes of the Commission, 1993.

Our Approach to the Study of Prenatal Diagnosis

Consistent with our recognition of the many issues raised by PND, we commissioned qualitative examinations by prominent ethicists, geneticists, and other scholars (see research volumes, *Prenatal Diagnosis: Background and Impact on Individuals*; *Current Practice of Prenatal Diagnosis in Canada*; and *Prenatal Diagnosis: New and Future Developments*). At the same time, in our public consultations, private sessions, and consultations with interested organizations and expert bodies, we were anxious to learn about issues and concerns surrounding PND and its use.   In addition, we commissioned studies on a range of PND topics: the history and evolution of PND; risk assessment of PND techniques; and the social context of PND, including attitudes toward persons with disabilities and ethical issues such as informed consent and choice.

Also commissioned was a series of field studies examining the actual delivery of PND in Canada today, both in genetics centres and in the referral system. Examples include a survey of genetics centres; a survey of referring physicians and their behaviour and attitudes toward PND; trends in the use of prenatal ultrasound; Manitoba's experience with its maternal serum alpha-fetoprotein screening program; and a demographic and geographic analysis of the users of PND services. We also examined women's experience of technology use during pregnancy; women's attitudes, perceptions, and experiences regarding PND; and the reactions of women to prenatal diagnosis of a genetic disorder leading to pregnancy termination.

Given the scope and complexity of PND, the Commission's objective was not limited to fashioning specific responses to specific problems. Instead, much of our approach to PND was predicated on the importance of providing a long-term perspective and situating PND within the larger context of health care in Canada.

Given rapid evolution of the technologies, we focussed on developing recommendations regarding a regulatory structure that would enable policy makers to deal not only with current techniques but also with future developments. Our approach has been to see beyond the origins and dissemination of specific diagnostic technologies and to consider how to create a more inclusive and systematic approach to the assessment, limitation, or introduction and use of prenatal diagnostic technologies in general.

Current Practice of Prenatal Diagnosis in Canada

This section outlines the current practice of PND in Canada. This includes at least four elements: the 22 genetics centres that provide the major diagnostic PND tests; the 10 000 or more general practitioners (GPs) and obstetricians who provide primary care of pregnant women, who may refer patients to genetics centres, and who play an increasing role in providing screening tests; the women and couples involved; and the programs and funding that support these services.

Genetics Centres

At the core of the PND services system in Canada are 22 genetics centres, which provide the three major categories of diagnostic PND tests

— amniocentesis, CVS, and targeted ultrasound. All three require highly specialized equipment and personnel to carry out the tests and interpret the results; hence, they are provided only to women at identified higher risk. To receive one of these tests, a pregnant woman must be referred to one of the specialized centres, usually by her family practitioner or obstetrician.

All the genetics centres are situated in urban areas — 16 are in university medical centres or tertiary care hospitals associated with university medical centres, and 6 are in large community hospitals. Prince Edward Island, New Brunswick, Labrador, the Northwest Territories, and the Yukon do not have a genetics centre. Women from these areas must be referred to the nearest centre, which may involve travelling considerable distances.

There are also 35 formal outreach sites associated with the genetics centres. The most extensive network is in Alberta, which has 18 outreach sites, compared to 8 in Ontario, 4 in the Maritimes, 3 in Newfoundland, and 6 in British Columbia. The services provided at these outreach sites vary. In some provinces, public health nurses at the outreach site provide routine referrals to the genetics centre for pregnant women who might not otherwise see a referring physician in time; in other provinces, amniocenteses are available at the outreach site, and the samples are shipped to the centre for analysis.

The laboratories associated with genetics centres analyze MSAFP samples taken at the centre, as well as MSAFP samples collected by other practitioners in the community. In 1990, 37 163 women were screened for MSAFP through laboratories associated with genetics centres, which often also provide the infrastructure for carrier screening programs.

We commissioned a survey of genetics centres to determine how many women are being referred and for which conditions; how many tests are being performed and what their results are; and, more generally, how the centres are operated. The detailed results are provided in the Commission's research studies, in the volume entitled *Current Practice of Prenatal Diagnosis in Canada*. We provide a brief summary here.

Referrals

In 1990, more than 22 000 women were referred for prenatal diagnostic services at genetics centres in Canada because of an identified higher risk of having a fetus with a congenital anomaly or genetic disease. The most common reason for referral was because the woman was over the age of 35 (known as "advanced maternal age"), which increases the risk of chromosomal disorder. Advanced maternal age accounted for about 78 percent of referrals (Table 26.4). The remaining 22 percent were referrals for a variety of reasons, including having had a previous child with a chromosomal abnormality (2.4 percent), a family history of chromosomal abnormality (2.3 percent), an abnormal MSAFP result (3.6 percent), abnormal ultrasound (3.1 percent), family history of single-gene disorder (1.6 percent), possible teratogen exposure (1.4 percent), and anxiety on the part of the pregnant woman about the health of the fetus (1.3 percent).

Table 26.4. Reasons for Referral to Genetics Centres for Prenatal Diagnosis	
Risk of chromosomal disorder	83.0%
Advanced maternal age	77.7
Previous chromosomal	2.4
Previous family chromosomal	2.3
Parental chromosomal	0.5
Chromosome marker abnormality	0.1
Risk of single-gene disorder	1.6
Risk of structural anomaly	10.6
Abnormal MSAFP*	3.6
Abnormal ultrasound*	3.1
Previous family neural tube defects	2.5
Teratogen	1.4
Pregnant woman's anxiety	1.3
Other	3.5

* May also indicate increased risk of chromosomal disorder.

Source: Hamerton, J.L., J.A. Evans, and L. Stranc. "Prenatal Diagnosis in Canada — 1990: A Review of Genetics Centres." In Research Volumes of the Royal Commission on New Reproductive Technologies, 1993.

Counselling

Women who are referred to a genetics centre receive counselling before being tested, in order to clarify the nature of their risk and to ensure that their choice to undergo testing is an informed one. The type of counselling and level of intensity depend on the reason for referral. Where the risks are well known and information is relatively straightforward to convey, as in the case of advanced maternal age, counselling is done by genetics associates at some centres (often nurses with special training in genetics), by family physicians, by obstetricians, or through group counselling. The average duration of a counselling session for patients referred to genetics centres for advanced maternal age was one hour, and partners were encouraged to attend.

Counselling for referrals because of family history are more complex, often requiring complicated statistical analysis and clinical interpretation.

This is done by medical geneticists. Such sessions are considerably longer and may involve repeat visits.

Tests Performed

After the counselling, some women decide not to proceed with the testing, particularly if they were referred for an invasive test, such as amniocentesis or CVS, which carries a small risk (less than 1 percent) of miscarriage. Almost 10 percent of patients referred for amniocentesis or CVS in 1990 declined the procedure. Some of these women (137) were offered targeted ultrasound, although ultrasound cannot pick up many of the chromosomal disorders for which the women would have been referred for invasive testing originally. Some women did not have a test for other reasons — for example, fetal death was discovered at the time testing was to have been done, or the woman miscarried before testing.

However, the majority of women referred to genetics centres did have a test (19 795 out of 22 222, or 89 percent). Of these, most had amniocentesis (15 454), while a much smaller number had either CVS (2 097) or targeted ultrasound (2 244) (Table 26.5). The latter number does not include all targeted ultrasounds conducted, because women are often referred to practitioners specializing in this procedure instead of to a genetics centre for this test.

Table 26.5. Amniocentesis, CVS, and Targeted Ultrasound Performed at Genetics Centres in Canada (1990)

Type of test	Number of women tested	% of women referred
Amniocentesis	15 454	69.5
Chorionic villus sampling	2 097	9.4
Targeted ultrasound	2 244	10.1
Total	19 795	89.0*

* Approximately 10 percent of referred women did not have a test, either because they decided not to undergo the test after counselling or for other reasons (for example, miscarriage before the test).

Source: Hamerton, J.L., J.A. Evans, and L. Stranc. "Prenatal Diagnosis in Canada — 1990: A Review of Genetics Centres." In Research Volumes of the Royal Commission on New Reproductive Technologies, 1993.

Of the 19 795 women who were tested in 1990, 95 percent received reassuring test results. However, a fetal disorder was detected for the remaining 5 percent of women tested — about 990 cases. Of these, 792 women (80 percent) decided to terminate the pregnancy. The decision to terminate is affected by many factors, including the severity of the disorder, its treatability (although in most cases the disorder detected is not treatable), the stage of pregnancy, and the circumstances and values of the individuals making the decision. The 792 constituted just over 3 percent of all women referred to genetics centres in 1990. To put this in perspective, about 6 percent of the 393 000 women who gave birth in Canada in 1990 were referred for prenatal testing; of the more than 92 600 therapeutic abortions performed annually in Canada, about 0.86 percent are done after PND.

Variations in Access

There were some marked regional variations in patient referrals. The rates varied from 7.0 percent of all pregnant women in Ontario to 1.5 percent in Newfoundland — a more than fourfold variation — as shown in Table 26.6.

Table 26.6. Referral Rates by Province (1990)

Province/region	% of pregnant women referred
Newfoundland	1.5
Maritimes	2.7
Quebec	5.9
Ontario	7.0
Manitoba	5.8
Saskatchewan	1.8
Alberta	4.1
British Columbia	6.1

Source: Hamerton, J.L., J.A. Evans, and L. Stranc. "Prenatal Diagnosis in Canada — 1990: A Review of Genetics Centres." In Research Volumes of the Royal Commission on New Reproductive Technologies, 1993.

There is a similar pattern for one specific category of referral — advanced maternal age. Although 52 percent of pregnant women aged 35 or over were referred across Canada, the number varied widely between provinces. The highest rate was in Quebec (64.5 percent); British Columbia, Manitoba, and Ontario were in the middle (between 49 and 57 percent); and in the other provinces the rates were much lower (30 percent in Alberta and the Maritimes, 23 percent in Saskatchewan, and 15 percent in Newfoundland) (Table 26.7).

In other words, there is more than a fourfold difference in referral rates between different parts of the country. Some of these differences may be the result of differences in women's choices; however, as discussed later in this chapter, data from our research and surveys of Canadians across the country suggest that regional differences in individual values or preferences are unlikely to explain this fourfold difference in referral rates. Values and preferences are very similar across the country, whereas physicians' attitudes were found to vary markedly between provinces.   There may also be practical considerations, however, such as the distance that may have to be travelled to have a test, that play a role in whether a physician deems it worthwhile for a woman to have a test. It may also be that women who are referred may balance the decision to have a test with the amount of inconvenience the trip would cause and their financial circumstances.

> Regional differences in individual values or preferences are unlikely to explain this fourfold difference in referral rates.

Table 26.7. Referral Rates for Advanced Maternal Age by Province (1990)	
Province/region	% of eligible women referred
Quebec	64.5
Ontario	56.7
British Columbia	54.6
Manitoba	49.3
Maritimes	30.7
Alberta	30.1
Saskatchewan	23.1
Newfoundland	15.0

Source: Hamerton, J.L., J.A. Evans, and L. Stranc. "Prenatal Diagnosis in Canada — 1990: A Review of Genetics Centres." In Research Volumes of the Royal Commission on New Reproductive Technologies, 1993.

It would seem, however, that at least part of the explanation lies in the referring practices of physicians. Family and general practitioners and obstetricians in some provinces are much more likely to offer referrals for certain indications than are their colleagues in other provinces.

There were also some variations in referral rates on the basis of place of residence, income, and education. A study done for the Commission showed that people in rural or northern communities were less likely to be referred to a genetics centre, as were people of lower income or education.

Unlike the practice of many infertility clinics (discussed in Chapter 20), there is no evidence that genetics centres deny access to any woman on the basis of factors such as income, education, or marital status. Those who are referred are accepted if they meet the genetic risk criteria (for example, they are 35 years of age or over). Variations in access arise, therefore, at the point of referral, because of the way physicians offer or withhold referrals, the way women accept or decline referrals, or how difficult it is to get to a centre.

> Fewer than expected family/general practitioners are referring women for prenatal diagnostic services, a problem that is magnified in rural and northern areas because they are usually the only physicians practising. The obverse of this is that the vast majority of obstetricians/gynaecologists (who make most of the referrals) are concentrated in the largest urban centres in every province. The implication is that women living in rural or northern communities who want prenatal diagnostic services may have to travel to an urban location just to get a referral. They will have to travel to yet another urban location for the prenatal diagnostic service itself.
>
> P. MacLeod et al., "A Demographic and Geographic Analysis of the Users of Prenatal Diagnostic Services in Canada," in Research Volumes of the Commission, 1993.

Guidelines and Accreditation

The Canadian College of Medical Geneticists (CCMG) established a system of guidelines and accreditation for the provision of PND services more than a decade ago, and the first genetics centres received accreditation in 1981. Centres satisfying the accreditation requirements are accredited for five years.

The criteria and written standards established by the CCMG cover such things as the availability of non-directive counselling, the adequacy of laboratory support, record-keeping practices, qualifications of the staff, and so on. Centres lose accreditation in a particular subspecialty if they do not have a CCMG-qualified staff person in that specialty. When the accreditation committee believes that problems it has identified can be rectified within a specific period, it may award provisional accreditation pending correction.

Accreditation is voluntary, however. Of the 22 centres, only 10 — all of them university-based — were accredited by the CCMG for the delivery of services in 1990. (The unaccredited university centres are at Memorial University, Dalhousie University, Laval University, the University of

Montreal, and the University of Saskatchewan.)   None of the general hospital centres is accredited, and none has applied for accreditation. Although lack of accreditation does not necessarily indicate a lower standard of service, it does make it impossible to evaluate, compare, and monitor the quality of prenatal diagnostic services across Canada, as this would depend upon the cooperation of all the centres.

Practitioners Involved

Although the size and composition of the 22 genetics centres vary, almost every centre has the following mix of professionals and related medical personnel: MD geneticists, PhD geneticists, MSc genetics associates, registered nurses, laboratory technicians, and ultrasound technicians (Table 26.8). Professional guidelines and qualifying exams exist for most of these personnel. The Royal College of Physicians and Surgeons of Canada developed a certification program in 1989, with CCMG input, for physicians who specialize in medical genetics; training requirements for PhD geneticists providing genetics services are set by the CCMG.

Table 26.8. Practitioners Involved in PND at Genetics Centres

Type of practitioner	Number
MD geneticists	60
PhD geneticists	41
Genetics associates	57
Total*	158

* Does not include radiologists or obstetricians who specialize in targeted diagnostic ultrasound for fetal anomalies, who often belong to radiology units that are separate from, but associated with, the genetics centres. It also does not include some community obstetricians who are associated with the genetics centres, and who may provide some routine counselling and testing.

Source: Hamerton, J.L., J.A. Evans, and L. Stranc. "Prenatal Diagnosis in Canada — 1990: A Review of Genetics Centres." In Research Volumes of the Royal Commission on New Reproductive Technologies, 1993.

The category of "genetics associate," which is relatively new, evolved as the demand for PND and genetics counselling grew faster than the supply of trained MD and PhD counsellors. Genetics associates have either a background in counselling, such as social work or psychology, and learn genetics on the job, or training in nursing, genetics, or other paramedical skills and learn the practical side of counselling on the job (Table 26.9).

As the number of genetics associates has grown, the need for formalization of their training and functions has been recognized. In response, a master's-level training program has been established at McGill University, and a second is being developed at the University of British Columbia. The Canadian Association of Genetic Counsellors has been incorporated and is currently developing guidelines for training and procedures for accreditation.

Table 26.9. Type of Training of Genetics Associates

Type of training	Number
Formal genetics counselling training	14
Master's degree in genetics	4
Bachelor's or Master's degree in nursing	16
Diploma in nursing	16
Other	7
Total	57

Source: Hamerton, J.L., J.A. Evans, and L. Stranc. "Prenatal Diagnosis in Canada — 1990: A Review of Genetics Centres." In Research Volumes of the Royal Commission on New Reproductive Technologies, 1993.

Referring Practitioners

In addition to the 200 or so medical professionals at genetics centres, there is a much larger network of practitioners involved in PND in Canada — namely, the 10 500 specialists and family and general practitioners who see pregnant women, and who may refer them to genetics centres for diagnostic testing. These practitioners constitute what might be termed the referral system that refers higher-risk patients to the genetics centres (Table 26.10).

As well as making referrals, an increasing number of practitioners also provide PND screening tests. For example, many now perform routine ultrasound in their offices, refer for routine ultrasound to a local facility, or take MSAFP samples.

Whether and how these practitioners offer referrals, give advice, or provide screening tests have a powerful effect on the evolution and provision of PND services in Canada. To understand how this larger referral system works, we commissioned two surveys. The first was a major nation-wide survey (which included obstetricians and family and general practitioners who had performed five deliveries or more in the year preceding the survey, radiologists doing obstetrical ultrasound, and paediatricians) that analyzed responses from 3 072 medical professionals involved in PND outside the genetics centres. The second survey analyzed information from 642 practitioners involved in Manitoba's MSAFP program (see research volume, *Current Practice of Prenatal Diagnosis in Canada*).

Table 26.10. Number of PND Practitioners Outside Genetics Centres* (1990)

Type of practitioner	Number in Canada
Obstetricians	1 528
GPs/family practitioners practising obstetrics	8 021
Radiologists doing prenatal ultrasound	991
Total	10 540

* Involved in PND through referring patients to genetics centres; doing preliminary counselling; providing routine ultrasound; taking MSAFP samples.

Source: Renaud, M., et al. "Canadian Physicians and Prenatal Diagnosis: Prudence and Ambivalence." In Research Volumes of the Royal Commission on New Reproductive Technologies, 1993.

Referrals: According to the first survey, almost all referrals to genetics centres were made by either obstetricians (56 percent) or general/family practitioners (40 percent) (Table 26.11). The role of general practitioners and obstetricians in referrals was found to vary according to local health care practices. For example, a GP may refer to an obstetrician who then refers to a genetics centre, or the GP may refer directly to the centre.

Significant provincial and regional variations in referral practices were found. Although obstetricians accounted for 56 percent of all referrals nation-wide, the figures ranged from over 80 percent in some centres (North York, Ottawa, and Saskatoon) to less than 25 percent in Vancouver. Similarly, while GPs accounted for 40 percent of referrals across Canada, the figures ranged from 72 percent in Calgary to 22 percent in St. John's.

Also, as noted earlier, there were very marked variations by province in the overall proportion of pregnant women referred by both obstetricians and GPs. These variations may reflect in part the fact that the relevant professional associations for GPs and obstetricians (the national and provincial medical associations and colleges of physicians and surgeons) have not adopted and promulgated policies about when doctors should offer referrals. The CCMG and the Society of Obstetricians and Gynaecologists of Canada (SOGC) have voluntary guidelines, but there is evidence that some referring physicians are basing their referral decisions on their own values, rather than medical need. For example, our nation-wide survey of referring physicians showed that 15 percent of respondents opposed abortion after PND, no matter how serious the condition or anomaly. At the other extreme, 16 percent responded that it is socially irresponsible for women at higher risk not to have PND and to give birth to an affected child. In addition, it was found that 40 percent of referring physicians believe that it is physicians, not women or couples, who should decide which fetal anomalies justify abortion; 51 percent said it would be inappropriate to offer amniocentesis to a woman who refuses to consider abortion if an anomaly is diagnosed.

Table 26.11. Source of Referrals to Genetics Centres (1990)

Type of practitioner	% of referrals
General or family practitioners	40
Obstetricians	56
Other*	4

* Includes referral by other physicians; referral through MSAFP program; self-referral; referral by public health nurses or fetal assessment units; referral through outreach programs.

Source: Hamerton, J.L., J.A. Evans, and L. Stranc. "Prenatal Diagnosis in Canada — 1990: A Review of Genetics Centres." In Research Volumes of the Royal Commission on New Reproductive Technologies, 1993.

These results show that a disturbing proportion of referring physicians do not accept the principle that patients should make their own informed choice about whether to have PND and whether to have an abortion after diagnosis of a fetal disorder. Moreover, when we examined regional variations in physicians' responses, we found that they closely matched the regional variations in referral rates. For example, respondents from Quebec were least likely to oppose the termination of pregnancy after a fetal disorder is detected by PND, while those from Saskatchewan expressed the highest level of opposition to aborting affected fetuses. The fact that pregnant women in Quebec are three times more likely to be referred to a genetics centre than women in Saskatchewan suggests strongly that many referring practitioners in Saskatchewan are basing their referral decisions more on their personal values than on medical indications. Our national survey did not show

> The CCMG and the Society of Obstetricians and Gynaecologists of Canada have voluntary guidelines, but there is evidence that some referring physicians are basing their referral decisions on their own values, rather than medical need.

regional variations in Canadians' attitudes toward PND sufficient to explain the difference in referral rates.

The nation-wide survey concluded that the more serious doctors consider anomalies to be, and the more they accept the option of abortion, the more likely they are to extend access to prenatal diagnostic procedures by providing referrals (and vice versa). This is of great concern to Commissioners, because respect for the pregnant woman's autonomy requires that it be her values and priorities, not the doctor's, that determine her decision to accept or decline PND testing.

> When we examined regional variations in physicians' responses, we found that they closely matched the regional variations in referral rates ... Our national survey did not show regional variations in Canadians' attitudes toward PND sufficient to explain the difference in referral rates ... Respect for the pregnant woman's autonomy requires that it be her values and priorities, not the doctor's, that determine her decision to accept or decline PND testing.

Referral rates are also affected by physicians' knowledge of these tests. For example, many of the physicians in the Manitoba study did not have accurate knowledge about the cut-off age for referrals, which may be leading to under-referrals to genetics centres.

Screening Tests: As well as providing referrals to genetics centres, an increasing number of practitioners in Canada also provide PND screening tests. Many now take blood samples for MSAFP screening, perform routine ultrasound in their offices, and/or refer for routine ultrasound to a local facility.

Here too, however, we found wide variations in the way services are provided. For example, the kind of information and counselling physicians provide before taking MSAFP samples varied greatly. In the Manitoba program (Manitoba is the only province with a MSAFP provincial program, although Ontario recently introduced provincial MSAFP screening as part of its triple-testing program), written information regarding the test was provided to physicians for distribution to patients. However, of the respondents to the Manitoba survey, only 30 percent provided this information to the woman before taking a MSAFP sample, 54 percent provided only oral information, and 6.6 percent provided no information at all. (About 10 percent did not respond to the question.)

There were also wide variations in the proportion of women to whom MSAFP screening was offered. In the Manitoba survey of practitioners, 3.5 percent did not respond to the question, 6.2 percent of GPs and obstetricians did not offer the test to any pregnant women, 11.1 percent offered it to pregnant women for specific reasons, such as positive family history, while the remaining 79.2 percent offered or provided it to all pregnant women. Among the 79.2 percent of practitioners who screened all pregnant women, there were wide variations in how the woman's consent was secured: 37.7 percent of doctors provided the test only if the woman gave her specific consent; at least 22 percent did the test without securing the patient's consent; and 19.4 percent provided the test unless the woman specifically declined — that is, the doctor did not seek specific consent, but if the woman asked what the test was for and then did not want it, she did not have the test.

Substantial regional variations were found in the way the other major screening test — routine ultrasound — is provided. For example, 89 percent of Quebec respondents in the national survey thought it appropriate to use ultrasound to screen for fetal anomalies, compared to 60 percent elsewhere in Canada. Further, while 40 percent of physicians in Manitoba and Alberta did not think it essential to order an ultrasound scan during pregnancy, only 4 percent of physicians in Quebec shared this opinion. (In part this reflects the policy of the Quebec health ministry, which has stated that ultrasound should be the PND screening test of choice in Quebec.)

> Substantial regional variations were found in the way the other major screening test — routine ultrasound — is provided.

Moreover, there is evidence that some physicians are overstating the capacity of routine ultrasound to detect fetal anomalies and to reassure patients that the fetus is healthy. Routine ultrasound (unlike the "targeted" ultrasound done at specialized centres) is not intended to screen for fetal anomalies, and it is not capable of identifying many structural anomalies, including some major ones. It may incidentally pick up some anomalies, but its efficacy as a screening tool in this regard is questionable (see discussion later in this chapter).

As with variations in referral practices, variations in the way prenatal screening tests are provided reflect the absence of established standards for the practices of GPs and obstetricians in this area, as well as the lack of monitoring of these practices. Although the CCMG has guidelines (also adopted by the SOGC) on when to refer patients to genetics centres, these are voluntary and often not adhered to. Standards regarding information provision, consent procedures, and counselling for MSAFP testing are needed, as are standards for routine ultrasound and referrals for both MSAFP testing and ultrasound. There are, moreover, no qualifying exams for GPs or obstetricians who wish to provide these PND services.

> It is in this large network of referring physicians, rather than in the genetics centres, that much of the variation in PND referral and testing practices occurs ... These variations raise serious doubts about whether women in Canada can expect to receive uniform, high-quality PND services, regardless of where they live and who their doctor is.

It is in this large network of referring physicians, rather than in the genetics centres, that much of the variation in PND referral and testing practices occurs. The data show that the level of knowledge and patterns of practice differ a great deal among physicians in the referral system. These variations raise serious doubts about whether women in Canada can expect to receive uniform, high-quality PND services, regardless of where they live and who their doctor is. In short, how a population is served depends not just on the presence of a genetics centre, but also on having knowledgeable practitioners providing primary care to pregnant women. The same is true, of course, of screening and referral in other areas of medicine.

Patients' Perspective

Three surveys of women's perceptions, attitudes, and experiences of PND were carried out for the Commission in which women were encouraged to discuss their feelings at length and in depth. The studies provide helpful insights into women's experiences and feelings as they undergo PND and face the decisions it entails. The three studies were quite different in design, samples, and methodology. In one study, 70 women referred for PND because of their age were interviewed before they received genetics counselling; they and an additional 52 women were also surveyed by questionnaire after counselling (total of 122, with a response rate of 91 percent).

Another study focussed on a selected group of 37 women (selected because they were not likely to be heard by the Commission in any other way) who had had a variety of experiences with PND, ranging from MSAFP screening to PND and abortion of an affected fetus. Based at a community health centre, the project recruited 5 teenagers, 10 immigrant and refugee women, 6 women with disabilities or deafness, 4 Aboriginal women, 3 parents of children with disabilities, and 9 single parents. Each woman had a semi-structured interview with the investigator, lasting from 1.5 to 4.5 hours; the women's recorded stories were analyzed to identify issues and common themes.

In the third study, two groups of women who had terminated a pregnancy after PND were interviewed at length by a psychologist at intervals ranging from six months to several years later. In one group were 76 women who had known they were at increased risk for a disorder (mostly because of their age) and who had received thorough genetics counselling before amniocentesis. The second group comprised 124 women who were not known to be at higher risk but who had had an unanticipated fetal disorder, detected by routine ultrasound, that was then confirmed by diagnostic testing. The two groups therefore differed in their preparedness for the test result and in the time available for decision making.

Several common themes, as described below, emerged from these three studies (see research volume, *Prenatal Diagnosis: Background and Impact on Individuals*).

Overall Approval

Overall, the majority of women had generally favourable views of PND testing, because the tests provided reassurance, identified problems, and helped them to manage their risk. Even women who had had stressful experiences because of false-positive MSAFP results said they would have the test with their next pregnancy. The women also felt ambivalence, however, describing the testing process as a benefit that has emotional costs attached. The women had to process complex technical information about risks, explore their attitudes toward disability and abortion, balance the desire to know as much as possible with acceptance of the pregnancy, and experience the discomforts of testing and the anxiety of waiting for results, while at the same time trying to enjoy the pregnancy.

Women had worries about the testing procedures, particularly the risk of miscarriage. Although the statistical risk is less than 1 percent, some women said they would feel guilty if they lost a healthy child as a result of having the test; indeed, as we have seen, some women decline amniocentesis for this reason. Anxiety while waiting for results and the length of the waiting period were also mentioned as sources of stress.

Referral and Counselling

Several other specific concerns were raised about the referral and counselling process. Some mentioned the incompleteness of the information provided by referring physicians about why they were being referred to a genetics centre, the nature of the tests, and other aspects of the process.

The women also thought counselling should go beyond the medical facts to include more discussion of their feelings about PND, disability, and abortion. Comments were made about the impersonal or detached attitudes of some practitioners, compared to the more open, supportive approach of other practitioners, and the need for "high-quality" interaction between practitioners and patients.

In one way or another, some women in each of the three studies perceived subtle pressures to have the recommended diagnostic test. In many instances, this was mainly because of the limited time available in which to schedule counselling sessions and tests. In other cases, however, particularly for some of the younger, less educated women, there was a sense of being swept along by an imposing process. There were no suggestions that overt coercion had occurred, although several referring physicians were reported to have asked why anyone would want the test if they would not abort an affected fetus. However, only one woman reported that her physician actively encouraged abortion if the fetus was found to be affected.

Deciding to Terminate a Pregnancy

For many women, a real appreciation of the seriousness of the PND process came only when the test result was abnormal, triggering a set of choices that required rapid decisions. No matter how supportive and non-directive the counselling, the task of sorting out what was right in light of their own values and priorities, evaluating risks and percentages, and weighing of options proved difficult and stressful for all the women interviewed, but more so for some than for others.

Women in the first two patient perspective studies expressed a range of views about having a child with a disability. Some were confident they could handle having such a child. Others said they would abort a fetus in the case of a very severe disability, but not for Down syndrome or spina bifida. Still others felt that to bring a child with Down syndrome into the world was not fair to the child.

In the third study, the great majority of women felt in retrospect that their decision to abort had been the correct choice for them. This decision is not easy with a wanted pregnancy, and a few of the women had had serious emotional or psychological problems, including guilt (10 percent). Four years later, some women reported that they still felt guilty. It was not possible, however, to design the study to show whether the frequency of psychological or emotional problems among the women in the study was higher or lower than in the general population or among women who decided to continue the pregnancy and have a child with a disability.

Even though most women felt they had made the decision that was correct for them, the experience of termination was difficult, particularly for those who had a fetal disorder detected unexpectedly during ultrasound late in the pregnancy: the women talked about the uneasiness of the ultrasound staff, the feeling of being a "number" as more scans were conducted, the shocking news, the urgency of making a decision, and the lack of personal support during the termination, as well as the lack of information about its aftermath and the sense of not being treated as parents who have just lost a much-desired child. We make recommendations later in this chapter with regard to support for those in this situation.

The Growth of Prenatal Diagnosis Services in Canada

Genetics centres are provincially funded, based on negotiation between the centres and provincial ministries of health, with some provinces having genetics advisory committees advising the minister of health regarding policy and funding in this area. Currently, there is a great deal of variation across the country in the methods of funding. Some provinces use global budgets, others use line-item budgets; some provinces pay personnel at the centres through salaries, others pay on a fee-for-service basis; some provinces separate PND from other genetics services, while others combine all genetics services into one budget category.

Such a funding situation makes it difficult to determine the precise amount spent on PND in Canada, or to compare the expenditures in different provinces. It is clear that expenditures are considerable, however, and increasing. All but one of the genetics centres reported a significant overall increase in the demand for PND services between 1985 and 1990 and predicted that such demands will rise further over the next five years.

The largest increase has been in referrals of pregnant women later in their reproductive years, for increased risk of chromosomal disorders. More women and more referring physicians are becoming aware of the guideline recommending that referral be offered to pregnant women who are 35 years of age or older, and this is leading to higher rates of referral. There are also more women in this age group because of the baby boom population.

In addition, as a result of scientific developments, more people are likely to be referred for DNA diagnosis of single-gene disorders in future. Demand is also likely to increase if screening tests continue to be developed or preventive strategies become available.

Dealing with increased demand will in turn require an increase in the resources available to genetics centres for laboratory and counselling services. In our survey, when asked to predict their staffing needs in five years, genetics centres projected a need for approximately 40 additional full-time MDs, 40 genetics associates, 20 outreach personnel, and smaller numbers of PhD geneticists and nurses.

These numbers are, of course, speculative and could change dramatically with changes in PND technology or with provincial funding decisions regarding development of screening tests. If current projections are accurate, however, there will be a shortage of trained genetics associates in the near future, since the training programs at McGill University and the University of British Columbia are not yet graduating large numbers.

The Views of Canadians

PND involves very personal and often difficult decisions by individuals and couples, but it also has implications for society more generally. This was brought home to Commissioners by the breadth, diversity, and intensity of views brought forward during our consultative and research activities. To come to a better understanding of public perceptions of PND, we collected information in two ways. First, we listened to Canadians (including users and providers of PND services, groups representing people who have some of the conditions detected through PND, persons with disabilities and groups representing them, and others concerned about the social and ethical implications of these technologies) through our public hearings, panel discussions, private sessions, and submissions. Second, to understand how Canadians in general view PND, we commissioned survey research on the values and attitudes of Canadians with respect to these activities.

Public Hearings and Submissions

Canadians have a wide spectrum of views on PND, and many of the oral and written presentations received by the Commission were insightful, thought provoking, and moving. The Commission is grateful for the time and effort put in by individuals and groups that made presentations to us.

Social and Ethical Dimensions

Interventions concerning the social and ethical dimensions of PND produced considerable debate during the Commission's hearings, reflecting the complexity of the questions involved and the difficult nature of the issues to be resolved. These issues included the potential impact of PND on attitudes toward abortion, the "medicalization" of pregnancy, societal attitudes toward people with disabilities, and the potential for discrimination against people who carry the gene for certain diseases.

Abortion: Women in Canada have the option of terminating a pregnancy if a fetal anomaly is detected through PND. Members of some religious and anti-abortion groups oppose this practice. They believe that to allow the abortion of fetuses with disorders reflects and perpetuates a lack of respect

> Testing benefits a pregnant woman by providing her with information about the status of her fetus and thus the option to terminate her pregnancy by early abortion or to carry the fetus to term while making necessary preparations for the accommodation of her child's needs. For those few disorders whose manifestations can be prevented, delayed, or ameliorated by interventions *in utero*, or by early delivery by Caesarian section or just by Caesarian section, testing provides an opportunity to reduce the magnitude of disability ... A universal prenatal screening program [without] adequate social supports for disabled individuals threatens to promote the public perception that women are expected to bring only perfect babies into the world. Such a perception hides the fact that it is society's responsibility to assist disabled children and their families throughout life. A program with a coercive and anti-disability bias would limit reproductive choice and must therefore be avoided.
>
> *K. Sandercock, Vancouver Women's Reproductive Technologies Coalition, Public Hearings Transcripts, London, Ontario, November 1, 1990.*

for human life. Representatives of these groups who conveyed their views to the Commission stated that using PND to identify fetuses affected with a congenital anomaly or genetic disease is appropriate only if it enables treatment of the disease *in utero* through fetal therapy, or if it enables parents and physicians to prepare for the birth and treatment of an affected child. They acknowledged that PND may be used in many cases by couples who would otherwise have terminated a pregnancy if testing were not available to provide evidence that the fetus was healthy.

> The message that it is not only permissible but preferable to abort any foetus that may be born with a disability resounds loud and clear from the advice given and the approach adopted by many within the medical community. Canadians who have a disability find this message repugnant and totally unacceptable. The implications for them in their day to day lives is to live in an environment of hostile and denigrating attitudes. The primary purpose of prenatal testing is to try to diagnosis disabling conditions in advance. The recommended "solution" to that diagnosis is abortion.
>
> *Brief to the Commission from the Canadian Association for Community Living, April 30, 1991.*

Many other groups and individuals felt strongly that if a fetus is affected by an anomaly or disorder, the choice of a course of action must be left entirely to the pregnant woman or couple. Other witnesses expressed concern that the availability of PND creates subtle pressures for abortion. We heard allegations that women or couples unwilling to consider abortion in the event that a fetus was affected were not offered PND services, despite the fact that PND in this instance might either reduce anxiety by showing that the fetus was unaffected or give them time to prepare for the birth of a child with a disability.

If such pressure occurs, it has obvious implications for individual autonomy in matters of reproductive health and well-being; it was therefore one of the aspects of PND on which we sought accurate data. Our research shows that any pressure for women to commit themselves to aborting an affected fetus comes from referring physicians, not from the genetics centres.

Medicalization of Pregnancy: The Commission received several representations concerning the effects of PND in medicalizing pregnancy; some argued that medicalization gives medical professionals and society at large increased power to control women's reproductive functions and choices. For example, some witnesses were concerned that the universal availability of PND would mean that it would become compulsory eventually, with possible repercussions — such as loss of hospital or medical insurance benefits — for those who declined to have testing. (See Part One, Chapter 2, for a more detailed discussion of the concept of medicalization and its relevance to new reproductive technologies.)

Attitudes Toward Disability:
Several intervenors spoke eloquently about the need for society
to examine what the use of PND
says about our attitudes toward
disability and members of society
who have disabilities.

Others questioned whether
the allocation of resources to PND
diverts attention from the non-
genetic causes of disability,
including accidents, socioeconomic status, and inadequate
prenatal care.

We were told that societal
supports are generally inadequate for women or couples who
have a child with a disability and
that, in these circumstances,
intervenors questioned whether
aborting the fetus or carrying it to
term was a real choice.

Potential for Discrimination:
Finally, intervenors expressed
concern that people who carry
the genes for certain diseases,
particularly those that begin to
affect an individual only later in
life, could be subject to
discrimination — in employment,
in access to health or life
insurance, or in other ways — if
the information revealed by PND
was not protected. This issue will
presumably grow in importance
as knowledge about the genetic
component of health expands —
for example, with respect to late-
onset diseases such as Huntington disease and Alzheimer disease, as well as with respect to
individual susceptibility to
conditions such as heart disease,
cancer, and a range of other
conditions. This topic is
discussed in Chapter 27.

There are many circumstances where
knowledge of the fetus's condition can
have a significant and beneficial
impact on the overall obstetric
management.

For example, if a woman is known to
be carrying a fetus with a non-lethal
structural abnormality such as an
intestinal obstruction in an otherwise
normal fetus, then arrangements can
be made in advance to optimize the
fetus's outcome by arranging for her to
deliver in a tertiary level centre with
immediate access to neonatology and
paediatric surgery. The couple will
also have time to emotionally and
psychologically prepare for the delivery
and the fact the child will be
immediately transferred to an intensive
care setting or undergo surgery.

*J. Johnson, Genetics Committee,
Society of Obstetricians and
Gynaecologists of Canada, Public
Hearings Transcripts, Toronto, Ontario,
November 19, 1990.*

Advocacy of termination solely on the
basis of race would be met with loud,
impassioned cries of protest, but
termination on the basis of gender is
dreamed of by some, and abortion on
the basis of a fetal abnormality is
considered the best thing to do. Best
for whom? Those of us who are
disabled question the criteria.

*M. Gibson, Spina Bifida and
Hydrocephalus Association of Ontario,
Public Hearings Transcripts, Toronto,
Ontario, November 20, 1990.*

The concern was also raised that employers or insurance companies might demand *post*-natal genetic testing as a precondition of being offered employment or insurance. The issues surrounding genetic screening in the workplace are important, but they lie outside our mandate, which is limited to prenatal genetic diagnosis as one of the new reproductive technologies. In countries where private insurance covers health care, PND does indeed become a key issue for insurance regulation. In Canada, however, where basic health care is guaranteed, this is less of a concern.

How Prenatal Diagnosis Is Delivered

Some of what we heard focussed on concerns about inequality of access to PND on the basis of socioeconomic status, education, or place of residence. Witnesses argued that the use of PND seems to rise with the level of income, education, and employment; that having a higher level of education seemed to make it more likely that a woman or couple either would be aware of PND or would be able to secure a referral if they wished to have testing.

Concerns were also expressed about the nature of counselling. Some witnesses thought that the counselling provided as part of PND services might fail to give prospective parents a full appreciation of their range of options, including the possibility of raising a child with a disability and an indication of the supports available, from an unbiased perspective free of stereotyping or prejudgement.

> We do not want to ignore or abolish medical technology — we want to use it. We want to ensure that women are given the information they need to enable them to make a choice around using it, and the necessary support for decisions which they need to make based on the use of that technology. We need to establish a true partnership between women and the practitioners who serve them.
>
> *Brief to the Commission from the Toronto Women's Health Network, November 30, 1990.*

We also heard calls for research into two principal areas concerning: (1) the long-term effects of the use of some of these technologies on women and children, and (2) efforts to improve the accuracy of diagnoses. The issues raised by Canadians are discussed at more length below.

Commission Surveys of Canadians

Two large surveys of Canadians carried out across the country for the Commission documented a high level of awareness of and support for PND. Responses to these surveys showed high levels of awareness of the existence of some prenatal diagnostic techniques, such as amniocentesis and ultrasound, but fewer respondents were aware of the full range of techniques available to assess the health of the fetus or of the nature and purpose of specific techniques. Levels of awareness are higher among women than among men, and among respondents with higher levels of formal education.

- The vast majority of those surveyed would be prepared either to use PND themselves (79 percent) or to allow others that option (81 percent). About 18 percent were opposed to either personal use or wider availability of PND services.

- A marked majority of those surveyed also support the availability of the option to terminate a pregnancy after PND, with only 16 percent opposed in all circumstances. The level of support depends on the severity of the disorder. For example, 73 percent of people surveyed strongly supported the availability of abortion if a disorder that is fatal early in life is diagnosed in the fetus, while approximately 60 percent supported the availability of abortion for disorders that make it almost certain that independent living will not be possible.

Sixteen percent of referring physicians believe that intentionally giving birth to a child with a genetic defect at the time when both PND and abortion are available is socially irresponsible. The existence of this view, even if only among a minority, supports the need to establish safeguards to protect the principles of autonomy and informed consent to PND.

Aspects of the Use of Prenatal Diagnosis in Canada

In thinking about the issues and in integrating a wide range of individual perspectives and experiences, professional orientations, and expert advice into a coherent set of policy recommendations that address them, we applied our guiding principles. The context of the ethic of care and the intent to prevent or avoid harm wherever possible directed our reasoning. The ethic of care seeks to empower *all* concerned, rather than some at the expense of others. Hence, we considered both what harms could be done to individuals and society by the use of PND, whether these can be prevented by safeguards and, if so, whether these are in place; and what harms could be done to individuals and society by *not* providing PND.

It is important to remember that harm can arise either way: that is, either by withholding or by providing PND. Withholding PND for severe disorders could cause harm to individuals and couples at higher risk of having an affected fetus. On the other hand, the technologies involved are too

We found that Canadians recognize the seriousness of the issues to be weighed in reaching these decisions and are willing to give others the opportunity to deal with the choices in the way they see fit.

complex and powerful to be provided without a context of adequate guidelines and safeguards to protect vulnerable interests (of individuals and of society). We therefore had three goals in mind: to safeguard against the inappropriate, unethical, or discriminatory use of PND; to remove obstacles to appropriate access; and to deal with deficiencies in the PND system that result in the (direct or indirect) withholding of appropriate services.

Our guiding principles require that both individuals and society be considered in reaching our recommendations. Individual women and couples who have PND testing are constantly searching for the choices that are "right" for them. Many of these choices will also be acceptable to society as a whole; choices can vary greatly between families without in any way transgressing the bounds of societal acceptability. We found that Canadians recognize the seriousness of the issues to be weighed in reaching these decisions and are willing to give others the opportunity to deal with the choices in the way they see fit.

The Commission's objective is not to render definitive or immutable answers but rather to recommend how the serious issues raised by PND can continue to be addressed in the years to come, guided by our ethical principles. We focus on four broad sets of issues in the remainder of this section:

- the counselling and decision-making aspects of the PND process;
- the moral and legal issues of confidentiality and liability;
- the relationship between disabilities and choices about whether to terminate a pregnancy; and
- access to prenatal diagnostic services.

Counselling, Information, and Support

Throughout this report we have been guided in part by the principle of autonomy and its corollary, informed choice. As discussed in Chapter 3, this ideal requires that individual women and couples have adequate information, support for decision making (for example, through counselling), and an adequate range of options from which to choose.

The Medical Genetics Counselling Process

Within the genetics centres, genetics counselling is provided at various levels of complexity, ranging from referrals for maternal age, where little work is needed to identify the risks and options involved, to referrals for a family history, which may require highly complex statistical analysis and clinical interpretation. Counselling is a very demanding process that often taxes the skills and professionalism of the counsellor and challenges and engages the individual woman's or couple's deeply held values. (See box, which outlines the goals of medical genetics counselling.)

The Medical Genetics Counselling Session

The aims of the counsellor are to

- provide estimates, in understandable form, of the probability of having an affected child, and of the risks and benefits of contemplated procedures;
- provide information about the nature, burden, and possible variability of the disorder and about what treatments and supports are currently possible for a child born with a particular disorder;
- try to allay anxiety based on misperceptions and help the woman or couple to deal with that which is well founded;
- try to appreciate the couple's perception of risk and burden and where they fit on the spectrum of views regarding abortion, the disabled, quality of life, and attitudes toward life (for example, are they optimistic, realistic, fatalistic?). Every family is different, and, recognizing this, counsellors must try not to project their personal views into the situation;
- try to help the couple, without being directive, to reach a decision best suited to their own situation, by pointing out pros and cons and acting as a sounding board and resource person. The counsellor wants to empathize with the couple or individual, yet must remain objective to be effective. It is a tenet of genetics counsellors not to be directive, fully recognizing that this is not easy.

Quality of Information

The provision of accurate information in an understandable format is a fundamental component of the broader counselling process. The Commission collected brochures and other informational materials provided to patients by Canadian genetics centres; many of the materials were found to be complex, technical, and difficult to read.

Thirty items of patient education material from 14 centres were analyzed for reading level, writing style, and visual appeal. Twenty of the 30 items tested required a reading level above Grade 12; 18 items were rated as having a "poor" writing style; and 16 had "poor" visual appeal. In terms of an overall rating, 26 items were rated either "poor" (16) or "fair" (10), while only 4 were rated "good" (2) or "excellent" (2). Written materials were not always available in the language of the people served, particularly in centres that served large immigrant populations.

Many of the individual items, however, had positive features that, taken together, could provide the basis for improving patient education materials provided by genetics centres. The Commission therefore recommends that

> **207. The Canadian College of Medical Geneticists coordinate a collaborative effort by genetics centres, with the input of concerned women's groups and organizations representing people with disabilities, to develop more appropriate educational materials on prenatal diagnosis.**

The Commission also recommends to provincial/territorial health ministries that

> **208. These materials be made available to women and the general public through physicians' offices, public health units, local hospitals with obstetrical units, community centres providing prenatal classes, and other appropriate means.**

and that

> **209. Centres with large immigrant populations ensure that written materials and, in particular, consent forms are available in the relevant languages, and that provincial/territorial health ministries ensure that funds are available for this purpose.**

Complexity and Time Constraints

Women and couples often find genetics counselling sessions helpful, and perhaps even comforting, but satisfaction is not universal. Several of the reasons for dissatisfaction are implicit in the nature of this counselling. The facts themselves may be unpalatable or threatening. People may have great difficulty accepting that they carry a gene for a deleterious condition or that their next child is at risk for a serious disorder.

In addition, counselling done before pregnancy or before testing can only provide probabilities — expressed, for example, as a 1 in 4 chance or a 1 in 100 chance that the next child will have the condition. But probabilities, no matter how precise, are unsatisfying. People being counselled would like to have simple yes or no answers, yet ambiguity is often unavoidable in genetics counselling situations.

In addition, even though a fetus is known to be affected, it is not possible to predict the severity for some disorders except in terms of range. This is because some particular disorders show a great range in severity.

For example, the gene for neurofibromatosis may be detected, but this does not predict how seriously the eventual child will be affected by the disorder, whose effects range from only minor skin changes in some to devastating disability and early death in others.

Moreover, many people being counselled have no first-hand knowledge of the disorder that has been diagnosed. For example, many people will never have encountered a child with cystic fibrosis, even though it is the most common single-gene disorder in Canada. This means that some prospective parents are almost entirely dependent on their counsellors for information about disabilities and may have difficulty imagining the various possibilities and options.

Because of the time constraints imposed by the PND context, women and couples may feel there is insufficient time to reach a thoughtful decision. The time frame for decision making may be particularly tight when the woman or couple wishes to consider termination if the fetus

> Firstly, concerning the way I see the multidisciplinary team: I see it among practitioners, physicians, or nurses, in the context of the hospital itself, when the woman is contacted and told, for example, that she is carrying a fetus with an abnormality.
>
> Before a decision is made about abortion, would it not be appropriate, in fact, to introduce a multidisciplinary team that discusses the prognosis of the child the woman is carrying? Of course, trisomy is a serious problem, a very severe abnormality, but it is well known that there is difficulty detecting the degree of severity — who knows? [Translation]
>
> *Y. Grenier, private citizen, Public Hearings Transcripts, Montreal, Quebec, November 21, 1990.*

is affected; the later in pregnancy an abortion is done, the more risk and trauma it involves for the woman. Although results are usually available earlier, in some cases they may not be received until the pregnancy has reached the twenty-first or twenty-second week of gestation (for example, cases where a test must be redone, which happens in 1.1 percent of amniocenteses). Even without re-testing, amniocentesis results may not be available until after the sixteenth week of gestation.

Counsellors at genetics centres are required by the CCMG guidelines to be non-directive. Non-directiveness is not always welcomed by those receiving counselling. Some women and couples find the information complex and overwhelming and ask the counsellor what he or she would do in their place. Some are frustrated when the counsellor insists that it is their decision.

Even with optimal counselling, it can be expected that some women and couples will feel frustrated and angry at the circumstances in which they find themselves.

In view of this, we believe that the counsellor should provide written summaries of genetics counselling sessions not only to the referring physician but also to the women and couples counselled (which we found was done by some centres). Reports of counselling carried out before testing could be of benefit to women and couples in deciding about PND; similarly, reports of post-test counselling could benefit women and couples with an affected

> We are concerned that the resources devoted to counselling may not be keeping pace with increasing demand for counselling services ... The need for more and different kinds of counselling resources will likely expand with growing diversity in Canadian society.

fetus who are considering their options. Even though in some cases there may not be time for them to be useful in that pregnancy, the family then has it on hand for future reference and decision making about reproduction.

We are concerned that the resources devoted to counselling may not be keeping pace with increasing demand for counselling services. As medical knowledge and PND technology develop further, more information will be available about the fetus at earlier stages of gestation, and the need for counselling will tend to increase as a result. The need for more and different kinds of counselling resources will also likely expand with growing diversity in Canadian society. Counselling must be adapted continuously to meet the needs of users and be sensitive to language, social, and cultural factors in addition to the other requirements already identified.

If these concerns are to be addressed, provincial/territorial health ministries will have to increase their funding for counselling. Genetics centres are often funded through global budgets, which include salaries for personnel. At present, resource allocation for PND counselling often fails to recognize its personnel-intensive nature and the time involved in providing genetics services. If testing is to be offered, health ministries must provide appropriate levels of support, and genetics centres should also use these resources as effectively as possible. For example, genetics counsellors, not physician geneticists, would be able to offer counselling when the reason for referral is that the woman is 35 years of age or older. The Commission recommends that

> **210. Provincial/territorial health ministries develop a formula for funding genetics centres based on caseload to ensure that adequate resources for counselling are available. For a given number of women and couples referred annually for counselling (and this is to be an agreed-upon mix of straightforward and complex cases), the ministry of health should provide funding for a**

given ratio of physician, genetics associate, and support personnel. Such a formula would allow more comparable care to be delivered across the country.

Supportive Counselling

We have particular concerns about the adequacy of supportive counselling to deal with the emotional and psychological needs of patients. We found that most genetics centres offer high-quality informational counselling before testing, to review testing results, and to re-evaluate recurrence risks. However, just as in any medical care, the genetics counsellor may not be sufficiently expert in the recognition or management of the complex psychological and emotional problems that may arise, particularly when a fetus is found to be affected.

When a severe disorder is diagnosed, the woman or couple involved faces very difficult decisions and may require additional supportive counselling. If a decision to terminate the pregnancy is made, follow-up counselling may be offered; several genetics centres offer social work, pastoral care, or psychological support services in such cases. Genetics associates often have significant involvement in follow-up and emotional support for the women or couples involved. However, genetics centres may lack adequate psychological, psychiatric, or social work resources to help provide care in complex situations.

> The mourning reaction (to abortion) should be anticipated and respected. A psychiatric consultation in the pre-termination period should be followed by a contact with the couple sometime later at home. Patients suggested that this contact be initiated by the medical team because people often do not feel comfortable contacting the psychiatric team themselves. Involvement with a parents' group or association could prevent the feeling of isolation expressed by many couples. Family members and friends often do not understand the sorrow as well as people who have had a similar experience.
>
> *L. Dallaire and G. Lortie, "Parental Reaction and Adaptability to the Prenatal Diagnosis of Genetic Disease Leading to Pregnancy Termination," in Research Volumes of the Commission, 1993.*

It is important to remember that women and couples undergoing a termination following PND may need support, just as parents whose child has died do. Hence, counselling support should be offered throughout the process. We found that there is a lack of personal support during the termination procedure and its aftermath. We believe that special attention should be given to the counselling needs of women and couples in cases involving termination following the discovery of a serious fetal disorder.

In addition, access or referral to self-help groups or associations of people who have had a child with the same disorder may help reduce the feeling of isolation and provide support and helpful advice. The Commission recommends

> **211. To the Canadian College of Medical Geneticists, the Society of Obstetricians and Gynaecologists of Canada, the Canadian Association of Genetic Counsellors, and all practitioners involved in prenatal diagnosis that steps be taken to ensure that the woman having termination because of a serious fetal disorder and her family receive support from medical and paramedical staff, just as those who lose a child after birth do, from obstetrical and ward personnel before, during, and after termination, as well as from genetics centre personnel.**

The Commission also recommends that

> **212. All centres providing prenatal testing have, within their centre or by referral, facilities to provide women with counselling, including grief counselling, appropriate to their situation. This should be a condition of licence.**

The Commission recommends further that

> **213. To help reduce the feelings of isolation expressed by many women and couples, referral to self-help groups or associations be offered (where they exist) to people who have experienced a termination because of a fetal disorder.**

Consent, Choice, and Individual Autonomy

Genetics counselling is part of a decision-making process that results, ideally, in a free and informed choice by women considering whether to undergo PND. How do women and couples make decisions once they have received all the information, counselling, and support that is available?

Our evidence shows that there is a distinction between problem solving (the search for the one correct technical answer, a process heavily dependent on the practitioner's expertise) and decision making (the balancing of probabilities and personal priorities, risks, and desires — a

There is no single "right" answer for all women and couples, only answers that are right for the individual woman or couple, based on personal circumstances and values.

process that centres around the patient's wishes) (see research volume, *Treatment of Infertility: Current Practices and Psychosocial Implications*). In the context of PND, informed consent and choice must be understood as matters of decision making, not problem solving. There is no single "right" answer for all women and couples, only answers that are right for the individual woman or couple, based on personal circumstances and values.

What is right for the woman or couple is often not immediately clear, either to the counsellor or to the people receiving counselling, whose perception of risk and burden may vary widely. The specific family situation may be crucial, and the woman or couple may have more day-to-day experience of a condition than the counsellor. For example, a couple may already have a child with cystic fibrosis or spina bifida. Some may equate aborting a fetus who has the same disorder with disloyalty and rejection of their loved child; others may reject the idea of bringing another such child into the world. A woman who has worked with children with Down syndrome may be much more anxious about her pregnancy than one who has not. A person with polycystic kidney disease that was entirely asymptomatic

The ultimate consequence of the genetic-risk standard and its associated discourse is a denial of abnormality, a fear of difference, and a reinforcement of couples' and women's narcissism, that is, the perception of the other as an extension of oneself, and even the projection of oneself, leading, ultimately, to an unwillingness to accept otherness. This, then, in short, defines how technology and science make the other into a tool and, as a corollary, how they make abnormality or handicap even more devastating. [Translation]

Brief to the Commission from M. De Koninck, Chaire D'Étude sur la Condition des Femmes, and M.-H. Parizeau, Professeure, Faculté de Philosophie, Université Laval, February 1991.

and discovered only on routine examination at the age of 30 may be much more willing to take the 50 percent chance of passing the gene on to a child than someone whose disease is more severe and who has already had a kidney transplant. Regardless of the decision of the woman or couple, counsellors should be expected to respect that decision and to provide support and help.

Issues of liability also arise with respect to gaining informed consent when performing PND procedures. As discussed in Part One (Chapter 4), physicians have a legal obligation to secure the informed consent of patients to all procedures, which requires disclosing the benefits and risks involved. The current legal status of informed consent rests on the principle that if the physician fails to inform a patient of what is termed a "material" risk or a "special risk with serious consequences" associated with the proposed treatment, the failure can give rise to a lawsuit for negligence. Hence, providers of PND must inform patients of all material risks associated with PND procedures (that is, risks that could affect whether the patient would agree to the procedure). Similarly, if a referring physician neglects to inform women 35 years of age or older about PND testing, and if an affected child is born, there could be a claim of negligence.

In the context of decision making, the principle of autonomy directs attention to questions of consent, options, and the social context for choice. Are women in fact free to choose whether they will have PND? If the fetus is affected, are they free to choose whether to have an abortion or whether to continue the pregnancy? Are there undue pressures from doctors, spouses, friends, relations, or other sources that influence their decisions? In assessing these questions, the Commission found that it is important to distinguish the genetics centres from the referral system.

Consent to Testing

Option to Refuse Prenatal Tests: Commission research found that women at the genetics centres recognize that they have the choice of accepting or declining testing. Indeed, approximately 10 percent of patients referred for amniocentesis or CVS do decline the procedure. This varied from about 20 percent in Ontario centres outside Toronto to 3.7 percent in Halifax. Newfoundland (17.3 percent) also had a relatively high percentage who declined; rates for Saskatchewan (7.7 percent), Manitoba (6.1 percent), Alberta (4.6 percent), and Quebec (4.4 percent) were lower.

These figures must be interpreted with caution, as record-keeping differences between centres may have influenced their accuracy. However, there is some indication that in areas where referral to a more distant centre is necessary, the women who are referred have usually decided in advance to have testing. The higher refusal rates in Ontario may indicate that when women do not have to travel as far for counselling and testing, they may be more likely to go to the centre for counselling and put off the decision about whether to accept the test until after the counselling (see research volume, *Current Practice of Prenatal Diagnosis in Canada*).

The fact that about 10 percent of women decline testing suggests that women do see refusal as an option. It is also important to remember that most women who object on principle to PND would not go to a genetics centre in the first place. Hence, we believe that informed consent to PND testing is being given at genetics centres.

This cannot be taken for granted, however; vigilance must be maintained to ensure that informed consent remains a reality. Overall, referring physicians are opposed to the coercive use of PND. In fact, mandatory testing would be resisted by genetics centres and the CCMG and would be unacceptable to the vast majority of people in any society that values individual autonomy. Indeed, it would probably be struck down as inconsistent with the *Canadian Charter of Rights and Freedoms*.

During our public hearings we heard it said that some women choosing PND have been told that they must commit themselves to an abortion if a disorder is found. Our data from across the country showed that this is not the case at genetics centres, and the CCMG guidelines (to which genetics centres must adhere in order to get CCMG accreditation) state clearly that such a commitment is not required. It is possible, however, that women are being told this by physicians who refer them to genetics centres.

Commitment to Terminate: During our public hearings we heard it said that some women choosing PND have been told that they must commit themselves to an abortion if a disorder is found. Our data from across the country showed that this is not the case at genetics centres, and the CCMG guidelines (to which genetics centres must adhere in order to get CCMG accreditation) state clearly that such a commitment is not required. It is possible, however, that women are being told this by physicians who refer them to genetics centres.

The policy of the centres, laid out by the CCMG, is that the woman or couple should have the right to make a decision when faced with the actual, rather than a hypothetical, situation, because people often respond differently in the two situations. Furthermore, even if a couple does not wish to consider terminating the pregnancy after a disorder is found, the information provided by PND may still help them prepare for the birth of an affected child and appropriate medical care for the fetus before birth and at delivery.

Our data did show, however, that at one centre with insufficient resources to do all the prenatal tests requested, women who would not consider abortion under any circumstances were advised against (though not refused) PND. This was to allow testing of more women who were leaving that decision until after the test.

We cannot take the principle of informed consent for granted. Evidence from our survey of referring physicians showed that approximately half supported the idea of requiring a commitment to abortion before providing PND. Moreover, 12 genetics centres have not applied for accreditation from the CCMG, so it is difficult to monitor their compliance with the CCMG guidelines. The Commission therefore recommends that

> **214. All genetics centres providing prenatal diagnosis services formally adopt an explicit policy (consistent with current Canadian College of Medical Geneticists guidelines) that agreement to terminate a pregnancy is not a precondition or requirement for undergoing prenatal testing. The Commission recommends further that adoption of such a policy be a condition of licence established by the National Reproductive Technologies Commission for centres providing prenatal diagnosis and genetics services.**

The Social Context for Choice

Most people in Canada think that the choice of whether to have PND when at risk for a serious disorder, and whether to have an abortion if a disorder is diagnosed, should be left to each woman or couple in accordance with their own values and circumstances (see research volume, *Social Values and Attitudes Surrounding New Reproductive Technologies*).

Various social pressures influence this choice. If a woman decides to terminate the pregnancy, some may view her decision as unethical. On the other hand, a woman who decides to continue a pregnancy and have an affected child may face disapproval from some members of the community who will view the decision as irresponsible. Another aspect she must consider is that the resources available for parents who choose to raise children with disabilities are limited, and that children with disabilities may be subject to prejudice and discrimination. For some individual women, economic and social realities make the possible alternative — raising a child with a disability — so formidable that it does not appear to be a genuine choice for them.

People receiving counselling should be fully informed, therefore, not only about the risks and the disorders involved, and about what the disorder means in terms of day-to-day functioning for the affected individual and lifelong consequences for themselves, but also about the social pressures they

Most people in Canada think that the choice of whether to have PND when at risk for a serious disorder, and whether to have an abortion if a disorder is diagnosed, should be left to each woman or couple in accordance with their own values and circumstances.

may experience, so that they have an opportunity to consider how such pressures might affect them (see research volume, *New Reproductive Technologies: Ethical Aspects*). These social pressures are important. We believe that women's capacity to make informed choices about PND would be improved if economic and social supports for families affected by disabilities were increased.

It is also important to realize that social pressures are not the only, or even the primary, factor in many decisions. For many families, lack of support or services is not the primary reason they do not wish to have an affected child. Although there is no question that increased support is necessary in the interests of social justice, this would not provide an acceptable alternative to PND and abortion of affected fetuses for many women and couples. To say that it would neglects the devastating impact of some mental and neurological disabilities, which require lifelong care, often overwhelm the parents' lives, and inflict suffering on the affected individual and, as a result, on family members and others who witness that suffering. In addition, parents — especially the woman, who often bears the primary responsibility for care — are left with few choices about pursuing other goals.

It is also important to realize that social pressures are not the only, or even the primary, factor in many decisions. For many families, lack of support or services is not the primary reason they do not wish to have an affected child.

Counselling and Informed Choice in the Referral Network

As noted earlier in this chapter, there are serious problems regarding counselling and informed consent within the referral network for PND. For example, given the demonstrated inadequacies with informed consent to MSAFP screening in Manitoba that our data show, we believe that women who consent to MSAFP screening should be required to sign a consent form that contains relevant information about the test.

Similar problems regarding informed consent arose in the context of referrals for women who were 35 years of age or over. In the Commission study of 70 such women referred to a genetics centre for PND, many were told that referral was "automatic" at their age (see research volume, *Prenatal Diagnosis: Background and Impact on Individuals*). Other Commission research found that some women do not realize that they can decline referral (see research volume, *New Reproductive Technologies: Ethical Aspects*).

Practising physicians, particularly obstetricians, tend to be much more directive than geneticists according to the evidence provided by our surveys.

Insofar as general practitioners and obstetricians do provide information, there are concerns about the directiveness of counselling. The Commission's survey of referring physicians found that 50 percent agreed with the statement that parents should have absolute right to freedom of choice regarding abortion, yet 40 percent thought that physicians, not parents, should decide which fetal anomalies justify abortion (see research volume, *Current Practice of Prenatal Diagnosis in Canada*).

Other findings were also relevant: for example, 16 percent of all physicians responding, and 27 percent of Quebec physicians, believed that it is a socially irresponsible act to have a child with a genetic disorder when PND is available. Similar proportions felt it would be justified to have laws to limit the transmission of genes causing severe disorders. Thus, practising physicians, particularly obstetricians, tend to be much more directive than geneticists according to the evidence provided by our surveys.

> It is urgent that we look critically at these technologies and consider the serious problems they create for women. We note, firstly, the intensive use of their bodies: the heavy reliance on treatments, the overmedication, the complexity of treatments, and the fact that they are increasingly numerous. Ultrasound is an example. Initially, this treatment was limited to women at risk; then, most women had one ultrasound during their pregnancy; later, they had three or four. And one of my colleagues was telling me this morning that, in some centres, women routinely had to have an ultrasound at every visit. So it has become routine in hospitals; it has become ordinary. [Translation]
>
> *A. Robinson, Groupe de recherche multidisciplinaire féministe, Public Hearings Transcripts, Quebec City, Quebec, September 26, 1990.*

The finding that many practising physicians (who determine whether and how referral for PND is offered) have attitudes that are less respectful of patient autonomy is an indication of the need for greater physician education and awareness in this regard. This has implications for medical school curricula, residency training, specialty examination content, and continuing medical education. The values and opinions of physicians must not be imposed on patients. The Commission recommends that

215. For women who consent to MSAFP screening, signed consent forms be required prior to taking blood for the test and that information about the test be contained on the consent form.

216. The Society of Obstetricians and Gynaecologists of Canada and the College of Family Practitioners of Canada encourage their members to pursue continuing medical education to increase their knowledge and understanding of the capabilities and limitations of prenatal diagnosis, the proper provision of accurate information, and the process of informed consent and choice.

and that

217. Specifically, increased efforts should be made in the continuing medical education of referring physicians to emphasize the right of individual women and couples to reproductive autonomy, to decide for themselves whether to have prenatal testing, and, if a serious disorder is detected, to decide whether to terminate or continue the pregnancy. These decisions must be based on the principle of informed choice, that is, with full knowledge of all the available options, benefits, and risks, and full and informed consent to undergo a prenatal diagnosis procedure.

Confidentiality

Disclosure of Genetic Information to Family Members

PND sometimes unexpectedly reveals sensitive information that, if disclosed, could benefit some individuals but harm others. This may give rise to serious ethical problems. For example, the test might reveal that the pregnant woman's partner is not the biological father of the fetus she is carrying.   In this situation, our data show that a woman's partner would not usually be told; rather, the woman would be told he is not the father and the decision about what to do left up to her. If DNA testing becomes used more often, such situations will

Doctors are under a legal duty to maintain the confidentiality of medical records. This legal duty is recognized in common law and civil law, as well as in various statutes and professional guidelines, and may even be protected by section 7 of the *Canadian Charter of Rights and Freedoms*.

arise more often.   Ideally, the pregnant woman should be informed in private, before she consents to testing, that the test may reveal paternity or, sometimes, that the partner is not the biological father of the child.

Dilemmas could also arise if testing revealed a chromosomal translocation carried by one of the partners, which would show that his or her near relatives were also at risk of having affected children. A lack of disclosure in this situation could harm the relatives, as they might wish to avoid having children affected by the disorder.

Generally speaking, doctors are under a legal duty to maintain the confidentiality of medical records. This legal duty is recognized in common law and civil law, as well as in various statutes and professional guidelines, and may even be protected by section 7 of the *Canadian Charter of Rights and Freedoms.*

However, there are three recognized exceptions to the duty of confidentiality: where there is consent by the patient, authorization of a court, or the risk of harm to third parties. For example, there are requirements to protect public health by reporting certain infectious diseases or an intentional threat to a third party. If a genetics counsellor wants to contact relatives at risk of having an affected child, it is not a question of public health or of avoiding intentional harm to another; rather, it is a question of providing third parties who are relatives with additional significant information they might not otherwise have.

A U.S. President's Commission (for the Study of Ethical Problems in Medicine and Biomedical and Behavioral Research) report in 1983 recommended that, in cases where there is a high probability of serious harm to an identifiable individual, a breach of confidence could be considered ethically acceptable if there were first a serious attempt to persuade the primary patient to allow the information to be divulged to identifiable relatives, if failure to inform could cause serious harm, and if the information released was limited to necessary genetic information. No court to date has rendered a judgement about such disclosures in the specific context of human genetics, so it is not known whether these guidelines would serve as a defence in the event of a suit by the person whose confidential records were disclosed without their consent or whether the failure to disclose would be considered negligent. Opinion varies among geneticists about how to deal with such problems,[1] but in general, as we have noted elsewhere (see Chapter 27), they believe that disclosure can usually be achieved by discussion, education, and tactful negotiation.

One other situation where full disclosure may raise ethical questions involves test results that are ambiguous; either the significance of test results is not clear (for example, mosaicism or an unusual chromosome that might, or might not, be a normal variant), or test results are conflicting. Even though disclosing such results could create so much anxiety that the woman might be better off not knowing, in our society full disclosure is now the norm. We consider failure to disclose paternalistic, as the assumption that a woman would not be able to deal with the information is disrespectful of her autonomy.

Protection of Privacy and Confidentiality

As noted earlier, concerns have been raised that information gained through PND may be wanted by insurance companies and employers.[2] Release of such information by the physician without the patient's consent would be a clear violation of the legal duty of confidentiality. Whatever the exceptions to confidentiality in civil or common law, they would not include a right to disclose information about the fetus to insurers or employers without the patient's consent.

PND records are protected by the same rights to privacy as other medical records. Indeed, the duty of confidentiality is particularly important here, given the private nature of the decision to have PND and the fact that information about the fetus and eventual child is involved, making consent to disclosure by the individual in question impossible. The records must therefore be protected from unauthorized access by third parties; we provide for this in our recommendations.

In the next chapter we briefly review the protections that now exist with regard to misuse of information about an individual's genetic make-up, but most of the concerns about the use of genetic information by employers or insurers relate to testing of individuals *post*-natally. This is an important issue but one that is outside the mandate of the Commission.

Liability

Physicians have a responsibility to inform pregnant women about their options with respect to managing the pregnancy. Offering at-risk women and couples the option of PND is considered a standard of care by the SOGC, the CCMG, and the American College of Obstetricians and Gynecologists. This has important implications for physicians. If a physician fails to inform an at-risk couple of the availability of PND and the woman subsequently delivers a child affected by a serious disorder that would have been detected by PND, that physician could be liable for damages in a civil suit for failure to inform them. In the United States, for example, physicians have been sued for failure to offer prenatal testing based on risks such as the woman's age, ethnicity, the

> Physicians have a responsibility to inform pregnant women about their options with respect to managing the pregnancy. Offering at-risk women and couples the option of PND is considered a standard of care by the SOGC, the CCMG, and the American College of Obstetricians and Gynecologists.

previous birth of an affected child, or exposure to teratogens such as rubella.

Whether the behaviour of a medical professional constitutes a fault, which can lead to a charge of negligence, or merely an error, which does not, will depend on how the act or omission measures up to the standards of the profession. According to the standards of medical geneticists, a genetics counsellor has a duty to explain the magnitude of a risk and the burden of the disorder, in a way that the woman or couple can understand, and to attempt to ensure that those being counselled do in fact understand the information provided (whether the person being counselled does comprehend is of course impossible to guarantee). If counsellors fail to inform patients adequately regarding the option of PND — or fail to provide preconception counselling if that is indicated — they can be sued for damages or injury. The purpose of such court actions is to get compensation — that is, to restore the patient, as far as possible, to the position they would have been in had the practitioner not acted negligently.

In the context of PND, the claim of negligence arises where there is misinformation or failure to supply information to a woman or couple who subsequently have an affected child that they would otherwise not have conceived or would have aborted. The claim for damages may be made by the parents or made on behalf of the child. As we will see, the courts have responded very differently to these two types of claims.

Wrongful Birth

Claims of damages by the parents have been referred to as involving "wrongful birth." The initial defence against such a claim was that the health care worker did not cause the damage; it was caused by a gene or, in some cases, a teratogen. However, negligence in establishing or imparting risk information has come to be seen by the courts as depriving women or couples of their right to prevent the conception or birth of a child with a disability, and failure to provide information has come to be seen as a direct cause of the injury.

There have been no reported cases in Canada of a wrongful birth claim arising from PND malpractice. Two Quebec cases arising from malpractice in sterilization are relevant to this issue, however. In *Cataford v. Moreau* (1978), a tubal ligation was done negligently, and a healthy eleventh child was born to the woman who had sought sterilization through tubal ligation. The parents were awarded medical and hospital expenses. However, the award with respect to the cost of rearing the child was modest, not only because of existing state support by way of family allowance but also because the court considered the birth of a child a benefit, if not a blessing.

In *Engstrom v. Courteau* (1986), a man with hereditary cataracts had a vasectomy after his first child was born with the disorder. No post-operative sperm count was done, and his second wife subsequently became pregnant and gave birth to another child with the disorder. The Quebec Superior Court allowed a claim for wrongful birth.

In the few PND-related wrongful birth suits in the United States, awards have generally been intended to cover the cost of raising an affected child over and above what would have been the cost of raising a child without the disorder. In other words, having a child per se is not considered a damage, even though the parents might not have had a child had they known the risk. The period of compensation may also extend beyond the age of majority, since parents have a moral and, in some jurisdictions, a legal obligation to support a dependent child beyond the age of majority. In some cases, awards were also made for the mental suffering of the parents.

Wrongful Life

Cases in which the child is the plaintiff in a suit brought by its parents on its behalf have been termed "wrongful life" claims. In general, the courts in both Canada and the United States have resisted making awards for wrongful life. For example, in the two Quebec cases mentioned above, the Quebec Superior Court rejected wrongful life claims on the grounds that there is no legal right not to be born; thus, having been born cannot be claimed as damage by a child. Among the reasons given for not allowing wrongful life claims are the following:

- Whereas parents have a right to control their reproduction, a child has no independent right not to be born. To accept such a right would imply that the physician was under a legal obligation to terminate the fetus's life (regardless of the parent's wishes).

- To accept the child's claim that it would be better off not to have been born is contrary to public policy, since it would devalue the life of an existing child and would thus be a violation of the sanctity of human life.

- Had the negligent action not taken place (that is, had the parents been warned), the child would not exist in order to sue. Since the aim of compensation is to restore the plaintiff (as far as possible) to the position they would have been in had the negligent action not occurred, "compensating" the child would seem to require returning it to a state of non-existence.

To summarize these two topics, wrongful birth suits brought by parents for reproductive risk malpractice are now widely accepted in U.S. jurisdictions. It is likely that such a suit would be allowed in Canada where avoidance of the risk could have been achieved by not conceiving the child or by aborting the fetus after PND. It is likely, however, that a wrongful life suit would be rejected in Canada.

As we also discuss in Chapter 30, "Judicial Intervention," the Commission is of the view that it would be wrong to permit wrongful life suits to be brought against women who bear a child affected by a disorder. We believe also that such suits would not be successful in Canadian courts. The Commission does not believe, therefore, that new legislation is needed to change the way Canadian courts are handling such cases.

The Commission is of the view that it would be wrong to permit wrongful life suits to be brought against women who bear a child affected by a disorder. We believe also that such suits would not be successful in Canadian courts. The Commission does not believe, therefore, that new legislation is needed to change the way Canadian courts are handling such cases.

Disabilities

If a severe disorder is identified prenatally, many women and couples decide to terminate the pregnancy. As we have seen, this has given rise to concerns that the current practice of PND is antithetical to the interests of people with disabilities and contributes to their marginalization in society. Some critics have also argued that PND is being used as a means of reducing the incidence of disabilities so as to reduce the "burden" on society of providing supports for people with disabilities. These concerns must be taken seriously and evaluated honestly. Among the questions on which Commissioners needed information were the following:

- What is the actual impact of PND on the frequency of disabling disorders in Canadian society? Is PND being done in order to reduce the incidence of such disorders in the population?

- How do individual women and couples, practitioners, and society deal with the question of the severity of a disability as it relates to PND?

- How do social attitudes and the availability of supportive programs for people with disabilities and parents of children with disabilities affect the decisions made by women and couples about PND and about terminating a pregnancy?

The Impact of Prenatal Diagnosis on Frequency of Disorders

There are two reasons why PND cannot eliminate or substantially reduce the overall incidence of genetic disorders and disabling conditions in the population.

First, the majority of congenital anomalies and genetic disorders cannot be detected by PND, nor is it possible to identify the majority of people at higher risk for these disorders and offer them diagnostic testing. Even for disorders for which population screening is offered in some parts of the country (for example, MSAFP testing for neural tube defects; carrier screening for thalassaemia), and even though the frequency of these particular disorders is reduced, these conditions account for only a very small proportion of all disorders. Furthermore, although the frequency of individuals with these disorders is reduced in the population, the frequency of the underlying genes is not altered.

Second, most disabilities are not genetic or congenital in origin. Most disabilities result from other factors, such as accidents, low birth weight, prematurity, viral or bacterial diseases, birth traumas, acts of violence, and aging. This means that using PND to test for genetic disorders may influence the frequency of particular categories of disorders, but it cannot be expected to and will never substantially decrease the overall incidence of disability in the population, because categories of disability affected by congenital anomalies account for such a small proportion of all disabilities.

PND is not designed to have a substantial impact on the incidence of disabilities in the population. Rather, it is designed to give those at higher risk of having an affected fetus options in dealing with their particular risk and to give them the same chance as other Canadians of having a healthy family.

The Effects and Severity of Disabilities

Prenatal diagnosis should be provided only to identify serious disorders. Some people are concerned that society's perception of what constitutes a serious disorder will change and that PND will, over time, lead to greater intolerance of even minor anomalies. It is important, therefore, to say something about what constitutes a "serious" disorder. A disorder can be serious because of the suffering it causes for the child and/or because of its emotional, physical, and financial effects on the parents and family. These are related but vary from one disorder to another.

Tay-Sachs disease, for example, is a particularly severe disorder in terms of the suffering it causes for the child; affected children have short and painful lives. Down syndrome can be burdensome for parents; though such children often lead long and happy lives, they may require constant care. If congenital heart disease is also present, Down syndrome can cause severe suffering for the child, but even in cases where the child's symptoms are not so serious, the child may be incapable of functioning independently.

Perceptions of the severity and impact of a disorder are, to some extent, subjective — they depend on the experiences and circumstances of the people involved. For example, a couple who has been trying for some years to have a child may view a given disorder or disability differently from a couple who did not plan the pregnancy and who already has several children. Genetics centres accept that since it is the parents who would have to care for an affected child, they are the only ones in a position to evaluate these factors.

Some disorders cause neither significant suffering to the child nor hardship for the parents — for example, webbed toes or extra digits.

Children with these minor anomalies do not suffer any ill health from them, and caring for them does not create any unusual hardship for the parents. Allowing PND and termination for such disorders would be unethical for several reasons. First, it reflects inappropriate views of disability, of the respect owed to human life, and of the nature and value of children and the parent-child relationship. It also violates the principle of appropriate use of resources, since it fulfils no real medical need.

It is important, therefore, that PND be used only to detect serious disorders. PND may incidentally reveal the existence of trivial disorders, but this is not the purpose of such procedures. It is not possible, however, to establish a definitive list of serious disorders. The severity and impact of a disorder can change over time, with changes in society and in the treatability of disorders. Moreover, we do not believe it is necessary to establish such a list; the literature and our own field survey show that couples usually do not seek PND for trivial reasons and that the likelihood of termination is related to the severity of the disorder identified. (The related question of PND to determine the sex of the fetus for non-medical reasons is discussed in Chapter 28.)

> The literature and our own field survey show that couples usually do not seek PND for trivial reasons and that the likelihood of termination is related to the severity of the disorder identified.

We heard from many genetics centres that they are having difficulty getting adequate funding from provincial governments to provide testing for serious disorders; requests for funds to provide a new PND test are often turned down or are accepted only after long and difficult negotiations. Examples of tests that are not funded in some provinces include metabolite measurements or enzyme assays for patients with certain inborn errors of metabolism and DNA mutation analysis for families at risk of Tay-Sachs disease. In at least one province, funding has to be negotiated case by case for testing of fetal chromosomes after routine ultrasound has picked up a physical anomaly, even though chromosomal testing in these circumstances is recommended by nationally recognized guidelines. Some geneticists try to provide these tests anyway, seeking reimbursement from the provincial ministry after the fact, or paying for them out of research budgets. However, this can create uncertainty, delays, backlogs, and anxiety for both practitioners and couples at risk. Given these circumstances, provincial health ministries seem unlikely to provide funds for testing intended to detect trivial disorders.

We see no evidence that Canadian women are seeking PND for trivial disorders, that genetics centres are offering PND for trivial disorders, or that provincial/territorial governments are funding PND for trivial disorders. This is an important issue, however, and one about which a tolerant and inclusive society cannot afford to be complacent. We believe, therefore, that this area of medical activity should be monitored and reported on, and that there should be more opportunities for public input on decisions about which PND tests should be provided. Greater public awareness is the best bulwark against the inappropriate use of PND for trivial disorders. Our recommendations later in this chapter are intended to establish such a system of public monitoring and debate.

> We see no evidence that Canadian women are seeking PND for trivial disorders, that genetics centres are offering PND for trivial disorders, or that provincial/territorial governments are funding PND for trivial disorders.

Public Policy and Social Attitudes Toward Disabilities

Support Programs for People with Disabilities: A frequent concern expressed at our hearings by people with disabilities was that providing resources for PND may divert money from programs providing support to people with disabilities and parents caring for children with disabilities.

We firmly endorse the importance of adequate social support for parents bringing up a child with a disability, both as a matter of justice for people with disabilities and as a matter of informed choice for the parents. Adequate support is essential if the decision to continue a pregnancy and have a child with a disability is to be a viable and socially accepted option. Moreover, recent medical advances in the treatment of children with disabilities have increased the need for social support. The deinstitutionalization of people with disabilities and the fact that people with disabilities are living longer often mean that parents (usually the mother) must care for a child well into old age. The economic and social costs of this can be substantial.

> We firmly endorse the importance of adequate social support for parents bringing up a child with a disability, both as a matter of justice for people with disabilities and as a matter of informed choice for the parents. Adequate support is essential if the decision to continue a pregnancy and have a child with a disability is to be a viable and socially accepted option.

We do not believe, however, that there is a trade-off between providing PND and providing support for people with disabilities. On the contrary, we believe that the two can go hand in hand.

For one thing, as noted previously, the incidence of disability in the population will be little affected by the provision of PND. Most childhood disability originates from other factors, and, as society ages, the overall proportion of people with disabilities is increasing. Statistics Canada figures for 1991 indicate that almost 16 percent of all Canadians reported some kind of disability, up from 13 percent in 1986.

It does not seem likely, therefore, that funding for PND will affect the funds available for social support for people with disabilities. Indeed, attitudes toward people with disabilities are changing as society becomes more informed about their needs and more aware of how constitutional and human rights protections must be reflected in public institutions and policies. The growing public profile of this issue is being reflected in increased attention to the needs of people with disabilities by all levels of government. Thus, concerns expressed about PND need to be placed in context of positive changes in Canadian policies and institutions with respect to disability and the participation of people with disabilities in all aspects of society.

The question of how best for society to provide support for people with disabilities is beyond our mandate. But we affirm our support for social policy and public education initiatives intended to provide adequate support for people with disabilities and to promote their equal treatment, acceptance, and participation in Canadian society.

Attitudes Toward People with Disabilities: Historically, Canadians with disabilities have faced significant prejudice and hostility, and society is still capable of such attitudes. Indeed, the Commission heard from some groups representing people with disabilities that as much suffering is caused by attitudes toward disability as results from the disability itself. Prejudice or hostility toward people with disabilities is unacceptable; the question is whether the existence and continuing development of PND technology promote such attitudes.

> We do not believe that there need be any conflict between the interests and needs of couples at risk and those of people with disabilities. To suggest that Canadians choose one or the other is an example of the adversarial stance that an ethic of care seeks to avoid, when in fact the aim should be to provide good care for all.

Some critics say that using PND to identify and abort affected fetuses is discrimination on the basis of disability, which in effect is prejudice against disabled persons in society. We do not accept this view. We believe it is possible to uncouple the issue of the availability of PND from issues surrounding society's attitudes toward and treatment of people with disabilities.

As explained earlier in this chapter, all couples face the possibility of having a child with a disorder or disability, even if the risk is low for most. If such a child is born, most parents feel emotionally committed to him or her. Almost all families love their children and do their best to respond to the challenges of child-rearing. But the commitment to value and nurture an existing child with a disability is not the same as the commitment to nurture a fetus where an anomaly has been detected. Lack of commitment to continue a pregnancy does not mean that commitment to an existing child or person is diminished.

Some people referred for PND are already caring for an affected child. These couples usually care deeply about their child, and many have struggled to improve social support and acceptance for people with disabilities. However, they may feel unable to cope with raising another affected child and so seek PND for future pregnancies. It is clear that these families are able to uncouple the issue of PND and possible termination of a pregnancy from their attitudes toward their existing child and toward people with disabilities in general. Many couples at risk wish to avoid having another child with severe disabilities. To assume that this desire represents hostility or prejudice toward existing children or adults with disabilities is, we believe, an oversimplification, both morally and psychologically.

Another concern we heard is that prospective parents may be given biased information about various disorders during PND counselling. Some representatives of people with disabil-

> To argue that the status of people with disabilities would be improved if PND were less available is misleading.

ities worried that doctors are providing parents with stereotyped and inaccurate information about living with disability. They claim that some doctors, particularly in the referring network, are telling parents that a child with cystic fibrosis or Down syndrome leads a painful or worthless existence. Many parents feel it would be selfish to abort an affected fetus solely on grounds of hardship to themselves; as a result, they believe, there may be a tendency to exaggerate the extent to which a disorder or disability causes suffering to the child.

Giving parents biased information would violate the principle of autonomy. It is therefore essential that information be as objective and accurate as possible. We have already recommended that the CCMG coordinate a collaborative effort by genetics centres to develop improved educational materials on PND and the disorders it can detect, and that groups representing people with disabilities be included in that effort. The Commission recommends further that

> **218. As part of its collaborative effort to develop appropriate counselling materials on prenatal diagnosis, the Canadian College of Medical Geneticists conduct a rigorous review of counselling protocols and information materials to ensure that disabilities and living with a disability are represented fairly and accurately. People representing those with disabilities, people at risk, and women should be included in this process.**

We must not let the availability of prenatal testing create the illusion that disabilities are avoidable — most are not. Disabilities will always be with us, whether PND is used or not. Society must offer support to people with disabilities. But to argue that the status of people with disabilities would be improved if PND were less available is misleading. Given that most disabilities are not congenital and cannot be diagnosed prenatally, it seems likely that society's approach to people with disabilities will not stand or fall on the availability of prenatal diagnosis services or the way they are provided. In fact, evidence suggests that in countries where PND is practised, there is greater rather than less interest in the welfare of people with disabilities as a result of increased medical and social awareness of their needs and rights.[3]

We do not believe that there need be any conflict between the interests and needs of couples at risk and those of people with disabilities. To suggest that Canadians choose one or the other is an example of the adversarial stance that an ethic of care seeks to avoid, when in fact the aim should be to provide good care for all.

Termination of Pregnancy

In the great majority of cases where a serious fetal disorder is diagnosed prenatally, no treatment of the fetus is available. The choice is usually between terminating the pregnancy or preparing for the birth of a child with a disorder or disability. As we have seen, most women in these circumstances decide to terminate the pregnancy.

This has raised the concern that the availability of PND might encourage the indiscriminate use of abortion. To assess this concern, we examined the likelihood of termination after PND, the way higher-risk families approach reproductive decisions in the absence of PND, and the views of Canadians about the termination of pregnancy in the context of PND.

Likelihood of Terminations

When a serious fetal disorder is detected by PND, approximately 80 percent of women decide to terminate the pregnancy. About 20 percent of women decide to carry on with the pregnancy, which suggests that the decision to terminate a pregnancy after a disorder is diagnosed is not taken lightly. Indeed, the decision to terminate is complicated, involving many factors. In particular, the severity of the disorder has a profound effect on the likelihood of a decision to terminate. As Table 26.12 indicates, the proportion of women in Canada who elected to terminate a pregnancy after a fetal disorder was detected varied greatly with the nature of the disorder.

The disorders in the last two groups listed have less serious or less predictable effects than disorders in the other two categories. In the case of Turner syndrome, the most frequent problems are short stature and infertility, but cardiovascular and other physical anomalies are also common.

Table 26.12. Pregnancy Termination After Diagnosis of Fetal Disorder

Type of disorder	% of women who terminated pregnancy
Trisomies 13, 18, and 21 (Down syndrome)	83
Neural tube defects	76
Turner syndrome	70
XXY, XYY, XXX syndromes, balanced translocations, mosaics	30

Source: Adapted from Hamerton, J.L., J.A. Evans, and L. Stranc. "Prenatal Diagnosis in Canada — 1990: A Review of Genetics Centres." In Research Volumes of the Royal Commission on New Reproductive Technologies, 1993.

Generally speaking, children with XXY, XYY, and XXX syndromes can be somewhat less intelligent than they otherwise would be and have certain learning and behavioural problems, but many such children exhibit only mild signs. The fact that fewer women choose to terminate a pregnancy when one of these disorders is detected shows that women and couples consider carefully the severity and burden of the disorder before making a decision to continue or terminate a pregnancy.

In short, PND is not inexorably linked to abortion when disorders are discovered. Information gained through PND may be used by one couple in a decision to terminate, while another couple may use the same information to prepare for the birth of a child with a disorder. It is evident that the decisions of women and couples are nuanced and situation-specific.

Coping with Higher Genetic Risk in the Absence of Prenatal Diagnosis

When discussing the relationship between PND and abortion, most people focus on the difficult decision women and couples face when a fetal disorder has been diagnosed. But this is just half the story; couples at higher risk also face a difficult decision when PND is not available. The desire to have children is deeply rooted, and most Canadians want to have children. Where PND is not available, a couple's knowledge that they are at higher risk for congenital or genetic disorders poses a serious threat to this goal.

Couples who want families are willing to take the usual risks that accompany reproduction. Studies have shown that when a couple does not realize that a congenital disorder is genetic in origin, they tend to have the same number of children as others in their community; as a result, they may have several affected children. When they know that the disorder has a genetic basis, unless PND with the option of termination is available, couples give up their plans to have children (or more children) rather than risk having an affected child. This is often deeply distressing to the couple, particularly if it is their first and only child who is affected.

When PND is made available to those who want it, higher-risk couples who had stopped having children often have repeated pregnancies at short intervals in order to have healthy children and a family of the desired size. Their family size increases to become similar to that of couples who are not at genetic risk.[4] For example, before PND was available for thalassaemia, couples with one affected child who knew about the one in four recurrence risk tried not to conceive. They avoided having further affected children but were unable to reach their goal of having a healthy family. In other words, PND allows high-risk couples to manage their risk and have the same chance as others to have healthy children.

Public Attitudes

Canadians' attitudes toward abortion are complex. Most support a woman's right to choose, but individual opinions vary widely about the personal circumstances in which abortion is appropriate. Most Canadians recognize that the diagnosis of a severe congenital anomaly in a wanted pregnancy is tragic and that it is with great regret that a woman or couple in these circumstances chooses to terminate the pregnancy.

Most Canadians do not feel they can tell others what they should do in these circumstances. A substantial majority (about three-quarters) say that if the fetus has a severe anomaly, the parents should have the option to terminate the pregnancy. Canadians recognize that termination in this situation is not a benefit but rather the opposite; nevertheless, they believe the option should be available.

Public support for having this option available to couples at risk is therefore a case of public respect for the extremely difficult situation of these couples — a situation in which all the options are difficult and none of the choices is easy. Commissioners believe that couples in this situation merit society's understanding and support, and we affirm our support for the availability of PND services to identify severe disorders and for the freedom of women and couples to choose among the options based on the information PND provides.

Access

Representations to the Commission on behalf of women's groups, people with disabilities, women of colour and members of visible minorities, professional associations, and others were eloquent about the need for women in Canada to have equal access to safe, high-quality PND services. As we have seen, however, there are substantial and worrisome variations in PND availability and use across the country. In this section, we examine some sources of variation in PND use: distance from a genetics centre; variations in referral patterns; and socioeconomic status.

Distance from a Centre

Utilization rates generally decline with distance from a genetics centre. In most provinces, genetics centres are located in one or two of the largest cities. Given the infrastructure and the skilled and experienced personnel needed, this makes sense from the perspective of functional requirements and appropriate use of resources. Like other medical technologies that depend on expensive infrastructure and skilled personnel, genetics centres should serve a catchment area of appropriate population size.

The further a woman lives from a centre, however, the less likely she is to use these services. The geographical distribution of referring obstetricians and gynaecologists also has an effect. As we have seen, they are more likely to make referrals than general practitioners, and, since they are concentrated in urban centres, a woman living in an urban centre is more likely to be referred. Women living in rural or northern communities who want prenatal diagnostic services may have to travel to an urban location to get a referral, then travel to yet another location for the actual PND service. This is a difficult, expensive, and time-consuming process. Women in remote communities may not in fact see a referring physician in time to get a referral for prenatal testing. Other women may be offered a referral but be unable to afford the time or money required to travel to the centre.

The problem is exacerbated in provinces with no genetics centre (Prince Edward Island, New Brunswick, the Northwest Territories, and the Yukon). Women from Prince Edward Island and New Brunswick are referred to Halifax for testing; women from the Northwest Territories are usually referred to Edmonton or Winnipeg, depending on which is closer (although some amniocenteses are performed in Yellowknife and the fluids sent to Edmonton for analysis); and women from the Yukon are tested in Vancouver.

Table 26.13. Geographical Distribution of Genetics Centres in Canada

Province	Population	Number of centres	Population/ centre
Nfld.	572 600 (2.2%)	1 (4.5%)	572 600
P.E.I.	130 500 (0.5%)	0 (—)	—
N.S.	890 200 (3.4%)	1 (4.5%)	890 200
N.B.	722 900 (2.7%)	0 (—)	—
Que.	6 749 400 (25.5%)	3 (13.7%)	2 249 800
Ont.	9 698 500 (36.6%)	10 (45.5%)	969 850
Man.	1 088 000 (4.1%)	1 (4.5%)	1 088 000
Sask.	1 000 400 (3.8%)	2 (9.1%)	500 200
Alta.	2 459 200 (9.3%)	2 (9.1%)	1 229 600
B.C.	3 120 600 (11.8%)	2 (9.1%)	1 560 300
Yukon/N.W.T.	79 800 (0.3%)	0 (—)	—
Canada	26 512 100 (100%)	22 (100%)	1 205 100

Source: Adapted from Sova, G. *1991 Corpus Almanac and Canadian Sourcebook*, 26th ed. Don Mills: Southam Business Information and Communications Group, 1990; and Hamerton, J.L., J.A. Evans, and L. Stranc. "Prenatal Diagnosis in Canada — 1990: A Review of Genetics Centres." In Research Volumes of the Royal Commission on New Reproductive Technologies, 1993.

Needless to say, having to travel out of province is difficult for many women. Some people have called for the establishment of more genetics centres to reduce these geographic inequalities. The existing distribution of centres generally makes sense, however, in terms of the size of the population each serves. As Table 26.13 shows, the average genetics centre in Canada serves a population of 1.2 million people, or roughly 4.5 percent of the total Canadian population. In this context, it would not be sensible or efficient to establish a genetics centre, for example, to serve the 79 800 people in the Yukon and Northwest Territories or the 130 500 people in Prince Edward Island.

Indeed, if we look at the distribution of genetics centres by region, rather than province, each region of the country appears to have its fair share of centres. For example, Atlantic Canada has 2 of the 22 centres across Canada (9.1 percent), to serve 2.3 million people (8.7 percent of the Canadian population); the Prairies have 5 of the 22 centres (22.7 percent), to serve 4.5 million people (17.2 percent of the population).

The solution to the problem of distance to genetics centres is not necessarily to build more centres. Rather, it is to improve the extent to which centres can reach out to remote areas — for example, through satellite clinics — and to improve the ability of women in remote communities to gain access to health care professionals who can provide referrals and to afford travel costs. Although we recognize the constraints facing provincial/territorial ministries of health, we believe that the importance of these choices — which may have lifelong consequences for the families involved — is such that access to services should remain a high priority in resource allocation decisions. The Commission therefore recommends that

219. **All pregnant women in Canada should have reasonable access to prenatal testing. Where this is difficult (as in rural and northern areas), genetics centres should establish outreach programs so that at least pretest counselling services can be available to all women closer to home. Funds for this purpose should be provided by provincial/territorial ministries of health. Further, provincial/territorial ministries of health should provide subsidies for those who want testing but are unable to afford the cost of travel from remote areas to a genetics centre.**

220. **In areas where obstetricians or family physicians are not available to provide referrals, there should be a designated individual in the public health system, such as a public health nurse, who is knowledgeable about prenatal diagnosis, so that women contemplating testing can obtain information close to home and, if they wish, be referred to the appropriate centre.**

and that

> **221. Interprovincial barriers to access to prenatal diagnosis services should be removed to allow women to receive prenatal testing at the most appropriate centre dealing with their particular risk. Samples should be taken locally and shipped for analysis to the appropriate centre, even if it is in another province. Funding in these cases should be provided by the ministry of health of the woman's province or territory of residence to the local centre to cover costs of taking a history and sample and shipping it to the centre doing the analysis, as well as for the analysis.**

Reasonable access also requires that women have the option of terminating or not terminating the pregnancy after PND, and that when termination is the choice, the procedure be accessible and covered in each province/territory as an insured health service.

Variations in Referral Patterns

As we have seen, there are wide variations in referral rates; for maternal age, for example, the rate ranges from 64.5 percent of eligible women in Quebec to 15 percent in Newfoundland — a more than fourfold difference. Similar variations exist for overall referral rates.

Commission surveys of people across Canada show that regional variations in attitudes toward PND cannot account for this fourfold difference. On the contrary, regional variations in people's willingness to use PND themselves were quite small (Table 26.14). Nor were there any regional variations in people's awareness of PND or their willingness to allow its availability for others.

As discussed earlier in this chapter, the more significant reason for these variations is that physicians in some parts of the country are less likely to offer referrals, whether because of lack of knowledge of the tests or their personal views about the appropriateness of using PND for certain disorders. The Commission's study uncovered extremely wide attitude disparities among physicians in different provinces. Disparities occurred in terms of when to use various tests, how grave certain conditions are considered to be, how directive physicians should be, and how readily they accept selective abortion. As a result, the study showed, the experiences of women who want prenatal testing depend on where they live; there seem to be provincial "cultures" that influence medical attitudes — and no doubt behaviours — and therefore the experience of pregnant women.

Table 26.14. Willingness of Canadians to Use Prenatal Diagnosis

Q: If you or your partner were expecting a child, would you use prenatal diagnosis of the fetus?

	Canada %	Maritimes %	Quebec %	Ontario %	Prairies %	B.C. %
Yes	69	70	75	65	67	66
Depends	7	7	5	7	8	10
Don't know	2	1	2	3	3	1
No	22	22	18	25	22	23

Source: Angus Reid Group Inc. "Reproductive Technologies — Qualitative Research: Summary of Observations." In Research Volumes of the Royal Commission on New Reproductive Technologies, 1993.

The wide divergence in attitudes among referring physicians is troubling in a country with a public health care system that has access as one of its basic principles. The Commission recommends that

> **222. Provincial colleges of physicians and surgeons and medical associations emphasize to their members that failure to discuss with patients the option of referral for a medically indicated prenatal diagnostic service is unethical and constitutes unacceptable medical practice. Information in this regard should be incorporated into medical school curricula and intern and residency training and examinations.**

Socioeconomic Factors

People of lower socioeconomic status are not referred for and do not use genetics services as often as higher-income women and women with higher levels of education, who are over-represented among those referred to genetics centres. Centres provide services to all women referred who have an indication of higher risk, so the reasons for this must lie in the referral process. We have outlined some factors that may underlie it — for example, the attitudes of referring physicians, the cost of travel, or the values of the individual women and couples. But it may also result from lack of awareness about what tests are available or difficulty understanding the issues raised throughout the PND process. As we have recommended, brochures and counselling should be understandable to people with varying levels of education and language skills, and these materials should be widely distributed to the public.

Overall, we found significant problems of access to PND services in Canada. Many women with legitimate medical indications for PND counselling and testing are not offered or do not have equal access to prenatal diagnostic services.

> Many women with legitimate medical indications for PND counselling and testing are not offered or do not have equal access to prenatal diagnostic services.

The solution is not to establish new genetics centres; rather, we need new ways of encouraging practitioners outside the genetics centres to work more effectively with the centres, to offer referrals to all women who have appropriate indications, and to ensure that women who want to make use of the services have access to them.

The Commission's Stance*

In this chapter, we have discussed several important and legitimate concerns about the use of PND and its implications for society. Having reviewed these concerns, the Commission concludes that, if provided in the proper way (with appropriate, unbiased counselling, leading to informed consent), using PND is both beneficial to individual women and couples at risk and consistent with social values regarding equality for persons with disabilities and respect for life.

> It is important that, as these technologies develop in Canada, we have a structure and process to decide whether we want to apply new technologies and, if we wish to apply them, to ensure that this occurs in a regulated and accountable way.

But this is not to say that PND should be allowed to develop according to a technological imperative or without boundaries. There are vulnerable interests of individuals and of society to be protected. The PND system requires monitoring and public input to ensure that PND is used in an ethical, safe, and beneficial manner. This is a rapidly changing area of technology, and it is important that, as these technologies develop in

---

* See Annex for dissenting opinion.

Canada, we have a structure and process to decide whether we want to apply new technologies and, if we wish to apply them, to ensure that this occurs in a regulated and accountable way. This needs to take into account the two quite distinct parts of the system — the genetics centres and the larger medical community. Our recommendations on how to ensure this are spelled out in the next two sections.

Using Prenatal Diagnosis Technologies Appropriately

The Role of Technology Assessment

The last two decades have seen rapid development and dissemination of PND technologies. Amniocentesis, CVS, and diagnostic ultrasound are all established components of the PND system in Canada; prenatal ultrasound is offered routinely in many provinces; MSAFP is emerging as a significant screening test; and new technologies now in development include using fetal cells in pregnant women's blood for PND, preimplantation diagnosis, and others.

As with any rapidly developing technology, our concern as a society must be that we are leading rather than being led by the existence of the technology. This requires the disciplined application of technology assessment. We need to have a clear understanding of how specific PND technologies work and how they are assessed as part of the process of ensuring appropriate use of these tests by practitioners. Resources for the provision of health care are not unlimited, and any new technology should be assessed for evidence that it is beneficial in terms of outcomes.

In addition, technology assessment provides information that is important in ensuring realistic public and patient expectations about what these technologies can and cannot do, what answers they can and cannot provide. Thus, technology assessment has a valuable role in curbing society's tendency to look to "miracle medicine" as a cure-all. Unrealistic expectations can lead to undue pressure (often patient-generated) to provide unproven technologies.

> As with any rapidly developing technology, our concern as a society must be that we are leading rather than being led by the existence of the technology.

Throughout this report we have emphasized the basic principle of evidence-based medicine — namely, that widespread use of medical treatments, procedures, or technologies should occur only after rigorous evaluation in clinical research trials. In this section, we examine how the technologies already in place (amniocentesis, CVS, ultrasound, and MSAFP) were assessed, as a way of identifying the lessons of this experience and developing recommendations about how this should be done in the future.

We begin with the major diagnostic tests (amniocentesis, CVS, targeted ultrasound), which are provided by the genetics centres in Canada; then we look at the major screening tests (routine ultrasound, MSAFP), which are being provided more widely; finally, we conclude with newer technologies (DNA analysis of fetal cells in a pregnant woman's blood, preimplantation diagnosis, and magnetic resonance imaging), which are at an earlier stage of development.

Diagnostic PND

Amniocentesis: Amniocentesis is currently provided in the second trimester of pregnancy, when the fetus is at 15 to 17 weeks' gestation. This is the most thoroughly studied and evaluated PND procedure. It is the most commonly used invasive PND procedure in the second trimester, with hundreds of thousands of amniocenteses having been done worldwide over the last 20 years, and it has been shown to be safe and effective. Success rates of up to 99.5 percent in obtaining a cytogenetic diagnosis have been reported in a study involving more than 7 000 cases.[5]

Life-threatening risks to the pregnant woman are almost non-existent; complications include leakage of amniotic fluid, transient vaginal spotting, and uterine contractions. Fetal injuries are rare. Fetal loss as a result of the procedure is in the order of 1 in 250. The risk of miscarriage for amniocentesis, as for other invasive prenatal tests, should be seen in light of the fact that approximately 8 percent of recognized pregnancies end in spontaneous abortion, and that the older a woman is, the more likely this is to occur, even if no testing is done.

In Canada, amniocentesis was assessed for effectiveness before being introduced widely as a service. Indeed, evaluation and standards-setting work with respect to amniocentesis, funded by the Medical Research Council of Canada and carried out by the CCMG and the genetics centres, helped set international standards in this area. The Commission found that the use of amniocentesis occurs in the context of written protocols detailing the appropriate indications for its use.

Chorionic Villus Sampling: Like amniocentesis, CVS was assessed for effectiveness before being used widely in Canada, and it is used in the context of written protocols detailing the appropriate indications for use.

The major drawback of amniocentesis is that it is performed relatively late in pregnancy. This led to research into CVS, a first-trimester procedure that allows for earlier diagnosis and decisions about the pregnancy. CVS is also more useful in detecting certain kinds of disorders, such as single-gene disorders. However, it is more difficult to interpret than amniocentesis and has slightly higher risks associated with it. For example, the need for retest with CVS is 7.5 percent, compared to 1.1 percent for amniocentesis.

Complications for the pregnant woman may include bleeding, cramping, and infection. Fetal loss rates as a result of CVS are slightly higher than those associated with amniocentesis. As yet, no study has examined whether there are any long-term effects of CVS, but some studies have been done on infants and children, and these have been generally reassuring. Recently, some concern has been raised about a possible relationship between CVS and limb damage when the test is performed very early in the pregnancy (before 10 weeks), but the available data are inconclusive, and more study is required to assess this possibility fully. Full information about this possible risk should be disclosed before consent to testing is obtained, and centres should ensure that this information is taken into account in decisions about the timing of CVS testing. The Commission recommends that

> **223. In view of recent reports of a possible relationship between early CVS and congenital limb deformities, data on all types of limb deformities in CVS-exposed infants be collected and analyzed to make more definitive outcome data available, and that the current state of knowledge on this risk be disclosed to all women contemplating the test.**

Early Amniocentesis: Research is being done to determine whether early amniocentesis (performed before 15 weeks' gestation) could provide the benefits of CVS (early detection) without its drawbacks (more difficult to interpret and higher risks). Recent studies suggest that early amniocentesis is associated with higher rates of fetal loss and amniotic fluid leakage than second-trimester amniocentesis,[6] but the differences in risks are not statistically significant; the risks are lower than those associated with CVS.

Although the safety of early amniocentesis has yet to be established definitively in clinical trials, some researchers believe that if its safety can be shown, early amniocentesis may eliminate the need for CVS.[7] Further evaluation, by means of a large multicentre randomized control trial, is needed to compare first-trimester amniocentesis and CVS as a basis for resource allocation decisions (see research volume, *Prenatal Diagnosis: Background and Impact on Individuals*) and before any introduction into routine practice in this country. For now, Canadian guidelines indicate that amniocentesis should be performed for routine indications between 15 and 17 weeks' gestation. Facilitation of such a multicentre trial should be considered a priority by the National Reproductive Technologies Commission as well as by agencies such as the MRC.

Targeted Ultrasound: Targeted ultrasound to detect fetal anomalies is provided by highly trained personnel using specialized equipment, usually in a facility associated with a genetics centre; the procedure can take up to an hour or more. (Routine ultrasound, discussed below, is often provided by obstetricians in their own offices and takes only a few minutes.)

The evidence shows that targeted ultrasound is quite effective as a diagnostic procedure, that is, to identify whether a suspected structural anomaly or malformation is present in the fetus. For example, a recent British study suggested that over 90 percent of major structural anomalies that are lethal or severely disabling can be detected through targeted ultrasound in referred high-risk pregnancies.[8]

The available evidence has shown no specific risks or biological consequences of targeted ultrasound.[9] The question of whether there are as yet undetected long-term effects has been raised, and it would be answerable by using data on exposed individuals, then using record linkage approaches to evaluate longer-term outcomes.

Targeted ultrasound carried out in referral centres, often associated with genetics centres, is used in accordance with written protocols developed by the SOGC, spelling out the appropriate indications for its use.

In summary, the Commission concludes that the major prenatal diagnostic tests provided at specialized genetics centres in Canada have been properly assessed for safety and efficacy and are now being provided for appropriate indications in the context of written protocols.

Screening Tests

The history of the assessment and use of PND screening tests (routine ultrasound and MSAFP) has been very different from that of the major diagnostic tests. Indeed, the Commission has serious reservations about the way screening tests have been assessed and provided. The number of physicians and personnel involved is much larger than for specialized tests done at genetics centres, making it more difficult to apply quality control or assessment.

> The Commission has serious reservations about the way screening tests have been assessed and provided.

Routine Ultrasound: Obstetrical ultrasound is now offered as a routine part of prenatal care — at least 80 percent of all pregnant women have this procedure in much of the Western world. It is offered to determine the gestational age of the fetus, to identify multiple pregnancies, and to look for placental abnormalities. As well, an increasing number of physicians use ultrasound to identify women who are at higher risk of having a fetus with a congenital disorder. However, the effectiveness of routine ultrasound to identify such fetuses is not at all clear. It varies greatly with the timing of the routine examination and the expertise of the ultrasonographer, with between a third and three-quarters of major malformations being detected.[10]   Many structural anomalies cannot be detected by routine ultrasound. Research conducted for the Commission suggests that, in some cases, routine ultrasound is being used inappropriately to reassure women that they are not carrying a fetus with Down syndrome. The value of routine ultrasound for this purpose is uncertain, and women might be given a false sense of security by apparently normal findings.

Even if routine ultrasound is not useful as a PND screening test, it might be appropriate for other reasons.   However, the effectiveness of routine ultrasound for these other purposes is also unclear. Although there is no question that routine ultrasound can help to date pregnancies and detect multiple pregnancies, we do not know how much of a difference this actually makes in terms of birth outcomes.[11]

Obstetrical ultrasound scanning has grown exponentially since its introduction and, as various authors have noted, the procedure spread before it was even evaluated ... Enthusiasm preceded any evidence of its effectiveness or safety. Although it is now a key component of prenatal care, there do not appear to be any explicit empirical standards that would warrant its routine use. Opinions differ on the number of ultrasound scans that should ideally be performed during pregnancy, and indeed on whether there is any valid clinical reason for doing them at all. Consensus conferences, it should be noted, have produced a variety of opinions. In France ... the consensus reached was two ultrasound scans per pregnancy. The U.S. National Institutes of Health, on the other hand, indicated in 1984 that there is no evidence justifying a firm and final opinion on this point.

M. Renaud et al., "Canadian Physicians and Prenatal Diagnosis: Prudence and Ambivalence," in Research Volumes of the Commission, 1993.

Despite the lack of evidence regarding effectiveness, there has been a massive increase in the number and cost of ultrasounds performed in Canada during the last 10 years (Table 26.15). The bulk of this increase (75 percent) is attributable to an increase in the per capita use of routine ultrasound, rather than an increase in the number of pregnancies (12 percent). It is essential to determine whether routine ultrasound is in fact effective in managing pregnancies more safely and effectively, because this has important implications for resource allocation and for medical practice.

If routine ultrasound does not help manage pregnancies more safely and effectively, the current number of tests is clearly too high. If routine ultrasound does achieve this purpose, however, the distribution of tests is seriously skewed (even if the overall number of tests is about right), because between 15 percent and 20 percent of women never receive screening.

Regional variations in the use of routine ultrasound account in part for this skewed distribution. According to the Commission's survey of referring physicians, 40 percent of physicians in Manitoba and Alberta do not consider it essential to order an ultrasound scan during pregnancy; in Quebec, only 4 percent of physicians share this opinion. In fact, Quebec physicians generally order two ultrasound scans per pregnancy, and it is only in Quebec that the great majority of physicians (89 percent, compared to 60 percent elsewhere in Canada) find it acceptable to use ultrasound to screen for anomalies. These variations in physician attitudes are reflected in provincial utilization rates — the percentage of all pregnant women having an ultrasound exam ranges from 97 percent in Quebec to 62 percent in Manitoba. These regional variations stem in part from the lack of formal guidelines regarding when it is appropriate for general practitioners and obstetricians to provide or to refer for routine ultrasound.

Table 26.15. Number of Obstetrical Ultrasound Procedures*		
Year	Number of procedures	Costs ($)
1982-83	358 722	21 174 894
1984-85	490 783	31 871 971
1986-87	636 515	43 748 019
1988-89	813 347	66 618 851
1990-91	998 492	74 649 481

* Number of ultrasound procedures associated with obstetrics and gynaecology and paid for under the provincial medical care insurance plans for Quebec, Ontario, Manitoba, Saskatchewan, Alberta, and British Columbia. Figures for the Atlantic provinces are not included, as ultrasound there is paid for under provincial hospital insurance plans, not medical insurance plans.

Source: Adapted from Health and Welfare Canada data, 1991.

Perhaps because of its non-invasive nature, the wide dissemination and use of routine ultrasound followed a very different pattern from introduction of the major diagnostic tests discussed previously. Unlike amniocentesis and CVS, the dissemination of routine ultrasound came well before any technology assessment of it and was not accompanied by formal guidelines regarding the appropriate indications for its use. Only in Manitoba do physicians providing ultrasounds have to be licensed and have a minimum of six months' training before they can meet the criteria for licensing.

It is essential to control this rapid proliferation of routine ultrasound and to determine whether the substantial funds now being devoted to it are justified. Two responses are called for. First, there is a need for further well-designed, sufficiently large

> The dissemination of routine ultrasound came well before any technology assessment of it and was not accompanied by formal guidelines regarding the appropriate indications for its use.

studies to evaluate the clinical effects of routine prenatal ultrasound. This would be a major undertaking, since a trial powerful enough to detect clinically significant effects of routine prenatal ultrasound on perinatal morbidity and mortality might require a sample size of over 12 000. We believe, nevertheless, that a major multicentre randomized control trial would help to determine the effectiveness and value of routine ultrasound as a procedure to help manage normal pregnancies. We therefore conclude that the National Research Technologies Commission should consider the pros and cons of underwriting some of the cost of such a trial. We would point out, however, that large amounts of money are already being spent to provide these services. If provincial/territorial ministries of health were to collaborate in developing the trial, and if they were to agree to structure their funding for routine ultrasound in such a way as to ensure that all service provision became part of the trial — for example, funding could be contingent upon appropriate data collection — the trial could be conducted for only the additional cost of data collection and analysis, instead of as an add-on to current service provision. Similarly, collaborative efforts at the international level could ensure that sufficient data on which to base judgements about effectiveness were collected quickly and at only a small additional cost relative to the current cost of providing services.

A second important aspect is that a program framework must be developed that will serve to contain both utilization rates and total costs for routine ultrasound. A Commission study of ultrasound use rates in British Columbia and in Ontario during the last 10 years showed clearly that the British Columbia approach, in which ultrasound can be provided only by licensed (hospital) facilities and is paid for out of hospital budgets, is far more effective in containing use and costs than is the Ontario system, which does not restrict practice location. This means that Ontario physicians with ultrasound equipment in their offices can bill for prenatal ultrasounds that they decide are needed and that they conduct in their own offices.

In the nine years preceeding 1991, expenditures for prenatal ultrasound increased twofold in British Columbia but fourfold in Ontario. While the number of hospital-based ultrasounds increased by only 16 percent in Ontario between 1983-84 and 1989-90, the number of non-hospital ultrasounds increased by about 300 percent. Thus, provincial health policy has implications for both the use and the costs of routine ultrasound. We believe that the British Columbia approach not only controls costs but makes possible quality control and the establishment of standards of training for personnel. It also eliminates the potential for self-referrals, which have been shown in many studies of medical practice to lead to unnecessary use. The Commission recommends that

> **224. Provincial/territorial ministries of health review the program framework within which routine ultrasound scanning during pregnancy is offered. The Commission concludes that requiring facilities that offer ultrasound to be licensed would promote women's best interests and best medical practice.**

and that

> **225. Provincial/territorial ministries of health eliminate potential conflicts of interest by ensuring that those ordering routine obstetrical ultrasounds do not usually provide them.**

Also, as discussed in greater depth in Chapter 28, ultrasound should not be used to identify the sex of the fetus, except for medically indicated reasons, before the third trimester. Commission research shows that it is highly unlikely that anyone would resort to abortion of a fetus of unwanted sex at this stage in pregnancy. The Commission recommends that

> **226. The Society of Obstetricians and Gynaecologists of Canada, the Canadian Association of Radiologists, and the College of Family Physicians of Canada review practice guidelines to ensure that practitioners using prenatal ultrasound do not perform ultrasound for the purpose of sex identification (except where medically indicated), and that they do not offer information on fetal sex except for medical reasons and upon request before the third trimester of pregnancy.**

MSAFP Screening: Alpha-fetoprotein is produced by the fetus; a higher than normal level of AFP in a pregnant woman's blood may indicate the presence of an abnormal fetal opening, such as a neural tube defect. This has led to the development of programs to measure the concentration of AFP in pregnant women's blood. It is a safe, relatively inexpensive, and easily performed method of screening pregnancies and identifying those at higher risk for neural tube defects.

The interpretation of test values is complex — results must be adjusted for the woman's age, weight, and race and the gestational age of the fetus, as well as for risks based on family history and population frequency; each laboratory conducting these tests must therefore establish normative values based on extensive testing experience. The results of MSAFP screening tests are expressed as probabilities. Since the test cannot determine with certainty whether the fetus is unaffected or affected, women with test results outside the normal range are offered further testing (targeted ultrasound or amniocentesis) to make a definitive diagnosis. The American Society of Human Genetics has developed guidelines for population-based MSAFP screening, which have been affirmed by the CCMG.

MSAFP screening is not a conclusive test. Several factors other than fetal anomaly may cause increased concentrations of AFP. Moreover, not every neural tube defect results in abnormally elevated MSAFP. The level of MSAFP may be above average but still within the "normal" range. In fact, deciding on the upper limit of "normal" MSAFP levels is very difficult. If the limit is set high, then some neural tube defects will be missed, with false-negative test results; if the limit is set low, resulting in false-positive test results, unnecessary amniocenteses will be performed. The cut-off values, therefore, are a matter of judgement in trying to achieve an optimal ratio.

In terms of safety, there have been no reports of complications arising from taking blood samples for purposes of MSAFP screening in the Manitoba program, although the further testing by amniocentesis entails the usual risks of that procedure. In Canada, MSAFP screening is offered as a province-wide program only in Manitoba (although the province of Ontario implemented a program, which includes MSAFP screening, offered to all pregnant women). The Manitoba program has proven effective in detecting neural tube defects — there has been a 50 percent decline in the incidence of liveborn infants with neural tube defects since the program was introduced in 1985. In 1989, about 60 percent of pregnant women in Manitoba were screened.[12] The results are comparable to those of similar programs in other countries.

There are some serious problems with counselling and informed consent in Manitoba's MSAFP program, discussed earlier in this chapter. In terms of sample analysis and follow-up, however, we believe that MSAFP screening is working effectively and being used appropriately in Manitoba's program. Written information is available for patients and physicians, the program has experienced laboratory personnel, and clear written guidelines are in place regarding how abnormal results should be followed up and by whom.

The same cannot be said with respect to the growing use of MSAFP screening in other provinces, which is marked by an absence of defined program guidelines and inconsistency in the availability of follow-up counselling. In Canada in 1989, 50 180 women were screened in eight provinces; somewhat fewer than 10 000 of these tests were done in Manitoba. Of the 37 825 MSAFP tests done in Ontario, 10 000 were done through private laboratories. British Columbia also had substantial numbers tested, but British Columbia does not have an established provincial program, and Ontario established its program only recently.

This proliferation of MSAFP testing outside established programs is worrisome. Our research suggests that the indications for which MSAFP testing is offered vary dramatically across the country. In some locations, MSAFP is being offered routinely by physicians; in other locations, it may be offered routinely or only to those at higher risk, depending on the physician.

The nature and quality of follow-up counselling also vary. In locations where a genetics centre analyzes the MSAFP samples, the centre also does follow-up counselling. But in other cases, particularly where private laboratories analyze the samples, counselling is left to the general practitioner or obstetrician, who may not have the knowledge or experience to provide appropriate counselling.

> The Commission believes that MSAFP should be used only as a routinely offered screening test where there is a program, funded by government, that includes well-designed information for women, education of physicians about the program, and the necessary facilities and resources to ensure accurate interpretation and follow-up, including counselling, when the results are abnormal.

As with routine ultrasound, these variations reflect the lack of clear guidelines and standards for providing MSAFP screening and counselling.

Given the problems associated with the proliferation of MSAFP, the Commission believes that MSAFP should be used only as a routinely offered screening test where there is a program, funded by government, that includes well-designed information for women, education of physicians about the program, and the necessary facilities and resources to ensure accurate interpretation and follow-up, including counselling, when the results are abnormal. Furthermore, given recent information emerging about the potential benefits of increased levels of folic acid in the diet of pregnant women in reducing the risk of neural tube defects, decisions about whether and how to extend MSAFP testing more widely should take into account how new knowledge about the effectiveness of this or other preventive strategies will influence the demand or need for MSAFP testing.

The decision about whether to offer MSAFP on a population basis is complex. We are not in a position to recommend what provinces should be doing in this regard, particularly as the technology is changing rapidly. This is one of the questions on which the Prenatal Diagnosis and Genetics Sub-Committee of the National Reproductive Technologies Commission may want to conduct assessments and make recommendations. We do believe, however, that if MSAFP is to be offered routinely, it must be in the context of a properly designed program within the public health care system. The Commission recommends that

> **227. MSAFP screening be offered on a population basis only within the confines of a program that adheres to the guidelines established by the American Society of Human Genetics and affirmed by the Canadian College of Medical Geneticists; that such programs be offered on the basis of informed choice and have the necessary laboratory, counselling, and prenatal diagnosis resources in place; and that such programs be affiliated with a licensed genetics centre.**

> **228. Where the resources to develop such programs and the associated counselling are not available, the test be offered by licensed genetics centres only to patients at high risk.**

and that

> **229. Provincial/territorial ministries of health not reimburse physicians or laboratories for MSAFP screening conducted outside such programs.**

Triple Testing: MSAFP was designed to look for abnormally elevated MSAFP levels. Recently, however, it has been shown that decreased levels of MSAFP are an indication of increased risk for fetal chromosomal abnormalities. The test is less accurate when used to detect Down syndrome than when used to detect neural tube defects, but accuracy rates have been improved by also measuring other biochemical markers that tend to be altered in the presence of some chromosomal disorders. These additional markers are the hormones human chorionic gonadotropin and unconjugated estriol; when the three tests are conducted together, the procedure is referred to as "triple testing." In addition to these hormonal markers, other biochemical markers may improve the efficiency of serum screening for certain obstetrical and genetic risks such as certain fetal anomalies and intrauterine growth retardation.[13]

It has been suggested that triple testing results could replace the use of advanced maternal age as the main indication for amniocentesis to detect chromosomal disorders, and that this would cost less, detect more disorders, yet require fewer amniocenteses.

While there are many potential benefits to triple testing and other tests being developed, it is vital that any maternal blood screening be offered on a population basis only within the context of a well-developed program with sufficient resources to permit the support and counselling that are essential accompaniments to informed choice.   Good planning, personnel and resource identification, funding allocation, and testing through pilot programs are necessary prerequisites.   In the absence of these factors — planning, resources in place for support, and counselling — population screening through testing could prove to be more harmful than beneficial.

Triple testing is one of several newer tests being developed; we discuss how such future technologies should be assessed and turn to our recommendations in the next section.

Assessing New Prenatal Diagnosis Technologies

Several prenatal diagnostic procedures either are under development or are already developed but so far in limited use (see box). We can assume that the pace of technology development is not going to lessen, because the desire for information about the fetus in higher-risk pregnancies, together with continuing scientific discovery, is likely to produce a steady stream of innovations. It is essential, therefore, to put in place the right kind of technology assessment model. In thinking about what this model should look like, we can draw certain lessons from the way PND technologies have been introduced and assessed in Canada previously.

As we have seen, the record of technology assessment in Canada is mixed. With regard to PND, we found that although the picture at the periphery has been quite different, among the genetics centres providing the major diagnostic tests there has been a high level of cooperation and discipline in the introduction of new technologies and a clear commitment that new technologies should not be made available except in the context of clinical trials until their safety and accuracy have been assessed. The assessment, introduction, and use of both amniocentesis and CVS have constituted good examples of technology assessment that give operational meaning to the broader concept of evidence-based medicine.

Canada has been a leader in the field of clinical testing of prenatal diagnostic techniques before their introduction to clinical practice:

- The first Canadian guidelines for the delivery of prenatal diagnostic services were published in 1974, as a joint effort of the Genetics Society of Canada (antedating the CCMG), the Canadian Paediatric Society, and the SOGC. This was the first attempt in the world to establish national guidelines for service delivery in this area. These guidelines were updated in 1983, 1991, and again in 1993.

- A collaborative multicentre trial of amniocentesis in 1976, supported by the MRC, demonstrated the safety and effectiveness of this technique and helped establish international standards for amniocentesis.

• Canada recently completed the first randomized clinical trial comparing CVS with second-trimester amniocentesis. This was made possible by a voluntary agreement among all Canadian genetics centres that CVS would be available only within the context of the trial.

• A proposal for a clinical trial comparing early amniocentesis with second-trimester amniocentesis has been developed with the cooperation of centres across the country, and funding for a trial is being sought before the procedure is offered as service.

Much of the credit for these achievements rests with the CCMG. As soon as amniocentesis was first provided in Canada in the early 1970s, it was evident that guidelines, quality control, procedures for accreditation of practitioners, and accredited training programs were needed. The formation of the CCMG in 1975 was intended to ensure that such services are delivered in a safe, effective, and non-directive manner.

The track record in Canada for assessing new prenatal diagnostic technologies at the centres has thus been very good. On the other hand, if we look at how PND testing provided in the larger medical community (such as routine ultrasound and MSAFP) has been introduced and assessed, a very different picture emerges. Routine ultrasound, for example, has simply proliferated, rather than being assessed and then introduced, showing that we cannot take for granted the disciplined introduction of technologies in the PND system. The same is true of MSAFP screening, which is being used in very different ways in different provinces. Only Manitoba has evaluated population screening before making it more widely available, although Ontario has recently embarked on a provincial program.

Why have these screening tests been allowed to proliferate without proper assessment? One reason is that, because these tests are non-invasive, they are relatively easy to administer — no special expertise is required to draw a blood sample or even to perform routine ultrasound, and the procedures pose few immediate risks to the pregnant woman or the fetus. As a result, many thousands of physicians in Canada could, if they so desired, provide these tests. By contrast, fewer than 100 medical professionals work at the 22 genetics centres. Needless to say, it is much more difficult to control the introduction and dissemination of new techniques under the former conditions.

The rapid and widespread adoption of routine prenatal ultrasound suggests that the lessons learned and models developed by centres in the past with respect to invasive tests have not been applied effectively to less invasive tests. This is very worrisome, as the extent of invasiveness and

New PND Technologies

Preimplantation diagnosis: Preimplantation diagnosis is an experimental form of prenatal diagnosis involving *in vitro* fertilization (see Chapter 20). Eggs are obtained from the woman, fertilized *in vitro*, and allowed to proceed through several cell divisions, after which one or more cells are removed for examination. If the chromosomal and/or genetic disorder in question is not discovered, the embryos can be placed in the uterus. This avoids the need to decide whether to terminate a pregnancy should PND reveal a genetic disease, since the diagnosis is made *before* the pregnancy is established. However, even if preimplantation diagnosis proves feasible, most couples at higher risk will likely continue to prefer prenatal diagnosis techniques such as amniocentesis, which are less invasive and more reliable. The survival rate for embryos implanted after testing by preimplantation diagnosis is around 20 percent, whereas it is over 99 percent for amniocentesis. Data on the safety and efficacy of preimplantation diagnosis are scant and continue to be collected. The available data indicate that preimplantation diagnosis is a difficult, invasive, expensive, and inefficient technique with very limited indications.

Prenatal diagnosis from fetal cells in maternal blood: Small numbers of fetal cells can be found in the blood of pregnant women. Because new techniques for amplifying DNA have opened up the possibility of making a diagnosis of genetic disease from very few cells, researchers are studying using these fetal cells for PND. Whereas other PND tests on maternal blood samples rely on biochemical markers, this tests the fetal cells themselves and thus the fetal chromosomes and genes. If successful, PND from fetal cells in maternal blood could provide a non-invasive, relatively safe, and economical method of detecting chromosomal and single-gene abnormalities at an early stage of pregnancy. This approach is still experimental, and its accuracy and effectiveness are not yet known. Clinical trials are under way in the United States and France, but PND by fetal cell analysis is not considered reliable enough for diagnostic testing at this time.

Magnetic resonance imaging (MRI): MRI is a way of viewing the body and its component parts. It is similar to ultrasound scanning in that it is non-invasive and capable of providing good tissue detail in normal and abnormal pregnancies. It is considered to have the potential to complement ultrasound scanning, in that an ambiguous finding could be clarified. However, MRI is very expensive and not widely available. At present, MRI technology still does not permit real-time imaging, and the equipment is not as portable as ultrasound equipment. Thus far, studies on the safety of MRI do not report any measurable adverse effects at levels used for diagnostic purposes. However, the potential biological effects on the fetus have not yet been examined sufficiently to justify recommendations about its use as a service.

Embryoscopy: Embryoscopy uses an endoscope to view the embryo. It is a very new technique still under development. Few data are available on risks associated with embryoscopy, but it appears that the risks are greater than those of amniocentesis and other prenatal diagnosis procedures, particularly loss of the pregnancy resulting from infection, bleeding, or spontaneous abortion. There is also a significant risk of preterm labour and delivery. Any use of embryoscopy constitutes research.

immediate risk should not be the primary factors determining whether technology assessment occurs before a technology comes into wide use. The use of non-beneficial technologies subjects people to unnecessary procedures and furthers inappropriate medicalization. Moreover, there are substantial opportunity costs involved in providing useless or non-beneficial technologies, which contravenes the principle of appropriate use of resources. For all these reasons, the use of non-beneficial technologies is unethical. This means that all tests, whatever their invasiveness or risks, should be examined against the same stringent, results-based criteria.

Moreover, the fact that a test is non-invasive or easy to administer says nothing about the often extensive laboratory and analytic resources required to provide meaningful results or adequate counselling about the results. A non-invasive test may be easy to administer, but the knowledge required to give appropriate counselling on abnormal results is not likely to be linked to the ability to administer the test. For example, if the analysis of fetal cells in pregnant women's blood proves feasible, this could mean that blood samples are taken widely before the resources and facilities for interpretation and follow-up are in place.

> The track record in Canada for assessing new prenatal diagnostic technologies at the centres has thus been very good. On the other hand, if we look at how PND testing provided in the larger medical community (such as routine ultrasound and MSAFP) has been introduced and assessed, a very different picture emerges.

What is required, therefore, is a conscious adoption of an evidence-based approach for all current and future PND technologies. The new PND technologies being developed vary in risk and invasiveness. It is likely that some of the more invasive, risky, and expensive tests (such as preimplantation diagnosis) will receive the same thorough assessment as amniocentesis and CVS before being introduced. In this regard, when evaluating proposals regarding the use of preimplantation diagnosis, the Assisted Conception Sub-Committee of the National Research Technologies Commission may wish to consult with the Prenatal Diagnosis and Genetics Sub-Committee, since it may have additional insights, based on its experience in the area of genetic testing. Most of the new PND technologies are being assessed according to what is sometimes called the "scientific consensus" model, that is, informal exchange of information, small pilot projects, and articles published in learned journals. This may lead to clinical research trials to establish whether a procedure is safe and effective, but often it is used widely before that assessment.

The scientific consensus model has served Canada well, at least for the assessment of diagnostic PND techniques. However, it would be desirable to develop a more formal process of technology assessment, to ensure that all new prenatal tests are assessed thoroughly. Such a process is needed particularly for those procedures offered in the wider medical community. A more formal process could also help to ensure that funding is available to conduct the large trials that are needed to produce the

> It would be desirable to develop a more formal process of technology assessment, to ensure that all new prenatal tests are assessed thoroughly.

information on which evidence-based medicine can be practised. For example, a large multicentre trial of routine ultrasound would cost several million dollars; given that up to $100 million is spent annually in Canada on these tests, however, it is important to determine whether they should continue to be offered.

It is important to recognize that clinical trials that seek to estimate small risks require such very large numbers of participants that the technologies being evaluated could almost be considered to be in general use. The significant differences are that (1) the collaborating centres agree to use the same protocols in the same way and to record their data in the same way; (2) if the trial is randomized the participating women must agree to randomization (randomization for purposes of a trial is ethical when a procedure is not known to be of benefit, because people with indications receive the procedure without participating in the trial); and (3) funding for testing comes out of research budgets.

To date, the MRC has funded the clinical trials that have been done in this area. However, the MRC does not have enough money to fund expensive new trials at this time, so the burden of funding trials will increasingly fall on provincial/territorial ministries of health. That is quite appropriate, since it is provincial/territorial ministries that are responsible for funding and managing the health care system, and technology assessment is part of that responsibility. However, not all provinces/territories are able to fund their own clinical trials, and this would lead to unnecessary duplication in any case. Hence, a formal process is needed to set priorities and coordinate the funding of clinical trials in this area.

There has also been a lack of involvement of ministries of health and community representatives in policy decisions about technology use. Again, a more formal process could respond to this concern. We believe that PND technology assessment requires the input of many groups, and that the appropriate forum for this process is the National Commission that we recommend be established. The Commission recommends that

> **230. The National Reproductive Technologies Commission establish and chair a Prenatal Diagnosis and Genetics Sub-Committee, with membership from relevant professional bodies, provincial/territorial health ministries, Health Canada, and groups and individuals**

representing the interests of patients, people with disabilities, and other key segments of the community,

(a)   to develop standards and guidelines for prenatal diagnosis technology assessment based on the principle that any new technology used at centres providing prenatal diagnosis and genetics services must be thoroughly assessed before its introduction and dissemination as a service;

(b)   to develop, fund (or coordinate funding from the provinces/territories), and implement a process for the regular and continuing identification and assessment of new prenatal diagnostic tests and procedures, for the purpose of determining the feasibility of use in service conditions; this should include trials of new prenatal diagnosis techniques provided not at centres but in the wider medical community;

(c)   to monitor and advise on all relevant issues relating to the prospective or retrospective assessment of prenatal diagnosis technologies and their introduction and dissemination; and

(d)   to ensure that all participating patients have full information on risks before they consent to take part in a clinical trial of a technology.

The assessment process we have just outlined will complement rather than compete with the technology assessment and resource allocation decision-making processes of provincial/territorial ministries of health. It is virtually impossible to prevent the proliferation of a technology once provinces/territories have agreed to fund or approve its acquisition and use (for example, by including it as an insurable service under provincial/territorial health insurance plans). Perhaps the single most important factor in preventing the inappropriate proliferation of PND technologies or procedures is the funding decisions of provincial/territorial ministries of health.

In the past, provincial/territorial ministries of health have often funded techniques before they were properly assessed, relying on the various professional colleges and medical associations to set guidelines and on the cooperation and self-discipline of individual practitioners to refrain from using them in unproven ways.

The experience with amniocentesis and CVS shows that such an approach is possible. But it is one thing to rely on the voluntary cooperation of 22 genetics centres and quite another to ensure the cooperation of more than 10 000 family/general practitioners and obstetricians. The proliferation of routine prenatal ultrasound shows that reliance on individual physicians to establish limits is inappropriate — it is not their role — and doing so may lead to rapidly increasing costs.

The decision not to fund technologies until they are properly assessed is especially important when a new technology or procedure has the capacity to be disseminated widely and used by a wide range of practitioners (for example, MSAFP screening and others that will come). Ministries of health should therefore demand and fund more rigorous technology assessment before agreeing to fund a service. This has been recognized in recent health care reforms in virtually all provinces/territories. Provincial/territorial health ministries and Health Canada have the capacity, even in times of financial restraint, to help stimulate and fund clinical trials of new technologies, and it is desirable that they do so.

> Ministries of health should therefore demand and fund more rigorous technology assessment before agreeing to fund a service.

The existence of a Prenatal Diagnosis and Genetics Sub-Committee within the National Reproductive Technologies Commission would be of great benefit to provinces as they grapple more actively with issues of technology assessment in this field. First, it would fund the most urgent clinical trials, thereby supplementing provincial/territorial technology assessment processes. The PND and Genetics Sub-Committee could also work with the Conference of the Deputy Ministers of Health to identify clinical trials (and pilot studies of programs) that should be organized cooperatively and funded jointly by provinces/territories. This would reduce unnecessary duplication of trials, since the results from one province or territory are likely to be more widely applicable. For treatments that are relatively unusual, this would allow provinces/territories to work together to obtain a sufficiently large sample size for a trial to give conclusive results. For other treatments, collaboration among the provinces/territories would allow a sufficiently large sample to be assembled much more quickly than could be done by a single province or territory acting alone.

In general, the standards- and guideline-setting and data collection functions of the Prenatal Diagnosis and Genetics Sub-Committee (discussed in more detail below) would provide essential information on which provincial/territorial health ministries could base resource allocation and other decisions. The Sub-Committee would provide information about what facilities and practitioners are doing and about the quality and results of these activities, as a basis for planning and resource allocation. This information would enable the development of appropriate standards of care and better information upon which to base decisions about new facilities and new technology acquisitions.

Without the country-wide data collection and assessment made possible by the existence of a Prenatal Diagnosis and Genetics Sub-Committee, some provinces/territories would be in a poor position to evaluate new PND technologies. Most provinces have only one or, at most, two genetics centres; without the context of comparative data from the entire country, it is difficult to assess quality and results at any individual genetics centre.

The data collection function and recommendations of the Sub-Committee would therefore provide important benefits to provincial/territorial ministries of health in managing an increasingly complex health care system. If a province or territory chose to make decisions about resource allocation that departed somewhat from the approach elsewhere, the health ministry would at least be in a position to know the baseline of services and standards from which it is departing and why it is doing so.

In short, the technology assessment process we propose, coordinated by the Prenatal Diagnosis and Genetics Sub-Committee, and the existing provincial/territorial technology assessment process are mutually reinforcing. The technology assessment promoted and monitored by the Sub-Committee would be for naught if provinces/territories agreed to fund technologies that have not been assessed properly; conversely, the provinces/territories would be unable to make informed resource allocation decisions without the data collection made possible by the Sub-Committee.

To promote this cooperation, a formal consultation process should be established between the Prenatal Diagnosis and Genetics Sub-Committee and the provincial/territorial ministries of health, through the Conference of Deputy Ministers of Health, and any existing provincial advisory committees or equivalent mechanisms. The Commission recommends that

> **231. Issues of technology assessment and use be the topic of at least annual consultations between the National Reproductive Technologies Commission's Prenatal Diagnosis and Genetics Sub-Committee and the Conference of Deputy Ministers of Health and other representatives of provincial/territorial ministries of health.**

An Accountable, Well-Managed System: The Genetics Centres

Canadian society is at a crossroads in terms of the management of techniques and resources applicable to PND. If common policies and clinical standards were adopted, then the various elements of PND we have examined could be made to function better to serve Canadians equitably and ethically across the country.

If this is not done, an increasingly inequitable patchwork of PND services will develop out of a series of piecemeal decisions — some taken by health care ministries under pressure from various interested groups; others taken by practitioners working in the absence of clear policy guidelines; some taken by professional organizations; and others taken by trial and error or by default. Not only would this situation be regrettable, allowing it to occur would be unethical, as it would create greater potential for harm to individuals and reduce the likelihood that safe, proven care is provided equitably and that resources are used responsibly. Given the social implications of misuse of these techniques and procedures and the vulnerable interests to be protected, there are cogent reasons for a coordinated response across the country.

We therefore present a blueprint for the further evolution of PND practices in Canada with the goal of achieving a more integrated system of services and standards across the country within boundaries established to ensure that only ethically and socially acceptable use occurs. As discussed throughout this chapter, there are two very different components to the provision of PND services in Canada: the genetics centres and the referring physicians. We begin with the reforms required in the genetics centres and the referral network before describing in more detail the role of the Prenatal Diagnosis and Genetics Sub-Committee of the National Commission.

> Canadian society is at a crossroads in terms of the management of techniques and resources applicable to PND ... We therefore present a blueprint for the further evolution of PND practices in Canada with the goal of achieving a more integrated system of services and standards across the country within boundaries established to ensure that only ethically and socially acceptable use occurs.

Our research shows that the genetics centres have, generally speaking, provided PND services safely and ethically. In large part, this has been a result of the efforts of the CCMG and the effectiveness of its guidelines regarding the accreditation of genetics centres, record keeping, the provision of non-directive counselling, the appropriate indications for testing, and training and accrediting service providers.

Participation in the CCMG accreditation process is voluntary; at present, 12 of the 22 centres providing PND have not applied for or received accreditation. The lack of accreditation does not necessarily mean lower standards, but only if all centres participate can we track what is happening in PND practices across the country and ensure that standards and quality control are maintained.

For example, CCMG guidelines state that, in the absence of any other indication, a pregnant woman's anxiety is not reason enough for PND testing; nevertheless, we found that some PND tests are being performed for this reason, including invasive tests that carry risks to the fetus and the pregnant woman. It is important to be able to identify such practices and take appropriate measures to prevent them. Similarly, although we found no evidence to support the charge that genetics centres are requiring a commitment to terminate a pregnancy as a precondition for access to testing, it is essential that decisions or policies involving such fundamental values not be left to the discretion of individual physicians.

In addition, Commission research uncovered variability in the quality and quantity of record keeping by genetics centres. For example, three centres reported that they did not routinely collect follow-up information on pregnancy outcomes after testing, and one other followed up only high-risk cases. If the continued development of prenatal services is to be monitored properly, data collection by the centres must be standardized.

In summary, the existing accreditation system, based on voluntary compliance, is inadequate in several ways. Since it is voluntary, we have no way of knowing whether appropriate guidelines are being followed consistently at all 22 genetics centres, as there is no way to require unaccredited centres to comply with the guidelines. There is no way to assess the training and expertise of counselling at all centres. We have no means of tracking the evolution of PND practice and ensuring that standards and quality control are maintained. The comprehensive data gathering necessary to support continuing technology assessment is not taking place. To remedy these flaws, we conclude that there should be mandatory licensing of genetics centres. However, before licensing, we recommend that the 12 genetics centres that are not accredited apply to the CCMG for review and prior accreditation so that the elements just enumerated can be assessed by that body, which has the experience and expertise to assess many aspects of service provision as well as the credentials of centre personnel. In addition, however, the Commission recommends that

> **232. All genetics centres or other facilities providing prenatal diagnosis for genetic disorders and congenital anomalies be subject to compulsory licensing by the National Reproductive Technologies Commission.**

As a condition of licence, genetics centres would have to comply with appropriate guidelines, to be established by the Prenatal Diagnosis and Genetics Sub-Committee of the NRTC. These would include such aspects as the qualifications of practitioners employed at the centre, record keeping, counselling, informed consent, and a code of practice. Breaching these conditions would be grounds for loss of licence.

The licensing process we propose carries forward the existing accreditation process developed and put in place over a decade ago by the CCMG. Indeed, we believe that it would be appropriate for the NRTC to build on the existing CCMG procedures and requirements in establishing its conditions of licence. CCMG members have the knowledge and have demonstrated the operational experience required for this task and should be heavily involved, but the NRTC, through its licensing process, should assume the ultimate approval authority.

It is essential that the current voluntary accreditation process be formalized in law under the aegis of the Prenatal Diagnosis and Genetics Sub-Committee. One reason is to ensure that accreditation is mandatory rather than voluntary and thus allow effective quality control and evaluation of outcomes. But bringing the accreditation process under the umbrella of the National Commission would also serve

> Bringing the accreditation process under the umbrella of the National Commission would also serve two other important goals: it would ensure that information on PND practices in Canada is available to the public; and it would provide a mechanism for public input into the formulation and revision of the guidelines governing those practices.

two other important goals: it would ensure that information on PND practices in Canada is available to the public; and it would provide a mechanism for public input into the formulation and revision of the guidelines governing those practices. To date, there has been little public input into the formulation of guidelines for the provision of prenatal diagnosis and little public information available about the practices of genetics centres in Canada. We believe that the public should have the opportunity to participate in the process of formulating guidelines and the opportunity to know whether guidelines are being complied with.

Licensing Requirements for Prenatal Diagnosis Services

The Commission recommends that

> **233. The compulsory licensing requirements for prenatal diagnosis services apply to any**

physician, centre, or other individual or facility providing prenatal diagnosis services for which the Prenatal Diagnosis and Genetics Sub- Committee of the National Reproductive Technologies Commission deems a licence necessary. In particular, we recommend that licence applicants be required to obtain prior accreditation by the Canadian College of Medical Geneticists. At this time, we recommend that the compulsory licensing requirement apply to the following prenatal diagnosis services:

(a)   amniocentesis

(b)   chorionic villus sampling (CVS)

(c)   any other prenatal testing of pregnant women aimed at obtaining information on the health status of the fetus with regard to congenital anomalies and genetic disease, other than provincial/territorial MSAFP screening programs or other provincial/ territorial programs involving testing of pregnant women's blood and provincially/ territorially licensed diagnostic ultrasound programs.

The Commission recommends that

234. Providing such prenatal diagnosis services without a licence issued by the National Reproductive Technologies Commission, or without complying with the National Commission's licensing requirements, constitutes an offence subject to prosecution.

and that

235. The Prenatal Diagnosis and Genetics Sub- Committee of the National Reproductive Technologies Commission develop, with input from relevant bodies, standards and guidelines to be adopted as conditions of licence.

The Distinction Between Recognized and Experimental Prenatal Diagnosis Procedures

In addition, the Commission recommends that the following requirements be adopted as conditions of licence:

236. Only procedures of proven safety and effectiveness for diagnosing the genetic disorder or congenital anomaly in question should be offered as routine testing. Procedures whose safety or effectiveness has not yet been clearly established should be offered only in the context of clinical trials.

237. Guidelines for determining which prenatal diagnosis procedures are of sufficiently proven safety and effectiveness to be offered as services, and which procedures remain experimental in nature, requiring further research, should be established by the Prenatal Diagnosis and Genetics Sub-Committee of the National Reproductive Technologies Commission.

238. In particular, the following should be considered experimental in nature, until their safety and effectiveness are more fully established:
    (a) chorionic villus sampling performed before 10 weeks' gestation;
    (b) early amniocentesis;
    (c) preimplantation diagnosis;
    (d) PND from fetal cells in the blood of pregnant women; and
    (e) embryoscopy.

239. **Prenatal diagnosis procedures that remain experimental in nature should be offered only in the context of research — most often as multicentre randomized clinical trials. Guidelines for carrying out such trials at licensed centres, including specific patient consent, record keeping, and other requirements and safeguards, should be established by the Prenatal Diagnosis and Genetics Sub-Committee of the National Reproductive Technologies Commission.**

240. **The Prenatal Diagnosis and Genetics Sub-Committee of the National Reproductive Technologies Commission should coordinate the data collection, monitoring, and research evaluation necessary to assign a given procedure to either the experimental category or the category of recognized treatment or diagnostic procedure.**

Impermissible Procedures

The Commission recommends that

241. **The Prenatal Diagnosis and Genetics Sub-Committee of the National Reproductive Technologies Commission have as part of its guidelines for licensing of genetics centres that no genetic alteration of a human zygote/embryo be permitted.**

242. We affirm the existing Canadian College of Medical Geneticists/Society of Obstetricians and Gynaecologists of Canada guideline that prenatal diagnosis to determine fetal sex for non-medical reasons not be offered, and adherence to this guideline should be a condition of licence.

Patient Information, Consent, and Counselling

The Commission recommends that

243. Prenatal diagnosis services should be provided in a manner that protects the patient's privacy and safeguards patient records from unauthorized access by third parties. Standard procedures and safeguards for ensuring the privacy and confidentiality of patient and medical records should be developed by the National Reproductive Technologies Commission.

244. Standard information materials and consent forms should be developed by the Prenatal Diagnosis and Genetics Sub-Committee of the National Reproductive Technologies Commission and should be distributed to all patients contemplating the use of prenatal diagnosis services.

245. Information materials should be in accessible language and format.

246. Consent forms should fully identify the specific procedures being consented to. Patients should be given ample time to discuss and fully

comprehend consent forms, and consent forms should be signed by the patient before any procedure is initiated.

247. The decision about whether to terminate a pregnancy should remain entirely with the woman; prior willingness or unwillingness to terminate a pregnancy should never operate as a precondition for prenatal diagnosis.

248. Genetics counselling should be an integral part of prenatal diagnosis services and should be provided by counsellors with appropriate training and expertise. For this reason, among others, we recommend that prior accreditation of a facility by the Canadian College of Medical Geneticists, which is equipped to assess this, be required.

249. Materials for patients about counselling and procedures should be developed by the Prenatal Diagnosis and Genetics Sub-Committee of the National Reproductive Technologies Commission. These should be designed to ensure that patients are fully informed of the probability, nature, burden, and possible variability of the disorder for which diagnosis or treatment is being provided, and that they are helped to reach a decision that best meets their particular situation and needs.

250. Counselling prior to and following termination of pregnancy, including grief counselling, should also be available, either on site or by referral.

Reporting, Licence Renewal, and Revocation of Licences

In addition to the specific conditions of licence outlined above, the Commission recommends that

> **251. Prenatal diagnosis services follow record-keeping, data collection, and data-reporting requirements established by the Prenatal Diagnosis and Genetics Sub-Committee of the National Reproductive Technologies Commission.**

> **252. Licensed prenatal diagnosis services report to the National Reproductive Technologies Commission on their activities, in a standard form, annually or in the event of any change substantially affecting the conditions of licence.**

> **253. Prenatal diagnosis services be required to apply to the National Commission for licence renewal every five years.**

and that

> **254. Licences to provide prenatal diagnosis services be revocable by the National Reproductive Technologies Commission at any time for breach of conditions of licence.**

These measures would ensure that services provided at the core of the PND system are consistent across the country and are monitored to ensure that they are provided in a safe and ethical manner.

The services and facilities that constitute the core of the PND system may change over time. With the increasing availability of non-invasive PND techniques, the need may arise for the licensing of facilities other than genetics centres. For example, private laboratories in Ontario with no affiliation to a genetics centre are offering MSAFP screening. We have recommended that at this time MSAFP be provided on a population screening basis only in the context of provincial programs administered in collaboration with genetics centres, which can provide the necessary counselling. We do not think any private laboratories should be providing population screening tests without this, as such laboratories do not have the counselling personnel and expertise necessary to follow up on test results.

In the future, it may become appropriate or necessary for some prenatal genetic testing to be provided by facilities unaffiliated with genetics centres. If this occurs, it is important that these facilities have the expertise and resources to provide the follow-up counselling and diagnosis required when results fall outside the normal range. Hence, the Prenatal Diagnosis and Genetics Sub-Committee should monitor the role of private laboratories and require licensing where necessary. One potential example is testing of fetal cells in maternal blood samples for genetic disease if this becomes feasible. Such testing should be available only through a licensed centre.

An Accountable, Well-Managed System: The Referral Network

Our research has documented several difficulties with the provision of prenatal diagnosis services in the larger network of physicians who see pregnant women, provide certain PND screening tests, and offer referrals to the genetics centres. These include:

- wide variations in physicians' knowledge about the availability of and appropriate indications for PND;

- failure by some physicians to offer referrals to all women who are eligible for testing;

- wide variations in the services offered to women in different provinces;

- variations in informed consent procedures for MSAFP screening and inadequate follow-up counselling;

- inappropriate use of routine ultrasound to reassure women about the absence of chromosomal disorders; and

- directive counselling and inappropriate attitudes on the part of some physicians with respect to women's reproductive autonomy and their right to choose or not to choose abortion following PND.

In short, there is a clear need for standards for clinical practice for practitioners in service settings other than genetics centres. At present, there is no mechanism to give patients some reasonable assurance of consistent standards of practice. This is a very difficult area to regulate, however, given the thousands of general/family practitioners and obstetricians who see pregnant women. Indeed, any physician can see a pregnant woman and refer her to a genetics centre; for example, an ophthalmologist could examine a pregnant woman's eyes, diagnose an X-linked disorder causing blindness, and refer her to a genetics centre.

It would not be realistic, therefore, to require that all service settings or medical professionals involved in providing PND-related services (other than those already enumerated) apply for special accreditation or licence. However, we support the provincial/territorial licensing of facilities providing routine prenatal ultrasound.   In addition, to ensure some standardization in the practices of referring physicians, better forms of self-regulation are required.   The relevant medical associations (such as the provincial medical associations and colleges, the Society of Obstetricians and Gynaecologists of Canada, and the College of Family Physicians of Canada) should develop and disseminate explicit written guidelines for their members with respect to the appropriate provision of PND-related services. There is also a need to ensure better knowledge of PND through physician education and training and to encourage more consistent standards of practice with respect to the use of tests and referrals.   We have already made several recommendations regarding specific aspects of these issues earlier in this chapter.   In addition, the Commission recommends that

> **255. The Society of Obstetricians and Gynaecologists of Canada, the Canadian Association of Radiologists, and the College of Family Physicians of Canada review practice guidelines to ensure that practitioners using prenatal ultrasound do not perform ultrasound for the purpose of sex identification (except where medically indicated) and do not deliberately examine for or volunteer information on fetal sex, except for medical reasons and upon request, prior to the third trimester.**

The Role of the Prenatal Diagnosis and Genetics Sub-Committee

We have already referred to the role of the Prenatal Diagnosis and Genetics Sub-Committee of the National Reproductive Technologies Commission in our earlier discussion of technology assessment and in our licensing recommendations for PND services. However, it is worth drawing these points together, because of the significant role the Sub-Committee will have in preserving the integrity of the PND system in Canada.

The Sub-Committee would be established and chaired by the National Reproductive Technologies Commission.   It would be one of six permanent sub-committees, along with those dealing with infertility prevention; assisted conception services; assisted insemination services; embryo research; and the provision of fetal tissue for research and other designated uses. Like National Commission members themselves, we recommend that at least half the members of the Prenatal Diagnosis and Genetics Sub-Committee be women, and that all members be chosen with a view to ensuring that they have a background and demonstrated experience in dealing with a multidisciplinary approach to issues, as well as an ability to work together to monitor developments in this field and propose policies in a way that reflects the interests and concerns of Canadian society as a whole.

The Prenatal Diagnosis and Genetics Sub-Committee would have several functions. It could decide to establish ad hoc working groups to deal with one or more of these functions, if appropriate:

- Setting and revising, from time to time, the licensing requirements for genetics centres (including guidelines for distinguishing between recognized and experimental procedures; guidelines for carrying out clinical trials; record-keeping requirements; and other requirements outlined in our recommendations), to be applied through the National Reproductive Technologies Commission hearing process. Professional associations, patient and other interested groups, and the general public would have input into this process. As noted above, CCMG review and accreditation would also be a specific condition of licence.

- Developing standard information materials, counselling materials, and patient consent forms to be used in the provision of PND services.

- Monitoring the assessment and introduction of new PND technologies; deciding which clinical trials of PND are most urgent; and funding or coordinating provincial/territorial funding for them. Annual consultations with the Conference of Deputy Ministers of Health would be an important part of this function.

- Gathering relevant country-wide data and information about facilities, technologies, and practices, which can be used as a basis for the Sub-Committee's guideline- and standard-setting activities, as well as by the provinces/territories in their own planning and resource allocation decisions. Publication of data on the provision and outcomes of prenatal diagnosis in Canada in the National Commission's annual report would facilitate understanding of the activities of each genetics centre within the national context and act as a uniform information base on which federal and provincial/territorial health ministries and relevant public authorities can base legislative, programmatic, or regulatory initiatives relating to the provision of prenatal diagnostic services in Canada.

- Discussing and setting policy on new issues and dilemmas as they arise, including identifying related training and education issues to bring to the attention of those responsible, monitoring the practices of private laboratories and other non-licensed PND providers, and ensuring appropriate levels of regulation on an ongoing basis.

- Working with other sub-committees of the National Commission on issues that relate to the mandate of more than one sub-committee, such as

  (a) embryo research;

  (b) preimplantation diagnosis; and

  (c) gene therapy.

- Disseminating information and promoting public awareness and debate regarding the provision of PND services in Canada, in part through the publication of the NRTC's annual report, as well as through periodic initiatives such as the preparation and/or publication of studies or position papers on emerging issues in the field of PND — for example, related to the development of new diagnostic tests or procedures. In addition, the Sub-Committee could sponsor public consultation initiatives, such as consensus conferences and wide circulation of position papers, to ensure the development of broadly based social consensus on potentially controversial issues surrounding the provision of prenatal diagnostic services and to discourage the use of prenatal diagnostic tests or procedures in ways that would undermine the confidence of the Canadian public in the prenatal diagnosis process.

The last function, disseminating accurate information on which to base a more informed public debate, is a particularly important part of the mandate we propose for the National Commission with respect to PND. We have emphasized the importance of public input in the formulation of licensing requirements governing the provision of PND services in Canada and public information about whether these are being adhered to. The measures we propose will ensure that the activities of the PND system are reported to the public in a timely and accessible way, so as to enable public discussion on policy making in this field. As we have suggested, the publication of the National Commission's annual report is an appropriate mechanism for this public reporting.

Accountability would also be promoted by the composition of the Prenatal Diagnosis and Genetics Sub-Committee, which should include a balance of NRTC and outside membership, ensuring broad representation of the various interests involved. This is why we have recommended that the Prenatal Diagnosis and Genetics Sub-Committee have a multi-disciplinary make-up, including membership from relevant professional bodies, federal and provincial/territorial health ministries, and individuals representing the concerns of patients, women, people with disabilities, and other key segments of the community. Where appropriate, the Sub-Committee should also consult directly with the public on issues under consideration — for example, by circulating draft policies or position papers for comment (see Chapter 5).

Finally, public education is needed to ensure more complete and accurate public under-standing of PND in Canada. As we have seen, the issues involved are complex, and there are many misconceptions about the nature and implications of PND and genetics testing.

In our view, these goals of public accountability and public education can be achieved only by including PND under the umbrella of the NRTC. Although other bodies, such as professional associations or genetics centres, often seek to involve the public in some aspects of their decision-making processes, only the NRTC can ensure a comprehensive system of public accountability and public education regarding PND.

> Disseminating accurate information on which to base a more informed public debate is a particularly important part of the mandate we propose for the National Commission with respect to PND ... Public education is needed to ensure more complete and accurate public understanding of PND in Canada. As we have seen, the issues involved are complex, and there are many misconceptions about the nature and implications of PND and genetics testing.

Indeed, the NRTC is needed to play a more general coordinating role, bringing all interested parties and perspectives to the same table. PND is a widespread and growing field of medical activity, one that impinges on the lives of many Canadians and has many social and ethical implications. It is vital to ensure that all those involved in the system — pregnant women and their partners, medical geneticists, community health care providers, physicians, provincial/territorial and federal health care funding agencies, and the general public — have the information they need for informed decisions and the opportunity to influence decisions that will affect them. The coordinating role of the Prenatal Diagnosis and Genetics Sub-Committee will help ensure that PND programs continue to develop appropriately and in the context of the values of Canadians. This is particularly important as well with regard to practice in the wider medical community. We have seen marked variation in practices with regard to consent and other aspects in the referral network, showing the importance of establishing and ensuring adherence to standards and guidelines. The Prenatal Diagnosis and Genetics Sub-Committee could assist the relevant professional bodies in bringing this about — for example, by providing appropriate information.

Conclusion

If we are to ensure that PND services are provided in a way that is both beneficial to individuals and couples and consistent with social values, certain changes are required. The reforms we have proposed would promote the autonomy of patients and the appropriate use of resources, while also protecting vulnerable interests of individuals and society and ensuring only ethical uses. In general, and in line with our ethic of care, one goal of our recommendations is to foster a spirit of cooperation among all participants.

In the system we envisage, some regional differences in the use of services would remain — reflecting levels of demand and budgetary resources — but we should see far less variation in referrals to genetics centres. Although there will still be differences between practitioners on various aspects of PND, there would be far less variation in adherence to clinical, counselling, and other standards of practice. There will be mechanisms for public input and public accountability with regard to the evolution of the system. Finally, there will be far fewer opportunities to introduce new diagnostic tests without appropriate assessment and monitoring, as well as far more in the way of disciplined across-Canada assessment and use of new technologies. These reforms will ensure that at-risk women and couples have equal access to a wide range of proven beneficial services.

> We believe that Canada has a unique capacity to put in place a structure for the provision of PND services that will serve Canadians now and adapt to the coming changes in technology and demand.

Is this vision feasible? We believe that Canada has a unique capacity to put in place a structure for the provision of PND services that will serve Canadians now and adapt to the coming changes in technology and demand. The necessary factors are in place: we have a strong history of voluntary cooperation by the genetics centres and the CCMG in the disciplined introduction of new PND technologies; there is good will among referring practitioners who have the interests of their patients at heart; we have a single-payer system of health care, which allows for control over the proliferation of new technologies; and we have strong incentives for cooperation on the part of provincial/territorial ministries of health, which are very cognizant of the need to manage the health care system more efficiently and of the need for better data on which to base planning and resource allocation decisions.

The reforms we propose offer the potential to manage more efficiently within existing resources and even to save resources. Although additional resources will be required to establish this structure and work through the first round of facility accreditation and quality assurance activities, there will be significant savings over time. This is because new technologies that do not work or do not provide benefit will not become part of the system. Thus, there are not only ethical but financial reasons for supporting the approach we propose. Canada has a unique opportunity to make this area of clinical practice a vibrant example of evidence-based medicine. PND in the framework we envisage would exemplify how the health care system should strive to work to the benefit of those who use and provide its services.

The track record of the medical genetics community has been impressive in terms of determining the efficacy and safety of the various prenatal diagnostic techniques *before* they are introduced widely. For example, the randomized across-Canada collaborative clinical trials of amniocentesis and chorionic villus sampling are models that other areas of medicine could do well to follow. Seldom have health care providers done as well in collaborating and limiting new technology until it is assessed — that is, in providing evidence-based services. Yet the public and various interest groups are relatively unaware of this.

At our public hearings and in submissions to the Commission, we noted a high level of suspicion and mistrust of services provided by the genetics community from some members of the public. We heard perceptions that prenatal diagnosis is being used as a "search and destroy" mission to "weed out defective fetuses"; we heard that prenatal diagnosis counselling is biased and predicated on the assumption that it is better to abort a fetus found to have an anomaly than to consider raising a child with a disability; we heard statements that some of the newer developments in this area are being used for eugenic purposes and that women were coerced into terminating pregnancies. These themes were raised by vocal and well-organized groups representing women, people with disabilities, and the pro-life movement, as well as some concerned individuals.

It has become evident that the genetics community needs to find better ways of communicating about how it carries out its work and needs to listen closely to what women are saying about their treatment experience. Not enough attention has been given to how patients view the experience or how the public perceives genetics services. There is a great deal of misinformation and a need for accurate, unbiased, and accessible information about genetics and about what

> At our public hearings and in submissions to the Commission, we noted a high level of suspicion and mistrust of services provided by the genetics community from some members of the public.

> It has become evident that the genetics community needs to find better ways of communicating about how it carries out its work ... There is a great deal of misinformation and a need for accurate, unbiased, and accessible information about genetics and about what services are actually provided, and in what ways, across the country ... The system we propose should make knowledge about activities in genetic medicine more open and accessible to the general public.

services are actually provided, and in what ways, across the country. The referral network of the physicians in particular needs to realize more clearly the need for providing full information and for respecting the autonomy and decision making of women.

The system we propose should make knowledge about activities in genetic medicine more open and accessible to the general public. Lack of knowledge leads to concerns about what "might be going on." Clear, open information is a much better basis for decisions about use of genetic knowledge, use in which the values of Canadians have an influence.

Appendix 1: Causes and Risks of Congenital Anomalies and Genetic Disease

This appendix lists the major causes of congenital diseases and early-onset genetic disorders and discusses who is at most risk of having children affected by these disorders. It shows that while some people are at much higher risk of having affected children, all of us are at risk, and it is often difficult to identify who is at higher risk.

Unknown Causes

The largest category of disorders comprises congenital anomalies whose origin or cause is unknown. Estimates reached by various studies of the proportion of anomalies that fall into this category range from 43 to 70 percent of cases. The exact percentage found in any one study depends to some extent on the expertise of physicians and on the diagnostic investigations done, but even in the most rigorous studies (such as Nelson and Holmes[14]) more than 4 congenital anomalies in 10 were of unknown origin.

Chromosomal Disorders

These diseases are caused by extra or missing chromosomes or parts of chromosomes. For example, people with Down syndrome (trisomy 21) have three copies of chromosome 21 instead of the usual two. Down syndrome is characterized by developmental retardation and various physical anomalies; other, more severe chromosomal disorders result in profound retardation and early death. These and other significant chromosomal abnormalities can arise during formation of the gametes (eggs and sperm) during fertilization, or during cell division in early embryonic development.

Every couple is at some risk of having a fetus with a chromosomal abnormality, but some couples are at higher risk than others. In particular, the risk increases in pregnancies later in a woman's childbearing years. The incidence of chromosomal abnormalities in the general population, based on studies of the chromosomes of consecutive newborns, is about 1 in 200 liveborn individuals (0.5 percent). However, the likelihood of a woman having a child with a chromosomal anomaly rises steeply from about age 35. For example, the risk of having a liveborn infant with an abnormal number of chromosomes is about 1 in 380 births when the woman is age 30, 1 in 180 at age 35, 1 in 60 at age 40, and 1 in 20 at age 45.[15] In some rare cases, chromosomal anomalies are inherited, so family history may also identify some women at higher risk. Still, the majority of infants with chromosomal anomalies are born following low-risk pregnancies, simply because most pregnancies are in women under the age of 35.

Single-Gene Disorders

Genes are responsible for producing the proteins that make human development and functioning possible. Changes in the sequence of chemical bases in a gene can mean that the particular protein is not made or does not function properly. If this is one of the proteins or enzymes essential to early development, the embryo or fetus will die *in utero*, be spontaneously aborted, or be delivered as an infant with severe anomalies. Indeed, the incidence of genetic anomalies is one of the reasons for the high rate of spontaneous abortion (see Chapter 7).

If the essential gene becomes important only in early childhood, an apparently normal infant will stop developing, become very ill, and die. For example, Tay-Sachs disease is a single-gene disorder in which the signs appear during the first year of life. The disease causes nervous system degeneration with blindness, severe mental retardation, seizures, and paralysis. Death usually occurs by five years of age.

Finally, an abnormal gene might cause a disorder only in later life. Huntington disease, for example, causes a progressive deterioration of the brain, typically starting in adulthood or middle age and leading to death, usually within 10 to 20 years.

Each single-gene disorder is relatively rare, with most recessive single-gene disorders having a birth incidence of 1 in 15 000 to 1 in 100 000. Even the most common such disorder in Western countries, cystic fibrosis, occurs in only 1 birth in 2 500. However, since there are approximately 4 000 known single-gene disorders, the combined likelihood of having one disorder or another is much higher. It is estimated that 1 in 277 liveborn individuals will have a single-gene disease that is evident before age 25.

Who is at risk of having a fetus with a single-gene disorder? In some cases, the gene responsible is a spontaneous dominant mutation, not found in either parent. There is no way to pinpoint who is at risk of having a fetus with a genetic disease caused in this way. In the majority of cases, however, the gene is inherited from one parent or both. The parents may not themselves exhibit any signs of a disorder, since (in cases of recessive diseases in both parents and X-linked diseases in the woman) the abnormal gene may be "covered" by a healthy gene. Although the parents are healthy, they are "carriers" of the abnormal gene and may pass it on to their children.

The Transmission of Single-Gene Disorders

Single-gene disorders are transmitted in one of three ways:

Recessive disorders: For recessive disease to occur, both genes in the pair — one received from the mother and one from the father— must be abnormal, since one normal copy of a gene is able to provide enough protein or enzyme to cover for its malfunctioning partner. If the parents each have only one abnormal member in the pair, they themselves are unaffected. Indeed, all of us probably carry at least one such gene that would be harmful in "double dose." However, when both parents carry the same defective gene, on average one-quarter of their offspring will have both genes faulty and thus be affected. Examples of recessive disorders are phenylketonuria (which results in retardation and seizures but can be treated by diet) and adenosine deaminase deficiency (which results in severe immune deficiency and early death). Another more widely known recessively inherited disease in Caucasian populations is cystic fibrosis, which leads to severe chronic respiratory and digestive problems and a reduced life expectancy.

Dominant disorders: In dominantly inherited disorders, only one member of the gene pair needs to be abnormal to cause the disease; the normal member of the pair is unable to cover for its malfunctioning partner. If the affected person reproduces, the abnormal gene will be passed on average to half their children, who will also be affected. Huntington disease is an example of a dominantly inherited single-gene defect.

X-linked disorders: In X-linked recessive disorders, the problem gene is located on the X chromosome. Since females have two Xs, if one is normal, that female will be healthy. Since males have only one X, if a male has the X-linked disease gene, he will be affected — there is no partner gene to "cover" it. In families where the mother has a gene for an X-linked recessive disorder, therefore, on average half the daughters will be healthy unaffected carriers of the gene, but half the sons will have the disease. An example of an X-linked, single-gene disorder is haemophilia. This bleeding disorder can now be partially controlled with injections of blood clotting factors.

Some people know that they are carriers of such genes, because of a family history of a particular single-gene disorder or, most often, because a previous child was born with that disorder. Others may know that they are at increased risk of being a carrier because of their ethnic descent. For example, Mediterranean populations are more likely to carry thalassaemia;

Ashkenazi Jews are at increased risk for carrying Tay-Sachs disease; black populations are more likely to carry sickle-cell disease; and Mennonite populations in Canada are at increased risk of carrying cystic fibrosis.

In the great majority of cases, however, people do not know that they are carriers of a single-gene disease. In fact, it is believed that everyone carries one or more abnormal recessive genes. If the disorder is recessive, the gene may be passed on for generations without producing a child with an observable disorder. Hence, even for those couples who have no reason to suspect that they are carriers of any particular genetic disorder, there is a small (though unknown) chance that both parents will carry the same genetic anomaly, and hence that the fetus may have a single-gene disorder.

The risk that an abnormal gene in the parent will result in a disorder in the child depends on whether the disorder is transmitted in a dominant, a recessive, or an X-linked way. If dominant, the risk that a child will be affected is one in two, even if only one parent has the gene; if X-linked, there is a one in two chance that male offspring will be affected; if recessive, and if both parents carry the gene, there is a one in four chance that the child will be affected.

Multifactorial Disorders

Multifactorial disorders result from complex interactions between environmental factors (which may include the chemical, social, and emotional environment) and the genes of an individual. Most of them are relatively mild and do not have an onset until adult life. Many adult-onset disorders fall into this multifactorial category; examples include some forms of diabetes, hypertension, heart disease, ulcers, thyrotoxicosis, and certain cancers. These disorders constitute by far the most frequent category. It is likely that most familial chronic diseases of adult onset fall into this group. However, some multifactorial disorders are congenital and can be quite severe — for example, neural tube defects (spina bifida and anencephaly).

Who is at risk for having a fetus with a multifactorial disorder? Because these disorders are partly the result of genes, they tend to run in families, so family history will identify some of those at greatest risk. A couple that has had a child with a multifactorial anomaly is identified as being at significant risk of recurrence. Evidence also suggests that some ethnic groups may be at higher risk of particular disorders — for example, Sikhs have higher rates of neural tube defects than the general population. However, a couple may be at risk of having an affected fetus even in the absence of a family history of the disease or anomaly; for example, one of the most frequent multifactorial disorders, neural tube defects, occurs in the general population in Canada at a rate of at least 1 in 820 births.

Teratogens

Another category of congenital anomalies arises as a result of the embryo or fetus being exposed to harmful agents or substances ("teratogens") *in utero*: for example, infections of the pregnant woman, such as rubella, toxoplasmosis, herpes, syphilis, and cytomegalovirus disease; diseases in the pregnant woman that affect the hormonal or metabolic milieu of the developing fetus, such as diabetes, phenylketonuria, and endocrine tumours; and other exposures, such as alcohol, inadequate nutrition, drugs, irradiation, chemical substances, and increased body temperature.   Evidence from animal research shows that genes may influence the susceptibility of the embryo or fetus to such agents, but this is difficult to demonstrate in human beings. Some examples of congenital anomalies and the agents associated with their genesis include those cases of cleft lip and spina bifida resulting from the pregnant woman's use of anti-convulsants; caudal dysplasia resulting from the woman's diabetes; and fetal alcohol syndrome resulting from excessive alcohol consumption by the pregnant woman.

There is a popular misconception that exposure to drugs or to chemicals in the environment is responsible for a large proportion of congenital anomalies. This belief results perhaps in part from the explosion of litigation, particularly in the United States, involving children with congenital anomalies. However, the evidence is that drugs and chemicals account for a very small percentage of anomalies.[16] Nevertheless, some exposures are an unavoidable risk in all pregnancies; for example, every woman is vulnerable to infection during pregnancy.

Uterine Factors

Some uterine factors can cause malformations in the fetus before birth — for example, an abnormality in the shape or size of the uterus may mean the fetus does not have enough space to develop normally.

General Sources

Adam, S., and M.R. Hayden. "Prenatal Testing for Huntington Disease: Psychosocial Aspects." In Research Volumes of the Royal Commission on New Reproductive Technologies, 1993.

Anderson, G.M. "An Analysis of Temporal and Regional Trends in the Use of Prenatal Ultrasonography." In Research Volumes of the Royal Commission on New Reproductive Technologies, 1993.

Baylis, F. "Assisted Reproductive Technologies: Informed Choice." In Research Volumes of the Royal Commission on New Reproductive Technologies, 1993.

Catano, J.W. "An Assessment of the Readability of Patient Education Materials Used by Genetic Screening Clinics." In Research Volumes of the Royal Commission on New Reproductive Technologies, 1993.

Chodirker, B.N., and J.A. Evans. "Maternal Serum AFP Screening Programs: The Manitoba Experience." In Research Volumes of the Royal Commission on New Reproductive Technologies, 1993.

Dallaire, L., and G. Lortie. "Parental Reaction and Adaptability to the Prenatal Diagnosis of Genetic Disease Leading to Pregnancy Termination." In Research Volumes of the Royal Commission on New Reproductive Technologies, 1993.

Deber, R.B., with H. Bouchard and A. Pendleton. "Implementing Shared Patient Decision Making: A Review of the Literature." In Research Volumes of the Royal Commission on New Reproductive Technologies, 1993.

Grant, K.R. "Perceptions, Attitudes, and Experiences of Prenatal Diagnosis: A Winnipeg Study of Women Over 35." In Research Volumes of the Royal Commission on New Reproductive Technologies, 1993.

Hamerton, J.L., J.A. Evans, and L. Stranc. "Prenatal Diagnosis in Canada — 1990: A Review of Genetics Centres." In Research Volumes of the Royal Commission on New Reproductive Technologies, 1993.

MacKay, I.F., and F.C. Fraser. "The History and Evolution of Prenatal Diagnosis." In Research Volumes of the Royal Commission on New Reproductive Technologies, 1993.

MacLeod, P.M., et al. "A Demographic and Geographic Analysis of the Users of Prenatal Diagnostic Services in Canada." In Research Volumes of the Royal Commission on New Reproductive Technologies, 1993.

Renaud, M., et al. "Canadian Physicians and Prenatal Diagnosis: Prudence and Ambivalence." In Research Volumes of the Royal Commission on New Reproductive Technologies, 1993.

Tudiver, S. "Manitoba Voices: A Qualitative Study of Women's Experiences with Technology in Pregnancy." In Research Volumes of the Royal Commission on New Reproductive Technologies, 1993.

Wertz, D. "Prenatal Diagnosis and Society." In Research Volumes of the Royal Commission on New Reproductive Technologies, 1993.

Specific References

1. Wertz, D.C., and J.C. Fletcher, eds. *Ethics and Human Genetics.* New York: Springer-Verlag, 1989.

2. Billings, P.R., et al. *Discrimination as a Consequence of Genetic Screening.* Boston: Harvard Medical School/Deconess Hospital, 1992.

3. Modell, B. "The Ethics of Prenatal Diagnosis and Genetic Counselling." *World Health Forum* 11 (2)(1990), p. 184.

4. Pembrey, M.E. "Prenatal Diagnosis: Healthier, Wealthier, and Wiser?" In *Bioscience-Society: Report of the Schering Workshop on Bioscience-Society, Berlin, November 25-30, 1990,* ed. D.J. Roy, B.E. Wynne, and R.W. Old. Chichester: John Wiley & Sons, 1991.

5. Benn, P.A. "The Centralized Prenatal Genetics Screening Program of New York City III: The First 7,000 Cases." *American Journal of Medical Genetics* 20 (1985): 369-84.

6. Elejalde, B.R., et al. "Prospective Study of Amniocentesis Performed Between Weeks 9 and 16 of Gestation: Its Feasibility, Risks, Complications and Use in Early Genetic Prenatal Diagnosis." *American Journal of Medical Genetics* 35 (1990): 188-96.

7. Neilson, J.P., and C.M. Gosden. "First Trimester Prenatal Diagnosis: Chorion Villus Sampling or Amniocentesis?" *British Journal of Obstetrics and Gynaecology* 98 (September 1991): 849-52.

8. Campbell, S., P. Smith, and J.M. Pearce. "The Ultrasound Diagnosis of Neural Tube Defects and Other Cranio-Spinal Abnormalities." In *Prenatal Diagnosis: Proceedings of the 11th Study Group of the Royal College of Obstetricians and Gynaecologists,* ed. C.H. Rodeck and K.H. Nicolaides. London: Royal College of Obstetricians and Gynaecologists, 1984.

9. Brent, R.L., R.P. Jensh, and D.A. Beckman. "Medical Sonography: Reproductive Effects and Risks." *Teratology* 44 (1991): 123-46.

10. Chitty, L.S., et al. "Effectiveness of Routine Ultrasonography in Detecting Fetal Structural Abnormalities in a Low Risk Population." *British Medical Journal* 303 (November 9, 1991): 1165-69.

11. Canadian Task Force on Periodic Health Examination. "Periodic Health Examination, 1992 Update: 2. Routine Prenatal Ultrasound Screening." *Canadian Medical Association Journal* 147 (5)(September 1, 1992): 627-33.

12. Wilson, R.D. "Survey of Canadian Centres Utilizing Maternal Serum Alpha Fetoprotein (MSAFP) Screening." *Journal of the Society of Obstetricians and Gynaecologists of Canada* 14 (February 1992): 63-72.

13. Ibid.

14. Nelson, K., and L.B. Holmes. "Malformations Due to Presumed Spontaneous Mutations in Newborn Infants." *New England Journal of Medicine* 320 (1)(January 5, 1989): 19-23.

15. Adapted from Hook, E.B. "Rates of Chromosome Abnormalities at Different Maternal Ages." *Obstetrics and Gynecology* 58 (3)(September 1981): 282-85.

16. Brent, R.L. "The Complexities of Solving the Problem of Human Malformations." *Clinics in Perinatology* 13 (3)(September 1986): 491-503.

Prenatal Diagnosis for Late-Onset Single-Gene Disorders and for Susceptibility Genes

The ability to identify genes through the use of DNA technology is increasing rapidly, and with it the need to assess its implications and consequences to ensure that any uses are ethical and beneficial. Evident in the testimony the Commission heard from Canadians were concerns that new capacities with regard to genetic identification held the potential for misuse and that rapid evolution of the field is making social oversight difficult. The fact that there are vulnerable interests to be protected — for example, against discriminatory uses of the technology by employers and insurers — makes this a matter for all of society to deal with.

DNA testing raises important social issues, and it is clear that public policy will be needed in a range of settings, but many of these applications are outside our mandate. In this chapter we consider DNA testing as it relates to reproduction and prenatal diagnosis for late-onset single-gene disorders and for susceptibility genes. We consider other uses relating to reproduction elsewhere. We evaluate current and potential prenatal uses of DNA testing and make recommendations about these uses in light of our ethic of care and guiding principles. Our goal is to ensure that uses of this technology will be principled and beneficial, and not driven by commercial goals or the mere existence of the technology.

We discussed the use of prenatal diagnosis for disorders that are present at birth (congenital) or begin in childhood ("early-onset") in Chapter 26. However, some single-gene disorders, and many multifactorial genetic disorders, do not manifest themselves until adulthood. Affected individuals may have a normal and healthy childhood before any signs of the disease become apparent — which may not occur until they are in their 30s or later. For some of these disorders, it has become possible, using DNA testing, to identify persons who have inherited the gene for a single-gene late-onset disorder such as Huntington disease. It has also become possible to identify, for a few disorders, persons who have inherited a gene that increases susceptibility to a late-onset multifactorial disorder. Both these uses of DNA testing have been called "predictive" testing, since the disease being tested for would not occur for many years, even decades. Testing for these, if carried out prenatally, could also identify fetuses carrying the relevant genes.

The term "predictive" testing is therefore confusing, because it can be used to refer to two very different types of testing. First, prenatal diagnosis can test for the presence of a gene or genes that increase susceptibility to certain multifactorial disorders. Multifactorial disorders, such as many types of cancer, cardio-vascular disease, and mental illness, result from a complex interaction of one or more genes and environmental factors. We know that these disorders have a partly genetic basis and that they tend to cluster in certain families. In some cases, scientists have discovered that the presence of a particular gene makes some individuals more susceptible to a disease than others in the general population. Having this "susceptibility gene" does not necessarily mean that the person will get the disease, because it also has an environmental component; some with the gene will not get the disease if they have a particularly healthy environment, diet, or way of life. Conversely, some people without the gene will get the disease if they are sufficiently exposed to the environmental factors that also play a role in causing the disease. We know, for example, that some women are at increased risk for breast cancer, given their family history, and it is becoming possible in some families to identify a gene that is responsible for this increased risk. But all women are at some risk for breast cancer, even if they do not have a susceptibility gene. Rather than use the term "predictive testing" for this type of testing, therefore, we use the term "susceptibility testing" to refer to the use of prenatal diagnosis to test for the presence of susceptibility genes in the fetus. No susceptibility testing is being done at present in Canada.

> Our concern is that if you institute screening without counselling and without the support necessary to launch screening, what you are going to end up with is a significant number of persons who are basically given information that only confuses them because you can't say for sure, yes they do have or don't have [the disorder] and at the same time you are not providing them with any kind of social support system to be able to deal with this kind of uncertainty.
>
> *M. Buchwald, Canadian Cystic Fibrosis Foundation, Public Hearings Transcripts, Toronto, Ontario, November 19, 1990.*

The second type of testing is for late-onset single-gene disorders. It is helpful to think of disorders with a genetic component as being on a continuum — at one end of the spectrum, having a particular gene makes a person somewhat more susceptible to an illness in some environmental circumstances; at the other end, having a particular gene makes it impossible for the individual to live and function normally beyond the age of onset, regardless of the environment. Along this continuum, however, the disorders generally fall into one of two broad, albeit somewhat artificial, categories: multifactorial disorders, described above, and single-gene disorders. Prenatal testing can also be used to detect the presence of the gene for a late-onset single-gene disorder.

Late-Onset Single-Gene Disorders

Huntington disease: Progressive mental deterioration (dementia) and uncontrollable jerky movements appear on average in the late 30s. Personality changes often occur in the early stages of the disease (which can last for many years) and may have devastating effects on the family. Individuals eventually become bedridden and unable to feed themselves in the later stages; the disease is fatal and has no known cure.

Adult polycystic kidney disease: Adult polycystic kidney disease causes a progressive reduction in kidney function. The disease has several genetic types; it is not fully penetrant, so that not all those with the gene become ill, but 85 percent will show abnormalities on ultrasound by age 25. Treatment can slow progress of the disease.

Familial adenomatous polyposis: Many benign growths occur in the intestine, some of which lead to cancer. The disease is fatal if not treated by removal of the colon; the risk of one or more of the adenomas undergoing malignant degeneration is virtually 100 percent.

Myotonic dystrophy: Myotonic dystrophy is an untreatable disease that results in variable degrees of muscle wasting and cataracts. The disease is highly penetrant but varies in severity. The prevalence in the Saguenay region of Quebec is 1 in 475 — about 30 to 60 times higher than the prevalence in other regions of the world; prevalence is estimated at 1/25 000 for European populations.

Retinitis pigmentosa: Several types of retinitis pigmentosa lead to progressive loss of vision in later life. No treatment is available.

Familial hypercholesterolaemia: Familial hypercholesterolaemia leads to early coronary heart disease (with onset of symptoms in the 30s or 40s) and other degenerative vascular problems. Early diagnosis allows treatment that can modify progress of the disease.

Single-gene disorders may be recessively or dominantly inherited. In dominant inheritance, the child of an affected person has a 50:50 chance of inheriting the responsible dominant gene. For many dominant disorders, presence of the gene equates with presence of the disorder — all those with the gene who live long enough will become affected. (Huntington disease is one such disorder.) However, some particular dominant disorders are not fully penetrant — that is, not everyone with the gene will manifest the disorder.

Unlike susceptibility genes, having a fully penetrant single-gene disorder is not a question of greater susceptibility or increased risk — presence of the gene equates with the eventual occurrence of the disease, even if no symptoms appear for many years. The relevant gene can be identified directly for some disorders; for others, closely linked genes or "markers" are still used instead, which makes prenatal diagnosis of the latter disorders less than 100 percent accurate. This situation will change in the coming decade, as it becomes possible to identify more and more disease genes directly using DNA technology. We therefore use the term "pre-symptomatic testing" to refer to the use of PND to test for the presence of genes for late-onset single-gene disorders (or their closely linked markers). PND of this type is currently being done for a few disorders in Canada, including Huntington disease.

Both susceptibility testing and pre-symptomatic testing raise important issues that do not arise with respect to PND for congenital disorders or early-onset disorders. We discuss these issues, as well as the current practice of pre-symptomatic testing and susceptibility testing, in the remainder of this chapter. It is important to bear in mind that we are concerned here with *prenatal* testing, which is done to help couples to decide how to manage a pregnancy. Children and adults can also be tested for susceptibility genes and late-onset single-gene disorders; in these cases, the objective of genetic testing is to provide information about the individual's own future health. This application of genetic diagnostic techniques is important, but it is outside our mandate. Throughout this chapter, therefore, the terms pre-symptomatic testing and susceptibility testing refer solely to testing done prenatally.

Prenatal Diagnosis for Late-Onset Single-Gene Disorders

Prenatal testing can be used to detect several dominantly inherited diseases of late onset (see box).[1] These disorders vary widely in their treatability and in their severity when not treated. As will be seen below, these differences in treatability and severity are reflected in people's decisions about whether to have pre-symptomatic testing and how they respond to the results.

Types of Tests

Most late-onset single-gene disorders are dominantly inherited — that is, if either the male or the female partner has the disorder, each child has a 50 percent chance of inheriting the gene from the affected parent. Until recently, couples had no way to determine whether a fetus had inherited the gene. New developments in DNA technology, however, have made it possible to use prenatal testing to determine whether a gene has been passed on; fetal cells are extracted through chorionic villus sampling or amniocentesis, and the DNA is analyzed. At present, this testing takes one of two forms: the test may look directly at the gene, or it may look for linked DNA markers. The latter approach requires study of family members as well.

For some disorders, it is possible to identify the gene that causes the disease and so ascertain with 100 percent accuracy whether the fetus has the gene. This is now possible for myotonic dystrophy, some forms of retinitis pigmentosa, Becker muscular dystrophy, and the Li-Fraumeni syndrome of multiple cancers.

The situation is changing rapidly as more genes are identified, but, in the interim, it is not yet possible to identify the gene directly in many disorders. Instead, tests are used to look for the presence of linked markers — that is, genes that are closely linked to the defective gene. Particular genes located close together on the chromosome (such as a disease gene and a nearby marker gene) are usually transmitted together to the offspring. By studying very large families with a history of a particular disorder, researchers have discovered linked markers that are almost always found together with the disease gene in a particular family. A marker for Huntington disease was discovered in this way in 1983. This made it possible to identify which offspring of an affected individual had inherited the marker gene and therefore to predict that the defective gene was also inherited. The presence of the linked marker was a very reliable indication of the presence of the defective gene — the correlation was over 95 percent for the Huntington disease marker — but it was not definitive. This has changed recently; in future, a linked marker will no longer need to be used now that the Huntington disease gene itself has been identified.

Although most pre-symptomatic testing for late-onset single-gene disorders relies on linked markers, such technology is transitional. Once genes and their mutations have been identified, testing for linked markers will be phased out. In the future, it will be possible to test directly for all dominant disorders. Such ability to identify the genes causing single-gene disorders is increasing rapidly, in part as a result of the Human Genome Project.

PND for late-onset diseases that relies on linked markers can take two forms: exclusion testing and so-called definitive testing (though this is a rather misleading term, since it is not entirely accurate). We will briefly describe the situation for Huntington disease, as this is the disorder on which the most information is available and it serves to explain the current role of markers.

"Definitive Testing"

So-called definitive testing involves detailed family linkage studies to identify the form of marker that accompanies the disease gene within the family. If a closely linked marker is found, this can be used to reveal the health status of both the parent and the fetus. For example, definitive testing may reveal that a woman did not inherit the Huntington disease gene from her affected father, in which case there would be no need to test the fetus. If the woman did inherit the disease gene, then the fetus could also be tested. If the fetus has the same marker, its risk is very high (98 percent); if not, its risk is very low (2 percent). Because it does not identify the disease gene directly, however, definitive testing is not 100 percent accurate. This kind of testing is not a simple process — gathering the necessary information from the family and doing the DNA analysis may take from several months to more than a year. Moreover, definitive testing is not always possible, because of difficulties in acquiring or analyzing the DNA. Before the gene for Huntington disease was identified, definitive testing was an option for about 75 percent of eligible couples.

Exclusion Testing

Exclusion testing is used when a parent does not know whether he or she will get a late-onset disorder, and does not want to know, but wants to avoid the birth of a child who would develop the disease. Exclusion testing makes it possible to determine whether a fetus is at low risk of a late-onset disorder by comparing the fetal genotype with that of one of the grandparents on the affected side of the family. If testing shows the fetus inherited the marker that came from the unaffected grandparent on that side, the fetus will be at very low risk for the disease — because only one gene of the pair the fetus receives can come from that side of the family. It does not give information on the parent's status, since he or she will have two genes from that side of the family. Exclusion testing, by contrast with definitive testing, requires DNA only from the fetus, the couple, and one grandparent on the affected side of the family.

As we have noted, these approaches will likely be phased out in coming years, although exclusion testing may still have some advantages if a parent does not want information about his or her own status.

Current Practices in Canada

Pre-symptomatic testing for late-onset single-gene disorders, whether for adults or prenatally, is relatively new and is currently provided in Canada for just a few disorders (Huntington disease, myotonic dystrophy, adult polycystic kidney disease, and others). This type of DNA testing pre-symptomatically has been available since the mid-1980s in Canada, and information is limited about the nature and implications of the practice. Most of the information available concerns one disorder — Huntington disease — which has been the subject of a continuing in-depth study known as the Canadian Collaborative Study of Predictive Testing for Huntington Disease.

The information emerging from the Canadian Collaborative Study is useful, since it illustrates issues common to all late-onset disorders. Prenatal pre-symptomatic testing for Huntington is currently provided at 14 of the 22 genetics centres in Canada; all 14 participate in the Canadian Collaborative Study. Since any one centre sees relatively few families with the disorder, the Canadian Collaborative Study was set up to collect data in a uniform way.

To help understand the practice of pre-symptomatic PND testing in Canada, and to evaluate the issues it raises, we commissioned two research studies in this area, both of which drew on information gathered through the Canadian Collaborative Study (see research volume, *Prenatal Diagnosis: New and Future Developments*). One study examined patterns of demand for pre-symptomatic or prenatal testing and the psychosocial aspects of prenatal testing. A questionnaire was used to obtain a sociodemographic profile of study participants and to ascertain their knowledge about and attitudes toward prenatal testing; it included questions, for example, about whether they chose to have prenatal testing and whether they knew the difference between exclusion testing and definitive testing. A psychosocial assessment of those who participated in prenatal testing was also done, and their reasons for decisions about pregnancy termination were explored.

> Prenatal testing for Huntington disease has now been offered in Canada for about five years. This ongoing national program has provided the opportunity to study the knowledge and attitudes of people at risk who choose or decline prenatal testing. During this period, over 425 people have participated in predictive testing. Of the 38 who became pregnant and were eligible for prenatal testing, 14 (37%) have entered the prenatal testing program. Of the 14, only 7 actually took the prenatal test. The other 7 withdrew, primarily due to miscarriage or not wanting to consider termination of pregnancy as an option. Clearly, the demand for prenatal testing for this late-onset, autosomal dominant disorder is lower than the expected demand.
>
> *S. Adam and M. Hayden, "Prenatal Testing for Huntington Disease: Psychosocial Aspects," in Research Volumes of the Commission, 1993.*

A second study discusses ethical aspects of predictive testing for Huntington disease, drawing on the experiences of the Canadian Collaborative Study as well as the relevant literature. Ethical issues covered include consent to predictive testing, the counselling process, and patient confidentiality; legal issues addressed include the concepts of wrongful birth and wrongful life, as well as physician liability.

The Canadian Collaborative Study has involved both adult and prenatal testing for markers linked to Huntington. In terms of prenatal testing, of the 47 couples enrolled in the study who became pregnant, 38 were eligible for prenatal testing. Of these 38 couples, 14 (37 percent) requested PND; 4 of these withdrew after pretest counselling, and for 3 others who withdrew termination of pregnancy was not an acceptable option. There were 7 remaining women (3 of whom had more than one pregnancy during the five-year study period) who underwent testing for a total of 11 pregnancies. From 11 prenatal tests, four pregnancies were designated low-risk; the remaining seven were found to be at high risk. Of the seven high-risk pregnancies, six were terminated.

The evidence suggests that prenatal testing for Huntington has been well received by the couples who have chosen it. Many parents at risk for developing Huntington want to avoid the birth of a child who will develop the disease. Shelin Adam explained to the Commission why a pregnant woman whose mother has Huntington disease sought PND:

> She knows what she has been through, living "at risk" for Huntington disease, and does not want to bring a child into this world that would have to go through that same sort of fear — every time she drops something, she thinks she has the start of the disease; every time she forgets something, she is worried. (*S. Adam, participant, Commission Colloquium on Prenatal Diagnosis, November 13, 1991.*)

For this woman, and for others in her situation, PND is seen as a valuable service, without which she would have given up the attempt to have children. But most eligible couples choose not to have prenatal testing. This is also true of prenatal testing for other late-onset disorders. In general, prenatal testing for late-onset single-gene disorders has a much lower utilization rate than testing for congenital anomalies or genetic diseases with their onset in childhood.

The utilization rate is also lower than was anticipated before the tests became available. Before testing was available for Huntington, studies surveying the attitudes of women with fetuses potentially at risk for Huntington indicated that between 32 and 65 percent would use prenatal testing. The actual utilization rate, at 18 percent, is

[A] cause for some alarm is the strong belief displayed by so many respondents that a cure for [Huntington disease] is in the pipeline. All the talk about genetics research and the Human Genome Project may well have engendered unrealistic expectations about progress in this and other diseases ... Appeals for public support need to be leavened with the truth, which is that it always takes longer than we've planned.

T. Powledge, reviewer, research volumes of the Commission, June 16, 1992.

thus outside the lower end of the anticipated range. There are several reasons for the low utilization rate:

- According to the results of the Canadian Collaborative Study, the most important reason for not having PND testing for Huntington is the belief that a cure will be found by the time the child reaches the age of onset. There is no effective treatment or cure for this disease at present, nor is one expected in the near future, but people may reason that the same DNA technologies that have enabled testing for Huntington will, with luck and with sufficient resources, lead to treatments or a cure.

- The uncertainty of the test has led some couples to decline testing. Although this is now changing, the test for Huntington relied on linked markers and so did not provide the same level of certainty as DNA tests that identify a gene directly. The 2 to 3 percent level of uncertainty is much greater, for example, than is the case for PND for chromosome disorders.

- Since the test for Huntington is relatively new, many couples at risk already have a child or children who were not tested and whose status is unknown. Some couples in this situation decline testing because they do not want some of their children to know their risk status while others do not.

- Many couples consider that a child can have an enjoyable and productive life for decades before symptoms of the disease begin to be troublesome. The late Woody Guthrie is often cited as an example of someone with Huntington disease who was able to enjoy life and contribute to society for many years.

Experience with other late-onset disorders for which prenatal testing is possible has shown that the proportion of couples who request PND declines as the seriousness of the disorder decreases and its treatability increases. For example, adult polycystic kidney disease is a late-onset single-gene disorder that varies in severity and is partially treatable with dialysis and kidney transplantation. Although PND using linked markers has been available for this disorder since 1986, very few families have taken advantage of it. A study conducted in Manchester, England, between 1988 and 1991 found that only 1 couple out of 40 with high-risk pregnancies requested prenatal testing. Another study in Australia showed a similar experience, with only one request for prenatal testing out of 46 eligible families over a three-year period.

The use of prenatal testing is even lower for those late-onset disorders where early intervention and treatment are possible. Familial hypercholesterolaemia (high blood cholesterol) is an autosomal dominant disorder that results eventually in heart attacks and strokes. However, diet and drug therapy have proven effective in reducing cholesterol levels. Even though prenatal testing using DNA probes is possible in families known to have the mutant gene, there have been virtually no requests for prenatal testing, presumably as a result of the success of treatment.

Issues in the Use of Prenatal Diagnosis for Late-Onset Single-Gene Disorders

The use of PND for late-onset disorders raises many of the same issues as the use of PND for congenital and early-onset disorders, discussed in the previous chapter. However, it also raises some important new issues, including the potential vulnerability of the child, the need for special counselling, and the disclosure of genetic information to family members. We examine these in turn.

Vulnerability of Children

The available evidence suggests that most of the small proportion of women who do seek PND for late-onset disorders choose to terminate the pregnancy if the disorder is detected. If they choose not to have an abortion, however, the resulting child who knows of his or her status may be placed in a very vulnerable position, for several reasons.

First, it is likely to be difficult to keep knowledge of the child's status a secret from other family members or from the child. Parents and other relatives who know that a child has the gene may perceive and treat him or her differently from siblings known to be at low risk. Needless to say, even if differential treatment is not conscious or deliberate, the effects on the child and his or her siblings could be very harmful.

There are also concerns for the child who knows he or she is at high risk. Since a very young child would not have the capacity to understand the information, it is only when the child is somewhat older that the implications of his or her status would start to become clear. This means that the child would have to deal with the information at a difficult time in the life cycle, when identity and self-image are being formed. The knowledge of being at very high risk could result in significant diminishing of self-esteem and self-worth for a developing child and many problems in adjustment, including anger at and resentment of parents and unaffected siblings.

It is not known how children and adolescents who have the knowledge that they are likely to develop a late-onset disease would deal with decisions about schooling, relationships, and marriage, but it is likely to place a severe burden on them. The potential for long periods of completely normal life could be destroyed by the knowledge that they will almost certainly begin to experience symptoms sooner or later, without them having chosen to have this knowledge.

A danger also exists that the genetic information revealed during PND testing could be disclosed by the family (deliberately or accidentally) to third parties, potentially leading to discrimination or stigmatization affecting the child's schooling or subsequent employment. When PND is used to detect congenital anomalies or early-onset disorders, the condition being tested for is clearly evident early in life; "normal" life for the child is life with the disorder. With late-onset disorders, however, the children have many years of life unaffected by the disorder, yet could still be deprived of a "normal" life if others learn that they will develop the disorder later on.

Hence, there are significant differences in the potential harms to children from prenatal testing for late-onset disorders and the potential harms to children from PND for congenital or early-onset disorders. Moreover, at present there is no way to use knowledge of the child's condition to improve the

> There are significant differences in the potential harms to children from prenatal testing for late-onset disorders and the potential harms to children from PND for congenital or early-onset disorders.

child's health. No treatment has been discovered or developed that might prevent or delay the onset of Huntington disease. Thus, their situation is unlike that for some congenital disorders, where knowledge that the disorder is present in the fetus can help in the medical care of the fetus and child and in preparing parents to care for the child, and where the disorder is evident early in any case.

The adverse effects of the knowledge for the resulting child may be great if the parents decide not to terminate after diagnosis of a late-onset disorder, and the benefits to the child are fewer than for diagnosis of a congenital disorder. For these reasons, many of those involved with Huntington disease (parents, relatives, and groups representing them, as well as testing practitioners) believe that prenatal testing should be refused in cases where parents are unwilling to consider terminating the pregnancy. This is the position of Canadian genetics centres participating in the Canadian Collaborative Study, as well as the position of the International Huntington Association and the World Federation of Neurology.

Commissioners agree that the decision about whether to offer testing where the parents are unwilling to consider termination is not easy. Given the potential harms of PND to the resulting child, we believe that testing for late-onset disorders is one instance where an exception can and should be made to the general prohibition on directive counselling. If termination is not a choice that the couple would be willing to make, counsellors should ensure that the potential harms to the child of knowing the PND test results are clearly outlined to parents. The facts usually act as a strong deterrent to having testing, and, when parents are unwilling to consider termination, counsellors should discourage testing and explain why they are doing so.

We do not believe, however, that parents should be asked for a commitment to terminate an affected pregnancy as a precondition for having the test. We believe the test should be available, after appropriate counselling, to all eligible couples who request it even if they say in advance that they will not terminate an affected pregnancy. Requiring a commitment to terminate is inappropriate for several reasons:

1. Most parents can be relied on to make sensible judgements in light of their own circumstances. In fact, the available evidence shows that after appropriate counselling, most couples who reject the option of abortion decide not to have pre-symptomatic PND testing. Commissioners believe that, after appropriate counselling, few if any who could not contemplate termination would be likely to want prenatal testing.

2. It is often difficult for people to know what they will do in a given situation as long as it remains hypothetical. As we noted with respect to PND for congenital anomalies, many women said that the PND decision-making process became "real" to them only when the test revealed a disorder. It is possible that some women and couples faced with an actual finding that the fetus is affected would opt for termination, even if they previously thought they would not do so.

3. There is no way to enforce a commitment to terminate a pregnancy. If a woman says that she plans to terminate an affected pregnancy, perhaps to gain access to the test, then decides to continue the pregnancy, she cannot be compelled to terminate. Moreover, it would be unacceptable to try to create a legal mechanism that could compel her to undergo an abortion.

4. Finally, the number of couples who might decide to have the testing even if they would not abort is extremely small. The evidence from the Canadian Collaborative Study suggests that this would occur in Canada, at most, only a few times a year. It is therefore important to keep this issue in perspective.

For these reasons, we believe that it is inappropriate to deny couples access to PND testing for late-onset disorders on the basis of their unwillingness to consider abortion. Principles such as individual autonomy and respect for people's ability to make decisions in line with their own circumstances and values preclude this.

It is desirable to protect children identified as being at high risk, who, as we have seen, are in a very vulnerable position. Hence, it is acceptable and appropriate for genetics counsellors to emphasize to the couple the potential harms to the resulting child of using PND in this context, and to discourage the use of PND by couples who are unwilling to consider termination.

We also believe, however, that it is desirable to protect children identified as being at high risk, who, as we have seen, are in a very vulnerable position. Hence, it is acceptable and appropriate for genetics counsellors to emphasize to the couple the potential harms to the resulting child of using PND in this context, and to discourage the use of PND by couples who are unwilling to consider termination.

Our position represents a departure from the usual practice in genetics counselling, which attempts to be non-directive. However, the clear potential for harm during a child's growing years and early adulthood makes it necessary to consider the interests of this vulnerable group. The same considerations do not apply in the case of PND for congenital and early-onset disorders. Hence, counselling practices need to be modified to reflect the distinctive needs of both parents and children when PND for late-onset disorders is at issue. The Commission recommends that

> **256. Provision of prenatal diagnosis for pre-symptomatic testing for late-onset single-gene disorders be restricted to genetics centres licensed by the National Reproductive Technologies Commission.**

and that

> **257. Pre- and post-test counselling for such disorders be rigorous and extensive in nature, with particular attention paid to the potential implications for any child born at high risk of developing a late-onset single-gene disorder, and that provision of such counselling be a condition of licence for all genetics centres providing such testing.**

Counselling and Support

Individuals who seek PND for late-onset disorders are generally well informed about the disorder in question. They have often lived with people who have the disorder and may be involved in caring for an affected parent. They still need intensive counselling and long-term support, however, often exceeding that normally provided in prenatal genetics counselling. For one thing, studies have shown that many individuals have difficulty understanding the technical aspects of the testing, particularly in the case of exclusion testing using linked markers. With respect to PND testing for Huntington disease, for example, Commission research showed that 89 percent of those surveyed for the study had difficulty fully understanding the technology because the current process of marker analysis was so complex (see research volume, *Prenatal Diagnosis: New and Future Developments*).

Given the complexity of both the testing and the counselling process, it is advisable that the DNA testing of parents and grandparents that is required as a basis for prenatal testing be carried out before the woman becomes pregnant. This provides sufficient time for the couple to assimilate information about prenatal testing. At present, many women who enter a prenatal testing program are already pregnant, which places them and the counsellors under severe time constraints. It is important, therefore, to educate the at-risk population about the desirability of carrying out DNA testing before pregnancy occurs.

Moreover, it is important to remember that couples undergoing definitive testing may be discovering their own health status, as well as that of the fetus. This can be a source of enormous stress. Discovering that one is almost certainly going to develop a serious and debilitating genetic disease is extremely difficult for any individual. Counselling is essential for individuals working through this situation.

In short, the significance of counselling in relation to PND for late-onset single-gene disorders cannot be overstated. This is recognized in the Canadian Collaborative Study, which offers parents a minimum of three counselling sessions before they get the test results. However, the Canadian Collaborative Study is being offered as part of a funded research program, and it is not clear whether similar funds for intensive counselling will be available when these tests are provided as part of provincial health insurance plans. We believe it is essential that adequate resources continue to be available to support families at risk in the future. The Commission recommends that

> The counselling alternative ... clarifies coexisting fundamental values, permitting a resolution that arises out of the experience of the participants in the dialogue rather than being imposed by referral to a third party.
>
> Heavy emphasis in counselling on what might be called value clarification may provide a model for the resolution of related issues in testing for other late-onset disorders. The need for in-depth counselling was also described with respect to fully informed choice.
>
> M. Cooke, "Ethical Issues of Prenatal Diagnosis for Predictive Testing for Genetic Disorders of Late Onset," in Research Volumes of the Commission, 1993.

258. Provincial/territorial ministries of health make available adequate resources for counselling in relation to prenatal testing for late-onset disorders.

Confidentiality and Access to DNA Test Results

Using PND testing for late-onset disorders raises many of the same concerns about confidentiality as PND for congenital disorders, but, in particular, there is concern about the potential for discrimination if this information is disclosed to third parties, including insurers, employers, and government agencies.

We refer to what we said in the previous chapter — namely, that the duty of confidentiality entails the obligation to protect information about an individual who has undergone genetic assessment and to ensure it is not released to others without the individual's explicit permission. Genetic information has the same legal protections as all other medical information; whatever the limits or exceptions to the duty of confidentiality are in civil or common law, they do not include a right to disclose information to insurers or employers without the patient's consent.

Some confidentiality issues, however, are unique to PND testing for late-onset disorders. As we have seen, most pre-symptomatic PND testing has so far used linked markers. This requires analysis of DNA from several relatives, including at least one with the disorder. The fact that PND for late-onset single-gene disorders often requires the involvement of other family members raises two kinds of issues: securing the consent of other members of the family to such testing; and regulating access to the results of such testing by other family members.

Consent to testing by other members of the family: Ethical difficulties may arise if a family member does not wish to be tested, but that particular individual's results are required to provide a diagnosis for a relative. Some ethicists believe that such individuals have a moral obligation to cooperate in a family linkage study — even at the risk of learning unwanted information — if their tissue sample is necessary to establish the pattern of inheritance that other family members need to know in order to establish their own risk and take steps that may be possible to safeguard their health or that of potential offspring.[2] All individuals have the right, however, to refuse treatment or investigation, even if some might wish that they would comply for the benefit of others.

Access to test results by other family members: Predictive testing takes place in a complex system of family inter-relationships, and the information revealed has a direct bearing on the health or reproductive risk of other family members. Ethical issues can therefore arise if the information generated through PND is withheld from other members of the family who might be affected. Do individuals have the moral right to withhold test results from family members?

Similar issues regarding the interaction of family members arise in the context of various chromosomal disorders. We believe that the only feasible approaches to these issues are tactful negotiation and common sense. The available evidence shows that the majority of such situations can be resolved through counselling.

The ethic of care reminds us that the counselling alternative is clearly preferable to a judicial process for mediating rights claims.

The alternative is to place more emphasis on judicial mediation between conflicting claims. For example, some people have proposed imposing a *prima facie* legal obligation on family members to cooperate in linkage studies, or a *prima facie* legal obligation on patients to share PND test information with other family members who may be affected. These obligations would have to be balanced against competing rights to confidentiality and privacy; this balancing process would be mediated by courts or other judicial tribunals.

The ethic of care reminds us that the counselling alternative is clearly preferable to a judicial process for mediating rights claims. Whereas judicial mediation promotes an adversarial stance between conflicting rights-bearers, counselling clarifies co-existing fundamental values, permitting a resolution that arises out of the experience of the participants in the dialogue rather than being imposed by referral to a third party (see research volume, *New Reproductive Technologies: Ethical Aspects*).

Full protection of individual privacy and confidentiality is already the practice with respect to PND in general. We reaffirm the importance of these principles with respect to prenatal testing for late-onset disorders and believe that counsellors should continue to pursue, through mediation counselling, consent by other family members to testing and access to test results by other potentially affected family members.

Employment: The Commission heard concerns about the potential for discrimination if employers or insurers had access to genetic information about prospective employees or candidates for insurance. These concerns appear to be based in part on the perception that such information would be readily available to parties other than the patients and their health care providers. As we have noted, however, several protections exist for this information, including the requirement to maintain the confidentiality of medical information unless the patient gives explicit consent to its release.

In addition, the federal *Privacy Act* allows government departments or agencies to collect personal information about individuals only if it relates directly to an operating program or activity of the department or agency in question. Personal genetic information would be unlikely to satisfy this criterion, so federal departments and agencies would not be able to justify collecting it. Further, the Privacy Commissioner of Canada has interpreted the act to mean that legislation must specifically authorize the collection of personal genetic information. However, the Privacy Commissioner's interpretation is open to challenge in a court, and thus collection of information may be justified without specific statutory authority.

Sections 7 and 8 of the *Canadian Charter of Rights and Freedoms* have been interpreted as offering a limited right of privacy against intrusions by federal and provincial governments. These sections could be interpreted as preventing federal government bodies from invading individual privacy by collecting genetic information. The section 15 equality provision of the Charter would appear to reinforce this protection by prohibiting legislation or policies that have the effect of discriminating on the basis of genetic traits related to race, colour, ethnic origin, or mental or physical disability.

Federal and provincial human rights legislation prohibits discrimination in employment on the basis of disability except in cases where being free of a particular disability is a bona fide occupational requirement for the job being filled. Given that genetic testing for diseases of late onset provides no indication of an individual's *current* health or disability status, employers would not be justified in asking for such information as a basis for deciding on a person's ability to do a job. However, one gap in human rights legislation is that a genetic susceptibility to a late-onset disorder might not be perceived by the law as a disability, and so such people may not have protection.

In summary, there appears to be considerable protection against discrimination in employment on the basis of genetic information. We recognize, however, that if genetic testing of adults comes into wider use, these protections could be challenged or eroded. For example, employers might seek to expand the definition of bona fide occupational requirements by claiming that the presence or absence of a given genetic trait would indicate a person's unsuitability for a particular job and to justify testing on this basis. These issues are outside our mandate, which relates to new reproductive technologies. We believe, nevertheless, that society must be prepared to address such questions in the context of a public policy response to the general issue of new and evolving genetic capabilities.

Insurance: Although the issues surrounding genetic testing and insurance are somewhat different from those related to employment, we heard similar concerns about the potential for discriminatory use of genetic testing results. Some provincial human rights laws exempt insurers from provisions prohibiting discrimination on grounds of disability. Insurers can therefore question applicants for insurance about disabilities that may be genetic in origin, as this helps them to assess risk and set premiums in consequence. They can also differentiate among applicants or deny them insurance because of a disability; differentiation or exclusion must generally be based, however, on "reasonable and bona fide grounds."

The growing availability of genetic testing for a wider range of conditions could therefore add to existing barriers to disability, life, and other types of insurance. These issues have attracted considerable attention in the United States because of refusals to provide health insurance to individuals or even to entire families on the basis of genetic testing of one member. With Canada's system of universal health insurance, no person would be denied basic health care, but genetic testing could result in a denial of disability insurance or other types of insurance.

In addition to the federal *Privacy Act*, human rights legislation, and the *Canadian Charter of Rights and Freedom*, other provisions found in data protection statutes, statutory torts legislation, the common law, and ethical and professional guidelines protect genetic information from being used to discriminate against a person or infringe on a person's right to privacy. For example, like the federal act, some provinces have privacy statutes that limit the collection, use, and disclosure of personal information. Furthermore, legislation exists that imposes obligations on physicians to maintain the confidentiality of health information in addition to their common law duty to do so.

However, there are gaps in these same laws and instruments, so that it is difficult to say for certain whether the law offers adequate protection of genetic information. For example, Quebec is the only province that has comprehensive data protection legislation that is currently being examined for possible extension to the private sector. Another gap in the protection offered by the law is where insurers are permitted to discriminate on the grounds of genetic disability. As well, because recent Supreme Court of Canada decisions affirm that the fetus under most applications of the law does not have legal rights, prenatal testing for susceptibilities or late-onset disorders may mean that, after the individual is born, he or she may be burdened with unwanted genetic information; if there are loopholes in the current protections with regard to access to test results or DNA samples, this information could be used as a basis for discrimination.

Thus, the precise level of protection offered by the law may not be apparent until cases pertaining to genetic privacy come before the courts. These general issues of protection of access to genetic information are outside our mandate, however, and should be addressed as part of a broader public policy response to the development of genetic science. We concur, however, with the perspective expressed by the Office of the Privacy Commissioner of Canada in a 1992 report, *Genetic Testing and Privacy*,[3] to the effect that insurers and other service providers should not be permitted to begin collecting information made newly available through genetic testing without a thorough review of the ethical and human rights implications of allowing this.

Prenatal Diagnosis for Susceptibility Genes

People with susceptibility genes are genetically predisposed toward multifactorial disorders, which differ from late-onset single-gene disorders in that they are caused by an interaction of genetic and environmental factors (such as diet and smoking). Although having a susceptibility gene increases the probability of getting the related disease, it does not necessarily lead to the disease; the relevant environmental factors may be absent or inoperative, or other genes may act to protect the individual from the disease.

Multifactorial disorders include some of the most common diseases in our society today, such as many types of cancer, cardiovascular disease, and mental illness. It has been estimated that up to 60 percent of adults will eventually suffer from a multifactorial disorder.[4] It has now become possible to identify susceptibility genes for some of these disorders through DNA testing. Examples include colon cancer, insulin-dependent diabetes mellitus, heart disease, rheumatoid diseases, and chronic obstructive lung disease (see research volume, *Prenatal Diagnosis: New and Future Developments*).

The ability to identify susceptibility genes raises the question of whether it is appropriate to test for them, a question on which the Commission heard a range of views from Canadians. For example, as with pre-symptomatic testing for late-onset single-gene disorders, susceptibility testing for multifactorial disorders could take place either prenatally or during adolescence or adulthood. In the latter case, individuals would be tested in order to evaluate their risk for a late-onset multifactorial disorder and provided with information that could help them manage that risk. In the prenatal case, a pregnant woman could have her fetus tested to determine its risk status, presumably with the intention of aborting a fetus that had the gene, as no prenatal treatment or prevention strategies are available.

No such prenatal testing for susceptibility genes is being done in Canada at present, but there is a limited amount of adult testing of members of families with a history of a disorder. Considerable interest has been shown in exploring susceptibility testing, both within the health care system and by commercial interests (see Chapter 24). The main health-related justification for such testing is that it might enable individuals at higher risk for a particular multifactorial disorder to take preventive measures or receive treatment earlier in their lives. Since the disorders are caused by a combination of genetic and environmental factors, it is possible, in principle, to modify a person's micro-environment with the aim of avoiding exposure to the factors that trigger the disorder. For example, people with a genetic susceptibility to coronary heart disease could alter their diet to decrease their cholesterol intake, increase their activity level, and have their cholesterol level checked more frequently to

> Canada has a window of opportunity to anticipate and shape developments in the area of susceptibility testing in accordance with our collective values and priorities. Guidelines and safeguards must be established to ensure that if any such testing takes place, it will be in an ethical and beneficial manner, and that our response as a society is not driven solely by technological imperatives or commercial goals.

enable earlier diagnosis and treatment. It has even been suggested that population screening programs be established to test all adults for certain common susceptibility genes, although no such program exists in Canada. As we will see in the next section, the likely health benefits of susceptibility testing programs, in terms of better prevention or earlier treatment, are not clear.

As with the case for single-gene late-onset disorders, the other reasons for the interest in susceptibility testing are not related to health care. For example, insurance companies offering life or disability insurance have a strong interest in identifying individuals who are at higher risk of developing multifactorial disorders, so as to minimize the insurer's exposure to risk. Employers may also wish to know the genetic susceptibilities of potential employees: healthy employees are more productive and less costly to employ. There are no programs in Canada at present to screen applicants for genetic susceptibility to disease for employment or insurance purposes. However, this is not what prevents access to medical records and test results by insurers — it is the physician's legal duty of confidentiality that prevents access without the patient's explicit consent. This may need to be made more explicit with regard to insurers in particular.

Given that commercial interests may wish to develop the concept of population testing for susceptibility genes, there are vulnerable interests to be protected, and governments should be considering what measures are needed to protect these interests. Canadians told the Commission that they are concerned about the use of DNA testing in harmful and discriminatory ways. Canada has a window of opportunity to anticipate and shape developments in the area of susceptibility testing in accordance with our collective values and priorities. Guidelines and safeguards must be established to ensure that if any such testing takes place, it will be in an ethical and beneficial manner, and that our response as a society is not driven solely by technological imperatives or commercial goals.

Before considering the possible uses of susceptibility testing, it is important to clarify what such tests would reveal. In the next section, we discuss what it means for an individual to have a susceptibility gene. We go on to consider the implications of susceptibility testing, both in the adult context and in the PND context.

What Does Susceptibility Testing Actually Tell Us?

Susceptibility testing is intended to provide individuals (or couples) with reliable information about the likelihood that they (or the fetus) will develop a multifactorial disorder later in life. The usefulness of this information is deficient in many important respects, however. First, many of the tests now available rely on linked markers, which means, as we saw earlier in this chapter, that the tests cannot establish definitively whether the relevant gene or genes are present. This will change as genes can be identified directly, but secondly, and more important, even when a susceptibility gene can be identified reliably, this does not mean that the individual will become ill with the disorder in question. It is essential to remember that the disorder will not appear in all people with susceptibility genes, and that not all people with a disorder will have particular genes. Environmental factors are also involved in the onset of multifactorial diseases, and these cannot be measured by DNA testing.

Susceptibility testing by itself, therefore, provides only limited information. Although someone with the gene may have an increased likelihood of becoming ill, the data are not usually good enough to answer accurately questions about how many people who have the gene actually get the disorder — is it 0.5 percent, or 5 percent, or 50 percent? We also need to know how this risk compares to that of others in the general population who lack the genes — does having certain genes increase one's disease risk by 5 percent, by 100 percent, or by 1 500 percent?

Answering these questions would require correlational studies that compare the clinical and natural history of those with a particular genotype to those in the general population who do not have the genotype. However, simply looking retrospectively at a group of people identified as ill with the disease in question and comparing them to a group of well people for differences in the frequency of the gene raise the problem of biased ascertainment, because such an approach does not provide a random sample of people with the gene — the sample would include only those with the gene who became ill. Moreover, since the disorders in question are of late onset, the data needed to conduct such studies must be collected over the long term. The study group may need to be followed over several decades to obtain the necessary information on outcomes. This imposes a considerable burden on participants, who must be willing to make themselves available for the full duration of the study, and creates difficulties for funding, since research agencies are often unable or unwilling to commit funds to such long-term projects.

We do not have good correlational data for the vast majority of susceptibility genes for multifactorial disorders. What we do know is that people with a particular multifactorial disorder often exhibit a particular genetic marker. But we also need to know how often these same genes are found in people who do not develop the disorder, or how much more likely people with the gene are to develop the disorder than people without the gene. In the absence of good information on the absolute risk for those

> Susceptibility testing by itself provides only limited information. Although someone with the gene may have an increased likelihood of becoming ill, the data are not usually good enough to answer accurately questions about how many people who have the gene actually get the disorder — is it 0.5 percent, or 5 percent, or 50 percent?

with the gene, as well as on the increased relative risk, susceptibility testing is likely to create unnecessary anxiety among those who have a susceptibility gene but whose risk is nonetheless quite low, and a false sense of security among those who lack a susceptibility gene but whose risk is nonetheless real.

For example, testing for the susceptibility gene for insulin-dependent diabetes mellitus (IDDM) would likely create unnecessary anxiety. There is no question that having the susceptibility gene for IDDM affects the likelihood of getting the disease — more than 95 percent of IDDM patients have the gene. However, although people with this gene are more likely to get IDDM than people without the gene, the vast majority of people who have the gene do not get IDDM. In fact, evidence suggests that only 1 person in every 150 who have the gene actually develops the disease. Most people with the susceptibility gene do not get the disorder because they are not exposed to the environmental factor or factors that trigger IDDM, or because they may have another gene that protects them. (The environmental factor involved is widely believed to be some sort of virus, although this has not been established definitively.) Telling people that they have the susceptibility gene for IDDM is therefore likely to cause unnecessary worry, even if they are also told that the likelihood of developing the disease is very low.

By contrast, testing for a recently identified susceptibility gene for breast cancer could create a false sense of security if the results are negative, as this genetic mutation accounts for only 9 percent of breast cancers.[5] As a result, being told that one lacks this particular susceptibility gene is likely to be misleading, unless it is also made clear that the vast majority of breast cancers are not associated with having this particular gene. In addition, there are probably other as yet unidentified susceptibility genes for breast cancer. People who lack the one identified gene may still be at significant risk for breast cancer, because they may have another gene or may be exposed to environmental factors that trigger the disease. In other words, the absence of the particular susceptibility gene being tested for does not mean that an individual lacks a genetic predisposition to the disorder. Furthermore, researchers are discovering that there are different genes that may indicate susceptibility to a particular disorder. Some individuals may have more than one of these, each of which changes the person's risk to a different extent. As a result, even the most sophisticated DNA susceptibility testing could miss a significant proportion of people with a genetic susceptibility. An understanding of these aspects of susceptibility testing is not easy to communicate, and they also mean that the benefits to be derived from this application of DNA testing are limited.

Finally, to complicate the picture still further, some people have what might be called "protective genes," which actually reduce their susceptibility to particular disorders. For example, protective genes have been identified for coronary artery disease and diabetes mellitus.

At its current state of development, therefore, susceptibility testing for multifactorial disorders on a population basis provides only very incomplete information on people's risks of developing them. It tells us only that some people have a greater risk (estimated with varying degrees of reliability) of developing a disease at some unpredictable point in the future.

The Implications of Adult Susceptibility Testing

In assessing the implications of allowing susceptibility testing, we need to consider the potential benefits, harms, and opportunity costs. We look first at adult susceptibility testing to establish a context for considering prenatal testing, the substance of our mandate in this area.

Potential Benefits

The major health-related benefit of adult susceptibility testing is that, in principle, it can allow individuals who know they are at higher risk of developing a particular multifactorial disease to avoid exposure to environmental factors that are known to trigger the symptoms of the disease and to seek earlier diagnosis and treatment. However, this presupposes that there is a proven treatment or prevention strategy for the disorder in question. People can derive some benefit from testing only if knowledge of their susceptibility allows them to avoid the disease. But, for most of these disorders, no effective intervention is available at present. For example, there is no known way to delay the onset of IDDM and hence no health benefit to individuals from knowing their genetic susceptibility.

The fact is that we know very little about the identity or inter-action of the specific environmental factors that trigger multi-factorial diseases. Moreover, some of the factors known to affect multifactorial disorders — such as the characteristics and quality of social relationships and human interaction — are very difficult to measure. Finally, it is likely that different environmental factors trigger different susceptibility genes for the same disorder. Hence, it is unlikely that a single prevention strategy would be effective in all cases of genetic susceptibility to a particular disorder.

> People can derive some benefit from testing only if knowledge of their susceptibility allows them to avoid the disease. But, for most of these disorders, no effective intervention is available at present.

Even if a prevention strategy is identified, how likely is it that individuals at risk would change their behaviour and follow the recommended prevention strategy? Experience shows that rates of compliance with medical treatment regimes are often quite low, even when people are already acutely ill.[6] In the case of susceptibility genes, where an illness is not yet present to serve as a motivating factor, compliance rates are likely to be lower still.[7] In the absence of specific strategies to provide continuing support and reinforcement, many people would find it difficult to follow a prevention regime for a disease that has yet to occur.

In summary, the ability of individuals and the health care system to react to and effectively use any information provided by susceptibility testing of the general population is likely to remain quite limited for a long time to come.

Potential Harms

Although the likely benefits of susceptibility testing for multifactorial disorders are quite minimal, the potential for harm is considerable. The use of susceptibility testing, like pre-symptomatic testing for single-gene disorders, creates a new category of people who are not ill but who know that they are susceptible to a specific illness. This could have a negative impact on people's self-image and sense of identity, as

> A caring society is one that does not impose special burdens or inequitable requirements on any of its members simply because they happen to have a particular genetic make-up.

well as on their family and other relationships. Moreover, people could be stigmatized by disclosure of their risk status. The likelihood of stigmatization would probably decline with the development of tests for a greater number of these genes and with increasing awareness that almost all of us carry genes that make us susceptible to one multifactorial disorder or another. When testing first became available, however, those who carried the genes that could be tested for might well encounter stigma or bias in their personal, school, or work lives.

Moreover, information from susceptibility testing, if obtained by third parties such as employers or insurers, could be used to discriminate against the individual; we discussed this issue in the context of PND in general. It would be essential, therefore, to ensure that information from susceptibility testing, like all other medical records, was protected from any disclosure without the individual's consent.

There are concerns that employers or insurers could demand that applicants undergo

> Would genetic screening be used in hiring and promotion? How will it affect access to health insurance, long term disability insurance and drug plans? To what extent will this technology impact negatively on the economic status of women? Will women's jobs become even more ghettoized than they have in the past?
>
> *N. Riche, Canadian Labour Congress, Public Hearings Transcripts, Toronto, Ontario, October 31, 1990.*

susceptibility testing as a precondition for gaining employment or buying life or disability insurance. The use of susceptibility testing in this context falls outside our mandate, but we are concerned about the potential for applying this technology for uses unrelated to health care. Unlike health care providers, employers or insurers would be under no obligation to respond to a diagnosis of genetic susceptibility with either therapeutic responses or preventive measures. The value of this information to employers and insurers would be based solely on financial considerations, not the interests of those being tested. For example, tests could identify actual or potential health care risks among employees or insurance applicants, thereby giving employers or insurers an opportunity to minimize their costs or liability. It would be neither the role nor the responsibility of employers or insurers to offer prevention, treatment, or even follow-up counselling for the individuals tested.

> We are concerned that women and men may be made more vulnerable economically because of the growth in diagnostic technologies ... The ability to screen for genetic disposition to conditions or illnesses will provide a tool that many employers, in their search for the perfect work force, are eager to use. Legislation has already been introduced in American jurisdictions permitting employers to demand and use the results of tests showing genetic disposition.
>
> *C. Micklewright, British Columbia Federation of Labour, Public Hearings Transcripts, Vancouver, British Columbia, November 27, 1990.*

We are very concerned about any use of susceptibility testing to identify employees or insurance applicants as health care risks, particularly when the ability of individuals and the health care system to respond would be quite limited. In our view, a caring society is one that does not impose special burdens or inequitable requirements on any of its members simply

> There is a need to review the legal protections now in place with respect to insurance and employment practices to determine whether they are adequate in an era of DNA testing, and we urge that this be done while the current window of opportunity is still open.

because they happen to have a particular genetic make-up. Despite being beyond our mandate, then, the issue of susceptibility testing in the context of the workplace or insurance is one that does require investigation and, possibly, a public policy response to ensure that information acquired through such testing cannot be used in discriminatory ways. Commissioners thus conclude that there is a need to review the legal protections now in place with respect to insurance and employment practices to determine whether they are adequate in an era of DNA testing, and we urge that this be done while the current window of opportunity is still open.

Opportunity Costs

The goal of avoiding the onset of multifactorial disorders is a worthy one. However, given the practical, ethical, and other difficulties of relying on susceptibility testing to realize this goal, we believe that alternative approaches would provide greater benefits and create fewer harms.

It is important to remember, for example, the potential effectiveness of environmental responses to multifactorial diseases. In the last several decades, mortality from cardiovascular disease has fallen by more than 40 percent, not as a result of identifying individuals who are at genetic risk but largely because of environmental change — such as changes in diet and smoking habits, increased physical activity, and changes in socioeconomic circumstances. Similarly, we know that improved prenatal care programs for pregnant women in disadvantaged circumstances will reduce the incidence of disease and disability throughout their children's lives.

Where environmental factors are associated with disease or ill health, then, it may be less effective to invest societal resources in discovering the individuals who are at genetic risk than to devote resources to changing the environment for everyone. In other words, the opportunity costs of emphasizing the genetic dimension of multifactorial conditions include the risk of diverting attention and research resources away from potentially more effective approaches, such as environmental change for communities or populations. Viewing diseases that have multiple causes as "genetic" tends to preclude remedies that attack the complex social determinants of health, which may well be equally or more important in causing the disease.

Genetic testing and disease prevention through improvements in the physical or social environment are not necessarily mutually exclusive undertakings. In fact, the purpose of identifying those with susceptibility genes is to permit environmental interventions that may allow them to avoid becoming ill. However, in assessing the costs of susceptibility testing, it is important to recognize just how expensive such testing would be if done appropriately and ethically. The cost would go far beyond the development and provision of the test, although this alone would be quite expensive. In addition, it would be necessary to establish and fund testing, counselling, and follow-up programs and to hire and train the personnel necessary to implement them. Susceptibility testing, if offered on a population screening basis, would identify many at-risk individuals, all of whom would require counselling. As we have seen, genetics counselling is personnel-intensive and time-consuming, because conveying risk information is complex and perceptions of risk differ widely. Unless appropriate counselling was provided, people could be lulled into a false sense of security or develop unnecessary anxiety about their risks, both of which could jeopardize rather than promote their future health. Quality control mechanisms for the laboratories that do the testing would also be necessary to minimize the possibility of errors, as would safeguards to protect the confidentiality of information generated through testing.

Commissioners believe that the resources needed to develop such screening programs would be better spent on prevention programs that focus on improving the social and physical environment for whole communities or populations. For the foreseeable future, widespread susceptibility testing would not be an appropriate use of resources — it would provide minimal benefits at too high an opportunity cost and has the potential to cause serious harm.

The Commission does recognize the value of continuing studies, for example, to track certain multifactorial diseases in large families with a history of a particular disorder. But these studies must be viewed as research, not clinical services, with all those involved receiving the full protection accorded participants in biomedical research in Canada today. All such studies involving human subjects would have to be based at a university or hospital and would have to be approved by research ethics boards, which follow Medical Research Council of Canada guidelines for research involving human subjects.

The time may come when population screening for particular susceptibility genes would be an appropriate use of resources. This is only a possibility at present, and many conditions would have to be met before such a program would be appropriate: the gene would have to be quite common in the population; reliable information would be needed about the actual risks posed by having the susceptibility gene; the disorder would have to be severe; an effective preventive strategy would have to be available; the gene would have to increase susceptibility by a significant amount; mechanisms for protecting the confidentiality of information and for assuring the quality and reliability of laboratory test results would have to be in place; and the appropriate forms of counselling and follow-up would have to be identified and funded.

> For the foreseeable future, widespread susceptibility testing would not be an appropriate use of resources — it would provide minimal benefits at too high an opportunity cost and has the potential to cause serious harm ... The time may come when population screening for particular susceptibility genes would be an appropriate use of resources. This is only a possibility at present, and many conditions would have to be met before such a program would be appropriate.

These conditions for a successful population-wide screening program are not currently in place (see research volume, *Prenatal Diagnosis: New and Future Developments*), and establishing them would be possible only if susceptibility screening were first tried out in research pilot studies. The danger is, however, that screening would not be done as part of a unified, well-planned public health program, based on the lessons of carefully monitored pilot studies, but would occur on an opportunistic and ad hoc basis. Consequently, Commissioners believe that safeguards should be in place to ensure that any transition from research to service be subjected to careful and rigorous review. In our view, programs for population screening of individuals for susceptibility to multifactorial diseases should not be funded or offered in the health care system. Studies aimed at tracking certain multifactorial diseases should be classified as research projects, not clinical diagnostic services, and all subjects involved in such studies should receive the full protection accorded participants in biomedical research.

The Implications of Prenatal Susceptibility Testing

We have outlined our concerns about adult susceptibility testing, which falls outside the Commission's mandate, in order to establish a context for the subject that is in fact within our mandate — susceptibility screening in the context of reproduction and reproductive technology. We believe that prenatal susceptibility testing is even less appropriate than adult testing, because the benefits are even fewer and the potential harms greater. Like prenatal testing for late-onset single-gene disorders, prenatal susceptibility testing puts children in a very vulnerable position if they are shown to be at higher risk. The potential harms to self-image and parent-child relations, which we discussed in the context of PND for single-gene disorders, apply equally to prenatal susceptibility testing, as does the potential for stigmatization and discrimination.

Although adults who agree voluntarily to undergo susceptibility testing may be willing and able to accept these potential dangers, it is not in the best interests of children to be subjected to them as a result of prenatal susceptibility testing. Moreover, there is little opportunity for parents to use information obtained prenatally about a child's genetic risk to help delay the onset of the disorder in question. As we have seen, few effective prevention strategies exist.

There has been no demand for the development and provision of prenatal susceptibility testing from couples with a family history of late-onset multifactorial

> The question has been raised whether society would approve of doing prenatal diagnosis to detect genes that have only an increased probability, not a certainty, of causing a serious disorder. Most geneticists would not approve, and existing guidelines suggest that it is not ethical. It might be concluded that prenatal testing for susceptibility genes is one possible use of prenatal diagnosis that has so many pitfalls and so few benefits that it should not be permitted.
>
> L. Prior, "Screening for Genetic Susceptibilities to Common Diseases," in Research Volumes of the Commission, 1993.

disorders. This is in sharp contrast to calls for PND for early-onset genetic disorders and congenital anomalies but similar to the situation with respect to prenatal testing for late-onset single-gene disorders, where tests have been developed but rates of use have been much lower than originally anticipated. There has been no identified demand for susceptibility testing.

Couples using PND want information about the health status of the fetus that is useful and relevant to the health and functioning of their child. Susceptibility testing is simply unable to provide this sort of information; having a susceptibility gene does not necessarily mean developing the disorder, the incidence of the disorder is affected by complex but potentially controllable environmental factors, and the disorders concerned do not develop until adulthood. Moreover, since everyone carries an unknown number of susceptibility genes, there is no way to ensure that children are free of all genetic susceptibilities — in fact, it is very unlikely that any of us are.

Given these limitations and potential harms, it is not surprising that demand for prenatal susceptibility testing has been negligible. Spending resources on prenatal testing for susceptibility genes would not be an effective or responsible investment of scarce health care resources. The Commission therefore recommends that

> **259. Prenatal diagnosis *not* be offered for genes that increase susceptibility to disease, and that this restriction be a condition of licence to provide prenatal diagnosis services established by the National Reproductive Technologies Commission.**

Conclusion

In our review of pre-symptomatic testing for late-onset disorders and testing for susceptibility genes, it is evident that many of the principles and recommendations developed in the context of PND for congenital anomalies and early-onset genetic diseases also apply to the provision of pre-symptomatic and susceptibility testing prenatally. We have not reiterated these here.

One distinctive issue arises when parents want prenatal testing for an adult-onset single-gene disorder but would continue the pregnancy regardless of what the test showed. As we have argued, the potential harm to the resulting child in this situation is such that testing should not be offered without full counselling emphasizing the lack of benefit to the child and the potential for serious harm.

To ensure that individuals and couples have the proper support to make the very difficult decisions regarding testing in the context of late-onset disorders, Commissioners believe that special efforts and resources must be provided to ensure that PND in this situation is accompanied by adequate and appropriate counselling. In the end, Commissioners find themselves returning to the basic logic underlying all PND — namely, that individual women and couples, when faced with difficult choices, are capable of making enlightened and appropriate decisions for themselves and their children when given proper and respectful support.

With regard to DNA testing for susceptibility to multifactorial disorders, despite its limitations, interest is substantial and will likely grow, particularly on the part of those with commercial interests. Many people look to the field of genetics to provide clear and understandable reasons for disease or ill health when in fact their determinants are very complex and include social, economic, and environmental factors. Susceptibility testing also has financial attractions for employers and insurers, and some biotechnology firms in the United States can see substantial profits in the future in the development and marketing of a range of test kits.

Given the commercial presence (both present and potential) in this area in other countries, and the vulnerable interests of individuals and society that therefore need protection, we believe that any pressure to introduce susceptibility testing in this country at this time should be resisted firmly and consistently. The premature application of susceptibility testing could be harmful to Canadians and would constitute a serious waste of resources. Given that we do not know how to use the limited information made available by such testing to improve prevention or treatment, susceptibility testing offers few benefits and creates many potential harms.

We have concluded, therefore, that susceptibility testing should not be provided prenatally (or on a population-screening basis) for the foreseeable future; although pre-symptomatic testing for single-gene late-onset diseases in families known to have the gene may be justified, testing for susceptibility genes on a population basis is not. Susceptibility testing should be provided to adults only in the context of research projects — such as family linkage studies or research pilot studies — with all the strictures and protections that entails.

Commissioners recognize that recommendations aimed at preventing or limiting the proliferation of susceptibility testing in the health care system are only part of the social response that is needed. Given that commercial interests may put resources behind developing and marketing DNA testing, there are vulnerable interests to be protected. Individuals do not have the expert knowledge to evaluate whether they need to be tested, and social harms may therefore result from widespread use of such testing. Governments should therefore ensure that these interests are protected. We do not find it likely that pressure for prenatal DNA testing for these categories of disorders will arise in the foreseeable future, and we have made recommendations in several chapters to limit the use of DNA testing and technology in other categories (see Chapters 26, 28, and 29). However, pressure to apply these tests could also arise in other areas of society — in the workplace or in the insurance industry, for example — that are outside our mandate. The use of susceptibility testing in the health care system is just one of the many significant issues posed by the emerging role of genetics in our society. Clear leadership and forward-looking policy responses to these issues are required from governments to ensure that the power of genetic science and technology is used in an ethical and beneficial manner wherever they may be applied. The Commission recommends that

> **260. The Prenatal Diagnosis and Genetics Sub-Committee of the National Reproductive Technologies Commission monitor developments in DNA testing as they relate to reproductive technologies, with a view to recommending regulations or limits if needed.**

Public information, consultation, and dialogue are the most effective bulwarks against misuse of these technologies in this rapidly changing field. The existence of a source for this information and a forum for consultation would help to ensure that the necessary dialogue takes place and that decision makers can develop policies that are both responsive to Canadians' social values and effective in achieving appropriate societal oversight and control of technology use.

General Sources

Adam, S., and M.R. Hayden. "Prenatal Testing for Huntington Disease: Psychosocial Aspects." In Research Volumes of the Royal Commission on New Reproductive Technologies, 1993.

Cooke, M. "Ethical Issues of Prenatal Diagnosis for Predictive Testing for Genetic Disorders of Late Onset." In Research Volumes of the Royal Commission on New Reproductive Technologies, 1993.

Guay, H., B.M. Knoppers, and I. Pannisset. "La génétique dans les domaines de l'assurance et de l'emploi." *Revue du Barreau* 52 (2)(April-June 1992): 185-343.

Holtzman, N.A. *Proceed with Caution: Predicting Genetic Risks in the Recombinant DNA Era.* Baltimore: Johns Hopkins University Press, 1989.

Prior, L. "Screening for Genetic Susceptibilities to Common Diseases." In Research Volumes of the Royal Commission on New Reproductive Technologies, 1993.

Specific References

1. McKusick, V.A. *Mendelian Inheritance in Man: Catalogs of Autosomal Dominant, Autosomal Recessive, and X-Linked Phenotypes.* 10th ed. Baltimore: Johns Hopkins University Press, 1992.

2. Capron, A.M. "Which Ills to Bear?: Reevaluating the 'Threat' of Modern Genetics." *Emory Law Journal* 39 (3)(1990), p. 685.

3. Canada. Privacy Commissioner of Canada. *Genetic Testing and Privacy.* Ottawa: Privacy Commissioner of Canada, 1992.

4. Science Council of Canada. *Genetics in Canadian Health Care.* Ottawa: Minister of Supply and Services Canada, 1991, p. 21.

5. Ibid., p. 25.

6. See, for example, Becker, M.H. "Patient Adherence to Prescribed Therapies." *Medical Care* 23 (5)(May 1985): 539-55.

7. Sackett, D.L., et al. "Randomized Clinical Trial of Strategies for Improving Medication Compliance in Primary Hypertension." *Lancet* (May 31, 1975): 1205-1207.

Sex Selection for Non-Medical Reasons

A child's sex is usually the result of chance — about half the time a girl is born and half the time it is a boy. However, some parents have tried to change these odds. Interest in trying to influence whether a boy or a girl is born is long-standing, and motivations for sex selection have varied over the centuries and from culture to culture. Numerous methods of sex selection have been proposed throughout history, including timing of intercourse, douching, and diet, as well as more exotic theories focussing on the phases of the moon, the direction of the wind, or even the direction of the bed.[1] Historically, interest has focussed on techniques to increase the likelihood of male offspring, since men have held a higher social, economic, and legal status in most societies.

These folk recipes have no proven effectiveness. In the past, most parents with a strong desire for a child of a particular sex would only be able to "keep on trying" until they had a child of the desired sex, sometimes having more children than they wanted in pursuit of their goal. However, recent technological developments have the potential to change the chances of having a child of one sex or the other. These new methods of sex selection are the focus of this chapter. Three distinct techniques are covered by the term "sex selection." These three methods are employed at different stages in the reproductive process, using different reproductive technologies.

First, *sperm treatment with assisted insemination* is used before conception and involves an attempt to influence which type of sperm cell fertilizes the egg. All eggs have an X chromosome, so if the egg is fertilized by a sperm that carries the Y chromosome it will lead to the birth of a boy (XY); if it is fertilized by a sperm that carries the X chromosome it will lead to a girl (XX). Semen is therefore treated in an effort to separate out the desired type of sperm, and assisted insemination using the treated semen is performed. Because the method is used before conception, it is sometimes known as "preconception sex selection" or "sex preselection"; this terminology has been used loosely, however, and has therefore become unclear, so we refer to this technique as "sex-selective insemination."

The second method, *in vitro* fertilization and preimplantation diagnosis, involves *in vitro* fertilization followed by preimplantation diagnosis to determine the sex of the resulting zygote. Only zygotes of the desired sex are transferred to the woman's uterus. We refer to this method as *sex-selective zygote transfer*.

These first two methods seek to influence the sex of the fetus before pregnancy is established. The third method, *prenatal diagnosis to detect fetal sex and sex-selective abortion*, involves identification of the sex of the fetus during the pregnancy using prenatal diagnosis, with abortion of the fetus of the undesired sex. Identification of fetal sex is possible by chorionic villus sampling, ultrasound, or amniocentesis between approximately 10 and 16 weeks' gestation. Therefore, if the fetus is not of the desired sex, a second-trimester abortion could be performed. We refer to this as "sex-selective abortion." (Future developments involving the examination of fetal cells in the pregnant woman's blood may allow fetal sex to be determined earlier in the pregnancy.)

Because the three techniques use different technologies and are employed at different stages in the reproductive process, they raise different issues and must be examined separately. It is important to remember, however, that sex selection techniques can be used for medical reasons, in situations where male offspring are at high risk of severe genetic disorders resulting from genes on the X chromosome (for example, Duchenne muscular dystrophy). As discussed in Chapter 27, most Canadians consider use of sex selection techniques to prevent the birth of male offspring at high risk of a severe genetic disorder to be an appropriate use of prenatal diagnosis. As well, the Canadian College of Medical Geneticists has long approved prenatal diagnosis to determine fetal sex as an appropriate option to offer to women or couples at risk of having male offspring affected by an X-linked disorder.

The focus in this chapter is the use of sex selection techniques in cases where a couple wants to have a child of one sex or the other for non-medical reasons, not because an X-linked disease is likely. When we speak of sex selection in this chapter, therefore, it is in this non-therapeutic context. After a brief survey of the views of Canadians on this topic, we discuss each of the techniques in turn, including their ethical and social aspects and our analysis and recommendations.

The Views of Canadians

Commissioners were informed by the discussion of sex selection during our public hearings and in written submissions, as well as by the views of Canadians across the country obtained through the Commission's survey research.

Public Hearings and Submissions

Most of the discussion in the public hearings concerned the use of prenatal diagnosis to determine the sex of the fetus and sex-selective abortion. This was an issue on which there is widespread agreement among Canadians. Almost all intervenors who commented on this form of sex selection were strongly opposed to it, except when it is used to avoid a serious sex-linked genetic disorder.

Representatives from a broad cross section of Canadian society — the medical sector, the community and social services sector, women's groups, religious groups, and concerned citizens — all voiced their opposition to sex-selective abortion because they believed it would have a discriminatory impact on women and/or because it involves abortion. A primary concern expressed by all these groups about sex-selective abortion is that the practice fosters, reinforces, and legitimizes discrimination on the basis of sex.

The Commission received testimony that the pressure to use sex-selective abortion to avoid female offspring is particularly strong for some women who are members of certain cultural or ethnic minorities. Representatives of these groups appearing before the Commission were especially concerned about the way clinics providing fetal sex identification target minority communities in their promotional activities. Particular concern was expressed about a clinic using ultrasound, established just across the U.S. border from Vancouver by a California physician. The physician is not licensed to practise in British Columbia, but witnesses told us that he has heavily promoted his service among Vancouver's large East Indian community. The response from the immigrant and visible minority community in Vancouver has been highly critical. At the Commission's public hearings in Vancouver, a representative of immigrant and visible minority women's groups denounced such clinics:

> Another cause for alarm is the misuse of pre-natal testing for the sex-selection of boys or girls. Given the preference in most cultures for male children, especially male first born children, boys will usually be selected over girls. This cross-culture preference for boys not only reflects the inequalities of the female role but further devalues the real lives of girls and women.
>
> *Brief to the Commission from Vancouver YWCA Board of Directors, December 1990.*

> We are opposed to having technologies directed against our communities that devalue women further and which are being legitimized in the name

of culture and tradition. We are opposed to this racist stereotyping of the Indo-Canadian culture and here today represent that tradition of resistance which is firmly rooted in our culture and which has fought against the devaluation of women for centuries. *(S. Thobani, Immigrant and Visible Minority Women of British Columbia, Public Hearings Transcripts, Vancouver, British Columbia, November 26, 1990.)*

The Commission's survey of ethnocultural community organizations subsequently confirmed these concerns. The Commission surveyed 312 organizations that represent or serve ethnocultural communities to help identify their views on new reproductive technologies. Most of these organizations did not have an official position on the use of reproductive technologies. However, not a single respondent supported the use of PND for the purposes of sex-selective abortion. Moreover, an overwhelming majority of respondents would be concerned if their community were to be the target of those promoting sex selection technologies (see research volume, *Social Values and Attitudes Surrounding New Reproductive Technologies*).

Many of the interventions the Commission heard assumed that the technique would be used, as it has been in some other countries, mainly to abort female fetuses. This led to concern that the widespread use of sex-selective abortion would lead to sex maldistribution, with a resulting preponderance of males in the population. Fears were expressed that sex maldistribution would have adverse effects on the most fundamental aspects of our society.

> Pre-natal diagnosis should be done only for medical reasons, not for sex pre-selection ... some cultures prefer male children, and there might be cultural pressures to abort female fetuses.
>
> *Brief to the Commission from the North Shuswap Women's Institute, March 24, 1992.*

A related concern was that sex-selective abortion would be used to ensure that the first-born child was a boy, who would then receive the emotional and financial advantages that are widely believed to accrue to first-born children.

Although virtually all intervenors opposed sex-selective abortion for non-medical reasons, no single preferred method to control the practice emerged from our public consultation process. Some groups wanted a legal ban on sex-selective abortions, but most groups, while critical of sex-selective abortions, believed that prohibiting such abortions would require authoritarian measures and place grave restrictions on women's autonomy and reproductive freedom. They felt it would require intrusive and ultimately futile attempts to monitor the actions of pregnant women who were informed of the sex of their fetus and to determine whether sex preference was the sole reason behind a woman's request for an abortion.

Most groups therefore favoured other approaches — for example, trying to ensure that PND is not used to identify the sex of the fetus except in cases where there is a risk of a serious sex-linked disorder, or encouraging broader social change and education to promote the valuing of males and females equally.

There was less discussion of the other two methods of sex selection — sperm treatment methods and sex-selective zygote transfer — perhaps because there is much less public awareness of them.   Our survey of people's attitudes toward the sex of their children, discussed below, showed a relatively low level of awareness of sperm treatment methods — less than one in four Canadians surveyed — and certainly a much lower level of awareness than for other aspects of our mandate, such as preconception arrangements, IVF, or PND.

> If sex selection is an option, boys will be chosen to be the first-born. What message does this give to daughters — second born, and second choice. Although experts have forecast profound social, psychological, and demographic consequences of sex selection, there is no unanimity on what exactly these consequences would be.
>
> *Brief to the Commission from*
> *L. Lavigne, St. Catharines, December*
> *13, 1990.*

Parental Preferences Regarding the Sex of Children and the Use of Sex Selection

To obtain a detailed analysis of Canadians' attitudes and views, the Commission undertook the first national survey of preferences regarding the sex of children and attitudes toward sex selection. The survey involved a random selection of more than 500 Canadians who intend to have children.   This research is described in our research volume entitled *Prenatal Diagnosis: New and Future Developments.*

The survey revealed that, contrary to what has been found in some other countries, a large majority of Canadians do not prefer children of one sex or the other.   Many intervenors in our public hearings assumed that Canadians have a pro-male bias with regard to family composition; we found that this assumption appears to be unfounded with regard to the Canadian population as a whole.

When asked about their preferences with respect to future children, 71 percent of respondents wanted equal numbers of boys and girls, 14 percent wanted more daughters, and 15 percent wanted more sons. For respondents who did not yet have children, the numbers were even more striking — 82 percent wanted an equal number of boys and girls, 10 percent preferred more sons, and 8 percent preferred more daughters.

There has been much speculation about the preferences of prospective parents regarding the sex of their first-born child. Our survey showed that for respondents who did not yet have children, the majority of respondents had no preference regarding the sex of their first child, while 26 percent preferred their first-born child to be a son and 21 percent preferred their first-born to be a daughter. Moreover, even those who did express a preference rated the importance of this preference as very low (1.8 on a scale of 1 to 5 for those who wanted a boy; 1.7 for those who wanted a girl).

In other words, most prospective parents expressed a weak preference for an equal number of sons and daughters, and a few expressed a weak preference about the sex of their first-born child. However, these preferences were generally seen as unimportant, almost trivial. The survey showed that virtually all prospective parents want, and feel strongly about having, at least one child of each sex.

> We feel that identifying sex for the purpose of embryo selection must be prohibited. At present, several studies have shown that embryos of the male sex would often be chosen, and the results are significant at the level of populations. When it is known, for example, that people the world over often prefer the first child to be a boy, we must see to what extent couples' and parents' social conditioning is now — must be controlled in this regard; there must be measures prohibiting embryo selection by sex. [Translation]
>
> *C. Coderre, Féderation des femmes du Québec, Public Hearings Transcripts, Montreal, Quebec, November 21, 1990.*

Previous international studies have consistently shown a significant difference between women and men in terms of their preferences regarding the sex of their children. According to most studies from other countries, fathers and mothers both express a pro-son bias, although the fathers' pro-son bias is usually much stronger. Our survey suggests that results of these studies cannot be generalized to Canada.

> Most prospective parents expressed a weak preference for an equal number of sons and daughters, and a few expressed a weak preference about the sex of their first-born child. However, these preferences were generally seen as unimportant, almost trivial. The survey showed that virtually all prospective parents want, and feel strongly about having, at least one child of each sex.

The attitudes of women respondents in our survey were almost perfectly sex-neutral — the average woman respondent wanted an equal number of boys and girls and had no preference regarding the sex of the first child. Male respondents did indicate a small pro-son bias: the average male respondent placed more importance on having at least one son than on having at least one daughter and on having a boy as the first child. However, the survey showed that each of these biases is slight, and it is clear that for men, as for women, biases in favour of either sex are trivial compared to the value of having at least one child of each sex.

Previous surveys of parental preferences have often assumed that people who express a preference regarding the number or order of sons and daughters would be likely to use sex selection techniques. We wanted to know whether this is the case. The likelihood of actually using sex selection techniques depends primarily on the importance people attach to their preference. As these preferences were often described as unimportant in our survey, it seems that few people would actually make use of sex selection techniques, particularly if they involve drawbacks such as moral conflicts, cost, intrusiveness, inconvenience, or delay.

This was borne out by the way respondents in our survey described their personal willingness to use sex selection techniques. None of the respondents would use sex-selective abortion if it was to be their first child. Fewer than 4 percent could imagine any circumstance in which they would use PND and abortion to avoid having a child of the undesired sex. Those few who would consider terminating the pregnancy would do so only if they already had one child or more of the same sex, and the fetus was also of that sex. Finally, this minority who would consider sex-selective abortion would do so only if the results of PND were available before the twelfth week of pregnancy (which is currently not the case). Thus, it is clear that very few Canadians would be prepared to contemplate a second-trimester abortion for sex-selective reasons.

> The solution to sex selection is not to restrict abortion, but to challenge the social and cultural conditions that create these pressures on women to make such a drastic "choice." We have to directly confront and challenge a social structure and culture from which such misogynist values spring.
>
> *Brief to the Commission from the Ontario Coalition for Abortion Clinics, May 1991.*

Canadians were more willing, however, to consider sperm treatment methods and sex-selective insemination. Approximately 21 percent of respondents could imagine some circumstance in which they might use such a technique. However, the survey data indicated that less than 2 percent would use sex-selective insemination for their first child. Somewhere between 6 and 9 percent of respondents said they would use sex-selective insemination either to have a girl after having one or more boys, or to have a boy after one or more girls. These situations — where sex-selective insemination is used with the goal of having at least one child of each sex — are the only circumstances in which a significant number of respondents said they would be willing to use sex-selective insemination.

The survey conducted for the Commission contradicts certain widely held beliefs about the preferences of Canadians with regard to the sex of their children. Yet the results of other recent surveys of Canadians are consistent. For example, a public opinion survey of 2 722 people across Canada, conducted for the Commission by Decima Research between December 1991 and July 1992, also showed no bias in the preferences of Canadians

The survey conducted for the Commission contradicts certain widely held beliefs about the preferences of Canadians with regard to the sex of their children. Yet the results of other recent surveys of Canadians are consistent.

regarding the sex of their children. Twenty-five percent agreed that it is very important to have at least one male child, while 24 percent agreed that it is very important to have at least one female child. The Decima survey also confirmed the overwhelming opposition in Canada to the use of sex-selective abortion. Only 2 percent of respondents approved of the termination of a pregnancy because the "sex of the fetus is not what the parents had hoped for," while 92 percent disapproved and 6 percent expressed no opinion.

It should be remembered, however, that answers to hypothetical questions on surveys may not be the same as actual behaviour. This is particularly the case if the technology were to be easily available and publicly countenanced.

Prenatal Diagnosis of Fetal Sex and Sex-Selective Abortion

The diagnostic techniques that constitute the core of PND — amniocentesis, chorionic villus sampling, and targeted ultrasound — are capable of providing a great deal of information about the fetus, including its sex. This has made it possible, in principle, for parents to discover the sex of the fetus and to terminate the pregnancy if they had hoped for a child of the other sex. In this section, we discuss the current regulations regarding the identification of fetal sex through PND and the issues it raises.

Current Situation

Intervenors at our public hearings expressed concern that prenatal testing to determine fetal sex for non-medical reasons is being done routinely at genetics centres. Our research shows that this is not the case. The joint guidelines of the Canadian College of Medical Geneticists and the Society of Obstetricians and Gynaecologists of Canada (CCMG/SOGC) state clearly that "Determination of fetal sex for nonmedical reasons, using either invasive or noninvasive means, is not considered to be appropriate."[2] The data obtained from our survey of genetics centres across the country showed that these guidelines are being adhered to.

The reason for this is straightforward: a prospective parent's desire to know the sex of the fetus is not a medical reason for providing access to PND, since sex is not a disease. As discussed in Chapter 26, the rationale for the PND system in Canada is to help couples at higher risk of having a child with a serious genetic disease or congenital disorder; identifying fetal sex to satisfy parental preferences falls entirely outside this approach to PND.

> Intervenors at our public hearings expressed concern that prenatal testing to determine fetal sex for non-medical reasons is being done routinely at genetics centres. Our research shows that this is not the case.

The Commission's research showed that women are sometimes referred to genetics centres by family physicians or obstetricians for prenatal testing to determine fetal sex for non-medical purposes. However, such referrals are rare and are strongly discouraged by the genetics centres. Women referred on this basis would typically be counselled by staff of the genetics centre but would not be offered PND testing. A survey conducted for the Commission found that genetics centres counselled 14 women in 1990 whose reason for requesting testing was sex selection — six in Quebec, five in British Columbia, and three in Ontario. In all but one case, which involved unusual circumstances, the centre refused to provide testing.

Our survey also showed that some centres receive inquiries from women by telephone regarding sex-selective abortion. These callers were rarely seen for counselling, although some centres would, if asked, provide the telephone numbers of U.S. programs that provide prenatal testing to determine fetal sex.

In short, there are few explicit referrals or requests for prenatal testing to determine fetal sex for non-medical reasons in Canada. Some women may indeed prefer to have a girl or a boy, quite apart from any socially generated pressure. In such situations, however, the social harm of providing testing is felt to outweigh the woman's or couple's preference, and the centres consider it reasonable to limit the woman's autonomy; these requests are therefore refused under CCMG/SOGC guidelines.

However, if women do have a valid medical indication for testing (for example, on the basis of their age or family history) and undergo the procedure, they will often be informed about the sex of the fetus at the same time as they are told about the presence or absence of a disorder or anomaly. The sex of the fetus is currently included in the laboratory report of test results sent to the genetics counsellor caring for the woman. This information is included even if it is not relevant to the genetic disorder being tested for, and generally it is made available to patients who request it. Some genetics counsellors in Canada reveal fetal sex routinely, while others reveal it only if the woman or couple ask specifically for that information.

The fact that fetal sex is often disclosed to patients who have been tested for a valid medical indication creates the possibility that someone who wanted to have a child of one sex could gain access to PND for this purpose, provided they met the medical indications. Testing might be warranted for medical reasons, yet the real reason for seeking testing might be to discover the sex of the fetus; for example, a 36-year-old woman who is eligible for PND because of her age might actually want testing to discover the sex of the fetus, not because of the risk of a chromosomal disorder.

> Genetic manipulation opens the door to control over embryo selection and quality. Here again, the long-term effect can be disastrous and this manipulation can have an effect on the genetic heritage. If many parents chose to have boys, for example, the result could be real demographic unbalance. [Translation]
>
> *Brief to the Commission from le Comité "Vieillir au féminin," de l'Université du troisième âge de l'Université de Moncton, January 18, 1991.*

Genetics centres are conscious of this potential for misuse of testing and do exercise control over the availability of testing, but there is no way to prevent such misuse entirely. Requests for PND that are intended to determine the sex of the fetus rather than disorders are difficult to identify; geneticists told the Commission that these probably occur in a few cases, but there is no evidence that the phenomenon is widespread. Indeed, as we discussed earlier, our public opinion surveys showed that the number of Canadians who would consider a second-trimester abortion for sex-selective reasons is very small indeed.

Despite the existence of professional guidelines discouraging prenatal testing to determine fetal sex for non-medical reasons, some practitioners in the PND community are ambivalent about the practice.[3] To determine how Canadian geneticists view this practice, the Commission conducted its own survey of the attitudes of 200 genetics counsellors in Canada. Half of this group were asked whether they approved of PND to determine sex for non-medical reasons. Only 2 percent of respondents personally approved of PND to determine fetal sex for non-medical reasons. However, a significant minority would attempt to accommodate a request for such testing, despite personal disapproval. The survey showed that 20 percent of the geneticists surveyed would recommend that their centre provide PND to determine fetal sex (if it were allowed) if a couple requested it, and 41 percent would be willing to give the couple the name of another centre that would do the test (see research volume, *Current Practice of Prenatal Diagnosis in Canada*).

Willingness to provide PND to determine fetal sex (if it were allowed) increased when the details of a hypothetical case were provided. The other half of the group of genetics counsellors was asked how they would respond to a request for PND to determine the sex of the fetus from a pregnant woman from a culture where the preference for sons is strong. In the hypothetical situation described, the woman already has three daughters, and her husband has told her he will send her back to their country of origin without her children if she has another daughter.

Under such circumstances, 14 percent of Canadian geneticists said they personally approved of providing the test; 26 percent would recommend that their centre provide the test; and 55 percent would refer the woman to another centre if their own centre would not provide it. On the other hand, many geneticists recognize that threats of divorce or abortion should not always be taken at face value. One recent study found that most geneticists view such threats as a bluff to gain access to prenatal testing for sex selection reasons.[4]

These findings are consistent with other information about the attitudes of Canadian medical geneticists. A minority would provide prenatal diagnosis to determine the sex of the fetus, particularly in difficult circumstances. For example, a 1985 survey showed that 30 percent of doctoral-level geneticists in Canada would perform PND for a couple with four daughters who wanted a son and who would abort a female fetus, and a further 17 percent would offer referral in this situation to another centre that offered the test.

> The Commission's surveys showed that only 4 percent would consider sex-selective abortion under any circumstances, and then only if the abortion could be performed in the first trimester. Since information about the sex of the fetus is not currently available before 10 to 12 weeks' gestation, there is every reason to believe that the number of sex-selective abortions in Canada is very low indeed.

Despite the existence of clear professional guidelines, the evidence suggests that a determined couple can gain access to the PND system to acquire information about the sex of the fetus, and that some referring physicians and geneticists would be willing to help such a couple, or at least would not obstruct them.

There is no reason to think, however, that this is a frequent occurrence in Canada. On the contrary, the Commission's surveys showed that only 4 percent would consider sex-selective abortion under any circumstances, and then only if the abortion could be performed in the first trimester. Since information about the sex of the fetus is not currently available before 10 to 12 weeks' gestation, there is every reason to believe that the number of sex-selective abortions in Canada is very low indeed.

Future developments in PND, however, may make information about the sex of the fetus more easily available. Ultrasound is already a widely used diagnostic technique, and future technical improvements may increase its capacity to reveal the sex of the fetus earlier in pregnancy. Similarly, research into the testing of fetal cells in the pregnant woman's blood may one day yield a reliable and non-invasive way of revealing fetal sex early in pregnancy. The relative simplicity of blood tests, coupled with the possibility of a first-trimester abortion, might reduce the existing barriers to sex-selective abortions. Moreover, taking blood or providing ultrasound — unlike chorionic villus sampling and amniocentesis — can in principle be performed more widely in the medical community rather than solely at specialized genetics centres. The existing CCMG/SOGC guidelines relate to activities at genetics centres and would therefore be inadequate to prevent misuse of these techniques. This suggests that guidelines covering these more broadly based activities would be needed if we determine that PND for sex selection should continue not to be available.

Issues and Recommendations

The Commission's public hearings and survey research revealed an overwhelming consensus against the use of PND and sex-selective abortion. More than 90 percent of those surveyed found it unacceptable to abort a fetus because the parents wanted a child of the opposite sex. Commissioners share this view for several reasons. First, sex-selective abortion offends the principle of respect for human life and dignity because it entails the deliberate termination of a pregnancy, for reasons related only to the sex of the fetus, at a stage when it is likely that the pregnancy would have resulted in a live birth. Our perceptions of the value of human life cannot help but be altered when a potential life at this stage of development is ended intentionally for no reason other than the sex of the fetus. Whether the procedure is used to select male or female fetuses — and even if it were used in a gender-neutral way — the devaluation of and disrespect for human life and dignity inherent in the practice make it morally unacceptable and ethically unjustifiable.

> Our perceptions of the value of human life cannot help but be altered when a potential life at this stage of development is ended intentionally for no reason other than the sex of the fetus. Whether the procedure is used to select male or female fetuses — and even if it were used in a gender-neutral way — the devaluation of and disrespect for human life and dignity inherent in the practice make it morally unacceptable and ethically unjustifiable.

In addition, the use of PND to determine fetal sex contradicts the very purpose and role of these procedures within the health care system — namely, to determine whether serious genetic diseases or congenital anomalies are present. Sex is not a disease, so the sex of the fetus is not medically relevant except in cases where a disease or anomaly is sex-linked. Acceptance of PND to determine fetal sex for non-medical reasons is contrary to the underpinnings of the PND system in Canada — the diagnosis and prevention of serious and untreatable genetic disease. Some are concerned that allowing sex-selective abortion could lead to easier acceptance of selective abortion on other grounds, such as height or skin colour, if this ever became feasible.

We believe it is important that the PND system be used only for the detection of serious genetic and congenital anomalies. We discussed why PND should not be used to test for trivial disorders in Chapter 26 — such use reflects inappropriate views of diversity, of the respect owed to human life, and of parenthood, and it violates the principle of appropriate use of resources, since it fulfils no medical need. Those arguments apply here with equal force.

Moreover, using PND in support of sex-selective abortion for non-medical reasons could violate principles of sexual equality. Indeed, some commentators have argued that sex-selective abortion for non-medical reasons could amount to wrongful discrimination under human rights law and the *Canadian Charter of Rights and Freedoms* if the practice is used in a way that reflects and perpetuates the subordinate status of women as a group in Canadian society. As the Canadian Research Institute for the Advancement of Women argued in their submission to the Commission,

> The philosophy behind sex selection is questionable in itself: what is more sexist than choosing a child purely on the basis of its sex? By increasing our emphasis on the importance of sexual difference, we can only create more rigid gender roles for men and women. *(Brief to the Commission from the Canadian Research Institute for the Advancement of Women, September 20, 1990.)*

We are aware that the preference for sons is strong among some Canadians, and that members of some ethnocultural groups in Canada value sons more highly. Indeed, those who make a business of providing diagnosis of fetal sex often justify their actions in terms of "respecting cultural minorities." It is important, however, to look more carefully at the nature and source of these cultural differences.

The preference for sons is strong in some countries, and PND and sex-selective abortion are used in those countries to abort female offspring. In India, for example, most PND procedures are performed for sex selection rather than the detection of genetic or congenital disorders (see research volume, *Prenatal Diagnosis: New and Future Developments*).

Some immigrants from these and other societies with a strong cultural tradition of preferring sons may carry these cultural values to Canada. However, as the Immigrant and Visible Minority Women of British Columbia emphasized during the Commission's public hearings, culture is neither monolithic nor static. On the contrary, traditional practices are often questioned and revised by the members of the culture, and culture generally is in a constant state of evolution. Many people in these countries have not discriminated against females in these ways and are in fact working actively to counter such tendencies.

The preference for sons is strong in some countries, and PND and sex-selective abortion are used in those countries to abort female offspring. In India, for example, most PND procedures are performed for sex selection rather than the detection of genetic or congenital disorders.

Moreover, many of the social and economic reasons underlying a cultural preference for sons in other countries do not apply in Canada. The economic and social reasons for preferring sons include, for example, the fact that a son is responsible for caring for parents in their old age; that a daughter seldom has the earning power to support aging parents; and that daughters represent a considerable economic burden in come countries because of the practice of paying dowries. However, selective abortion to avoid female offspring cannot be justified by such factors in Canada; rather, in this country it would be a matter of satisfying a parent's preference for sons — a preference that would perpetuate the devaluation of women.

We are aware that the preference for sons is nonetheless strong in some sectors of society. As a result, some women may still face considerable pressure to have sons. It has been argued by some that providing PND to determine fetal sex would help these women cope with family pressure to have sons.

As we have seen, a significant number of geneticists in Canada said that they believe it appropriate to provide PND in the case of a woman whose husband is threatening to break up the family if she does not produce a son. It is under-

To allow couples to identify and abort female fetuses because of a cultural preference for sons would devalue all women and jeopardize the achievement of sexual equality in this country.

standable that genetics counsellors would feel sympathy for patients in such difficult circumstances. As well as our concern for the individual woman trying to satisfy family or cultural demands, we must also take into account, however, justice for all women. The provision of PND to determine fetal sex might ease the plight of one woman temporarily. However, to allow couples to identify and abort female fetuses because of a cultural preference for sons would devalue all women and jeopardize the achievement of sexual equality in this country.

Providing PND to determine fetal sex in this situation does not solve the problem that put the woman, and other women in her community, in this difficult position in the first place. On the contrary, it perpetuates and reinforces the problem — it ultimately harms the status of women in her community and, indeed, in Canada as a whole. Moreover, she herself will continue to be regarded and valued for her ability to produce sons.

It is therefore shortsighted to accommodate a woman's request for PND and sex-selective abortion of female fetuses in order to alleviate family pressures on her. If the reason for the preference for a son is the existence of sexist pressures within the community, then fulfilling such a request will provide little long-term benefit for the woman. Indeed, reinforcing these pressures will only harm the woman later on, as well as her sisters, daughters, and granddaughters. As one analyst has commented,

> Arguments that sex selection will lead to a better quality of life for families, children, or women are comprehensible only in the context of a sexist society that gives preferential treatment to one sex, usually the male. *(D. Wertz, "Prenatal Diagnosis and Society," in Research Volumes of the Commission, 1993.)*

It is important, therefore, to ensure that the ideal of respecting cultural differences is not used to rationalize coercion against vulnerable members of the group or the oppression or subordination of women generally. Respect for cultural differences is a valuable, indeed defining, characteristic of Canada. However, respect for cultural diversity must be situated within the context of Canada's fundamental principles, including its constitutional and international commitments to the protection and promotion of human rights. These principles include respect for sexual equality and the protection of the vulnerable.

This view is supported by the Canadian Medical Association in its discussion of sex selection:

> Nor is the Association persuaded that the mere fact that a particular outlook is culturally entrenched establishes the ethical acceptability of that outlook. The disenfranchisement of women in some cultures is a case in point ... Another way of putting that is to say that Canada insists on maintaining the pre-eminence of certain fundamental principles as a condition of membership within Canadian society itself.[5]

The Commission therefore rejects the use of PND with sex-selective abortion as inconsistent with our guiding principles — respect for human life and dignity, sexual equality, protection of the vulnerable, and the balancing of individual and collective interests. Finally, sex selection for non-medical purposes is also a misuse of collective resources. To allow allocation of scarce health care resources to provide PND with sex-selective abortion would clearly be unethical. This applies even where those services would be purchased in a private market because, as explained elsewhere in this report, such services virtually always entail significant costs to the public purse as well.

For all these reasons, Commissioners reject the use of PND with sex-selective abortion. It violates the Commission's ethical guidelines and distorts the underlying premises of the PND system. Commissioners are strongly of the view that PND to determine sex and sex-selective abortion have no role in the health care system.

We believe that the existing CCMG/SOGC guideline, which states that fetal sex determination for non-medical reasons is an inappropriate practice, is an important starting point for the regulation of this form of sex selection. Because of this guideline, patients requesting PND to determine fetal sex for non-medical reasons have usually been denied access to the services of genetics centres in Canada. To ensure that the guideline continues to be followed by all genetics centres providing PND, adherence to this guideline should be made a condition of receiving a licence to provide PND services. The Commission therefore

The Commission rejects the use of PND with sex-selective abortion as inconsistent with our guiding principles — respect for human life and dignity, sexual equality, protection of the vulnerable, and the balancing of individual and collective interests. Finally, sex selection for non-medical purposes is also a misuse of collective resources.

> **261. Affirms the existing Canadian College of Medical Geneticists/Society of Obstetricians and Gynaecologists of Canada guideline that prenatal diagnosis to determine fetal sex for non-medical reasons not be offered. Adherence to this guideline should be a precondition of securing and maintaining a licence to provide prenatal diagnosis services from the National Reproductive Technologies Commission.**

As noted earlier in this chapter, the CCMG/SOGC guidelines may be inadequate to cover future developments in PND, such as ultrasound to identify fetal sex or testing of fetal cells in pregnant women's blood. It is possible for these newer, non-invasive tests to be provided outside licensed genetics centres and hence outside the reach of the CCMG/SOGC and the National Reproductive Technologies Commission. Indeed, private clinics specializing in the use of ultrasound to determine fetal sex already exist in the United States. The possibility exists that private "fetal sexing" clinics could be established in Canada in the future, using ultrasound, blood tests, or other technologies.

We resolutely oppose the establishment of private clinics or physicians' practices providing detection of fetal sex for a fee. To prevent this, we recommend that any clinic or practice providing PND to determine fetal sex be defined as providing a "genetic service" and hence be required to obtain a licence from the National Reproductive Technologies Commission. This will prevent clinics or practitioners from using these newer techniques to determine fetal sex for non-medical reasons, since a condition of licensing will be adherence to the CCMG/SOGC guideline. The Commission recommends that

> **262. The requirement that all clinics and physicians providing prenatal diagnosis be licensed by the National Reproductive Technologies Commission extend to any clinic or physician providing services aimed at identifying fetal sex (including the use of ultrasound or blood tests on pregnant women). The Commission recommends further that adherence to guidelines prohibiting the use of prenatal diagnosis to determine fetal sex for non-medical reasons be a condition of such licence.**

Disclosure of Fetal Sex After Testing for a Genetic Disease

A more complicated issue concerns the disclosure of fetal sex to patients who have a valid medical reason for undergoing PND. For example, every pregnant woman over 35 years of age has a legitimate entitlement to prenatal testing and could use this entitlement to obtain information about the sex of the fetus. Knowledge about fetal sex may have some influence on abortion decisions among women having PND because of their age, especially if the pregnancy was not intended (see research volume, *Prenatal Diagnosis: New and Future Developments*). There may be cases, for example, where a genetic anomaly not linked to fetal sex is discovered, but information about the sex of the fetus might "tip the balance" in making a decision about termination.

In many cases, the woman prefers not to know the sex of the fetus. However, in cases where the patient does want to know, many geneticists feel ambivalent about whether to provide this information. On one hand, many counsellors believe that knowledge of fetal sex can add to the pleasure parents derive from a pregnancy, helping to personalize the fetus, and thereby strengthening bonding. Also, many geneticists believe, as a general principle, that doctors should disclose all information in the patients' records that the patient requests to know. Anything other than full disclosure is viewed as paternalistic and possibly a violation of the patient's legal right to know information in his or her medical records. On the other hand, many geneticists do not feel comfortable disclosing the sex of the fetus except in cases of a sex-linked disease, because this information is not relevant to the health of the fetus.

It is not clear whether a legal duty to disclose fetal sex exists in either the United States or Canada, as the courts have not yet tackled this question directly. In the United States, some practitioners of PND refuse to provide information about the sex of otherwise healthy fetuses until the legal ambiguity of this issue is clarified; other practitioners provide full disclosure, to avoid potential legal problems.

In Canada, current practice is to disclose the sex of the fetus if asked. However, it is not clear whether any legal requirement to comply with such a request exists. Generally speaking, patients have a right to the information in their medical records but not to the documents themselves. In the province of Quebec, for example, an individual has a statutory right of access to personal medical information. In other provinces, some of which do not have statutes dealing specifically with access to medical information, the same general principle applies: the individual has a right of access, upon request, to the medical information in his or her medical records.

> We strongly support the general principle of full disclosure of medical information in support of informed choice, which is an integral part of the shift away from a paternalistic model of the physician/patient relationship to a partnership model. We do not wish to weaken that principle. The issue, however, is not simply whether patients have a right to the information in their medical records; it is also important to discourage misuse of non-medical information that is revealed by genetic testing.

However, the exact scope of this legal principle is unclear — including its application to the disclosure of non-medical information regarding the sex of the fetus — as there have been relatively few court cases to date. In one province, Manitoba, the PND centre had a policy in the late 1970s of not revealing the sex of the fetus until the twentieth week of gestation. In the early 1980s, in view of increasing human rights activity and legislation, the hospital's legal advisers suggested that this practice should be changed, and that patients probably had a legal right to this information. The current policy in Manitoba, as elsewhere, is to give information on the sex of the fetus if requested. In all centres there must be valid medical indications for having the test in the first place.

We strongly support the general principle of full disclosure of medical information in support of informed choice, which is an integral part of the shift away from a paternalistic model of the physician/patient relationship to a partnership model. We do not wish to weaken that principle. The issue, however, is not simply whether patients have a right to the information in their medical records; it is also important to discourage misuse of non-medical information that is revealed by genetic testing.

We believe, as a general principle, that prenatal testing should not be seen by either physicians or patients as a mechanism simply for identifying the sex of the fetus. If the reason for prenatal testing is to detect disease, then it is the presence or absence of disease that is relevant. Information on the sex of the fetus is not medically relevant — it does not tell the physician or the patient about the health of the fetus (except in cases of X-linked diseases or diseases that affect one sex more severely than the other). Because this information is not medically relevant, and because it can be misused for sex-selective purposes, we considered the possibility that it should be withheld from the patient. This could be done in various ways.

One possibility would be to amend the legislation governing access to medical records and to create an exception in the case of information regarding the sex of the fetus. We believe that this would create a dangerous precedent, and that even a well-crafted exception could be misused. Since our studies have shown that very few Canadian women would consider undergoing sex-selective abortion, the risks of limiting the right of patients to their records seem greater than the risk that the information will be misused.

Another possibility would be to allow access to information about the sex of the fetus, but to make that information more difficult to get. For example, the laboratories that perform prenatal testing could be instructed not to include information about the sex of the fetus in the report they forward to the genetics counsellor or referring physician (except where medically relevant). The laboratory would identify and record the sex of the fetus — this is part of the standard testing procedure and is inherent in the notation system used to record chromosomal findings; it is also used as a quality control measure (the sex identified by testing can be compared with the sex of the child born). However, the laboratory would not forward that information to the genetics centre. The counsellor or physician would then be able to inform the patient whether a genetic disease was present or absent, but would not be able to inform her of the sex of the fetus. If the patient was determined to find out the sex of the fetus, she could contact the laboratory directly, which would disclose the information to her. To do this would require a certain amount of effort and inconvenience on the woman's part — it would make access to information about fetal sex more difficult, but not impossible.

There is some merit in this idea. It would reinforce the idea that the purpose of PND is to detect disease, not to satisfy parental preferences about the sex of their children. And since the capacity of genetic testing to uncover information about the fetus will likely expand in the future, it would be important to establish the principle that the only legitimate purpose of genetic testing is to diagnose health-related information.

> It would be important to establish the principle that the only legitimate purpose of genetic testing is to diagnose health-related information.

Since this would constitute a change of practice, it would be important to tell patients that prenatal test information would not include the sex of the fetus, unless it is medically relevant. Patients would then be tested knowing that fetal sex would not be disclosed. If patients were genuinely concerned about detecting fetal disorders, rather than sex selection, this change in policy would not affect their wish to undergo PND for valid medical reasons.

Although we considered this proposal seriously, we concluded that it was not practical. Laboratories would receive calls from women who were simply curious about the sex of the fetus but who would have no intention of using that information prenatally, as well as from women who were determined to know the sex of the fetus and who might be inclined to have a sex-selective abortion. This would shift responsibility from physicians to the laboratories and increase their costs without preventing some potential misuse of this information; laboratories are not set up to deal with these sorts of requests — they rarely deal directly with the public and do not have the personnel and financial resources to verify and respond to such requests.

There is no simple and foolproof way of guaranteeing that couples do not misuse information regarding the sex of the fetus. However, given the evidence that very few Canadians are prepared to contemplate sex-selective abortion, particularly in the second or third trimester, we believe that the danger of misuse is quite low. We are willing to put our trust in the humanity and good judgement of Canadian women and couples.

Yet we cannot ignore the possibility that inappropriate pressures may be applied to women within some segments of Canadian society. Nor can we ignore the possibility that future developments in PND testing — which may be capable of providing information about fetal sex earlier in pregnancy — could lead more Canadians to consider sex-selective abortion.

Clearly, this is an issue that deserves further study and continuing monitoring. We believe that the Prenatal Diagnosis and Genetics Sub-Committee of the National Reproductive Technologies Commission should actively monitor the situation in Canada for evidence that information regarding the sex of the fetus is being misused. If such evidence is found, the National Commission should consider whether a legal mechanism should be put in place to limit the patients' right to access to information in their medical records. The Commission recommends that

> **263. The guidelines established by the National Reproductive Technologies Commission for licensed prenatal diagnosis clinics indicate that information on the sex of the fetus be given to the woman or referring practitioner only upon direct request. Patients should be informed prior to testing that the usual practice is to reveal this information only if it is medically relevant to the health of the fetus.**

Regulating the disclosure of fetal sex during routine ultrasound to monitor pregnancy is even more difficult. Particularly when ultrasound is used later in pregnancy, the practitioner (or even the patient) may become aware of the sex of the fetus as the image appears on the ultrasound screen. Because the practitioner/patient interaction is not mediated by laboratory testing, the possibility of disclosure of fetal sex is greater.

Although it may rarely be impossible to avoid the inadvertent disclosure of fetal sex during routine ultrasound examinations, we think it is important to ensure that appropriate guidelines and standards of practice exist for physicians providing prenatal ultrasound — whether it is an obstetrician, a radiologist, or a general practitioner — stating that the sex of the fetus should not be evaluated intentionally or disclosed intentionally to the patient before the third trimester. The current standards of the Canadian Association of Radiologists pertaining to ultrasonography practice do not address the issues of fetal sex determination or disclosure of fetal sex.

> The adoption of guidelines would prevent practitioners from intentionally offering fetal sex detection and acquiring patients on this basis. Equally important, such guidelines would also support practitioners who do not wish to disclose fetal sex to patients earlier in pregnancy, but who find it difficult to turn down patients' direct requests.

Adoption of such guidelines would prevent practitioners from intentionally offering fetal sex detection and acquiring patients on this basis. Equally important, such guidelines would also support practitioners who do not wish to disclose fetal sex to patients earlier in pregnancy, but who find it difficult to turn down patients' direct requests. Patients know that practitioners using ultrasound often can tell the sex of the fetus and may ask for this information out of curiosity. It is sometimes difficult for practitioners not to comply with such requests, particularly in close physician/patient relationships, unless they have recourse to an explicit professional guideline or standard that fetal sex is not to be examined for and disclosed.

It is highly unlikely that a woman would request or obtain a sex-selective abortion during the third trimester, however, so there is little reason not to disclose fetal sex if ultrasound at this stage of pregnancy incidentally reveals this information. We do not believe that the use of ultrasound at any stage simply to detect sex is justified; nevertheless, because knowledge of the sex of the fetus is of interest to families and can help promote bonding between the woman and fetus, we believe disclosing the sex of the fetus, if it is observed incidentally during the third trimester and requested by the woman, should be allowed. The Commission recommends that

> **264. The Society of Obstetricians and Gynaecologists of Canada, the Canadian Association of Radiologists, and the College of Family Physicians of Canada review practice guidelines to ensure that practitioners using prenatal ultrasound do not perform ultrasound for sex identification (except where medically indicated) and do not deliberately examine for or volunteer information on fetal sex, except for medical reasons, and upon request, prior to the third trimester.**

Sex-Selective Zygote Transfer

The second currently known method of sex selection is sex-selective zygote transfer. This is an invasive, expensive, and technologically complicated procedure involving both *in vitro* fertilization and preimplantation diagnosis.

The woman's eggs are retrieved through laparoscopy, the eggs are fertilized *in vitro* with her partner's (or a donor's) sperm, and the sex of the resulting zygotes is determined through preimplantation diagnosis, which can detect whether the zygote has an XX or an XY chromosome complement. Only zygotes of the desired sex are then transferred to the woman's uterus. Although this technique is different in important respects from the use of PND and sex-selective abortion, Commissioners believe that it, too, is unethical and medically inappropriate, for many of the same reasons.

First, sex-selective zygote transfer is not an appropriate use of resources. It uses a sophisticated, expensive, stressful, and inefficient diagnostic procedure for what is clearly a non-therapeutic objective. It is difficult to imagine many couples wishing to follow this route simply to have a child of the preferred sex. Both the IVF procedure and the preimplantation diagnosis test are expensive, adding up to thousands of dollars per cycle. Similarly, using preimplantation diagnosis to detect the sex of the zygote for non-medical reasons distorts the role of preimplantation diagnosis, which is to identify the presence of severe genetic diseases at a very early stage in the development of the zygote.

Sex-selective preimplantation diagnosis also carries risks for the woman involved, from the use of ovulation induction drugs to the egg retrieval procedure. Subjecting women to medical procedures involving risk is unethical except where there is a clear therapeutic purpose — that is, to treat disease and promote health. In actual practice, preimplantation diagnosis is likely to be pursued very rarely, because of its intrusive nature and expense.

Use of preimplantation diagnosis to identify zygotes of a particular sex also conflicts with the principle of respect for human life and dignity. As we discuss in Chapter 22, zygotes do not have the same moral status as embryos or fetuses; they do not have a fixed and individuated identity or a central nervous system, and the probability that they will result in a liveborn individual is low — perhaps one in five in those situations where both partners are likely to be fertile. Nonetheless, zygotes are not just human tissue; the potential they embody means that refusing to transfer a zygote solely on the basis of its sex is inconsistent with the respect owed to it.

In the view of Commissioners, these objections are such that any use of preimplantation diagnosis for purposes of non-medical sex selection is not justified and should be prohibited. Since preimplantation

> Any use of preimplantation diagnosis for purposes of non-medical sex selection is not justified and should be prohibited.

diagnosis requires the use of IVF technology, it is currently carried out in IVF clinics. We have concluded that all proposals to use preimplantation diagnosis on zygotes should be approved by the Assisted Conception Sub-Committee of the National Reproductive Technologies Commission. We further recommend that the guidelines covering IVF clinics prohibit the use of preimplantation diagnosis to determine fetal sex for non-medical reasons. Even though it is very unlikely practitioners or couples would be willing to pursue preimplantation diagnosis for this purpose, it is important we reassure Canadians that it is not occurring, by making adherence to these guidelines a condition of licensing by the National Reproductive Technologies Commission. The Commission recommends that

> **265. The National Reproductive Technologies Commission guidelines for licensed *in vitro* fertilization clinics prohibit the use of preimplantation diagnosis to determine fetal sex for non-medical reasons. Adherence to these guidelines should be a condition of licensing by the National Reproductive Technologies Commission.**

Sex-Selective Insemination

Current Practices

The various methods of trying to influence the sex of a child before conception can be grouped into two categories. First, there are "natural" methods, such as timing of intercourse, altered coital position, alteration of vaginal acidity, and dietary changes to alter the content of cervical secretions. The reliability of these methods is unknown. Some research has tested whether particular timing of intercourse relative to the time of ovulation has an effect on the sex of resulting offspring, but recent studies have generally not confirmed this.[6]

Our focus in this section is on the other group of methods, which involve laboratory treatment of sperm. Several sperm separation methods have been designed in the last 20 years to separate the two kinds of sperm — those carrying the Y chromosome (leading to male offspring) and those carrying the X (leading to female offspring). Taking advantage of presumed differences in density and motility, sperm separation attempts have been performed by electrophoretic, flow fractionation, and cell-sorting techniques. Immunological techniques have also been used in an effort to separate the two kinds of sperm.

It is difficult to assess the effectiveness of these techniques. The results of studies have been inconclusive, and the studies have been criticized for poor follow-up and lack of control groups.[7] However, many reviews of the evidence have come to the same general conclusion: while theoretically possible and clinically feasible, none of these sperm separation techniques has proved very reliable. Some have proved just effective enough to encourage continued research and development and the establishment of commercial clinics offering sex-selective insemination.

The best-known and most widely used technique was developed by an American researcher, Ronald Ericsson, in 1973. It is based on evidence that Y-bearing sperm swim faster than X-bearing sperm. The technique involves washing the sperm and layering it on increasingly thick albumin protein, through which some sperm swim faster. This technique has been used to retrieve sperm samples rich in Y-bearing sperm for assisted insemination. Ericsson claims a 72 percent success rate in producing male children (rather than the usual 52 percent), but this claim has not been verified independently.[8]

Producing X-bearing sperm is more difficult. The slower sperm left over from Ericsson's albumin test cannot be used, because the sample will include a high percentage of abnormal Y-bearing sperm as well as healthy X-bearing sperm. The most promising technique for producing samples rich in X-bearing sperm is a filtration technique developed originally to prepare semen samples with better sperm motility. Researchers discovered incidentally that the method also enriches the proportion of X-bearing sperm by up to 22 percent. Because isolating X-bearing sperm is more difficult, and because there is some evidence that the use of fertility drugs to induce ovulation may increase the chances of having a girl, drugs such as clomiphene are often used in conjunction with this filtration technique. This also results in an increased frequency (8.5 percent) of twins. Various other combinations of sperm-sorting techniques and ovulation induction drugs have been used in the hope of increasing the likelihood of conceiving a girl. Ericsson claims a 69 percent success rate for couples seeking a girl, although independent confirmation is not available.

The effectiveness of this or any similar sperm separation technique is an open question, as they have not been confirmed independently. What objective data are available suggest that the child is of the desired sex well under 80 percent of the time for both boys and girls,

> The procedure is intrusive and may need to be repeated, as any given insemination with treated sperm has a less than 10 percent chance of resulting in a liveborn child.

compared to the usual chance of about 50 percent.[9] In the absence of better data, these forms of sex-selective insemination must therefore be seen as experimental, not proven techniques. The procedure is intrusive and may need to be repeated, as any given insemination with treated sperm has a less than 10 percent chance of resulting in a liveborn child. Despite these limitations, it is likely that some sperm separation method will eventually be able to influence the likelihood of having a boy or girl fairly reliably.

Whatever the current effectiveness of sperm separation techniques, entrepreneurs have judged that there is a market for sex-selective insemination. Private clinics have been opened in the United States, the United Kingdom, Canada, and elsewhere to provide this service for a fee. Private clinics are particularly active in the United States, where the Ericsson technique has been franchised to over 50 clinics through a business firm. In the United Kingdom, the establishment of private clinics offering sex-selective insemination has led to the Human Fertility and Embryology Authority's consultation initiative on sex selection. Here in Canada, one sex-selective insemination clinic using the Ericsson technique has been in existence in Toronto since 1987, and a second one recently opened in Toronto. The procedure is not covered by provincial medical insurance plans, and the charge is about $500 per insemination.

Issues and Recommendations

Trying to influence the sex of offspring before conception raises different issues from either sex-selective abortion or sex-selective zygote transfer. For example, sorting sperm does not raise the same issues of respect for human life as aborting a fetus or discarding zygotes because of their sex. However, the practice does raise important questions regarding both the potential for discriminatory use that would offend sexual equality principles and the appropriate use of resources.

Sexual Equality

For reasons discussed earlier, Commissioners find it unacceptable for sex-selective insemination to be used in a way that undermines or jeopardizes equality — that is, to select first-born sons, to select families with more sons than daughters, or to perpetuate the cultural devaluation of women. There is strong evidence, however, that sex-selective insemination would not likely be used in this way in Canada. The marked preference for boys that may have characterized public opinion in Canada in the past has clearly eroded. Although some parents have a weak preference regarding the sex of their first-born child, fewer than 2 percent of Canadians say they would actually consider using sex-selective insemination to try to satisfy that preference. Instead, the use of sex-selective insemination in this country is more likely to be directed to enabling couples to have at least one child of each sex in their family. As we saw earlier in this chapter, this is very important to most Canadians — indeed, it is the only desire regarding the sex of children that Canadians feel strongly about and are willing to take steps to fulfil. This is still only a minority, however — 8 percent of couples with two sons would consider sex-selective insemination to have a girl, rather than continuing to have children in the hope that one would be a girl. A similar number of couples with two daughters would consider using sex-selective insemination to have a son.

Our survey of parental preferences therefore suggests that sex-selective insemination, if used, would be used in a gender-neutral way by most people in this country. This is consistent with the experience of Ericsson's clinics in the United States. According to Ericsson, a survey of 7 000 couples at his clinics revealed that less than 1 percent wanted to use the service for their first-born. Instead, couples used it for their last child, to have a child of the sex they did not already have. In fact, Ericsson says that 51 percent of requests at his clinics are for girls.[10] But the technique for conceiving females involves taking fertility drugs and is therefore more complicated and expensive; more services are in fact provided to try to produce boys.

> The use of sex-selective insemination in this country is more likely to be directed to enabling couples to have at least one child of each sex in their family. As we saw earlier in this chapter, this is very important to most Canadians — indeed, it is the only desire regarding the sex of children that Canadians feel strongly about and are willing to take steps to fulfil.

A 1989 study by Nan Chico, a professor of sociology in California, found that couples who contacted Ericsson's clinics for more information about sex-selective insemination already had an average of two children of the same sex and were seeking "mixed families." Her study of 2 505 letters to Ericsson's clinics found that those desiring a first-born male accounted for 1.4 percent of the total, and that there was nearly a 50:50 balance in requests for boys and girls.[11]

We believe that the use of sex-selective insemination by couples to have a child of the sex they do not already have is not necessarily sex-discriminatory. As the CFAS/SOCG note, this reason for seeking sex-selective insemination "implies that parents are expressing less of a gender preference *per se* and more of a desire to enhance family development with the sort of unique relationship that only a brother/sister or mother-daughter/father-son interaction can afford."[12] Boys and girls are different, and the widespread desire to have at least one child of each sex reflects the fact that parents find joy and delight in these differences. The desire to have a son after two daughters, or a daughter after two sons, is a natural one that reflects a desire to enjoy children of both sexes, not a bias in favour of one sex or a devaluation of the other.

> There are important differences between the male and female experience, and the desire to have the distinctive relationships that come from having sons and from having daughters is not, in and of itself, evidence of sexism.

Of course, it is possible that some couples could be motivated by sexist stereotypes, such as the wish to pass on a family business to a son rather than a daughter. We recognize that such stereotypes exist in society. But the existence of sexism in our society is not grounds to conclude that this technology would necessarily be used for sexist reasons. There are important differences between the male and female experience, and the desire to have the distinctive relationships that come from having sons and from having daughters is not, in and of itself, evidence of sexism.

Another aspect to be taken into account is whether sex-selective insemination would significantly affect the overall sex ratio in society at large. If many couples used sex-selective insemination to select boys, while few couples used it to select girls, the resulting inequality in the sex ratio in the general population could have serious social repercussions. Our research suggests, however, that there is little danger of this occurring, for several reasons.

First, our surveys showed no significant pro-son (or pro-daughter) bias in the population; therefore, sex-selective insemination is likely to leave the sex ratio unchanged. Second, even if there were a pro-son or pro-daughter bias in parental preferences, this is unlikely to have a significant impact on the sex ratio, because relatively few couples would actually act on their preference. As we have shown, preferences about the sex of children tend generally to be weak. Few couples attach enough importance to it to undergo substantial inconvenience, expense, or risk to try to increase the chance of having a child of the desired sex. Undergoing sex-selective insemination is intrusive, unproven, expensive, and tedious. A sperm sample must be delivered to the clinic, the woman must time her visit to the clinic to coincide with ovulation, and the couple must abstain from intercourse during this time. The process usually has to be repeated several times, since establishing a pregnancy usually takes several cycles.

> The kinds of sex selection methods that significant numbers of people would be willing to use are ineffective at present, while those that are effective are unacceptable to all but a handful of people. There is no reason to believe this will change in the foreseeable future.
>
> *M. Thomas, "Preference for the Sex of One's Children and the Prospective Use of Sex Selection," in Research Volumes of the Commission, 1993.*

It is not surprising, therefore, that sex-selective insemination is not very popular even in countries where it is widely available. One other possibility should be considered, however. As discussed in our research volume entitled *Prenatal Diagnosis: New and Future Developments*, if the sperm separation method for selecting one sex were much more reliable and easier to use than that for the other sex, then an imbalance in the sex ratio could occur because that method would be used more. The possibility that differences in the techniques for selecting boys and girls could alter the sex ratio should not be ignored. On the other hand, given that only a relatively small number of people appear to be willing to use sex-selective insemination, the potential for a sudden change in the ratio is very small.

We believe, therefore, that certain uses of sex-selective insemination are not inherently inconsistent with the principle of sexual equality and may be gender-neutral in their motivations and implications. Nonetheless, other aspects must also be taken into account in coming to our recommendations. First, there are segments within the Canadian population where males are valued more highly, putting pressure on women to undergo such techniques for discriminatory, sexist reasons. This would have to be protected against if sex-selective insemination were allowed. We would also need to ensure that it was not used in a gender-biased way in terms of the order and number of sons (or daughters) in each family.

Some have proposed that these problems could be overcome by establishing a system to limit access to couples who already had at least two children of one sex and none of the other and who wanted to use sex-selective insemination to have a child of the other sex. This would ensure that sex-selective insemination could not be used to have a first-born son, or to have more sons than daughters, but only to have at least one child of each sex.

We gave this proposal very serious consideration. However, we rejected it for several reasons. Although Commissioners recognize and sympathize with the strong desire of many couples to have at least one child of each sex, we do not believe that society should lend any substance to the notion that families in which all the children are of the same sex are less than ideal. Society should not promote the view that a family of all girls — or all boys — fails to meet some arbitrary

> Certain uses of sex-selective insemination are not inherently inconsistent with the principle of sexual equality and may be gender-neutral in their motivations and implications. Nonetheless, other aspects must also be taken into account in coming to our recommendations ... We do not believe that society should lend any substance to the notion that families in which all the children are of the same sex are less than ideal ... Moreover, using sex-selective insemination could have a detrimental effect not only on a child of the opposite sex born despite the procedure, but on earlier children.

standard of what constitutes the ideal family. The availability of even tightly controlled sex selection would signal approval of it, which may in turn promote change in the current attitudes of Canadians that the sex of a child is of little importance. Moreover, using sex-selective insemination could have a detrimental effect not only on a child of the opposite sex born despite the procedure, but on earlier children. If a couple with two daughters used sex-selective insemination to have a boy, the girls could well interpret this as reflecting on their adequacy in their parents' eyes, as could a girl born after a procedure that did not "work."

Appropriate Use of Resources

In addition to all the caveats just enumerated, the principle of appropriate use of resources must be considered.

Sex-selective insemination is not a medically necessary service. It is not intended to treat or avoid disease or to promote human health. In addition, having a child of a particular sex is not so important in people's lives as to justify the use of public resources to achieve it. Helping couples who are infertile or helping couples at high risk of passing on a genetic disorder to have a healthy child are legitimate aims on which to spend public resources, whereas satisfying parental wishes to have children of each sex is not.

It might seem that allowing private clinics to offer sex-selective insemination for a fee would not constitute an inappropriate use of public resources, since it would then be consumers, not the provincial insurance plan, who would pay for the service. However, as we saw in Chapter 20, the activities of private clinics often impose costs on the public health care system. In the case of private IVF clinics, these costs are substantial. In the case of sex-selective insemination, they would be less significant. Nevertheless, these clinics could generate such costs; for example, the initial medical examination of clients and laboratory testing of the male partner's sperm (before sperm-sorting techniques are used) could be charged to the public health insurance plan. Similarly, in the case of techniques aimed at conceiving a girl, the use of fertility-enhancing drugs could be charged to provincial drug plans or to private supplementary health insurance (although most provinces do not cover drugs such as clomiphene for any purpose).

More important in this case, however, is that ensuring that sex-selective insemination was being provided in private clinics in a safe and ethical way would require a strict system of licensing and monitoring. This alone would present significant costs to the public purse, and Commissioners would be strongly opposed to the use of scarce public resources for this purpose. Although a scheme might be devised to recoup some of these costs through licensing fees, given the potential harms we identified earlier, we believe that there is no legitimate reason to allow these services to be provided at all.

Similarly, unproven sex-selective insemination techniques should not be defined as "medical research." To define these techniques as medical research implies that they should be funded out of medical research budgets and that, if their efficacy becomes proven, these techniques should be considered for funding as medical services within the public health care system. The Commission believes, however, that it would be a serious distortion of the health care system, and an inappropriate use of public funds, to view sex-selective insemination as a medical service.

In summary, we believe that sex-selective insemination for non-medical reasons should not be allowed, for the following reasons:

- It would constitute an inappropriate use of public resources to provide this service. Even if it is provided in private clinics for a fee, the only way to ensure it is not used in a sexist way (for example, as a result of pressure on women to use it to have male children) would entail significant public resources (for example, monitoring, data collection, and analysis), which would constitute an inappropriate use of resources.

- Although people who choose to use the technique might well do so in ways that are not inherently sexist (for example, to have a child of each sex), its availability would nonetheless reinforce the message that the composition of a family, in terms of the sex of the children, is important.

- Even if use of the technique were restricted to situations where the couple was trying to have a girl after two boys (or vice versa), the existing children could feel that their own sex is not valued as much as the other, as could a child born after a procedure that did not "work."

- The technique is unproven, and, although it could be verified and improved by additional research, to spend research dollars to prove that it works would be inappropriate given other priorities for medical research.

Private clinics offering sex-selective insemination currently fall outside systems of accountability such as ethical review boards and professional organizations. In Chapter 19 we recommended that any clinic or physician offering assisted insemination with sperm treated with the aim of separating X- and Y-bearing sperm be required to obtain a licence from the National Reproductive Technologies Commission; we also outlined the conditions of licence for offering assisted conception services. The Commission recommends further that

> **266. As a condition of licence for offering assisted conception services, sperm treated with the aim of separating X- and Y-bearing sperm be provided only for individuals who have a clear medical indication (for example, X-linked disease). In such cases, there should be**
> **(a)   disclosure of objective information to patients about the lack of reliability of any technique used; and**
> **(b)   record keeping and annual reporting to the National Reproductive Technologies Commission with respect to the sex of the children resulting from insemination following such sperm treatment.**

Conclusion

We have looked at three techniques that could be used to influence or select the sex of children: prenatal diagnosis with sex-selective abortion; preimplantation diagnosis with sex-selective zygote transfer; and sperm treatment with sex-selective insemination. Each of the three techniques raises different ethical and social issues. At the same time, all three techniques raise concerns related to fundamental values and the kind of society Canadians want to live in. For example, groups representing women from minority communities were concerned about the use of reproductive technologies, particularly sex selection, to exploit stereotypical attitudes associated with race or culture. Commissioners took these concerns very seriously in coming to our recommendations. We support the efforts of these groups to resist pressures for sex selection within their communities and to promote wider adoption of fundamental values such as sexual equality. In so doing, we recognize the importance of protecting these values in the larger Canadian community as well by ensuring that they are not undermined or compromised by our recommendations.

More specifically, Commissioners view the practice of PND and sex-selective abortion for non-medical reasons as contrary to the Commission's guiding principles and incompatible with generally held Canadian values. This practice violates the principles of respect for human life and dignity, sexual equality, protection of the vulnerable, and the appropriate use of resources. Moreover, it has the potential to distort the role of PND within the health care system, which is to identify serious disorders in the fetus or zygote and to avoid the birth of a child with a serious genetic disease or congenital anomaly.

Existing CCMG guidelines disapprove of the use of PND to determine fetal sex for non-medical reasons, and to date these guidelines have generally worked to ensure that PND is not misused for this purpose. However, further action is required to remove any ambiguity about the legitimacy of this practice and to ensure that safeguards are in place to deal with future developments in PND technology.

The challenge has been to translate the broad public consensus against sex-selective abortion for non-medical reasons into measures that will not create other, more difficult problems. Any attempt to limit abortion for sex-selective reasons would prove impossible to enforce and would risk eroding other aspects of women's reproductive autonomy. Instead, Commissioners decided upon a two-part approach: first, NRTC-licensed PND centres should be prohibited from providing PND to determine fetal sex for non-medical reasons; second, when prenatal testing is done for a medical reason, information on the sex of the fetus should be given to the patient only on direct request or if it is medically relevant. Commissioners believe that this approach will prevent PND from being misused for sex-selective purposes, without infringing on women's privacy and reproductive autonomy or violating the principle that patients should have access to their medical records.

Where prenatal testing is done outside genetics centres, through ultrasound or blood tests administered by obstetricians, radiologists, or general or other practitioners, the same general conditions and standards of practice should apply. We have recommended that professional guidelines be reviewed and amended if necessary to ensure that practitioners do not provide prenatal detection of sex for non-medical reasons and do not deliberately examine for or volunteer information on fetal sex before the last trimester of pregnancy except for medical reasons.

We believe that an approach based on licensing centres is also appropriate to prevent misuse of the second technique — preimplantation diagnosis and sex-selective zygote transfer — as preimplantation diagnosis for non-medical reasons will not be allowed.

With respect to the third technique — sperm treatment and sex-selective insemination — evidence suggests that the great majority of Canadians do not have a gender bias with respect to the sex of their children and that they would consider using sex-selective insemination only with the aim of having at least one child of each sex. We are sensitive to and empathize with the desire to have at least one child of each sex and to establish the unique family relationships that come from having both sons and daughters. We believe that sex-selective insemination, if used in support of these goals, is not in itself unethical, although it is not a medical service. It may be consistent with sexual equality, if used in a gender-neutral way.

We have shown clearly, however, that additional factors must be taken into consideration in deciding whether sex-selective insemination should be permitted. These include questions such as whether permitting this practice would reinforce the view that the sex of a child is important; whether it would make existing children feel that their own sex is lacking in some way; and whether it would involve the appropriate use of resources. In addition, because the technique is unproven, it would be unethical to offer the procedure in the absence of research aimed at determining its effectiveness and safety; however, such research is not of sufficient value to justify devoting scarce research dollars to it.

These considerations led us to conclude that sex-selective insemination services should not be available in Canada, and our recommendations reflect this view. We recommend that sex-selective insemination services be provided only where there is a medical indication, and only in licensed settings with corresponding requirements for informed consent, data collection, and reporting.

Finally, Commissioners conclude that all three techniques raise important issues that must be addressed at the international as well as the domestic level. The opening of fetal sexing clinics just across the border in the United States, aimed in part at attracting Canadian clients, shows that these issues cannot be addressed solely in a domestic context. As we have discussed at several places in our report, we believe that the National Reproductive Technologies Commission should promote and participate in efforts to develop international guidelines on new reproductive technology-related issues of international importance. These should include guidelines relevant to sex selection for non-medical purposes.

General Sources

Thomas, M. "Preference for the Sex of One's Children and the Prospective Use of Sex Selection." In Research Volumes of the Royal Commission on New Reproductive Technologies, 1993.

Wertz, D. "Prenatal Diagnosis and Society." In Research Volumes of the Royal Commission on New Reproductive Technologies, 1993.

Specific References

1. For a historical review, see Schaffir, J. "What Are Little Boys Made Of? The Never-Ending Search for Sex Selection Techniques." *Perspectives in Biology and Medicine* 34 (4)(Summer 1991): 516-25.

2. Canadian College of Medical Geneticists and the Society of Obstetricians and Gynaecologists of Canada. "Canadian Guidelines for Prenatal Diagnosis of Genetic Disorders: An Update." *Journal of the Society of Obstetricians and Gynaecologists of Canada* 15 (Suppl.)(March 1993), p. 38.

3. Burke, B.M. "Genetic Counselor Attitudes Towards Fetal Sex Identification and Selective Abortion." *Social Science Medicine* 34 (11)(1992): 1263-69; Evans, M.I. "Attitudes on the Ethics of Abortion, Sex Selection, and Selective Pregnancy Termination Among Health Care Professionals, Ethicists, and Clergy Likely to Encounter Such Situations." *American Journal of Obstetrics and Gynecology* 164 (4)(1991): 1092-99.

4. Wertz, D.C., and J.C. Fletcher. "Fatal Knowledge? Prenatal Diagnosis and Sex Selection." *Hastings Center Report* 19 (3)(May-June 1989): 21-27; Kaye, C.I., and J. La Puma. "Geneticists and Sex Selection." *Hastings Center Report* 20 (4)(July-August 1990): 40-41.

5. Kluge, E.-H.W., and C. Lucock. *New Human Reproductive Technologies: A Preliminary Perspective of the Canadian Medical Association.* Ottawa: Canadian Medical Association, 1991.

6. See Gray, R.H. "Natural Family Planning and Sex Selection: Fact or Fiction?" *American Journal of Obstetrics and Gynecology* 165 (6)(Part 2)(December 1991), p. 1984; France, J.T. "Characteristics of Natural Conceptual Cycles Occurring in a Prospective Study of Sex Preselection: Fertility Awareness Symptoms, Hormone Levels, Sperm Survival, and Pregnancy Outcome." *International Journal of Fertility* 37 (4)(1992), p. 244.

7. Jaffe, S.B. "A Controlled Study for Gender Selection." *Fertility and Sterility* 56 (2)(August 1991), p. 254.

8. Beernink, F.J., W.P. Dmowski, and R.J. Ericsson. "Sex Preselection Through Albumin Separation of Sperm." *Fertility and Sterility* 59 (3)(February 1993): 382-86.

9. Jaffe, "A Controlled Study for Gender Selection," p. 257.

10. Mickleburgh, R. "Sex Selection Controversy Renewed: Second Canadian 'Sperm Firm' to Offer Choice of Offspring." *Globe and Mail*, September 3, 1992, A1.

11. Plevin, N. "Parents Take a Thorny Ethical Path in Quest to Select Sex of Children." *The Los Angeles Times*, June 14, 1992, Part B, p. 7.

12. Canadian Fertility and Andrology Society and the Society of Obstetricians and Gynaecologists of Canada. Combined Ethics Committee. *Ethical Considerations of the New Reproductive Technologies*. Toronto: Ribosome Communications, 1990.

Gene Therapy and Genetic Alteration

Twenty years ago, geneticists invented procedures for isolating single, identifiable genes and for "splicing" those genes into a foreign chromosome in such a way that the inserted gene would become functional and would duplicate in the process of cell division. This ability has given rise to various applications in agriculture and pharmaceuticals and is the basis for much of the biotechnology industry. It is also an ability that is evolving rapidly, giving rise to concerns about the development of technology outstripping society's capacity to make reasoned decisions about its acceptability and use. We heard these concerns and many other related to genetic alteration in our public consultations.

As we saw in the previous three chapters, developments in DNA technology have also enabled the identification of some of the specific genes responsible for particular genetic diseases. The potential of "gene splicing" to treat genetic disease in human beings was immediately evident. Generally speaking, there are few effective cures for genetic diseases, whether they are of early onset or late onset; this is why most couples decide to terminate a pregnancy when PND reveals that the fetus is affected by a severe genetic disorder. However, these recent scientific discoveries mean that it may become possible to treat some severe genetic disorders by altering the gene in question. This field of research is known as human gene therapy.

The Commission's mandate did not ask us to examine and make recommendations on all uses of genetic knowledge; it asked us to examine genetic manipulation and therapeutic interventions to correct genetic anomalies in the context of human reproduction and to make recommendations in the public interest with respect to them. Our concern in this chapter, as with the technologies examined in the previous chapters, is on the use of gene therapy and alteration in the reproductive context. Thus, our examination does not focus on therapy or alteration used after birth, but many of the issues are similar. To conduct our review of these issues, we listened to Canadians, commissioned research and analysis, and considered the issues through the prism of our guiding principles and our evidence-based approach to technology assessment. Given that the field is developing so rapidly, with the exact direction of those developments still uncertain, this area will need continued public discussion to guide appropriate policy development.

Human gene therapy involves the insertion of genetic material into a human being with the intention of correcting a particular genetic defect. Specifically, a genetic defect resulting from an alteration in the DNA of a particular gene is corrected by inserting a normal DNA sequence for that gene into the individual's cells. One approach to inserting this genetic material is to remove cells containing the genetic defect from the individual, alter them in culture by adding the normal gene, then return the altered cells to the body. Another approach is to use altered viruses to deliver the gene — for example, into the respiratory tract if that is where the defect is expressed (as in the case of cystic fibrosis).

Gene therapy may be the only hope for some severely affected individuals who would otherwise die or be very severely disabled by a genetic disease. In addition, the knowledge that some severe genetic conditions may be amenable to gene therapy may broaden the options open to couples at risk of passing on a genetic disease. For disorders that are not treatable by any other means except gene therapy, the availability of this treatment could encourage some people who might otherwise terminate a pregnancy to continue it to term.

This is a new and rapidly developing field, but it has taken two decades of laboratory and animal studies to test the safety and feasibility of this approach and to develop the appropriate techniques for human application. The first approved clinical trials involving human gene therapy began in September 1990,[1] in the United States, and research has moved rapidly since then. A recent survey listed 15 research protocols involving 59 patients at nine different institutions in the United States, France, Italy, and China.[2] Gene therapy is, however, still very much an experimental technique.

At present, no gene therapy research involving human subjects is being done in Canada. However, several research centres in Canada are doing laboratory or animal work related to gene therapy. For example, groups at the Royal Victoria Hospital in Montreal, Mount Sinai Hospital Research Institute and the Hospital for Sick Children Research Institute in Toronto, and the Terry Fox Laboratory in Vancouver are investigating the use of retroviruses to transfer genes into blood-producing cells. Physical methods of DNA transfer into cells are being researched, and the use of electroporation is being examined at the Toronto General Hospital.

The development of gene therapy has created both hopes and fears. As one researcher commented in a study (see research volume, *Prenatal Diagnosis: New and Future Developments*) prepared for the Commission,

> The prospect of using directed genetic alteration to treat serious inherited disorders ... raises the hopes of patients and their families, but also the fears of those who perceive it as tampering with the secrets of life, or at least creating unknown hazards. (*L. Prior, "Somatic and Germ Line Gene Therapy: Current Status and Prospects," in Research Volumes of the Commission, 1993.*)

As we will see, there are reasons for these divergent responses, since gene therapy does indeed contain both significant potential benefits and unknown risks.

In evaluating these benefits and risks, it is important to keep in mind that the term "gene therapy" has been used to cover a wide range of procedures that are used for different purposes and in different contexts. The term gene "therapy" is misleading; as we will see, in some cases it is more accurate to call it gene "alteration," because no treatment of an individual with a disorder is involved. There are two major categories of genetic alteration: the first, somatic cell gene therapy, involves the introduction of the corrective DNA into the somatic cells (the non-reproductive body cells) of an affected individual. Since the altered genetic material is not inserted into the reproductive (germ) cells, the alteration is not passed on to subsequent generations. The second category involves the introduction of the corrective DNA into the germ cells, with the result that the genetic change can be passed on to subsequent generations.

There are two possible purposes for genetic alteration. The genetic alteration may be intended to treat disease, or it may be intended to enhance particular desired qualities, such as height or intelligence. Only the former is appropriately called gene therapy, since the term "therapy" implies the treatment of disease. Although enhancement is often discussed under the term "gene therapy," this is inappropriate, as its aims are entirely different. To emphasize this important distinction, we refer to it as "non-therapeutic genetic alteration" or "genetic enhancement" and treat it separately in this chapter.

Genetic alteration can be performed during adulthood, childhood, or prenatally on zygotes and fetuses. Although all of the current gene therapy research involving human beings is done on children or adults, if post-natal gene therapy proves effective, prenatal treatment may be considered. For example, a fetus diagnosed as having a severe single-gene disorder could potentially be treated through somatic cell gene therapy *in utero*. Similarly, if it becomes feasible to identify zygotes with genetic disorders through preimplantation diagnosis, the suggestion may arise that they be treated through genetic alteration *in vitro*. If this were done early in development, it is probable that the cells giving rise to the testes or ovaries (the "gonads") in the resulting fetus would also be altered. This is not "germ-line therapy" per se but zygote therapy that may also alter the germ line as a side effect.

The Views of Canadians

Some indication of public views and attitudes can be gained from the input the Commission received at hearings and in submissions, although much of that input was on use of genetic knowledge in general. Recent surveys in the United States also provide some relevant information.

Public Hearings and Submissions

The topic of gene therapy received less attention in our hearings and submissions than some other aspects of our mandate. However, what was said was thoughtful, and a wide range of positions on the medical and ethical acceptability of gene therapy was expressed. For example, we heard from many people whose lives have been touched by severe genetic disorders; for them, somatic cell gene therapy is seen as a valid response to severe genetic diseases that cannot be treated effectively at present.

Although there was general support for the provision of somatic cell gene therapy for disease, there was more scepticism about the concept of altering a zygote's DNA at a time when the gonads would also be affected. These reservations reflect concerns about the unknown consequences of changing the DNA of cells when these changes may be passed on

> As a member of a family affected by a genetic disease and as a representative of other families affected by genetic diseases, I would like to emphasize that we are greatly affected by the policies or guidelines established in this area of reproductive technology. Many of our families are benefiting from the existing technology in the area of prenatal diagnosis ... Ultimately, our families look forward with profound interest to the day in the future when advances in this area and the area of gene therapy remove the death sentence now imposed on children afflicted with Tay-Sachs and the allied diseases ... it is important to note that the ideal solution in the eyes of a parent such as myself who was told that their baby was dying would be for the medical technology to be there to save my baby's life ... Should research into the areas of gene therapy be stopped or slowed down? No. This is not gene therapy to raise a child's IQ or change a child's looks. In my eyes, as in the eyes of the parents in our group, we ... just wanted our children to live.
>
> *H. Reiter, National Tay-Sachs and Allied Diseases Association of Ontario, Public Hearings Transcripts, Toronto, Ontario, October 31, 1990.*

to the next generation, the risks of permanent alterations in the human gene pool, the ethical implications of research involving human zygotes, and the potential for discriminatory use of technology.

Among those who discussed the topic, there was unanimous opposition to the concept of enhancement genetics intended to "improve" normal levels of human intelligence, strength, beauty, or other personal characteristics. This is seen as highly discriminatory in intent and totally antithetical to the values of Canadian society.

There was also strong agreement that all forms of gene therapy should be regulated on a national basis and that there should be national regulations prohibiting non-therapeutic gene alteration or genetic enhancement.

> We must refrain from trying to design or redesign human beings or perfect them according to our own notions ... The technologies we are discussing may have a place in alleviating suffering and combatting disease but should never be used as a means of seeking to reinvent human beings.
>
> *P. Marshall, The Evangelical Fellowship of Canada, Public Hearings Transcripts, Toronto, Ontario, November 20, 1990.*

These views are in line with the emerging international consensus on the acceptability of gene therapy. An international survey of 20 policy statements issued between 1980 and 1990 by legislative bodies, government agencies, professional organizations, and religious bodies concluded that

> Without exception, all 20 of these policy statements accept the moral legitimacy of somatic cell gene therapy for the cure of disease. Evaluations of germ-line genetic intervention for the cure or prevention of disease are mixed, with a majority of the policy statements opposing such intervention. None of the 20 statements supports the enhancement of human capabilities by genetic means.[3]

It is important to note, however, that some Canadians appearing before the Commission expressed opposition to all forms of gene therapy and recommended an outright moratorium on any such techniques. This opposition was based in part on broader reservations about the safety and wisdom of genetic manipulation technologies.

Surveys of Opinion

Most information on public attitudes toward gene therapy comes from the United States, where several public opinion surveys have been conducted. Since the mid-1980s, public reaction in the United States to gene therapy has been characterized consistently by high levels of approval for the use of gene therapy, but low levels of actual knowledge and information about the procedure.

For example, a survey of attitudes toward gene therapy conducted in April 1992 found that Americans were "at once deeply enthusiastic about the new science of gene therapy, in which patients receive healthy copies of genes they lack, but admittedly ignorant of any details about who might benefit or how. For example, 89% said they approved of using the novel approach to thwart genetic disorders, yet 60% confessed that they [had] heard almost nothing about the technique."[4] The same survey also revealed that a sizable minority approved of the use of genetic alteration for non-therapeutic enhancement as well as for treating disease. For example, 42 percent said that they approved of genetic alteration to improve the intelligence of children.

Such a high level of approval for gene therapy arises in part, no doubt, from the nature of media coverage of the topic. As we will see, there are serious technical and ethical limitations to the use of genetic alteration. These difficulties tend to be downplayed by the media, which have focussed instead on the glamour of high-tech medicine and the possibility of "miracle medicine" breakthroughs. This is perhaps inevitable, given the space and time limitations imposed by media coverage formats, as well as the complexity of the technology and the issues surrounding it. In an under-standable desire to establish for media audiences the link between the discovery and the ultimate application or treatment, the intervening development processes and difficulties are usually minimized; the length and uncertainty of the stage between initial discovery and clinically useful application are often compressed or ignored. In addition, the range of potential applications of gene therapy is treated as large and ever-increasing — gene therapy is presented as revolutionizing wide areas of medical practice in the near future. Such an approach to covering these subjects also contributes to an oversimplified body-as-machine, doctor-as-mechanic view of disease, in which the genetic causes of disease are emphasized at the expense of the complex web of causation involving social and cultural factors, as well as physiological and immunological factors.

> We recommend that techniques involving the reshaping of human genes in any way be limited to the very narrow sphere of prevention and cure of specifically identifiable genetic diseases associated with human suffering and misery, and not extended in any way to positive eugenic programs of species improvement.
>
> *Brief to the Commission from the Mennonite Central Committee Canada, December 18, 1990.*

It is essential to develop a more informed and balanced public debate about the merits and limits of gene therapy. We look first at the most developed form of gene therapy — somatic cell gene therapy. We then consider the more speculative (and troubling) forms — gene therapy of a zygote that may alter the germ line, or genetic alteration of the germ line in adults with the goal of prevention, and non-therapeutic genetic alteration. Our major focus, however, is on the possible uses of gene therapy in the reproductive context.

Somatic Cell Gene Therapy

Somatic cell gene therapy is the form of gene therapy on which research is most advanced and is an active area of biomedical research. It is still highly experimental, however, and its ultimate usefulness in the treatment of genetic disease is unknown.   We examine the range of conditions potentially amenable to this form of therapy, then consider the issues it raises.

Potential Uses of Somatic Cell Gene Therapy

Genetic disorders differ very widely in the extent to which they could be corrected by existing or foreseeable gene therapy procedures.   For example, chromosomal disorders (such as Down syndrome) are not amenable to gene therapy.   These disorders involve the absence or duplication of fragments of chromosomes or entire chromosomes; as a result, the chromosomes have many extra or missing genes. Because no techniques are available to insert or remove sufficient DNA to correct such large defects, gene therapy does not apply to chromosomal disorders.

Similarly, most multifactorial disorders — which are the most common category of genetic diseases and include, for example, much cardiovascular disease — are beyond the reach of somatic cell gene therapy at its current level of development.

Genetic therapy on embryos, fetuses and adults with serious genetic defects (such as cystic fibrosis or Tay-Sachs Disease) would be of great good to humanity and particularly to women in our capacity as primary caregivers on a global level. The darker side of genetic engineering is its potential to damage the human gene pool and to link with eugenic ideology and practice on a more powerful scale than has been possible previously ... If the human gene pool is understood as the collective property of humanity, then control of interventions in it and the judgement of risk and benefit are a public matter and need the participation of people who are not medical doctors, research scientists, lawyers, or statisticians. In addition to the need for representation by medical interests on the national ethics board, the [Canadian Advisory Council on the Status of Women] strongly recommends the inclusion of women's and labour group representatives, community health activists, and other lay people.

Brief to the Commission from the Canadian Advisory Council on the Status of Women, March 1991.

Multifactorial disorders are determined by a combination of genetic predisposition and interaction with the environment. As we saw in the previous chapter, the genetic components are not understood sufficiently to warrant serious contemplation of genetic intervention.

Gene therapy is therefore relevant primarily to single-gene disorders. However, even within the category of single-gene disorders, there are wide differences in the potential usefulness of gene therapy. Recessive disorders (for example, Tay-Sachs disease) are much more amenable to gene therapy than dominant disorders. Recessive disorders can, in principle, be corrected simply by inserting a normal gene somewhere in the chromosomes of an affected cell (this is called "gene insertion"), without replacing or repairing the defective gene. Dominant gene disorders, on the other hand, are manifested even though the person has only a single copy of the defective gene. This is because defective dominant genes often alter the proteins that are the body's building blocks, which results in structurally abnormal tissues, so that normal function is not possible. Adding a normal gene in this case is not enough, because the aberrant gene product interferes with the ability of the normal gene product to form normal tissue. This means such disorders usually can be corrected only by repairing the defect in that dominant gene itself or by replacing it with a normal gene. (This is called "gene replacement.") This may involve replacement of the entire gene or of the aberrant nucleotides within the gene. For simplicity, we will speak of replacing genes, although in some cases only a part of the gene is replaced.

This is an important difference because, at present, only gene insertion is feasible in human beings. It is possible to insert a normal copy of the gene that is defective, which will then supplement the defective gene, but it is not yet possible to correct the mutation itself. To replace or repair the defective gene itself would require the ability to "target" the inserted genetic material with precision, so that it could be inserted in place of the original defective material. Such targeting is not currently possible, and, although research is proceeding, there is no guarantee that the required precision will be achieved in the near future.

As a result, only recessive single-gene disorders are amenable to gene therapy at present. As explained in Chapter 26, recessive disorders are manifested only if a person inherits a "double dose" of the defective gene. A person who has one copy of the defective gene will be healthy (although he or she will be a carrier of the genetic disease), because the normal gene can "cover" for the defective gene, producing enough of the protein for normal functioning. Inserting one copy of the normal gene into someone with a double dose of the defective gene may, therefore, be enough to restore health, even without trying to alter the defective genes. Some examples are severe combined immunodeficiency syndrome resulting from adenosine deaminase deficiency; deficiencies in liver enzymes; and some recessive central nervous system disorders like Tay-Sachs disease. The first approved clinical trial of gene therapy, begun in September 1990 at the

National Institutes of Health in the United States, involved such a recessive single-gene disease. The gene for the enzyme adenosine deaminase was inserted into children with severe combined immunodeficiency. This trial is continuing, and the inserted genes appear to be succeeding in increasing the children's immune response.[5] However, even if the trials for some recessive disorders prove successful, it is doubtful that somatic cell gene therapy will prove effective even for all recessive single-gene diseases, as many technical problems remain to be solved. The three most pressing of these technical problems are insertion methods, accessibility of the tissue, and regulation of the gene product.

> Genetic manipulation should be limited at present to corrective measures ... to work aimed at the eradication of abnormalities significantly impairing the capacity for or the quality of life. We would see this type of corrective genetics limited to somatic-line therapy, which would have an impact only on individuals affected by the disease. On the other hand the use of germ-line therapy which would produce a permanent alteration in the gene human pool should be implemented only after a full discussion and general agreement within our society.
>
> *M. Buchwald, Canadian Cystic Fibrosis Foundation, Public Hearings Transcripts, Toronto, Ontario, November 19, 1990.*

Methods of Insertion

Inserting genetic material into a human cell in such a way that it becomes integrated into the genome and becomes functional requires the precise identification and manipulation of submicroscopic amounts of genetic material. Current methods have not proved entirely satisfactory, with the result that the challenges associated with delivering healthy DNA sequences to the appropriate somatic cells remain formidable. The absence of appropriate methods of inserting genetic material constitutes a major impediment to the use of somatic cell gene therapy for some recessive diseases for the foreseeable future.

Accessibility

Another limitation to gene therapy is that the target organ for the genetic material must be accessible. This is not so much of a problem when the genetic disease manifests itself in changes in a protein or enzyme that circulates throughout the body — these diseases can be addressed by inserting the gene into any appropriate accessible tissue, as this will change the circulation level of that substance. But for other genetic diseases that affect particular tissue types, the usefulness of gene therapy will depend on the accessibility of the tissue. Gene therapy may be possible if the clinical consequences of a disorder arise from changes occurring in a single accessible tissue, such as bone marrow or liver. However, several gene disorders affect relatively inaccessible tissues such as brain tissue (for example, Tay-Sachs disease), and these are not currently amenable to gene therapy.

Regulation of Gene Product

It is not enough for the genetic material to be inserted. The product of the inserted gene must also be regulated properly — that is, the gene must produce its particular protein at the proper time and in the proper amount. Too much of a protein may be as harmful as too little. Therefore, genes that require very precise regulation of expression are poor candidates for gene therapy because the current understanding of gene regulation is insufficient to ensure such precise control.

In summary, the present technology largely limits the use of gene therapy to single-gene recessive disorders where there is an accessible tissue and little regulation of the gene product is required. This means that gene therapy is relevant at present to only a small fraction of the total number of recessive disorders, which in turn is a fraction of the total number of single-gene disorders, which in turn is a small fraction of the total number of disorders in which genes are important. Although somatic cell gene therapy research is moving quickly, there is still a long way to go with respect to its feasibility. Even if some of these technical difficulties are solved, as some undoubtedly will be, there is no reason to think that gene therapy will ever become a miracle cure for genetic disease in general.

The Commission's particular interest is in the prenatal use of somatic cell gene therapy on fetuses *in utero*. Many of the limitations just mentioned apply with particular force to the prenatal use of gene therapy; for example, accessibility is an even more serious obstacle when dealing with a fetus *in utero*.

There are also additional risks in applying somatic cell gene therapy prenatally. If done at a very early stage of development — for example, when the zygote is accessible *in vitro* after preimplantation diagnosis — there is the risk that the insertion of somatic cells may result in de facto germ-line gene therapy; that is, that the entire range of cells in the zygote, germ-line as well as somatic, will be affected. Thus, any gene therapy done before the body organs begin to develop could result in germ-line gene alteration. Rather than alter the zygote at this early stage, it seems more appropriate not to transfer those zygotes diagnosed as affected by the disorder in question.

The other stage when the developing fetus could be treated is after PND by CVS or amniocentesis (that is, after at least 10 weeks' gestation). At that stage of development it would be possible to "see" and reach the tissues of the fetus using ultrasound guidance. Such procedures would pose risks for the pregnant woman, both from the invasive nature of the procedure and from unintended consequences of inserting new genetic information into the fetus. Given these risks, many couples would probably opt to terminate the pregnancy if the fetus was found to be affected with a serious disorder.

Given the greater obstacles and risks of prenatal treatment, as well as the current state of knowledge about the results of post-natal treatment, little research is being conducted into fetal applications at present, even in animal models. Somatic cell gene therapy on the fetus *in utero* would be the only way to treat some genetic diseases, however. Some disorders could be treated only if they were corrected during fetal development, before they have caused irreversible damage. This is true of Lesch-Nyhan syndrome and some other severe central nervous system disorders. (Many in-born errors of metabolism can be dealt with after birth, since the mother's metabolic system usually keeps the circulating level of the substances normal in the fetus, but single-gene conditions that result in congenital anomalies must be dealt with earlier.) In addition, some tissues may be more amenable to effective gene insertion during the rapid growth that takes place during fetal development than they are after birth. Hence, fetal gene therapy, while currently speculative, may come to play a valid, if very limited, role in the treatment of genetic disease.

Issues Raised by the Use of Somatic Cell Gene Therapy

There seems to be no reason to object in principle to somatic cell gene therapy, which can be seen as a natural extension of commonly used medical procedures. For example, people with diabetes who are unable to produce normal amounts of insulin are given this missing gene product by daily injection.   If the insulin-producing gene could be inserted into someone with diabetes, the effect would be the same as the daily injection, except that gene therapy would provide lifetime relief. The same permanent result would occur if the diabetic received a tissue or organ transplant, which would also provide cells containing the normal gene. By itself, then, the idea of somatic cell gene alteration does not seem to raise any new moral problems. Although somatic cell gene therapy is not inherently objectionable, its actual application does raise several important issues, including risks, informed consent, confidentiality, and appropriate use of resources.

Risks

The methods used to insert genetic material may expose the patient to infectious viruses and increase the risk of cancer. At the current state of the technology, it is not possible to control how or where the inserted DNA integrates into the host cell. Thus, there is a risk that the random integration of inserted genes could result in the activation or deactivation of genes that influence susceptibility to cancer or promote the body's ability to suppress the development of tumours. This could increase the possibility that the person would subsequently develop cancer, although the probability is quite small. A risk of cancer resulting from treatment is not unique to gene insertion — it also occurs in other life-saving treatments, such as anti-rejection medications used in kidney transplant patients.

Another risk is that if genetic material integrates successfully but the treatment is insufficient, the procedure may simply prolong a severe disorder, without actually curing the disease or even alleviating the suffering.

Given these risks at this time, the use of somatic cell gene therapy is appropriate only for diseases that lead to severe debilitation or death and that cannot be treated successfully by any other means.

In the case of fetal applications of gene therapy, as well as unintended consequences of the insertion of new genetic information into the fetus, there are additional risks to the pregnant woman, resulting from the intrusiveness of the procedure. If post-natal gene therapy proves safe and effective in the future, however, the use of gene therapy *in utero* could be considered for fetal conditions that cause irreversible damage before birth.

Informed Consent

As with all medical research, an individual's involvement in gene therapy should be informed and voluntary. The person should be fully informed about the nature and risks of treatment and should make the decision about whether to participate completely free of any pressure. Sufficient information must therefore be provided about the proposed treatment and the patient's role in it, in a form that can be understood, to enable the patient to decide whether to participate. The patient should also know that it will remain unknown for many years whether adverse long-term effects occur. The level of disclosure should be proportionate to the likelihood and scale of possible harm, but even the remote possibility of adverse consequences should be disclosed.

Several problems arise with respect to informed consent for gene therapy. First, gene therapy is irreversible (just as most surgery is), so the right to revoke one's consent is less meaningful than for continuing medical treatment. It is particularly important, therefore, to ensure that the highest standards of informed consent are met.

Second, in reproductive contexts, both the fetus that receives the DNA alteration and the pregnant woman are being treated. The woman's decision about whether to consent to treatment must therefore be based not only on information about potential risks and benefits to the fetus but also on potential harms to herself. In-depth counselling should be provided to ensure full review of the state of knowledge concerning the risks of changing the DNA in the fetus — what the known risks are as well as what is unknown — the relative risks and benefits of alternative treatments, and the reversibility of any side effects.

Confidentiality

As with PND and genetic testing, information obtained during somatic cell gene therapy research trials could be prejudicial to individuals being treated or to their families. Any information obtained must therefore be reported in a manner that conceals the identity of individuals being treated. No one outside the research team should be permitted to handle data that could reveal patient identity. Identifying information should be disclosed only with the individual's express authorization. There may be problems in maintaining anonymity, since there is widespread interest in gene therapy among the public, as well as in scientific, government, and other communities. The potential for wide publicity may make it difficult to assure people's privacy, since there could be many ways for the media to identify who is being treated. Acknowledgement of the risk of media exposure should be part of the process of informed consent.

Appropriate Use of Resources

Somatic cell gene therapy is expensive. If the procedure proves effective, costs will likely decline as techniques are refined and treatment becomes more widely available. It will always be a relatively expensive procedure, however, since considerable expertise and expensive laboratory support are required. But there are also substantial costs associated with treating children born with a genetic disease, who often require procedures that are as expensive or invasive. For example, children with immuno-deficiency may have several bone marrow transplants, which are likely to be more expensive than gene therapy if the latter becomes part of clinical practice. Commissioners therefore believe that it is appropriate to provide public funding for research into somatic cell gene therapy for serious disorders for which there are no alternative treatments.

Of course, researchers should not neglect the development of other possible treatments for the genetic diseases in question. For example, some success has been achieved in treating adenosine deaminase deficiency through the drug PEG-ADA. Clearly, the appropriateness of funding further research into gene therapy for this disorder or other disorders will depend on the success of drug treatment.

Regulating Somatic Cell Gene Therapy

Commissioners believe that the therapeutic intent of somatic cell gene therapy is broadly consistent with the ethic of care. However, further research or future clinical application in this area must be managed in a socially responsible way. At present, any proposal for somatic cell gene therapy research in Canada would be carried out within the context of the

Medical Research Council of Canada's *Guidelines for Research on Somatic Cell Gene Therapy in Humans.*[6] The MRC applies these guidelines to all researchers who receive MRC funding for medical research involving somatic cell gene therapy. These guidelines are also applied by a wide range of hospitals, funding bodies, and universities in Canada. For the foreseeable future, then, any gene therapy project in Canada would originate from an institution that is covered by MRC guidelines.

These guidelines cover many of the issues we have identified as important for the ethical application of gene therapy, including informed consent, confidentiality, and limiting gene therapy to serious diseases for which no alternative treatments are available. Commissioners believe that the MRC's guidelines on somatic cell gene therapy research provide a solid foundation for the management of this research in Canada. However, they need to be implemented fully and supplemented in several ways, as discussed later in this chapter.

One key feature of the MRC's guidelines involves the recommendation that these guidelines be applied in a two-tiered fashion, first at the local level by research ethics boards of hospitals and universities and then, in the case of a positive review by the local research ethics board, in a second review by a national committee. A similar two-step process has been established in the United States for federally funded gene therapy research, with review both at the local institutional level and by the Recombinant DNA Advisory Committee of the National Institutes of Health.

However, the national review committee proposed by the MRC has yet to become a functioning reality. There has not been a pressing need for this committee to date, because research in Canada has not yet involved human subjects. However, this will soon change. Commissioners believe that the national review committee

> The national review committee proposed by the MRC should be established immediately, to provide assistance to local research ethics boards and to ensure consistent national treatment of gene therapy research activities.

proposed by the MRC should be established immediately, to provide assistance to local research ethics boards and to ensure consistent national treatment of gene therapy research activities.

Somatic cell gene therapy has the capacity to generate scientifically difficult and ethically demanding questions that might place an unfair burden on the resources of local research ethics boards and that would benefit from the broader perspective and additional analytic resources implicit in a national review function. Also, a national review committee would maintain consistency of treatment of these potentially highly controversial research projects across Canada. It is unreasonable to expect the system of locally controlled, volunteer-based research ethics boards alone to provide an adequate framework for protecting either research subjects or the national interest in monitoring the evolution and application of gene therapy.

We also believe that the MRC guidelines need to be supplemented in two important ways. First, public reporting should be an essential element of any national review function, given the growing public interest in therapeutic advances and strong public concerns about potential abuses of this technology. A high level of public availability of information must be associated with the process of approving and funding research involving human beings. Commissioners believe it will be important for the MRC's proposed national review committee to report publicly on somatic cell gene therapy research in Canada on a regular basis — both the failures and successes — perhaps in the MRC president's annual report.

Second, with regard to matters within its mandate, Commissioners believe that special safeguards are required for fetal applications of somatic cell gene therapy. Any research projects involving fetal applications of somatic cell gene therapy should be undertaken only with the greatest of care, given the vulnerability of the recipient, the technical difficulty of the procedure, and the need to respect the autonomy of the pregnant woman.

> Proposals for fetal gene therapy research must be assessed carefully to ensure that they do not promote development of an adversarial relationship between a woman and her fetus, and that they constitute an appropriate use of resources.

Commissioners view the potential development of fetal gene therapy with considerable misgivings. To the extent that these developments encourage increased interest in and capacity to support the health of the fetus, they are useful. To the extent that the possibility of performing somatic cell gene therapy condones coercion or undermines the autonomy of women, however, some very real concerns must be addressed. Proposals for fetal gene therapy research must therefore be assessed carefully to ensure that they do not promote development of an adversarial relationship between a woman and her fetus, and that they constitute an appropriate use of resources.

To ensure this careful assessment, Commissioners believe that gene therapy research and/or subsequent clinical treatment involving fetuses should be approved by the Prenatal Diagnosis and Genetics Sub-Committee of the National Reproductive Technologies Commission, as well as by the MRC's proposed national review committee on gene therapy. While the MRC review process is invaluable, medical and scientific perspectives predominate, both at the local research ethics board level and nationally. Moreover, the few representatives of the general public are often drawn from a narrow range of professional groups, with little reflection of women's groups, the community health sector, or other relevant interests.

The National Commission, by contrast, would embody a wider range of perspectives and would be more publicly accountable than the MRC's national review committee. Hence, the MRC national review committee and the National Commission Prenatal Diagnosis and Genetics Sub-Committee would provide complementary forms of assessment, based on their different expertise and perspectives. The MRC national committee would apply expertise primarily to the scientific merits of research proposals, while the National Commission Sub-Committee would focus primarily on social and ethical issues.

Moreover, approval by the Prenatal Diagnosis and Genetics Sub-Committee of the National Commission would help integrate fetal gene therapy with the larger PND system in Canada. If and when fetal applications of somatic cell gene therapy prove clinically feasible, it will be important to ensure that there is close cooperation between the prenatal diagnosis system, which may reveal to at-risk couples that their fetus is affected by a genetic disease, and the practice of gene therapy, which would be available as an option for treating that disease. The Commission therefore recommends that

> **267. Any proposal for somatic cell gene therapy research involving human fetuses as subjects be reviewed and approved by the Prenatal Diagnosis and Genetics Sub-Committee of the National Reproductive Technologies Commission, following review and approval by the Medical Research Council national review committee for gene therapy.**

and that

> **268. The National Reproductive Technologies Commission develop guidelines concerning the appropriate indications for fetal applications of somatic cell gene therapy as the field evolves, with a view to increasing the National Reproductive Technologies Commission's regulatory involvement if the need arises.**

Germ-Line Genetic Alteration

Potential Uses of Germ-Line Genetic Alteration

The term "germ-line gene therapy," although widely used, is in fact misleading. "Therapy" implies treatment of an individual (a person or a developing fetus) for a disease that has been identified. Genetic alteration aimed specifically at the gonads to alter the gametes is therefore not therapy — there are no existing affected individuals. It is quite incorrect, therefore, to refer to genetic alteration done in adults with the aim of altering the germ cells as "therapy" — it is a "preventive" strategy. For purposes of analysis, it is important not to describe this, misleadingly, as "therapy," as there is much less willingness to undertake risk (both individually and societally) in order to prevent disease than to do so for therapeutic purposes.

It is possible, however, to consider genetic therapy involving the zygote or the fetus — that is, genetic alteration aimed at curing disease in that zygote or fetus. If done very early in development during the zygote stage, this could affect the germ line. There are two windows of opportunity during which the developing entity is theoretically accessible for genetic therapy before birth. The first is after IVF and preimplantation diagnosis have shown that the zygote is affected. If gene insertion were done at this stage, before the process of cell differentiation and the development of body organs (organogenesis), then the genetic change would be present in most or all cells — and could thus affect the germ line of the resulting fetus as well. Some have argued that this not only would treat that particular zygote but might prevent the transmission of the gene to future generations. However, rather than taking the risk of altering genes that will be passed on to the next generation, there is the less risky option of simply not transferring affected zygotes.

> Rather than taking the risk of altering genes that will be passed on to the next generation, there is the less risky option of simply not transferring affected zygotes.

The next window of opportunity (before birth) is much later, after organogenesis; treatment of an affected fetus at that time would be unlikely to affect its germ line. A major reason for interest in gene therapy before birth is that it might be able to treat certain genetic diseases that are not amenable to therapy after birth — for example, diseases that cause irreparable harm early in fetal development or that affect multiple body systems.

Germ-line genetic alteration has also been discussed (under the misnomer "germ-line therapy") in terms of relevance to adults who either have, or are carriers of, a genetic disorder. But if an adult manifests a genetic disease, then altering his or her germ cells would not treat that disease, which would continue to affect the body cells; it would mean simply that the disease gene would not be passed on to offspring. It is incorrect to call this therapy — the aim is preventive, not therapeutic. The difficulties associated with altering the gametes or gonads of adults are enormous, to the point where few proponents of germ-line alteration consider this a viable option. Germ-line genetic alteration is much more complicated than somatic cell gene therapy. Whereas somatic cell gene therapy uses gene insertion, germ-line therapy would require gene replacement (which is not feasible in human beings at present) of all the germ cells affected. If a normal gene were simply inserted, without removing the defective gene, then the genetic disease could still be passed on to future generations.

Research with animals has demonstrated that inter-generational transmission of genetic information inserted into zygotes (so the gonads contain the altered gene) is possible.

> Genetic alteration intended to affect the germ line is both unnecessary and unwise.

However, the failure rate of insertion and transmission to offspring is high. Moreover, animal germ-line alteration is done for different purposes than human germ-line alteration would be. Germ-line genetic alteration in animal zygotes is not done to treat disease, but to create "transgenic" breeding lines of animals, either to establish an animal model of a human disease that will be inherited, enabling the production of animals that can be used in research, or to produce animals that make commercially valuable proteins. Neither of these purposes applies to human beings. At present, therefore, genetic alteration in human beings that affects the germ line is a wholly untested procedure. Moreover, as discussed in the next section, genetic alteration intended to affect the germ line is both unnecessary and unwise.

Issues in the Use of Germ-Line Genetic Alteration

Many of the issues raised by somatic cell gene therapy would also apply to germ-line genetic alteration — for example, requirements for informed consent and confidentiality. However, in addition, several unique and very troubling aspects of germ-line genetic alteration distinguish it from somatic cell gene therapy.

First, the risks associated with germ-line alteration are much greater than those surrounding somatic cell gene therapy. As we have seen, it is not possible to target an inserted gene precisely to a specific chromosomal site, raising the possibility that an inserted gene could interfere with other vital gene functions or even activate genes related to cancer development. The consequences of random insertion, while serious, are less severe in the case of somatic cell gene therapy, since a "mistake" would affect only a single target cell or tissue. In genetic alteration of the zygote, however, this "mistake" would be incorporated into most or all its cells.

Moreover, there is no reason to risk these consequences, for there is an easier and less risky alternative to treatment of the zygote. Treating a zygote at a stage when the germ line would be affected first requires determining which zygotes have a genetic disorder, which means that preimplantation diagnosis would have to be performed. It would therefore be possible not to transfer the zygotes found to be affected and to transfer only those found to be unaffected. Couples who are at risk of passing on a genetic disorder have a very good chance that at least one of their zygotes will not have the defective gene, although the exact odds depend on the kind of genetic disorder. (Recall that preimplantation diagnosis would be done on more than one zygote at a time, since multiple eggs would normally be retrieved for fertilization and preimplantation diagnosis during *in vitro* fertilization procedures.)

For example, if four eggs have been retrieved and fertilized *in vitro*, and if both parents are carriers of a recessive gene, then the odds are that three of the four zygotes tested by preimplantation diagnosis will turn out to be healthy and unaffected by the genetic disease. On average, one of the four zygotes will be diagnosed as having the genetic disease, but it does not have to be transferred to the woman's uterus; three healthy zygotes can be transferred, without any need for gene therapy. There is therefore no justification for performing gene therapy on affected zygotes when healthy zygotes can be obtained for transfer.

Similarly, if one parent has a dominant disorder, the odds are that two of four zygotes tested through preimplantation diagnosis will turn out to be healthy and so can be transferred without gene therapy. Even in the very rare instance that both parents have a dominant disorder, there is still a 25 percent chance of producing a healthy zygote.

Finally, if the genetic disease is X-linked, half the zygotes with a male chromosomal complement will be affected. Preimplantation diagnosis can be used to identify the female zygotes and the unaffected male zygotes, which will be healthy and can be transferred.

In all these cases, then, preimplantation diagnosis can be used to identify healthy zygotes for transfer. Hence, it is difficult to envision the real-world situations in which genetic alteration involving a zygote at an early enough stage of development to affect the germ line would be an appropriate response. Few couples are likely to prefer transfer of an altered zygote to not transferring those affected.

> It is difficult to envision the real-world situations in which genetic alteration involving a zygote at an early enough stage of development to affect the germ line would be an appropriate response.

The only situation in which preimplantation diagnosis could not be used to identify normal zygotes is if both members of the couple are affected by a recessive disorder (and are not just carriers of it). In this case, it is virtually certain that all their zygotes will be affected by the disease. This would be extremely rare, however, as the average incidence of a recessive disorder is 1 in 20 000. The random likelihood that two affected individuals would mate is therefore exceedingly small. Moreover, even if they do, if both are healthy and functional enough to achieve pregnancy, the condition affecting them cannot be among the most devastating of the genetic diseases. Indeed, such diseases are likely to be relatively mild (for example, deafness) and certainly not devastating enough to warrant attempting manipulation of the DNA of a zygote. Further, couples in this situation could also consider using donor gametes.

The same logic applies to the possibility, mentioned earlier, that germ-line genetic alteration could be applied to the gametes of an adult who is a carrier of a genetic disease. It is not currently feasible to perform genetic alteration of sperm or eggs. But, even if it were to become possible, in order to alter the carrier sperm the sperm carrying the disease would have to be distinguished from those that do not, or else *all* the sperm would have to be altered.

A misguided argument has been made that gene therapy on zygotes that also affects the germ line is desirable, even if other options are available to avoid or treat affected offspring, because it has the advantage of serving a preventive function, by reducing the transmission of genetic disease to future generations. Fetuses that have been treated by somatic cell gene therapy, or zygotes from high-risk couples that have been tested by preimplantation diagnosis and found normal, do not have a genetic disease, but some are still carriers of the disease and so risk passing it on to future generations. DNA alteration of such zygotes would eliminate the risk. (The same preventive argument is made for research into germ-line genetic alteration on adult gametes or gonads.)

For example, it has been argued that "society should pursue the development of strategies for preventing or correcting, at the germ-line level, genetic features that will lead to, or enhance, pathological conditions" as a way of ensuring that present and future couples can "exercise their rights to reproductive health."[7]

The idea of eliminating the risk of transmitting genetic disease may sound attractive, but it is in fact based on a misunderstanding of human genetics. All of us are carriers of various recessive genetic disorders — that is, we all carry genetic mutations that, if found in a double dose, could be deleterious, even fatal. To set as our aim the elimination of all risk of passing on genetic disease would involve genetic alteration of the gametes or gonads of all adults.

For example, if a recessive disorder occurs in 1 in 10 000 live births, which is relatively frequent for a recessive disorder, then approximately 1 individual in 50 is a carrier for that disorder, although that individual will be quite normal and healthy. To prevent this 1 in 10 000 chance of a recessive disorder, one would have to alter the DNA of 1 individual in 50 — and this would have to be done for all the hundreds of recessive single-gene disorders that exist.

The fact is that all human beings carry a few genes that would be deleterious if passed on to offspring in a double dose. The risk of passing on genetic disease is inherent in the human condition; it makes no sense to try to alter this in this way. Not only is the goal of a genetically "perfect" human being impossible to achieve, but human beings in all their diversity have value in themselves.

Moreover, even if it were feasible, it is not necessarily desirable from an evolutionary perspective. The fact that we all possess a certain amount of genetic mutation is what provides the reservoir for the species to adapt to changing environmental circumstances. The risks of genetic alteration of the germ line therefore do not affect just the individual involved. The human genome has evolved over millions of years, in complex and subtle homeostasis with the environment. For example, we know that having carriers of certain genetic disorders is beneficial to a population. The best-known example is the gene for sickle-cell anaemia, which provides greater resistance to malaria. Many other examples are suspected as well. We simply do not know enough to contemplate intentionally changing the human genome in the way required for a germ-line prevention program to have any appreciable effect.

It is important, however, not to exaggerate the possible impact of germ-line genetic alteration on the DNA of the species as a whole. Many medical treatments affect the

> The behaviour of humanity has always had consequences for the composition of the gene pool.

likelihood that particular genotypes will be passed on — it can be argued that the gene pool of the next generation is altered by any medical treatment or social support that allows people with a disease with a genetic component, who would formerly have died at an early age, to survive and reproduce. We do not withhold treatment of individuals for that reason. The behaviour of humanity has always had consequences for the composition of the gene pool. For example, technological innovation and cultural change affect the human gene pool. As one observer put it,

> ... it seems to me that the possibilities for what can be accomplished directly through genetic engineering are being exaggerated. After all, the human gene pool is enormous; there are over three billion human beings, and a large percentage of them at any given time are fertile. To effect a really significant change in a gene pool of that size through genetic engineering would call for delicate microsurgery on a lot of people. If we wanted to introduce far-reaching and practically irreversible changes into the shape of human life, we could do so far more effectively in the old-fashioned ways, by technological innovation and cultural change.[8]

It is nonetheless important to note that germ-line genetic alteration would be unique in that it involves intentional interference in human evolution. This imposes a greater responsibility to consider the impact of decisions regarding it on our species and on the interests of future generations.

Commissioners are of the opinion that the question of the impact of technology on future generations is one that touches on gene therapy, susceptibility testing, and other new reproductive technologies, and thus should be treated in a disciplined manner over the long term by setting up a framework to clarify what is prohibited, how activities will be regulated, and how decisions will be made.

It is nonetheless important to note that germ-line genetic alteration would be unique in that it involves intentional interference in human evolution. This imposes a greater responsibility to consider the impact of decisions regarding it on our species and on the interests of future generations.

Regulating Germ-Line Genetic Alteration

It is clear that germ-line genetic alteration is inconsistent with the Commission's guiding principles. There are many risks and potential harms, without any clear benefit to any individual. It is not an appropriate use of resources, and it jeopardizes, rather than protects, those who are vulnerable. Since any foreseeable germ-line genetic alteration would involve embryo research, it would be covered by the legislative and licensing mechanisms we propose in Chapter 22. However, we believe it is important to emphasize the unacceptability of germ-line genetic alteration by including it in the licensing conditions for infertility clinics, which in practice would be the source of human zygotes (or eggs) in Canada. The Commission therefore recommends that

> **269. No research involving alteration of the DNA of human zygotes be permitted or funded in Canada. This prohibition would be monitored and enforced by the Embryo Research Sub-Committee of the National Reproductive Technologies Commission.**

and that

> **270. The Prenatal Diagnosis and Genetics Sub-Committee of the National Reproductive Technologies Commission have as part of its guidelines for centres licensed to provide PND and genetics services that no genetic alteration of a human zygote be permitted.**

Non-Therapeutic Genetic Alteration

Genetic enhancement involves the attempt to enhance or improve an already healthy genetic structure by inserting a gene for "improvement." This non-therapeutic use of genetic technology might take the form of altering either somatic cells or germ cells.

Like gene therapy, the scope of genetic enhancement feasibility is quite narrow. Genetic alteration to improve complex human traits, such as beauty, intelligence, vigour, and longevity, is far beyond our technical capabilities and will be so for the foreseeable future. These complex traits are multifactorial in nature; that is, they are a function of complex interactions between genetic and environmental factors. As a result, enhancement of any particular gene is not likely to have the desired effect.

Genetic enhancement may be possible in principle for some simpler physical characteristics, such as height. However, the risks involved are totally disproportionate to any benefits that might be gained. These risks include not only all the risks discussed earlier with respect to somatic or germ-line gene alteration (such as inducing cancer), but others that are unique to genetic enhancement. As one scholar has commented,

> Any alteration or addition [to the normal genome] is likely to have deleterious, not beneficial results. Any gene acts on the background of many other genes that also have evolved over millennia.[9]

For example, although attempts to increase the size of mice by inserting growth hormone genes have succeeded in increasing their size, they have also led to a variety of deformities and functional disturbances.

Moreover, the motivation for non-therapeutic gene alteration requires close examination. Proponents argue that genetic enhancement is really no different from cosmetic surgery, and that the desire to improve oneself is natural and commendable. However, comparing enhancement genetics to cosmetic surgery or to other ways of helping individuals "make the best of themselves" is misleading and neglects the potential harms. We see three major types of risk in connection with genetic enhancement:[10]

- *Social risks*: A caring society values people for themselves and for their uniqueness. Our ethical principles tell us that all individuals should be valued equally. Genetic enhancement raises the prospect of a society where some people would be accepted only if they were "improved" — they would not be acceptable as themselves. This is a form of commodifying individuals — people are treated as things that can be changed according to someone else's notions of human perfection. This shows a lack of respect for human life and dignity and intolerance for human diversity, which is likely to lead to discrimination against and devaluing of certain categories of people. Any use of genetic enhancement raises troubling and potentially discriminatory judgements about what sorts of enhancement would be allowed and who would have access to them. In the case of gene therapy, the issue of who should receive the alteration is clear — those with a severe disease should be eligible for medical treatment. But in the case of genetic enhancement, the selection process, by definition, cannot be based on medical need. It must therefore be based on other, as yet unspecified, criteria. Would it be a lottery or, more likely, those most able to pay?

As there is no therapeutic objective, the goal of such alteration would be to pursue non-medical objectives, which might be economic, social, cultural, ethnic, or other. What are these objectives, and whose objectives are they? There is also the danger that people might be pressured to undergo such a procedure and be subject to discrimination if they refused. Finally, use of technology in this way might promote a social program of eugenics or indeed change our concept of what it is to be a human being.

- *Medical risks*: Many of the risks of cosmetic surgery are documented, but we do not know the risks of inserting genetic material, such as the risk of disrupting a tumour suppressor or activating a cancer-related gene.

- *Opportunity costs*: The non-therapeutic use of genetic alteration technology would draw away needed resources and skilled personnel from real medical problems. To allow DNA alteration in healthy individuals when there are so many other pressing calls on social attention and resources would be irresponsible and unethical.

The desire to improve the longevity, talents, and vigour of ourselves and our children is not inherently objectionable. However, this can best be achieved by improving the social and environmental factors that shape our daily lives — such as improved education or a healthier environment — rather than through the risky and potentially discriminatory use of genetic enhancement by those with the money or power to gain access to the technology.

In short, Commissioners find any non-therapeutic use of gene alteration unacceptable both in principle and in practice. It is not clear who would benefit or at what cost; there is the great risk of discriminatory use; and it is unacceptable to impose serious risks on healthy individuals for unclear benefit.

Our recommendations earlier in this chapter on somatic cell gene therapy have already made clear that research on genetic alteration in human beings is appropriate only for the treatment of serious diseases when no alternative treatment exists. Any non-therapeutic use of genetic alteration technology is also inconsistent with the existing MRC guidelines, which we have endorsed and supplemented with our recommendations.

It is extremely doubtful that any use of this technology for individual enhancement would ever be proposed by a genetics centre; but, if this ever did occur, the National Reproductive Technologies Commission would be able to turn down any such proposal.

It is important to remain vigilant about the possible misuse of technology that can change DNA, and it is important for the general public to become more aware of the issues it raises. Although these areas are outside our mandate, and the uses of genetic technology in general (for example, to "improve" individuals) are outside the span of new reproductive technologies and the National Reproductive Technologies Commission, we believe that a mechanism for keeping a watching brief on this area is desirable. Hence, we conclude that the National Council on Bioethics in Human Research (NCBHR) should consider this to be an area that warrants continued attention. The Commission recommends that

> **271. No research involving the alteration of DNA for enhancement purposes be permitted or funded in Canada. Proposals for any such project should be refused by the Medical Research Council national review committee on gene therapy.**

and that

> **272. The National Council on Bioethics in Human Research address the question of non-therapeutic genetic alteration and monitor developments in this field.**

Conclusion

The widespread and intense interest in all aspects of DNA technology that can alter genetic make-up includes both ardent hopes for the development of cures for severe, often fatal, genetic diseases and equally intense concerns about the potential abuses of science's increasing capacity for genetic manipulation. Our recommendations take into account the potential uses of these technologies in the context of human reproduction. Other applications of DNA technology are outside our mandate; we believe, however, that their implications for society warrant continued vigilance and public dialogue on whether and under what circumstances such applications might be permitted. This is why we have recommended that existing bodies charged with various review responsibilities maintain a watching brief and promote the necessary dialogue through publications, discussion papers, and other public education tools.   In addition, Commissioners believe that the current stage of development of DNA technology in Canada provides a unique window of opportunity for enlightened policy responses that, if adopted now, will help set the future course of how our new capacity to alter genetic make-up is used in this country.

With respect to both germ-line genetic alteration and enhancement genetics, Commissioners are of the opinion that the risks associated with any such research on human zygotes or human subjects are completely out of proportion to any potential benefits, and that publicly funded research of this type should not be conducted in Canada.

> With respect to both germ-line genetic alteration and enhancement genetics, Commissioners are of the opinion that the risks associated with any such research on human zygotes or human subjects are completely out of proportion to any potential benefits, and that publicly funded research of this type should not be conducted in Canada.

Somatic cell gene therapy in general is outside our mandate. Nevertheless, to ensure appropriate limits on those aspects of somatic cell gene therapy that are within our mandate (that is, its use in the reproductive context), and to ensure that such uses, if permitted, can be appropriately regulated, we believe that a broader approach is necessary. Only if a mechanism is in place to review all proposals for somatic cell gene therapy can we ensure that the oversight we recommend for prenatal or reproductive uses occurs.   This would mean that the following division of responsibilities should be in place with respect to somatic cell gene therapy:

- The Medical Research Council would continue to regulate human gene therapy research in general and immediately establish its recommended national review committee to review all proposals for somatic cell gene therapy research involving human subjects.

- Any proposal for the application of somatic cell gene therapy to fetuses would also be subject to approval by the Prenatal Diagnosis and Genetics Sub-Committee of the National Reproductive Technologies Commission.

- As part of its regulation of research involving human zygotes, the National Reproductive Technologies Commission would prohibit any genetic alteration of human zygotes, as such alteration may affect the germ line.

- The National Council on Bioethics in Human Research would address the question of the use of DNA technology that alters genetic make-up (for example, non-therapeutic uses or "preventive" uses) with respect to the ethical and social implications, including consideration of the interests of future generations.

We believe that this division of responsibilities will serve Canadians well, now and in the future, with regard to DNA technology that alters genetic make-up, both by overseeing present-day research and by stimulating an informed and reasoned public debate about any future uses of DNA alteration technology in health care, or indeed any other use that is proposed.

General Sources

Prior, L. "Somatic and Germ Line Gene Therapy: Current Status and Prospects." In Research Volumes of the Royal Commission on New Reproductive Technologies, 1993.

Specific References

1. The first administration of genetically altered material into human beings occurred in 1980. However, this experiment was premature and not an approved clinical trial. It was quickly stopped, and the researcher was censured. A voluntary moratorium was in effect regarding human gene therapy between 1980 and 1990, although laboratory and animal research continued.

2. Adapted from "Human Gene Transfer/Therapy Patient Registry — Summary." *Human Gene Therapy* 3 (6)(December 1992), p. 729.

3. Walters, L. "Human Gene Therapy: Ethics and Public Policy." *Human Gene Therapy* 2 (2)(Summer 1991), p. 117.

4. Angier, N. "Many Americans Say Genetic Information Is Public Property." *New York Times*, September 29, 1992.

5. Blaese, R.M. "Development of Gene Therapy for Immunodeficiency: Adenosine Deaminase Deficiency." *Pediatric Research* 33 (Suppl.)(1)(1993): 49-55.

6. Medical Research Council of Canada. *Guidelines for Research on Somatic Cell Gene Therapy in Humans*. Ottawa: Minister of Supply and Services Canada, 1990.

7. Zimmerman, B.K. "Human Germ-Line Therapy: The Case for Its Development and Use." *Journal of Medicine and Philosophy* 16 (1991), p. 593.

8. Porter, J. "What Is Morally Distinctive About Genetic Engineering." *Human Gene Therapy* 1 (4)(Winter 1990), p. 423.

9. Prior, L. "Somatic and Germ Line Gene Therapy: Current Status and Prospects." In Research Volumes of the Royal Commission on New Reproductive Technologies, 1993.

10. For an exploration of these issues, see Anderson, W.F. "The First Signs of Danger." *Human Gene Therapy* 3 (4)(1992): 359-60.

Judicial Intervention in Pregnancy and Birth

The use of legislation and court decisions to control a pregnant woman's behaviour in situations where a fetus is thought to be at risk* — that is, judicial intervention in pregnancy and birth — provides an example of how technological developments can raise new ethical issues for society. The increasing incidence of judicial intervention has occurred in part because recent technological and medical developments have contributed to the ability to visualize, and hence to conceptualize, the fetus as an entity separate from the pregnant woman.

Technology, by enabling us to "see" the fetus, in particular through clearer and more detailed ultrasound images, provides a graphic depiction of the fetus that was previously not possible. Other medical technologies have reinforced this impression among medical practitioners and in society generally: prenatal diagnosis contributes to the perception of the fetus as a separate being with a specific medical condition that can be detected before birth; the ability to sustain newborns of lower and lower birth weight outside the womb changes perceptions of a fetus at the same stage of development *in utero*; and the emerging capacity to perform fetal surgery for certain conditions reinforces the view of the fetus as a separate patient. This new way of conceptualizing the fetus is even apparent in popular media images and illustrations portraying the fetus as an isolated entity suspended in an unidentifiable medium — seldom acknowledging the presence of the pregnant woman's body, without which the fetus cannot exist.

---

* Legislation and policies that apply specifically to pregnant women and women of childbearing age in the workplace (for example, exclusionary or protectionist laws and policies concerned with exposure to harmful substances in the workplace), while relevant to our mandate, are covered in Chapter 13, "Exposure to Harmful Agents in the Workplace and the Environment and Infertility."

The tendency to see the fetus as a separate entity is evident in a good deal of legislative and judicial activity in jurisdictions across North America. Although this is more evident in the United States, the tendency exists in Canada as well. The province of New Brunswick has extended its child protection law to include the fetus in its definition of "child," and in 1989 the Law Reform Commission of Canada proposed a new category of "crimes against the fetus." In one reported Canadian case, a woman was required to undergo a Caesarian section considered necessary for the health of the fetus, and in another a woman who was 8-1/2 months pregnant was ordered to remain in a hospital ward until she had given birth. A woman's consumption of alcohol during pregnancy was also characterized by a court as physical abuse — in other words, existing child welfare legislation was construed to apply to the fetus. (See box for developments in the United States.)

**Judicial Intervention in Pregnancy and Birth:
Recent Developments in the United States**

One major area of legislative activity in the United States involves the extension or creation of criminal offences to deal with the infliction of harm on a fetus. General homicide provisions have been extended to include the unlawful killing of a viable fetus, and a new offence of "feticide" has been created in several states. As well, offences relating to fetal abuse or neglect have been developed, including the offence of failure to provide the necessities of life, such as food and medical care, to a child conceived but not yet born. As an indication of the degree to which the criminal law is being employed in this context, the American Civil Liberties Association reported that in the first six months of 1990, South Carolina prosecuted 18 women for criminal neglect arising out of drug use during pregnancy.

Another use of the criminal law involves the sentencing of pregnant women who are charged with offences to "protective" incarceration in the belief that prison would provide a safer environment for their fetuses. Women who have been convicted of child abuse or related offences have also been ordered to use contraceptives or offered sterilization as a condition of probation.

In addition to the use of the criminal law, judicial intervention in the United States has taken the form of forced blood transfusions over the religious objections of a pregnant woman in the interests of the fetus, and court-ordered Caesarian sections. Advance directives declining medical treatment in case of supervening incompetence ("living wills") have been deemed to be of no force and effect during pregnancy. As well, courts have suggested that a child could sue the mother for damages arising as a result of the mother's actions during pregnancy.

Changing ideas about the fetus, fostered by technological development, have the potential for both positive and negative consequences. On the positive side, for example, society has become increasingly aware of the effects on the health of the fetus of nutrition and tobacco and alcohol use during pregnancy. Information gained through prenatal diagnosis can allow fetuses with certain anomalies to be treated at birth, and, in much rarer cases, treatment prenatally can lead to the birth of a healthier child.

At the same time, society must be aware of the ethical and legal difficulties inherent in regarding the fetus as a patient who is separate from the pregnant woman. Considering the interests of the fetus in isolation from those of the woman has the potential to establish adversary relationships that, at their extreme, can lead to efforts to force the pregnant woman to act in the interests of this "separate patient." This may mean that a woman's right not to be subject to unwanted interference with her physical integrity is taken away from her, with serious implications not just for that woman, but for all women who become pregnant.

Judicial intervention tends to occur when the ethic of care has broken down — situations that the Commission seeks to prevent. What should society do to protect the fetus? Should it empower the courts to over-ride a pregnant woman's refusal of health care? Should it enact legislation of some kind? Or are other measures more appropriate? In the next few pages we consider the issues raised by judicial intervention in pregnancy and birth. We outline the views of Canadians and discuss the issues from both a legal and an ethical perspective, with a view to reaching conclusions and recommendations that reinforce or re-establish the ethic of care in such cases.

Judicial Intervention Defined

Our mandate directed us to examine "judicial interventions during gestation and birth." This examination involved considering how legislation and court decisions are or may be used to control a pregnant woman's behaviour. Such judicial intervention usually occurs when a woman is believed to be endangering the fetus she is carrying by refusing medical treatment believed necessary for fetal health, by abusing drugs or alcohol, or by engaging in behaviour such as prostitution. The matter is typically brought before the courts by a children's aid society, a health care facility, or, in some cases, a physician.

Judicial interventions during gestation and birth can take several forms. Canadian courts, for example, have ordered pregnant women to refrain from specified behaviours and to undergo certain medical procedures considered necessary for the health of the fetus. (See box for how Canadian law has been used as the basis for judicial intervention.) U.S. courts have issued similar directives, ordering women to engage or not to engage in certain behaviours during pregnancy, to undergo Caesarian section and other medical treatment, and to be incarcerated until they had given birth.

Judicial Intervention in Canada

Several legal avenues have been used to justify judicial intervention in pregnancy and birth, but most cases have involved child welfare law. These cases are considered by many legal scholars to be exceptional, and the use of the law for this purpose has been heavily criticized. If such uses continue to be repeated in future, they will no doubt give rise to court challenges under the *Canadian Charter of Rights and Freedoms*.

In *Re Children's Aid Society for the District of Kenora and J.L.*, the Ontario Provincial Court ordered Crown wardship of a child born suffering from fetal alcohol syndrome. The Court held that the child was "in need of protection," within the meaning of the provincial child welfare act, both *prior to* and after its birth, on the grounds that the mother's excessive consumption of alcohol during pregnancy constituted physical abuse of the child and that her refusal to seek treatment during pregnancy endangered the child's health. Although the apprehension occurred after birth, this case is significant in its characterization of prenatal abuse and in its finding that existing child welfare legislation could be construed to apply to a fetus.

Another case had a different outcome. In *Re A. (in utero)*, which involved an application for Crown wardship of a fetus, an interim order was sought subjecting the fetus to the supervision of the Children's Aid Society. The terms of the order would have required the mother to submit to prenatal medical supervision or, in the event of her refusal, to be detained in hospital until the birth of the child and undergo all medical procedures deemed necessary for the well-being of the fetus. The court noted that the Society had legitimate concerns for the welfare of the fetus, but it refused the application on the basis that Ontario's child welfare legislation does not accord a fetus the right to protection. The court also held that its *parens patriae* jurisdiction did not authorize judicial intervention on behalf of the fetus, stating:

> ... here the child is actually inside of the mother. It is, therefore, impossible in this case to take steps to protect the child without ultimately forcing the mother, under restraint if necessary, to undergo medical treatment and other processes, against her will. I believe that the *parens patriae* jurisdiction is just not broad enough to envisage the forcible confinement of a parent as a necessary incident of its exercise. Even if it were, however, the court should be very wary about using its powers in such instances, as its routine exercise could possibly lead to some abuse of pregnant mothers.

The criminal law has also been used as a basis for judicial intervention.

(continued in next box)

Judicial Intervention in Canada (*continued*)
Canadian Cases

Criminal Law
The criminal law was used to intervene in pregnancy in *R. v. McKenzie*, a case where a pregnant woman was convicted of communicating for the purpose of prostitution and failing to appear in court. The judge stated "... the only way to protect this child is to have this child born in custody ..." Accordingly, he sentenced the woman to 60 days in jail and ordered that she remain in a hospital ward until the child was born.

Constitutional Issues
Constitutional arguments have been raised in only one reported Canadian case of judicial intervention. *Joe v. Director of Family and Children's Services* involved an appeal of an order made under the Yukon *Children's Act*. The act provides that where a fetus is subject to a serious risk of fetal alcohol syndrome or other injury as a result of a pregnant woman's use of addictive or intoxicating substances, a judge can order the woman to participate in supervision or counselling. The court concluded that the section interfered with the pregnant woman's right to liberty under section 7 of the Charter and that the term "fetal alcohol syndrome" was so vague as to result in a lack of substantive fairness. Because Ms. Joe had complied with the order by the time of the appeal, however, this issue was moot.

Few cases have reached the courts in Canada, because the women most likely to encounter this situation are often in no position to resist and therefore they comply with the wishes of a physician or child welfare authority. An examination of the cases that have been reported shows that the women most likely to be subjected to judicial intervention are disproportionately poor, Aboriginal, or members of a racial or ethnic minority — all factors that influence their capacity to resist intervention. Whether overt discrimination is at work or whether the life circumstances of these women are such that their behaviour during pregnancy is more likely to come under scrutiny is difficult to disentangle.

Judicial intervention is an issue for all women in Canada, however, regardless of socioeconomic status, because its implications go beyond the consequences for an individual woman; it is an issue for women more generally if becoming pregnant means that they waive the constitutional protections afforded other citizens.

The Views of Canadians

An understanding of these issues was evident in the testimony Commissioners heard. It was clear, for example, that Canadians are aware of the difficult situations that give rise to attempts at judicial intervention and would like to find a way of responding to these situations that is respectful of women's autonomy and constitutional rights while also providing the means to demonstrate concern for at-risk fetuses. Thus, we heard from Canadians both a concern that women not be coerced or their rights infringed and a concern for society's responsibilities in relation to the well-being of the fetus. The Commission also heard thoughtful recommendations about what society's response should be in these situations.

The Canadian Bar Association, for example, stated that "The fetus should be protected by the provision of medical, social, and educational services to pregnant women and to women at risk generally in society." In a similar vein, the British Columbia Association of Social Workers wrote,

> Any state efforts to protect the fetus must recognize that the well-being of the fetus is best protected by ensuring pregnant women have adequate socio-economic resources. This means social programs and social policies should attend to the well-being of women before, during and after pregnancy. The conditions of pregnant women's lives cannot be ignored in the context of society's compelling interest in fetal well-being. *(Brief to the Commission from the British Columbia Association of Social Workers, February 1991.)*

The Manitoba Association for Childbirth and Family Education summed up the concerns of many witnesses:

> [We] would certainly agree that women who are willingly pregnant have a moral obligation to safeguard their unborn babies to the best of their ability. However, we feel that judicial intervention in pregnancy and childbirth is a very poor way to achieve this ... [P]unishing a woman for abusing drugs, failing to get medical attention or otherwise endangering her fetus places all the responsibility for the well-being of the unborn on the shoulders of the mother without offering any concrete support to her. A punitive approach doesn't address the poverty or social problems which may have created the abusive situation [in the first place]. *(A. Basham, Manitoba Association for Childbirth and Family Education Inc., Public Hearings Transcripts, Winnipeg, Manitoba, October 23, 1990.)*

Legal Issues*

Much of the recent debate about judicial intervention has centred on the legal status and rights of the individuals involved and the status of the fetus. Two points are particularly relevant. First, under Canadian law, a fetus does not have independent legal or constitutional rights; whether we look at Anglo-Canadian common law or Quebec civil law, a human being

---

* See Annex for dissenting opinion.

does not acquire legal rights until he or she is born alive. It follows that a third party cannot volunteer to defend the "rights" of a being that has no legal existence.

Second, women have constitutionally protected rights to equality, liberty, and security of the person, as well as the right to refuse medical treatment. These constitutional rights of women, which are set out in the *Canadian Charter of Rights and Freedoms* and interpreted through court decisions, are fundamental to human dignity and autonomy, for they are basic concepts in human rights. Like other women and men, pregnant women therefore have a constitutional right to refuse unwanted medical treatment or control that threatens their bodily integrity or interferes with their ability to make independent decisions about their medical care.

It follows that compelling a pregnant woman to conform to certain standards of behaviour, or requiring her to undergo surgery or other invasive procedures, would constitute an unacceptable violation of her individual rights and her equality rights. It would also have adverse effects on the rights of women generally in Canadian society by imposing on pregnant women a standard of behaviour not required of any other member of society. As the Supreme Court of Canada has confirmed, discrimination on the basis of pregnancy constitutes sex discrimination.

Permitting judicial intervention therefore has serious implications for the autonomy of individual women and for the status of women collectively in our society. All individuals have the right to make personal decisions, to control their bodily integrity, and to refuse unwanted medical treatment. These are not mere legal technicalities; they represent some of the most deeply held values in society and form the basis for fundamental and constitutional human rights.

> Permitting judicial intervention therefore has serious implications for the autonomy of individual women and for the status of women collectively in our society.

A person can be found mentally incompetent to make these decisions under provincial mental health laws only in a very narrow range of circumstances; drug and alcohol addiction (whether during pregnancy or not) would rarely, if ever, qualify as such a circumstance. The use of mental health legislation to commit or treat a pregnant woman against her will, even where the language of the statute appears to be applicable, would clearly offend Charter principles.

Moreover, the legal consequence of being found mentally incompetent is simply the appointment of a legal guardian to make decisions on one's behalf. That guardian must, in all cases, make those decisions in the best interests of the incompetent person in question, and not in the perceived best interests of some third party, such as the state or the fetus.

As numerous intervenors pointed out in their testimony before the Commission, women do not give up their right to control their own bodies or to determine the course of their medical treatment just because they are pregnant. A woman has the right to make her own choices, whether they are good or bad, because it is the woman whose body and health are affected, the woman who must live with her decision, and the woman who must bear the consequences of that decision for the rest of her life. In this respect, pregnant women are no different from any other responsible individual; to treat pregnant women differently from other women and men, or to impose a different standard of behaviour on them, is neither morally nor legally defensible.

Canadian Case Law: The Status of the Fetus

In its 1989 decision in *Tremblay v. Daigle*, the Supreme Court of Canada held that the fetus is not a legal person under Quebec civil law, the Anglo-Canadian common law, or the Quebec *Charter of Human Rights and Freedoms*. The Court also rejected the argument that the potential father had the right to veto the pregnant woman's decision with respect to the fetus, or that a parent or third party could volunteer to defend the rights of the fetus, which has no legal existence.

In considering the general issue of fetal rights, the Court stated that "A foetus would appear to be a paradigmatic example of a being whose alleged rights would be inseparable from the rights of others, and in particular, from the rights of the woman carrying the foetus." In its subsequent decision in *R. v. Sullivan and Lemay*, the Court also held that the fetus is not a person for purposes of the *Criminal Code*.

In its decision in *Borowski v. Attorney General of Canada*, the Saskatchewan Court of Appeal held that the fetus is not protected under section 7 of the Charter and so does not enjoy a constitutional right to "life, liberty and security of the person." The U.S. Supreme Court came to a similar decision under the U.S. *Bill of Rights*. Legal recognition of the fetus has also been rejected in Britain and Australia and under the *European Convention*.

The Ethical View

The Commission's position on judicial intervention in pregnancy and birth, while consistent with the legal and constitutional considerations just described, relies primarily on our ethical stance and guiding principles, which we have applied throughout our report and in our recommendations. Although many legal and constitutional arguments can be made, our conclusions with respect to judicial intervention

> Although many legal and constitutional arguments can be made, our conclusions with respect to judicial intervention rest largely on our ethical reasoning.

rest largely on our ethical reasoning. In our view, it is ethically (as well as legally) wrong to suggest that pregnant women's rights to make decisions about their medical care and treatment should be changed or lessened because they are pregnant.

Canadian Case Law: The Rights of Pregnant Women

In its 1988 decision in *R. v. Morgentaler*, the Supreme Court of Canada ruled that, by interfering with their bodily integrity and subjecting them to serious psychological stress, the abortion provisions of the *Criminal Code* (section 251) violated women's rights to liberty and security of the person. The Court found that the abortion provisions impaired women's rights under the *Canadian Charter of Rights and Freedoms* (section 7) and could not be seen as "reasonable limits" that are "demonstrably justified in a free and democratic society" (section 1).

In her decision, Justice Wilson characterized section 251 as a violation of pregnant women's constitutional rights on the basis that "In essence, what [the section] does is assert the woman's capacity to reproduce is not to be subject to her own control. It is to be subject to the control of the state. She may not choose whether to exercise her existing capacity or not to exercise it. This is not, in my view, just a matter of interfering with her liberty in the sense ... of her right to personal autonomy in decision making, it is a direct interference with her physical 'person' as well. She is truly being treated as a means — a means to an end which she does not desire but over which she has no control."

In its 1989 decision in *Brooks v. Canada Safeway Ltd.*, the Supreme Court also ruled that discrimination based on pregnancy constitutes sex discrimination, which is prohibited under federal and provincial human rights law and under the Charter. In his judgement, Chief Justice Dickson asserted that "it is difficult to conceive that distinctions or discriminations based upon pregnancy could ever be regarded as other than discrimination based upon sex."

Consistent with the ethic of care — which is concerned with preventing conflicts instead of trying to resolve them after they arise — we begin by asking questions about how to ensure the best possible prenatal health and the maximum degree of well-being for both the pregnant woman and the fetus. Regardless of whether a fetus is a "person" with "rights," it is clear that the interests of the fetus are worthy of protection: what transpires before birth — the behaviour of the woman during pregnancy, the provision of medical treatment to her and to the fetus — can seriously affect the health and well-being of the child that is eventually born. Society therefore has an interest in promoting the prenatal health and well-being of the fetus and of the woman carrying it.

From the woman's perspective, however, considering the interests of her fetus separately from her own has the potential to create adversary situations with negative consequences for her autonomy and bodily integrity, for her relationship with her partner, and for her relationship with her physician. Judicial intervention is bound to precipitate crisis and conflict, instead of preventing them through support and care. It also ignores the basic components of women's fundamental human rights — the right to bodily integrity, and the right to equality, privacy, and dignity. Importantly, as we will see, such measures are also unlikely to be effective and may not in fact protect the fetus.

If we impose a legal obligation upon a woman to care for her fetus — even if it were possible to legislate a caring and nurturing relationship — the potential for curtailing women's choices and behaviour becomes staggering. The kinds of substances and activities that could pose a danger to the fetus are many, varied, and increasing: cigarettes, alcohol, drugs (both legal and illegal), environmental pollutants, strenuous exercise, saunas, and inadequate nutrition. As scientific knowledge develops, the list is becoming longer. Many women's management of pregnancy could be subject to challenge and scrutiny, and pregnancy could become the source of potential liability suits against women who failed to comply with certain standards of behaviour. In some cases, fearing a less-than-perfect outcome, a pregnant woman might feel compelled to seek abortion instead of care.

> [There are] questions about the relationship of the pregnant woman to the fetus. That relationship should, surely, be regarded as being different, both legally and morally, from the relationship of the health care facility, of reproductive researchers, and of corporations, to the fetus. When the fetus is within the woman's body, the maternal/fetal relationship may arguably be regarded as a unity, and the competent woman's informed decisions about the fetus and her pregnancy should prevail ... the goal should be to protect and enhance the health of both the fetus and the pregnant woman without infringing upon the woman's reproductive autonomy. Ensuring that a child does not suffer from events that occurred while it was a fetus need not require treating the fetus as a patient, or according the fetus a status independent of the pregnant woman.
>
> *C. Overall, reviewer, research volumes of the Commission, August 19, 1992.*

Moreover, the threat of judicial intervention could have significant negative effects on fetal and maternal health. If women knew that they could be confined against their will, forced to submit to medical treatment, or charged with criminal offences, they might well avoid seeking medical care. Unfortunately, those who might avoid seeking care would likely be those who need it most — for example, women who are dependent on drugs or alcohol. As a result, health problems would escape detection and treatment — precisely the opposite effect sought by those who would use judicial means to intervene.

Physicians and Judicial Intervention

Several professional associations have prepared reports concerning a physician's responsibility to a pregnant woman and her fetus. The Royal College of Physicians and Surgeons of Canada has suggested that where the physician's view of what is in the best interests of the fetus conflicts with the view of the pregnant woman, the role of the physician is to provide counselling and persuasion, but not coercion.

The American College of Obstetricians and Gynecologists has also taken the position that it is important for the physician to avoid a coercive role, noting that coercion violates the principle of informed consent and threatens the doctor/patient relationship. The College concludes that resort to the courts is counterproductive and almost never warranted. The American Medical Association has reached similar conclusions and has also suggested that criminal sanctions or civil liability for behaviour by a pregnant woman that could be harmful to the fetus are inappropriate.

The resort to judicial intervention also has serious implications for the relationship between a pregnant woman and her physician. If the physician is perceived to be potentially coercive instead of a caregiver, the woman might begin to withhold information or stop seeking prenatal care, with detrimental consequences for her health and that of the fetus. These dangers are recognized by many professional associations of physicians. Moreover, experience with judicial intervention has shown the uncertainties inherent in diagnosis and treatment; in several cases of judicial intervention, the medical treatment deemed essential by the courts later turned out not to have been necessary. For example, a woman who went into hiding in defiance of a court order to undergo a Caesarian section later gave birth vaginally to a healthy child. Thus, medical and judicial judgements — even those made with the best of intentions — can be mistaken. In addition, the very limited time frame within which most such decisions must be made and acted upon makes the process of judicial intervention unlikely to lead to fully considered, principled, or constitutional conclusions.

Finally, judicial intervention both emerges from and reinforces a social perception of the role of women in reproduction that instrumentalizes them and devalues their humanity and individuality. At the core of the impulse toward judicial intervention in pregnancy and birth is the view that pregnant women are the means to an end — the birth of healthy children. To the extent that judicial intervention reinforces the notion that a pregnant woman's role is only to carry and deliver a healthy child, it denies her existence as an autonomous individual with legal and constitutional rights and is dangerous to the rights and autonomy of all women.

In summary, judicial intervention offers no satisfactory answer to ensuring the well-being of the fetus: it precipitates crisis and conflict, it ignores women's fundamental constitutional and human rights, it contributes to an instrumentalized view of their role in reproduction — with adverse consequences for women individually and as a group — and, most important, it is not effective in achieving its goal of protecting fetal well-being.

Society cannot care for a fetus, in the absence of the pregnant woman's cooperation, without taking control of the woman herself.   The physical relationship between the fetus and the pregnant woman and the dependency of the fetus on the pregnant

Judicial intervention offers no satisfactory answer to ensuring the well-being of the fetus: it precipitates crisis and conflict, it ignores women's fundamental constitutional and human rights, it contributes to an instrumentalized view of their role in reproduction — with adverse consequences for women individually and as a group — and, most important, it is not effective in achieving its goal of protecting fetal well-being.

North American Case Law: Right to Refuse Medical Treatment

The right of individuals to have control over their own bodies is a longstanding principle of Canadian law. An important aspect of this principle is the right to refuse unwanted medical treatment. This right is set out clearly under the Quebec *Civil Code*, as discussed in the 1992 Nancy B. case, which held that a patient has the right to refuse respiratory support. This principle is also protected under Anglo-Canadian common law, as discussed in the 1990 *Malette v. Shulman* case.

In the 1991 case of *Fleming v. Reid*, involving involuntary psychiatric patients, the Ontario Court of Appeal held that the right to be free from non-consensual invasions of one's bodily integrity and to make decisions with respect to one's medical treatment are also protected under section 7 of the Charter.

In its 1990 decision in *In re A.C.*, the District of Columbia Court of Appeals discussed the specific situation of pregnant women in the following terms: "[I]t would be an extraordinary case indeed in which a court might ever be justified in overriding the patient's wishes and authorizing a major surgical procedure such as a caesarean section ... Indeed, some may doubt that there could ever be a situation extraordinary or compelling enough to justify a massive intrusion into a person's body, such as a caesarean section, against that person's will."

Any limits imposed on the rights of pregnant women to refuse unwanted medical treatment would amount to a violation not only of their right to security of the person under section 7 of the Charter, but also, in accordance with the Supreme Court of Canada decision in *Brooks v. Canada Safeway Ltd.*, of their right to sex equality under section 15.

woman for sustenance make this impossible. By forcing medical intervention, society would be requiring pregnant women to do something that is asked of no other individual: to undergo medical treatment for the benefit of another. Even a living child has no right to force a parent to undergo medical procedures for the child's benefit, however morally compelling the case might be. This infringement of bodily autonomy and physical integrity is not justified on any grounds.

This imperative will not change even as research pushes the boundaries of what can be done to treat a fetus *in utero*. For example, if and when surgery on a fetus moves beyond the research stage for a range of conditions, there may be increasing pressure on pregnant women to consent to such procedures. Whether these techniques remain experimental or move into the realm of accepted practice, they must be offered only in the context of the ethical and legal considerations set out in this chapter — that is, in the context of the pregnant woman's autonomy and with her informed consent, based on full knowledge of the nature and risks of the proposed treatment.

An Approach Based on Support and Care

If we reject judicial intervention in pregnancy and birth on moral, practical, and legal grounds, we must return to the question of how to ensure the health and well-being of the fetus and the pregnant woman. How should society respond to a situation where a woman is not caring for her fetus or engaging in behaviour that may harm it? In the Commission's view, the answer lies in examining the reasons for that behaviour and seeking solutions that address them.

Some of the situations that give rise to attempts at judicial intervention are among the most difficult and tragic imaginable. The potential for harm is evident; the dangers to a fetus of alcohol abuse, drug addiction, or sexually transmitted diseases are real and potentially devastating. These situations are all the more distressing because the caring and nurturing assumed to be inherent in the relationship between woman and fetus appear to be absent.

Although many cases involving refusal to follow medical advice or to accept surgical or other medical treatment have involved drug or alcohol abuse, a woman's reasons for choosing a particular course of action may include her socioeconomic circumstances, her educational level, her religious convictions, her cultural beliefs, her fears, or other deeply held values or personal beliefs. Of relevance in this regard is the fact that most of the women who have been subject to judicial intervention to date have been Aboriginal women and women of colour.

Whatever the circumstances, judicial intervention does not provide a solution, because it does nothing to address the circumstances that bring about attempts to intervene or to create the social conditions and support that help to ensure a successful pregnancy and healthy outcome for both the woman and the child.

In reaching this conclusion, Commissioners are acutely aware of the tragic nature of some of the situations that give rise to efforts to intervene in a pregnancy. As members of the

> Whatever the circumstances, judicial intervention does not provide a solution, because it does nothing to address the circumstances that bring about attempts to intervene or to create the social conditions and support that help to ensure a successful pregnancy and healthy outcome for both the woman and the child.

helping professions, physicians and child welfare workers face situations that call on their basic human instinct to help where possible — an impulse that is rightly very difficult to resist because it is so fundamental to who they are and the job they do. The decision to respect a woman's autonomy and physical integrity and not to intervene must surely be one of the most difficult decisions any human being would ever be called upon to make. That is why the Commissioners' decision in this matter was reached through long and careful deliberation and consideration of the issues from all sides. We made this decision not because harm to a fetus is acceptable or even tolerable, but because the dangers posed by judicial intervention far outweigh any benefits that a given individual intervention might yield.

In line with the ethic of care, we believe that the best approach is to seek ways to ensure that the needs of both the woman and the fetus are met — in other words, to prevent a situation developing in which child welfare, medical, or other authorities might consider judicial intervention appropriate or necessary. The ethic of care offers a means of avoiding the conflicts inherent in judicial

> A societal interest in pregnancy and birth — to maximize the chances for the birth of a healthy child — is a goal Commissioners strongly endorse; it is an important and worthy goal. But our examination of the legal, ethical, and social implications of judicial intervention leads to the inescapable conclusion that judicial intervention is neither an acceptable nor an effective method of achieving that goal.

intervention by promoting two fundamental values: respect for the rights and autonomy of the pregnant woman and concern for the health and well-being of the fetus. The best way to accomplish this is not by compelling pregnant women to behave in certain ways, but by providing a supportive and caring environment in which they can make informed decisions and choose from among realistic options before and during pregnancy.

The situations that lead to judicial intervention are inherently distressing because of the commitment we, as a society and as individuals, have to respect human life and dignity — the life and dignity of the pregnant woman, expressed through her autonomy, and that of the fetus, as a potential person. Judicial intervention sacrifices the human dignity

and rights of one for the
potential well-being of the other.
Taking the alternative route of
care and assistance means that
the human life and dignity of
both woman and fetus are
respected — and it may even
accomplish what legislation or
court decisions cannot:
establish a caring and nurturing
relationship.

Taking the alternative route of care
and assistance means that the human
life and dignity of both woman and
fetus are respected — and it may even
accomplish what legislation or court
decisions cannot: establish a caring
and nurturing relationship.

Clearly, the vast majority of women will act in a way they believe to be
in the best interests of their fetus. The best way to promote prenatal health
is therefore to provide the information and support necessary to enable
pregnant women to make healthy choices for the well-being of themselves
and their fetuses and informing them — in non-coercive, non-judgemental
ways — about the implications of their decisions. This includes providing
safe and accessible contraception and abortion services; offering accessible
and culturally appropriate prenatal care and social services to pregnant
women; counselling pregnant women about healthy lifestyles and ensuring
they have the means to make these choices, including financial assistance
where necessary; and providing information, outreach, and supports in the
forms pregnant women need to make informed choices and realistic
decisions about care and treatment, particularly for addictions.

The Canadian Bar Association pointed out, in its brief to the
Commission, that recourse to judicial intervention should be seen as a
failure — a failure to provide policies and programs that sustain a woman's
right to manage her pregnancy and to support her decisions with
appropriate services and resources in the community. By itself, prohibiting
judicial intervention does not fulfil our responsibility as a society to
promote the health and well-being of pregnant women. Meeting this
responsibility also requires appropriate programs, services, and outreach
designed specifically to support pregnant women who are in the difficult
circumstances we have outlined. This is not the case at present. In fact,
overall, the behaviour that attracts judicial intervention may be less
threatening to fetal and neonatal health than the well-documented effects
of poverty on a much larger number of pregnancies.

As we discuss in Chapter 14, a variety of appropriately designed
supportive programs for pregnant women can at the same time help to
ensure the well-being of the fetus. In particular, with respect to pregnant
women who endanger the health of their fetuses by using alcohol or drugs,
the Board of Trustees of the American Medical Association has
recommended that "[p]regnant substance abusers should be provided with
rehabilitative treatment appropriate to their specific physiological and
psychological needs." Similar conclusions have been reached by this
Commission and by others studying the problem of drug use during
pregnancy. What is required is ready access to facilities and services that

provide outreach, counselling, and treatment designed specifically for pregnant women that are appropriate to their needs.

Conclusion and Recommendations

In summary, trying to use the law and the courts to protect fetal health can only be counterproductive. Such laws may, on the surface, have appeal, because we all support the goal of the well-being of the fetus, and enacting them may appear to be a logical extension of society's interest in the health of the fetus. But there is nothing in our experience to demonstrate that such laws work in practice. Indeed, there is strong evidence to the contrary, particularly because the instruments available to the courts — forcing action under penalty of fines or incarceration — are brutally blunt and patently unsuited to the goal of promoting anyone's health or well-being. Clearly, if protecting the fetus is the goal, other methods are needed.

A societal interest in pregnancy and birth — to maximize the chances for the birth of a healthy child — is a goal Commissioners strongly endorse; it is an important and worthy goal. But our examination of the legal, ethical, and social implications of judicial intervention leads to the inescapable conclusion that judicial intervention is neither an acceptable nor an effective method of achieving that goal. Because the woman's consent and cooperation are needed to ensure a positive outcome for the fetus, it follows that the most effective way of caring for the fetus is through appropriate support and caring for the pregnant woman. The Commission therefore recommends that

> **273. Judicial intervention in pregnancy and birth not be permissible. Specifically, the Commission recommends that**
> **(a) medical treatment never be imposed upon a pregnant woman against her wishes;**
> **(b) the criminal law, or any other law, never be used to confine or imprison a pregnant woman in the interests of her fetus;**
> **(c) the conduct of a pregnant woman in relation to her fetus not be criminalized;**
> **(d) child welfare or other legislation never be used to control a woman's behaviour during pregnancy or birth; and**
> **(e) civil liability never be imposed upon a woman for harm done to her fetus during pregnancy.**

274. Unwanted medical treatment and other interferences, or threatened interferences, with the physical autonomy of pregnant women be recognized explicitly under the *Criminal Code* as criminal assault.

and that

275. All provinces/territories ensure that they have in place
  (a) information and education programs directed to pregnant women so that they do not inadvertently put a fetus at risk;
  (b) outreach and culturally appropriate support services for pregnant women and young women in potentially vulnerable groups; and
  (c) counselling, rehabilitation, outreach, and support services designed specifically to meet the needs of pregnant women with drug/alcohol addictions.

In conclusion, it is the Commission's view that almost all pregnant women will take steps to maximize their chances of a healthy birth if they have ready access to the information, prenatal care, social services, and income support necessary to do so. In the Commission's view, extending care to the fetus by giving the pregnant woman the support she needs provides the best hope for enhancing the health and well-being of both the fetus and the woman carrying it.

General Sources

Rodgers, S. "Juridical Interference with Gestation and Birth." In Research Volumes of the Royal Commission on New Reproductive Technologies, 1993.

Uses of Fetal Tissue

♦

The most widely known use of fetal tissue, largely as a result of extensive media coverage, is in trials of transplantation treatment that may some day prolong and enhance the lives of thousands of Canadians. Therapeutic use of fetal tissue could result in considerable alleviation of human suffering. The treatment now under research may improve the daily lives of people with such diseases as Parkinson, Alzheimer, and diabetes and many other problems; it may one day enable these patients to move their bodies freely, to remember, or to discontinue insulin injections as the transplanted fetal tissue supplies what is needed. Using fetal tissue transplants to correct these diseases is possible in theory, but whether fetal tissue transplantation research will realize these expectations is simply not known. This means that all the usual ethical concerns about research involving human beings must be applied, and the potential for benefit must therefore be weighed against the fact that the treatment may prove not to work.

It is also essential to recognize that this field of research raises serious social and ethical issues to be considered and addressed. The only reliable source of fetal tissue for transplantation is elective abortions. To some, this makes fetal tissue transplantation inherently wrong; others are concerned about the dangers of commodifying fetal tissue or creating pressure on women to have abortions in order to donate fetal tissue. The possible risks of coercion, commercialization, and promotion of abortion must be evaluated and taken into consideration in deciding whether the use of fetal tissue should be allowed and, if so, under what circumstances.

Transplantation is only one of many medical and scientific uses of fetal tissue, and, although this research has received the most publicity, it represents only a small fraction of the use of fetal tissue at present. Fetal tissue from both spontaneous and elective abortions is studied to learn about normal and abnormal fetal development, as well as the genetic or environmental causes of congenital diseases, and it is used in the diagnosis of viral diseases and the development of vaccines, in the testing of new pharmaceutical products, and in the education and training of medical and health professionals. Indeed, the use of fetal tissue in medicine goes back at least to the 1920s, and fetal tissue procurement organizations in the United States and Britain have been distributing fetal tissue to researchers for 30 years.

The other uses of fetal tissue raise many of the same ethical issues as fetal tissue transplantation, so that transplantation should be situated in the broader context of fetal tissue use. Although fetal tissue transplantation was mentioned specifically in the Commission's mandate, we looked for information pertaining to all existing and potential uses of fetal tissue. Whether or not fetal tissue transplantation proves successful, society must address the question of the ethical uses of fetal tissue.

In approaching the task of deciding whether to endorse, condemn, or limit the use of fetal tissue in research, the Commission considered many aspects and questions. If the Commission were to endorse some uses of human fetal tissue, should a woman's

> In approaching the task of deciding whether to endorse, condemn, or limit the use of fetal tissue in research, the Commission considered many aspects and questions.

informed consent be required before tissue from an aborted fetus could be used for research? Or by terminating her pregnancy, would she also have relinquished whatever interests she might have had in the tissue? If her consent were required, what should the timing of it be — could the choice to abort be kept separate from the decision to donate tissue from the fetus? How could society ensure that a woman's consent to either abortion or use of tissue was not coerced? Should specification of the recipient for the tissue be prohibited, to remove any possibility that a woman might conceive with the idea of using the tissue for a specific recipient?

The Commission also needed to consider the potential for financial exploitation or coercion. If research shows that fetal tissue transplants treat disease effectively, what safeguards would need to be in place to ensure that women would not be under pressure to donate fetal tissue? Also to be considered is that increasing demand for fetal tissue could prompt Canadians to look abroad for supplies in jurisdictions where international guidelines on obtaining human tissue are ignored.

These are just a few of the concerns raised by the use of fetal tissue. If fetal tissue transplantation research proves to be successful and matures into more widely used practice, it will be even more important that a clear framework for only ethical use be in place. The Commission's research and Canadians' input to us have shown the importance of establishing a legislative and regulatory framework for this activity. Moreover, this framework must be national in scope because the interests to be safeguarded transcend provincial boundaries.

In this chapter we document what we learned from Canadians across the country and from our research into the current and future uses of fetal tissue, both in Canada and abroad. We then review some of the laws, regulatory mechanisms, and government policies that have restricted or shaped research and treatment in this field, in Canada and in other jurisdictions. In light of this background, we go on to outline the ethical, legal, and social implications of fetal tissue use. Our recommendations for policy development in this area conclude the chapter.

The Views of Canadians

Commission Surveys

Early in our mandate, the Commission conducted two surveys on the views of Canadians on new reproductive technologies. The results of the first, a qualitative study involving personal interviews and group discussions held in 1990, helped us to understand how much Canadians knew about fetal tissue use and the issues it raises. The second, a telephone survey of approximately 1 500 Canadian adults, gave us some additional insight into Canadians' views and opinions on the subject (see research volume, *Social Values and Attitudes Surrounding New Reproductive Technologies*). Then, between December 1991 and July 1992, we undertook a values survey; questionnaire responses from 7 664 Canadians randomly chosen from across the country were analyzed. In all, more than 9 000 Canadians were asked for their opinions on this topic.

Results from these surveys suggest that fetal tissue transplantation is less familiar to Canadians than other medical procedures in our mandate, such as *in vitro* fertilization and prenatal diagnosis. In the 1990 telephone survey, fewer than half of those interviewed (42 percent) were aware of research using fetal tissue to treat disease. In the 1992 values survey, 62 percent said they were aware of the use of fetal tissue in medical research, although only 18 percent said they were well informed about it.

Although the overall level of awareness of fetal tissue transplantation research was not high, many survey respondents viewed it as a positive development that could be of benefit to society because it might result in treatments or cures for debilitating diseases. In the 1990 telephone survey, for example, 84 percent of respondents stated that the use of fetal tissue to treat fatal diseases should be allowed, while only 12 percent opposed it. Respondents who endorsed fetal tissue transplantation often likened it to organ donation. When asked whether they personally would want to undergo treatment using fetal tissue if they were suffering from a serious disease, 72 percent said that they would.

There was also widespread support (77 percent) for the use of fetal tissue in medical research, while 16 percent opposed it. In both the 1990 and 1992 surveys, the level of support for the use of fetal tissue in treatment or research was slightly higher among men than among women (a margin of four to nine percentage points) and among individuals with higher levels of education.

As shown in Table 31.1, there was widespread agreement (77 percent) that fetal tissue should not be used for non-medical, commercial purposes. Respondents feared that permitting this use of fetal tissue would promote the commercialization of human reproduction. During the personal interviews, the need for regulation and control emerged as a key concern; participants predicted that any prospect of financial gain could increase the demand for fetal tissue and prompt the creation of financial inducements for women to initiate and terminate pregnancies. Participants also objected if the proposed use was purely cosmetic, which they considered trivial by comparison with curing neurological disease and advancing scientific knowledge.

Table 31.1. Permissibility of Using Fetal Tissue

Use	Allow	Do not allow
To treat disease	84%	12%
Medical research	77%	16%
Commercial purposes	18%	77%

Source: Angus Reid Group Inc. "Reproductive Technologies — Qualitative Research: Summary of Observations." In Research Volumes of the Royal Commission on New Reproductive Technologies, 1993.

Submissions to the Commission

The Commission also heard a wide range of views from experts and interested parties, laypersons, and interest groups at public hearings and through written submissions and telephone calls. Some anti-abortion, family, and religious groups argued that fetal tissue should not be used in research or therapy because this may promote abortion. Some stated that the use of fetal tissue from miscarriages and ectopic pregnancies was ethically acceptable, but that the use of tissue from elective abortions was not. Some felt, for example, that women might be more likely to abort a pregnancy if they believed they were thereby contributing to medical research.   Concerns were also raised that the demand for human fetal tissue would create social pressures encouraging women to abort pregnancies about which they were ambivalent. Some people also believed that if fetal tissue research expands, doctors might encourage women to abort in order to secure an adequate supply of fetal tissue. Others thought that the care of women having an abortion could be compromised because of researchers' desire to obtain tissue at a specific stage of fetal development. Some speculated that commercialization of fetal tissue would occur and would encourage women to initiate and terminate pregnancies in response to financial incentives.

Others were concerned that women might initiate a pregnancy in order to recover fetal tissues for a particular recipient, such as an aging parent with Parkinson disease or a child in need of organ or tissue transplantation.   At least one case has been reported in the medical literature (in Hungary) where a pregnancy appears to have been terminated expressly to provide fetal tissue for transplantation.

> No woman, professional/lay person, or medical personnel [should] receive any inducement or reward, monetary or otherwise, for making fetal tissue available or to terminate a pregnancy.
>
> *Brief to the Commission from the Canadian Baptist Federation, October 29, 1990.*

Some objections to the use of fetal tissue for transplantation hinged on the misperception that the tissue used is taken from fetuses that are still alive. This misperception may result from the fact that after a fetus (or an adult human being) dies, the various tissues of the body die at different times — some cells and tissue remain alive (or "viable") for several hours.   Fetal cells taken after fetal death may be viable for some time and, if placed in an appropriate culture medium *in vitro* or if cryo-preserved, may remain viable for months or years.   Some fetal tissue research requires that the tissue be viable in this sense, just as research with tissues taken from an adult may require it.   It is important that this use of viable or living fetal tissue not be confused, however, with the use of a viable or living fetus.

> We urge the Canadian government to: outlaw buying and selling of human fetal tissue; nationalize such tissue; [and] appoint a Government Board to oversee the acquiring, distribution, use, and disposal of such tissue. Membership should be appointed from the medical, scientific, religious communities, and half should be female. The Blood Bank is a good model to follow in running this organization.
>
> *Brief to the Commission from the Halifax Monthly Meeting [Quakers], December 20, 1990.*

Commissioners heard a full range of views on these issues. From representatives of Alliance for Life in Montreal, we heard:

> Scientific research should not be conducted on embryos or on fetal tissue resulting from induced abortion, nor should such tissue be utilized for transplantation into other people suffering from disease. Such uses would legitimize abortion [and] have the potential of encouraging acceptance of it, and of increasing the type and numbers of abortions, as well as the gestational age at which [abortion] is performed. In all cases of induced abortion it is impossible to get proper informed consent. (*A. Kiss, Alliance pour la vie, Public Hearings Transcripts, Montreal, Quebec, November 21, 1990.*)

We also heard from representatives of the Canadian Abortion Rights Action League in Halifax, who said:

> It is argued that women will be forced to become pregnant and to abort. We point out that there is no evidence to support this theory. Women in society in general need to be vigilant against coercion of any kind for any reason. It is argued that commercialization of fetal tissue will proliferate. Again, this is an example of scare-mongering. Canada has no tradition of commercializing donated blood or body parts ... It is said that women will be asked to delay abortions to maximize chances of success for recipients. However, where research is underway, there is a clear policy to separate the abortion procedure from fetal tissue transplant therapy.

> Finally, opponents argue that fetal [tissue] transplantation shows disrespect for life and a disrespect for fetuses. This argument can only be made by people who wish to grant legal status to the fetus. In fact, such an argument grants a greater status to fetus[es] than to people, inasmuch as research on human cadavers is an established part of medical education and practice and does not imply a disrespect for human life nor for human beings. (*K. Holmwood, Canadian Abortion Rights Action League, Public Hearings Transcripts, Halifax, Nova Scotia, October 18, 1990.*)

These two views summarize a great deal of the input Commissioners heard on this issue. What we found most interesting about the written and oral submissions was that, apart from the obvious difference of opinion about the status of the fetus, the values expressed by participants had much in common. No one favoured the commercialization of fetal tissue. All opposed the exploitation of vulnerable women, the deliberate undertaking of a pregnancy to produce fetal tissue for a particular use, and the use of abortion methods that were not in the best interests of the pregnant woman.

Thus, despite the range of views, there was also a significant degree of congruence on some aspects of these issues. Indeed, it seems that many of the concerns and disagreements among Canadians about fetal tissue use stem from a shortage of information about this research, about the feasible sources of fetal tissue and its alternatives, and about the mechanisms for regulating research. To help address this lack of information, we commissioned a series of studies examining research involving the use of fetal tissue, its future directions, its current conduct in Canada and abroad, the

Apart from the obvious difference of opinion about the status of the fetus, the values expressed by participants had much in common ... Thus, despite the range of views, there was also a significant degree of congruence on some aspects of these issues.

source of fetal tissue, and current regulations in Canada and abroad. (For a brief review of policies in other countries, see Appendix 1.) We focussed particularly on research into whether fetal tissue can be used to alleviate disease, since this is the aspect that generates most public concern. Our findings are discussed in the next few sections.

Uses of Fetal Tissue

Fetal tissue has a wide variety of uses, including experimental transplantation treatment, basic medical research, the development and testing of pharmaceutical products, pathology testing, viral diagnostics, and medical education.

The best-known use of fetal tissue involves research into the development of experimental treatments, such as fetal tissue transplantation for Parkinson disease. However, fetal tissue is also used in basic research to increase knowledge about human functioning and disease processes. This may involve, for example, the study of the form and structure of organs or cells using dead tissue. Other basic research involves *in vitro* culture of living tissue or cells to study the biochemical and physiological processes of fetal development and the genetic or environmental bases of various diseases. Disciplines involved in this research include anatomy, pathology, genetics, cytogenetics, endocrinology, biochemistry, and molecular biology.

Fetal tissue can also be transplanted into animals to create animal models of various human diseases. For example, fetal blood-generating cells (haematopoietic stem cells) have been transplanted into a strain of mice that are unable to reject the cells because the mice have an inherited immune deficiency. The cells give rise to human blood cells in the mice, offering an animal model in which disorders of the human blood system (including leukemia and AIDS) can be studied.

Fetal tissue has also been used for many decades in the development and production of pharmaceutical products, such as vaccines against polio, measles, rubella, and other diseases. The 1954 Nobel prize for medicine was awarded for work on the polio vaccine using fetal kidney cell cultures.

It has been reported that fetal cells in culture are also used to screen new pharmaceutical products for toxicity or to identify carcinogens or agents causing congenital anomalies. For example, the U.S. National Institutes of Health funded research examining fetal tissue to determine the carcinogenicity of tobacco smoke from active and passive smoking.

Fetal tissue is also used in the diagnosis of human viral diseases, including hepatitis, influenza, and HIV. Cultures prepared from fetal tissues allow a more accurate and rapid diagnosis of certain viruses than any other method, and some viruses can be isolated only in spongioblasts derived from fetal brain tissue.

However, the most frequent category of fetal tissue use is for pathological examination or testing. Fetal tissue from spontaneous abortions is subject to a routine pathology examination in hospitals. Abnormalities may be identified, helping to diagnose the cause of the pregnancy loss. This is part of normal patient care and helps physicians care for and advise women on future pregnancies. Fetuses from therapeutic abortions are also examined by hospital pathology services. Hospitals in Canada have a general policy of examining all tissue removed surgically, as part of quality assurance, and indeed this is required under provincial/territorial legislation. In the case of therapeutic abortions, the pathology examination is used to verify the pregnancy, to ensure that fetal tissue has been evacuated during the abortion, and to check for any abnormalities in the fetal tissue.

> The most frequent category of fetal tissue use is for pathological examination or testing ... Hospitals in Canada have a general policy of examining all tissue removed surgically, as part of quality assurance, and indeed this is required under provincial/territorial legislation.

Finally, fetal tissue and fetal specimens are used in the education and training of medical, nursing, and other health sciences students so they can learn about normal human development and the disease processes that may affect it.

Some commentators include all these uses of fetal tissue under the general heading of "research." Indeed, circumstances do exist in which each of these uses of fetal tissue could be part of an experiment or research project. However, it is important to realize that most of these uses of fetal tissue have been routine for many years, an everyday part of clinical practice, pharmaceutical methods, or medical education. Although some uses of fetal tissue involve research and experimentation, to describe all uses of fetal tissue as "research" ignores the extent to which certain uses of fetal tissue are well established in the health care system. Taken together, these diverse uses of fetal tissue have provided invaluable new knowledge about human health, have prevented much human suffering (for example, from polio), and have led to greater understanding of disease processes.

Potential Usefulness of Fetal Tissue for Transplantation

The particular use of fetal tissue that has received the most public attention is transplantation. In the past two decades, human organ transplantation and tissue replacement using organs and tissues (from adults and children) have found a valuable role in medical care. Transplant recipients' survival rates have increased significantly. Better procedures and new anti-rejection drugs have revolutionized the therapeutic potential of transplanting human organs and tissues. As a result, procedures once considered experimental, such as corneal and kidney transplants, have become recognized and valuable medical procedures.

Fetal tissue has certain unique biological properties that make it particularly valuable for transplantation. Because of these advantages over adult tissue as a transplant material, there appears to be a strong possibility that some forms of fetal tissue transplantation could become recognized medical practice in the next few years. The advantages of fetal tissue as a transplant material include

- its capacity for growth and differentiation;

- its ability to survive culture and manipulation *in vitro*;

- its different immunological properties; and

- its potential to restore function in a transplant recipient.

Growth and Differentiation

In general, fetal tissue cells, both human and animal, exhibit a remarkable capacity for change and differentiation; they are also more able to migrate and form new intercellular connections and to extend new fibres both in transplant recipients (*in vivo*) and in the laboratory (*in vitro*), making them particularly useful for transplantation.

Differentiation refers to the process whereby cells become more and more specialized — in both form and function — to do a particular job in the body. The capacity for differentiation is greatest at early stages of fetal development and diminishes as the fetus develops; the capacity is largely lost in many tissues by the end of fetal development. Once this has happened, each cell has assumed its lifelong assignment — for example, to be a skin cell — and there is very little possibility of its changing function — to become, for example, a bone cell (redifferentiation).

Culture *In Vitro*

Fetal cells are more resistant to damage, both during *in vitro* manipulations and after transplantation. One reason is that they are able to survive at lower oxygen levels than adult tissue cells. Another is that immature fetal cells are less strongly attached to one another than adult tissue cells are, making fetal cells less likely to rupture while they are being separated and prepared for transplantation.

Cells in early fetal tissues may continue to divide in the laboratory, while the cells from many adult tissues, such as brain and heart cells, do not. Fetal cells also divide more rapidly and more often than those adult cells, such as liver cells, that will multiply under appropriate laboratory conditions. Selection of specific cell types *in vitro* may be aided by this robustness.

The capacity of fetal cells to divide and grow *in vitro* has led to research interest in the development and maintenance of cultured fetal cell lines. If these cell lines could be frozen and thawed successfully, they could provide a secure source of material for both research and therapy, reducing the need for continuing access to new sources of fetal tissue.

Immunogenicity

The most important obstacle to successful transplantation is the rejection of transplant material by the recipient. The host immune system recognizes the transplanted material as genetically distinct from itself — as it does with infectious bacteria or viruses — and initiates a destructive immune response.

In recent years, transplant results have been improved dramatically by the use of more advanced methods of matching potential donor tissue with that of the recipient, and by the use of drugs, such as cyclosporin, that suppress the body's immune response. Immunosuppression is not always successful, however, and tissue and organ rejection remains a major problem. Serious side effects from immunosuppressive drugs are frequent, and patients are more susceptible to infections that can result in death. Moreover, the drugs often must be taken for a lifetime.

The proteins on cell surfaces (antigens) that provoke an immune response begin to appear only as development proceeds in various tissues, so that fetal tissues may provoke less immune response. In addition, fetal tissues do not contain cells that elicit graft-versus-host disease (where the cells in the graft harm the host), which makes them more desirable for transplantation.

Restoration of Function in Transplant Recipients

Extensive animal studies have looked at the growth and functional capacity of transplanted animal fetal cells of various types. It has been found that these fetal cells may produce high levels of certain substances in their host — including factors that induce blood vessel formation and neuron survival — that can enhance their growth as grafts and that may also facilitate regeneration by surrounding tissues in the recipient.

Animal studies indicate that there is demonstrable and clinically significant growth and functional recovery by transplanted fetal cells in animal models for Parkinson disease and Type I (juvenile or insulin-dependent) diabetes. Such studies provide the rationale for clinical trials using fetal tissue transplantation in human patients when conventional treatments fail.

Given all these characteristics of fetal tissue, it is not surprising that researchers in the area of transplantation have looked to fetal rather than adult tissue as a source of transplantation material. Indeed, the use of human fetal tissue for transplantation is not new. The first attempts at transplanting fetal pancreas tissue to treat diabetes occurred in the 1920s. However, recent scientific developments mean the number of potential disorders that may be treatable through fetal tissue transplantation has increased. Studies in the Commission's research volumes outline the disorders being explored for possible treatment in this way. Most research to treat the diseases is at an early stage and is often theoretical or involves animal experiments, but fetal tissue has been used in human subjects in Parkinson disease, Alzheimer disease, and diabetes mellitus, among others. However, the only research in Canada using fetal tissue transplantation in human subjects at present is one trial for Parkinson disease, at the Victoria General Hospital in Halifax (see Appendix 2).

Future Directions in Fetal Tissue Research and Treatment

It is difficult to predict what the future of this research will be, but hopes are that fetal tissue transplantation will be useful in treating a range of disorders. For example, fetal neural tissue transplants may be used in the near future to treat Alzheimer disease. It has also been speculated that patients with other neurological disorders may benefit in the more distant future. Similarly, fetal liver tissue transplants may be used in the future to treat diseases currently treated through the use of bone marrow transplants; many blood disorders are theoretically future candidates for this approach. It has been speculated that eventually fetal liver tissue might be able to be used to restore function that has been depleted by anti-cancer therapy, thereby allowing use of higher doses of anti-cancer medication or irradiation. (For further information on future directions for fetal tissue transplantation, see research volumes.)

Fetal tissue may also be used more in future to create models of human disease in animals, so they can be studied more easily, and to produce antibodies for therapeutic purposes. It is important to remember, however, that many of these future uses of fetal tissue are quite speculative, and some are many years away from being investigated.

Information on Uses of Fetal Tissue in Canada

Although the future uses of fetal tissue remain speculative, Commissioners wanted to know how fetal tissue is being used in Canada today. We discovered, however, that relatively few data were accessible regarding the use of fetal tissue in this country; in part, this is because of the large number of sites at which medical research takes place and because of the range of funding sources for medical research, including both governmental and non-governmental sources. As a result, data on research projects and uses of fetal tissue in research are not centralized in one location.

Non-governmental sources have supported various forms of fetal tissue research in Canadian laboratories, including fetal tissue transplantation research. For example, The Parkinson Foundation of Canada helps fund the clinical trial of fetal tissue transplants for Parkinson disease in Halifax.

The leading federal agency supporting research in the health sciences, including fetal tissue research, is the Medical Research Council of Canada, which provides about 30 percent of the funds for medical research in Canada. Our consultations with Canadian scientists suggested that the MRC has provided funds totalling several million dollars over the last three decades for research using fetal tissue. This research has investigated a wide range of subjects, including the regulation and effects of fetal hormone secretion, the normal and pathologic development of fetal organs, the chromosomal make-up of cells from normal and abnormal fetuses, and aspects of fetal tissue metabolism, including generation or elimination of toxic or therapeutic compounds. The research has been directed to understanding fetal health and disease, as well as health and disease in pregnant women; in fact, Canadian research has made significant contributions to knowledge that has provided the foundation for advances in reducing illness and death in newborns.

The Minister of the Department of National Health and Welfare stated in the House of Commons in July 1988 that federal funds would not be used for research involving the use of fetal tissue transplantation in human beings.[1] Since then, the MRC has received no requests for funding for such research.

The U.S. government banned federal funding of transplantation of tissue from elective abortions in 1988; the ban was rescinded by President Clinton in January 1993. The Canadian decision regarding federal funding of fetal tissue transplantation research will not likely be revisited until the Commission has reported.

In summary, it was not possible to obtain complete data on the use of fetal tissue in research in Canada. This is not the case in Britain, where a centralized fetal tissue bank collects and distributes fetal tissue to researchers and publishes annual reports listing the research projects that receive fetal tissue from the bank.

It is clear, nevertheless, that many research groups in Canada have used human fetal tissue for their investigations during the last three decades and that many studies are currently in progress. As far as we can determine, these research projects have been carried out at universities, hospitals, or other non-profit institutions, using tissue collected from local hospitals. In recent years, they have been conducted with institutional research ethics board approval, in accordance with the 1987 MRC *Guidelines on Research Involving Human Subjects*, which have been adopted by all schools of health sciences in Canada and their affiliated teaching hospitals and research institutes.

However, these research projects are just one aspect of the handling and use of fetal tissue in Canada. As we noted earlier, fetal tissue is used in many other ways, such as pathology testing and medical education, and we felt it was important to get Canadian data on the entire spectrum of fetal tissue use. We wanted to know how much fetal tissue is collected and who has access to it, for what purposes, and according to what guidelines. To get a sense of this larger picture, we surveyed every health care facility from which fetal tissue could be obtained. This was one component of a larger study intended to identify how all reproductive tissues obtained in these facilities are used or handled. (The results of this survey as they pertain to the handling of gametes and zygotes/embryos were discussed in Chapter 22.)

Health Care Facilities, Abortion Clinics, and Medical Laboratories in Canada

As detailed in our research volume entitled *Background and Current Practice of Fetal Tissue and Embryo Research in Canada*, a survey of Canadian health care facilities offering obstetrical or gynaecological services was conducted for the Commission between November 1991 and February 1992. Among the 642 facilities on which the survey results are based, 80 reported that they did not handle abortuses or fetal tissue. Of those that did, most reported that they disposed of fetal tissue after it had undergone routine pathology testing. However, 83 facilities said they provided tissues to other institutions, laboratories, or individual researchers, while 5 facilities said they retained these tissues, at least in part, for in-house research.

The research team conducting the survey thought some of the respondents might not have been aware of how their facility handled reproductive tissues, or of the purpose for which tissues were distributed to outside agencies. To get a clearer picture of the overall use of fetal tissue, the Commission undertook a follow-up survey in May and June 1992 of the 60 medical laboratories identified in the previous survey as recipients of reproductive tissue, including fetal tissue. Of the 48 medical laboratories that responded, 31 reported handling abortuses/fetal tissues in particular. Of these, all used fetal tissue for pathology analysis. This is clearly the most common use of fetal tissue in Canada. After examination or testing, nine laboratories disposed of the fetal tissue in-house, while others sent tissue to medical waste firms for disposal. Only one laboratory reported using fetal tissue in research.

To complete the picture, the Commission surveyed 23 medical waste firms identified as receiving reproductive tissues. None of these firms reported any use of fetal tissue other than disposal.

These surveys revealed a pattern of fetal tissue use in Canada; the most common, and indeed routine, use of fetal tissue is the examining of tissue from spontaneous and therapeutic abortions in the pathology laboratory, followed by disposal of the tissue through incineration. The pathology testing is done in hospitals and in laboratories; the disposal may be done by hospitals, laboratories, or medical waste firms.

In the relatively few facilities (either hospitals or laboratories) that do conduct research using fetal tissue, a considerable range of projects is being carried out: one example is a study to develop simple, long-term methods of assessing the health of the fetus during pregnancy; another is the clinical trial of fetal tissue transplantation treatment for Parkinson disease being conducted in Halifax. This latter project will play a significant role in establishing international standards for assessing the usefulness of fetal tissue transplantation treatment for this disorder (see Appendix 2).

Our survey indicated that scientists obtain fetal tissue for research either directly from hospitals and abortion clinics or from other investigators who themselves obtain the tissue from a hospital or clinic. No payments are involved, except for the service of transporting the tissue.

Although the survey was comprehensive in its coverage, its results may be incomplete and inaccurate in various ways. One of the more interesting results was that many hospital administrators were not aware of how reproductive tissues were handled and disposed of in their facility. The respondent filling out the questionnaire in each facility may not have been aware of some studies in the facility using fetal tissue samples from abortuses, and there may be no one within the facility who formally collects such data. Another finding was that one-third of the hospitals or clinics handling fetal tissue and disposing of fetal tissue reported having written protocols; two-thirds did not.

Moreover, there may have been differences in the way respondents interpreted the term "fetal tissue research." For example, someone who examines the chromosomes of cells from spontaneous abortions as part of a larger project on chromosomal genetic disorders might think of themselves as engaged in "cytogenetics research," not "fetal tissue research." No standardized terminology is used to discuss and categorize the different uses of fetal tissue.

We believe it is important for Canadians to have accurate and reliable information about the use of fetal tissue in Canada, and that proper record keeping and reporting mechanisms must therefore be in place. Our recommendations at the end of this chapter address this issue.

Pharmaceutical Manufacturers and Biotechnology Companies in Canada

Cell lines in culture, derived from human fetal tissue, have been used for several decades by pharmaceutical and biotechnology companies in the development of vaccines such as the human polio vaccine. Fetal cell lines have also been used to develop various pharmaceutical products and diagnostic tests. We felt it was important, therefore, to determine whether private sector companies in Canada were using fetal tissue.

The Commission surveyed all 67 member companies of the Pharmaceutical Manufacturers Association of Canada in 1992 to assess their use of human fetal tissues in research and development. Of the 55 pharmaceutical companies that responded, none reported any use of fetal tissue, although some believed that the industry may in future invest in research using fetal tissue related to the treatment of Parkinson disease.

The same questionnaire was sent to 26 biotechnology companies that were identified as potential users of human reproductive tissues. Of the 20 biotechnology companies that responded, only 1 reported research related to fetal tissue. It uses human cell lines originally developed from fetal lung fibroblast in the late 1950s and 1960s.

It would appear that there is little use of fetal tissue by the private sector in Canada, although no information is available on the differences between the companies that responded and those that did not. When asked to explain why there was not more interest in fetal tissue, respondents cited concerns about the expense involved and the potentially controversial nature of such research. It is important to note, however, that this survey dealt with the use of fetal tissue in Canada. There is some evidence, discussed below, that fetal tissue is used by pharmaceutical and biotechnology firms in other countries, including firms whose Canadian subsidiaries responded to the Commission's survey.

The Use of Placental Tissue

As part of our survey, we also examined the handling and use of placentas. The research use of placental matter does not raise the same ethical concerns as research involving zygotes, embryos, and fetal tissue. Indeed, placental matter is usually seen as a waste product and is treated in the same way as other waste products of medical procedures.

However, the handling of placental matter has come to public attention as a result of recent newspaper reports that placentas are being sold by Canadian hospitals and exported to France, and that no consent is obtained for this. Our investigation showed that more than 100 hospitals in Canada sell placentas, for about 35¢ each, to one medical waste firm (Bocknek Ltd.), which then forwards them to the Institut Mérieux in Lyon, France. The Institut Mérieux uses placentas to produce various pharmaceutical products, such as human albumin, polyvalent immune globulins for intramuscular use, and histamine-protective immune globulin, all used in the care of patients. The Institut Mérieux processes between 3 000 and 4 000 tons of placentas each year, collected from 8 000 hospitals worldwide; between 1 and 2 percent of this material comes from Canada. This is the only case we discovered of human reproductive tissue of any kind being exported from Canada.

Some people have expressed concern that the placentas exported to France are used in the production of cosmetics.

> Those tissues going to medical waste firms were simply being disposed of, with the one exception of placentas ... The placentas sold by health care facilities are forwarded by the medical waste firm receiving them to the Institut Mérieux in France for production of pharmaceutical products such as vaccines, gamma globulin, and other therapeutic agents.
>
> Provincial human tissue gift acts in Canada forbid the selling of human tissues for medical or therapeutic research. It is evident that placentas are not viewed by these hospitals as coming within the acts but are seen as a waste by-product of childbirth and are classified as "discarded human body material" that would otherwise have to be incinerated.
>
> *SPR Associates Inc., "Report on a Follow-Up Survey of Use and Handling of Human Reproductive Tissues (Survey of Medical Laboratories and Medical Waste Disposal Firms)," in Research Volumes of the Commission, 1993.*

Indeed, some of the surveyed hospitals that sold the placentas listed cosmetics among the end uses of the material. So far as we can determine, however, placental material exported from Canada to the Institut Mérieux is used only to produce pharmaceutical products. In the past, a subsidiary of the Institut Mérieux did make cosmetics from human placental tissue using placentas collected in France. When contacted, however, the Institut Mérieux was most emphatic that this is no longer done.

This is not the only use of placental matter; our survey revealed that eight health care facilities retained placental tissue, and nine medical laboratories reported they used placentas for research purposes. Our survey identified more research projects in Canada using placentas than projects using zygotes, embryos, or fetal tissue. Placentas are of great scientific interest because they are the point of connection between the fetal blood vessels and those of the pregnant woman.

We have serious reservations about the current practice of selling placentas to the Institut Mérieux without the woman's consent. We do not object to the selling of placental material per se. It would cost money to dispose of placental material through incineration, like other medical waste products, a cost that would have to be borne by the public health care system. If these costs can be saved, and if the waste tissue is used to produce pharmaceutical products that are of benefit, this is appropriate. However, we believe that women should be informed that placentas are used in this way and should be given the option of having their placental material disposed of through incineration, if they object. Some women may have religious or other objections to the possible use of their placentas in creating pharmaceutical products, and these should be respected. The Commission recommends that

> **276. Hospitals obtain consent from women, by means of written consent forms, regarding the disposal of placentas.**

Uses of Fetal Tissue in Other Countries

There are few firm data regarding the use of fetal tissue in other countries. Few countries have centralized registries or have conducted national surveys. Arrangements to obtain fetal tissue for study are usually negotiated on an individual basis between researchers and hospitals or clinics in most countries.

An exception is Britain, which since 1957 has had a centralized fetal tissue bank in London, run by the United Kingdom Medical Research Council. Between 1981 and 1986, 124 researchers received fetal tissue from the bank, which distributes between 4 000 and 5 000 tissue samples each year, derived from some 800 fetal specimens. Of these projects, most involved virology (27 percent), molecular biology and genetics (23 percent), immunology (17 percent), tissue culture (15 percent), descriptive embryology (7 percent), haematology (3 percent), and bacteriology (2 percent). Little research is being done into transplantation — the bank has not supplied any fetal tissue for research into transplantation since 1983. Fetal tissue is obtained from local obstetricians, who receive no payment for the tissue. The woman's permission is required before fetal tissue is sent to the bank. The tissue is then distributed to researchers at no cost, except transportation charges. A requirement is that the research for which the tissue is sought has obtained the approval of a local institutional ethics committee.

Similar details regarding fetal tissue use are not available for other countries. However, some information can be gleaned from funding agencies, agencies that obtain fetal tissue for distribution, and published studies.

In the United States, the National Institutes of Health is the major source of federal funds for medical research. It provided more than $11 million in funding in 1987 for 116 projects involving fetal tissue. These projects used fetal tissue for a variety of purposes: to study the genetic basis of certain diseases (for example, retinoblastoma); the carcinogenicity of tobacco smoke; the process of lung maturation; the transmission of AIDS; and the development of cell cultures used to study disease resistance. As noted earlier, in 1988 the U.S. government imposed a ban, since rescinded, on federal funding of transplantation research using fetal tissue from elective abortions.

A substantial amount of private sector research that involves fetal tissue is also being conducted by U.S. biotechnology and pharmaceutical companies. However, no reliable information exists on the number of companies using fetal tissue or the nature of their research. Examples of private sector research include the development of cell lines for toxicity testing, particularly for medical products that may be used by pregnant women, the development of vaccines, and the development of techniques for transplantation therapy.

Very little is known about how U.S. companies acquire fetal tissue. In some cases, tissues are acquired from specialized procurement agencies. For example, the International Institute for the Advancement of Medicine, a non-profit tissue procurement agency that is the largest U.S. distributor of fetal tissue for research, has supplied fetal tissue to 86 institutions, 19 of which were for-profit corporations. However, private companies in the United States may also receive tissue through informal arrangements with abortion clinics. A 1988 survey by the National Abortion Federation, with responses from more than half its 300 U.S. clinic members, revealed that 11 clinics provided fetal tissue for research programs, which in two cases were carried out by commercial laboratories.

The Council of Europe recently released a report on the use of reproductive tissue, including fetal tissue, in Europe. According to the report, research using fetal tissue is going on in the areas of pathology/testing, viral identification and vaccine development, anatomy/embryology, molecular genetics, the development of animal models of human disease, and transplantation. The Council of Europe report also notes a "persistent rumour" that human fetal tissue is used by European cosmetics firms, but states that this rumour is "without foundation." Animal fetal tissue is used by some French cosmetics firms, and human placental material has been used by cosmetics firms in the past; there appears to be no evidence, however, that human fetal material has been used or is being used by cosmetics firms.[2]

There have been other rumours regarding the commercial use of fetal tissue. In a book on global traffic in commodities, for example, James Ridgeway stated that human fetal tissue has been shipped from South

Korea to Fort Detrick, Maryland, for use by the U.S. Army in investigations of haemorrhagic fever, and that "100 000 fetuses a year end up in research laboratories" around the world. This has been cited as evidence

> The solution is to ensure that any fetal tissue used in research is obtained in a controlled, accountable, and ethical way.

of "a rapidly growing market for human fetuses." However, the Commission was unable to establish the basis for this claim, which remains unsubstantiated.[3]

Nevertheless, we take very seriously the possibility that fetal tissue could become commercialized and the object of international trade. We believe that the solution is not to ban the use of fetal tissue — since this would deprive society of valuable medical research and treatment, and could also drive the activity underground. The solution is to ensure that any fetal tissue used in research is obtained in a controlled, accountable, and ethical way. This is one of the goals of our recommendations later in this chapter.

Obtaining Fetal Tissue

To be suitable for most research uses, including uses in transplantation research, fetal tissue must have viable cells, be free of significant genetic anomalies, and be uncontaminated by infectious agents — bacterial, viral, or fungal. Some research projects can be carried out with tissue that does not meet these requirements, but others, particularly transplantation research, cannot be. These criteria must therefore be considered when evaluating the potential sources of fetal tissue.

Current Sources of Tissue

Some research questions can be answered using fetal tissue from spontaneous abortions — in fact, research on such tissue has provided insights into the causes and consequences of disease processes that affect the fetus. We know, for example, that approximately half of early spontaneously aborted fetuses have chromosomal abnormalities; this knowledge was gained by studying the chromosomes in their cells. Scientists have also learned about the development of fetal anomalies from the study of tissues from spontaneous abortions.

Other research questions cannot be answered by studying fetal tissue from this source. For example, fetal material from spontaneous abortions cannot be used for transplantation research. Difficulties in obtaining this material include the unpredictable timing of the event, and tissue death and degeneration. In addition, the tissue from spontaneous abortions is often infected. This, coupled with the high incidence of chromosomal abnormalities, renders tissue from spontaneously aborted fetuses largely unsuitable for many research projects, including transplantation. For these reasons, fetal tissue from spontaneous abortion is rarely used for clinical research applications.

For reasons associated with tissue viability, condition, and availability, elective first-trimester abortion provides more suitable fetal tissue for some kinds of research, particularly research involving transplantation to treat disease.

More than 90 000 abortions are performed annually in Canada (92 665 in 1990).[4] About 90 percent of these take place within the first trimester. The overwhelming majority of these procedures are performed between the fifth and twelfth weeks of gestation, usually by vacuum aspiration. Fetal tissue from these procedures, although fragmented, is generally usable and can be collected without contamination. Tissues at these stages of development are useful for many types of research and optimal for some. Fetal tissue used in the transplantation research project being carried out in Halifax is from fetuses aborted in the first trimester.

Altering the method of abortion may allow collection of tissue better suited for use in transplantation research. For example, researchers in Sweden have used other techniques, such as forceps or a manual syringe under ultrasound guidance, to obtain less fragmented fetal tissue. Similarly, a modified vacuum aspiration technique has been used in the United States. These are experimental techniques, and their safety for the woman undergoing the abortion has not been established. We make recommendations with regard to this later in this chapter.

Some areas of fetal tissue transplantation research (for example, fetal pancreatic tissue transplants) must use tissues from second-trimester abortions. The most common method of abortion at this stage is the dilation and evacuation technique. This procedure is considered to be the safest for the pregnant woman, and tissue obtained from this procedure is generally usable.

Termination of pregnancy later than the second trimester is unusual and is almost always done only when a severe abnormality has been discovered in the fetus at this stage of pregnancy. It can be performed by replacing the amniotic fluid with a concentrated saline solution or by stimulating uterine contractions with drugs (for example, prostaglandins). Tissue from fetuses at this stage of development is less usable for most research purposes, as it is more differentiated and mature, and because there is often a genetic anomaly. Moreover, these methods of abortion

> Fetal material from spontaneous abortions cannot be used for transplantation research. Difficulties in obtaining this material include the unpredictable timing of the event, and tissue death and degeneration. In addition, the tissue from spontaneous abortions is often infected.

rarely yield viable fetal cells — almost never in the case of saline injection and only rarely in the case of prostaglandin induction.

Alternative Sources of Fetal Tissue for Transplantation and Other Research

Many of the ethical and legal issues raised by using tissue derived from therapeutic abortions could be avoided if it were possible to use alternative material. Several possibilities are therefore under investigation — some more promising than others. However, their practical clinical use is likely many years away.

Ectopic Pregnancy

In an ectopic pregnancy the embryo implants in a woman's fallopian tube instead of in her uterus. The condition is life-threatening to the woman unless the fetus aborts spontaneously or is removed surgically. Between 40 and 64 percent of ectopic pregnancies abort spontaneously in the first trimester. This material is rarely recognizable or viable in culture and therefore is generally not usable for fetal tissue transplantation or other research.

Ectopic pregnancies that do not abort spontaneously require surgical removal of the fetus to save the woman's life. The surgically removed fetal tissue is usually normal and thus more useful than the fetal tissue from spontaneously aborted ectopic pregnancies. However, the low incidence and unpredictable occurrence of ectopic pregnancies restrict the availability and usefulness of this source of tissue. Moreover, because surgical removal of the fetus often damages the woman's fallopian tube, the recent trend has been to abort ectopic pregnancies non-surgically through the use of a local injection of methotrexate in an effort to preserve the fallopian tube. This procedure renders the fetal tissue unsuitable for research and transplantation.

Human Fetal Cell Lines

Continuously propagated cultures (cell lines derived from fetal tissue) have obvious advantages as a potential source of fetal tissue for transplantation. Theoretically, cells from a few fetuses might be made to proliferate *in vitro* to provide a virtually limitless supply of transplantable tissue. There are several serious difficulties with this scenario, however. Fetal tissue cell lines currently in existence continue to grow and divide only because they have been specially treated to behave this way. As a consequence, the cells are also likely to keep dividing after transplantation, possibly resulting in tumours. Because of the length of time they are kept in culture, fetal tissue cell lines may also develop abnormal antigens that make them identifiable as foreign by the recipient and which are likely to lead to their rejection.

In the future, it may be possible to avoid rejection, as well as the potential spread of cancerous cells, by implanting fetal cell lines that are "encapsulated." Other approaches to the propagation of non-cancerous lines of human endocrine, neurological, or stem cells by various means, including treatment with growth factors, are under development. It is unlikely, however, that fetal tissue cell lines will be able to replace fetal tissue in the near future in transplantation research. Even if cell lines can be used to replace fetal tissue for transplantation in the future, cell lines will not be able to replace fetal tissue for all other research purposes — for example, cultured cells would not be useful for basic research into fetal development.

Umbilical Cord Blood

Umbilical cord blood obtained from normal placentas at birth is a readily available potential source of blood stem cells. These could, in theory, replace the transplantation of fetal liver cells in the treatment of certain blood disorders. Indeed, at least two children with a rare inherited blood disease have been treated by transplantation of cord blood from compatible newborn siblings. However, umbilical cord blood is useful only for compatible recipients, because the cells in it are more immunologically mature than fetal tissue cells and they may recognize the host body as "foreign," going on to mount a catastrophic graft-versus-host reaction.

Non-Human Fetal Tissue

Non-human fetal tissue has also been considered for transplantation into human beings. However, species differences greatly limit the usefulness of this approach. All cells express species-specific antigens that can be recognized as foreign by the recipient, so survival of grafts across species requires that they be protected from rejection. Grafts from other species have been considered for clinical application, but the potential toxic effects of prolonged use of the immunosuppressive drugs now available have discouraged pursuit of this approach.

Microencapsulation

Microencapsulation of animal tissues, allowing useful products to leak out of the capsule while preventing antibodies from getting in, is one approach being worked on. It may prove useful eventually in treating endocrine or metabolic disorders through implantation. Where direct contact between graft and host cells is needed for neurological

> Despite active research into alternative materials for transplantation, it seems that, for the present, fetal tissue from elective abortion provides the only reliable source of tissue for transplantation research.

or other applications, it may be less useful, although researchers at Brown University in the United States, working with a commercial company, are awaiting government approval to begin clinical trials for patients with Parkinson disease on a newly patented capsule containing dopamine-producing rat tumour cells.[5] Several other laboratories are pursuing this line of work, and several U.S. companies have recently been formed to use similar approaches.

Despite active research into alternative materials for transplantation, it seems that, for the present, fetal tissue from elective abortion provides the only reliable source of tissue for transplantation research. Alternative therapies that do not involve transplantation may also be developed — for example, the development of new drugs to treat Parkinson disease or to improve disease prevention.

Potential Availability of Fetal Tissue

Given that elective abortion currently provides the only reliable source of fetal tissue for transplantation research, it is relevant to know how the present availability of fetal tissue from this source is related to the potential demand for it, should transplantation treatment prove effective.

Fetal tissue is currently collected for research and therapeutic use from about 1 percent of induced abortions performed in Canadian hospitals. Present research thus uses only a small fraction of the available fetal tissue. U.S. studies have found more than 90 percent of women undergoing abortion would consent to the use of tissue for research or transplantation, and some Canadian observers believe the same would hold in Canada. It is probable that fetal tissue could therefore be collected from most of the abortions performed annually in Canada.

We can compare this potential availability of tissue with the estimated annual incidence of the diseases most likely to be treatable by human fetal tissue transplantation in the near future. Approximately 8 000 new cases of Parkinson disease and 4 000 cases of insulin-dependent diabetes mellitus are diagnosed in Canada each year. However, since other methods of treatment work for all but the most serious cases, less than 10 percent of such patients would be possible candidates for fetal tissue transplants in the near future. The annual number of new cases of leukemia and congenital immunodeficiency disorders is approximately 4 000, and about 100 cases of Huntington disease occur each year, but the availability of other methods of treatment means the use of fetal tissue would be indicated only in some of these cases. The figures therefore suggest that the tissue available from therapeutic abortions would be more than sufficient to accommodate the need for tissue for therapeutic uses in the foreseeable future.

It is impossible to make accurate longer-range predictions. On one hand, some speculative future applications of fetal tissue transplantation could involve many more patients. On the other hand, the development of preventive measures, alternative treatments, or alternative sources of transplantable tissue could eliminate much of the potential future demand for fetal tissue. Another factor in any longer-term prediction is change in the incidence or methods of abortion. For example, if the use of RU-486 became widespread, the supply of fetal tissue usable for research or treatment would diminish. These factors render attempts at longer-range prediction largely futile.

Regulations Relevant to Fetal Tissue Use in Canada

On the basis of the evidence we have reviewed, we judge that there is a real possibility that research involving the use of fetal tissue could result in considerable alleviation of human suffering. It is also evident to us that, at present, elective abortion provides the only practical source of fetal tissue for such treatment. Even if transplantation proves largely unsuccessful, a wide range of other research, diagnostic, and educational uses of fetal tissue can and already do provide important health benefits to society.

We are very conscious of the need to address the many ethical and social questions raised by fetal tissue use and to safeguard against the possible risks of coercion, commercialization, and the promotion of abortion. We need to determine whether it is possible, through legislation or other regulatory mechanisms, to eliminate these risks while allowing society to realize the benefits. In approaching this question, we looked first at the current system of laws and professional guidelines that relate to fetal tissue use in Canada.

At present, the principal laws governing the research use of human tissue are the provincial tissue transfer laws. These are based largely on the 1971 *Uniform Tissue Gift Act*, developed by the Conference of Commissioners on Uniformity of Legislation in Canada (the Uniform Law Conference of Canada). The act requires obtaining the consent of living persons for the transplantation of their tissue into another person.

> Strict guidelines [should] be formulated under the Health Act specifying under what conditions fetal tissue can be obtained for research; and that the effectiveness of fetal tissue transplants [should] be monitored by a national committee on bioethics. Monitoring and guidelines should: (a) prevent abuse of the technology, such as ensuring that no fetus is aborted solely to provide transplant tissue; [and] (b) ensure that the abortion method used is one that is best suited to the welfare of the woman involved, rather than for the optimal preservation of the fetal tissue for transplant.
>
> *Brief to the Commission from the Provincial Council of Women of British Columbia, July 24, 1990.*

It is not clear whether many of the provincial human tissue gift acts (HTGAs) include fetal material in the definition of "tissue." Two clearly do not. The acts of Manitoba and Prince Edward Island specifically exclude fetuses from the definition of tissue. On the other hand, the wording of the Quebec *Civil Code* may be broad enough to regulate transplantation of fetal tissue. If fetal material is covered under the *Civil Code* and other provincial acts, their provisions will require asking the woman from whom a fetus is removed for her consent to the use of the tissue. If that consent is not given, the tissue cannot be used for transplantation.

Even if fetal tissue is not interpreted as "tissue" under various HTGAs in the common law provinces, it may well be considered "body parts." HTGAs generally prohibit the sale of body parts as well as tissue. This is consistent with laws prohibiting the sale of human organs in the United States and most of Western Europe. The acts provide procedures that can be used to secure the donor's consent for the use of body parts after the donor's death for use in therapy, research, or education. The acts also appear to leave it open to use procedures other than those set out in the acts to obtain body parts for use in transplantation.

If a court or legislature ultimately decides that the transplantation of fetal material is not regulated by HTGAs, the common law or civil law will apply. Historically, there was a common law presumption that when a patient entered a hospital, he or she implicitly abandoned to science any tissue or body parts removed during surgery. This abandoned material might then be used for research or education. That presumption of abandonment might be rebutted if the patient expressed a specific interest in retaining the body part.

However, recent developments in the United States suggest that this presumption may be changing. In *Moore v. Regents of the University of California*,[6] physicians used a patient's spleen, which had been surgically removed for health reasons, to develop a highly profitable cell line. They did not inform the patient that they were intending to use the spleen for this purpose. The Supreme Court of California concluded that a physician must disclose personal interests unrelated to the patient's health in order to satisfy the physician's fiduciary duty and to obtain the patient's informed consent to the medical procedure. In *Moore*, Mr. Justice Panelli concluded as follows:

> Even if the splenectomy had a therapeutic purpose, it does not follow that [the physician] had no duty to disclose his additional research and economic interests ... [T]he existence of a motivation for a medical procedure unrelated to the patient's health is a potential conflict of interest and a fact material to the patient's decision.[7]

The findings in this case are not, of course, binding on Canadian courts, and the facts can be distinguished from the situation of using fetal tissue for transplantation, education, or non-commercial research. Still, the reasoning in this case suggests that the legal thinking in this area may be evolving. In addition, the requirement of full and informed consent in the medical treatment context (as well as for research or other uses) is consistent with constitutional law principles relating to human dignity and autonomy. It can therefore reasonably be assumed that consent should be sought for use of tissue or body parts, including fetal tissue, taken from patients if the intended use is not routine pathological examination but research, creation of cell lines, banking, treatment (including transplantation), or education.

However, the form and timing of this consent have not been legally defined, and the practice of hospitals in terms of seeking such consent varies. The most common practice in Canada is to ask patients who enter hospital to sign an admission form containing a general waiver regarding the use of tissue removed during surgery. The wording of this waiver varies. For example, it may ask the patient to give the hospital authorization to "dispose" of tissues and body parts. Some hospitals treat the patient's consent to dispose of tissue as implicitly including authorization to use the tissue in research or education. In other cases, the hospital admission form may simply include a more explicit reference to the possibility that surgically removed tissue may be used for research purposes. Most hospitals in Canada operate on the assumption that the general waiver signed by patients when they are admitted to hospital is sufficient for legal purposes. Only the revised Quebec *Civil Code* (in force January 1, 1994) specifically provides that consent must be obtained for any research on human cells, tissues, and substances.

Some hospitals seek consent to the use of tissue removed during a particular operation, rather than (or in addition to) a general waiver regarding the use of any and all tissue that may be removed during the course of the patient's stay in hospital. This operation-specific consent may take two forms. Hospitals may include a clause regarding the use of removed tissue in the consent form for the particular operation. This is common in the United States, where standard consent forms for elective abortions contain a clause asking for consent to the use of fetal tissue for research or education. One standard formulation of this clause is as follows: "I further understand that in accordance with applicable law, any tissue removed may be examined and retained for medical or educational purposes and may be disposed of in accordance with the custom practised."

More rarely, patients may be asked to sign a separate consent form regarding the use of removed tissue, in addition to the consent form for the surgery itself. This makes it clear that consent to the procedure does not require consent to the particular use of the tissue.

In short, considerable uncertainty surrounds the legal status of fetal tissue and the state of the law regarding the need for consent to the use of removed fetal tissue for transplantation, research, or education. There is also some lack of uniformity across Canada in provisions governing commerce in human tissue and body parts, which likely includes fetal material.

Some groups suggested to the Commission that fetuses are not legally parts of the pregnant woman's body, but rather persons in their own right. In this view, any legal obligation that may exist to obtain informed consent would require the fetus itself to consent to the use of its tissue (through some proxy). As we have discussed in Chapter 30, although the Supreme Court

Considerable uncertainty surrounds the legal status of fetal tissue and the state of the law regarding the need for consent to the use of removed fetal tissue for transplantation, research, or education. There is also some lack of uniformity across Canada in provisions governing commerce in human tissue and body parts, which likely includes fetal material.

of Canada has not yet ruled on the status of the fetus under the *Canadian Charter of Rights and Freedoms*, it has decided that a fetus is not a person under Quebec civil law, the Quebec Charter, common law, or under the Canadian *Criminal Code*. It is therefore very unlikely that the Court would find that a fetus has independent rights under the Canadian Charter. This means that no consent or other legal obligations would be owed to the fetus. The consent that would be required, if any, is therefore that of the woman.

In addition to these possible legal requirements, the Medical Research Council's *Guidelines on Research Involving Human Subjects* govern fetal tissue acquisitions. Compliance with these guidelines, adopted in 1987, is necessary where the research in question is funded by the MRC, but the guidelines have also been adopted widely by research institutions, universities, hospitals, and other granting agencies in Canada. The guidelines state that the woman's permission to use "separated tissue and placental material" in research should be sought "wherever possible." In research designed to use fetal tissue from therapeutic abortions, the guidelines also state that the research protocol must not

The use of tissues or cells obtained from elective abortions [should be acceptable] in research designed to improve understanding of health and disease, or to provide means of treating intractable disease, [provided that]: research requirements must exert no influence on any aspect of the abortion, including the decision to abort, the timing and the procedures used; consent of the mother to use the tissues or cells must be obtained; [and] the research protocol must be approved by a Research Ethics Board as outlined in the [MRC] Guidelines [on Research Involving Human Subjects].

Brief to the Commission from the Medical Research Council of Canada, April 1991.

influence the choice of procedure used for the abortion.

However, like the common law, the MRC's requirement of "consent" is unclear. The MRC guidelines do not provide much guidance regarding the extent, form, or timing of this informed consent. For example, what kind of information should be given to the pregnant woman, and when should her consent to tissue donation be sought? Is it enough to include a general waiver within a hospital admission form or a clause within the consent form for the abortion procedure?

We believe that the pregnant woman's consent to the use of fetal tissue should be separate from the consent to hospital admission or to the abortion procedure. A clause in the abortion consent form may be overlooked by patients who are focussing on the risks and benefits of a surgical procedure. Unless there is a separate form, the woman may not realize that her consent to the abortion does not require her to consent to the use of the tissue. Moreover, this clause does not provide enough information to allow the woman's informed consent to use of the tissue. For example, it does not provide information regarding protection of her anonymity or the possible need for serological testing of her if the tissue is to be used specifically for transplantation.

Hence, we believe that a separate consent form should be required for uses of fetal tissue other than for the routine examination of the tissue that is a part of the medical care of the patient. All other uses of fetal tissue — including education and research — should require the separate consent of the woman undergoing the abortion. We discuss the requirements of informed consent further below.

> We believe that the pregnant woman's consent to the use of fetal tissue should be separate from the consent to hospital admission or to the abortion procedure.

Canadian legislation and guidelines also have other gaps. For example, there is no guidance regarding who should be allowed to obtain and distribute fetal tissue or who should have access to it. There should also be guidelines outlining whether the timing or method of abortion can be modified, as well as guidelines with respect to the timing of request for permission to use fetal tissue in research. Such guidelines are common in other countries and are needed in Canada (see Appendix 1, The Regulation of Fetal Tissue Use in Other Countries).

Issues and Recommendations

We have grouped our recommendations into five areas of concern: the ethical uses of fetal tissue; obtaining tissue and informed consent; the commercialization of fetal tissue; the funding of research using fetal tissue; and accountability.

The Ethical Uses of Fetal Tissue

Commissioners heard arguments that the use of fetal tissue in research (whatever the source) violates the principle of respect for human life, since it treats fetuses as a means. In the Commissioners' judgement, this is not the case. Research and other use of tissue and organs from children and adults who have died are allowed. Most Canadians accept that organ transplantation and research on human cadaver tissues for valid scientific purposes are consistent with respect for human life; by analogy, we conclude that research on human fetal tissue is acceptable under controlled conditions. Indeed, attending to the ethic of care would suggest this research not only should be permissible but should be pursued, if it appears to hold the best likelihood of leading to effective treatment. However, this should be done only in circumstances that ensure tissue is obtained with safeguards against coercion, commercialization, and unethical use in place and is used for purposes that respect human life and dignity. In light of these considerations, the Commission recommends that

> The range of current and future applications of human fetal cadaver gives evidence of the importance of these applications for the advancement of knowledge and the improvement of medical therapy. However, increasing use of this tissue will also have ethical, legal, and social implications.
>
> *A. Fine, "Human Fetal Tissue Research: Origins, State of the Art, Future Applications, and Implications," in Research Volumes of the Commission, 1993.*

> **277. The provision of human fetal tissue for use in research, or for any purpose not related to the medical care of the woman herself, be subject to compulsory licensing by the National Reproductive Technologies Commission.**

In the next few pages we outline some of the aspects of regulating fetal tissue provision that we believe should be part of the conditions under which facilities obtain and hold a licence to provide fetal tissue.

Respect for human life clearly imposes certain limitations on research using fetal tissue. It is important to ensure, for example, that fetal death has been determined before tissue is taken. Concerns have been raised that fetuses might be kept alive artificially to improve the chances of securing more viable tissue. We found no evidence of this. When the standard vacuum aspiration technique is used to terminate a pregnancy in the first trimester, this would not be a concern, as only fragmented tissues, not intact fetuses, are recovered. If other abortion methods (such as saline or prostaglandin inductions or low vacuum procedures) are used, however, it is possible that an intact fetus would be recovered; to guard against the possibility of abuses in such cases, the determination of fetal death should be made by someone other than the researcher who is to use the tissue. The Commission recommends that

> **278. When abortion methods other than standard vacuum aspiration in the first trimester are used,**
> **(a) research use of fetal tissue be permitted only after fetal death has been established; and**
> **(b) fetal death be established by a physician not associated with subsequent use of the tissue.**

We found that there are no Canadian guidelines establishing appropriate criteria for fetal death. Because the fetus is at a much earlier developmental stage, the criteria for death focussing on brain function that have been developed for newborns are not necessarily applicable. Since it would be unethical to use tissue from a living fetus, appropriate definitions of fetal death are required and must be developed with input from those with relevant expertise. The Commission recommends that

> **279. Determination of fetal death be based on national standards of fetal death, and that these be developed by Health Canada in conjunction with the provinces/territories, relevant professionals, and ethicists.**

Respect for human life precludes the use of fetal tissue for any purpose other than scientifically valid research intended to improve understanding of human functioning and disease, or to provide improved means of diagnosing and treating disease. Accordingly, the Commission recommends that

> **280. Fetal tissue use in research be permitted only if the research is directed to understanding human functioning or disease, or to diagnose or treat disease.**

Obtaining Tissue and Informed Consent

There is no empirical evidence to support the claim that permitting research using fetal tissue encourages abortion. For example, we found no reports of changes in the incidence of abortion in locations where well-publicized clinical trials of fetal tissue transplantation are under way. Nevertheless, this possibility should be guarded against by establishing a structure that creates a clear separation between the clinical care of the pregnant woman and her decision-making processes, and the researchers using fetal tissue. This separation is important in guarding against the possibility that researchers who want to obtain fetal tissue could influence a woman's decision to have an abortion. This safeguard will ensure that abortion is not encouraged by caregivers and will take into account respect for human life. Such a separation is also required by respect for the woman's autonomy, since it will ensure that women will not be subject to pressure or coercion to terminate a pregnancy, to modify the abortion method used, or to consent to the use of fetal tissue in research. The precise mechanisms for separating the decision to terminate a pregnancy from consideration of any subsequent tissue use are discussed below.

Separating Consent to Abortion from Consent to Tissue Use

Any request or discussion of use of fetal tissue for research should be deferred until after the woman gives informed consent to an abortion. This would apply to all settings where the option of abortion is discussed, including family practices, genetics clinics, family planning clinics, abortion clinics, and specialists' services. Only after a woman has chosen to abort a pregnancy, and has consented in writing to the procedure, should she be informed about the possible uses of fetal tissue. Women should not be pressured in any way to give consent, which is why it is important that the issue of fetal tissue use not be raised at all until after her decision is made. It should also be made clear that her decision regarding consent to the use of fetal tissue will not in any way affect the quality of her clinical care. Each decision — to have an abortion, and to consent to tissue use — should be made independently of the other.

The method for seeking consent to fetal tissue use should be in keeping with the principles of full disclosure and autonomy. The woman should also be informed of the provisions to protect the anonymity of donors. If the tissue is to be used for research involving transplantation into a human patient, she should be informed of the need for serological testing, including HIV testing. (Such testing is not necessary for research not involving transplantation.)

It is possible that a potential commercial application may emerge after some time; for example, a cell line derived from fetal tissue may on further study turn out to have unanticipated or commercially useful purposes. The woman should be informed of this possibility, and her consent should include the understanding that she will not receive any benefit from such use.

We believe that consent procedures of this type will help to guard against the possibility that researchers who want to obtain fetal tissue could influence a woman's decision to have an abortion. The Commission recommends that

281. (a) Any use of fetal tissue (other than routine examination or tests as part of medical care) requires the informed consent, in writing, of the woman undergoing therapeutic abortion.

(b) This consent must be obtained separately from, and subsequent to, her decision to terminate the pregnancy.

(c) Consent to fetal tissue use must be sought in a manner that makes it clear that the woman's decision with respect to the use of fetal tissue will not affect the quality of her medical care.

(d) Consent to the use of fetal tissue in research and education should be obtained When the tissue is to be used for research involving transplantation into a human patient, specific authorization for this use should also be obtained; in this case, the woman should be informed and consent to serological testing, including HIV testing.

(e) The woman should be informed that, if a project has commercial potential, no commercial or other financial benefit will accrue to her.

We believe that these recommendations will ensure the necessary separation of the decision to terminate a pregnancy from consideration of whether and how the tissue will be used. It will help ensure that the possible donation of fetal tissue does not affect the woman's decision to terminate the pregnancy or the medical care provided by her physician. To protect this separation even further, we believe several other steps are also required relating to protection of the woman's privacy, the method of abortion, the designation of tissue recipients, and co-authorship credit.

Anonymity

Privacy must be respected in any research project. Once the tissue has been collected, any information that would allow either the woman or her partner to be identified should be removed. Non-identifying information about either partner could accompany the tissue, but only if needed and only if specified in advance in the research protocol.

For example, a researcher involved in transplantation research may need to know certain facts about the woman and her pregnancy (for example, her age, medical history, HIV status, the stage of pregnancy, the sex of the fetus).   The researcher would list such parameters in the research protocol, and this information would then be included with the tissue.   However, information about the personal identity of the woman would never accompany the tissue. The Commission recommends that

> **282. No personally identifying information regarding the woman accompany fetal tissue.**

Method of Abortion

A decision to permit use of fetal tissue in research should not alter a woman's health care in any way; in particular, it should not influence the choice of abortion method. As noted earlier, prolonging a pregnancy or altering the abortion method can increase the likelihood that resulting fetal tissue will be more suitable for transplantation purposes. However, the method of abortion should be chosen on the basis of what is best for the woman and never on the basis of the suitability of fetal tissue for transplantation research. Any method used must have been demonstrated not to increase the risk for the woman in any way and must not involve prolonging the pregnancy.

At present, Canada has no uniform guidelines or legislation concerning the permissibility of modifying abortion procedures expressly to facilitate recovery of fetal tissue.   We are of the view that this situation is undesirable. The Commission recommends that

> **283. The abortion method and timing be chosen solely to protect the health and interests of the woman involved.**

Prohibiting Designation of the Recipient of Fetal Tissue

Given the current availability of fetal tissue from therapeutic abortions and the relatively limited use of it, it does not seem likely that in the foreseeable future there will be heightened pressure from researchers or potential transplant recipients for women to donate fetal tissue for research. However, in specific cases where compatible tissue would be of possible benefit in transplantation, there might be pressure to consent to a donation, particularly from near relatives.

At present, Canada has no law that would prevent such "directed" donations, and the issue of directed donation is not mentioned in the MRC guidelines. This means it would be possible for a woman to consent to donate fetal tissue on condition that it be used to treat someone she designates.

Permitting fetal tissue to be used to treat a designated person creates the possibility that a woman might initiate a pregnancy deliberately to produce fetal tissue for transplantation to a loved one, or that she might be persuaded to terminate a wanted pregnancy in order to benefit someone important to her. This is using a fetus as a means to an end and would contradict the principle of respect for human life. It would devalue human reproduction and, consequently, human life. Indeed, we found that most Canadians are deeply uncomfortable with and reject the idea of a woman becoming pregnant for these reasons.

> While women undoubtedly are entitled to access to abortion, there may be some ethically justified limitations on their freedom to determine the use of embryonic and fetal tissue. Analogously, blood donors are not free to specify to what use their blood is put. And no one has the freedom to compel clinics to make use of their excised organs.
>
> *C. Overall, reviewer, research volumes of the Commission, May 29, 1992.*

We conclude that regulations should prohibit health professionals or facilities from any role in facilitating the use of fetal tissue in a designated or intrafamilial recipient; this would ensure that pregnancies were not undertaken with the intention of providing fetal tissue for a designated recipient. Women undergoing abortion should not know the identity of recipients of fetal tissue participating in research trials or therapy, nor should recipients know the source of the tissue. The Commission recommends that

284. Designation of recipients of fetal tissue by women undergoing abortion be prohibited.

In Britain, a centralized fetal tissue bank (analogous to a blood bank) has been established to receive fetal tissue and distribute it to approved research projects. This tissue bank serves as an intermediary, guaranteeing that there is no contact between the woman and the recipient of fetal tissue. Because of the limited extent of fetal tissue use in transplantation at this time, we do not believe it is necessary to recommend a centralized structure of this type. However, this issue should be re-evaluated by the National Reproductive Technologies Commission if fetal tissue transplantation use proves effective and expands in the future.

Benefits from Providing Fetal Tissue

Finally, to protect the separation of clinical and research responsibilities, we believe that the supplier of fetal tissue should not derive benefit from doing so. A supplier should not receive funding from research grants involving the use of fetal tissue or derive any other indirect financial benefit as a result of tissue provision. This prohibition should not prevent cost recovery for providing processing, transportation, or services such as microbiological testing of the tissue. In addition, a supplier of fetal tissue should not be given co-authorship credit for this role in any publications that emerge as a result of the research use of fetal tissue if this is the only contribution to the research. According to a survey, 30 percent of doctors in Canada accepted the idea of co-authorship credit for the supplier of fetal tissue.[8] Nevertheless, Commissioners believe that this creates a conflict of interest, and it means that the obtaining of consent to abortion may be subtly influenced. The Commission recommends that

> **285. Physicians supplying fetal tissue do not receive co-authorship credit for this role in publications resulting from the research use of that fetal tissue, or any direct or indirect financial benefit.**

Commercialization and Patenting

The non-commercialization of reproduction is one of our guiding principles. Apart from its threat to human dignity, the commercialization of fetal tissue could open the door to exploitation of poor women, especially in developing countries, who might be persuaded to begin and end pregnancies for money. It is therefore important to develop measures to limit the possibility of trade in fetal tissue.

In 1989, the World Health Assembly, concerned about commercial trafficking in human organs, adopted a resolution to prevent the purchase and sale of human organs. It called on member states to introduce, as part of their organ transplantation policies, a set of guiding principles,[9] including the following:

* Giving or receiving payment (including any other compensation or reward) for organs should be prohibited.

* Advertising the need for or availability of organs, with a view to offering or seeking payment, should be prohibited.

* Physicians and other health professionals should be prohibited from engaging in organ transplantation procedures if they have reason to believe that the organs concerned have been the subject of commercial transactions.

- Organs should be made available to patients on the basis of medical need, not on the basis of financial or other considerations.

We believe that these principles should also apply to fetal tissue. As we have noted, laws prohibiting the sale of human organs are now in place in Canada, the United States, and most of Western Europe. However, not all of those laws in Canada include fetal tissue explicitly or implicitly. This is why the Commission recommended that the commercial exchange of fetuses and fetal tissue be prohibited under threat of criminal sanction (see Chapter 5). The Commission recommends further that

> **286. Provincial human tissue gift acts be amended specifically to prohibit the sale of fetal tissues and any payment to the woman from whom the tissue is obtained.**

A further step is needed to ensure that any Canadian use of fetal tissue obtained in countries without laws or guidelines dealing with tissue and organ donation does not encourage unethical or harmful practices in those countries. Given the dearth of relevant legislation in much of the world, we believe that importation of fetal tissue by Canadian research facilities, including biotechnology and pharmaceutical companies, should be regulated.

Although it is our conclusion that the sale of fetal tissue should be prohibited, medical facilities that recover fetal tissues, preserve, differentiate, and diagnose them; prepare them for transportation; and transport them should be able to recover the costs of such services, as is the case with organ transplants. These service charges (as distinct from commodity sales) are permissible under the World Health Assembly's ethical guidelines and should continue to be allowed. (Since these expenses are not incurred by the woman giving permission to the use of fetal tissue, no financial payment should ever be made to her.)

No profit should be made on these services, however; they should be provided only on a cost-recovery basis. One U.S. company that provides fetal pancreatic islet cells free of charge for use in diabetes clinical trials is planning to market these cells in the next few years. Proposed service charges for the acquisition, preparation, storage, and transportation of these cells would make the company a profitable business. The company estimates that there is a potential $8 billion market worldwide for the treatment of diabetes.[10] We believe that so-called "service charges" should not provide a source of profit for private industry dealing with fetal tissue, since this would amount to the commodification of fetal tissue. Service charges in this country should be set at appropriate levels, that is, simply to recover costs. The Commission recommends that

287. The prohibition of the commercial exchange of fetuses and fetal tissue extend to tissue imported from other countries, so that no fetuses or fetal tissues are used in Canada for which women have received payment, or where a profit has been made by an intermediary.

and that

288. The costs of handling fetal tissue be recoverable only on a not-for-profit basis.

Resolving the issue of commercialization of fetal tissue still leaves the more complicated question of the appropriateness of patenting products or processes developed through research on fetal tissue. For example, researchers may discover a new way to culture fetal neural cells, discover and maintain a particular cell line that produces a therapeutically useful product, or discover a way to treat cultured cells that increases their production of neurotransmitters. Transplanted neural tissue that has been cultured in this way might be particularly useful in treating disease; alternatively, the substances produced by the altered cells might be of use in treatment. Developing and perfecting such techniques might require significant financial investment, however, and governments may be unable or unwilling to develop and support this research. Pharmaceutical, biotechnological, or other companies might invest in the development of potentially beneficial products or processes, but only if there is a reasonable expectation of profit. The possibility of profit may depend on the existence of intellectual property protection, such as patent or copyright.

We discussed the issues raised by patenting such innovations in Chapter 24. To recapitulate, Commissioners believe strongly that fetuses should never be an appropriate subject for patents. However, if they are intended to benefit human health, and if the safeguards we have recommended for obtaining and using fetal tissue are in place, innovative products and processes using fetal tissue as a source may warrant some limited form of patent protection. However, this is an area we have identified as requiring further study before policies are made, bearing in mind the principles we outline in that chapter.

> Commissioners believe strongly that fetuses should never be an appropriate subject for patents. However, if they are intended to benefit human health, and if the safeguards we have recommended for obtaining and using fetal tissue are in place, innovative products and processes using fetal tissue as a source may warrant some limited form of patent protection.

Funding of Fetal Tissue Research

A variety of public and private agencies provide funds for research projects involving fetal tissue use. The largest source of public funds for this research is the Medical Research Council. However, as noted earlier, the MRC decided not to fund a particular type of fetal tissue research — transplantation research using tissue from elective abortions — after the Minister of the Department of National Health and Welfare objected to such funding in 1988.

We believe that there is clear justification for public funding of many forms of research using fetal tissue, including both basic research and research into transplantation. Basic research involving fetal tissue has had a proven record for many decades and has played an important role in the development of vaccines and antibodies, in the diagnosis of viruses, and, in general, in understanding many facets of human health and disease.

Whether fetal tissue transplantation research will result in the development of beneficial and efficacious treatments is not known; however, we believe that funding of this research is justified. The potential benefits are substantial, particularly in terms of reducing the human suffering caused by disease. The ethic of care means we must avoid or prevent this suffering if possible. Obviously, many of the most important benefits cannot be measured in economic terms, but if we consider the impact on medical care, productivity, and other factors, their impact could be enormous.

In supporting research that may lead to effective treatment of disease in the future, it is important not to neglect the immediate needs of those currently affected by these diseases — both must be taken into account in resource allocation decisions. Nor should promising research into alternative treatments or prevention strategies for these diseases be neglected. Fetal tissue transplantation is unlikely ever to replace the need for more conventional approaches and treatments.

The recent situation in the United States suggests what can happen when public funding for fetal tissue transplantation research is withdrawn. Rather than adopting legislation to control fetal tissue transplantation research, the U.S. federal government withdrew funding in 1988, as a result of pressure from the anti-abortion lobby, thereby creating a legislative and regulatory vacuum. Despite the unanimous recommendation of a government-appointed advisory committee that the funding prohibition be lifted, the Bush administration subsequently extended the ban until 1992. (As previously noted, the ban was lifted by the Clinton administration.)

This funding prohibition had several unintended effects. Rather than being halted entirely, some fetal tissue transplantation research continued with private funding, which meant that it escaped the review and accountability mechanisms that accompany public funding. The United

States also lost some highly qualified researchers to other countries, including Canada.

The U.S. experience shows the pitfalls of trying to ban public research funding or allowing research to go on in a regulatory vacuum. We believe that MRC's ban has discouraged other agencies from funding such work in Canada (as did the ban in the United States). We believe that federal funding of fetal tissue transplantation research would support potentially life-saving research, while also providing, through accountability for the use of public funds, a mechanism to monitor and regulate the ethical use of fetal tissue. The Commission recommends that

> **289. Research projects using fetal tissue (including those related to transplantation in human beings) be eligible for public funding by the Medical Research Council of Canada and other agencies, provided they meet applicable ethical and scientific research standards and tissue is obtained in accordance with the recommendations of the Royal Commission on New Reproductive Technologies.**

Accountability

In the absence of national or provincial laws or guidelines governing the use of fetal tissue, research proposals are reviewed by hospital, clinic, or university research ethics boards. These differ in composition, expertise, and approach and operate without the benefit of a common set of detailed guidelines. Moreover, private sector research involving fetal tissue is not necessarily subject to research ethics board review and approval. To date in Canada, there has been no way of approving or accrediting individual physicians or clinics as sources of fetal tissue or to ensure that appropriate records on the collection and distribution of fetal tissue are kept.

The experience of such agencies as the National Disease Research Interchange in the United States and the Medical Research Council Tissue Bank in Great Britain suggests that there are advantages to a government-supported central organization for monitoring fetal tissue use. The ethical, safety, and record-keeping standards of these organizations are clearly superior to the unregulated and undocumented individual arrangements through which Canadian researchers currently obtain such tissue. A key advantage of centralized oversight is that it can also bring the private sector under legislative and regulatory control; another is that information can be made available for the public on the use of fetal tissue.

Licensing will ensure that use of fetal tissue for research or education taking place in both the public and private sectors uses only tissue that has been obtained in compliance with the ethical guidelines we have recommended with respect to informed consent, the determination of fetal death, the separation of clinical and research responsibilities, and the absence of designated donation, among other matters. As a condition of licence, fetal tissue would be provided only to

> As a condition of licence, fetal tissue would be provided only to researchers/users who have obtained research ethics board approval for the use ... Clear guidelines set by the National Reproductive Technologies Commission should be used by these boards.

researchers/users who have obtained research ethics board approval for the use. Since some research ethics boards may not have broad representation, and to help ensure consistency of approach, clear guidelines set by the National Reproductive Technologies Commission should be used by these boards in their decisions on any research project proposing to use fetal tissue. Taken together, these measures will ensure that the use of fetal tissue is for legitimate purposes, related to education or improving human health, and is obtained in an ethical way. It will also enable information to be collected that allows the public to know about the use of fetal tissue in Canada, thus enhancing accountability.

The specific details of the licensing scheme we recommend are set out below.

Licensing Requirements for the Provision of Human Fetal Tissue to Users

The Commission recommends that

> 290. **Compulsory licensing be required for the provision of human fetal tissue by any physician, centre, clinic, or other individual or facility providing human fetal tissue for research (including transplantation research) or for any purpose other than medical care of the woman, routine pathology testing, or disposal.**

> 291. **Providing fetal tissue without a licence issued by the National Reproductive Technologies Commission, or without complying with the National Reproductive Technologies**

Commission's licensing requirements, as outlined below, constitutes an offence subject to prosecution.

and that

292. The National Reproductive Technologies Commission establish a permanent Fetal Tissue Sub-Committee to monitor the supply and use of fetal tissue, to develop standards and guidelines to be adopted as conditions of licence, and to oversee the implementation of the licensing program.

The Commission recommends that

293. In particular, the following requirements be adopted as conditions of licence:

(a) Unless obtained using first-trimester standard vacuum aspiration, only fetal tissue from fetuses that have been pronounced dead by a physician not associated with the subsequent use of the tissue can be provided for use in research.

(b) The full and informed consent of the woman, sought independently of and subsequent to the decision to abort, and including specific consent for use of fetal tissue in research involving transplantation, must be obtained in relation to any fetal tissue provided for use.

(c) Donation of fetal tissue to designated recipients should not be permitted.

(d) The exchange of fetal tissue should not occur on a for-profit basis; payment should be limited to the reasonable costs of handling, transporting, or testing of such tissue.

(e) The use of fetal tissue in research (or any other use) should be permitted only if the research is directed to understanding biological mechanisms with potential medical relevance or treating disease.

(f)   Fetal tissue should be provided only for projects that meet ethical research guidelines developed by the Fetal Tissue Sub-Committee of the National Commission and that have received prior institutional research ethics board approval, including scientific and ethical review. Written documentation of such approval must be obtained before any fetal tissue is provided for use and must be held on file by the provider for five years.

(g)   Licensed individuals or facilities providing human fetal tissue for use would be required to comply with record-keeping, data collection, and data reporting requirements established by the National Reproductive Technologies Commission.

(h)   Licence holders would be required to report annually to the National Reproductive Technologies Commission in accordance with requirements established by the National Commission with respect to the form and content of information, including information on the number and type of projects for which fetal tissue has been supplied.

The Role of the Fetal Tissue Sub-Committee

We referred to some of the functions of the Fetal Tissue Sub-Committee in the licensing conditions set out above. However, in light of the key role the Sub-Committee will play in ensuring the ethical and accountable use of fetal tissue in Canada, it is also important to note the Sub-Committee's other functions here.

The Fetal Tissue Sub-Committee would be established and chaired by the National Reproductive Technologies Commission. It would be one of six permanent sub-committees, along with those dealing with infertility prevention; assisted conception services; assisted insemination services; prenatal diagnosis; and embryo research. Like National Commission members themselves, we recommend that at least half the members of the Fetal Tissue Sub-Committee be women, and that all members be chosen with a view to ensuring that they have a background and demonstrated experience in dealing with a multidisciplinary approach to issues, as well as an ability to work together to find solutions and recommend policies to address the issues raised by the use of fetal tissue in research in a way that meets the concerns of Canadian society as a whole.

As well as setting and revising the licensing requirements for the provision of human fetal tissue to users, the Fetal Tissue Sub-Committee would

- develop ethical research guidelines to be applied by institutional or local research ethics boards in reviewing and approving projects involving the use of fetal tissue and ensuring that such guidelines are applied in an appropriate fashion;

- compile, analyze, and report to the public (through the National Commission's annual report) information documenting the use of fetal tissue in Canada and documenting that local research ethics boards are applying the National Commission's guidelines in an appropriate fashion; and

- monitor developments in the area of research using fetal tissue with a view to keeping the public informed, promoting public dialogue, and anticipating or proposing the need for further regulatory involvement in this field.

Conclusion

Transplantation is only one subcategory of fetal tissue use in research; only a very small proportion of fetal tissue currently used in research is used for transplantation research. Many important and far-reaching health benefits have been gained, however, from other studies and research using fetal tissue.

At present, virtually all use of fetal tissue in transplantation constitutes research. Indeed, fetal tissue transplantation is considered the treatment of choice in only one instance — to treat DiGeorge syndrome, a rare inherited immunodeficiency disease for which fetal thymus tissue transplantation is the recommended treatment.

Fetal tissue transplantation may be found to be of little or no therapeutic value — in which case there is not likely to be any increase in the demand for fetal tissue for this purpose. On the other hand, if these techniques are found to be of benefit in treating disease, significant increases in the demand for fetal tissue could result. If treatment based on cell lines was found to be as effective as the direct use of fetal tissue, this, too, would alter the situation. We cannot predict what will happen in the future as research evolves. What we must do instead is to ensure that, whatever the outcome of research, we have already set in place limits and boundaries to prevent misuse and coercion and, within those limits, have put in place a regulatory system and licensing to ensure only beneficial and ethical uses of fetal tissue.

The progress in adult organ transplantation over the last two decades, as well as early results in fetal tissue transplantation, suggest that there is a reasonable possibility that some forms of transplantation will move from research to clinical practice in the next few years. The possibility of benefit to people suffering from disease

> The use of fetal tissues or cells is acceptable in research designed to improve understanding of human functioning and to explore means of treating human disease. We judge it important, however, that any use of human fetal tissue be in the context of the boundaries, regulatory system, and guidelines we have outlined.

means we have an ethical obligation to pursue it — if it can be done without harm to others. The regulatory system we have outlined offers a means of ensuring this and is a response to issues of national importance.

In summary, the Commission concludes that the use of fetal tissues or cells is acceptable in research designed to improve understanding of human functioning and to explore means of treating human disease. We judge it important, however, that any use of human fetal tissue be in the context of the boundaries, regulatory system, and guidelines we have outlined. If fetal tissue transplantation is found in future to be more effective than other therapies for the treatment of a disease, its use should be permitted — provided the tissue is collected, distributed, and used in the ethical manner we have outlined. We would also encourage research, however, into alternatives to treatments using fetal tissues.

Appendix 1: The Regulation of Fetal Tissue Use in Other Countries

For background information on the use of fetal tissue, we examined the regulation of this research in other jurisdictions, including Australia, Germany, Holland, France, the United States, Sweden, and the United Kingdom, as well as the Council of Europe.

In Australia, it is legal to use fetal tissues from therapeutic abortions in research involving transplantation with the consent of the woman and, where practical, her partner. Research protocols must be approved by a properly constituted ethics committee, and the abortion procedure must be totally separated from the research. The woman's specific consent is required if tissues or cells are to be propagated in culture or transplanted into a human recipient. The decision about whether to approach a pregnant woman about the possible use of fetal tissue for such research lies with the woman's clinician, not with the researcher. The information sought through the proposed research must not be available through research using non-human fetal tissue, nor should any element of commerce be involved in the transfer of fetal tissue.

In Germany, the law permits research use of tissues obtained with consent, but the 1987 Clinical Code relating to the use of embryos and fetal tissue was reformed to criminalize the taking of these materials without consent.

In Holland, there are clear rules on the use of fetal tissue for research. When an abortion clinic is asked for tissue, it must ensure that the research project is scientifically valid, that it has been approved by an ethics committee, and that the clinic and the research institute have a written agreement.   The woman's consent is always obtained.   It is understood that any tissue retrieved will be destroyed, unless consent to any other use is obtained. The clinic may not receive any financial or other inducement to provide fetal tissue. There can be no direct link between the doctor performing the abortion and the prospective researcher, and the researcher may not influence the method of abortion. No tissue may be released for research or other uses related to cosmetics.

In France, the National Ethics Consultative Committee for Life and the Health Sciences issued an opinion in 1984 stating that the use of fetal tissue for transplantation should be limited to exceptional cases where the disease being treated is rare, there are no equally effective alternative treatments, and the intended beneficiary would receive a manifest advantage (such as survival). Only tissues from fetuses of less than 20 weeks' gestational age should be used, and only after death has been confirmed. Maintaining the fetus artificially in order to remove viable tissue is not permitted. The decision to donate tissue should not influence the timing or method of abortion. The woman and her partner have a right to veto the use of fetal tissue if the abortion is for medical reasons. However, in cases of abortions without medical indication, the woman's consent to use of the tissue for transplantation is not required because this might be seen as legitimating the abortion. No commercial or industrial use of fetal tissue is allowed, and public authorities restrict research involving fetal tissue to institutions that can demonstrate they have the necessary competence and facilities.

In 1986, the Parliamentary Assembly of the Council of Europe adopted Recommendation 1046 regarding the research use of human embryos and fetal tissue. It is essentially identical to the French guidelines, except that it requires the consent of the woman and her partner even in cases of elective abortion.[11]

In the United States, fetal tissue use is regulated primarily at the state level. Between 1969 and 1973, all 50 states enacted legislation based on the *Uniform Anatomical Gift Act*, which allows the donation of fetal tissue or organs provided that there is documented consent from either the woman or her partner and the other partner is not known to object. It also allows the donor to designate the recipient of the tissue, which could be a patient, researcher, or institution, although this provision is widely criticized. The *Uniform Anatomical Gift Act* prohibits the physician who certifies death from participating in the removal or transplantation of tissue. Several states have passed laws that place additional restrictions on fetal tissue research. For example, nine states prohibit the use of fetal tissue obtained from therapeutic abortions in research.[12]

The Swedish Society of Medicine issued provisional guidelines approving the use of fetal tissue for transplantation research in 1985 (and reaffirmed them in 1990). These guidelines state that tissue can be taken only from dead fetuses; that the woman must have given her informed consent after a "reasonable period of counselling" (to allow for consultation of close relatives); that the decision to donate tissue should not in any way affect the method or timing of the abortion; that there should be no communication between the woman and the recipient; that only isolated cells of nerve tissue may be used for transplantation; and that approval for every project involving fetal tissue transplantation should be given by a regional research ethics committee.[13]

The British Medical Association produced interim guidelines in 1988. They are similar to the Swedish guidelines, but also state that there should be no financial reward for donating fetal tissue and that the generation of a pregnancy solely to produce fetal tissue for donation is unethical.[14] In 1989, a government committee recommended that a government organization be responsible for procuring and distributing fetal tissue, to ensure that there is a complete separation between the researchers who receive the tissue and the physicians who manage the pregnancy and abortion.[15]

By comparison with practices elsewhere in the world, then, there is relatively little regulation of the use of fetal tissue in Canada. Canada has no legislation or professional guidelines dealing with such issues as the separation of research and clinical care, modifications to abortion procedures, artificial maintenance of fetal life, the designation of tissue recipients, or the appropriate aims of fetal tissue research. The Commission believes, however, that the use of fetal tissue in transplantation research, and fetal tissue research more generally, is appropriate only if governed by clear principles and safeguards with respect to these and other issues.

Appendix 2: The First Canadian Research Using Fetal Tissue Transplantation in Human Beings

In June 1991, the Commission met with researchers and administrators at Dalhousie University and Victoria General Hospital where the first Canadian clinical trial of fetal tissue transplantation was begun. This trial is the only clinical fetal tissue transplantation research in Canada and concerns the treatment of Parkinson disease. One of the objectives of the meeting was to learn what process the hospital followed before approving the trial. Among those present were the Dean of the university's medical school, the President of the hospital, and the Chair of the ad hoc committee established by the hospital's Board of Commissioners to examine the information and recommend a decision-making process.

The two-year approval process involved several stages of review. Although the medical faculty's research committee had endorsed the scientific validity of the proposed research, the hospital's own research review committee chose to send the proposal to independent experts around the country for external scientific review. The Research Review Committee at the Victoria General Hospital unanimously endorsed the scientific validity of the study. Next, the committee sent the proposal to three independent reviewers at Canadian bioethics centres.

The result of both the scientific and ethical reviews was a recommendation by the research review committee to the hospital administration that the proposal be considered acceptable on both scientific and ethical grounds.   It then fell to the hospital's lay Board of Commissioners to make the ultimate decision to approve or not to approve the proposal. The board struck a three-member ad hoc committee, whose task was to examine in detail the background information forwarded by the research review committee and to recommend to the full Board how the decision would be made.

For four months the committee studied various aspects of the proposal and sought additional information about the costs and funding of the proposed research. We heard from the chairperson that the most difficult aspect of the committee's decision dealt with the relationship between the transplantation process and the source of the fetal tissue. Meanwhile, the proposal was being considered by yet another internal organization, the hospital's Ethics Consultation Service. Comprising nurses, social workers, psychologists, a lawyer, and a minister, the service considered the pros and cons of the proposed research from the perspective of the patient with Parkinson disease, the woman undergoing the abortion, and the fetus.

From the moment the proposal became public and throughout the years of decision making, the hospital and the university were besieged with telephone calls and letters from people opposed to fetal tissue from therapeutic abortions being used in the research. Demonstrations outside the entrance of the hospital were commonplace; some individuals contacted the hospital to say they would withhold financial pledges to the hospital if the research project went ahead.

In 1990, following the longest and most detailed assessment of any research proposal in its 131-year history, the hospital approved the trial. The Board of Commissioners expects a status report in 1994. In the meantime, it follows the project's progress informally.

General Sources

Angus Reid Group Inc. "Reproductive Technologies — Qualitative Research: Summary of Observations." In Research Volumes of the Royal Commission on New Reproductive Technologies, 1993.

Begley, S., et al. "Cures from the Womb: Fetal Tissue Promises New Hope for Incurable Diseases and Beguiling Questions of Science." *Newsweek*, February 22, 1993: 49-51.

Decima Research. "Social Values and Attitudes of Canadians Toward New Reproductive Technologies." In Research Volumes of the Royal Commission on New Reproductive Technologies, 1993.

de Groh, M. "Key Findings from a National Survey Conducted by the Angus Reid Group: Infertility, Surrogacy, Fetal Tissue Research, and Reproductive Technologies." In Research Volumes of the Royal Commission on New Reproductive Technologies, 1993.

Dickens, B.M. "Legal Issues in Embryo and Fetal Tissue Research and Therapy." In Research Volumes of the Royal Commission on New Reproductive Technologies, 1993.

Fine, A. "Human Fetal Tissue Research: Origins, State of the Art, Future Applications, and Implications." In Research Volumes of the Royal Commission on New Reproductive Technologies, 1993.

Gunning, J. *Human IVF, Embryo Research, Fetal Tissue for Research and Treatment, and Abortion: International Information.* London: HMSO, 1990.

McLaren, A. "Human Embryo Research: Past, Present, and Future." In Research Volumes of the Royal Commission on New Reproductive Technologies, 1993.

Medical Research Council of Canada. *Guidelines on Research Involving Human Subjects.* Ottawa: Minister of Supply and Services Canada, 1987.

Mullen, M.A. "The Use of Human Embryos and Fetal Tissues: A Research Architecture." In Research Volumes of the Royal Commission on New Reproductive Technologies, 1993.

SPR Associates Inc. "Report on a Survey of Use and Handling of Human Reproductive Tissues in Canadian Health Care Facilities." In Research Volumes of the Royal Commission on New Reproductive Technologies, 1993.

SPR Associates Inc. "Report on a Follow-Up Survey of Use and Handling of Human Reproductive Tissues (Survey of Medical Laboratories and Medical Waste Disposal Firms)." In Research Volumes of the Royal Commission on New Reproductive Technologies, 1993.

Specific References

1. Canada. House of Commons. *Debates*, July 15, 1988, p. 17613.

2. Council of Europe. Select Committee of Experts on the Use of Human Embryos and Foetuses. *Report on the Use of Human Foetal, Embryonic and Pre-Embryonic Material for Diagnostic, Therapeutic, Scientific, Industrial and Commercial Purposes.* Strasbourg: Secretariat, Council of Europe, 1990.

3. Ridgeway, J. "Fetuses." In *Who Owns the Earth.* New York: Macmillan, 1980. A similar report of "the alleged sale of 12 000 pairs of fetal South Korean kidneys to a U.S. source for $15 a pair" is attributed to the *Sunday Times* of London, England; see Scott, R. *The Body as Property.* New York: Viking, 1981; and Fine, A. "Human Fetal Tissue Research: Origins, State of the Art, Future Applications, and Implications." In Research Volumes of the Royal Commission on New Reproductive Technologies, 1993.

4. Wadhera, S., and J. Strachan. "Therapeutic Abortions, Canada and the Provinces." *Health Reports* 4 (2)(1992): 210-11.

5. Fellman, B. "New Hope for the Body Betrayed." *Brown Alumni Monthly* (February, 1992): 21-24.

6. *Moore v. Regents of the University of California.* 793 P. 2d 479 (Cal. 1990).

7. Ibid., p. 486.

8. Weber, S. "Doctors Accept Use of Fetal Tissue ... in Theory." *The Medical Post*, November 10, 1992, p. 48.

9. World Health Organization. *Human Organ Transplantation: A Report on Developments Under the Auspices of WHO (1987-1991).* Geneva: WHO, 1991, pp. 7-11.

10. Hillebrecht, J.M. "Regulating the Clinical Uses of Fetal Tissues." *Journal of Legal Medicine* 10 (2)(1989): 269-322.

11. Council of Europe. Parliamentary Assembly. "Recommendation 1046 (1986) (1) on the Use of Human Embryos and Fetuses for Diagnostic, Therapeutic, Scientific, Industrial and Commercial Purposes." September 24, 1986.

12. However, these laws do not preclude the use of fetal tissue from elective abortions for therapeutic purposes. Hence, if and when fetal tissue transplantation becomes accepted therapy, rather than experimental research, these laws might not apply.

13. Swedish Society of Medicine. Delegation for Medical Ethics. *Guiding Principles for the Use of Fetal Tissue in Clinical Transplantation Research.* Stockholm: The Society, 1990.

14. Vawter, D.E., et al. *The Use of Human Fetal Tissue: Scientific, Ethical, and Policy Concerns.* Minneapolis: University of Minnesota, 1990.

15. United Kingdom. Committee to Review the Guidance on the Research Uses of Fetuses and Fetal Material. *Report* (The Polkinghorne Report). London: HMSO, 1989.

Part
Three

Overview of Recommendations

Overview of Recommendations

As a society we need to create a situation such that individual Canadians can make decisions about their involvement with new reproductive technologies in the knowledge that their ethical, legal, and social aspects and their safety and effectiveness have been given due consideration. Given this goal, we have made recommendations that set boundaries around the use of the technologies and that establish a National Reproductive Technologies Commission to license and regulate those activities in this field that are permissible. This would not be its only function, however; it would also play a facilitating and coordinating role, bringing together, learning from, and giving policy direction to provincial/ territorial ministries of health and professionals working in this field.

In this third and concluding part of our report, we have grouped together the recommendations we made in Part Two, according to who would be responsible for implementing them. In the preceding 31 chapters, we discussed individual technologies in a detailed way and made recommendations flowing from our ethical and scientific analysis of the data we gathered. In this final part we give an overall picture of the way we propose that new reproductive technologies be managed in Canada and an overview of our recommendations. Simply providing a comprehensive list of recommendations would not highlight what we consider to be the most important recommendations, clarify how they are intended to work together, or identify who is responsible for implementing them or for their cost. It also would not highlight how our recommendations can contribute to preservation of our publicly supported health care system by their evidence-based approach.

Many of our recommendations are quite detailed or technical and require the context of our data and reasoning to render them meaningful to readers. Therefore, we believe it is more helpful to step back from our detailed recommendations and to concentrate instead on the overall picture, focussing on the role of the essential partners we have identified and the responsibilities we envisage for them. At the same time, we provide numbered cross-references so that readers can easily refer back to Part Two for the context and details of our recommendations and summaries of licensing requirements.

As we have seen throughout our examination of the conditions, technologies, and practices encompassed by our mandate, both potential benefits and potential harms are associated with the use of new reproductive technologies. The Commission therefore concludes

> It is the role of governments as guardians of the public interest to ensure that individuals and society as a whole are not harmed by inappropriate use of reproductive technologies.

that it is essential, in a field where individuals may lack the knowledge necessary to protect their own interests, that these vulnerable interests be protected through rules and regulations established by society, which will also serve to protect the vulnerable interests of the wider community. As a society we all have an interest in the character and values of the community in which we live and responsibility to ensure that the community is one in which people are not treated as commodities and technologies are not used in ways that offend human dignity. It is the role of governments as guardians of the public interest to ensure that individuals and society as a whole are not harmed by inappropriate use of reproductive technologies.

Given the potential harms to women and children and to important social values, to allow Canada's response to new reproductive technologies to be delayed or fragmented by the existing web of jurisdictional and administrative arrangements would be, in the Commissioners' view, a mistake of enormous proportions. We believe that the national regulatory framework we propose is essential, but by itself it is not sufficient. If we are to deal with new reproductive technologies appropriately in our society, strong leadership and cooperation will be required among governments, researchers, and professionals involved in new reproductive technologies, as well as many other sectors of society. Taking an evidence-based approach to the provision of permissible technologies is the only way to achieve the goals of effective treatment of people, avoidance of harm, and efficient use of resources. It is quite clear that no one group or organization can act effectively in isolation — partnership and cooperation between the federal government, provincial/territorial governments, professional organizations, patient groups, and other affected interests are critical.

All these partners have a necessary and interactive role: for example, provinces are essential partners with several ministries involved (provincial family law regimes must take into account the situations created by the use of new reproductive technologies; provincial ministries of education must grapple with the real and necessary role they will play in preventing infertility; and so on); professional organizations must ensure that their members receive the necessary training in preventing, diagnosing, and treating infertility; researchers and organizations funding research have a responsibility to ensure that all research receives ethical and social evaluation before being funded and carried out; health and social service workers will have to take into account the unique needs of the new types of families created by the use of new reproductive technologies; and individuals have the responsibility to inform themselves as fully as possible before making any decisions.

It is clear, then, that many sectors of society beyond the health care sector and public institutions beyond the federal government will have crucial roles to play.   Concerted action and cooperation by the provinces/territories, the professions, and other key participants in the context of the proposed national framework are the only way to ensure ethical and accountable use of new reproductive technologies in Canada — now and in the future. This cooperation will enable provinces/territories to harmonize and standardize the delivery of new reproductive technologies in their respective jurisdictions, allow more effective strategies aimed at preventing infertility, and let Canadians know that their interests are being protected in a comprehensive and open way.

We recognize that implementing our recommendations will take considerable public and political will. By grouping our recommendations according to who should have responsibility for implementing them, we hope not only to assist those who are responsible but also to assist advocacy groups, individuals, and others who will be monitoring development in this field and monitoring progress in implementing our recommendations.

Recommendations by Area of Responsibility

We outline the general structure of the approach we recommend by focussing on the various "actors" responsible for implementing our recommendations with regard to infertility and new reproductive technologies. These actors include the federal and provincial/territorial governments, the health professions, private sector interests, and various advocacy and public interest groups. The detailed recommendations in Part Two reflect our view about how these institutions and groups should act and interact in the sphere of new reproductive technologies.

By focussing here on the main responsibilities we envisage for the principal actors, we hope to clarify the overall structure of our recommendations and to identify clearly who is accountable for implementing them. However, numbered cross-references to specific recommendations are provided for readers who wish to look up the details of the recommendations or the data and reasoning that led to them.

Consistent with our mandate from the federal government, with the call we heard from Canadians for a national response, and with the constitutional obligation of the federal government to legislate for the peace, order, and good government of Canada, many of our recommendations are addressed to the federal government. We look first at the role we have recommended for the federal government, before considering the important roles of the provincial/territorial governments; the health care professions; private sector interests; and other interested groups.

Federal Government

The recommendations we address to the federal government fall into three general categories: first, recommendations regarding the need for criminal legislation to set boundaries around the use of new reproductive technologies in Canada; second, recommendations regarding the establishment and operation of a National Reproductive Technologies Commission to manage new reproductive technologies within those boundaries; and third, other recommendations addressed to existing federal departments and agencies. We look at each of these categories in turn.

Criminal Legislation

We have judged that certain activities conflict so sharply with the values espoused by Canadians and by this Commission, and are so potentially harmful to the interests of individuals and of society, that they must be prohibited by the federal government under threat of criminal sanction. These actions include human zygote/embryo research related to ectogenesis, cloning, animal/human hybrids, the transfer of zygotes to another species [184], or the maturation and fertilization of eggs from human fetuses; the sale of human eggs, sperm, zygotes, fetuses, and fetal tissues [192, 286, 287]; and advertising for or acting as an intermediary to bring about a preconception arrangement, receiving payment or any financial or commercial benefit for acting as an intermediary, and making payment for a preconception arrangement [199].

We also recommend that unwanted medical treatment and other interferences or threatened interferences with the physical autonomy of pregnant women be recognized explicitly under the *Criminal Code* as criminal assault. To ensure that medical treatment never be imposed upon a pregnant woman against her wishes, we also recommend that the criminal law, or any other law, never be used to confine or imprison a pregnant woman in the interests of her fetus, and that the conduct of a pregnant woman in relation to her fetus not be criminalized [273, 274].

Establishing the National Reproductive Technologies Commission

The legislative prohibitions we have recommended will protect against certain egregious threats to human dignity and to women's equality and freedom. However, criminal legislation is not flexible enough to regulate the day-to-day provision of new reproductive technologies. To ensure that new reproductive technologies are provided in a safe, ethical, and accountable way within these boundaries, we recommend that the federal government establish an independent National Reproductive Technologies Commission, charged with the primary responsibility of ensuring that new reproductive technologies are developed and applied in the national public interest [1]. In particular, we recommend that the National Commission be composed of 12 members appointed by the Governor in Council, at least 6 of whom, including the president, are appointed on a full-time basis. We recommend that National Commission members be appointed for an initial five-year term, with a possible one-, two-, or three-year renewal of their terms, to allow for the staggering of new appointments. We are of the view that these numbers and terms of appointments will permit the development of a high level of expertise while allowing for sufficiently diverse representation of interests and a close working relationship among National Commission members.

We believe that women should make up a substantial proportion of the National Commission's members, normally at least half. In addition, membership of the National Commission and its sub-committees should always include persons knowledgeable about the interests and perspectives of those with disabilities, those who are infertile, and those who are members of racial minority, Aboriginal, and economically disadvantaged communities. A range of expertise should also be represented, including reproductive medicine, ethics, law, and social sciences. In other words, Commissioners see the need for a broad mix of views in the membership of the National Commission and are confident that there are many Canadians, both women and men, who are fully qualified to take on these responsibilities and from among whom such appointments can be made.

Given the range and diversity of its mandate, we believe that the National Commission can best fulfil its responsibilities if it establishes six permanent sub-committees devoted to different aspects of new reproductive technologies. These six sub-committees would focus on infertility prevention; assisted conception; assisted insemination; prenatal diagnosis and genetics; human zygote/embryo research; and the provision of fetal tissue for use in research. We recommend that each of these sub-committees includes both National Commission and non-National Commission membership, and that outside members include people representing the views and interests of governments, relevant professional bodies, consumers, and other groups with particular interest in the area of the sub-committee activity in question. Like National Commission members themselves, we recommend that at least half of sub-committee members normally be women, and that all members be chosen with a view to ensuring that they have a background and demonstrated experience in dealing with a multidisciplinary approach to issues, as well as an ability to work together to find solutions and recommend policies to address the difficult issues raised by new reproductive technologies in a way that meets the concerns of Canadian society as a whole. The sub-committees would therefore serve as important forums for public input and community representation. The functions of each sub-committee are summarized below.

Infertility Prevention Sub-Committee

We recommend the establishment of a permanent sub-committee of the National Reproductive Technologies Commission, with primary responsibility in the field of infertility prevention and reproductive health promotion [61]. It will serve to promote and coordinate public education and research in the area of reproductive health and infertility prevention both in Canada and internationally. Among the functions of the Infertility Prevention Sub-Committee would be the following:

- promoting and supporting consultation and cooperation among federal and provincial/territorial departments of health, labour, and the environment; among agencies such as the Canadian Centre for Occupational Health and Safety and the Canadian Centre on Substance Abuse; provincial workers' compensation boards; and other governmental bodies with responsibilities related to the field of reproductive health;

- consulting with the provinces/territories, directly or through the Conference of Deputy Ministers of Health, on matters related to infertility prevention and reproductive health;

- advising the federal and provincial/territorial governments on legislative and regulatory issues related to infertility prevention and reproductive health promotion, including in the areas of environmental protection and occupational health and safety;

- consulting with health care professionals, community and public health personnel, educators, family planning organizations, and others involved in public education efforts in the field of reproductive health;

- promoting, on behalf of the federal government, international co-operation in research, information gathering, and public health initiatives related to infertility prevention (see, for example, our recommendation with respect to a cooperative international effort to assess existing data on workplace and environmental exposures that may represent risks to reproductive health) [41]; and

- promoting public awareness and discussion about the causes, incidence, and preventability of infertility in Canada, in part through the National Commission's annual report.

Assisted Insemination Sub-Committee

We recommend that the National Commission establish an Assisted Insemination Sub-Committee with responsibility for licensing the collection, storage, distribution, and use of sperm in connection with assisted insemination; for setting the standards and guidelines to be adopted as conditions of licence; and for monitoring developments in the field of assisted insemination [84].

The compulsory licensing requirements would apply to any individual or facility either engaged in the collection, storage, distribution, and use of sperm in connection with the assisted insemination of a woman other than the social partner of the sperm donor or using sperm having had sex-selective treatment for insemination even if for the social partner. Sperm collection, sperm storage and distribution, and the provision of assisted insemination services would constitute three distinct licensing categories, although one facility could apply for a licence in more than one category [83, 85].

The Assisted Insemination Sub-Committee would develop, with input from relevant bodies, standards and guidelines to be adopted as conditions of licence [83-103]. The recommendations of the Royal Commission on New Reproductive Technologies should serve as a basis for these guidelines.

In particular, we recommend that the conditions of licence for facilities involved in sperm collection ensure [88]:

- screening of donors and testing of donor sperm for infectious diseases (including a six-month quarantine on donated sperm to allow for human immunodeficiency virus [HIV] testing of donors);
- informed consent of sperm donors (including standardized information and consent forms and counselling);
- compensation to donors is for inconvenience only, with no financial incentive;
- sperm is forwarded only to licensed sperm storage facilities; and
- proper record keeping, and that identifying and non-identifying information on the donor accompany sperm sent to a licensed storage facility.

For facilities involved in sperm storage, we recommend the following conditions of licence [94]:

- all sperm stored or distributed by a sperm storage and distribution facility must be obtained from a licensed sperm collection facility;

- applications for sperm should be accepted only from an individual or facility licensed to provide assisted insemination services or from an individual woman seeking sperm for self-insemination (without discrimination on the basis of factors such as sexual orientation, marital status, or economic status);

- informed consent of women receiving sperm for self-insemination is obtained (including a signed statement that the sperm is for her own use, that she has received, read, and understood information materials outlining the risks, responsibilities, and implications of donor insemination, and that she consents knowingly to using the sperm);

- non-identifying information about the sperm donor should accompany sperm distributed to qualified applicants;

- there must be proper record keeping enabling the necessary linking of donor, recipient, and the child(ren), to ensure that there are no more than 10 live births from a single sperm donor, and that the donor or the child(ren) can be contacted in the event of serious medical need (for example, discovery of a serious disease in either the child or donor that would have implications for the other); and

- identifying information regarding the donor should be kept confidential and forwarded to the National Reproductive Technologies Commission for secure storage. It should be released only in the event of serious medical need as determined by a court of law.

For facilities providing assisted insemination services, we recommend the following conditions of licence [99]:

- only frozen sperm from licensed storage and distribution facilities should be used;

- the importing of sperm is not permitted;

- a licence is required to perform insemination at any site other than the vagina even if the recipient is the social partner;

- access should be determined by legitimate medical criteria, not on the basis of social factors such as sexual orientation or marital or economic status;

- standard information, counselling, and consent forms should be completed and signed by all recipients before any treatment;

- at the time of the insemination, the recipient should be provided with donor information (identified only by the donor information code number); and

- there must be proper record keeping, which would involve the completion of a form by the recipient to be returned to the sperm storage and distribution facility in the event of a live birth.

We also recommend that licensed facilities providing assisted insemination not be permitted to use sex preselection techniques — that is, sperm treatment methods designed to separate X- and Y-bearing sperm — except for individuals who have a clear medical indication for this procedure (for example, X-linked disease) [93]. Patients with these indications should also be provided with objective information about the lack of reliability of any technique used, and data allowing estimation of success rates should be kept and forwarded annually to the National Reproductive Technologies Commission [100, 266].

All three types of licensed facilities should be required to report annually to the National Reproductive Technologies Commission [89, 96, 101], and all should operate on a non-profit basis [88(p), 94(m)].

Assisted Conception Sub-Committee

We recommend that the National Commission establish an Assisted Conception Sub-Committee with responsibility for setting the standards and guidelines to be adopted as conditions of licence and for monitoring developments in the field [105].

The compulsory licensing requirements for assisted conception services would apply to any physician, centre, or other individual or facility providing any of the following services or any other service related to assisted conception [104, 130]:

- *in vitro* fertilization (IVF)
- embryo transfer (either to the woman who was the source of the egg giving rise to the embryo or to another woman)
- gamete intrafallopian transfer (GIFT)
- zygote intrafallopian transfer (ZIFT)
- preimplantation diagnosis
- insemination at sites other than the vagina
- direct egg/sperm transfer (DOST) [130].

The Assisted Conception Sub-Committee would develop standards and guidelines to be adopted as conditions of licence, with input from relevant professional bodies and individuals and groups representing patients and other key sectors of the community [132].

The recommendations of the Royal Commission on New Reproductive Technologies should serve as a basis for these guidelines [130-159]. In particular, these guidelines should ensure the following:

- informed choice (including the provision of standard information materials and consent forms; non-directive counselling) [115-120, 146-151];

- standardized calculation of success rates, based on live births per 100 treatment cycles initiated [110, 112, 152, 153];

- consistent record keeping according to specified criteria (including the protection of patient confidentiality and the use of standard forms to allow record linkage) [155-157];

- annual reporting to the National Reproductive Technologies Commission (including success rates and side effects) [111, 113, 155, 156];

- the establishment of staff qualifications and expertise consistent with specified criteria [114];

- offering only drugs and procedures of proven effectiveness for the infertility condition in question as treatment; offering procedures whose effectiveness has not yet been clearly established only in the context of clinical trials [133-136];

- transferring a maximum of three zygotes to a woman's uterus in any IVF attempt [108, 143];

- basing access to IVF treatment on legitimate medical criteria, without discrimination on the basis of factors such as marital status, sexual orientation, or economic status [121, 141, 145];

- not operating assisted conception services on a for-profit basis [154]; and

- offering IVF only after infertility investigation of both the male and female partner, and only after less intrusive/costly options have been considered [137, 138, 142].

The guidelines developed by the Assisted Conception Sub-Committee should also prohibit the provision of assisted conception procedures in support of a preconception arrangement [202] and the use of prenatal diagnosis to determine fetal sex for non-medical reasons [265].

The Assisted Conception Sub-Committee would also develop standards and guidelines governing egg and embryo donation in licensed clinics [182]. We recommend that the guidelines ensure that

- no designated donation of eggs or zygotes occurs [167, 172];

- women who have experienced menopause at the usual age not be candidates to receive donated eggs or zygotes [162, 173];

- egg retrieval procedures solely for the purpose of donation not be performed [166, 174];

- informed consent is sought for both donors and recipients, including provision of standardized information materials and counselling [160, 164, 165];

- zygotes are disposed of in accordance with the wishes of the gamete donor(s), expressed in writing before the gamete retrieval [170, 175, 180, 181];

- zygotes are not stored for more than five years from the date they are frozen, and zygotes stored for a couple's own use only are stored up to the death of either partner [171, 180];

- record keeping is uniform and consistent with specified criteria (including identifying and non-identifying information on donor, and reporting to the National Reproductive Technologies Commission) [163, 176];

- donor anonymity is protected (access to information about the donor should be the same as for assisted insemination, discussed above) [176(b)];

- donors are screened and tested to prevent the transmission of infectious diseases (including a six-month quarantine on donor zygotes to allow for HIV testing of donors) [161, 177, 178]; and

- egg and zygote donors are not compensated in any way [168, 179].

In addition to its licensing functions, the Assisted Conception Sub-Committee would also

- facilitate and monitor randomized control trials of unproven drugs and procedures such as GIFT or IVF for endometriosis [63, 74, 107, 124-127, 135, 136];

- monitor the promotional activities of pharmaceutical companies in the marketing of fertility drugs [71];

- analyze the data reported to the National Reproductive Technologies Commission by the clinics; regulate access to coded information in this data base by qualified researchers; and issue an annual report based on the data [75, 76, 78, 81];

- consult annually with the Conference of Deputy Ministers of Health;

- monitor the assessment and introduction of new assisted conception technologies [109]; and

- develop guidelines for prescribing fertility drugs within licensed clinics, including the provision of standard information materials and consent forms [69, 72, 73] and standardized record keeping and reporting [75, 76, 78, 80].

Embryo Research Sub-Committee

We recommend that the National Reproductive Technologies Commission establish a permanent Embryo Research Sub-Committee, with responsibility for licensing facilities engaged in research using human zygotes, for developing standards and guidelines to be adopted as conditions of licence, and for monitoring developments in this area [197].

The licensing requirements for zygote/embryo research should apply to any physician, centre, or other individual or facility using human zygotes in research.   Both experimental and "innovative" therapies for human zygotes should fall under the rubric of research [193, 195].

The Embryo Research Sub-Committee would develop, with input from relevant bodies, standards and guidelines to be adopted as conditions of licence [197].   The recommendations of the Royal Commission on New Reproductive Technologies should serve as a basis for these guidelines [195-198].

In particular, we recommend that the following requirements be adopted as conditions of licence:

- all approved research must be restricted to the first 14 days of development of the human zygote [183, 198(a)];

- research involving genetic alteration of human zygotes or embryos is not permitted [185, 198(i), 269];

- informed consent of the persons who have donated the gametes used to create the zygote (including standard gamete donor information materials and consent forms) is essential [186, 187, 198(b), (d)];

- objectives of research on human zygotes should be achievable only through the use of human zygotes [198(h)];

- research must be directed at understanding human health and not be undertaken for commercial gain [198(g)];

- the creation of human zygotes specifically for research purposes is permissible, but invasive procedures specifically to retrieve eggs for purposes of creating zygotes for research is not [188, 198(c)];

- human zygotes that have been subject to manipulation of any kind for research purposes cannot be transferred to a woman's body without the specific approval of the National Reproductive Technologies Commission, and then only in the context of a clinical trial [189, 190, 194, 198(f)];

- any research project involving the use of human zygotes undertaken by a licensed researcher or facility must be approved by a local research ethics board, based on national guidelines developed by the Embryo Research Sub-Committee [198(j)];

- there must be proper record keeping (including confidentiality of information on donors) [198(e)]; and

- there must be annual reporting to the National Reproductive Technologies Commission [198(k)].

Prenatal Diagnosis and Genetics Sub-Committee

We recommend that the National Reproductive Technologies Commission establish a permanent Prenatal Diagnosis and Genetics Sub-Committee, with responsibility for licensing facilities providing prenatal diagnosis services, for developing standards and guidelines to be adopted as conditions of licence, and for monitoring developments in this area [230].

The compulsory licensing requirements for prenatal diagnosis services should apply to any physician, centre, or other individual or facility providing the following prenatal diagnosis services [232, 233]:

- amniocentesis
- chorionic villus sampling (CVS)
- any other prenatal testing of pregnant women aimed at obtaining information on the health status of the fetus with regard to congenital anomalies and genetic disease, other than provincial maternal serum alpha-fetoprotein (MSAFP) screening programs or other provincial programs involving testing of pregnant women's blood and provincially licensed diagnostic ultrasound programs.

The Prenatal Diagnosis and Genetics Sub-Committee would develop, with input from relevant bodies, standards and guidelines to be adopted as conditions of licence [235]. The recommendations of the Royal Commission on New Reproductive Technologies should serve as a basis for these guidelines [233-254]. In particular, facilities seeking a licence would have to obtain prior accreditation by the Canadian College of Medical Geneticists [233, 248].

We recommend that the following requirements be adopted as conditions of licence:

- fully informed consent is obtained (including the provision of standard information materials and consent forms, and non-directive counselling) [214, 215, 244-250];
- prior willingness or unwillingness to terminate a pregnancy should never operate as a precondition for prenatal diagnosis [214, 247];
- counselling prior to and following termination of pregnancy, including grief counselling, should also be available, either on-site or by referral [212, 213, 250];
- no genetic alteration of a human zygote/embryo is permitted [241, 270];
- record keeping is according to specified criteria (including the protection of patient confidentiality) that would allow outcomes to be assessed [243, 251]; and
- there must be annual reporting to the National Reproductive Technologies Commission [252].

We also recommend that special safeguards be in place for the prenatal diagnosis of late-onset disorders [256]. Licensing guidelines should provide that

- special counselling be available for prenatal diagnostic testing for late-onset single-gene disorders [257]; and

- prenatal diagnosis should *not* be offered to detect so-called susceptibility genes [259].

We also wish to prevent the misuse of prenatal diagnosis for sex-selection purposes. The Prenatal Diagnosis and Genetics Sub-Committee guidelines should therefore also specify that

- prenatal diagnosis to determine fetal sex for non-medical reasons should not be offered [242, 261, 262]; and

- where prenatal diagnosis has been provided for a medical reason, patients should be informed prior to testing that the usual practice is to reveal information on the sex of the fetus only if it is medically relevant to the health of the fetus. Information on the sex of the fetus should be given to the woman or referring practitioner only on direct request [263].

In addition to its licensing functions, the Prenatal Diagnosis and Genetics Sub-Committee would also

- provide guidelines and monitor clinical trials of procedures that remain experimental in nature [237-239];

- determine which prenatal diagnosis procedures are of sufficiently proven safety and effectiveness to be offered as services, and help ensure that procedures whose safety or effectiveness has not yet been clearly established should be offered only in the context of clinical trials [236, 238, 240];

- consult annually with the Conference of Deputy Ministers of Health [231]; and

- monitor developments in deoxyribonucleic acid (DNA) testing as they relate to reproductive technologies [260].

The Prenatal Diagnosis and Genetics Sub-Committee would also be responsible for monitoring developments in gene therapy in the reproductive context. We therefore recommend that the Sub-Committee develop guidelines concerning the appropriate indications for fetal applications of somatic cell gene therapy as the field evolves, and that any proposal for somatic cell gene therapy research involving human fetuses be reviewed and approved by the Prenatal Diagnosis and Genetics Sub-Committee, following review and approval by the Medical Research Council national review committee for gene therapy [267, 268].

Fetal Tissue Sub-Committee

We recommend that the National Commission establish a permanent Fetal Tissue Sub-Committee to monitor the supply and use of fetal tissue, to develop standards and guidelines to be adopted as conditions of licence, and to oversee the implementation of the licensing program [292].

Compulsory licensing would be required for the provision of human fetal tissue by any physician, centre, clinic, or other individual or facility providing human fetal tissue for research (including transplantation research) or for any purpose other than medical care of the woman, routine pathology testing, or disposal [277, 290].

The Fetal Tissue Sub-Committee would develop, with input from relevant bodies, standards and guidelines to be adopted as conditions of licence [292]. The recommendations of the Royal Commission on New Reproductive Technologies should serve as a basis for these guidelines [290-293].

In particular, we recommend that the following requirements be adopted as conditions of licence:

- full and informed consent of the woman, sought independently of and subsequent to the decision to abort, and including specific consent for use in transplantation, must be obtained in relation to any fetal tissue provided for use [281, 293(b)];

- fetal death must be determined before use of fetal tissue in research [278, 293(a)];

- donation of fetal tissue to designated recipients should not be permitted [284, 293(c)];

- there is no compensation to the physician supplying fetal tissue, except to cover costs of handling the tissue [288, 293(d)];

- the woman is informed that no commercial benefit or other financial benefit will accrue to her from use of fetal tissue [281(e)];

- the research is permitted only if it is directed to understanding human functioning or disease, or to diagnose or treat disease [280, 293(e)];

- fetal tissue is provided only for projects that meet ethical research guidelines developed by the Sub-Committee and that have received prior institutional research ethics committee approval, including scientific and ethical review [293(f)];

- records must be kept according to specified criteria [293(g)];

- no personally identifying information regarding the woman accompanies fetal tissue [282];

- physicians supplying fetal tissue do not receive co-authorship credit for this role in publications resulting from the research use of that fetal tissue or any direct or indirect financial benefit [285]; and

- there must be annual reporting to the National Reproductive Technologies Commission [293(h)].

Federal Departments and Agencies

In the Commissioners' view, the most urgent responsibility of the federal government is to set boundaries around the provision of new reproductive technologies, through the criminal prohibition of certain activities, and to establish the National Reproductive Technologies Commission to regulate new reproductive technologies within those boundaries. However, we also recommend that federal departments and agencies undertake several other important activities, in some cases in conjunction with other governments and non-governmental bodies.

In particular, we see an active role for the departments of Health, Human Resources and Labour, and the Environment, as well as the Medical Research Council of Canada. We look at each in turn.

Health Canada

We believe that Health Canada should take a leadership role in initiating and coordinating public health education campaigns for the prevention of infertility. This would include:

*   conducting surveys of reproduction and of reproductive behaviour every five years, and ensuring that these surveys include a measurement of the prevalence of infertility, using a standardized definition so that infertility can be tracked over time [2];

*   updating every five years the *Canadian Guidelines for the Prevention, Diagnosis, Management and Treatment of Sexually Transmitted Diseases in Neonates, Children, Adolescents and Adults* (1992), and ensuring that a free copy of the guidelines is available to all primary care physicians, obstetricians/gynaecologists, urologists, sexually transmitted disease (STD) clinics, provincial and territorial nurses, community care clinics, nurses in school settings, educators teaching STD management at nursing and medical schools, and nursing and medical students [18, 19];

*   funding the Canadian Task Force on the Periodic Health Examination or a similar body to compile, update, and publish its findings in a practical guide for primary health care workers on useful preventive services and ensuring that the guide include STD prevention [20]; and

*   if results of a current study show they have an effect, requiring manufacturers to include on all containers of alcoholic beverages health warnings about the risks of alcohol consumption, including risks to the fetus [50].

We also recommend several initiatives that involve consultation and coordination between Health Canada and provincial/territorial ministries of health and education. Working in conjunction with provincial/territorial governments, Health Canada should

- ensure that goals and objectives for health education incorporate information about the effects of severe dietary restrictions and severe weight control on health and fertility [45];

- review and evaluate existing programs to reduce alcohol consumption among young people and, where necessary, develop new or improved initiatives to accomplish this objective [49];

- develop school-based and public education programs for young people concerning drug use [54, 55]; and

- develop specific programs targeted at high-risk individuals such as drugs users, prostitutes, and street youth regarding drug use, and, in particular, ensure that counselling and treatment programs are made available to help women who become pregnant while abusing drugs to stop using them [56].

Other recommendations will require Health Canada to work not only with provincial/territorial governments, but also with a wide range of other sectors. This is particularly true of our recommendations regarding sexual health education and anti-smoking campaigns.

Health Canada is currently assessing the national Guidelines for Sexual Health Education, developed by a multidisciplinary advisory committee involving federal, provincial, professional, and community input. We endorse these guidelines, which call for a collaborative effort of a range of sectors: family, education, medicine, public health, social services, and all three levels of government. We therefore recommend to Health Canada, and to all parties involved, that sexual health education programs be based on the national Guidelines for Sexual Health Education [4, 5]. We recommend further that

- sexual health programs offer help and support for parents to play an active role in providing sexual health education to their children [3];

- sexual health education programs be designed and presented in recognition of the fact that individuals engage in a range of sexual behaviours (including abstinence, delay, sexual activity) and that they need accurate information pertinent to all these choices [8, 9];

- sexual health education programs convey the message that young people who are sexually active need to protect themselves in two ways, that is, against both pregnancy and sexually transmitted diseases [10];

- sexual health education programs be designed to help individuals identify and evaluate the sexual messages conveyed by the media, to understand what these messages mean for individual and societal sexual health [11];

- initial funding for sexual health education programs include funding for an evaluation component [6];

- national surveys and other research be undertaken regularly (at least every five years) to document the knowledge, attitudes, and experience of youth and adults regarding sexual health and sexual behaviour [14]; and

- agencies involved in public health education develop sexual health programs and services designed specifically to target hard-to-reach populations [15].

The federal government, including Health Canada, has been actively involved in anti-smoking campaigns through the Steering Committee of the National Strategy to Reduce Tobacco Use, whose membership includes federal, provincial, and territorial governments and eight national health organizations. We endorse the guidelines developed in support of the National Strategy to Reduce Tobacco Use [23], which emphasize the need for all levels of government and many non-governmental organizations to coordinate their activities. Hence we recommend to Health Canada, and to all the parties involved, that this strategy be supported. We recommend further that

- public education efforts endorsed by the Steering Committee of the National Strategy to Reduce Tobacco Use in Canada include informing women of the evidence regarding the effect of cigarette smoking on ability to conceive, in addition to the adverse effects on pregnancy and the health of the fetus [27];

- public education efforts include messages that encourage men to stop smoking to maximize the chances that their female partner will be able to conceive and have a healthy pregnancy and birth [28]; and

- prenatal classes include information and support with regard to the importance of smoking cessation [30].

We have also made recommendations directed to the Drugs Directorate, a unit of Health Canada, to improve its system of drug approval and post-marketing surveillance:

- Canadian specifications be required for the evaluation of drugs used in assisted conception [65];

- the Drugs Directorate consult with experts who have clinical and research experience with fertility drugs, to ensure that the benefits and risks of new drugs have been evaluated comprehensively [66];

- up-to-date criteria be developed appropriate for screening the safety and efficacy of new biotechnology products, including recombinant fertility drugs [67]; and

- any trial of a fertility drug be reviewed by the research ethics board of a major hospital or university [68].

Finally, we recommend that Health Canada develop national standards of fetal death, in conjunction with the provinces, relevant professionals, and ethicists [279]. We also recommend that they require pharmaceutical companies marketing fertility drugs to contribute funding for clinical trials to test unproven uses and for studies to follow up on post-marketing reports of adverse effects [64, 74]. Given that pharmaceutical companies benefit from fertility drug sales, they should be required to contribute to the appropriate evaluation of these drugs.

Department of Human Resources and Labour

We believe that the federal Department of Human Resources and Labour should also play an important role in the prevention of infertility, particularly in terms of delayed childbearing and occupational health and safety.

Some of our recommendations will require close cooperation between the federal Department of Human Resources and Labour and its provincial counterparts. In conjunction with provincial/territorial departments responsible for labour, the Department should

- inform employers about and encourage them to adopt work-related policies and programs that help employees balance work and family responsibilities [32];

- review legislation, policies, and programs to ensure that these provide adequate time for paid parental leave and that they protect employment opportunities, seniority, and work-related benefits for women who leave the workforce temporarily to have children [33];

- work toward establishing uniform standards in occupational health and safety across the country, in particular in relation to reproductive hazards [37];

- develop programs to monitor the exposure of workers in various occupations to known reproductive hazards, with the aim of developing appropriate control and prevention measures [42]; and

- introduce a comprehensive strategy for child care that addresses the need for licensed and affordable child care services [34].

Environment Canada

Environment Canada has a particular responsibility in the area of environmental threats to reproductive health. We therefore recommend that

- reproductive health experts be asked to examine existing and proposed regulations under the *Canadian Environmental Protection Act* and make appropriate recommendations to ensure that they take into account reproductive health risks [39];

- Environment Canada specifically include consideration of the issue of reproductive health in all actions undertaken to protect the environment [40]; and

- the federal government organize and provide funding to a working group of Canadian experts in the field of reproductive health and workplace and environmental exposures, to work with the World Health Organization to initiate a cooperative international effort to critically assess the existing data on occupational and environmental substances that may represent risks to reproductive health [41].

Medical Research Council

The federally funded Medical Research Council (MRC) provides some 30 percent of the funds for medical research conducted in Canada. Its funding decisions help determine which health problems are researched in Canada and which experimental treatments are tested. We believe that the area of reproductive health, particularly the prevention of infertility, should be a greater priority and receive a higher level of research funding.

We therefore recommend that the Medical Research Council

- consider making basic and applied research on sexual and reproductive health, including sexually transmitted diseases, a higher priority [21];

- consider targeting funding to the training of epidemiological researchers as part of an overall approach to assigning higher priority to applied research on sexual and reproductive health [22];

- support research studies on the impact of designated substances and families of chemicals that are suspected of causing adverse reproductive health effects [43]; and

- consider how to increase the pool of trained researchers qualified to conduct research in the area of occupational and environmental reproductive health effects [44].

We believe that research involving human zygotes and the use of fetal tissue is ethically acceptable, under certain conditions, and can provide important health benefits. We therefore recommend that

- research projects involving the use of human zygotes and carried out in licensed facilities be eligible for public funding [191]; and

- research projects using fetal tissue (including those related to transplantation in human beings) be eligible for public funding by the Medical Research Council of Canada and other agencies, provided they meet applicable ethical and scientific research standards and tissue is obtained in accordance with the recommendations of the Royal Commission on New Reproductive Technologies [289].

We believe, however, that research in humans involving the alteration of DNA for enhancement purposes would not be ethically acceptable, and that any proposal for such research should be refused by the Medical Research Council review committee on gene therapy [271].

Although the MRC is the largest source of federal funds for medical research, these recommendations should also apply to other federal research funding organizations, such as the National Health Research and Development Program of Health Canada.

Other Federal Action

Two final areas for federal action relate to patenting and to adoption.

We believe that patenting in this new and changing area is a topic that requires further study before specific policy can be recommended. We therefore recommend that Industry and Science Canada (Canadian Intellectual Property Office), in conjunction with the National Reproductive Technologies Commission, undertake further study of the issue of intellectual property protection in the area of new reproductive technologies with a view to making recommendations to the federal government for any necessary amendments to the *Patent Act* [206]. In our discussion of this issue, we outlined the principles and goals that we conclude should underlie such policies.

We believe that adoption is an important alternative to the use of new reproductive technologies. We therefore recommend that the federal government, in conjunction with provincial/territorial governments, undertake a joint review of adoption in Canada, with a view to addressing such issues as the relative merits of public and private adoption systems in promoting the best interests of the child and in meeting the needs of the other parties involved; access to adoption and barriers to access; cost; record keeping and disclosure; counselling and consent; the advantages and drawbacks of interprovincial/territorial harmonization of policies, services, and practices; and issues in relation to international adoptions [62].

National Council on Bioethics in Human Research

We recommend that the National Council on Bioethics in Human Research monitor evolving knowledge and potential developments in the field of non-therapeutic genetic alteration (that is, outside the field of reproduction itself) with a view to considering whether and what types of measures may need to be put in place in the future [272].

Provincial/Territorial Governments

Many of the recommendations we have made to the federal government can be achieved only through consultation and cooperation with the provincial/territorial governments. Provincial/territorial governments will be a vital partner in implementing our recommendations. For example, the federal government must work together with provincial/territorial governments on issues such as sexual health education and other public health education campaigns that relate to infertility prevention, occupational health and safety, and adoption policy. We are impressed by the cooperation shown in the development of the national Guidelines on Sexual Health Education, and in the work of the National Strategy to Reduce Tobacco Use. These examples show that the various levels of government can work together very effectively toward common goals when the health and well-being of Canadians are involved.

Provincial/territorial governments, because of their role in health care, are also essential partners in the six sub-committees of the National Reproductive Technologies Commission, and provincial/territorial input will be crucial in the formulation of standards and guidelines governing the provision and licensing of new reproductive technologies. Moreover, annual interactions between the National Reproductive Technologies Commission and the Conference of Deputy Ministers of Health are important in promoting information sharing and the development of common approaches in this area. This partnership with regard to reproductive health care will enable more effective, evidence-based management of this part of the health care system.

In addition to working together with the federal government in these and other ways, provinces/territories should take the initiative in several areas to protect and promote the best interests of Canadians. These areas include aspects of health education in schools, workers' compensation, family law, funding of the delivery of new reproductive technologies through the publicly supported health care system, support for clinical trials of unproven techniques, and reform of human tissue gift acts.

In the area of health education in schools, we recommend that provincial/territorial ministries of education

- mandate health education that includes smoking prevention for all young Canadians in elementary and high school grades [25];

- ensure that health curricula and school programs, in conjunction with community programs, focus on the benefits of a smoke-free life as a means of preventing and reducing smoking among young people [26]; and

- mandate the provision of comprehensive sexual health education sequentially from the beginning of elementary school through to the end of high school [7].

In the area of workers' safety, we recommend that

- workers' compensation boards establish their employer contribution rates using penalty assessments based on observed hazards or health and safety audits. This approach should be adapted to include specific provisions for reproductive hazards [36]; and

- occupational health and safety legislation be amended to provide more equal participation by employers and workers with a view to reducing workplace hazards [38].

In the area of family law, we recommend that provincial/territorial legislation be amended (by those provinces/territories that have not already done so) to reflect the reality of assisted conception. In the context of sperm donation, we recommend that legislation be passed to ensure that [82]

- the donor's rights and responsibilities of parenthood are severed by the act of sperm donation;

- the married or cohabiting male partner of a donor insemination recipient, if he has given his written consent at the time of insemination, is considered the legal father of the child;

- if the legal mother of the child has no male partner, the child has the legal status of "father unknown"; and

- if the female partner of a donor insemination child's mother acts as a parent toward the child, such a relationship be recognized by the courts in determining the best interests of the child for purposes of custody, access, and support, or in the event of the death of the child's mother.

Similarly, provincial/territorial legislation should clarify legal parenthood in the case of egg donation, with the woman gestating and giving birth being declared the legal mother of the resulting child [169].

In the matter of preconception agreements, as well as the criminal prohibitions we have recommended, provincial/territorial legislation should specify that:

- all preconception agreements, whether or not they involve payment, are unenforceable against the gestational woman [200];

- a woman who gives birth to a child is considered the legal mother of the child, regardless of the source of the egg [203];

- as in the case of adoption, the birth mother should be allowed to relinquish her maternal rights only after a minimum waiting period following the birth of the child [204]; and

- in any dispute over custody, the best interests of the child should prevail over the interests of the adults involved [205].

The funding decisions made by provincial/territorial ministries of health will play a vital role in determining how new procedures are disseminated, how accessible they are, and whether appropriate counselling and information are provided. It is important that provinces/territorial ministries make these decisions in accordance with the precepts of evidence-based medicine, equal access, and the importance of informed choice.

In terms of evidence-based medicine, we recommend to provincial/territorial ministries of health that

- *in vitro* fertilization for bilateral fallopian tube blockage be an insured service under provincial medicare programs, but not for other indications [128, 129];

- the program framework within which routine ultrasound scanning during pregnancy is offered be reviewed; facilities that offer ultrasound should be licensed in order to promote women's best interests and best medical practice [224];

- potential conflicts of interest be eliminated by ensuring that those ordering routine obstetrical ultrasounds do not usually provide them [225]; and

- physicians or laboratories should not be reimbursed for MSAFP screening conducted outside coordinated provincial MSAFP screening programs [229].

In terms of promoting informed choice and equal access to reproductive technologies offered through the publicly supported health care system, we recommend that adequate funds be provided by provincial/territorial ministries of health for the following purposes:

- making available appropriate educational materials on the technologies to women and the general public through physicians' offices, public health units, local hospitals with obstetrical units, community centres providing prenatal classes, and other appropriate means; centres with large immigrant populations should ensure that written materials and, in particular, consent forms are available in the relevant languages [208, 209];

- the establishment of outreach programs where necessary so that appropriate information and referrals are available to all women closer to home [219];

- in areas where obstetricians or family physicians are not available to provide referrals, a designated individual in the public health system, such as a public health nurse, should provide information and referrals, so that women contemplating technology use can obtain information closer to home and, if they wish, be referred to the appropriate centre [220];

- interprovincial barriers to access to assisted conception and prenatal diagnosis services should be removed to allow women to receive services at the most appropriate centre [221]; and

- standards for funding based on caseload be developed to ensure that adequate resources for counselling are available. This would allow more comparable care to be delivered across the country [210, 258].

Provinces/territories also have an important role in protecting the autonomy of pregnant women against the threat of judicial intervention and providing support to pregnant women whose fetuses may be at risk. We therefore recommend that

- child welfare or other legislation never be used to control a woman's behaviour during pregnancy or birth; and that civil liability never be imposed upon a woman for harm done to her fetus during pregnancy [273(d), (e)];

- information and education programs be directed to pregnant women so that they do not inadvertently put a fetus at risk [275(a)];

- outreach and culturally appropriate support services be provided for pregnant women and young women in potentially vulnerable groups [275(b)]; and

- counselling, rehabilitation, outreach, and support services be designed specifically to meet the needs of pregnant women with drug/alcohol addictions [275(c)].

Finally, we recommend two further provincial initiatives:

- existing legislative measures designed to discourage tobacco use among teenagers should be strengthened and rigorously enforced [24]; and

- human tissue gift acts should be amended specifically to prohibit the sale of fetal tissues and any payment to the woman from whom the tissue is obtained [286]. The prohibition on the commercial exchange of fetuses and fetal tissue extends to tissue imported from other countries [287].

Health Care Professions

Health care professionals are equally vital partners in the implementation of our recommendations. For example, professional bodies will be represented on the various sub-committees of the National Reproductive Technologies Commission, and their input will help the sub-committees formulate their standards and guidelines. In the case of the Prenatal Diagnosis and Genetics Sub-Committee, given the demonstrated experience and record of the Canadian College of Medical Geneticists in evaluating centres, we have recommended that accreditation by the College be a precondition for licensing of genetics centres by the Prenatal Diagnosis and Genetics Sub-Committee [248].

In addition to their participation in the National Reproductive Technologies Commission, we have also made various recommendations regarding the education, training, and practices of health care professionals in Canada. We believe that many health care professionals are not well informed about issues relating to the prevention and treatment of infertility or to the uses and limits of prenatal diagnosis, and that some patients are therefore not receiving appropriate advice, referrals, or treatment.

To ensure that health care professionals practising outside licensed clinics are able to advise their patients properly regarding sexually transmitted diseases, we recommend that

- the Royal College of Physicians and Surgeons of Canada, the College of Family Physicians of Canada, and the Canadian Nurses Association propose standards for the content and duration of sexually transmitted diseases training provided by medical/nursing schools for various levels of clinical practice [16]; and

- continuing medical education courses be offered by faculties of medicine for obstetricians/gynaecologists, infectious disease specialists, and general practitioners, and by nursing faculties and community colleges for nurses, on the diagnosis, treatment, and counselling of individuals with sexually transmitted diseases [17].

To ensure that patients are not subjected to unnecessary or inappropriate infertility treatments, physicians and other health care workers should assess and counsel patients about their possible risk factors. In particular, we recommend that physicians and health care workers

- routinely evaluate women or couples seeking infertility treatment to determine whether smoking, eating habits, excessive exercise, alcohol consumption, or illicit drug use might be a contributing factor in their infertility. Patients should be informed about the effect of these factors on their fertility. If one or more of these factors is present, patients should be encouraged to modify their behaviour accordingly, and counselling and support to help them accomplish this goal should be available. This should be a first step before any form of infertility treatment is attempted [29, 31, 46, 47, 51, 52, 53, 57];

- ensure that women who have endometriosis know about the possible implications of the disease for their fertility so that they can take this information into account when making their childbearing plans [48];

- counsel couples considering surgical sterilization to ensure that they view the decision as permanent, and inform them of the likelihood of pregnancy after reversal of tubal ligation or vasectomy [58];

- counsel young women (and men) who are not in long-term monogamous relationships about the need for dual forms of protection against pregnancy and sexually transmitted diseases — in particular, that oral contraceptives should be used in conjunction with a barrier form of contraception to protect against not only pregnancy but also sexually transmitted diseases [59]; and

- inform women about the protection against sexually transmitted diseases provided by various forms of contraception and whether their use may be associated with a delayed return to fertility after contraceptive use is discontinued [60].

Once infertility has been properly diagnosed, it is important that the physician be able to provide treatment in a safe and effective manner or be able to provide an appropriate referral. If the treatment is provided within a licensed assisted conception clinic, standards of care will be determined by the guidelines established by the Assisted Conception Sub-Committee of the National Commission. If the treatment is provided outside a licensed clinic, however, there must be professional guidelines.   We therefore recommend that

- the College of Family Practitioners of Canada and the Society of Obstetricians and Gynaecologists of Canada develop and disseminate guidelines for use by practitioners prescribing fertility drugs outside the context of licensed clinics. In particular, these guidelines should recommend against the prescribing of drugs where safe use requires specialized expertise and hormonal monitoring of women taking the drugs [70]; and

- a practical referral guide for general practitioners be developed by the College of Family Physicians of Canada and distributed widely [122, 123].

In the context of prenatal diagnosis, we believe that improvements can be made in the way patients are counselled, both within and outside centres. We recommend with regard to prenatal diagnosis that

- the College of Family Practitioners of Canada and the Society of Obstetricians and Gynaecologists of Canada encourage their members to pursue continuing medical education to increase their knowledge and understanding of the capabilities and limitations of prenatal diagnosis, the proper provision of accurate information, and the process of informed consent and choice. Specifically, increased efforts should be made in continuing education of referring physicians to emphasize the right of individual women and couples to reproductive autonomy, to decide for themselves whether to have prenatal testing, and, if a serious disorder is detected, to decide whether to terminate or continue the pregnancy [216, 217];

- the Canadian College of Medical Geneticists coordinate a collaborative effort by genetics centres, with the input of organizations representing patients, people with disabilities, and concerned women's groups, to develop accurate, understandable, and clear educational materials on prenatal diagnosis that fairly portray living with the disabilities diagnosed [207, 218];

- provincial colleges of physicians and surgeons and medical associations emphasize to their members that failure to discuss with patients the option of referral for a medically indicated prenatal diagnostic service is unethical and constitutes unacceptable medical practice. Information in this regard should be incorporated into medical school curricula and intern and residency training and examinations [222]; and

- relevant professional associations emphasize to their members that a woman having pregnancy termination because of a serious fetal disorder, together with her family, should receive support from medical and paramedical staff [211].

The licensing scheme we propose will help to ensure that prenatal diagnosis provided within genetics centres will not be misused for sex-selection purposes. It is also important to avoid such misuse outside the clinics, and to that end we recommend that the Society of Obstetricians and Gynaecologists of Canada, the Canadian Association of Radiologists, and the College of Family Physicians of Canada review their practice guidelines to ensure that practitioners using prenatal ultrasound do not perform ultrasound for the purpose of sex identification (except where medically indicated) and do not deliberately seek or offer information on fetal sex except for medical reasons prior to the third trimester of pregnancy [226, 255, 264].

Given that these tissues must be disposed of, we do not think the practice of selling placentas for use in the production of pharmaceutical and therapeutic products should be discontinued. However, we recommend that hospitals seek written consent from the mother for any use of the placenta other than disposal [276].

Finally, we believe that professional associations must ensure that their members are not facilitating preconception arrangements. We therefore recommend that all self-regulating professional bodies, such as provincial colleges of physicians and surgeons and provincial law societies, adopt strict codes of conduct, disciplinary measures, and severe penalties, including loss of licence to practise, against members knowingly involved in brokering or performing assisted insemination, *in vitro* fertilization, or zygote/embryo transfer to facilitate a preconception arrangement [201].

Patients and Other Affected Groups

Organizations representing individuals and groups affected by new reproductive technologies (such as women, people who are infertile, people at risk to have affected children, and people with disabilities) have important roles to play and perspectives to bring. In particular, we have recommended that such groups be represented on the relevant sub-committees of the National Reproductive Technologies Commission. For example, groups representing people with disabilities and patients at risk of genetic diseases should be included on the Prenatal Diagnosis and Genetics Sub-Committee. Moreover, the input of these groups will help the sub-committees formulate their standards and guidelines.

We have also recommended that organizations representing people with disabilities, people at risk, and women work with the Canadian College of Medical Geneticists in developing counselling protocols and information materials to ensure that disabilities and living with a disability are represented fairly and accurately [218].

We also believe that an important role for these groups is to pressure other bodies — particularly the federal and provincial/territorial governments and the health professions — to implement the recommendations we have made. Indeed, we hope that by summarizing our recommendations here by area of responsibility, we will help advocacy groups and the general public identify who they should look to, and hold accountable, for action on these recommendations.

Commercial Interests

We have already addressed the need to protect vulnerable interests of individuals and of society from commercial interests in some of the recommendations listed above. In some cases, commercial interests have been excluded entirely from activity in an area. For example, facilities involved in assisted insemination or assisted conception must operate on a non-profit basis, and commercial surrogacy agencies are prohibited [88(p), 94(m), 154, 199]. In other cases, we have recommended that the activities of commercial interests be tightly monitored. For example, we have made recommendations regarding the sale of products that may pose risks to fertility, including restrictions on the way tobacco is sold and required warning labels on alcohol products [24, 50], and we have recommended that those physicians ordering routine obstetrical ultrasound testing do not usually provide it [225]. The promotional activities of companies marketing fertility drugs in Canada will be monitored by the Assisted Conception Sub-Committee [71], and we have recommended mechanisms for ethical review of any clinical trials funded by pharmaceutical companies even if these occur outside universities or university-affiliated hospitals [68]. We have made recommendations that will enable outcomes of drug treatment to be evaluated more effectively and to limit unproven use of drugs for infertility treatment [63-67].

We believe that pharmaceutical companies should be required to contribute to the cost of conducting the clinical trials needed to assess the safety and efficacy of fertility drugs even after these are on the market. We therefore recommend that the federal government require those pharmaceutical companies marketing fertility drugs to contribute funding for clinical trials for unproven uses, as well as for studies on them identified as necessary by Health Canada based on post-marketing reports of adverse effects. This funding should be administered at arm's length by national research funding agencies, but the studies should be facilitated and overseen by the National Reproductive Technologies Commission [64, 74, 79].

Employers

Some of our recommendations regarding workplace safety will affect employers whose workers may face reproductive hazards [see, for example, 36-38]. We also believe that the presence of workplace reproductive hazards should not be used to discriminate against women. We therefore recommend that control of workplace hazards not be sought through discriminatory personnel policies, and that reduction of hazards be sought through the use of engineering and workplace design controls wherever feasible [35].

School Boards

School boards have a pivotal role in the provision of sexual health education. They can help ensure that requirements for teachers delivering sexual health education in schools are in accordance with the criteria outlined in the Guidelines for Sexual Health Education [13], as we recommended earlier.

We recommend further that school boards consider the benefits of making contraception more accessible to young people who are sexually active — for example, through condom dispensers in high schools and referral to appropriate health services [12].

Conclusion

The recommendations summarized here are the product of three and a half years of research, analysis, consultation, and conscientious deliberation. Commissioners spent untold hours weighing evidence and considering the various positions and points of view presented to us by Canadians. We were conscious throughout that the recommendations we made would affect the day-to-day lives of many thousands of Canadians and that we could not take this responsibility lightly. Our goal was to seek a way that Canada, as a society, can obtain the benefits of technology for its members while also protecting them from potential harms through its abuse or misuse.

Each of the technologies, conditions, and practices in our mandate had potential harms and benefits that had to be considered. There were no easy solutions, no obvious yes-or-no answers, to many of the complex social, ethical, and legal issues they raised. Their complexity and differences in potential use meant that we could not take a simplistic all-or-nothing approach to their evaluation. We therefore listened to Canadians; we assessed new reproductive technologies in light of exhaustive evidence and data and analyzed their implications using explicit ethical principles, an understanding of Canadian social values and attitudes, and a belief that medical treatment should not be offered without evidence that it works. We reached three major conclusions. First, there is an urgent need for boundaries around the entire field of new reproductive technologies, and some technologies must remain outside the boundaries of the permissible. Second, within those boundaries, accountable regulation of permissible activities is needed to protect the interests of all involved. Third, we concluded that permanent mechanisms should be put in place to provide a flexible and continuing response to issues concerning new reproductive technologies as they evolve further.

We have set out a blueprint for how Canada, with its unique institutions and make-up, can approach new reproductive technologies, regulate their use, and ensure that future development is in the public interest. Our blueprint is detailed and involves the participation and commitment — financial, temporal, and moral — of many different sectors of society. The approach we propose is feasible and practical, and we have laid out a detailed plan for how it can be accomplished. In our view the reasons for taking such action are compelling: the potential for harm to individuals, and the need to protect vulnerable interests of individuals and of society. Implementing our recommendations will enable Canada to use scientific knowledge to better the lives of many Canadians: it will demonstrate that we care about each other's well-being and that we recognize collective values with respect to the importance people attach to having children. At the same time it will ensure only ethical and accountable use of technology is made with the awareness that there are potential harms that must be guarded against. Implementing our recommendations will enable Canadians to take pride in our collective ability as a society to demonstrate wisdom, compassion, and decency in the way we choose to use technology.

At the beginning of our mandate we made a commitment to keep Canadians apprised of what we were doing so that they could benefit from the information and discussion generated by our activities. In that spirit, in this concluding part of our report, we have outlined who should be responsible for taking action on our recommendations, so that it will be equally possible for Canadians to see whether and how well our recommendations are being implemented. We have done our job in as caring and conscientious a way as we know how. The next steps are not ours — they belong to governments, the professions, and individual Canadians.

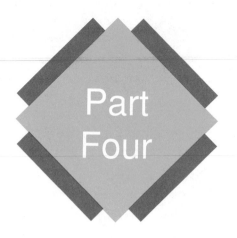

Part
Four

**Annex
Glossary
Appendices**

Commissioner Suzanne Rozell Scorsone:

Six Dissenting Opinions

Preamble

The supplementary statements made here must be taken in the overall context of my agreement with the vast majority of the recommendations of the Royal Commission on New Reproductive Technologies. The areas of disagreement are few, indeed only six: educational strategies for STD prevention, access to new reproductive technologies, embryo research, termination as an appropriate response to the prenatal diagnosis of a disorder, the genetic link in donor insemination, and judicial intervention.

Under the Chairmanship of Patricia Baird, our discussion as Commissioners was free and wide-ranging, all concerns and perspectives brought to the table. The presence of these few supplementary differences of opinion as part of the unitary final report witnesses to the liberty given to the expression of viewpoints. That the areas of disagreement are serious should not be taken to reflect in any way on the rest of the report, since in other areas of similarly serious import we have been able to reach a mutual, collaborative view and common recommendations, if in a minority of instances out of different reasoning. These questions are matters of great debate in Canadian society at large; that there would be some degree of respectful difference of opinion on a Commission called together out of diverse backgrounds and expertise to examine these issues on behalf of Canadians is precisely what one would expect. The overall unanimity on all other recommendations witnesses to the fact that they arise out of genuinely achieved and viable agreement.

The presentation of these arguments is necessarily complex and lengthy, but it reflects only the great complexity of the long process of discussion and research in which we have engaged together. The volumes upon volumes recording the testimony we have heard and the research undertaken for the Commission are witness to the amount of evidence, analysis, and reasoning on which each conclusion and recommendation is based.

The Commission report is capable of a short-form presentation of reasoning because each point is a conclusion based on far more complex assumptions and analyses. Unfortunately, to argue persuasively toward different conclusions on these few subjects, more of that background has to be made explicit and examined.

The most essential points and recommendations are presented in this section, and the reasoning on which they are based is in the following section. Those readers with little time may wish to concentrate on the former, while the latter will be of interest to those others who wish to examine in greater detail why and how these conclusions have been reached and to explore their implications.

It remains for Parliament and the people of Canada, along with the various levels of jurisdiction and the organizations and individuals concerned, to assess the persuasiveness of arguments and to decide upon the implementation of recommendations. Now that our deliberations have ended, and both our many common and our few differing conclusions reached, it is time for the next stage of the democratic process.

I. Educational Strategies for STD Prevention

I agree that education in sexual health should be available to all. There is, however, no national consensus on the value context of such education. The present freedoms and jurisdictional roles of the parents of minor children, provinces, school boards, hospitals, and social services, particularly those mandated and sponsored by religious or other value-based groups, in determining the approaches and value contexts of sexual education should therefore be preserved. However thorny and difficult the issues, Canada, by tradition and constitution, honours legitimate differences in values and approach.

The Guidelines for Sexual Health Education generated in response to a recommendation by the Expert Interdisciplinary Advisory Committee on Sexually Transmitted Diseases in Children and Youth (EIAC-STD) and the Federal/Provincial/Territorial Working Group on Adolescent Reproductive Health ought not to be adopted at the national level. These guidelines contain some elements that constitutionally protected separate, denominational, and dissentient schools could not implement without breaching their moral codes and mandates. The guidelines, moreover, discuss "sexual health" without mentioning such key concepts as commitment, childbearing, children and child-rearing, marriage, or love; the focus is the behaviour, knowledge, motivation, and choice of the individual which, important as they are, do not suffice. The ethic of care, the prism of the Royal Commission's understanding and clearly imbued with the concepts of relationship and commitment, is not inherent in the guidelines themselves. It would not follow them into national adoption were the Guidelines for Sexual Health Education not to be amended and revised from their foundations in accord with the ethical guidelines laid out by this Commission.

The requirements for those teaching sexual health education should not be based on those recommended in the Guidelines for Sexual Health Education. The mandating of the requirements for persons delivering sexual health education in schools should promote the enabling of every classroom teacher, not only of specialists. Properly resourced classroom teachers have an important role, following that of parents, in the provision of family life education. Particularly in Grades 1-8, it is important that education and example in this intimate and relationship-based area be mediated primarily through people with whom a child has an ongoing and supportive relationship and who are in a position for follow-up and clarification.

The membership of the recommended Infertility Prevention Sub-Committee should be broadened to include parent groups, ethicists, representatives of religious and other groups engaged in the sponsorship of schools, and others. A full range of viewpoints representative of those in the Canadian population should be ensured.   The principles for participation in the full National Reproductive Technologies Commission are broad and representative. As the list for this particular sub-committee now stands, however, containing as it does, beyond the necessary professionals, the advocacy groups of only one sort of overlapping network, only one possible viewpoint in a highly controverted field would be likely to have effective representation.   In an influential national body, a narrow perspective would be inappropriate.

Finally, I would give key prominence to parents, particularly those of minor children. The Commission report rightly underscores the importance of their capacities, but nonetheless places agencies, government bodies, and other outside organizations in all explicitly mentioned primary decision-making roles, portraying parents as a promising but adjunct resource.   It is instead the case that the legal rights and primary responsibility of parents for the medical and educational care of their minor children are both inherent in and essential to their role.

This includes their responsibility for notification and consent for medical treatment related to contraception. Schools should not be engaged in making unilateral referrals of minors for medical treatment, including contraception, without the consent of parents. This is an unjustified expropriation of the normal custodial role and jurisdiction of the responsible parent. The issue is not a simple one of the autonomy of minors, since the custodial role of parents is rooted in the empirically observable and normal incompleteness of minors' process of development of the capacity for fully competent and responsible autonomy, whether in their own best interests or those of others. Mechanisms exist for dealing with overtly dysfunctional or neglectful family or other social situations; the treatment of all families as though they were dysfunctional and hence targets for state intervention is highly inappropriate.

The generation of all programs of STD prevention directed at young people should also have primary involvement of parents and their representative groups from the earliest stages. It is parents who have the primary responsibility and right to determine the nature of the values education of their minor children, and parents who, on the ground, provide the most prevalent support systems for their children of any age in living with and coping with the results, both positive and negative, of their sexual choices.

Legitimate diversity is essential to fundamental human freedoms.

II. Access to New Reproductive Technologies

The vast majority of the recommendations of this Commission maintain a fine and humane balance of the complex medical, ethical, social, and legal factors which form their context. On very few points do I feel obliged to object that this balance has not been maintained. This is one. On this issue a single perspective is being taken as normative, whereas a multiplicity of perspectives are not only present among Canadians but are, in my view, a matter of legitimate and necessary freedom.

Had the Commission report recommended simply that, in a pluralistic society, the provision of new reproductive technologies to persons living in a broad range of social situations is acceptable so long as the best interests of the child are maintained, this dissent would not have been written. Such a recommendation would have permitted diversity and freedom of both thought and action for all those involved. I cannot agree, however, with a recommendation which would impose on all health care institutions and personnel the use of a single and solely medical set of criteria, to the absolute exclusion, always and everywhere, of other factors.

While medical criteria are one key and essential component of determining access to *in vitro* fertilization (IVF), donor insemination (DI or AID) and other new reproductive technologies, there are also social and diverse ethical questions surrounding them which ought not to be dismissed. Health care institutions have latitude in setting their policies concerning access to new reproductive technologies, but there should be no absolute requirement of provision without regard to "factors such as marital status, sexual orientation or social and economic status." Such a requirement might appear to reduce the decision to solely objective criteria. It does not. To consider such factors relevant or irrelevant is, either way, a social/ethical opinion and choice. Those who consider them relevant, particularly but not only because of their impact on the best interests of a child and/or for reasons of conscience or religious belief, must not have the contrary view imposed upon them with no possibility of legitimate diversity.

Nor can I agree that the exclusion of all but medical indications should be a condition of the licensing of any assisted conception facility. Such a condition would discriminate against religious groups and board-electing communities which did not accept this perspective; health care facilities sponsored by such groups and communities would be denied the capacity to offer direct oocyte/sperm transfer (DOST), gamete intrafallopian transfer (GIFT), IVF, donor insemination, or any other of the licensable treatments.

It would also have the unintended effect of reducing access to assisted conception for the great majority of those seeking it, as the imposition of such a requirement would cause existing fertility clinics in health care facilities sponsored by some such groups and communities to close.

Licensing requirements have a legitimate purpose in the maintenance of high medical, record-keeping, and research standards. They should not be used as a mechanism of social engineering. Yet this is what the licensing and its inherent advocacy of the activity of those holding only one set of moral and ethical values and the exclusion of all others, particularly when their views reflect those of the majority of Canadians, would be. The Commission report agrees that religious institutions exist and should not be forced to contravene their religious beliefs, seeking to demonstrate this by saying that they have no intent to force any practitioner or clinic to provide new reproductive technologies if they do not wish to do so. Yet the erection of government licensing structures implementing a policy that one may believe as one wishes so long as one absents oneself or accepts being excluded from the public forum, from a public service, and from an activity would itself be a contravention of religious freedom or freedom of any other sort of conscientious opinion. It closes the field to all those who hold any but one set of ideas. This does constitute discrimination based on religion.

The imposition by government of a single view would have implications far beyond new reproductive technologies, since it would be a precedent of state override of diversity arising from religious belief and other values. This would have implications, not only in many fields of religiously sponsored health care and education, but in the social services, including adoption.

Policy with respect to access should be set by the boards and/or organizational owners (for instance charitable organizations, religious orders or religious bodies) of the respective health care facilities. Boards and/or organizational owners should set these policies in accord with their mandates and ethical policies, bearing in mind the guidelines of the relevant professional associations, within the guidelines, regulations and legislation of provincial government, and in dialogue with the values and concerns of the surrounding community of the ultimate providers, the taxpayers.

Conflicts over the applicability of a policy to individual cases should be resolved as such conflicts are resolved in other fields of medicine, of law, and of social service to children and families. It would be unreasonable and impracticable for each criterion "to be specified in law." Such prior legislative specification is not made in cases of child protection or home assessment for adoption or other aspects of child welfare, or, on another level, of legitimate variation in mandate, policy, and practice between and among secular and religiously sponsored institutions. The variability of human situations is too great, and the effect of any one factor may vary, compensated for or rendered more serious depending upon the concomitant existence or severity of others. The blunt instrument of legislation centralizing inflexible criteria for assessments is unwarranted and would itself have negative consequences. Arguments in the Commission text appealing to the Charter are a matter of opinion expanding the interpretation of its application well beyond what has been or is likely to be established.

The principle of the best interests of the child, clearly recognized in law, should take precedence over any other interest; this is clearly justified in a free and democratic society. Similarly, the freedom of conscience of individual professionals, physicians, nurses and others must be upheld. The freedoms of health care institutions sponsored by religious bodies or communities must be preserved. They are and must remain free to set policies in accord with the moral codes inherent in their mandates as a matter of fundamental human rights.

III. Embryo Research

I accept and endorse, not only the great majority of the recommendations of the final report of the Royal Commission on New Reproductive Technologies on the subject of *in vitro* fertilization, but many of those dealing with embryo research and with directly associated aspects of IVF. I cannot, however, accept others; my dissent and my reasoning are laid out here.

Experimentation and other forms of non-therapeutic research on viable human zygotes or embryos should not be permitted at any point in development. Still less should human zygotes or embryos be deliberately brought into being for the purpose of research. Such experimentation instrumentalizes the human, and is incompatible with commonly accepted ethical norms for research on human subjects. It would set precedents which would have implications far beyond embryo research, implications which would be counterproductive for the sick, the disabled, the elderly, and for anyone else who may not be accepted by or convenient to some other individual or group.

Researchers should not be permitted to fertilize ova taken from ovaries removed from women having hysterectomies, nor (the Commission makes no recommendation on this latter point) from the ovaries of women who have died. This would make the instrumentalization of the human, woman and embryo, still more grave, first because of the impersonal objectification involved. Second, the numbers of ovaries potentially available from hysterectomies and/or cadavers, as well as the ease with which sperm can be procured, carry the risk of the creation of a vast industry (even if non-profit) utilizing such embryos, most likely for experimental research rather than for conceptions in the treatment of infertile women, to the dehumanization of both the embryos and the adult individuals involved and of society as a whole. There are already so many supernumerary ova and embryos remaining from IVF that some are used for research; let these be used for donation to other infertile women if they appear to be healthy.

That research on viable zygotes/embryos would yield useful information is no doubt true, but the same could be said of many sorts of experimentation on human subjects which are deemed unacceptable. Human dignity, non-maleficence, respect for life, and the protection of the vulnerable are higher values.

Research into infertility treatments which do not generate supernumerary embryos and treatments which do not submit a woman to the stress and risk of hormonal ovarian stimulation and superovulation should be pursued as a matter of high priority in policy and funding. I fully endorse the recommendation in which the Commission report encourages such research; the only difference is the primary priority I would prefer to see it given. Treatments of this sort would not only be unambiguously in the health interest of the woman and the intended child. They would also free medical facilities from any suspicion that access to embryos for research would be a priority driving or structuring some modalities of infertility treatment. In accord with the principles enunciated many times by the Commission, the choice of any treatment modality must be unambiguously in the interest of the particular woman and the intended child.

Any viable embryos which have been generated *in vitro* and which are not transferred to the mother immediately should have the possibility of normal life and development, whether by being cryopreserved for subsequent implantation, or by immediate transfer to the uterus of another woman in what may be viewed as a sort of prenatal adoption.

If embryos have been cryopreserved and the male parent dies, it should be the choice of the woman whether or not to have the embryos transferred to her uterus. No external entity, whether a physician, a clinic, a regulatory body or the state, has the right to oblige her to be bereaved at once of her spouse and of their expected, already-conceived children.

Embryos cryopreserved for the time limit allowed by the National Commission, or of whom the female parent has died (given that the male parent cannot gestate them), or who are the subject of irresolvable dispute such as might exist where the male and female parents have died or have divorced, should not be destroyed; rather they should be offered for prenatal adoption to an infertile woman in a manner parallel to the adoption of born children who are wards of the Crown.

With respect to the patenting of cell lines derived from embryos or fetal tissues, the Commission report lays out very real dilemmas, recommending further study. While seeing the strength of the report's arguments from the need for investment, I view the patenting of cell lines derived from human tissues, specifically those of embryos and fetuses, as unacceptable. If lacunae in the law with respect to patenting of "microbial life forms" now permit such patenting, they should be closed. Patenting of the inventive processes of cell line cultivation or distribution by pharmaceutical companies of the biochemical products (such as insulin or dopamine) derived from such cell lines would be acceptable, but the cell lines themselves are and remain human tissue, with the full, distinct, and individual human genome. Other modes of investment should be developed to ensure research and non-profit access.

The licensing and monitoring structure recommended by the Commission's final report presents a highly useful mode of avoiding abuse and commercialization, of ensuring that all treatments are in the primary interest of the specific woman and intended child, and of assuring high standards of research practice and record keeping. It should, however, permit only research which uses unfertilized gametes or non-viable embryos certainly incapable of human life or development, such as those with three or more pronuclei, or those which will clearly develop into a hydatidiform mole. Some researchers already do very useful work based on observation or manipulation of embryos known to be nonviable.

The approach of Germany, which prohibits all embryo research including research between sperm penetration and syngamy, is exceedingly careful to avoid even the possibility of exploitation of an intrinsically or potentially human subject. An empirically-based and quite reasonable argument can also be made for research on ova which have been penetrated by sperm but in which the separate chromosome-containing pronuclei of sperm and ovum have not yet fused at syngamy. This question deserves further careful examination.

The task of the recommended Sub-Committee structure is licensing and monitoring; the Commission has not recommended that it engage in the active promotion and expansion of embryo research. It is, however, a common tendency of human groups to become agents of facilitation for the activity with which they are concerned — indeed promotion is rightly part of the recommended mandates of other Sub-Committees, such as that on infertility prevention. That promotion is not part of its task should be made explicit in the mandate of the Sub-Committee on Embryo Research.

IV. Aspects of Prenatal Diagnosis

No part of the text of this report which would state or imply that termination is an appropriate response to a prenatal diagnosis finding of a disorder has my support or assent. The pain and great difficulty which the parents of a child with a severe early-onset disorder face should be met by society with greatly increased resources for social support, care, and research into treatment. The knowledge that a person bears a gene for a disease of late onset says nothing about the value of the life of that person before — or after — that onset.

For each of us death will inevitably come, although most of us do not know when or how. Not knowing the time or the length and difficulty of the process of dying does not make one person's life more significant than the life of a person who does know or whose parents know. Termination, whether for disorders of early or late onset, seems to me to be a final discrimination against the disabled and the sick, a prenatal form of direct euthanasia.

It does not follow that prenatal diagnosis should be opposed as a matter of policy. That many do terminate pregnancies after the finding of some types of disorder does not invalidate the investigation itself. The decisions that people make upon receiving the information may be of greatly differing kinds.

Uncertainty, under circumstances of advanced maternal age or a family history or other likelihood of a disorder, would once have caused physicians routinely to recommend abortion or would have led fearful couples to abort; the availability of PND and the reassuring result most receive cause many to continue their pregnancies to term.

Prenatal diagnosis may prepare a family to receive a disabled child. It may increasingly permit treatment, at the time of or even before birth, of many disorders, such as spina bifida revealed by testing for MSAFP or even some single-gene disorders such as cystic fibrosis or ADA deficiency. Given recent explorations of the genesis of beta-amyloid protein with relation to both trisomy 21 (Down syndrome) and some chromosome 21-associated forms of Alzheimer disease, it may not even be too much to hope for a future treatment for Down syndrome. Recent statements by Dr. Teepu Siddique, head of a research team very recently reported as having identified the defect in a "free-radical" combatting enzyme associated with one form of amyotrophic lateral sclerosis, offer a similar, if still distant, hope for the late-onset disorder commonly known as Lou Gehrig disease.[1] Many other examples are possible. Such treatments would be eagerly desired by many parents.

The structures, norms of information and consent, medical standards and counselling requirements recommended by the Commission are highly constructive overall. Canada does not have a law limiting or regulating the criteria for abortion, although law and precedent do — and must continue to — recognize the freedom of physicians and health care institutions not to participate in it, and should further recognize that freedom as the right of nurses and others. The Commission report's recommendations concerning even-handed, objective presentation of all relevant information and options, including social supports, care, treatment, and the non-directive exploration of personal values in the making of decisions, if fully implemented, will do much to help people to understand clearly the implications of the decisions they ultimately make, and to encourage at least some people to bear and care for their disabled children.

For these reasons, I give my general acceptance and support to the recommendations of this Commission on prenatal diagnosis.

V. The Genetic Link in Gamete Donation

The Commission has made a highly significant contribution to the question of gamete donation in the recommendations on medical and informed consent standards, record keeping, and the rejection of commercialization. While not all Canadians accept the deliberate and health-care-system-facilitated engendering of children without a personal knowledge and a committed bond between their genetic parents, the widespread existence of the practice and its acceptance by others necessitate its regulation in the best interests of all those involved, particularly the children born. The implementation of most of the recommendations would make great strides toward the care and protection of all parties.

I differ, however, with the recommendation that the children of ovum or sperm gamete donation be denied access to identifying information concerning their progenitor(s) except after a court process and under conditions of serious medical need. Even this would be great progress over the present situation, in which the lack of adequate — or any — record keeping denies the offspring any information, non-identifying or identifying, about his or her progenitor. The Commission report has recommended great progress in procedure and record keeping and it eloquently sketches the negative effects of secrecy, but it does not follow its insight through to completion. The recommendation of a continuing near-universal barrier fails to recognize the rights of the child at the age of majority to have access to his or her own personal information, information which is of great importance to the identity of many people and which is of great social and cultural significance to both individuals and groups in this country.

The donor's right to privacy if he or she does not wish to be known can be protected, and the donor's wish not to bear legal responsibility and obligations toward the child can be given formal and binding recognition without the erection of absolute barriers to identification and contact if both parties are willing.

The right and need of the nurturing parent(s), both social/genetic and solely social, to have full care of and legal custody of the child until adulthood can also be protected. Adoption, with the recognition of rights, needs, and viable protections now evolving in that field, is a very relevant exemplar of the same valid concerns.

If the activation of the disclosure process were to require the child's having reached adulthood, the possible disruption of the process of bonding and rearing within the custodial family mentioned in the report would not arise.   The gamete donor could be able to state intent at the time of donation but be further able to change that decision either way at any subsequent time.   This is the model most commonly followed in adoption.

The assumption that the rights of an adult child of gamete donation to information on the specifics of his or her heritage can be negated rests upon definitions of the parent-child bond which would deny the importance of the perduring genetic link, that aspect of his or her identity which is genetically based.   In this respect the Commission report has gone beyond affirming social definitions of relationships to absolutizing social definitions, making them the fundamental and sole criterion of ethical and legal recognition, irrespective of the existence of other salient and inherent realities.   The determination of these social definitions has been set solely on the wishes of the engendering or receiving adults and, even more, on the fiat of the state; this nullification of the rights of the offspring appears to me to be unjustified on any social or empirical ground.

In any case, reaching conclusions on the nature, structure, and legal definition of the family and of the parent-child link as such is outside the mandate of this Commission.   It has not been the subject of the sort of extensive exploration which has rightly been devoted to such mandated subjects as the circumvention of infertility.   Such absolute conclusions based on such far-reaching assumptions are therefore unwarranted.

On one other question I also have practical concerns which have implications for the principles we have unanimously affirmed.

Even the general norm that outcome be reported by sperm recipients — unless that reporting is confirmed by confidentiality-maintaining health record data bank linkages — is likely to weaken record keeping to the point that many of the recommendations made in our report would be difficult or impossible to fulfil, given the known low rate of return on questionnaires of any sort.   There is a further strong possibility that encouragement of self-insemination, particularly if sperm banks were to operate on a carry-out basis, would undercut the application of the principles at which we have arrived.   Of greatest concern here would be questions of record keeping, of medical and other history, and even of commerce.   Sperm for self-insemination should be therefore used in a comfortable and well-appointed room provided on the site of the clinic or sperm bank, and should not otherwise be taken out of the facility.

VI. Judicial Intervention in Pregnancy

I do not concur with the recommendation that judicial intervention in pregnancy not be permissible, nor do I concur with the associated legislative measures.   Words like "never" are, in my view, far too absolute. Intervention is generally inadvisable, but should not be entirely precluded.

The existing possibility of recourse to the courts, a disinterested forum with accepted legitimacy for mediation and resolution of conflict in matters of human welfare, remains necessary in an area so fraught with ambivalence on the part of all parties in very specific and particular personal difficulties.

Nor would I support a departure from the normal protections of all individuals from medical or other intervention, whatever their sex. Application of the severe sanctions of the criminal law uniquely to interventions directed at pregnant women appears to me to be unjustified. Intervention in pregnancy is not fundamentally different from other forms of medical or social intervention, and women are not so different from men in their essence or before the law that the protections and sanctions governing them should be of different orders.

Such an absolutization could, moreover, have negative and discriminatory implications, calling into question the equality of men and women before the law.

There are many issues in which attention to the collective status of women and the autonomy of women as women would be of proportionately overriding importance; this is not one of them. The consequences for individual vulnerable human beings, both woman and child, are too severe and personal, and the variability of circumstances is too great to be resolved by an absolutized application of a general principle without the possibility of review of individual cases.

The resolution of the situations of individuals should be determined in the best interests of those individuals and of those whom they affect. Their cases should not be predetermined in service to the interests of some other or larger aggregate group, such as women, whose cause (or rather one available sociopolitical interpretation of whose cause) that individual has not explicitly embraced, since no one may be used as a means to an end, however worthy that end.

There may be instances in which judicial intervention would enable and defend a woman's best interests, her actual consent and autonomy against the coercion arising from some particular factor in her situation. One such example would be the case of a severely addicted woman who states clearly and explicitly that she wants her child to be healthy but whose withdrawal symptoms would demonstrably drive her to seek the drug she abuses were she not in mandatory treatment. Since only judicial review and possible intervention would allow the nature of her most fundamental consent and the actual expression of her choice and autonomy to be ascertained and enabled, even autonomy would in some instances require the continued existence of the possibility of judicial intervention in pregnancy. The Commission report itself, in what appears to me to be a contradiction of its own position, refers to the appointment of a legal guardian for a person found mentally incompetent. Such a finding and appointment requires court examination of the case and would therefore in fact constitute judicial intervention.   It is precisely the ineradicable need for the availability of objective assessment such as this in grave cases that is the point of this dissent.

Questions of the existence or non-existence of independent legal or constitutional rights of the fetus are irrelevant to the issue. The state has been declared by the Supreme Court of Canada to have an interest in the fetus, which means that this interest must have some possibility and venue of exercise. The principle of the requirement of consent to treatment, including treatment in the interests of another of any age or relationship, is accepted both in ethics and in law, which means that a woman is protected in general from non-consensual intervention. Positing that the fetus "has no legal existence" and that no third party can volunteer to defend the rights of such a being is therefore neither strictly accurate in law nor necessary to the ordinary protection of women.

I do fully concur with my fellow Commissioners, however, in recommendations which would maximize education, service, and care extended to all women, especially to those who are vulnerable or addicted, so that risk to both woman and fetus can be avoided.

Detailed·Reasoning on the Dissenting Opinions

Educational Strategies for STD Prevention

I am in full agreement with my fellow Commissioners with respect to most recommendations on STD prevention, including the conviction that education in sexual health should be made available to all. There is, however, no national consensus on precisely what the content of such education should be. The essential biological facts about sexual function, reproduction, its control, and dysfunctions such as sexually transmitted diseases can be effectively rendered within a variety of value contexts. Value contexts are of crucial importance to those who hold them, but those contexts, while they overlap in some respects, will in some degree be mutually exclusive. There should be full freedom for the presentation of information within those differing value contexts.

Accordingly, I do not endorse the recommendation of adoption at the national level for sexual health education programs of the Guidelines for Sexual Health Education generated by a working group convened by the Sex Information and Education Council of Canada (SIECCAN) at the initiative and under the auspices of EIAC-STD and the Federal/Provincial/Territorial Working Group on Adolescent Reproductive Health. While the guidelines acknowledge differences in value systems, they nonetheless focus on certain components of sexual education as to be required. Many schools, notably the Catholic separate public schools — but also those sponsored by many Protestant, Jewish, Muslim or other religious groups — could not comply with certain aspects of those guidelines and remain true to their mandates. As just one example, such schools cannot, within their value mandates, "affirm individuals who make either choice" in their approach to "adolescents" who "may elect abstinence while other adolescents may not."[2]

The Royal Commission on New Reproductive Technologies, through its commitment to the ethic of care, does take a fundamental stance throughout that the treatment of all human beings should be viewed through a prism of connectedness, commitment, benevolence, and relationship. Were the Guidelines for Sexual Health Education to be adopted as they are at the national level, however, they would not be viewed or implemented through the prism of this Commission but entirely independently unless they were extensively revised from their foundations using the ethical principles of the Commission. The ethic of care, then, cannot be assumed as the prior context of implementation.

The Guidelines themselves, while endorsing choice among a range of behaviours which would be contrary to the belief systems of many parents and religious schools, are silent on such key aspects of the context of sexual health as commitment, childbearing, child-rearing, marriage, or even love. The approach focusses almost entirely on the autonomous individual;

relationships are presented only as something potentially positive about which the individual may wish to make decisions. Sexual expression seems to be the primary given, with relationships a secondary and optional adjunct.

There are many who, consistent with the ethic of care, would see a primary setting in relationships, particularly as a component of the education of children and adolescents, as absolutely essential to the formation of sexual and broader human responsibility. This is the context and the human reality of personal decision. The guideline makes clear that it does not adopt particular strategies, perhaps because it seeks to leave room for the information desired by virtually any age or value or behavioural group. Its very abstinence from any value stance, however, leaves little of practical substance said, and that little highly impersonal. The absence of a value stance is, after all, as much a statement of value judgement as the presence of one. It is a statement of indifferentism and moral relativism. Some people hold this view, as is their right, but it is not in any sense objective or value neutral. Its imposition at the national level would be the imposition of one available view upon all who hold other views.

The guidelines present parents, including the parents of minor children, as one resource among many, rather than as those with the primary responsibility and right with respect to the education and custody of their children in these deeply value-laden areas. In my view and in that of many Canadians, responsibility for the sexual and family life education of minor children is not primarily collective, as these guidelines present it as being. Rather, schools and other agencies of the state function as the delegates of parents. Yet these guidelines, in defining comprehensiveness, lump together in "shared responsibility" virtually anyone who may have some influence, "parents, peers, places of worship, schools, health care systems, governments, the media, and a variety of other such institutions and agencies."[3]

One wonders, moreover, what form of new constitutional social structure is envisioned under the categories of "Integrated" and "Co-ordinated."[4] It seems that in the recommended system "learning in formal settings such as schools, community health systems and social service agencies are [sic] complemented and reinforced by education acquired in informal settings through parents, families, friends, the media and other sources," and that "the various sources of sexual health education work collaboratively with each other and with the related health, clinical and social services to maximize the impact of such education."

In such a system, then, the schools, community health systems and social services would have the primary role, and be "reinforced" by parents, who are just one source among families, friends, the media and others. This negates the primary responsibility and jurisdiction of parents with respect to minor children. Yet, as the Commission report clearly and rightly acknowledges, it is they who provide the most effective sex education when they are actively involved and who provide the most enduring and most deeply imprinted role models to their children. It is they who are most likely to be called upon, before or beyond any state-provided services, to support and help their children, both minor and adult, in whatever may develop out of their sexual relationships and behaviour.

If all these very diverse "sources" are to "work collaboratively," who, precisely, is to coordinate or direct them? Who is to ensure that formal and informal systems really do say the same thing, particularly when we know that many of them at this time (parents, peers, the framers of these guidelines, and various segments of the entertainment and other media) hold widely differing views on these subjects? Surely this model is not intended to be an elevation of statism to a level hitherto undreamt of in Canada. If it is not, then what is being suggested as integration and coordination is not realizable, and one wonders whether it constitutes more a notional ideal than a practical and implementable program of education in sexual health. One may, then, question its appropriateness as a set of coherent guidelines to be adopted at the national level.

The guideline approach also assumes a fully adult, rational, consequence-aware mode of decision making in all sexual matters. It makes reference to age level or cognitive development, but makes few practical distinctions in that light in its discussion of information to be transmitted or behaviour which is appropriate. Whether this is entirely applicable to youth is highly questionable.

The methodology of contraceptive protection, moreover, tends to call upon modes of perception which most young people are still developing and tend to exercise inconsistently. This suggests that other methodologies, such as the presentation of a value-consistent world view which includes the postponement of sexual activity until marriage, have an important role to play. This implies making, at some point, a set of value judgements, not an element of the guideline approach. Teenagers tend to have, as a normal aspect of their developmental stage, an incomplete sense of cause and effect, action and consequence. This is particularly so when the effect is separated from the cause by an indeterminate time, as sexual activity, STD infection, and later infertility inevitably are. Risk and probability are consequently also less than fully comprehensible to many teenagers, the population most at risk for STD-based infertility, since they tend to have an age-based sense of invulnerability and immortality.

Research has repeatedly shown that, however much young people report they know about contraceptive use and STD avoidance, many or most who are sexually active do not use the protections they know about, either consistently or at all. Yet effective STD prevention, condom-based contraception, or family planning of any sort all require precisely the systematic skills and perceptions of planning, cause and effect, and reality-recognition. One may question whether simply multiplying the information and contraceptive provision which is already being done — and of which virtually every teenager is well aware — is necessarily the most effective approach. Others must not be precluded. Nor is a stress on communication, self-esteem, and assertiveness enough, as important as they are for the avoidance of exploitation, coercion, or simple misunderstanding. Getting their messages straight is not sufficient if what two teens communicate and agree about is nonetheless unsafe and uncommitted premature sexual activity.

Much sex education aimed at teenagers, including that suggested by the guidelines, seems to assume that most are at present or imminently to be sexually active, and that most parents take little or no primary responsibility in preparing their children for responsible sexual health. This is true of some. It is not true of the majority of parents or the majority of young people under the age of 18 years. It is simply not the case that, as the Commission report text claims: "most" 15-19 year olds are sexually active. The evidence is quite otherwise.

The terminology used suggests that the vast majority are engaged in present and frequent sexual activity. The studies available to date do not indicate that such an overgeneralization is appropriate. Distinctions have to be made on grounds of age cohort, of the presence of activity, of the degree of activity, and of other factors such as region and social group.

The *Canada Youth and AIDS Study* tabulates those who have had intercourse at least once in their lifetimes as being 31% of males and 21% of females in Grade 9. In Grade 11, the percentage of those who have had intercourse at least once in their lifetimes rises to 49% for males and 46% for females. These numbers are far higher than one would wish, certainly, but it is not a majority, let alone "most" of those in the population, and, since a single incident at any time in the past counts for tabulation purposes, the actual present activity of respondents is not conveyed. This study goes on to make that distinction; this is helpful because, while even one incident carries a risk, a young person who had sexual intercourse once or twice, at some indefinite time in the past, and who is not sexually active now presents quite a different risk profile altogether from that of a young person who is having sexual intercourse with multiple and shifting partners weekly. The educational and other approaches appropriate to reach the two young people effectively are just as different.

The study indicates that those Grade 9 males were comprised of 11% who had had intercourse once, 13% who had had it a few times, and only 7% who had it often, this last group being a closer representation of those who "are sexually active." For females, the percentages for Grade 9 were 6% once, 9% a few times, and 6% often. For Grade 11, the numbers rise, but still do not convey a majority activity phenomenon. Some 9% of males and 7% of females reported sexual intercourse once; 24% of males and 18% of females reported it as occurring a few times; while 16% of males and 21% of females reported it as occurring often. It is with dropouts (to whose behaviour school-based sexual education programs are irrelevant) that the numbers of those engaged in frequent sexual activity rise precipitately, to

52% of males and 47% of females. These numbers are even higher than those for university and college students, as high as those are.

Let us turn the numbers around, however. In Grade 9, 69% of males and 79% of females report themselves to be virgins. In Grade 11, 51% of males and 54% of females also report themselves never to have had sexual intercourse. Even among university and college students, legal adults who are no longer involved in school-based sexual education programs, 23% of males and 27% of females report themselves as not having yet had sexual intercourse in their lifetimes.[5]

This seems to vary, moreover, not only by study, but by region. A study of girls and young women under the age of 18 years, carried out by Insight Canada Research for Ortho-McNeil, Inc. and endorsed by the Society of Obstetricians and Gynaecologists of Canada, indicated that in 1992 a full 64% of 1 024 respondents had never had sexual intercourse. This rose to 70% among Toronto respondents and 68% among Vancouver respondents, while 55% of Montreal respondents said they had not yet had sexual intercourse.[6] One does not know what the figures for smaller cities and towns or for rural areas would be, nor do these figures cover the Maritime or Prairie provinces or the Territories. One might expect further variation. There is variation also by other characteristics which would be of particular relevance to those framing family life education in separate, denominational, or dissentient schools. The *Canada Youth and AIDS Study* cites church attendance and positive relationships with parents (these two factors themselves found to be linked) as associated with significantly reduced risk-taking behaviours of various kinds, not only sexual activity, but use of alcohol, cannabis, or tobacco, as well as low self-esteem or wishing to leave home.[7] This would tend to support arguments that the different approach of religiously based schools and homes has positive results, that not all populations have the same profile or the same needs, and that not every program need be — or ought to be — geared to the worst-case scenario.

The sexual activity of students under 18 years of age is therefore a minority phenomenon in no way comparable to that of legal adults aged 18 or 19, either in frequency or in its social or psychological meaning. They should not be lumped together. It is at those younger people that sexual education in the schools is directed. The behaviour of the majority should be reinforced, not taken as exceptional and non-normative at their age level. Moreover, mechanisms exist to deal with the hard cases of parental neglect or the information needs and behaviour of troubled minors. To frame all of sexual education in terms appropriate to the hard cases runs the risk of making them normative, of appearing to condone and hence of fostering, for some, the very mindset and activity which it intends to counter.

I do not endorse the recommendation that "requirements for teachers delivering sexual health education" be "in accordance with the criteria outlined in the Guidelines for Sexual Health Education." This would mean that sex education could only be provided by specialists or the small minority of classroom teachers who have already received specialized training, rather than primarily by the properly resourced classroom teacher who knows the children and is available for follow-up and for an ongoing relationship with parents.

Curricula exist which give teachers and students the materials required for a consistent and well-informed program in sexual and relationship education. One such is *Fully Alive*,[8] a curriculum activating and resourcing parents, teachers, and students, written on the basis of wide grass-roots consultation and collaboration with teachers, students, and parents in every Ontario diocese under the sponsorship of the Ontario Conference of Catholic Bishops. This curriculum is enhanced by in-service workshop training, but does not require expert credentials to present it. The program already covers Grades 1-8; secondary school texts and resources are in preparation. Other such programs exist or could be written.

Family life/sex education is not so different from the other subjects in the curriculum that it requires a different and more elite structure for its presentation. Training of teachers is an excellent thing, and the availability of specialists to help classroom teachers is to be supported; sexual education components can be built into the programs preparing new teachers for the classroom. Neither funding nor personnel exists, however, for the training of the entire body of teachers. As of this writing, indeed, the continuing struggle with public debt has meant that new teachers are experiencing great difficulty in finding employment, and many school boards are facing the grim possibility of staff reductions. For the foreseeable future, requirements of specialized training not already in the background of existing personnel would necessarily mean the removal of responsibility for sex education from most classroom teachers and its lodging with existing specialists and outside speakers.

I would not wish to see sex education dominated by the certainly useful but too often isolated parachuting of an external "expert," such as a sex education consultant or a public health nurse, into the classroom or auditorium for a quick session largely divorced from a larger value or relationship context. Sex and family life education, by its nature, deals with intimacy and relationships rather than impersonal information (the standard "plumbing" lecture) and unfamiliar persons. It should therefore be done, insofar as possible, and particularly in Grades 1-8, by parents and by teachers who have an ongoing and supportive relationship with the child.

As valuable as qualifications are, there is a well-known professional-izing tendency, identified elsewhere in our report, of specialists to believe that they and their colleagues are the only and most appropriate providers of whatever their given activity might be. It is particularly ironic that professionalization should become a factor in something so universally human as the transmission of values in sexual and family life education.

If only specialists are capable of competent transmission in this area, the entire world has been in a very bad way for many thousands of years, and the existence of any healthy families or supportive and loving relationships, or the births of many billions of children themselves are all highly inexplicable.

This is not to speak of the interest involved in making the services, resources, and training which one particular viewpoint-group provide mandatory for a vast population of other educational professionals serving literally millions of clients (i.e., Canadian children).   Education is an industry, if an industry of a particularly altruistic, non-profit, and highly regulated sort, and, as in any industry, the nature of regulations and credentialling requirements affects not only the interests of consumers (students and their parents) and of suppliers (teachers), but also of the suppliers of the suppliers (those who engage in the provision of credentialling courses and other resources). Umbrella groups comprising numbers of persons involved in sex education, credentialling, and resource production can be very fertile sources of expertise and insight. Qualifications required for classroom teaching of sex education, however, should be determined by school boards and provincial ministries of education.

I do not endorse the recommendations that schools provide information, condom machines, and referral of young people to clinical facilities for contraception. Children tend to pass through puberty between the ages of about nine and fifteen; all such individuals are minors. For schools to make unilateral provision or referrals without parental knowledge or consent would violate the rights and responsibilities and the religious freedoms of parents. The statement in the text that "in our view, laws related to the age of consent for medical treatment should not preclude teenagers from obtaining contraception on their own behalf" makes the intent to bypass parental knowledge and consent explicit, at least for minors aged thirteen to fifteen. I am not one of those referred to as being of this view.

Extending mechanisms of the override of parental responsibility, which may be appropriate in exceptional cases of neglect or dysfunction, to cover the entire population of families is to extend state intervention far beyond its rightful and constructive role. The schools and family planning clinics would not and could not be there to support the young people in coping with the results of sexual activity they would be being encouraged to make or at least condoned in making. That would be left to the parents whose responsibility and even awareness of the existence of risk had been circumvented and denied.

Decisions on questions of sexual education, moreover, rest with the parents and other taxpayers who elect trustees, even of secular, non-religiously mandated schools and school boards. What may be in accord with the views and values of one community may not be in accord with those of another. Community values should be manifest in the care and education of the young. Parents and individual students who wish a particular approach are free to choose their school, bearing in mind the values that it promotes.

A requirement that schools provide non-judgemental information, availability of condoms, and referrals to health services with respect to students of any age, minors or older, would also violate the religious freedoms of denominational, separate, and dissentient schools. These are recognized and protected, both under long-held Canadian law and tradition and under Sections 15 and 29 of the *Canadian Charter of Rights and Freedoms*. The Commission report is more careful than the guidelines in its wording, recommending only that "school boards consider the benefits of making contraception readily accessible ..." This is not a new question for any school board given the three decades and more of the debate; it is certainly not a new question for the denominational, separate and dissentient schools. Boards are and must remain free to have policies consistent with their own value mandates and the wishes of the communities who elect their trustees.

I disagree with the linked statements in the report that approaches that promote or give information on only a single approach such as abstinence offer nothing to those who become sexually active, and that programs *should* reflect the "reality that society is characterized by a range of sexual attitudes and behaviours." There are two objections here, one of accuracy and one of constitutional rights and freedoms.

First, accuracy. No group of which I am aware teaches abstinence only, which sounds like a bleak requirement of universal and life-long involuntary celibacy. Many do teach the postponement of good and healthy and satisfying sexual activity until the commitment of mutually faithful marriage. As the Commission report insightfully acknowledges, there is no question that doing this will prevent sexually transmitted diseases, indeed more effectively than any other method. In any case, it is entirely possible to present information on contraceptive methods — what they are, how they work and also their drawbacks — in a context that informs but does not condone non-marital sexual activity. Those who are sexually active would have the information in the context of encouragement to cease that activity. Promotion of the maintenance of sexual expression within marriage is best done, not on a base of ignorance as this report seems to imply, but on a base of full awareness of its constructive appropriateness. Fertility awareness training, including discussion of natural means of family planning as compared with other means, given in many programs, does this. It may be argued that people need to know what a thing is in order to decide not to do it, particularly when it is as socially pervasive as the non-marital sex/birth control message is today. *Fully Alive* presents such information for Grade 8 in a clear fertility-awareness and marital-sexual-expression value matrix.

The need for an elaborate and expensive campaign to train educational personnel and teenagers in the specifics of birth control methods is questionable in any case, even from the perspective of those who look upon them as important to reductions in STD and pregnancy rates. Any North American teenagers who are unaware of condoms or other methods of birth control must live in a most improbable isolation, not only from their parents and peers, but from television, billboards, pharmacy displays, and mass circulation magazines and other forms of media. Sexually active teens who are capable of decoding the operational instructions for complex audiovisual machinery can also read the instructions on a box of condoms. The semi-literate, who unfortunately are not few, can readily understand the pictorial instructions. The problem is not ignorance but attitude. What is needed is not information that teens already have, but perspective and motivation toward healthy relationships and behaviour. This will of necessity involve value perspectives; these do vary in sometimes mutually exclusive ways, meaning that one approach cannot be imposed upon all.

Beyond that problem of accuracy, however, is the far deeper problem of constitutional rights and freedoms. The requirements and recommendations under discussion are incompatible with the beliefs and the derived moral codes of particular religious groups. Any requirement that a particular essential religious or other mandated moral teaching should be replaced by an incompatible one would be a direct violation of religious freedoms. It would also be a violation of the freedoms and responsibilities of provinces, school boards (both separate and non-separate), private schools, and those social service agencies and health care institutions that serve adolescents out of a particular religious or other value mandate.

Catholic separate school boards, or other religiously mandated schools, or other providers of sex education, whether Protestant, Jewish, Muslim, or any other, are highly unlikely to consider it consistent with their mandates to be obliged by some outside body or guideline to present, as the report suggests, "the range of sexual attitudes and behaviours" that occur in our society as equally legitimate or condoned, or as part of a "variety of options for maintaining sexual health." Many would hold that they could not act consistently with their moral values by telling teenagers, for example, that "sexual activity in life-committed, monogamous marriage is an option, but if you choose such other options as 'delay' (time and criteria unspecified) or 'sexual activity' with a series of 'caring and respectful' partners here are some suggestions, such as 'dual protection,' to make them 'safer' as your 'path to sexual health.'" What of the rest of the possible "range of sexual behaviours and attitudes" not mentioned in the parenthetical examples, since surely those are not the only sexual attitudes and behaviours in society's range? Could such schools maintain the recommended public education norm of being "non-judgemental," suggesting condom use for those who choose promiscuous — or even commercial — encounters? The purpose of religiously mandated schools is to present education within a belief system and its associated value system. This necessarily entails value judgements.

There remains also the delicate question of homosexuality. The Roman Catholic Church which sponsors the Roman Catholic separate public schools teaches that persons who are of homosexual orientation must be welcomed with respect, compassion, and sensitivity, and that one must avoid any sign of unjust discrimination in their regard, but it does not give approbation to homosexual activity, believing that homosexual persons are called to chastity.[9] Many other religious groups — as well as many people whose opinions have a non-religious base — believe and teach from a similar perspective. The Guidelines for Sexual Health Education would oblige all schools explicitly to contradict that perspective.

The Commission report takes as an exemplar the third study by Orton and Rosenblatt. Let us leave aside for the moment the methodological weaknesses of that study. If their work is to be taken as representative of what religious groups may expect, it is enlightening to look at their fourth study, *Sexual Health for Youth: Creating a Three-Sector Network in Ontario*.[10] Since the Commission report does not cite it, the Commission has given no approbation to this aspect of its content. Its mention here, then, is useful rather because this study makes explicit the conflict over values and with religious freedom which has been hitherto under the surface of the debate.

In this publication, distributed by Planned Parenthood of Ontario, the authors target the Catholic Separate School System. They object explicitly not only to its existence, which would be problematical enough, but to certain of the specifics of the belief system of Catholicism — not only with respect to sex education but with respect to its sacramental theology and ecclesiology. While acknowledging that students in Roman Catholic separate schools have more consistent access to family life education than do students in public schools, they object explicitly to the religious values in its content. They represent Catholicism as incompatible with Canadian democracy, which would come as a disenfranchising surprise, both to the voters among the near-half of the Canadian population who are Catholic and to the many who have served or are now serving in public office. The democratic process initiated by the Ontario Bishops in the generation of *Fully Alive* is not mentioned. Even Catholicism's international character is the subject of opprobrium, since the Church is "centrally based in another country." They recommend that the State act in support of change in the belief system of the Church. The intolerant rhetoric is reminiscent of the "no Popery" diatribes of the last century. Since the writers are faced with the existence of a separate school system, they recommend that Catholic schools be permitted to teach according to their beliefs in religion class but be obliged to present Orton and Rosenblatt's agenda (essentially identical in its specifics to that of the Guidelines for Sexual Health Education) in health class. They also state that the same difficulties exist with respect to Catholic children's aid societies.

All of this is clearly incompatible with the freedoms and rights of separate, denominational, and dissentient schools, which exist as fully integrated educational environments. The statements in the report with respect to the belief system of the Catholic Church would, if made governmental policy, constitute a severe invasion of the religious freedoms of both individuals and groups. In a publication purporting to propose a structure coordinating the educational, social service, and public health systems under provincial jurisdiction for sex education, this is of major concern. The authors have the freedom to hold any opinion they choose about values, personal religious beliefs, and the educational strategies they prefer. In a free and democratic society with constitutionally protected freedom of religion and of separate, denominational, and dissentient schools, one may question whether it is either appropriate or a matter of right for them to recommend that government deny that same freedom to others, in this case to Catholic persons and their institutions.

Fortunately, it is highly doubtful that such an intervention to violate religious rights and freedoms would be taken up as the policy of any level of government. Yet, since Orton and Rosenblatt's agenda and their recommended imposition of their methods on all schools and social service agencies are essentially similar to the agenda of the Guidelines for Sexual Health Education recommended by the Commission report, it is important to note that the Orton-Rosenblatt recommendations have only brought explicitly to the surface the conflict with religious belief systems which the imposition of those agendas would necessarily entail.

Those of that opinion would without doubt have much the same disagreements with the belief systems and educational policies of many religious groups drawn from among those of Protestant, Jewish, Muslim, or Hindu faith, as well as others. Many such groups have private schools that educate within provincial ministry guidelines. Some already receive public funding in some provinces; whether such schools will also receive funding parallel to that of the Catholic separate public schools is the subject of a court case ongoing in Ontario as of this writing. Whether religiously based schools are public or private, however, it is clear that, were such methods to be imposed on all schools and other institutions giving sexual health education, the freedom of religion would indeed become a major issue, of grave concern to many Canadians of many backgrounds and faiths.

There is indeed a role for educational strategies targeted directly to populations, such as drug users, street youth, and prostitutes, clearly engaged in high-risk activities. For this reason I entirely support the recommendations fostering programs to reach these groups. There is also a role for one-on-one counselling of individual students who have demon-strably and irrevocably chosen to take repeated sexual risks. Such strategies are not, however, appropriate for the classroom, the role of which is the development of a value-consistent view of sexuality, not damage control to deal with attitudes and behaviours which are already dysfunctional. Parents of minor children and adults on their own account are free to choose to be served by institutions whose philosophy and approach are consistent with their own. They should remain so.

A case in point is the Baltimore pregnancy prevention program taken as another exemplar in the Commission report.[11] That program involved schools in a high-poverty inner city region of a city similar to no city existing anywhere in Canada in its industrial decline, unemployment, and associated urban problems. Pregnancy rates were elevated well above the national average, beginning in junior high school. Nine out of ten of the junior high school students and three out of four of the high school students in the study were from families of such low incomes and at such risk of malnutrition that they qualified for the government-provided free lunch.[12]

The control group of schools did not have other types of information, counselling, or service programs; they had no programs at all. It is not surprising that the program produced some considerable rate of positive results, since anything under such severe circumstances may more than reasonably be expected to be an improvement over nothing. On the other hand, the study and the methods of the program provide no valid comparison with other sorts of program, since no others were tested. It seems likely, indeed, that the class presentations and group discussions were far more important than individual counselling or clinic use in delaying first intercourse and in reducing pregnancies, since 72.7% of students were exposed to class presentations and 50.6% to group discussions, while only 19.7% had any individual counselling and 14.5% (most of them girls) made even a single medical visit.[13] Classroom presentations and group discussions are elements in virtually any sort of family life education programs.

One may question, at the same time, whether a model used in this near-crisis context, atypical even of communities in the United States, is necessarily an appropriate model for every school in every city, town, and village across this very different country.

That the Baltimore articles conclude that provision of and school-based referral to medical facilities for contraception is nonetheless a good thing is also unsurprising, not to say predictable. The authors are associated with the Johns Hopkins Department of Obstetrics and Gynaecology, which is deeply involved in research and information-dissemination publications on international provision of birth control. *Family Planning Perspectives*, in which the articles are published, is an organ of the Guttmacher Institute, which has a similar focus. The publication is at least in part funded by pharmaceutical companies through full-page advertisements of contraceptive drugs and devices. These sources represent only one segment, albeit an important one, of a far wider field of discussion and debate.

Conclusion

In sum, the appropriate jurisdictional bodies, institutions, and, in the case of adults and parents of minor children, individuals should remain free to choose the approach they will take to sound and full education in sexual health, both in general and with specific reference to the prevention of the sexually transmitted diseases which can damage or destroy fertility.

Some may assume the prior, inevitable and value-neutral existence of a broad range of sexual practices and seek to provide information, drugs, and devices to reduce the risk. Others see it as their role, their right, and their mandate to reduce the development of the more risk-bearing forms of sexual behaviour by educating young people in committed, respectful, life-giving, and stable relationship formation as a prerequisite for healthy sexual activity. This varies by community, by school, and by other factors. The freedom to choose an approach — and for parents to choose the approach suitable for their children — must remain. Insofar as separate, denominational or dissentient schools — and the parents and taxpayers who support and entrust these schools with their children — take the latter approach as a necessary component of their fulfilment of their mandates, their right and responsibility to do so are constitutionally protected.

No governmental body at any level should attempt to impose conformity with the former view in this highly controverted area.

Any governmental body, including the proposed Infertility Prevention Sub-Committee, with a mandate to foster STD prevention and education in sexual health should have among its members people with a broad range of representative viewpoints, rather than advocacy and service provision groups chosen only from among those with a narrow range of interests and perspectives. Essential among members should be representatives of religious and other value-mandated groups which sponsor educational institutions and other sources of sexual health education such as social services and health care facilities. The Sub-Committee should have a prominent, indeed primary, component of representatives of parents and their groups.

When and if future evidence indicates that one or another approach is vastly more effective and supportive of human flourishing than any other, it will be adopted voluntarily by most. Until that time and beyond, the full and legitimate diversity of views and methods must be preserved and fostered as a matter of fundamental human freedoms.

Access to New Reproductive Technologies [14]

One source of the difficulty arising around access to new reproductive technologies is that, in this field perhaps more than many others, medical, social, legal, and ethical considerations overlap. It is precisely for this reason that the Commission was called into being with its given mandate. In most fields of medicine, treatment is provided on medical grounds utterly irrespective of the social context. There are certain situations in which aspects of the social context may impinge upon medical considerations, as for example the presence or absence of family caregivers, or the presence of a social network fostering substance abuse. Even in these cases, however, the primary concern and the only criterion of indications for treatment would almost invariably be medical and primarily focussed on the individual.

The social, particularly the social service, and the legal spheres are in many respects different in that regard, since human relationships and personal capacities and attributes are by definition an intrinsic factor in any assessment, therapeutic program, or legal relationship in the undertaking of social and legal roles. Where in medical practice the focus is the relatively isolated individual, in the social, social service, and legal spheres the focus is on relationships linking varying numbers of individuals, the characteristics of one necessarily having an impact on all the others and on the nature and functioning of their relationship. Social factors are a crucial element in whether or not a social or legal relationship is likely to be functional or enduring. If such relationships are set up without regard to those factors, harm, sometimes great harm, may ensue for all involved, and particularly for the most vulnerable. These separate spheres, then, have tended to have somewhat differing ethical approaches to criteria for access. Assessment of one or another among a broad range of criteria, such as marital status and stability, personality profile, or income and stability of employment, can under limited circumstances be considered not only acceptable but necessary in determining the appropriateness of access to many sorts of service or relationship, both personal and wholly contractual. Examples could include adoption, admission as a client to a specific sort of social service therapy group or program, employment as a Children's Aid Society foster parent, or, as with income and employment, the taking out of a mortgage.

New reproductive technologies are not focussed solely on the isolated individual patient, but necessarily affect others, principally the child who is to be born, over a lifetime. They also affect the human relationships which are the subject of much of the content of value systems held by individuals and groups, not only of patients, but of practitioners and health care institutions and the body politic comprising the taxpayers and their governmental institutions. In my view, given the broad interaction of social and legal factors in the medical practice of provision of new reproductive technologies, the reduction of the multifaceted ethics of the social, social service, and legal spheres to the single-factor ethics which appropriately characterize the medical sphere would not only be inappropriate in itself, but would also have negative consequences of many sorts. It is with these that this dissent is largely concerned.

It is one thing to say that people may do a thing if they consider it appropriate. It is another thing entirely to say, as the Commission report recommendation does, that they must do it whether or not it is in accord with their moral and ethical convictions, on pain of being excluded from any capacity to provide that type of service to anyone.

The recommendations of this Commission report would not, indeed, overtly and actively force a physician or a religiously sponsored medical facility to provide new reproductive technologies against their consciences; it would simply face them with an invidious choice. They would be obliged to provide licensable technologies under circumstances that would conflict with their mandates and ethical codes, or they must withdraw from providing them altogether. This would, in effect, discriminate against such religious individuals and institutions, since it would bar them from the provision of new reproductive technologies to anyone. The fact that their views would be in accord with those of the majority of Canadians would not protect them from being excluded from the field of reproductive technologies. For example, a physician who would not give a prior commitment to provide assisted insemination to unmarried or lesbian women would be barred from receiving a licence to provide it to the majority of those seeking it, those already in stable and committed heterosexual relationships. The same would be true of physicians or clinics whose fertility practice consisted largely of licensable hormonal treatments of anovulatory or irregularly ovulating married women or of IVF or GIFT or DOST to women in stable heterosexual couples. That unmarried or lesbian women would be unlikely to seek such treatment would be irrelevant, were an explicit commitment to use only medical criteria and exclude any social factors nonetheless a condition of every licence issued by the National Commission. If he or she were already in practice, the choice for a physician would be between conscience and the abandonment of developed expertise and livelihood. A hospital which could not accept such a policy in principle would be barred from seeking to provide licensable reproductive technologies, and, if it were already providing fertility therapy, would be obliged to close its existing facilities.

The non-use of any but medical criteria should therefore not be made a condition of the licensing of fertility clinics/sperm banks. Such a condition would be discriminatory in that it would prohibit the provision of reproductive technologies by hospitals and clinics sponsored by religious groups or community-elected boards which hold another moral/ethical perspective. It would also be counterproductive with respect to overall access to provision of assisted conception. There are at this time in Canada a certain number of such health care facilities providing one or more of the licensable treatments, such as DOST, GIFT, IVF, and donor insemination. They may have a mandate and character arising from Salvation Army, Roman Catholic, or some other affiliation or community value base. Some health care facilities and sponsoring organizations would be certain to decide that they could not both comply with such a requirement of licensing and act consistently within their mandates. This licensing requirement would have the concrete effect, then, of causing health care institutions sponsored by some religious bodies or working in board-electing communities viewing some non-medical factors as legitimate and essential to close down existing assisted conception facilities rather than act in contravention of their own consciences and mandated ethical perspectives. It is ironic that a requirement which seems directed toward increased access would have the actual effect of reducing it for the great majority of the population of those seeking assisted conception.

Licensing requirements can be exceedingly constructive in maintaining high standards of medical practice, record keeping, and research. It is on this base that I am in accord with their establishment. They should not, however, be used as a mechanism of social engineering. To use such licensing as a basis of enfranchising and conferring legitimacy upon only those practitioners and others who espouse one set of values, thus setting precedents for other areas and forms of practice and excluding those who hold other sets of values, does, in my view, constitute social engineering, whether or not those making the recommendation intend it to be so. If that were to become a feature of the purpose and function of licensing requirements, inseparable from their other, legitimate purposes, I would oppose them. Permitting diversity in practice is one thing. Forcing uniformity of practice in a conscientiously controverted and value-laden area, against the clearly stated values of the majority of Canadians, is quite another.

The exceedingly important principle of equality is cited in the Commission report with respect to access to new reproductive technologies, but it is implicitly equated with autonomy. This individual autonomy is an extension of the single-factor ethics of medical indication which the Commission report has taken into the social sphere on this issue, duplicating there its focus on the individual. People are considered equal only if they receive the same service if and as they autonomously choose. This is not, in my view, a valid equation. A person may be fully equal with all other persons, and have all the rights and obligations of citizenship, without having a right to demand the activation of every available service of society to facilitate each of his or her social choices.

We may look for parallels to other fields of social life. Marriage is a great good, and the freedom to marry is as fundamental a human right as the right to seek to bear or beget children, but a person cannot demand that the state provide him or her with a spouse if there are no volunteers. A person may wish to be employed in a high-income position, and must be free to seek such a position, but he or she cannot expect to be hired without certain social characteristics such as the relevant ability, training, and experience, and even then a given employer is not obliged to choose that individual if another, more qualified applicant is at hand. The government, for its part, is not called upon to provide or guarantee another such position. Yet the unmarried person is equal as a human being and as a citizen to any married person in the land, and the person who must seek another job is equal as a human being and a citizen to the other who was, in the event, hired for the specific position.

The absolutization of the principle of autonomy, which is what is chiefly at issue here, would risk or require the non-fulfilment or the contravention of other principles, such as those of the best interests of the child, the constitutional and other appropriate jurisdictions of the various levels of the health care system and social service systems, the freedom of individual health care providers not to be obliged to act against their consciences, and the freedom of religiously mandated health care institutions to follow the moral codes inherent in their nature.

The recognition by the Commission report that there may indeed be some circumstances in which provision of new reproductive technologies would not be appropriate is very much welcome. Yet reproduction is not so different from the other fields of medicine and, with respect to the best interests of a child, of family law and of the social services that the ordinary modes of resolution of conflict over the applicability of health care facility policy to particular individual cases should be replaced by the blunt instrument of prior specification in law of some list of criteria for discretion. Such a requirement would be unwieldy and unreasonable, given the great variability of human situations. What may be a factor of limited weight in one situation may, in combination with others, have quite a different significance.

The best interests of the child, a principle clearly recognized in law, should take precedence over any other interest, as all Commissioners agree. As will become clear, however, we disagree as to the probable effects of various non-medical factors on those interests. As with any other dispute surrounding the application of policy or the assessment of what would constitute appropriate action, appeal may be made, as for example to institutional boards of ethics, to boards of directors, or to the courts. To substitute for this a list of criteria emanating from the federal or provincial legislature would constitute a major shift of the locus of decision making with respect to individual indications for treatment and service from the local institution and jurisdiction where the treatment or service takes place to the legislative functions and offices of the upper reaches of government. This would be contrary to the principle of subsidiarity, that decisions should be made as close to the level of application as reasonably possible, authority being accorded to each successively higher level of jurisdiction only as necessary for the effective functioning of society and for the mutual respect, protection and service, both of those directly concerned and of all.

A centralized, governmental, legislative specification, at either the federal or the provincial level, of a list of such criteria would be insensitive to the complexities of human situations. It is quite true that individual physicians or social workers or other such front-line personnel may err in their assessment of such a situation; it is for this reason that appeals may be made. It does not follow that they always err, or that they err in any but a minority of instances. The entire system of child protection, for example, is predicated on the assumption that in a majority of instances social service personnel, properly trained and supervised, will only intervene when there is sufficient reason, and that it is better to risk intervening unnecessarily in some cases than to risk the results of failing to act upon an assessment indicating serious cause. It is also true that only such front-line, trained persons are in any realistic position to perceive and analyze what may be very complex and difficult human situations. Even where appeals occur, they are usually accompanied by yet more analyses of often ambiguous and always complex human situations through the perceptions of other front-line persons with specialized expertise.

To replace the best judgement of a physician, associated social service personnel, and the whole process of boards and appeals with a legislated list is tempting because it may appear to cut the Gordian knot. By ancient legend he who untied the convoluted knot tied by King Gordius of Phrygia would rule all Asia. Alexander the Conqueror did indeed take direct and apparently simplifying action, slicing the knot in two with his sword. He did not, however, untie it; he merely left its severed strands in a heap on the ground. He did defeat the armies of diverse societies until he crossed the Indus River in what is now Pakistan, but he had little inclination to create or foster administrative structures which, to be effective in dealing with human complexity, diversity and ambiguity, are necessarily somewhat tedious. He promptly died, and his brief empire quickly came to resemble what his over-simple and control-taking action had made of the knot.

It appears to me likely that replacing front-line perception, decision, and due appeal to established structures with a blunt, legislated list of permissible criteria could do less good and more damage by its insensitivity to individual situations and to legitimate variation than would ever have been done by the modalities and entities it seeks to replace.

Even from the perspective of the adults seeking service, access to reproductive technologies is not a simple question of autonomy rights. Reproduction is not entirely a private act, even under the usual circumstances. It affects the community, and the community is called upon to exercise energy and resources supporting the adults and children involved. For this reason we publicly license, witness and register marriages, register births, assess and register adoptions, pay to educate children, and bring to bear all the provisions of family law where necessary. The act of conception and the choices around reproduction, however, are so very personal that they are essentially private except insofar as they necessarily call upon the resources and activity of the public sphere. Ordinarily they do not. When, however, a person or two persons seek the help of new reproductive technologies, the acts have taken on a more explicitly public character. Instead of proceeding on their own, without interference or help from society, individuals or couples are seeking to mobilize the health care system, its institutions, its personnel, and public funding to bring about a conception. The choice is no longer primarily private, but in some large, even predominant degree, public. At this point, others are being asked to act to enable an action. They, too, have choices.

Reproductive rights are negative rights; that is, no one may interfere to prevent individuals from making the reproductive decisions they choose to make, whether or not the actions may be deemed wise, moral, or functional, so long as no publicly demonstrable harm is done to others and all actions are consensual. Reproductive rights are not, however, positive rights, or entitlements.

First of all, as this Commission has underscored, a child is a person, not an object to which another person has a right. The child is an end in himself or herself. This is an issue, not just in the relatively new field of new reproductive technologies, but in the established field of adoption, in which social criteria are very much part of the home study assessment in the best interests of the child. Again, people have a negative right to seek to have children, not a positive right to demand that government and its agencies act to provide access to another person. It is the child who is the end, to be cared for by the adults who derive their satisfaction and fulfilment from enabling the child, not by using the child for their own rights-fulfilment.

It is entirely appropriate to apply human rights theory and law on non-discrimination to access to goods, services, and equal opportunity in the educational and occupational life of an individual. That individual, however, cannot demand that the same characteristics which must be ignored in giving him or her access to things also be ignored when he or she seeks access to persons, particularly when one or more of those characteristics would in some way limit the best interests of or jeopardize the other person or persons.

As just one obvious example, age is a prohibited ground of discrimination under human rights law, but the adoption of a child by a person or couple over the age of, say, 50 would make the orphaning of that child before the age of majority a distinct possibility, not to speak of the natural, progressive diminution of the sheer physical energy required to care for a young child or adolescent. There are instances of post-menopausal women seeking egg donation by IVF so that they can bear a child; it is not only for medical but also for social reasons that this is unwise, in the best interests of the child. The unanimous recommendation of this Commission that post-menopausal women not be candidates to be recipients of egg donation is therefore, in my view, wise and justified, not only on the cited biological and medical grounds, but on social, psychological, and other grounds as well. This is just one among the illustrations possible of a situation in which the social context ought to be an important factor in the formation of policy and/or in the right of a physician to refuse treatment. This would clearly not be consistent with the recommended rarity of instances of refusal on non-medical grounds. Similarly, the presence or absence of significant marital conflict if a person is in a partnership is irrelevant to and should not be a factor in job applications or advancement unless it demonstrably affects job performance; it is highly relevant to the environment in which a child will be raised, to the point that it becomes a factor in what is, in effect, the capacity of an individual or couple to fulfil the parental role. This is recognized under child welfare legislation and jurisprudence, as the presence of grave marital conflict can become one element in cases of child protection.

As a further example, Sweden, a very liberal culture with its acceptance of a high out-of-wedlock birth rate and its strong emphasis on individual human rights, is only one of many countries which require that both *in vitro* fertilization and donor insemination be provided only to stable heterosexual couples. It requires, moreover, that insemination must be performed in a public hospital. Sweden goes further in specifying that only the gametes of such partners (rather than donated gametes) be part of IVF therapy, and in requiring that only those willing to make a commitment to disclosure of their identity when the child reaches adulthood be permitted to donate sperm.[15, 16] That some social criteria have a legitimate component role in access to reproductive technologies has ample precedent, then, not only in practice and health care institution policy in this country, but in both practice and law in various other countries.

Both age and marital stability or conflict are part of the overall question of the ability to parent. On one level, some social criteria as related to parenting are parallel to job qualifications and ability, assessment of which is not deemed discriminatory. On a far deeper level, however, it is a question of whose welfare and interests are the focus of decision making; family law reflects the broader principle that it must be primarily those of the child.

Second, those providing even a highly valuable but nonetheless not medically necessary service have a right to choose whether or not they can in conscience perform any act. Childbearing is a very deep part of our humanity, and infertility is a physical and therefore a medically definable condition. It is a great good to give the medical help necessary to enable a wanted conception. Yet an infertile person is not in personal, physical danger. A person who is fully fertile but who wishes access to new reproductive technologies to bring about a pregnancy for the essentially social reason that there is no partner of the opposite sex is still less at any discernible medical risk. I do not think there is an absolute requirement to provide a medical service to a person who is not, effectively, in physical danger, although providing it may be a good thing. There is no positive requirement at all, in my view, to provide that service if the person has no medical indication as such. Nor, from the testimony I have heard and the material I have read, am I alone in this view. A difference of opinion clearly exists on whether or not the ethical principle of an obligation to rescue is operative here. Differences of opinion and therefore, when it comes to the point of action, differences of conscience may therefore exist on either entirely secular or religious grounds.

A person or a pair of persons, while they may request facilitation of their wishes, do not have the right to oblige others to facilitate or act to bring about what they wish, even against the will, conscience or better judgement of those others.   Government funding, and hence taxpayer funding, of new reproductive technologies is a prudential choice, in my view not only a good but a wise one, since among other things it brings them under a regulatory and record-keeping framework and avoids both commercialization and a two-tier system of health care. It is for this reason that I fully support related recommendations of this report. Such funding is not, however, a matter of strict entitlement.

Society cannot interfere, then, in most personal reproductive activities even in circumstances under which those activities may be thought to be dysfunctional, ill-considered, or contrary to the moral views of some or even most individual members of the body politic. Society is not, however, obliged to enable and fund all such reproductive activities. That is a choice, like many other questions of social policy, which society must make. This should usually be on a local institutional basis and ordinarily with responsiveness to the community being called upon to fund the policies and activities being undertaken. This is in accord with the principle of subsidiarity.   The freedom of conscience of individual professionals, both physicians and nurses, and the freedoms of religiously mandated and sponsored health care institutions must also be preserved as a matter of fundamental human rights.

Social considerations become concerns, indeed they become moral questions, not solely but largely because they have a practical impact on the welfare of human beings. Let us take the instance of marital status. There are legitimate and well-documented concerns about the difficulties faced by the children of single-parent families. Certainly, love and stability are even more important than family structure. A loving and stable single-parent family is a better environment for a child than a two-parent home filled with severe and irresolvable conflict or even abuse. Single mothers often labour heroically and successfully to raise their children healthily and well.

Their task, however, is more difficult than that of a two-parent family, for both economic and psychological reasons. Children in single-parent families are, much as we wish it were otherwise, more at risk than are children in stable two-parent families for lower school achievement, a higher rate of psychological difficulties requiring treatment, and dysfunctional behaviour, including involvement with the justice system. This is, be it noted, only an increased risk, not an absolute prediction for every individual case, but the increased risk has been repeatedly demonstrated statistically. It is real.[17]

As a society, and as the relatives, friends and neighbours of single parents, we are called upon to be as supportive as possible to those who find themselves raising children alone, and to recognize and value their achievements. Nonetheless, whether we are required to act, or to fund the health care system to act, deliberately to set up this higher-risk situation from the outset is a question which may legitimately be asked.

Income is another question. Concerns, valid concerns, have been raised in the report about the tendency of those couples recorded as having received infertility treatments to be of the upper income brackets. Insofar as this is due to the cost of treatment, it is a compelling argument for government funding of the procedures. It is likely, of course, that some of the skewing by income status has to do with the known tendency of those with higher education to be aware of and to seek out and trust technological solutions to this as to many other setbacks or challenges they experience.

Nonetheless, beyond the immediate question of treatment funding, there is the question of the resources available for the child's ongoing security and upbringing. A child of a non-affluent but nonetheless financially secure, solid, loving family is as well off on the human level as the child of a similarly stable but affluent family. Discrimination against the non-affluent would be contrary to justice, and our recommendations seek to counter it. In the probably rare case in which the income of a woman or couple seeking new reproductive technology assistance is exceedingly low, however, or were the income to be dependent upon social assistance (welfare), one may question whether either the best interests of the child or fiscal responsibility would be consistent with *requiring* a practitioner to provide infertility treatment or donor insemination. Again, absolutizing even a good principle is frequently imprudent, excluding the fulfilment of other principles.

There are many reservations expressed by Canadians about the appropriateness of provision of new reproductive technologies in cases which do not concern a committed marital partnership or in which there are doubts about the capacity of an individual adequately to care for a child. The Commission report cites a survey of clinics, reporting that a number of non-medical criteria are often used in determining access at many facilities. These may range from such factors as the ability of a mother to stay home with the child to psychological immaturity, or doubtful ability to parent, with lack of a partner, low income, sexual orientation, and country of residence among them.

First, the questions raised in the survey of clinics are very different in their import. In a society in which the majority of mothers of young children do work outside the home, at least in part because the costs of raising children now often require a double income, it would seem inconsistent for a health care facility policy to exclude women who are in the workforce. New reproductive technologies, we must remember, if successful, aid in the birth of newborn children. This is quite distinct from the situation of adoptions of children who are older than newborns; the disruption they have experienced may make the full-time, consistent availability of an adoptive parent at home a therapeutic necessity as it would not be for a newborn whose sense of trust and bonding is still in healthy formation and has not been traumatized. Country of residence or low income may have quite a different practical import, whether for the child or for the publicly funded health and social service systems. Sexual orientation and marital status touch both upon social values and upon differing views of the best interests of the child.

Second, the Decima survey entitled *Social Values and Attitudes of Canadians Toward New Reproductive Technologies*, carried out for this Commission, demonstrates that Canadians do share some of these concerns. While 74% supported new reproductive technology use by a couple unable to "conceive unless the egg and sperm are brought together outside the body and placed in her womb," with only 6% opposed and 15% neither supporting nor opposing, a very substantially lower 30% supported the proposed scenario of a "single woman who is inseminated with an anonymous donor's sperm so she can have a child," with 46% opposed and 23% neither supporting nor opposing. The proposed scenario of "a lesbian couple who have one of them inseminated with an anonymous donor's sperm so she can bear a child" was supported by 11% and opposed by 71%, while 13% neither supported nor opposed it. They were not asked directly about their views on the ability to parent.[18] It seems, then, that the Canadian population does not equate all situations of family formation. It would seem clear that many Canadians do consider at least some social criteria to be relevant and applicable to the use of new reproductive technologies.

Taking the issue from a different angle, more indirectly related to the use of reproductive technologies, the survey found a similar variation. When asked their attitudes toward various groups having or adopting children, 39% were supportive of a single woman deciding to have children outside of a marriage or common-law relationship, while 35% were opposed or strongly opposed and 25% were neither. Some 33% were supportive of a single man doing so, with 43% opposed or strongly opposed and 23% neither. A homosexual co-residential couple having or adopting children was supported or strongly supported by 16%, opposed or strongly opposed by 65%, with 18% neither supporting nor opposing. Only 15% supported or strongly supported having or adopting children on the part of a married couple on welfare, while 63% were opposed or strongly opposed and 22% were neither.[19]

This would clearly indicate, again, that many Canadians consider some social characteristics to be relevant to family formation. It would seem that this constitutes a considerably more widespread and more definite and analytical societal view than is suggested by the report phrasing that "some Canadians are uneasy about family forms that might be facilitated by such access to AI." It is not a vague emotion of unease; it is an opinion and a fairly consistent set of social values. It is unlikely that respondents as a representative sample of voters and taxpayers would wish to fund services, or would wish their government and publicly supported health care institutions to be required across the board to provide services which would deliberately bring about situations which they do not support or which they oppose.

The argument against the applicability of the opinion of the Canadian public as framed in the Commission report is interesting. It affirms that "society's approach to new reproductive technologies should be governed by the social values of Canadians." It goes on, however, to make a distinction between "social values" and "individual opinions," which appears to mean that the opinions of even a majority of Canadians are not their real social values. The report states that "the social values held by Canadians are reflected in the *Canadian Charter of Rights and Freedoms*, and the prohibitions on discrimination it contains must be our guide in this matter."[20] There are various levels on which the implications asserted to be covered by this statement can — indeed must — be examined and questioned.

First, the stated view of the nature of non-discrimination is only one among many possible interpretations of the Charter on this question. Up to the present, no court has ruled that the Charter is in fact to be interpreted in such a way that the prohibited grounds would take precedence over the best interests of a child or of the freedom of conscience and religion in matters of doctrinal and the derived moral import.

Nor is it readily apparent that all the grounds mentioned in the Commission report are in fact subsumed under the grounds prohibited under the Charter. Even marital status, sexual orientation, and income are given only as examples of an unspecified range of non-medical criteria to which the Commission report refers. Of yet more fundamental importance, the Charter does not disallow the use of criteria which affect the capacity to fulfil a function or a job description.

I do not see how the views of an overwhelming majority of Canadians can be construed as not being an authentic representation of the social values of the country. The survey done for this Commission of Canadians on their attitudes toward new reproductive technologies delineates the problem clearly. Half again as many respondents opposed single women's use of reproductive technologies as supported it. Nearly three-quarters were opposed or strongly opposed to the use of reproductive technologies by homosexual couples, a tiny minority supporting it. Nearly two-thirds opposed a couple on welfare having or adopting children. Respondents were not asked their opinion of new reproductive technology use by such a couple, but, on the clear pattern emerging on the other questions, one would expect greater opposition to action by the public health care system to bring about a situation that respondents do not support. The responses cited here have specifically to do with marital status, sexual orientation, and income, the three examples of an unspecified range of non-medical criteria which the Commission recommends not be used as criteria of access. If this survey validly reflects a cross section of the views of the population, and every indication seems to confirm that it does, how can their stated opinions on appropriate family structure and on inappropriate uses of health-care-system-provided new reproductive technologies be said not to reflect or constitute the "social values of Canadians"?

One interpretation among the diverse existing interpretations of the Charter is taken in the Commission report to be the real and only reflection of the social values of Canadians. Do not the views of a strikingly large proportion of its citizens have a role to play in defining what the social values of a country are, and in the intimately related interpretation of what, under the Charter, is "justifiable in a free and democratic society"? Do the views of the people, the *demos*, not have an essential role in defining the values and therefore the shape of a democratic society? Quite an interesting — and probably rather heated — discussion of the nature of democracy, representation and responsible government could be focussed on this question.

It is, moreover, the right of health care professionals to follow their consciences in matters of health care provision. As of the present time, that right is recognized for doctors; it should also be clearly recognized for nurses and others who are closely involved. Social considerations in the provision of therapy which is not a matter of entitlement even if it is publicly funded may also be questions of conscience. That some of those social considerations are indeed matters of conscience is clear enough from their being the subject of ethical and moral codes in virtually every society of the world.

Questions such as whether those codes ought to be altered in some way, or whether the services should be provided within such a code under one circumstance or another, and the salience of the effect of that choice on others, including the child, are part of a moral and ethical argument, not a medical one, no matter what the opinion of a particular speaker one way or another may be. This is even more the case with donor insemination than it is with IVF, since the provision of donor insemination to a woman not in a committed marital or common-law relationship with a man is an instance of medically delivered circumvention of a social problem. On the medical level the woman herself is probably fertile, which means that the procedure is not, in essence, a medical treatment at all. If recent developments in the technological capacity to fertilize a woman's ovum with the single sperm of her husband become widely successful, donor insemination or IVF using donor sperm within marriage could become almost completely obsolete, used only in cases of total azoospermia, or lack of sperm, on the part of the husband. The field of donor insemination, then, including the formal structures recommended by this Commission, would be almost entirely concerned with provision of sperm to fertile women with no male partner.

Let us leave aside the surrounding prudential judgements about the financing of DI services and structures if demand from married couples (the majority of present cases) were to be greatly reduced. Let us rather focus directly on the existence of a significant social component in the question. Access to new reproductive technologies, particularly DI, then, is now and, in a probably increasing degree will be, a medically mediated circumvention of a social, not a physical, problem.

In a pluralistic society, the available provision of such a circumvention is acceptable, so long as the best interests of the child are of primary concern. The framing of an absolutized national requirement that no social/moral questions can be brought to bear on the provision of a primarily socially conditioned service is not acceptable. It could not help but be an interference with the consciences of those health care providers who object, either in general principle or under specific circumstances, to doing so.

The incompatibility of such a recommendation with the essential freedom of religiously mandated health care institutions is also quite clear. Hospitals and other health care institutions run under the auspices of religious groups, whether they be Catholic, Jewish, Salvation Army, or any other, are protected (as collective expressions of individual religious freedoms) under the religious freedom provisions of the Charter. These freedoms have their foundation, not only in fundamental human rights, but in Canadian law and jurisprudence since the *Quebec Act* of 1773 and the *British North America Act* of 1867. Religiously sponsored health care and other institutions are and must remain free to set their policies in accord with the moral codes inherent in their mandates. This means that they must continue to be free to expect, not only that their co-religionists among the staff will be personally free, but that the institution as a whole will, through the decisions of its board of directors, remain free to set policy to be followed by all staff in accord with the principles, religious laws and values of the sponsoring religious group. No national commission or agency has the right or jurisdiction to deny that freedom.

This is of utterly essential importance far beyond the field of new reproductive technologies. If once the policy of a national or any other secular body were to be given effective jurisdiction to overrule religious principle and were to be made binding on a religiously based institution, this would have the effect of denying the freedom of religious health care, social service, and other institutions. The precedent would be as applicable in hospices for the terminally ill or in chronic-care facilities for the frail elderly, emergency wards, and intensive care units, or in the adoption services of social service agencies as in departments of obstetrics and gynaecology.

This is not alarmism, but the consequence of the application of a certain controversial school of thought about the nature of the definition of equality under the Charter. This school of thought would seek to erase religion — among other value systems — as a foundation of legitimate diversity of practice in public institutions. There is discussion in some circles, for example, of viewing as discriminatory the placement of a child for adoption in accord with the religion designated by the mother and in accord with the mandate of religiously sponsored adoption agencies. This would mean that a Christian or Jewish or other religious organization sponsoring an adoption agency could not place children according to the religion of the mother who had approached them on her child's behalf, and that a mother could not designate the religion in which her child would be raised should she approach a secular agency. This, in my view, would violate the freedom of religion of the mother and the legitimate mandates and policies of the agencies concerned. The imposition of this and other, similar policies in adoption would also, I am certain, cause still more young mothers to avoid situations of adoption placement in which they would have their newly-won role in the choice of adoptive setting for their children taken away from them again.

I am fully in accord with the Commission recommendation that there be a review of adoption in Canada. It is clear from the text, however, that this is one of the issues which would be examined under the heading of "equality or non-discrimination in access." This illustrates the fact that the ruling out by government of any social factors, including religious belief, with respect to provision of new reproductive technologies would set a precedent with application in a far wider range of fields than would be at first apparent.

The fields of application are broad. A precedent would have been set by which Christian moral and ethical principles, or Jewish moral and ethical principles and rabbinic decisions on the application of Halakha to health care — or any other moral system basic to a religiously-sponsored facility — would no longer be matters of right in religiously-based institutions. They would have been preempted by governmental fiat at the federal or provincial level. If they operated at all they would do so only at the pleasure of government. In these days of reductions in available funding and of discussion of triage, treatment priorities, and even euthanasia, it is essential that religiously based institutions remain free to interpret their ethical policies according to their mandates.

I gravely doubt that the removal of the freedoms of religiously-sponsored institutions with respect to new reproductive technologies, or the setting of the associated precedents for other institutions would be in accord with the intent or the policy of the federal government or of most decision makers within provincial governments; I also gravely doubt that it would survive a court challenge. It would certainly be a question of crucial import to the religious communities. This set of recommendations should not, therefore, be supported.

In our pluralistic society there is a clear diversity of perspectives on how best to apply even universally-held human values, as well as the well-known respectful disagreements on what the approach to other values should be. Religiously sponsored institutions, whether in health care, education or the social services, pioneered the foundation of these services in Canada. They carried the bulk of the responsibility during much of the history of our country until changes in scale, demographics, and technology made the transfer of funding responsibility and some — but not all — other functions to the secular government necessary and appropriate.

Religiously-based service institutions have a great and constructive contribution to make, both in today's complex society and in the developing future. They must continue to be free to present their vision and to be available to those who seek their services, amid the evolution, and/or the waxing and waning, of opinion, philosophical theory, and political approach in other wings of those sectors.

Those who hold that only medical criteria should impinge on access to new reproductive technologies are working as much out of a philosophical, ethical, political, and moral position as are those who see consideration of some social factors as appropriate, whether they hold that contrary view for secular or religious reasons or both. There is no purely or minimalistically "scientific" or "objective" approach to these questions; all approaches entail value judgements based upon a set of ethics arising out of a world view, whether the person holding them has reflected systematically on them or not. Even agnosticism and atheism are theologies; on the secular level even the avoidance of ethical/social evaluation entails an ethical/social evaluation. A public forum that excludes the ethical values and the contribution of religious communities, comprising as they do large sectors of the citizenry of this country, and that excludes the service institutions they sponsor, has not opted for the removal of value judgements from the process. It has merely imposed one set of value judgements, those absolutizing autonomy whatever its characteristics or impact, on everyone and removed other voices from the service of the people.

Nor is it clear to me that even health care institutions not sponsored by religious groups need necessarily exclude social characteristics or criteria entirely from their consideration of policies on access to new reproductive technologies. They are certainly free to exclude some, most, or all social characteristics as factors. Some already do, on a general policy basis or in response to individual circumstances on the basis of physician discretion. They are, however, in some degree responsible to the communities who pay the taxes supporting their services. Some communities might be in full overall agreement with the exclusion of social criteria from the question. Other communities might exclude some but consider others relevant. As has been pointed out, the data from the general cross-section survey of Canadian opinion found considerable variation in the importance given to one social factor and another by respondents.

The boards of such particular hospitals should not only consult with a broad range of persons of expertise, such as ethicists, social scientists and the members of community groups, but maintain an open dialogue with their surrounding communities; the setting of policies with respect to access to new reproductive technologies should then rest with those boards. Again, this should be a local institutional decision, bearing in mind the appropriate professional association guidelines and within the guidelines, regulations and legislation of the appropriate provincial bodies.

Conclusion

It might not seem that so apparently small and inclusive-sounding a thing as recommending a requirement that access to new reproductive technologies be confined to medical rather than any social criteria would raise such broad and fundamental questions. Nor would the brief discussion of the reasons given in the report for it seem to bear so many unexamined presuppositions and implications. The reality, rather, however unintended it may be, is a radical exclusion. Its purpose and mode of operation are specifically to exclude health care personnel or institutions — and the communities of citizens who host and fund and are therefore the ultimate providers of infertility treatment — from the exercise of their choices based on differing ethical priorities and/or their religious freedoms. It is to oblige them to act in ways in which they have a right to choose not to act.

In a free and democratic society, one would expect recommendations which would permit variation of practice in accord with legitimately differing value systems. Instead, the recommendations impose one ethical view upon all, excluding those, the majority, who hold any different and legitimate ethical view from the process and from practice. The Commission report clearly would not have any intent whatever to jeopardize the best interests of children, but there is ample evidence to support arguments that the giving of near-absolute primacy to the autonomy rights of adults in this sphere would jeopardize those interests nonetheless.

The question of access to new reproductive technologies therefore cannot fail to raise just such fundamental questions of human rights and hence of the Constitution of this country.

Embryo Research

To place so serious a concern before the Government and people of Canada, I must also place before them my reasoning with respect to the ethics of experimentation on human subjects, with respect to the clear difference between this question and the issue of abortion, and with respect to what an embryo (sometimes termed in its earlier stages a zygote) is. I shall then lay out the justifications we as a Commission have heard for the use of human embryos for experimentation, and the reasons why I find these justifications both unpersuasive and deeply disturbing as carrying implications which range far beyond our actions toward human embryos.

In my view the only experimentation on a human embryo which should be permitted is that which would be of therapeutic benefit to that specific embryo in order to avoid or treat a severe disorder. Since, at the present stage of animal embryo research, it does not seem that such therapy could be done on human embryos with a reasonable expectation of success, even this should not be attempted, now or in the immediately foreseeable future.

The norms for research on human subjects accept only research which is for the benefit of, or at the least non-harmful to, the research subject. No human subject is subjected to substantial risk in experimentation for the benefit of others, however possibly enlightening that research might be. Embryo research is the only form of present-day research on human subjects in which those norms are disregarded. Up to the present, therapy on human embryos is not, as far as I am aware, being attempted; all research on embryos now done is for other purposes. Experimentation on embryos which will necessarily die from the intervention or be destroyed thereafter is clearly not for their benefit; the risks to them are absolute.

The question of experimentation on embryos is not related to, nor an extension of, the question of abortion. Experimentation on embryos involves no removal of a conflict between the embryo and the desires, aspirations, welfare, or health of a woman. There is no question of the balance of conflicting rights between an unborn and an adult human being. Those, including myself, who view humans at any stage of development to be full (though perhaps unrecognized) persons would of course hold experimentation on embryos to be a lethal offence against human rights. There are many others, however, who do not share this view of the unborn who would nonetheless oppose experimentation on embryos. Where conflict with the woman is absent they would hold the embryo and the fetus to be of great human significance and value. Indeed many of the public opponents of embryo research are pro-choice feminists. Each one of us begins life as an embryo. There are many with diverse opinions on abortion who agree in viewing experimentation on embryos with deep misgiving or outright opposition, seeing in it the instrumentalization of the human.

The question of acceptance or prohibition of experimentation on embryos presupposes a clear understanding of the point at which an embryo comes into existence. Gametes do not, by themselves, have the amplitude of the human genome, which requires the union of both sperm and ovum; gametes are not on their own capable of human development. There is not, therefore, what the Commission report posits as being an undifferentiated continuum of human life from gamete to embryo to fetus to born child. The continuum begins with fertilization. Only with the joining of two gametes does the full genome of a human individual come into being; without that joining no human life, no human development and no human individual can be possible. Experimentation, observation and the future development of preconception diagnosis using gametes would therefore, with due safeguards and respect, be legitimate, as the Commission report states if for other reasons. The absence of an ethical problem with research on gametes does not relativize or diminish the ethical problem once two gametes have joined and an embryo has come into existence. Key to the point at which ethical problems arise, then, is the point at which two gametes fuse to become a single human embryo.

Much popular or even political or bioethical discussion on the subject assumes that the genetic materials of the sperm and of the ovum fuse at the point of penetration of the ovum by the sperm. Much literature speaks of a "single cell." It appears, however, that the single cell of the fertilized ovum contains the two pronuclei, the still-separate envelopes of maternal and paternal chromosomes. They do not fuse until the chromosomes have replicated and segregated, migrating along the spindle and separating into the two cells of the first cleavage.[21] In the mouse, expression of paternal gene-derived proteins is first found at the two-cell phase,[22] suggesting that, if the process in humans is similar in this respect to that in the mouse, the genes of the embryo as an entity become operational after syngamy. The joining of the two gametes, or syngamy, then, is a process which may take a range of estimated time spans, perhaps 24 hours.

Whether sperm penetration of the ovum or full syngamy is the point of existence of an embryo is a question which still requires careful scientific, philosophical, and ethical examination. At penetration, the single cell contains the full genetic complement received from sperm and ovum, but they only fuse and interact together at syngamy. So is the penetrated ovum a zygote? Or is it still an ovum through which the envelope containing the genetic complement of the sperm, still a separate entity, is travelling toward the envelope containing the genetic complement of the ovum, the zygote only coming into existence at syngamy?

If syngamy is the point at which the zygote (the early embryo) comes into existence, it is possible that some of the forms of observation or intervention (such as prenatal — or preconceptional — diagnosis using the third polar body, or the so-called "hamster test" for sperm function) are legitimate so long as they are ended before syngamy takes place. The hamster test does involve, and the finding of a severe abnormality by polar body analysis presumably would involve, termination of the penetrated ovum before syngamy. However these questions are resolved, after syngamy an embryo certainly exists, with all the ethical issues which surround it.

If an embryo is dead, these questions do not arise. If there are such severe abnormalities that development is impossible, and the zygote is non-viable, as in the case of three pronuclei or an entity which will certainly become a hydatidiform mole, it could be argued that what exists is not truly a human embryo. An entity with three pronuclei or a hydatidiform mole has no inherent capacity to be or to become a human being or individual.

The ethical issues surrounding the treatment of embryos do not appear to me to be raised in these cases either. I do not, therefore, object to those research projects which involve non-viable embryos or tissues which are certainly developing into a mole. They may yield much information about fertilization and early development and metabolism which may be both medically and scientifically useful, yet without the exploitation of viable human subjects. It is, however, precisely the living and normal embryo, with its full inherent being and its capacity for development, upon which the report of the Commission would allow experimentation.

This Commission has adopted certain ethical principles within an overarching ethic of care, among which are non-maleficence, protection of the vulnerable, informed consent, and respect for life. I do not see how these principles can be consistent with experimentation on embryos ending in their death. Human embryos are alive, they are certainly vulnerable, and they cannot consent to being the subjects of non-therapeutic research.

Surely non-maleficence is incompatible with a course of experimentation and destruction; this, for its subjects, is harm.

Surely respect for life has to do with its preservation, not with its use and termination with some sort of due solemnity.

Nor can the protection of vulnerable human embryos be accomplished by their use and resultant destruction.

If it is others who are to benefit from the non-maleficence, protection, and respect, then we are using one human directly and deliberately for the benefit of another. The other who will benefit is not only someone other than the research subject; it is not even the woman who is receiving the fertility therapy which allows the retrieval of the ova. The research would benefit the scientists who gain information from the research, and perhaps at some future time it may (or may not) yield application to infertility treatment. The research is not, however, to be of any direct therapeutic benefit to either of the subjects concerned.

This use is, in my view, far more problematical than the use of fetal tissue from elective abortions for therapeutic transplantation to victims of such disorders as Parkinson disease. Those transplants, as thus far performed in Canada and as recommended by this Commission, would be separated by elaborate systems of decision and personnel from the elective abortions on which they thus far depend. It is our recommendation that no fetal tissue be taken unless the fetus is already dead.

The results of the survey of the attitudes of Canadians done for this Commission indicate that, even among those who were opposed to the termination of an unplanned pregnancy, only 18% considered it wrong to use fetal tissue in medical procedures. A somewhat larger proportion, 26%, approved of the use of fetal tissue, and 56% were uncertain.[23] It seems, therefore, that opposition to termination does not necessarily carry with it opposition to the use of fetal tissue in medical procedures if there is no link to the abortion decision.

Moreover, in my view other alternatives can be and ought as a high priority to be developed which would avoid these ethical problems and the current systemic dependency upon ongoing elective abortion. This, too, accords with the response of Canadians to the Decima poll. Some 31% overall would support the research if the fetus would be aborted anyway, but 48% said they would support research if the fetus were "miscarried." Again, 18% opposed it under any circumstances.[24] This strongly suggests that 66% of Canadians would prefer alternatives which would involve no ongoing dependence on terminations of pregnancy. Such alternatives could include autologous grafts of treated tissues from some other part of the patient's body, retrieval and storage of tissue from ectopic pregnancies, cultivated cell lines, or animal tissue which is rendered immunologically mute, as well as further research in drug therapy. Use of fetal tissue for transplant has been and can be further divorced from both individual and systemic complicity in the death which produces the tissue, at least until the day when it can be fully replaced by other effective treatments which raise no such ethical difficulties.

By contrast, while the parental decision to donate embryos could be separated from the experimental activities of staff performing the experiments, the acts which bring about the embryos' demise cannot. The doctor/researcher who does the one does the other. The experimentation and the termination are parts of a single action, or the termination follows the experimentation. In either case, the experimentation is the inseparable reason for the termination. In the case of creation of embryos from sperm and ova, not as supernumerary results of *in vitro* fertilization but for the express purpose of experimentation, the decisions and acts of use and destruction would be deliberate from the very outset. I cannot see experimentation on embryos as anything but a lethal exploitation in varying degrees of premeditated severity.

Various arguments have been used to justify the use of embryos; I shall outline here why I do not find them persuasive. I do not in the least doubt the sincerity and good will of those who use these arguments. My fellow Commissioners and I are fully agreed on the centrality of an ethic of care; many others who use these arguments are also of good intent. The disagreement has to do with how and to whom the ethic of care is to be applied in a situation in which the interests of all cannot be gathered into a single solution.

Some say that knowledge concerning biological processes and potential therapeutic applications can be gained. This argument presupposes that the end justifies the means. That great knowledge could be gained would be true of any number of experiments on human subjects which could be — or have been — performed and which are now universally agreed to be unethical.

Whether or not *in vitro* fertilization has shown sufficient empirical promise of success that the sacrifice of embryos would yield any significant improvement is still uncertain. Whether any practical benefit is particularly likely to result is only one criterion of the ethical evaluation of any sort of scientific enquiry. That benefit might result does not *by itself* justify any action; other conditions must also be satisfied which I do not see as having been satisfied here.

Some follow the utility argument further, saying that, since we have supernumerary embryos, we might as well use them rather than allowing them to go to waste. This reasoning does not by itself justify any action either. It has been used for activity ranging from the entirely legitimate and constructive use for transplant of organs taken from people who have died in traffic accidents to the atrocity of using the bodies of the victims of genocide as resources for hair cloth and soap. The use of any part of a human body is only legitimate and ethical if the means of gaining access to it involve consent, and no exploitation or complicity in the death.

It seems to me that we neither need generate spare embryos nor, if we have generated them, need we put them to such use. Other alternatives for infertility treatment are available or should be pursued, such as fertilization of the single ovum of a natural cycle, in the form of IVF or, better still, combined with fertilization within the body of the woman, as in GIFT or DOST. All of these allow infertility treatment without leaving supernumerary embryos. Such techniques would remove the ethical ambiguity of supernumerary embryos. In the case of natural cycle IVF or DOST, in which the single ovum of a natural cycle is retrieved and transferred in the same cycle, the absence of hormonal intervention would entail lesser stress and risk for the woman and very likely would also raise the likelihood of successful implantation in a normally developed endometrium.

Once cryopreservation of ova has become feasible, there will be no justification for the fertilization of more than the number of embryos, normally three, appropriate for a single transfer. Supernumerary ova for subsequent transfer, research, or disposal, or ova retrieved from a stimulated cycle for transfer in an unstimulated cycle, would replace supernumerary or stored embryos, and would present few of their ethical dilemmas.

Were such techniques to be developed to a point of effectiveness equal to or superior to that of hormonally stimulated *in vitro* fertilization, there would be no further reason for the production of supernumerary embryos outside the body.

If supernumerary embryos already do exist *in vitro*, the alternatives of cryopreservation for implantation in the mother, or of adoption for gestation by a second woman, while presenting associated difficulties of their own, offer at least a chance of normal life and do not involve the exploitation and destruction which are inherent in experimentation. This should be the alternative if a couple choose not to have more than a certain number transferred, or if they have not chosen to have cryopreserved embryos transferred during the time limit (the Commission report suggests five years) specified at the outset by the fertility clinic. The Commission report has recommended that only ova, not embryos, be used in pregnancy-generating infertility treatment of non-ovulating women unless there is a medical problem in both spouses. Yet, since the purpose of generating embryos through IVF is to bring them to birth, not to provide a resource for research, ruling that supernumerary embryos are, for that sole reason, to be consigned only to use as research subjects and/or disposal appears contradictory. In my view the adoption of embryos is, in terms of relationship, parallel to the adoption of a born child, and is hence acceptable.

A widowed man cannot himself gestate the embryos he and his wife have conceived and caused to be cryopreserved. He should therefore also offer them for prenatal adoption, as difficult as giving them up might be, since the only mode by which he could cause them to be gestated to birth and parent them himself would be some form of gestational contract arrangement, commonly called gestational surrogacy, or to marry another woman and cause her to gestate the embryos of the first wife; neither of these scenarios would be ethically acceptable because of their implications for the woman.

This difference depending upon the gender of the surviving spouse is not, as the Commission report suggests, discriminatory; it is derived from the physical realities of sexual dimorphism. This Commission has recommended a prohibition on a single man's contracting the ovum-producing and gestational services of a woman to generate his own genetic child (preconception contracts, or "surrogacy"), while recommending that single women be permitted contractual access to the sperm of a man to generate her own genetic child. It therefore seems that, in principle, this Commission holds that, where the physical realities of gender would give rise to differing social consequences of apparently parallel actions, a difference in policy is legitimate and non-discriminatory. Permitting a widowed woman to gestate the embryos she and her husband had already conceived while not permitting the surrogacy option to a widowed man is a precisely similar application of the principle. Universal deprivation is not a necessary or appropriate response to sexual difference.

Nor is it the case that the limit "does not deprive people of an option that most people have." That would be true of posthumous insemination, which, as we shall see, has its own legal and social ambiguities. It is not true of embryo gestation. The embryo exists. "Most people," if what is meant by this is those who do not require or have not already made use of new reproductive technologies, would indeed not have access to insemination by their husband if he had died. If, however, there existed already-conceived embryos, "most" women would be pregnant and would be free to carry the pregnancy through to term. It would be surprising, indeed, if they did not wish to do so. We do not oblige a pregnant widow to abort, however early the stage of pregnancy, even though the birth will take place after her husband's death. Some women would view an external intervention to prevent them from gestating their own embryos after the death of their husbands in much the same light.

It seems contradictory to permit donor insemination of single women, an entirely *de novo*, technologically established single parenthood, while seeking to prohibit the completion of the birth of existing embryos already initiated with the wish of both parents. The mother would be a single parent and the birth would no longer take place within a couple which did previously exist; if the first sort of single parenthood is acceptable to this Commission, it is strange that the second would not be.

It seems doubly ironic that the Commission recommendation would prevent a woman from gestating embryos she and her much-loved and committed husband had already conceived, while the same widow could, under the Commission's recommendations, approach a sperm bank/ infertility clinic and gain access to a stranger's sperm and IVF for her ova as infertility treatment with no social or marital status questions asked.

If embryos have been cryopreserved and the male parent dies, it should be the choice of the female parent whether or not to have the embryos transferred to her uterus. No external entity, whether a physician, a clinic, a regulatory body, or the state, has the right to oblige her to be bereaved at once of her spouse and of their expected children. It seems inconsistent that the report recommends, on the one hand, that "embryos should be disposed of in accordance with the wishes of the gamete donors," while, on the other hand, recommending that embryos not be stored beyond the death of one "gamete donor," irrespective of the wishes of the other, or of both.

Yet such embryos were conceived by a couple, whatever the technological help they may have received, in order that they might have the hope of bringing to birth a wanted child or children. In the absence of evidence to the contrary, it should be assumed that the survival of the embryos would also be in accord with the wishes of the man who has since died. This may well be the only hope the woman has of ever having a child.

Some are of the view that the completion of the gestation of such embryos would be harmful to existing siblings. This is unpersuasive, for at least three reasons. First, most couples who seek the help of an infertility clinic do so because they have no children already born. There are likely to be no siblings to disrupt; in fact, this may be the woman's only chance of having any children at all. Second, if there were children already born, it could equally be argued that the knowledge that the state or a clinic had intervened to destroy their embryonic siblings when their father died would be as or even more disruptive for them on the psychological level.

Third, Canada's social structure is not inheritance bound. In a society with a lingering tradition of hereditary social status, of impartible or entailed estates passed down a single lineage, perhaps by primogeniture, and of agriculture based on inherited ownership or tenure, the number and birth order of siblings might well be salient, whether or not it was just. Such considerations contributed to a parallel recommendation in the Warnock Report, coming as it did out of the history and society of the United Kingdom. Inheritance is not this sort of economic or social factor in Canadian society, structured as it is around social mobility, achieved status, education, or other forms of skill, and independent employment or entrepreneurship, largely in occupations not bound in any way to the land or to hereditary tenure of any form. It is unlikely that any unfairness or undue dislocation to siblings already born would result from the birth of another. If "legal reform to ensure clear succession and inheritance rights" is necessary to expedite the settling of estates and to protect the "interests of already existing children" (in the unlikely event that there are any), so be it. This Commission has recommended the passing of much clarifying and regulatory legislation; this is merely one addition to what is desirable.

It may be doubted whether the courts would uphold such a stricture on embryo transfer to a widowed woman after the death of her husband in any case. A California case has been reported concerning the right of a man to have the authority in his will to determine what may be done with his cryopreserved sperm after his death. The woman who is designated in the will as able to choose whether or not to be impregnated had been his lover rather than his wife; there exist two adult children from a previous marriage who have sought to have the vials of sperm destroyed. The California Supreme Court, upholding a lower court decision, ruled that the Court did not have the authority to make a value judgement as to whether or not it is better for such a potential child to be born. Nor did the state have an interest sufficient to justify interference with an individual's decision about the use of his own sperm, although the child, if born, would be unlikely to have rights in the existing estate. Any further challenge to the will proceeds on other grounds.[25, 26] No parallel case has reached the courts in Canada as yet as far as I am aware. What the effect of the precedent would be in this different jurisdiction remains to be seen. Nonetheless, in this one instance even the posthumous use of sperm by a woman who is not a marital partner has been ruled as a matter of the choice of the man from whom it came and the woman who would be inseminated, even over the objections of adults who would become the child's half-siblings. The implications for the upholding of the far less problematical choice of an established couple in the transfer of embryos already conceived by mutual act, where there are no pre-existent siblings or without objection from existing siblings, seem clear enough.

Whether or not this decision will be repeated in other jurisdictions is not yet known. A reasonable countervailing argument could be made that the initiation of hitherto non-existent offspring after the death of one parent goes beyond the usual social meaning and mutuality of reproduction. We shall see whether rights in one's gametes will in the end be established as a question of absolute autonomy. Even were the Canadian courts not to take reproductive autonomy quite so far, however, it is unlikely that they would uphold strictures on the right of a woman to complete the gestation of her and her husband's own embryos. The conception has already occurred by the act of both persons, and the embryos do exist; what remains is to complete a process already mutually begun, not to begin a process de novo. The woman has already begun her part of the action, and the only aspect of it which the man was capable of contributing has already been completed. One would expect a court to uphold her right to complete that part of the reproductive action which would have been solely hers even if her partner were still living.

In the absence of evidence to the contrary, the husband's wish for the embryos to reach birth and to be raised would be assumed from the very fact of his having joined with his wife in conceiving them and causing them to be cryopreserved. The reproductive decisions of a couple, and indeed of an individual, are personal and a matter of fundamental human rights. In this sort of case the decision is not only shared throughout its joint history by the couple and held by the woman; its realization is already in process in the existence of the conceived embryos. Whether a court would uphold an interventive policy or act of any external individual or body contravening and halting the progress of such an initially shared and now individual decision is at least highly dubious.

Death is grievous, but it is a natural part of life. Its sundering does not contaminate. We should not, in our modern fear of death, invent new taboos surrounding it which would prohibit a woman from making a decision about her own embryos and her own relationships which would under other circumstances be viewed as belonging in her hands as a matter of right.

One person might, as I have heard it argued, view as morbid a choice to gestate the embryos conceived with a husband who has since died. Another might view it as a transcendence of one aspect of death and a triumph of the couple's love through bringing forth, loving, nurturing, and educating to adulthood a child they had both wanted and conceived before death intervened unlooked for. The child would be an end in himself or herself, not a mere means of coping with mourning or a replacement for the lost spouse. The point, however, is that a woman may choose to keep the death that thwarted her in her marriage from thwarting also her (their) desire for parenthood and a familial future.

It is for the woman, not for others, to choose. If after a reasonable period, perhaps 18 months or two years allowing for mourning and the making of decisions, she has decided not to have them transferred to her own uterus, they should be offered for transfer to a woman who is infertile, again in a form of prenatal adoption. Such embryos need not be destroyed or used for research.

There is something of a potential for conflict of interest in the collaboration of infertility clinics with embryo research projects, a conflict which perhaps the establishment of a licensing body may help to reduce but cannot eliminate. A clinic which cooperates with or incorporates experimentation on embryos may indeed be using the research to aid in the understanding of both fertility and infertility. Simultaneously, however, it may experience a disincentive to developing modes of treatment, such as natural cycle IVF or DOST, which, although they may cause less hormonal stress on the woman and involve less surgical intervention, will also produce no embryos to supply the other research arm of the facility. It is a principle of this Commission that a woman's treatment should be in her primary interest and in the interest of her future child; in such a case the setting of research priorities may not allow for the development of treatments which could potentially be most in the interest of the subjects involved.

The very reverse of the development of infertility treatments which do not expose embryos to use in research, or which cannot be used as sources for the deliberate creation of embryos for research, would be the utilization of ova taken from the ovaries of women having hysterectomies for reasons entirely removed from infertility treatment, or from the ovaries of women recently dead. Given the well-established use of other types of cadaveric organ donations, the latter question requires the attention, not only of the relevant National Commission sub-committee, should Government establish it, but of other concerned professional bodies, ethicists, and Canadian society as a whole.

Neither of these sources of ova for embryo conception should be permitted, in my view, as they would take the instrumentalization of the human to an even greater extreme. Such use is quite distinct from the legitimate transplantation of the healthy organ of a cadaveric donor or the blood or bone marrow of a living donor to save the life of someone at risk. Instead of the personal gift of the part of one recently dead person being used and maintained in saving the life of a specific (even if unknown) other person, an entire embryonic human entity would be raw material for use and disposal for some more remote, putative, and impersonal benefit. From the perspective of the woman, living or now dead, what is being used is not her body part but what will be, after fertilization, her offspring, removed from her in a procedure entirely unconnected to her own procreation. The embryos created under such circumstances would come into existence with no human relationship, no generative relationship at all; this essential aspect of our humanness and human reproduction would be deliberately absent.

Given the numbers of hysterectomies (and accidental deaths of women of childbearing age), the supply of such ovaries could be vast. Sperm are readily procurable. This Commission has taken a strong stand against the commercialization of any aspect of reproduction. Yet the instrumental-ization of the human remains instrumentalization, whether or not it reaps a commercial profit. Indeed, not all industries are commercial; some, such as most medicine, publicly sponsored education, or the services of government itself, comprise a substantial proportion of the activity of a nation's economy with the incentives taking a non-profit form throughout. Were researchers to be permitted to utilize such ova, a similarly vast resource industry could be created, at first for (non-profit) research purposes and perhaps subsequently for the production of substances found through the research. That a source of supply for research is a principal purpose of the expansion of ovum retrieval to include ovaries removed during hysterectomies is made explicit in the Commission report chapter on embryo research, in the discussion of the *in vitro* creation of zygotes.

The result of permitted and expanded experimentation on human embryos would be the dehumanization, not only of the embryos, but of the adult human beings, the researchers, and the women and men asked to donate their gametes, who act to bring this about. A society which permits it suffers a great loss of its humanity. We would all become less by consenting to our society's permitting human embryos to be treated, not as the gift of human life or as individual entities with intrinsic human significance, but as a large, aggregate-volume resource.

Research on embryos has, of course, many sub-fields. One of these is the development of cell lines. With respect to the patenting of cell lines derived from embryos, or, for the same reasons, from fetal tissues, the Commission report lays out the very real dilemmas, recommending further study. In my view, the patenting of cell lines, whether derived from embryos, fetuses or other, including adult, human tissues, is a means which is not justified by its end. The Commission report has dealt overall with questions of commercial interests in a highly insightful, balanced, fair, and ethically acute fashion; it is only on this one point, on which the report leaves a specific question open for further examination, that I wish to differ by stating a firm and decided position.

While seeing the pragmatic strength of the arguments from the need for investment, I view the patenting of cell lines derived from any human tissues, including those of embryos and fetuses, as unacceptable. If lacunae in the law with respect to patenting of "microbial life forms," clearly intended to refer to lower life forms such as viruses or bacteria, now permit such patenting of the cells, not only of higher life forms, but of human beings, they should be closed. Patenting of the inventive processes of cultivation or distribution by pharmaceutical companies of the biochemical products (such as insulin or dopamine) derived from such cell lines would be acceptable, but the cell lines themselves are and remain human tissue, with the full, distinct and individual human genome.

Non-profit, university, and hospital-based modalities of cultivation, with appropriate cost recovery and salary remuneration, should suffice to ensure access. Even if pharmaceutical corporations were to become involved, perhaps in collaboration with research-ethics-board-monitored, university-related hospitals, in developing the patentable inventive processes and in distributing the derived biochemical products, the cell lines themselves are human tissue like all other similar human tissue and should not be patentable.

It is unquestionably true that cell lines may prove therapeutically very useful and that commercial interests might be more inclined to propagate them if there were expanded patent protection for their profits. This is also true of all the other uses of technology for which we have recommended a prohibition of commercial interest or for which commercial interest has already been prohibited in law. It is precisely because they would otherwise be attractive to commerce that commercialization is prohibited with respect to certain things considered too closely allied to our fundamental humanity.

Returning to the general question, it may be that by refusing to experiment on human embryos we will forego certain sorts of knowledge and some derived treatments. The same is true of our refusal to do any other sort of experimentation deemed unethical. Most of the objectives of embryo research enumerated in the Commission report can be largely realized through the use of animal embryos, or even the aforementioned human cell lines. Some specific applications of that general information, however, would doubtless be available only through the utilization of human embryos. There are many types of information for purposes of medicine and human biology (or social science or psychology) which we will never have, whatever their potential utility, because we cannot, for example, do the same sorts of controlled experiments which are possible with non-human subjects. We do not permit laboratory drug trials in which human subjects are chosen, confined, controlled, and ultimately "sacrificed" for observation of the drug effects. Such trials using animals are unquestionably more scientifically precise than anything which is done with free human beings, but the knowledge which might be gained from the use of human subjects in such controlled experiments is, as all agree, clearly less important than the dignity, welfare, and freedom of human subjects.

The Commission report has argued that the implantation of therapeutically treated individual embryos without prior testing of the techniques on populations of sacrificed human embryos would have an unacceptable level of risk. Beyond the risk that the offspring could have some disorder or that the pregnancy might not survive, the nature of the risk is unclear; risk to the mother is mentioned, but what that might be beyond psychological stress and the risks of any pregnancy has not been specified.

I would argue in return that any application of an innovative drug or other medical treatment to human subjects after animal trials involves a certain level of uncertainty and risk. We do not use that risk and uncertainty to justify the treatment of some intermediate human population as we would laboratory animals. Rather we accept the known level of uncertainty and hedge it round with ethical safeguards and limitations, such as, for example, the testing of somatic gene therapy first on those who had no other viable hope. The known uncertainties involved in transfer of any therapy from animal to human subjects does not justify the treatment of the initial human subjects like laboratory animals; this is as true for human embryos as for fetuses, born children, or adults. Since, however, there is no indication that successful therapy on embryos (of any species) will be possible in the near or foreseeable future, arguments on the question are necessarily hypothetical. If, moreover, the uncertainties around a procedure are unreasonably great and cannot be elucidated without exploitation, it ought not to be done. This might mean that some couples would not be able to have children genetically their own. This would be grievous, but not so grievous as using unethical means to attempt to deal with their difficulty. Nor would society be harmed.

Human knowledge is exceedingly valuable and useful, but it is not of absolute value. Human dignity, non-maleficence, the respect for life and the protection of the vulnerable are higher values. If they and the search for knowledge cannot together be accommodated, human dignity, life, avoidance of harm and protection take precedence.

Some argue that the human embryo is not yet a human being or a person, and therefore the respect for life and protection of the vulnerable due to human beings are not due to it. This is usually framed around one or more of four justifications, that individuation is not observed to be complete, that it is not implanted in the mother's endometrium, that there is a considerable rate of embryonic wastage, and that an embryo becomes the focus of care and nurturance to and beyond birth because someone, usually the physician guiding the choice of the mother, decides to confer that status — all other embryos are deemed not to have this social role and therefore not to be due those forms of care.

As I have said, both those who are pro-life and many who are pro-choice object to experimentation on embryos. The flaws I see in these four justifications would also be, I think, of common concern to many who may differ with one another on the issue of abortion, because of the implications of the locus of decision for the fundamental determination of the human rights of anyone, not only for embryos. There will be many people who, whatever they may or may not consider the moral status, the nature, value or rights of the human embryo to be, will find broader implications for human rights of these four rationales deeply disturbing.

The key difficulty with all these arguments is that, in one way or another, they rest on defining inclusion among those having humanity, rights, and value in terms of the perception or desires of others, not in terms of what the one under definition is in himself or herself. The application is to the human embryo, but there is no reason given or implied which would limit these principles to the embryo.

It is indeed the case that science must work from empirical observation; it would be, however, a serious mistake to confuse what we can know or observe of another with what is. Each thing or person in the universe has a reality in itself, himself, or herself. We observe, we perceive, we form a portrait (or, in science, many overlapping portraits) of that reality, but those portraits are necessarily incomplete and may shift over time with changing information and with the perspective of the observer. The portrait is not the reality. The portrait is only a more or less accurate representation of the reality. The reality has an existence in itself, herself, or himself which is prior to any perception by others, any social relationship, or any role.

It is also true, on the social level, that our relationships are a vital, indeed essential, part of our humanity; it would be deeply unjust, however, to define human beings solely by those relationships and roles. Would any one of us wish to have our validity as human beings contingent upon our being known or accepted by someone else? Has not each of us had the experience of being negated or refused acceptance by another or an entire group of others? Our freedom and human dignity are contingent upon the fact (and it is to be hoped also our awareness) that we are valid and real and endowed with human worth and dignity in ourselves, prior to and irrespective of the presence or absence of relationships with — or acceptance by — others. Only upon that foundation of intrinsic human validity and dignity can we then build effective human relationships. Acceptance by one or more others may be a criterion of our entry into various sorts of structured groups. It is not the criterion of our reality and dignity as human beings.

We cannot negate or create one another, conferring or denying existence and reality by some exterior acknowledgement or dismissal.

In the case of human embryos, we as external examiners cannot yet in our present state of knowledge *observe* individuation until the primitive streak appears or until we are certain that twinning will not occur; it may well be, however, that the processes which determine individuation have been established long before we can observe them. Indeed they must have been, in order for the cells to be sorted into the differentiated placement which the subsequently visible primitive streak embodies. In any case, to say that two human individuals may exist in the future, as in the case of identical twins, is not to say that what is present now is not a human individual. Before twinning, the embryo is nonetheless a human entity, someone. The embryo is not a nothing before the rare event of twinning is no longer possible. The embryo is human, and has his or her full individual genome (including gender) from the beginning, long before someone else, with the amazing but nonetheless limited and extrinsic capacities of science for observation, can see the primitive streak. That an embryo is a human reality is not made true by what we can perceive or say of it, but by what it — he or she — is.

Arguing from implantation is considerably further yet from the definition of the embryo by what it is in itself. Implantation, which begins at approximately the seventh day and is complete by the eleventh or twelfth,[27] is the commencement, not of an identity of the embryo, but of one aspect of the relationship of physical contact with the mother. In other words, arguments from implantation argue from relationship, not from identity — from one form of direct encounter with the mother, not from the reality of the embryo itself. The choice of implantation as the beginning of that relationship is so arbitrary as to seem perhaps at least in part political.

Even the aspect of physical contact is not consistently followed through in these arguments, since implantation begins around the seventh day. Cutoff dates for experimentation at the fourteenth day utilize the later point of completion of implantation around day 11 or 12, plus an extra 2, not the actual establishment on day 7 of the process of physical envelopment in the lining of the maternal uterus. (I have not seen reasoning that would justify the extension of the 12 days to 14, and can only wonder whether it may conveniently round the calendar workweeks for decision-making bodies and researchers.) The existence of the embryo has been within the mother, receiving the sustaining environment from her from the outset; more than half of its genetic identity (given the maternal transmission of the mitochondria) comes directly from her. Hormonal signals between the embryo and the mother have been mediating subtle physical interactions. The physical relationship of the embryo with the mother has been a reality since the outset, and does not begin at day 7, let alone at day 14. To define an embryo as being the focus of care once fully implanted, then, is to define her or him by relation to another, not in herself or himself, and in terms of only one, relatively later-occurring aspect of the relationship at that.

Those who argue from the rate of embryonic and fetal wastage appear to me to pursue a perspective of trivialization which is difficult, upon examination, to support. This is so even when it is argued that embryos fertilized *in vitro* should be suitable subjects for research because they have an higher rate of wastage than those fertilized *in utero* and hence a lower likelihood that any given individual embryo would have the capacity to live and develop fully. To say the probability that many embryos would not live justifies termination of some who are now alive seems to imply that those with a high probability of death are *for that reason* legitimate subjects for use and termination.

Given other differences in gene expression between superovulated and normally ovulated ova,[28] the relatively high rate of lethal chromosomal abnormalities observed in embryos fertilized *in vitro* very likely does not reflect natural rates so much as side effects of the forced ripening of ova by superovulatory drugs. Since human embryos naturally fertilized are ordinarily unavailable for examination, it is difficult to be certain what the natural rate of embryonic death would be; estimates tend to vary widely and the assumptions upon which extrapolations are based tend not to be made explicit by the writers who make them. Some rate of natural embryonic death does nonetheless occur, difficult as it may be to measure.

Except in the presence of observable malformations, however, it is impossible to know which embryos under observation *in vitro* would live and which would, if transferred to the woman's uterus, nonetheless undergo a natural death. Whether the probable embryo death rate would have been a third or a half or nine-tenths or any other given estimate, the other proportion, the two-thirds, the half, the tenth or whatever it might be, *would* have lived had they been in the nurturing maternal environment. Arguments seeking to justify experimentation on embryos which show all observable signs of being alive and normal on the grounds of their *possible* death seem to be saying "they might die anyway, so it is all right to kill them."

Again, the rationale specifies no reason why it could be applied only to embryos. Infant mortality rates in some countries today — and in our own only a century and more ago — may run as high as some estimates of embryonic and fetal death. Some infants are born with diseases which make their early deaths probable or certain. The same can be said of adults under circumstances of epidemic, war, or specific diagnosis of disease, and at any age. That he or she may die, whether by the strength of probabilities or by the certainty of diagnosis, does not make anyone less worthy of care, or less human in himself, or in herself. For that matter, for each of us the mortality rate over the long term is 100 percent. On a historical or geological or astronomical scale, our lives are many and brief. Most of us will be forgotten in a generation by all but our immediate families, and few indeed will be remembered by anyone three generations hence.

Yet each of us is of infinite dignity and worth. That our existence on earth is ephemeral does not diminish our worth by one iota, since it is not derived from lifespan or impact but from our intrinsic human dignity. The most vulnerable and the weakest of us may also have an unlooked-for effect on others: even an embryo, like a poor child, or a sick adult, or a frail elderly person, by his or her very existence obliges others to make decisions, to act, to be or to refuse to be, toward another in ways which affect who they themselves become. Those who have a faith believe they know from Whom this dignity comes and to Whom we go, but many others who do not believe in a God nonetheless see and hold fast to the dignity of all human beings and the justice and care that are due them in this short life.

That human individuals, embryo or young adult or octogenarian, are likely to die, then, does not mean that *this* specific individual before us will die soon or what would happen if we provided care. Still less does it mean that we are justified in doing anything which will bring that death about. Human dignity perdures in the face of even the certainty of our death; the possibility or the fact of coming death diminishes it not at all. Rates of embryo or fetal death are not relevant to the question of experimentation on them as human subjects.

The fourth argument for the legitimacy of use of embryos as human subjects is that, until a doctor designates an embryo as healthy and a woman chooses to have the embryo transferred to her uterus, the embryo is not yet the focus of the parent-child relationship and care which derive from that choosing. This is an extension of the same exclusively relationship-based, recognition-based definitional reasoning implied in taking implantation as a benchmark, and has the same flaws. The choice or designation argument only makes the ground of the definition that much more explicit. The embryo is ascribed a status based on the perception and the choice of others, not on anything intrinsic to itself. Indeed, it is acknowledged by those of this view that fully healthy embryos may not be so designated and may therefore be used as experimental research subjects — or even be brought into being expressly for that purpose; the key point is the extrinsic choice of someone else, not the intrinsic reality of the one chosen or refused.

This calls to mind the ancient Greek and Roman practice of presenting the newborn to the *paterfamilias*. If he explicitly recognized the child as part of the family, the child lived and was cared for; if not, the child had no status within the group, was what we might today call an unperson, and was exposed to die on a hillside if not found and fostered by someone else. In terms of social structure, the principle of an inclusion contingent upon the desire of another is the same; only the persons making the decision and its point in time are different.

It is for all these reasons that I dissent on the question of the use of viable human embryos for experimentation or arbitrary disposal. The use itself is, in my view, an exploitation of human subjects. The justifications commonly used for it I find unpersuasive because they rest on assumptions which have broad, negative, and thus far largely unexamined implications for society, for law, and for ethics.

"You're nobody 'till somebody loves you."[29] A subjectively emotive line in an old torch song this may be. It is a highly dubious principle in law, in philosophical anthropology, or in social or medical ethics. Our individual reality, our human validity is not contingent upon the will or the recognition of other human beings; when it is made so, as has happened all too often to many individuals and groups in human history, the result is injustice.

Conclusion

I have no doubt that those, and certainly my fellow Commissioners, who advocate experimentation on or a policy of destruction of viable human embryos wish to do what is constructive and to avoid harm. My purpose here is not to question their intent.

For all the reasons I have laid out, however, I am of the view that the establishment of non-therapeutic research on viable human embryos would have two overarching wrongful results. First, it would be a lethal exploitation of human entities. Second, it would set precedents for hitherto unaccepted principles of medical ethics and of experimentation on human subjects. The associated definition of who is of human significance and who is therefore worthy of protection and care would have implications far beyond embryo research. These implications would be counterproductive for the human rights of the disabled, of the terminally ill, and of any individual or group whom another individual or group does not wish to recognize. A dehumanization not only of embryos and the adults who participated in such research but of all society would be among the consequences, however unintended.

The recommended National Commission structure for licensing and approval of research, then, appears to me to be appropriate and potentially effective for the maintenance of standards and protection of all parties from unmonitored or commercial exploitation. Without the establishment of such a body, the absence of regulation and monitoring, particularly outside institutions which have ethics review boards, would leave the field open to the possibility of shoddy research, inadequate record keeping, commercialization, and other forms of abuse.

This structure, however, should permit research only on gametes and non-viable embryos with abnormalities, such as having three pronuclei, intrinsically incompatible with human life or development. A strong and reasonable argument can also be made for allowing research on ova after the penetration of sperm but before syngamy, although the careful, because experienced, approach of Germany, which prohibits experimentation even at the pronuclear stage, is more certain of avoiding any possibility of exploitation of human subjects.

All viable embryos resulting from fertility treatment should be given an opportunity to develop normally, whether by implantation in the mother, by cryopreservation for future implantation in the mother, or by adoption by another woman to whom they are transferred.

The creation of embryos for the express purpose of utilizing them for research, whether by means of the deliberate fertilization of supernumerary embryos in fertility treatment or the creation of embryos from stored sperm and ova retrieved from cadavers or during hysterectomies, should be expressly prohibited. I am in full accord with the Commission recommendation that the use of ova from fetuses be prohibited.

The Genetic Link in Gamete Donation

Rights, Choice, Identity, and Disclosure

I fully endorse the recommendations in this Commission report having to do with non-commercialization, standards of medical practice, and informed consent, and record maintenance in cases of ovum or sperm gamete donation, as well as the recommendations having to do with the giving of non-identifying social, physical and medical information to the gamete recipient, with the hope that this will be transmitted to the child.

I differ with the report's recommended limitation of identifying information to cases of serious medical necessity. The searches of some adult adoptees for birth parents have been met with increasing legal recognition and the formation of registries facilitating contact between them if both parties agree. The similar searches increasingly undertaken by children of donor insemination indicate that there is a common need. It appears to me that there is no valid justification for refusing to meet it with the same recognition.[30]

Medical history, of course, is important; it has received the bulk of research attention until recently because most geneticists are physicians or work with physicians in the tracing and treatment of disorders. It is, however, a backward tracing of the role of genes from the sketching of dysfunction, rather than an understanding of the normally functioning genome. Just as the physical and social meaning of the genetic link is far broader than the transmission of disease, people may clearly have legitimate reasons other than a documentable fear of a disorder for wishing to know the identity of their progenitor(s).

Beyond the compelling nature of specific medical or other reasons for seeking information, this is, in my view, a human right. Individuals should not have to approach some external tribunal or authority to plead their case for fundamental information about themselves which is theirs by right. A child, at least once having reached the age of majority, has a right to know the identity of his or her progenitor(s) if the progenitor(s) agree. Not all children of gamete donation and certainly not all gamete donors will, when the moment of the majority of the child comes, wish to know the identity of or be in contact with one another. The parallel to adoption would no doubt be apparent in this also. Both parties have rights to privacy which should not be violated. If, however, both wish to be known to one another, externally imposed prohibitions on that identification seem gravely arbitrary at best. There is a strong argument that such prohibitions constitute a violation of the rights of the individual to his or her own records and to his or her own personal information, information which is only one but nonetheless a fundamental component of his or her identity.

Concern is expressed in the Commission report that attention to the identity of a progenitor would belittle or disrupt the bonds of the child with the family of rearing. These are parallel to the objections once raised in cases of adoption to the identification of progenitors even once the child had reached adulthood. Yet the bonds of social rearing are exceedingly strong and deeply imprinting. They exist in their own right. Knowledge of the identity of a genetic progenitor cannot replace those bonds; it cannot disrupt them if they are founded in consistent love, commitment, support, and the bonding which arises from a long history of shared life. The identification of a progenitor could not bring about a fundamental disruption, although it may become an element in the expression of a disruption if one existed in some serious form already.

Many adoptive children who have found their progenitors simultaneously find their ties to their adoptive families affirmed as the realities they are even as the ambiguities and unknowns are replaced with clarity and knowledge. There is no reason to expect that the experience of the adult children of gamete donation would greatly differ, all the more since one parent is genetically linked.

Progenitors' choice with respect to identification would, of course, necessitate some offspring having access to that information and others not having it. This does not constitute discrimination as the Commission report alleges. It is one of the normal consequences of the operation of human freedom. Adoptive children and their progenitors have to deal with the reality of similar freedom to permit or refuse identification and contact on the part of the other. So do all people who wish to pursue any sort of human relationship. This does not justify a merely apparent equalization by the utter denial of identification and/or contact to all, including those who mutually wish it. State-sanctioned, uniform deprivation is not a solution to differences in access which arise from personal, individual human choices.

I disagree with the Commission report's view that the gamete donation family is so fundamentally different from the adoptive family that the child should lack rights that the child of an adoptive family would have. That one parent is genetically related does not negate the fact that there remains another genetic link which is not part of the social family. Indeed, the case of adoption of the genetic children of one partner by a subsequent spouse not genetically related to them does not entail a legally defined or enforced denial or obscuring of the identity of the former spouse or partner who co-engendered the child. Some adoptive families, then, are precisely parallel in their structure to some families formed by gamete donation, yet function with identification of the genetic parent without any denial of the child's right to know the identity of the progenitor, custodial and jurisdictional questions being clearly resolved under the law.

That the parentage of some children in the general population is not accurately reported is unfortunate, but it is a result of private actions and decisions which the state cannot investigate and in which the state cannot intervene. The state remains passive in tolerating a private deception or a private refusal of identification. This is not parallel to and does not justify the overt action of the legislative and recording function of the state and the public health care system and its personnel to obscure information of fundamental importance to the person whom it most concerns, the adult offspring of gamete donation.

It is also probable that the courts would find as valid the right of the adult child of gamete donation to information concerning the perduring link itself, the field of adoption being one — but not the only one — providing ample precedent in Canada and other jurisdictions. There are also such precedents as a California ruling that a gestational surrogate was a "genetic stranger" to a child conceived from the ovum and sperm of the contracting couple.[31] Surrogacy of any sort is exploitative and unacceptable, as the Commission report elsewhere makes clear with full unanimity. What is relevant here, however, is that, when the court was faced with an already-existing case of gestational surrogacy, the genetic link was recognized and given primacy when the best interests of the child did not involve a social bond with the surrogate which the child had not yet had time to form. No case directly seeking a ruling on the nature and force of the genetic link as distinct from the social link has yet come before the Canadian courts. If, however, an adult offspring of gamete donation were to seek mutually consensual identifying information on a perduring genetic link, it is probable that the existence of such a right would not be denied.

Sweden has taken a very strong stand, in my view the ideal one, in allowing to donate their gametes only those who are willing to be identified, should the child wish it upon reaching "a mature age." The approach acknowledges the reality of the genetic link from the perspective of both donor and child, while preserving the family of rearing from undesired legal or social/psychological complication during the child's upbringing. In the consultative framing of the legislation, the Prime Minister at the time, Olaf Palme, was determined that the law should not be "founded on a lie." He placed emphasis on the results of many international studies which demonstrated that children want to know their biological parents. The new law, passed in 1985, was framed to meet the need of children to know their biological background. This has reportedly greatly reduced the number of students donating sperm; after an initial drop the sperm supply subsequently returned almost to the previous level, estimates being 80-90 percent. The donor profile, however, changed to one of married men with children, donating out of a knowledge of what engendering children means and a conviction of social solidarity.[32, 33]

It is argued by those concerned with provision that this lessens the overall supply. No doubt it does, in some degree. On the other hand, this approach does require that people know clearly what they are doing and deal truthfully with all aspects of it, including that of all their relationships, without evasion. The rights of all are protected. Nothing is imposed upon the unknowing or the unwilling, since all provisions are known before the choice is freely made to enter upon the action.

Gamete supply is not, in my view, the most important priority. Nor is the engendering of children irrespective of the associated costs in personal conflict and denial of rights and identity, not to speak of the denial or obliteration of what is, in fact, true. The end, however important to those seeking it, does not by itself justify the means. If people may not wish to do a thing when all of its realities are known, one may question whether the solution is to ask the state and its health care system to act to hide the realities so that people will be more inclined to do it.

In our investigations and hearing of testimony, as the report eloquently relates, we learned that ambiguity and deception have their costs. It is quite true that donor insemination is a frequently-used procedure. I am not, however, aware of the existence of any large, random-sample controlled study of the long-term results of gamete donation which would tell us what the rates of various sorts of psychological and sociodynamic outcome tend to be. The studies brought before us, and the testimonies of those addressing us, were powerful but they were qualitative and anecdotal; we cannot yet know how representative they were. Many supported gamete donation. Nonetheless, they give rise to concern.

A frequent theme was conflict, even marriage breakdown, after, and reportedly in some degree because of, donor insemination. This conflict can occur, not only within the emotions and relationships of the offspring and of those receiving the donation, but within the psyche and subsequent relationships of the donor, when the fact of having "children out there somewhere" begins to acquire emotional significance for the donor or, a little-noted complication, for the donor's subsequent partner. The secrecy which protects the "reputation" for fertility of a man or woman may be, in its own way, a time bomb, not only for the child who may learn of his or her origins later, but for the relationship of the man and woman who rear the child. The fact of having made use of donor insemination may not be a matter of secrecy for a single heterosexual or lesbian woman who visibly has no existing male partner; the erasure of the identity of the progenitor will not, however, keep a child from knowing of the existence of the fathers of other children, that he or she must have had one on at least the physical level, and wondering who he was and what he was like. The presence of a male partner and the identity of the progenitor can be blocked, but the void left cannot. It seems that many people — often with the instruction or encouragement of their physicians — who engage in gamete donation deal with the resultant questions by an avoidance which results, not in simplification, but in ambiguity and consequent interior and interpersonal conflict.

The main difficulty of the Swedish approach lies in the permanence of the commitment to disclosure, the fact that the adult offspring may or may not choose to act upon it notwithstanding. The permanence of the donor's commitment is not a valid objection — indeed it is in my view the ideal — in principle, once granted the fact of gamete donation. Our family-related commitments are public and remain permanently so, even when relationships break down and contact ceases. Divorce does not expunge the fact and the identities of a marriage from the public record; nor does relationship breakdown between parents and an adult child erase a birth certificate. Even such relatively less momentous acts as purchasing property or building an addition on a private house leave public records which remain after the property is transferred to another owner and the individuals have left. For an adult donor to make a commitment to something of such significance as the deliberate, health-care-system-facilitated generation of a child is at least as serious and public an act as many others which remain in the permanent public record as a matter of course.

In this respect gamete donation should be still more open to disclosure than adoption, which is based on the resolution of previously existent, difficult and often unintended human situations, even tragedies, as donation is not. If donors know what engendering children means and know before they make that commitment that it will be permanent, it is entirely reasonable to expect them to regard it as such, particularly when no legal requirements of nurture or financial support go with it. Even when identification is made, contact is no more obligatory than is any other voluntary human contact. If the life situation and relationships of the donor at the time are not favourable to contact — or, as in the Swedish case, to continued relationship after an initial contact — there need be none. That is a choice. All the commitment to disclosure does is remove the mask, causing all those involved to deal directly and truthfully with the realities of the persons and the action.

In Canada, however, at this point it would be a major accomplishment even to allow mutual identification with full protection for the ability to change the statement of intent for or against disclosure at any time. Such a system would also allow the mutual identification of those very few existing donors and their adult offspring whose medical records have been sufficiently complete to permit it. Given that even the adequate record keeping recommended in our report will constitute a considerable change in gamete donation practice, a process parallel to that of adoption disclosure registries would be a major breakthrough for the adult children of gamete donation, and for their progenitors.

Gamete Donation and the Nature of the Genetic Parent-Child Link

The genetic and social aspects of the link between parent and child ordinarily exist and function together. The physical father and mother not only engender but nurture and rear the child to independent adulthood. Under serious circumstances, in the best interests of the child, these two aspects of the parent-child link can be separated, as in adoption, the genetic aspect of parenthood being overridden and all legal and social functions of parenthood being exercised by a person or persons who are not genetically linked to the child.

An essential genetic link, however, does perdure. Approximately half of the genes of any given individual come from each genetic parent. As is becoming increasingly clear, the genetic heritage of a person has, while not a determining role, nonetheless a crucially important role in that person's functioning and in his or her identity. This affects not only physical features and physical health, but aspects of function which are related to personality, perceptions and other important components of the self.

It is, moreover, only in very recent times, and chiefly in North America, that a segment of a culture has appeared which places little emphasis on ancestral ties and histories. In part this is an effect of the relativization of descent and inheritance as sources of social status and occupation. Adoption within a recognized legal framework has a relatively short history in Canada, the first province legislating its establishment in 1873 and other provinces following suit over several decades well into this century. Before that the genetic tie was the only mode of descent, as well as the primary mode of inheritance.

Observed from an anthropological perspective, adoption was made possible in part by the industrial revolution and wage or salaried employment or entrepreneurship based on education, skills and a mobile labour market. Now that hereditary status and land tenure are no longer vital to a prospective heir's livelihood in Canada, ascribed filiation, that is legal relationships of descent which are based on decision rather than on claims to genetic relationships, have become matters of preference which radically threaten no one. They therefore are legally unchallenged (and unchallengeable) by those collateral relatives who would have inherited from a childless couple or by those siblings who would have had a larger share of an estate had a child not been adopted.

The perception of adoption has greatly evolved over this century (more or less, by province) of experience, and questions of "real" ties become matters of social bonding rather than validity of claims to property. As the adoptive bond emerged as psychologically, legally and socially enduring in itself, and genetically-based disputes over property faded to utter obsolescence, even the social reasons to deny the desire for mutual identification became uncompelling. Now, in effect, both those involved in adoptive relationships and the state which authorizes them can afford to recognize the genetic link because it does not threaten the psychological, social, or legal attributes of the adoptive link in any effective way. There is no longer any need to deny or block the genetic link.

In the case of donor insemination, as in adoption in earlier stages of its history, defining social parenting as being the only "real" bond has been an attempt, not only to affirm the social bond, but to deny, or at least block, any continuing salience or existence of what was commonly called the "blood tie." There is also, however, a movement among some groups in society to elevate the socially ascribed definition of social roles to the position of sole determiner of social structure and legal rights. The objective is to allow their preferred redefinitions of some of the more fundamental terms of social structure, including — or perhaps principally — those defining marriage and the family. On the conceptual level, from that theoretical perspective, if a social role can be "deconstructed" to negate any objective reality value of any of its definitions, components, relationships, or attributes, then it can be viewed as being no more and no less than what someone says it is. At that point it can be redefined as being virtually anything that a particular group or ideology would have it, without reference to any inherent physical characteristic or any appeal to the "nature" of any relationship.

That much about social structure is culturally defined is indisputable; some societies are matrilineal while others are patrilineal and still others are both (ambilineal); some assign status entirely by descent and inheritance while others assign it primarily by occupation or education. The role of relative income in status varies greatly by society and by subsegment in any larger society.

It does seem, however, when we look at the cross-cultural ethnographic record, that every culture has a form of marriage and of descent of some sort, and that the basis of that form is an agreed-upon type of relationship between male-female couples and the children they engender. The social and genetic aspects of the parent-child bond may under certain circumstances be distinguished in varying ways in various societies, and the relationships of male and female may be formalized in similarly varying ways. Families may function as co-residential multigenerational units or as scattered extended families with widely varying degrees of cohesiveness. In the vast majority of circumstances, however, societies are comprised of structures based on enduring male-female pairs and their children. Even those traditional societies giving formal recognition to same-sex relationships, societies which, though not numerous, do exist, give them a status which is distinct from that of marriage.

This would seem to be related to, among other things, the recognition that any conception requires the action of a male and a female. Even the circumventing technologies which we are considering, however the ova and sperm may be redistributed, nonetheless require a male and a female whose gametes join and who have a physical genetic relationship with the resulting child. The anonymization inherent in sperm banking and the medicalization of donor insemination (or of ovum donation, although it requires surgery to bring it about) is in a very real sense a modality of masking the human relationships which exist even as they are being bypassed. A physician and/or a sperm bank intervenes so that a specific woman and a specific man do not have to "know" or acknowledge one another, in either the relational or the physical sense.

There is that about the capacity to engender children which is so primordial and inherent in the male-female and parent-child interactions, bonds, and relationships that this bond cannot be solely socially defined, or redefined, without reference to those realities. It is problematical and contradictory enough to attempt to separate the adult personal male and female components in generation even when two persons may not meet one another. It is impossible to separate the child from the genetic link with either parent, since he or she carries those genes, with all their effects, for life — in all likelihood passing them on to children of the next generation in turn.

Even on this continent, there is no consensus that the parent-child link can be restructured at will. Indeed the reverse has been universally taken as axiomatic until very recently. While social and economic mobility have made the inheritance of property and occupation of little practical importance, the sense of rootedness and personal connectedness in genetic ancestry tends to remain. The solely social definition of the parent-child link is actually supported by a fairly small segment of the population.

While the opinion surveys done by this Commission did not directly explore the definition of the genetic link after gamete donation, the genetic link is clearly held to be important by many Canadians of all ethnic backgrounds. It is held to be all the more so by Canadians of cultural and/or religious backgrounds which strongly emphasize lineage. Examples such as the genetic link being required for the fulfilling of the Jewish mitzvah of engendering male and female children capable themselves of engendering children, and the Chinese reverence for ancestors, are only two of many which could be brought forward. For that matter, the very fact that many of those who use donor insemination seek to do so in secrecy is itself a paradoxical reflection of the value which genetic ties are held to have in the population as a whole. We should be leery of redefinition of precedent-setting social and legal roles based on premises which intrinsically deny or relativize values and self-definitions held by many, or even most, Canadians.

There is an important and insufficiently explored role of the genetic parent-child link in the development of the self-definition, the identity, of many people. The Commission report, indeed, insightfully acknowledges it. That this is true where the genetic and social parent-child links remain intact is patently obvious. What family — and what individual — does not make reference to the relatives who share, not only eye shape or hair colour, but also aspects of personal interest and temperament?

Studies of separated twins indicate that these commonalities are not only matters of nurture, the environment, and education of the child, but have a genetic component. That genetic commonalities are unpredictably assorted does not lessen the fact, and perhaps even more importantly the perception among both parents and children, that they exist and are a component of a reflective self-understanding. In the old nature versus nurture debate, it is increasingly clear that both are of essential importance — along with the large part of every individual which is utterly unique. The same questions that arise among individuals in intact families necessarily also occur to those whose genetic and social links have been severed, however appropriate that severing may have been at the time.[34]

One may question whether it is wise to frame social definitions and the derived legal definitions and applications of the parent-child link solely on conceptualizations which recognize only one ascribed aspect of that link, ignoring empirically observable inherent genetic continuities (which are also perceived and given a social value by most in this society). It is one thing to frame the law in a way which balances the acknowledged rights of individual parties who may differ in their wishes. It is another to frame the law in terms of monofactorial principles of social structure which are not held by consensus and which may be an imposition of one social view on those Canadians who hold another view, whether as individuals or as groups.

Self-Insemination Within the Health Care Facility Setting

It is possible that widespread encouragement of self-insemination (SI), if sperm banks were to operate on the recommended carry-out basis, would undercut the application of some of the principles at which we have arrived. Of greatest concern here would be questions of record keeping and of medical and other history, and even of the possibility of commerce. It seems somewhat contradictory to set up an elaborate formal structure for standard setting and record keeping in donor insemination, while simultaneously stating that "where possible, both heterosexual couples and women without a male partner should be encouraged to avoid the costly and medicalized aspects of clinical DI programs by choosing SI," the recipient(s) being instructed in thawing and administering the sperm elsewhere. This would encompass the vast majority of donor insemination recipients. It refers to all but those who would require specialized interventions such as intrauterine insemination or sperm washing and concentration, techniques which are usually used for insemination by husband in any case. In my view, the intent that comprehensive record keeping and certain other standards not be compromised is, on the practical level, unrealizable with SI.

Once a private citizen has taken sperm out of a sperm bank, moreover, there is no certainty whatever that it was used by the person herself, or that it was not passed on, even for unrecorded for-profit payment, to someone else whose identity, medical history, etc., are unknown to — and perhaps would even have been of grave concern to — the sperm bank or fertility clinic. Given the large number of inseminations which are sometimes necessary for a conception, plus the possibility of seeking subsequent children by the same means, a private individual could distribute a considerable quantity of sperm to an indeterminate number of people over time without the awareness of the sperm bank or clinic, or of the national registry. Return of information on live births and other aspects of outcome, of course, would not be accurate or, as is far more likely, would not occur at all. If, however, the report recommendation that this information be routinely returned on a form by the parents of DI children were also to become practice, the non-return of information from these individuals would not arouse suspicion either.

The return of information on a form forwarded solely by the receiving parties, including by those who use it as intended, is a problem in any case, given the known low return rates on voluntary forms of any kind. This is particularly so in the case of forms which must be kept and remembered for a considerable period of time before being filled out and returned. The information gathered would also be skewed toward the optimistic, as those who experienced miscarriage or the birth of a child with a disorder would be still less likely to fill in and mail the forms. Viable follow-up would have to be made possible by confidentiality-maintaining data base linkages to other medical records. If, then, sperm is widely distributed on an informal, carry-out basis, there is no certainty that it has been used by those who present themselves as having used it or that the ethical standards and accurate record keeping which have been recommended would be maintained. In some significant proportion of instances they may not be.

Even when, as in the probable majority of SI cases, the sperm is used by those who undertake to use it, even as prescription drugs are used by patients outside a medical office, record keeping would be compromised. That many of those who receive prescription drugs do not use them correctly or completely, or do not use them at all, is well known. Drug trials routinely require formal follow-up to be able to ascertain both the successful administration of the drug and the outcome. If one objective of record keeping is to know the success and risks of donor insemination, shifting the majority of donor inseminations to a largely informal self-insemination model will be unlikely to accomplish that objective. The birth, the records and the identity of a child are arguably also of even greater importance than the prescription of a drug, since the individual who does not comply with the physician's prescription instructions risks only himself or herself, while in the case of SI a child is also involved.

One can understand the desire that conception take place in the known surroundings of the home. Once the public health care system is being approached for donor insemination, however, some level of intimacy has already been sacrificed. Allowing SI outside the clinic setting would undercut the associated recommendations in this report and the principles they embody for the welfare of the child and all others concerned. The requirement that insemination occur only in hospital facilities has ample precedent, not only in Canada but in other countries, Sweden being only one.[35]

Sperm for self-insemination should be therefore used in a private, comfortable, and well-appointed room provided on the site of the clinic or sperm bank, and should not otherwise be taken out of the facility.

Conclusion

While the existence of gamete donation is accepted by many Canadians, other Canadians are not in accord with the practice. Asking that public regulation be given to it does not presuppose universal condoning or national consensus. Individuals, health care personnel and health care institutions are — and should remain — free to choose whether or not to participate in or to provide it. Some may argue, with considerable persuasiveness, that they would prefer that their tax monies not be devoted to a practice which they oppose. Others will argue, however, as we of this Commission have done, that bringing what is already a permitted practice under the umbrella of the governmental health care system allows it to be supervised and regulated. Only in this way can abuses such as commercialization, grossly multiple donation or use of medically dangerous fresh sperm, which, as this Commission has found, exist not only in other countries but in Canada, be avoided and standards and records be maintained in the best interests of all parties, the child foremost.

Judicial Intervention in Pregnancy

The role of law is largely to protect the rights of individuals, and, in cases of conflict, to balance those rights. Where there is a question of legal intervention, then, there are two related questions. What is the evil which the law is to remedy, and does any given remedy create more problems than did the original evil itself? The possible evils we must consider exist at a minimum of two levels. The more obvious is the individual level, as between the life-long harm to a fetus and the limitation of a woman's autonomy. The second is the societal, as between the potential effects of judicial intervention in pregnancy on the collective status and autonomy of women and, by contradistinction, the potential effects on both equality and the nature of the rule of law arising from the absolute preclusion of such intervention.

Judicial intervention in pregnancy is a question which only arises because of situations which are tragic in the conflicts which they embody. In this I am in full accord with my fellow Commissioners. No matter what the disposition of an individual case, there will be results which one wishes had not occurred. To intervene means to save the child at the cost of coercing an unwilling woman into surgery or close supervision or imprisonment to control her harmful behaviour. Not to intervene means to leave the woman free to act in any way whatever at the cost of accepting preventable but almost certain harm, handicap, or death for her child. One cannot regard any resolution of the question without ambivalence.

The questions which must be resolved are many and complex. I do not believe that there has been sufficient reflection on them, by Canadian society as a whole or by the relevant expert disciplines, to warrant any categorical statements by this Commission on the most humane and constitutionally consistent approach. The arguments adduced here will have to suffice for the present, as the Decima survey done for this Commission did not ask the Canadian public their views on this question, confining itself to new reproductive technologies per se. Given the importance of its broad implications, this is a question on which the views of Canadians should be actively and representatively sought before any legislative change is even contemplated.

My task here is not to resolve the issue but to raise questions as to whether there are not other, still greater evils which arise if we hold that a woman must not or cannot ever, in principle, have her autonomy limited in these ways. Unless we are certain — and I am one among many who are not — we should not take premature action to alter the existing legislative and other protective structures.

The Dilemma

As presented to us, judicial intervention in pregnancy seems chiefly to arise under two sets of circumstances, those of harmful lifestyle at any point in pregnancy or those of medical emergency, usually at the point of birth. Intervention in the first set of circumstances, in the rare instances in which it occurs, takes the form of measures to alter the substance abuse or other harmful behaviour, whether by mandatory supervision, treatment or incarceration. Intervention in the second set would chiefly take the form of court-ordered Caesarian sections. There has been discussion of court-enforced surgery to correct a disorder in the fetus *in utero*, but this seems to be a hypothetical concern rather than a concrete situation. A related question is that of whether a woman would be liable for civil damages or would be subject to criminal charges for damage done to the fetus after the child is born.

I am in full agreement with my colleague Commissioners that the question of judicial intervention in pregnancy arises when the ethic of care has broken down, and that our primary concern must be to provide such social, educational, economic and medical supports to pregnant women that such conflicts may be avoided. Most pregnancies are models of the ethic of care in action, first on the part of women, and with their partners, relatives, friends, and societal institutions providing all possible support.

A lapse in this manifesting of care does, however, sometimes occur. Our task, then, is to find a way to deal with something that everyone wishes had not happened. The ethic of care has broken down and we are faced, unavoidably, with a conflict of rights which an appeal to mutual and universal care will not resolve.

The fetus is vulnerable, and is certainly in no position to help herself or himself. One question, then, is whether the woman should be obliged to give the help, obliged, that is, to follow the principles of care for the vulnerable and respect for life, or whether her autonomy is of such prior importance as to be sacrosanct, even in a case in which most people would choose otherwise and would wish that she, too, would choose otherwise. A second question is what the broader implications of either conclusion would be.

The Courts and the Defence of Actual Consent and Autonomy

The recommendation that judicial intervention in pregnancy not be permissible assumes that the courts would necessarily be oppressive and coercive in overriding a woman's consent. Yet we must consider the possibility that in some cases the courts, in mandating treatment, could be acting in defence of a woman's best interests, actual intent and consent, and thus her authentic autonomy, against the coercion she experiences from some other factor in her life, such as severe drug addiction.

The only practical mode of determining whether this is or is not so is to carry out the examination of the particular case. It follows, then, that judicial review and possible intervention would have to remain a possibility in order to determine what the exercise of her best interests, intent, consent, and hence actual autonomy would be and to mandate measures which would enable it. Precluding judicial intervention in pregnancy, then, could in some cases militate against the very autonomy which the Commission report wishes to protect.

I agree that in general a woman's refusal to consent to treatment should not be overridden; this is not because she is a woman but because she is a human being. Since the one patient is inside the other, he or she can only be reached by intervention in the body or the behaviour of the non-consenting other. We do not force a person to undergo invasive treatment for the sole benefit of another (as in living donation of a kidney), even when the other would die without the intervention. Nor do we force those of sound mind to accept medical treatment for themselves, even if we consider their judgement to be in error, or when non-treatment is likely to result in their death.

The principle of the requirement of consent would seem to mean that in general a pregnant woman ought not to be coerced into treatment against her will. The Commission report, however, appears to assume exceptionless, perpetual and unambivalent, unambiguous, consistent and rational choice on the part of the woman. In some cases as they actually occur in practice there may be doubt as to the competence and hence the nature of the consent of an individual woman. This may be so if she is drug-impaired or in a state of drug withdrawal which would cause her to say or do anything to get a fresh supply, whatever her deeper intent for her fetus might be. Perhaps a clinician is faced with a woman whose statements of intent are shifting because of some emotional state or panic, or because of some form of lack of capacity to understand that treatment is the only mode of bringing about the outcome she has explicitly said she wants, the birth of a healthy baby.

There may, therefore, be a question as to what her most fundamental choice actually is. Is she acting as a rational, choosing adult, having decided that drug ingestion is more important to her than the welfare of her fetus? It seems that the Commission report predicates its interpretation of autonomy only on this assumption. Or does she in fact intend good for her fetus but is being coerced at one irrational moment by the urgency and desperation of her drug withdrawal to say and do things which in another, rational moment, she would not wish to say or do? In such cases it may be that some form of objective assessment of her intent is necessary, not only in the child's interests but in her own. Would a court be coercing her, or would it be protecting her from coercion?

The weighing of consent or refusal of consent on the part of a woman under conditions of medical emergency and distress is not as straightforward as it might be were she deciding calmly over a period of weeks on whether or not to donate a kidney. The consent or refusal of a woman chronically under the influence of alcohol or drugs is similarly difficult to determine. If we as a society are ambivalent about such situations, it is highly likely that any given woman in that position would be far more so.

Society recognizes that diminished competence diminishes the capacity for informed consent. Our own Commission concludes that informed consent must go beyond mere acceptance to informed choice, which seems to me to presuppose not only full information, and awareness of alternatives and implications, but also sufficient rational capacity to choose. At what point does some state of impairment or incoherence or panic or incapacity so diminish competence that a disinterested party must become involved?

Our society accepts the principle that, while the mentally ill should in general be hospitalized only with their consent, well-founded fear that a person will harm himself or herself or someone else can warrant committal. Because of the human consequences of either a narrow or a broad interpretation of that harm, the point at which this principle would apply is the subject of ongoing debate, or indeed struggle. The principle itself, however, is accepted and there is clear recognition that the dilemma is real. The question must arise whether severe drug addiction resulting in incoherence or uncontrollable compulsion is sufficiently parallel to or cognate with severe mental illness in some respects that similar approaches are appropriate.

The Commission report asserts that "the use of mental health legislation to commit or treat a pregnant woman against her will, even where the language of the statute appears to be applicable, would clearly offend Charter principles," but it does not give any reason why this should be so. One would assume, rather, that mental health legislation is applicable to both sexes, and is not suspensible solely because a person is female or because she is pregnant. If a woman is not mentally competent to determine the nature of her own consistent choice or her own best interest, even prior to consideration of the welfare of another, help may be needed as in many other instances of grave impairment.

The Commission report seems, indeed, to contradict itself on this point. It states that the "legal consequence of being found mentally incompetent is the appointment of a legal guardian to make decisions on one's behalf." Precisely. This requires judicial intervention, whether a person is pregnant or not, and even if the best interest of the woman were considered the primary or even the sole consideration. It may well be that treatment or behaviour which would protect the fetus would also be in her best interest with respect to her own health, were she found, under the principles of mental health legislation, likely to do herself severe and irretrievable harm. It would certainly be in her best interest with respect to her future life of responsibility for the care and custody of a child who could, were there to be the action of a guardian or some other modality of treatment, be born without handicaps burdensome, not only to the child, but to the woman.

It is in the face of these dilemmas that the application of ethical principles, social analysis, medical diagnosis and therapy, and the role of the courts come to overlap.

The courts are a disinterested forum with accepted legitimacy in our society for the resolution of what will necessarily be grave doubts, ambiguities, and conflicts. Any other body, such as an ethics committee, or another individual, such as an ombudsman or even a mediating social worker, designated to take responsibility for these conflicts will rapidly find themselves exercising what amount to quasi-judicial functions. Yet the mandates of such bodies and persons are not, in fact, judicial; ambiguities may remain and time-limited emergency conditions may compound the urgency of finding a resolution. The final forum in our society is, and must be, the courts.

Women as an Aggregate

Arguments opposing judicial review in individual cases on grounds of a posited effect on the collective status of women or on the autonomy of all individual women seem to me to have serious internal contradictions, and to leave insufficient room for sensitivity to these specific individual women's interests and situations.

The assumption appears to be that no claim should exist which might limit the autonomy of any woman. This has many political, constitutional, and other implications.

The individuals, women and children, who are caught in these tragic situations are not being treated in these arguments as ends in themselves but more a secondary means to a separate and arguably unrelated political end, an end concerning which the individual women in these conflicts may have no — or some other — personal awareness or commitment. It is they, the individual women, however, who will be left with the care of the handicapped child, or with the bereavement, which follows non-intervention.

Judicial intervention in rare instances of grave circumstances does not in any way reinforce "the notion that a pregnant woman's role is *only* [emphasis mine] to carry and deliver a healthy child" or for that reason deny "her existence as an autonomous individual with legal and constitutional rights," hence being "dangerous to the rights and autonomy of all women." Every person has a multiplicity of often overlapping roles. To define any person in terms of only one of them — or to posit, as the Commission report does, that unspecified other people define and may be further encouraged to define all members of a group in terms of only one of them — is reductionist. Indeed I know of no group anywhere on any contemporary political or philosophical spectrum which claims that the delivering of a healthy child is a woman's — or a pregnant woman's — only role. When the subject is raised, the notion is universally condemned. It is hence a red herring, however politically potent the slogan.

Women and men both, as adult human beings, have formal and informal rights and responsibilities arising from each of the roles they undertake. This may be, to take just a few of the more commonly experienced examples, as employer, employee, spouse, friend, contractor, contractee, parent, child, and, yes, gestating woman. Gestation toward the goal of delivering of a healthy child is not the only role a pregnant woman has, as any woman who has been pregnant and any other person who has lived or worked with a pregnant woman knows. It is, nonetheless, one of the roles she does have, and the responsibilities which go with it exist as the responsibilities which arise from any other of her roles exist.

It is certainly true, as the Commission report points out, that a caring and nurturing relationship cannot be legislated. Society does, however, quite routinely legislate the minimum fulfilment of the formal responsibilities and obligations of various social roles, including those, such as the parent-child or the marital role, which are best generated and supported by the informal and strong bonds of affect, caring, and commitment. This is because it is often upon the fulfilment of social roles that the essential welfare of others depends.

If, as must be the case, women are to be deemed equal, women must be deemed to have the full responsibilities which accompany full rights. We expect every adult to act responsibly with respect to the roles they freely undertake, and with respect to the persons to whom they have undertaken both the rights and the obligations which characterize those roles. To expect that pregnant women act as responsibly as we expect every other adult to act is to uphold and defend the rights of women as competent, free and full participants in society. It is the negation or the waiving of those responsibilities which, in my view, would be "dangerous to the rights and autonomy of all women."

Those who argue against judicial intervention in pregnancy in order to protect or advance a gender-based, aggregate, absolute autonomy may be viewed, particularly if they are themselves women, as being in a conflict of interest. Whatever resolution is reached by society with respect to these situations, it should be primarily for the welfare of the principals, the specific woman and the specific child. It should not be in aid of positions on any other issue, or in aid of the separate and different interests of the members of any larger group.

Many of those who subscribe to the collective status argument would never intend to use individuals as means to an end; this nonetheless seems to me to be the other side of the collective status coin. The issue of judicial intervention in pregnancy should not be caught in, or be treated as a strategic element in, a larger and distinct political struggle, however important and worthy some of the issues in that struggle may be.

Such arguments may, moreover, by placing women either or both above or beneath the law, be ultimately counterproductive to furthering the equality of men and women within our common humanity. This, as I shall suggest, would be a far greater evil than would a continued wrestling with these agonizing conflicts on a case-by-case basis.

Responsibility, Equality, and the Constitution

We must deal with the question of a woman's accountability for her actions. The case of judicial intervention in pregnancy is different from that of abortion, in that the child is to be born and, if surviving, he or she will have to live with whatever the consequences of the conflict turn out to be. Fetal alcohol syndrome, brain damage from oxygen deprivation at the time of birth, and the results of being born with cocaine or heroin addiction are among the more common of such consequences.

Again, we must deal with this question not only in pragmatic terms but in principle. There can be no doubt that the inconvenience or loss of mobility or other effects experienced by a woman of mandatory but temporary care or treatment would be far less severe than the effects of an entire lifetime of mental and/or physical handicap on the child who is to be born. This is a very important question of proportion. On the practical level, however, were women to be systematically threatened with lawsuits or criminal penalties when their addictions or choices had damaged their children, some pregnant women might well, as the Commission report rightly points out, avoid medical care for themselves and for their children, or perhaps abort out of fear of sanctions. This would obviously be counterproductive from the perspective of the good of the fetus along with that of the mother.

The concerns expressed in the Commission report that "the potential for curtailing women's choices and behaviour becomes staggering" and that many women's pregnancies could become "subject to challenge and scrutiny" nonetheless seem to me to be alarmist. It would be not only repugnant and totalitarian but simply impossible to set up some sort of science-fictional infrastructure to enforce the compliance of every woman who did not seek adequate prenatal care or who did not follow her doctor's advice. Equally repugnant and bureaucratically impossible would be the assessment of every newborn for possibly matrigenic (parallel to iatrogenic) damage, and the resultant laying of charges. A significant segment of the literature on the subject paints just such bizarre scenarios representing judicial intervention in pregnancy as the harbinger of some total and coercive (male) medico-governmental dictatorship over women.

The painting of such extremes, however, or rather the setting up of such straw men, tends to obscure the rather more prosaic but far more probable scenarios in the instances one finds on the ground. Specific children are born severely damaged in ways which were entirely preventable and which were entirely within the responsibility of the mother. Once the children are born there is no question that they are legal persons. Laws exist which allow them to sue for damage done — or to inherit — through events which occurred before they were born, so long as they are subsequently born alive. It would probably be imprudent, counter-productive and impracticable to sue women for the developmental and other handicaps children may suffer because of what their mothers did while they were *en ventre sa mère*. Yet we may ask whether women are not responsible in principle, and therefore what the implications of the question itself are for the status of women before the law.

The Commission report says that pregnant women "are no different from any other responsible individual; to treat pregnant women differently from other women and men, or to impose a different standard of behaviour on them, is neither morally nor legally defensible." It should be clear by this point that I agree. Where we disagree is on the application. Autonomy is a necessary good, but it is not an absolute. All of us have, as the report says, the right to make our own choices, but rights necessarily entail responsibilities; where our choices may or do harm others, our choices are, in fact, limited, and we are held accountable, whatever our gender. It is the suspension of that accountability with respect to pregnant women which would constitute the setting of a different (and lower) standard of behaviour.

An employer who chooses to employ people in his or her factory or office is responsible before the law to provide them with a safe environment. If one of them is injured in some way for which the employer is responsible, the injured person can sue or the employer may be charged with offences related to negligence, up to and including negligent homicide.

A woman, unless she has been raped, has in some measure willed her pregnancy, at least to the degree that she consensually participated in the sexual union which initiated it. If family planning was not used, she participated in that choice also. Is she not to be deemed responsible for the environment she provides the one who is there at her initiative, even as the employer is responsible for the environment he or she provides for the employee who is there at his or her initiative? A householder who is liable for injury suffered by a person on his or her hazardously maintained property provides yet another parallel.

To some it may appear that a woman should not be held responsible in a manner parallel to the responsibility of an employer or a householder. Yet let us look at the questions raised by such an exemption. It seems to me that the rationale would have to be that a woman is either above or beneath the law on grounds of gender and pregnancy, assertions which one may question.

If the argument is that a woman must not be held responsible because she is a woman and it is her choice, this seems to me to imply that a woman is above the ordinary application of the law because she is a woman. I have not yet seen a clear, let alone persuasive, argument as to why this should be true.

Be it granted, only a woman can become pregnant, as only a man can produce sperm. Neither fact is discriminatory; they are simply an empirically observable given, a function of the highly adaptive, population-variability-maintaining sexual dimorphism that human beings share with most organisms above the evolutionary level of the worm. Granted, too, given the unique human capacity for awareness and, with that, the development of the philosophy and ethics of social and legal responsibility, that there may therefore be modes of exercise of responsibility which are possible only for a woman, as there are other modes of exercise of responsibility which are possible only for a man.

The standard of behaviour, however, is the same. While one *ought* to act in accord with the principles of benevolence and care, that is in ways which are supportive of and helpful to others, at a minimum one is free to act as one wills so long as one acts in ways which do not harm others. As only a woman can, by her own drug abuse or other actions, severely handicap someone for life, only a man can rape. That only one gender can do one or the other form of harm does not make accountability for either discriminatory. The single standard of behaviour pertains to both. The difference in culpability has to do with the probable social circumstances of such a woman and the physiological and psychological burden of addiction, as compared with the improbability of any credible mitigating factors in rape. The difference, however, has to do with an independent assessment of the capacity of the individual to choose not to do harm, and hence an assessment of competence; it has nothing to do with gender discrimination.

If the argument is that any woman in this sort of situation is vulnerable, has arrived in her unfortunate situation for reasons utterly beyond her control and ought not to be burdened with the ordinary application of the law, this seems to imply that she is beneath the law because she is incapable of the responsible, rational choice which underpins all adult participation in the society as framed by the law, again because she is a woman. It appears to me that a blanket application of this to all cases involving all women would be to return women to the patronizing and disenfranchising protections once offered to "women, children and the insane."

That all persons are to be assumed mentally and morally competent and capable in the absence of evidence to the contrary is essential to their full, adult participation in a democracy. Placing this in doubt with respect to women as a group rather than with respect to particular individual women appears to me to be highly counterproductive.

The argument from aggregate seems to suppose that if any woman is judged incompetent, all women are by extension judged incompetent. Conversely, it seems to suppose that if all women are to be viewed as full legal and moral persons, every woman must be assumed under any and all circumstances to be wise, objective, and rational (and right "for her") in everything she does.

I would not make the assumption that if women are not deemed universally competent, they are condemned to being deemed universally incompetent as a class or group. They are individuals. Most would fall into the rational, decision-competent, responsible category, at least most of the time, not because they are women but because they are adult human beings. Some individual women, like some individual men, however, do have diminished responsibility which is due to temporarily, chronically, or permanently impaired judgement. If this is so in individual cases, then the question of the protections and treatments — and the controls — which ordinarily apply to those of seriously impaired capacity must arise. Otherwise, freedom requires that women, adults indistinguishable from men on that ground, are assumed to be competent, and hence both responsible and accountable.

We must, as women, beware of overusing arguments claiming protections and privileges on grounds that we will otherwise be victims. Victims are victims because they are weaker than those seen as victimizing them. The unspoken correlate of such arguments is that women are, in fact, the weaker vessel, and that we cannot stand on our own taking full responsibility for our actions. It is *because* I see women and men as equal that I cannot accept arguments from collective victimization. Some individual women are victims as some individual men are victims, and protections must be constructed accordingly. Arguments for protections and exemptions from responsibility on grounds of what amounts to a collective victim status, however, negate and undermine the collective and individual equality of women.

State Interest in the Fetus

The question of the personhood of the fetus is irrelevant to that of judicial intervention in pregnancy. By extension so, too, is the question of the treatment of the fetus as a separate patient, although in my view it is no more than a recognition of reality, whatever rights that patient may or may not be deemed under the law to have.

Even were the fetus to be recognized as a full person before the law, the ordinary protections of one person, the woman, against medical intervention or confinement for the sole benefit of another would still exist. If they apply with respect to aid to those already born and physically independent of the prospective donor, they will certainly apply with respect to aid to those located physically within another.

The Commission report raises the fact that the fetus has not been recognized to have the independent legal or constitutional rights of a person under the law. The woman is seen from this perspective by the report as having no legal obligation to undergo intervention since there is, in effect, no rights-endowed legal person whom she has an obligation not to harm. The report goes on to say that no third party can "volunteer to defend the 'rights' of a being that has no legal existence."

Many questions are raised by this approach.

The Supreme Court of Canada, in the Morgentaler decision, recognized a state interest in the fetus. The decision of the Court and the opinions of all but one Justice made no distinction between levels of advancement. Instances of judicial intervention in pregnancy have in any case for the most part arisen in later pregnancy.

Since such a state interest in the fetus does exist, one wonders what meaning it would have were that interest not to be of any force or effect even when a child is about to be born or is viable and the removal of the mother's access to drugs or alcohol or so very routine a medical procedure as a Caesarian section would be sufficient to save his or her life and health. If an interest exists it must have application in some set of circumstances. If that interest were not applicable in these extreme circumstances it would be applicable in no conceivable circumstances which involved a conflict with the woman carrying the child.

Since the Morgentaler case focussed on abortion, which does indeed involve a conflict between the mother and the child *en ventre sa mère*, it is precisely in the welfare of the fetus in the event of some measure of conflict with the mother herself that the Court saw the state to have an interest, rather than in some conflict with another party, such as some individual committing assault on the mother or some corporate entity polluting the available drinking water with teratogenic effects on the fetus.

To argue, then, that a woman in principle has the unlimited right to endanger her fetus in any way she wishes at any stage before birth and that no third party, which would include the state, can defend the fetus is to argue that the Court, in finding a state interest in the fetus, had enunciated an absurdity, which I doubt.

The Question of Criminalization

I do not see sufficient reason for the recommendation that unwanted medical treatment and other interferences or threatened interferences with the physical autonomy of pregnant women be recognized explicitly under the *Criminal Code* as criminal assault. Making an action an offence under the *Criminal Code* implies that the action is unequivocally and clearly repugnant to the Canadian body politic, so much so that other remedies are neither sufficient to control it nor capable of a sufficient degree of symbolic censure. One must ask, then, whether all intervention in pregnancy fulfils those conditions.

First, as I have argued above, intervention in pregnancy under some very limited circumstances is not unequivocally repugnant to all members of Canadian society on either the symbolic or the practical level. Second, it appears to me that intervention in pregnancy can be and now is effectively controlled by more moderate and gender-neutral means. Third, there are internal difficulties with the recommendation itself.

One would assume that what is being suggested is that intervention without benefit of judicial warrant be criminalized. Judicial intervention itself could not, of course, be criminalized, since a judge cannot be charged or penalized for decisions he or she makes on the bench. To seek sanctions against judges for reaching particular decisions would strike at the roots of the independence of the judiciary and hence of the rule of law.

That a person has the right to refuse invasive treatment or detention by a physician or other professional is accepted both in ethics and in law. Protections already exist. The Commission has been told that the main remedy in the case of non-consensual medical intervention is in the form of *tort* law, claims of civil damages when suit is brought by the claimant. Malpractice is a parallel instance. One may ask whether the criminal sanctions with respect to assault would also already apply. They may; if so, their focus is the protection of persons, not of women as a separate group.

It is unclear to me why intervention in pregnancy would be more heinous than any other sort of medical or social/psychological intervention without consent. If it is at the same level of seriousness, then I do not see why it should be singled out so that a different and more severe set of sanctions should apply. Non-consensual intervention in a situation which is by definition confined to women is not more invasive than intervention in others which could occur in both men and women, such as kidney failure or removal of bone marrow for transplantation. An argument that confinement of or surgery on women is more serious than confinement or surgery which pertains to both sexes would be discriminatory; such an argument would privilege women on grounds of their sex and hence deny equality. I therefore cannot see justification for making the offence and the sanctions different in kind from those pertaining to all medical procedures or other interventions.

Even the criminalization of intervention in pregnancy would not remove the possibility of judicial intervention. In judicial intervention, it is the judge, not the physician or other professional, who is the prime actor, mandating the actions of others. A judge can authorize police to search premises or to seize property — or remove children — for sufficient cause. A judge can also authorize detention for certain grave reasons. These activities, without such authorization, would be criminal. Criminalization of medical and other forms of intervention would therefore affect only the activities of doctors or other professionals acting on their own, not judicial review and intervention itself. If the present sanctions are adequate deterrents to professionals' acting on their own, and if judicial intervention can take place whatever the sanctions, I can see no practical effect of a new measure of criminalization.

Nor does the number of instances of judicially mandated intervention in pregnancy seem to present sufficient concrete cause for concern. The small handful of cases which have come to appeal in Canada, and the fact that they have often been overturned, would seem to suggest that the present system is functioning to discourage judicial intervention in pregnancy. If the present system seems to be producing the outcomes desired by the Commission report, and if there is no evidence of an epidemic of such interventions, let alone of interventions for less than grave cause, I do not see any practical reason for an escalation of sanctions or for altering the judicial modes by which decisions are reached.

I grant that the workings of the Canadian judicial system may be imperfect, as the workings of any system are imperfect. If, however, we were to assume that all courts would make oppressive, biased or erroneous decisions, and that women require protection from them by removing from the courts the capacity to review and decide such questions, we cast into doubt the entire system our society has created for the resolution of disputes and harm-causing ambiguity with no viable replacement.

Nor is the argument from the claim that medical or judicial judgements may err, citing one selected case, convincing. To take the possibility of error as an argument for never acting upon expert advice under any circumstances whatever is an extreme which would paralyze all social action. Our own report in another place has made the point that all of medicine carries some level of risk. Physicians offer expertise, not omniscience. The same is true of judges. In this they are like all human beings; beyond this they bear the same heavy responsibility as all those in positions of particular social trust.

On these questions as in all others within the body politic, within medicine and within the social services, evidence must be examined, prudence and caution exercised, but some degree of uncertainty is simply a reality of the human condition. It does not absolve us as a society, or the judges who act as the arbiters for our society under grave circumstances, of the responsibility to weigh what can be known of fact, expert advice and concern, to take care that any intervention will avoid doing serious or disproportionate harm to any party, and then to make decisions. Argument that those delegated by society should absent themselves entirely from doing so because of the possibility of error would be, were this accepted in principle and universally applied, to abdicate all active and governmental or custodial forms of human social responsibility. If it would be absurd to apply it universally, one may question the applicability of the argument to this one field.

It appears to me to be more reasonable to accept that judicial review may, in very rare and serious cases and with all due caution and attention to interests and evidence, take place at the time the question arises, before the decision on whether or not to take action is made. It should, however, be very clear that the ordinary protections against non-consensual intervention apply in cases of pregnancy as in all others.

Social Context

A woman's social context can certainly dispose toward the sorts of conflict we are considering, so it is largely through the social context that we as a society can seek to prevent them.

It seems that the majority of cases in which these conflicts arise are associated with poverty. It has been alleged by some (and is implied as a distinct possibility in the text of the Commission report) that the high proportion of cases of judicial intervention in pregnancy which involve the poor and members of visible minorities is due to racism and class discrimination in the medical and judicial systems. This is easy enough to assert, and carries a potent political impact. We as a Commission have not, however, been given a fully documented social analysis of such cases, including adequate evidence corroborating bias. We have not seen, for instance, a retrospective random or universal sample study of judicial decisions rendered to middle-class/working-class as compared with poor women, or white and visible minority women. I would not, as a social scientist, say that such bias has been demonstrated. There may well be individual judges whose outlook is biased; this must be dealt with on that individual level. The remedy, however, is neither a restructuring of the jurisdiction of the courts nor an attribution of bias to the entire judicial system.

Applying Occam's razor, looking for the simplest explanation for the available data, it is more probable that it is poverty which is the root cause. Poverty is associated with the low levels of education and consequent low awareness of the importance of prenatal care, the low recourse to the health care system, the fear of complex, high-tech procedures and the alienation and addictions which tend to foster these conflicts. While in Canada the majority of poor women are not members of visible minorities, minority women are over-represented among the poor for their proportion in the general population, an inequity which must be remedied on its own terms. It is not necessary to assume — or to imply — that all doctors and judges who have mandated supervision or treatment for poor women are biased.

There is, moreover, no evidence that any causal relationship should even be suggested between the "religious convictions ... cultural beliefs ... or other deeply held values or personal beliefs" of Aboriginal women and women of colour on the one hand and cases of judicial intervention in pregnancy related to the "refusal to accept surgical or other medical treatment or to follow medical advice" on the other.

First, there are no grounds on which to make such a collective connection. Aboriginal women and women of colour come from highly diverse social, ethnic, religious and other traditions, since their ancestors were born in lands spanning not only the wide expanse of Canada but the globe itself. If there are groups who do hold refusal of medical treatment and advice as a value, we have not had evidence of it brought before us. Even if a specific group or groups did hold such a view, however, it could not be generalized to all Aboriginal women or women of colour. Each group and individual should be able to speak for themselves in this regard.

Second, we have had no concrete instances brought before us of judicial review or intervention in a case of refusal on principle or on grounds of culture, deeply held personal values or belief. It is certainly hypothetically possible that instances of such refusal might arise, parallel to the refusal of Jehovah's Witnesses to accept blood transfusions or of Christian Scientists to seek various sorts of medical technology. There may also be some women who wish to give birth within a "women's circle," with a group-chosen "wise woman" or unlicensed midwife rather than a medically credentialled practitioner. It may be that the defence of such latter groups against feared requirements of professional medical supervision is related to some significant segment of the feminist concerns which dominate discussion of this issue. No cases of judicial intervention on grounds of culture-based values or principle, however, whatever the ethnic or other context of the woman, appeared in the evidence with which we have been presented.

Third, as the report acknowledges, cases of judicial intervention in pregnancy usually involve abuse of drugs, alcohol or both. Still others involve often-related activities such as prostitution. Both substance abuse and prostitution carry a serious risk of violence and disease (such as AIDS, the toxic effects of cocaine, or the effects of alcohol on the brain) which damage and can kill both mother and child. Alcohol and drug addiction or prostitution are not part of the "cultural values" or "religious beliefs" of any Aboriginal or other visible minority groups, whatever the enmeshment of those dysfunctional behaviours with social conditions.

The testimony we as a Commission heard from Native groups emphasized the great and positive cosmic value placed on women and on their bearing and bringing forth of life as part of the work of the Creator. Many other groups hold equally positive views of the importance of a woman's nurturance of her child, including before birth. Many Aboriginal and other ethnocultural groups are engaged in movements to revitalize aspects of their traditional cultures, bringing them to bear on their contemporary lives by integrating today's realities with a strong sense of identity, dignity and values arising from centuries of experience understood through elements of their own tradition. One of the many purposes of this revitalization is to heal individuals affected by precisely those same sorts of behaviour which give rise to judicial review. Women, whatever their culture or ethnic background, do not "choose a particular course of action," refusing treatment or refusing to follow medical advice which would divert them from engaging in the substance abuse and prostitution which have in actual cases drawn the scrutiny of the courts, on grounds of their "deeply held values or personal beliefs."

The ethnic or cultural origin of a woman is therefore not a root factor in her behaviour in any case of judicial intervention in pregnancy of which I am aware. The courts have not scrutinized cases where rejection was based on principle, and those cases in which the courts have intervened have concerned dysfunctional behaviour unrelated to and indeed antithetical to the cultural, religious and other beliefs of all women, including Aboriginal women and women of colour. If some Aboriginal or visible minority women have been among the tiny handful of Canadian cases of judicial intervention in pregnancy, it is due to disproportionate rates of marginalization and poverty, not to the cultural or religious beliefs or values of the groups from which these specific women come.

I would agree with the Commission report that judicial intervention does not change the circumstances that bring about the attempts to intervene, or at least it does not change them directly. That the Commission report would object to judicial intervention in pregnancy on those grounds seems to me to be somewhat inconsistent, however. That an approach may not cure a problem, only circumventing it and changing its practical outcome, seems elsewhere to be presented in this report as acceptable and constructive. Circumvention and outcome alteration are, after all, precisely the modality of several of the approaches to infertility which this Commission accepts, with due safeguards. The social context is, of course, very different, but the logical structure of the approach is the same.

I would disagree, moreover, with the report's view that intervention provides no solution. Any solution of such cases will probably be imperfect — indeed, non-intervention is itself concerned with avoidance of engagement, not with offering a solution of any sort. The very point, however, of those rare instances in which intervention is appropriate is to "create the social conditions and support that help to ensure a successful pregnancy and health outcome for both the woman and the child."

For example, a woman required to reside for a period of time in a treatment centre, well-fed, with access to counselling, peer support and referral to services to upgrade her education and prospects of employment, and free of the ready availability of the substances to which she is addicted (and which may elsewhere be pressed upon her by her companions) has precisely those social conditions and supports conducive to a "healthy outcome," if this is taken to mean the withdrawal of the woman from drug dependency, her reception of other forms of prenatal and perinatal care, and the absence of mental and/or other permanent disabilities in the child. The supports would indeed be temporary; the woman could later return to a dysfunctional pattern of life if she chose to. Yet there would be concrete benefits, not only to the child but to the woman. The child would not have been harmed; that particular systemically devastating source of harm would have been avoided and, for that child at least, could not recur. The woman herself would have been given the opportunity, the supports and the access to resources to choose to make a definitive and permanent change in her mode of life toward social and economic independence; she would also herself benefit from the fact that the child for whom she would have maternal responsibility and care would be unimpaired by the multiple severe disabilities which are the reason for the concern which gives rise to judicial intervention.

Middle-class and working-class women of all races and cultures in this country tend to have had knowledge of and relatively ready access to prenatal care, and to have been sufficiently aware of the need to avoid substance abuse and other harmful behaviour, particularly during pregnancy, that they would have been unlikely to have come to a judge's attention in the first place. If poverty is associated with the root conditions for much of the tragedy and conflict in society, the fact that the poor are those whose consequence-ridden turmoil comes before judges is precisely what one would expect.

The effective remedy to the problem, then, would lie in combatting poverty, not in removing the capacity of judges to review and adjudicate the conflicts of the poor.

Prevention

If, then, we seek to avoid these conflicts, the place to start is in outreach to women in low-income and any other vulnerable groups. There are many possible strategies, many or all of which could be used in concert. They dovetail with the concerns which have emerged over and over again in our work as a Commission.

Family life education is the first point of prevention, transmitting a strong awareness of responsibility, of pregnancy and of prenatal care and birth long before a girl or woman becomes pregnant.

Outreach to women (and men) with substance addictions is already a priority, but more is needed. In a sense, any social and economic and job training program which gives people hope and a means of building a constructive life is, directly or indirectly, contributing to primary prevention of addictions and to rehabilitation of those who have been addicted.

If many poor women do not receive adequate prenatal care, even in this society in which care is universally offered, perhaps innovative strategies to reach them should be attempted. Public health departments are already engaged in much work of this kind. Public health consultations should be encouraged with a random sample of poor women from all groups at risk, with public health personnel, with anthropologists and sociologists, and with community groups; such consultations could perhaps give rise to new or improved ways of bringing mobile prenatal care, combined where appropriate with addiction treatment, in their own settings, cultures, and languages, to women who do not spontaneously seek out care in large hospital institutions or in stationary private medical offices.

Programs of this type would be helpful, not only to those who would be at risk of conflicts which could come to the point of judicial examination, but to all women at reproductive risk of any kind. They complement efforts to prevent or control STDs, to avoid adverse outcomes of pregnancy from any cause, and to further maternal and child care.

It is probable that no program can eliminate all situations of conflict. The principles we have discussed will, in rare instances, have to be brought into play. Judicial interventions in pregnancy and birth are nonetheless already very few; if, in our overall support for women, we can answer most needs before they reach the point of conflict, judicial review and intervention in pregnancy can in large degree be avoided.

Conclusion

The judiciary provides the final forum with the broadest scope and accepted legitimacy for the assessment and resolution of otherwise irresolvable dilemmas. For the hard cases which we are discussing, there is no superior mode of seeking, with the full range of testimony and expert advice, the real intent, consent and interests of the individual woman, even if these are placed prior to the recognized, affirmed and supported interests of the child within her. Some nightmarishly vast system of supervision of every pregnant woman would obviously be both repugnant and operationally impossible. It does not follow that rare cases cannot exist in which judicial intervention would be feasible, appropriate, and reasonable.

The unvaried assumption that a woman, because she is one of the class of women, must always be deemed to be fully and unambivalently certain at each given moment of what she intends and of its full implications, isolated from the context of her other expressions of intent, could well leave many individual women with the consequences having been allowed by default to abandon a positive intent under conditions of impairment or some other transitory state. So too would an assumption that, for broader reasons of the collective interests of women, even if a woman is not fully competent she must be treated as though she is. The same would be true of the opposite assumption that a woman, because she is a woman, should be taken solely at her word in such a moment, because she is so constrained by victimization, circumstance, and addiction that she is not responsible for the results of her actions and that those consequences, therefore, do not matter.

The women in such cases would then be left, not only with sorrow and guilt, but with a handicapped child. It is these women, not their doctors, not the members of hospital bioethics committees, nor yet the members of this Commission, who would have the burden of caring for their damaged children for what could be a lifetime, a burden which would be only partly alleviated by services provided by the state or by turning the children over for full-time state institutional care. The children would be left with those handicaps, not just as a burden, but as an overriding reality of life.

No system can guarantee that this would never occur. Only the availability of the objectivity of judicial assessment in cases of manifest ambivalence or impairment, however, will allow flexibility and sensitivity to individual women and their situations. If the wellbeing of a woman and the wellbeing, health and very life of a child depend upon that sensitivity, the absolutization of an approach which would preclude it would seem to me to be a deeply inadequate response.

Moreover, many of the arguments or recommendations against judicial intervention in pregnancy or for the imposition of criminal sanctions distinct from the ordinary, non-gender-related sanctions against non-consensual intervention are premised on assumptions which are, in my view, at odds with the fundamental principles of human equality and of full participation, irrespective of gender, in a free and democratic society. To accept them would ultimately be counterproductive for women and for children, and also for men. By identifying rights, protections and interests with membership in a group, such as the aggregate of women, rather than with universal human identity, responsibilities and protections, it would raise questions about the constitutional structures which underlie our polity itself, with implications which have yet to be examined.

For all these reasons, I see grave difficulties with, and would generally wish to discourage, overriding a woman's refusal of consent to surgical or behavioural intervention in pregnancy. Like my fellow Commissioners, I see every effort at prevention before these tragic situations arise as being the most constructive mode of approach. For both ethical and constitutional reasons, however, I see neither the absolute preclusion of judicial intervention in pregnancy nor the imposition of new sanctions distinguishing the protections of women from those of men as being justified.

Respect, Debate, and the Political Process

On most issues on which diverse opinions exist in society, the flourishing of human freedom, including the freedom to act according to those ideas, must be defended. This is fundamental to human dignity and welfare. There is a point, however, at which the life, welfare, and human dignity of human beings is at such serious risk that society is obliged to act in a universal fashion. It is on this principle, indeed, that we as a Commission have recommended prohibitions of such practices as preconception contracts or uses of technology which bear unacceptably high medical risks.

The majority of my expressions of dissent from our common report, therefore, have to do with the avoidance of absolutized single-perspective resolutions to complex dilemmas and the preservation of the legitimate freedoms of individuals and groups. The case of research on viable embryos, by contradistinction, appears to me to have such far-reaching and negative consequences, both for them and for society at large, that prohibition is the justified response.

In all of these cases, however, a common thread exists. When some, be they embryos, religious groups sponsoring education, women whose complex compulsions and ambivalences about their pregnancies may require judicial elucidation, or anyone else, are made objects subordinated to the collective or individual interests or opinions of others, there is ground for grave injustice, even when the intentions are good. It is better not to drive ahead in ways which, for some, place freedoms and welfare at serious risk or which obliterate those freedoms or that welfare altogether, even when benefit to some others might result or when those who hold a particular view might have the satisfaction of seeing their convictions implemented as universal practice. To do so would be, at its root, both a negation of human rights and, at worst, exploitation. The imposed narrowing of permissible opinion and practice, moreover, would reduce the variability out of which creative insights, adaptations and innovations come.

In a pluralistic society, there are many different views on all of these issues held by highly conscientious people of integrity. This is true among those who have intervened before our Commission; it is true within the

Commission itself. Those of my colleague Commissioners who take a different view from that expressed here would never, I am utterly certain, wish to see any form of negation of human rights or exploitation. On most subjects we are in overall agreement. Where we differ, we do so, not on our ethical principles, but on the conditions and relative priority of the application of them to specific situations, and on the probable results. We differ while sharing a complete and mutual personal warmth and respect.

It is important that this be explicitly stated, because so often the debate on issues of this importance and political controversy tends to slide from substantive toward *ad hominem* arguments, serving neither fairness to persons nor elucidation of the questions. It is one of the achievements of this Commission that questions of such substance have been investigated and debated to the point of final public presentation in an atmosphere of the quest for sound evidence and regard for both the views and the humanity of all. "In needful things, unity; in doubtful things, liberty; in all things, charity." This saying emerging from the Middle Ages is today no less wise.

It is for the Parliament and people of Canada, for the various jurisdictional levels concerned, and for the courts to read the arguments, assessing the persuasiveness of each in deciding the actions it is best for society to take.

References

1. *The Toronto Star*, Friday, August 20, 1993, p. A3

2. Expert Interdisciplinary Advisory Committee on Sexually Transmitted Diseases in Children and Youth (EIAC-STD) and the Federal/Provincial/ Territorial Working Group on Adolescent Reproductive Health: Guidelines for Sexual Health Education, Principle 3, Guidelines, Segment 6 (Pagination varies by printed format.)

3. Ibid.: Principle 2, First Paragraph

4. Ibid.: Principle 2, Second and Third Paragraphs

5. King, Alan J.C. et al.: *Canada Youth and AIDS Study*; Queen's University at Kingston, pp. 83, 85

6. Barnes, Alan: "Fewer Metro girls sexually active, 3-city poll finds"; *The Toronto Star*, Tuesday, November 24, 1992

7. King, op. cit.: pp. 18, 32-34

8. Santin, Sylvia, Gen. Ed.: *Fully Alive*; Maxwell Macmillan Canada, Don Mills, Ontario, 1988-1992

9. *Catechisme de L'Église Catholique*; (Français) Mame-Librairie Éditrice Vaticane, Paris, 1992, Sections 2357-9, p. 480; (Latin) Libreria Editrice Vaticana, Citta del Vaticano, 1992

10. Orton, M.J. and Rosenblatt, E.: *Sexual Health for Youth: Creating a Three-Sector Network in Ontario*; distributed by Planned Parenthood, Ontario; 1993, see particularly pp. 154-6. Dr. Orton is a Research Associate at the Faculty of Social Work, University of Toronto; the Faculty did not publish the study.

11. Zabin, Laurie Schwab, et al.: "The Baltimore Pregnancy Prevention Program for Urban Teenagers: I. How Did It Work?; II. What Did It Cost?"; in *Family Planning Perspectives*, Vol. 20, #4, July/August 1988, esp. p. 186

12. Zabin, Laurie S., et al.: "Evaluation of a Pregnancy Prevention Program for Urban Teenagers"; in *Family Planning Perspectives*, Vol. 18, #3, May/June 1986, esp. pp. 119 and 123

13. Zabin: 1988, p.185

14. The segments of the Commission report discussed are to be found principally in Part Two, Chapter 12, "Adoption" (Access to Adoption and An Adoption System in the Best Interests of Children); Chapter 15, "Assisted Insemination" (Access to Treatment, Alternatives to the Medical Setting, Familial and Societal Implications of DI, and Recommendation #4 under Assisted Insemination Services); and Chapter 16, "IVF" (Decision-Making About IVF, Access to Treatment, and Recommendation #16, Impermissible Barriers to Treatment).

15. Bischofberger, Erwin; Member, National Ethics Committee, Sweden, Personal Communication

16. Bischofberger, Erwin B., J. Lindsten and U. Rosenqvist: "Sweden", in Dorothy C. Wertz and John C. Fletcher, eds.: *Ethics and Human Genetics: A Cross-Cultural Perspective*; Springer-Verlag, Berlin, New York; 1989; pp. 339-352

17. As examples from a vast literature:

> Featherstone, Darin R.; Bert P. Cundick; Larry C. Jensen: "Difference in School Behaviour and Achievement Between Children from Intact, Reconstituted and Single-Parent Families"; in *Adolescence*, Vol. 27, #105, Spring 1992

> Capaldi, Deborah: "Step Families: An American Perspective"; in *Family Policy Bulletin*, June 1992, Family Policy Studies Centre, London, England

> Bronfenbrenner, Urie: "Principles for the Healthy Growth and Development of Children"; in L. Eugene Arnold, ed.: *Parents, Children and Change*, pp. 243-9, Lexington Books, D.C. Heath and Co., Lexington, Mass., 1985

> Bronfenbrenner, Urie: "Effects of Divorce on Mothers and Children", ibid., pp. 424-6

18. Decima Research: *Social Values and Attitudes of Canadians Toward New Reproductive Technologies*, 1993; Figure 24, p. 85

19. Ibid.: Figure 11, p. 36

20. Commission report: Part Two, Chapter 15, Assisted Insemination, Access to Treatment

21. Sadler, T.W.: *Langman's Medical Embryology*, 6th ed.; Williams & Wilkins, Baltimore, 1990; p. 29

22. Erickson, R.P.: "Gene Expression in Preimplantation Embryos", p. 204; in Yury Verlinsky and Anver Kuliev: *Preimplantation Genetics*, Plenum Press, New York, 1990, pp. 203-211

23. Decima Research: *Social Values and Attitudes of Canadians Toward New Reproductive Technologies*; A Report to The Royal Commission on New Reproductive Technologies, May 1993 Draft; Section: Fetal Tissue Research, Table 33; p. 83

24. Ibid.; Section: Fetal Tissue Research; p. 82

25. Reed, Christopher: "US Court Upholds Individual's Right to Decide in Ruling that Dead Man's Sperm May Be Used to Father Children"; in *The Guardian*, Monday, June 21 1993

26. No Byline: "Ruling Left Intact in Sperm Bequest"; AP, *New York Times National*, Sunday, Sept. 5, 1993

27. Sadler: op. cit., p. 41

28. Erickson: op. cit., pp. 206-7

29. Morgan, Russ; Larry Stock; James Cavanaugh: "You're Nobody 'Till Somebody Loves You"; Southern Music Publishing Co., New York, 1944

30. See also Daly, Kerry J., and Michael P. Sobol: *Adoption in Canada*, University of Guelph, 1993, pp. 63-4

31. *Globe and Mail* coverage in reverse date order, most recent status first:

>   Campbell, Murray: "Court Rules Against Surrogate Mother of Child Conceived Outside Womb" (California Court of Appeals): Wed., Oct. 9, 1991, p. A15

>   Campbell, Murray: "Woman Loses Bid to Be Parent: Child Not Genetically Linked to Surrogate Mother"; Oct. 23, 1990, p. A14

>   No Byline: "US judge will rule Monday in bitter surrogate-mother case"; Thurs., Oct. 18, 1990, p. A20

>   No Byline: "Custody trial told of surrogate's boasts: Woman expected millions, witness says"; Wed., Oct. 17, p. A13

>   Campbell, Murray: "Treat surrogate as natural parent, custody case told: Woman giving birth has rights despite absence of genetic link, ethics expert says"; Wed., Oct. 10, 1990, p. A9

>   Campbell, Murray: "US case stays unresolved: Genetic parents awarded temporary custody of infant"; Fri., Sept. 28, 1990, p. A12

>   Campbell, Murray: "Premature baby sets a legal precedent: California judge delays hearing for a week as surrogate mother sues her employers for custody"; Sat., Sept. 22, 1990, p. A10

No Byline: "US court to decide on custody of fetus: Definition of 'parent' could be raised"; Tues., Sept. 18, 1990, p. A1

32. Bischofberger, Erwin; Member, National Ethics Committee, Sweden, Personal Communication

33. Bischofberger, Erwin B., J. Lindsten and U. Rosenqvist: op. cit., pp. 339-352

34. Daly, op. cit., p. 60

35. Bischofberger et al.: op. cit.

Glossary*

♦

A

AFP: alpha-fetoprotein. See **MSAFP**.

AI: See **assisted insemination**.

AID: An abbreviation for **assisted insemination** by donor. To avoid confusion with **AIDS**, the term **donor insemination (DI)** is used.

AIDS: Acquired immunodeficiency syndrome. A disease defined by a set of signs and symptoms, caused by the **human immunodeficiency virus (HIV)**, transmitted through body fluids (e.g., **semen**, blood) and characterized by compromised immune response.

AIH: Assisted insemination homologous. Term for **assisted insemination** when **sperm** from the woman's husband or partner is used. Also known as *assisted insemination by husband*.

Adhesions: Rubbery bands of scar tissue resulting from the body's attempt to repair damage caused by **endometriosis**, by surgery, or by previous infections. Such bands, if in the **fallopian tubes** and **ovaries**, can obstruct the tubes and prevent **fertilization**. Adhesions may be removed by a minor surgical procedure, but major surgery is necessary to eliminate dense and fibrous adhesions.

Alpha-fetoprotein: See **MSAFP**.

---

* Boldface terms used in these definitions are also defined in this glossary.

Alzheimer disease: A progressive, abnormal cognitive impairment, manifested as a loss of memory, language, and other intellectual capabilities, accompanied by a general diminishment of competence and resulting ultimately in death.

Amenorrhea: The absence of menstruation (which usually occurs from puberty until menopause) in a woman of menstrual age.   In primary amenorrhea, the woman has never had a menstrual period by this age.   In secondary amenorrhea, menstruation stops after having started.   When menstruation is irregular or scanty, rather than absent, the term **oligomenorrhea** is used.   There are many causes of amenorrhea and oligomenorrhea, some of which may be associated with **infertility**.

Amniocentesis: A procedure in which a needle is used to withdraw a small amount of the amniotic fluid that surrounds the fetus in the **uterus**.   **Ultrasound** monitoring is used to guide the needle through the woman's abdomen into the amniotic sac.   The fluid can be tested for **alpha-fetoprotein**.   In addition, since the amniotic fluid contains fetal cells, these cells can be grown in cell culture and analyzed for a variety of genetic disorders.   This takes two to four weeks.   Amplification of the genetic material can shorten the time needed to obtain results.   The test is usually done at 15 to 16 weeks' **gestation** but can be done as early as 12 weeks.

Amnion: The membrane that forms a fluid-filled sac surrounding and protecting the **embryo** or **fetus**.

Anencephaly: A **neural tube defect** resulting in severe lethal deformity of the brain, caused when the neural tube fails to close.

Aneuploidy: Any deviation from the usual number of **chromosomes** (46 in human beings).   For specific examples, see **Down syndrome**; **Turner syndrome**.

Anorexia nervosa: An abnormal aversion to food.   Individuals with the condition have an eating pattern that leads to dangerous weight loss.   When a female's body weight falls below a critical level, **ovulation** and menstruation may fail to start or they may cease.   **Fertility** may be affected.

Anovulation: Absence of **ovulation**.

Antibody: A protein produced by white blood cells in response to the presence of a specific foreign substance (antigen) in the body, with which it interacts.   See **antisperm antibodies**.

Antisperm antibodies: Antibodies to **sperm** found in either member of an infertile couple, which may interfere with sperm movement or ability to interact with the egg.   They may be present in the reproductive tract fluids of the female, or the serum or seminal fluid of the male.

Assisted insemination: See **AIH**; **donor insemination**; **IVF**; **intrauterine insemination**.

Assisted reproduction: See **DOST**; **donor insemination**; **embryo transfer**; **GIFT**; **IVF**; **ZIFT**.

Autosome: A **chromosome** other than a sex chromosome. Human beings have 44 autosomes (22 pairs).

Azoospermia: Absence of living **sperm** in the **semen**; may be caused by congenital abnormality or by an infection-related blockage of the duct that carries sperm, or by environment- or occupation-related impairment in sperm production. See also **oligospermia**.

B

Blastocyst: A fluid-filled sphere of cells — a stage of development of the **zygote**. A small cluster of cells in the centre of the sphere gives rise to the **embryo**, and the outer wall of the sphere gives rise to the **placenta** and supporting membranes.

Bromocriptine: A synthetic compound that interferes with the **pituitary** gland's ability to secrete **prolactin**, a **hormone** that effects **ovulation**. It may be prescribed for an infertile woman whose pituitary makes too much prolactin.

C

CVS: See **chorionic villus sampling**.

Caesarian section: (also Cesarean) Surgical delivery of a baby through an abdominal and uterine incision. Also called *C-section*.

Cervical mucus: Mucus produced by the **cervix** that undergoes complex changes in its physical properties in response to changing **hormone** levels during the **menstrual cycle**. The cervical mucus guards the upper reproductive tract against the entry of bacteria and against **sperm**, except for the days around **ovulation**. Around ovulation, the mucus becomes clear and watery and the number of antisperm white blood cells in the mucus drops. These changes aid the sperm in surviving and in moving up the female reproductive tract toward the egg. Vaginal infections may adversely affect the cervical mucus, creating an unfriendly environment for the sperm. For testing with respect to **infertility**, see **sperm-mucus cross test**.

Cervix: The lower portion of the **uterus** that opens into the **vagina**.

Chimera: An individual whose cells derive from different **zygotes**. They may arise naturally, as where blood-forming cells are exchanged *in utero* between dizygotic (produced by two separate eggs and sperm) twins, or they may be deliberately engineered in animals. A chimera differs from a **mosaic**, in which the two genetically different cell lines arise by a change in the genetic material of a cell within an individual, or in culture.

Chlamydia: The bacteria *Chlamydia trachomatis* causes a common **sexually transmitted disease**. In women, infection may cause **pelvic inflammatory disease (PID)** of the upper genital tract, leading to **infertility**. It is difficult to cure and as well as causing infertility it may cause an increased risk of **ectopic pregnancy**, stillbirth, premature birth, and eye infection and pneumonia in a resulting infant. In males, chlamydia may cause inflammation of the **urethra**, which, if untreated, can reach the epididymis, where **sperm** are stored.

Chorionic villus sampling (CVS) or chorionic biopsy: A procedure for obtaining fetal tissue. A small amount of chorion (outer membrane surrounding the **embryo** and **fetus**) tissue is removed through the pregnant woman's abdominal wall or **cervix**, using a catheter (small tube) under **ultrasound** guidance. Like **amniocentesis**, CVS can be used to detect biochemical, **DNA**, and chromosomal problems, and for sex determination, but it cannot detect **neural tube defects**. CVS can be done as early as the eighth or ninth week of pregnancy, and the results are usually known within a week (although confirmation after cell culture is advisable).

Chromosomal disorder: A disorder resulting from an addition or deletion of an entire chromosome (**aneuploidy**) or part of one. For examples of aneuploidy, see **Down syndrome**; **Turner syndrome**.

Chromosome: Thread-like structure in the nucleus of a cell, containing **DNA**, the hereditary material (i.e., **genes**). The normal number of chromosomes in humans is 46: 22 pairs of **autosomes** and two **sex chromosomes**.

Clinical trial: An evaluation of a new intervention, treatment (e.g., a drug), or procedure (e.g., a surgical approach) to see how well it works, as compared to known treatments or procedures or to no treatment. Ideally, patients would be assigned at random to one group or the other (randomized trial), but this sometimes may raise difficult logistical or ethical problems. A clinical practice is said to be *non-validated* where its safety and efficacy have not been established.

Clomiphene citrate: A fertility drug used primarily in women with menstrual irregularity. It is like **estrogen** and binds to estrogen receptors in the brain, thereby fooling the **pituitary** into releasing the

hormones necessary for **ovulation**. Its possible adverse effects include dry **cervical mucus**, an increased risk of **multiple pregnancy**, ovarian enlargement, and, sometimes, **infertility** by affecting the woman's **menstrual cycle**. It is also used in *in vitro* **fertilization** as an **ovulatory stimulant**.

Cloning: The process of producing a group of cells (clones), all genetically identical to the original ancestral cell. This may be achieved by asexual reproduction (without union of egg and **sperm**), as in plant cuttings. Another type of cloning is achieved by nucleus substitution (also called *nuclear transplantation*). The nucleus is removed from an unfertilized egg cell and replaced with a new nucleus taken from a donor embryonic cell. A third method, also used in agriculture, is by embryo division. In **gene** technology, cloning is the process of producing multiple copies of a single gene or segment of **DNA**. See also **genetic engineering**.

Conceptus: A fertilized egg and, later, the **embryo**, **fetus**, **placenta**, and membranes. After the egg has been fertilized, the cells begin to divide. Some of these cells will become the embryo. Other cells will become part of the membranes and placenta that nourish the developing embryo.

Congenital anomaly: An anomaly that is present at birth. It may be caused by: genetic factors (chromosomal or gene defects); injury by infectious disease during pregnancy (e.g., rubella); other environmental factors, such as drugs (e.g., thalidomide), chemicals (e.g., mercury), or radiation; or combinations of hereditary and environmental factors. The majority of congenital anomalies are of unknown cause.

Conjugated estriol: A mixture of the sodium salts of the sulphate esters of estrogenic substances, principally estrone and equilin, that are of the type excreted by pregnant mares, occurring as a buff-coloured, amorphous powder; the actions and uses are those of **estrogens** administered orally.

Contraception: A means of preventing conception (**fertilization** of an egg by a **sperm**). For possible effects on **fertility**, see **IUD**; **oral contraceptive**. See also **sterility**, surgical.

Corpus luteum: Literally, *yellow body*. **Follicle** cells left behind in the **ovary** when the egg is released. Its maintenance and function depend on stimulation by **luteinizing hormone**, and it produces **hormones** itself, the most important of which is **progesterone**. Progesterone prepares the uterine lining for implantation of the egg. If pregnancy does not occur, the corpus luteum regresses and menstruation occurs.

Cryopreservation: Preservation of tissues such as **sperm** or **zygotes** by freezing them at extremely low temperatures in liquid nitrogen. For example, in *in vitro* **fertilization**, more eggs may be fertilized than can be implanted. These "extra" zygotes may be placed in serum and a cryoprotectant (a substance that helps to protect tissues when frozen for storage). The tissue may be used later, after thawing.

Cystic fibrosis: An autosomal **recessive** disorder with variable expressivity, which is most common in Caucasians. The secretory glands do not function normally, and abnormal mucus builds up in the lungs and digestive system, which can lead to death in early adulthood. The **gene** has been mapped and the missing protein identified. It can be detected prenatally in the majority of cases.

Cytomegalovirus: A virus that may be transmitted sexually. The effects are host-specific (i.e., depending on the age and the immune status of the infected person, the virus can cause a variety of clinical symptoms). A pregnant woman who is infected may infect her **fetus**, causing stillbirth or growth retardation and nervous system defects in the resulting child.

D

DES: Diethylstilbestrol. A synthetic **estrogen**, given to pregnant women, mostly in the 1960s, to prevent **miscarriage**. It was not proven effective in preventing miscarriage and has been found to cause cancer and genital tract and uterine anomalies, and thus decreased **fertility**, in some individuals exposed *in utero*.

DI: See **Donor insemination**.

DNA: Deoxyribonucleic acid. The genetic material contained in the **chromosomes** and mitochondria, which codes for hereditary characteristics. It consists of a double spiral, in which the two strands are held together by substances called *nucleotides*. There are four nucleotides, and each can pair with only one other; therefore, the sequence on one strand is complementary to that on the other.

DNA probes: See **gene probe**.

DOST: Direct ovum and sperm transfer. A technique of **assisted reproduction** in which retrieved eggs and **sperm** prepared by washing are transferred through the **cervix** into a woman's **uterus** using a catheter (small tube).

Danazol: A synthetic derivative of the male hormone **testosterone** used in treatment of **endometriosis** in women. It often has masculinizing effects.

Deoxyribonucleic acid: See **DNA**.

Diabetes mellitus: A disturbance in body metabolism that causes abnormal elevation of blood sugar levels and other destructive effects. In men, diabetes may cause retrograde ejaculation (see **ejaculate**). See also **fetal tissue transplantation** for experimental treatment of the juvenile type.

Diethylstilbestrol: See **DES**.

Dilation and curettage (D&C): An operation that involves stretching the cervical opening (dilation) to scrape out the lining of the **uterus** (curettage). It may be done, for example, after a **miscarriage** or to terminate a pregnancy. It may increase the risk of **infertility** through infection or scarring.

Direct ovum and sperm transfer: See **DOST**.

Dominant: Each body cell has two copies of the **gene** at any specific locus, one inherited from the mother and the other inherited from the father. A dominant gene is one that is expressed, regardless of the nature of its companion gene. A person with a dominant condition will have inherited it from one of the parents unless the person has a new **mutation**. Each child of a person with a dominant condition will get either the normal or the abnormal gene and so has one chance in two of being affected. Compare with **recessive**.

Donor insemination: Introduction of **sperm** into a woman's **vagina** for the purpose of conception (**fertilization** of an egg). If it is put into the **cervix** it is called intracervical insemination. The insemination is timed to fall just before or on the expected day of **ovulation** (egg release) to maximize the chance of fertilization.   Intravaginal insemination is technically simple and can be done without medical aid (sometimes called **self-insemination**). However, there may be a risk of infectious disease. See **donor screening**. For a more complex method of insemination, see **intrauterine insemination**.

Donor screening, microbial: Screening of **sperm** or egg donors by direct culture of the **semen** or **cervix**, or by a blood test of the donor, depending on the infectious disease being screened, in order to protect the recipient and the resulting child. These infectious diseases or disease-causing organisms include **chlamydia, cytomegalovirus, gonorrhoea**, hepatitis, **herpes**, **HIV, mycoplasma**, and **syphilis**. For HIV, this screening will not detect newly infected donors. To do this, the sperm or fertilized eggs must be frozen and the donor retested for HIV in six months.

Down syndrome (trisomy 21): A chromosomal disorder caused by the presence of an extra **chromosome** 21. The frequency of the disorder increases with greater maternal age, beginning to rise more sharply at around age 35.

Duchenne muscular dystrophy: A severe disorder that begins during early childhood and leads to progressive wasting of the leg and pelvic muscles, heart disease, and death by early adulthood.

E

Ectopic pregnancy: A pregnancy that occurs when a fertilized egg implants and begins development outside the **uterus**, usually in a **fallopian tube**. Frequency is increased in **in vitro fertilization** pregnancies. Ectopic pregnancies are more likely to occur in women with tubal damage and in women who have had certain **sexually transmitted diseases**. Ectopic pregnancies end in **miscarriage** because tissues other than the uterus cannot support a **fetus**. If the ectopic pregnancy ruptures, this may result in a medical emergency and permanent tubal damage.

Egg donor: A woman who donates eggs to another woman. This may be a healthy volunteer or one undergoing sterilization, **hysterectomy**, or **egg retrieval** for her own reproduction. Such an individual is the genetic mother of any offspring resulting from **fertilization** of the egg.

Egg recipient: This might be a woman with no accessible eggs or one who is a carrier for an autosomal **dominant** or **X-linked** condition but who is capable of gestating. The donated eggs could be fertilized with **sperm** from the egg recipient's partner before implantation into her **uterus**.

Egg retrieval: Removal of one or more mature eggs from the **ovary** after administration of an **ovulatory stimulant** for **in vitro fertilization**, using **ultrasound** guidance, or for **gamete intrafallopian transfer**, using **laparoscopy**.

Ejaculate: The seminal fluid expelled by ejaculation and normally containing **sperm**. Ejaculation involves a two-part spinal reflex: first the emission phase, when the semen moves into the **urethra**, and then the ejaculation proper, when it is propelled out of the urethra at the time of orgasm. Ejaculation is said to be *retrograde* when **semen** flows into the bladder rather than through the penis. When a man has a spinal cord injury, electrical stimulation of the nerve that controls ejaculation may be used to obtain semen for **assisted insemination**.

Embryo: In humans, the term used to describe the organism during the stages of growth from about the second through the eighth week after **fertilization**. During this period, the brain, eyes, heart, upper and lower limbs, and other organs are formed. From fertilization up to this point (14 days after fertilization) the organism is referred to as the **zygote**. From eight weeks to birth it is termed a **fetus**.

Embryo donation: Transfer of a **zygote** to a woman or couple for **implantation**. This may occur where more zygotes are created *in vitro* than can be used in a treatment cycle or where frozen zygotes are no longer needed by those who created them.

Embryo flushing: See **uterine lavage**.

Embryo freezing: See **cryopreservation**.

Embryo transfer or replacement: The procedure by which one or more **zygotes** obtained from *in vitro* **fertilization** or by **uterine lavage** are placed, or replaced, into the **uterus** of a woman, using a catheter (small tube) passed through her **cervix**. For specific techniques, see **GIFT**; **ZIFT**.

Endocrine system: Network of organs, including the adrenals, pancreas, **pituitary**, **ovaries**, **testes**, and parathyroid glands, which produce and secrete **hormones** directly into the bloodstream for transport to specific target organs, where they exert their effects.

Endometrial biopsy: Removal (for subsequent microscopic examination) of a sample of cells from the endometrium (lining of the **uterus**), usually just before menstruation, to evaluate ovulatory function. The procedure is done without an anaesthetic, using an instrument placed through the **cervix**. If the cells show the characteristics of normal cells at this point in the **menstrual cycle**, **progesterone** production is considered adequate.

Endometriosis: Presence of endometrial tissue (the normal uterine lining) in abnormal locations, such as the **fallopian tubes**, **ovaries**, or peritoneal (abdominal) cavity. Endometriosis can interfere with nearly every phase of the reproductive cycle. It may cause intercourse to be painful, may result in **adhesions**, and is associated with **infertility** in severe cases.

Endometritis: Inflammation of the lining of the **uterus**.

Epidemiology: Study of the frequency and distribution of disease in human populations.

Estriol: A reduction product of estradiol and estrone, having relatively weak estrogenic activity. It is detectable in high concentrations in the urine, especially human pregnancy urine. The official preparation, rarely used clinically, is a white, microcrystalline powder, to be administered orally.

Estrogen: A class of steroid **hormone**s, produced mainly by the **ovaries**, having a variety of functions. The estrogen estradiol is necessary for complete maturation of eggs during a woman's **menstrual cycle**. Synthetic estrogens, produced in laboratories, are similar in chemical structure to naturally occurring estrogens. They are used to alter or interfere with the production of menstrual cycle hormones.

F

Fallopian tubes: A pair of tubes that conduct the egg from the **ovary** to the **uterus**. **Fertilization** normally occurs within the tubes. Blocked or scarred fallopian tubes are a major cause of **infertility** in women. See **adhesions**; **endometriosis**; **pelvic inflammatory disease**; **salpingitis**. In some cases, surgical excision of the diseased area and reconnection of the tubes (salpingotomy) may restore fertility. Investigative tests include **hysterosalpingogram** and **laparoscopy**.

Fecundity: The capacity (degree of ability) to conceive or impregnate, whether or not this capacity has been fulfilled. Contrast **fertility**.

Fertility: The ability to produce offspring. In demographic terms, it is a statement of the actual number of births. Contrast **fecundity**. See also **infertility.**

Fertilization: Union of an egg and a **sperm** to produce a **zygote**, which may then develop further to the **embryo** stage.

Fetal therapy: A term that includes the established procedure of intrauterine blood exchange for Rh incompatibility, and experimental drug or vitamin treatment of an inborn error of metabolism (a genetically determined biochemical imbalance in which a specific enzyme defect produces a metabolic abnormality).

Fetal tissue research: Use of fetal cadaver tissue to study, for example, **congenital anomalies**, carcinogenesis, and infectious disease. Potential sources are **ectopic pregnancy**, **miscarriage**, stillbirth, and pregnancy termination. The latter renders the most usable source of tissue. See also **fetal tissue transplantation**.

Fetal tissue transplantation: Use of fetal cadaver tissue, for example, to treat infants in need of organ replacement, children with juvenile **diabetes mellitus**, and adults with **Parkinson disease**. Use of these tissues, such as liver, thymus, neural, and pancreatic tissue, is still experimental, with the exception of thymus transplant for infants with DiGeorge syndrome (absent thymus). Fetal tissue has major advantages for this purpose, over adult tissue.

Fetus: The developing entity from eight weeks after **fertilization** until birth. The two prior stages are **zygote** and **embryo**.

Follicle: A fluid-filled structure within the **ovary** that contains the developing egg. At **ovulation**, the follicle breaks through the surface of the ovary and the egg is released.

Follicle-stimulating hormone (FSH): A **pituitary hormone**, which, along with other **hormones**, stimulates maturation of the **follicle** in the **ovary** in women and formation of the **sperm** in the **testes** in men.

G

GIFT: Gamete intrafallopian transfer.   A technique of **assisted reproduction** in which a woman's mature eggs are removed by **laparoscopy** or by a catheter (small tube) under **ultrasound** guidance and then reintroduced with **sperm** into the **fallopian tubes**.

Gn-RH: Gonadotropin-releasing hormone.   Also known as **luteinizing hormone releasing hormone (LH-RH)**.   The **hormone** released from the **hypothalamus** that causes secretion of gonadotropins from the **pituitary** gland. It can be pulse-injected to stimulate ovarian function in women with **infertility** caused by deficient gonadotropins. However, there is a risk of **hyperstimulation** of the **ovaries**.

Gamete: The mature male or female reproductive cell, which contains one set of 23 **chromosomes** rather than the two sets found in **somatic** (body) **cells**. In a man, the gametes are **sperm**; in a woman, they are eggs.

Gamete intrafallopian transfer: See **GIFT**.

Gene: The physical and functional unit of heredity; an ordered sequence of nucleotides (substances that make up the **DNA**) situated in a particular position on a particular **chromosome** and having a particular function.

Gene probe: A segment of single-stranded **DNA** or **RNA** containing the DNA sequence for part of a particular **gene**, labelled with a radioactive or chemical marker and used to identify a specific region of the **genome** by binding to the complementary sequence for that gene.

Gene therapy: Therapy aimed at curing a disease due to a defective **gene**, either by insertion of a normal gene or by correction of the abnormal one. It is called *somatic gene therapy* if it applies to the cells of the body other than the **germ cells** (eggs or **sperm**), and *germ line gene therapy* if it applies to the germ cells. See **genetic alteration, directed**; **genetic engineering**.

Genetic alteration, directed: Changing the structure of a particular **gene** in a controlled way. It includes **gene therapy** but also applies to hypothesized alteration of the **DNA** for non-therapeutic purposes, as in enhancement of supposedly superior traits. See **genetic engineering** for the kinds of techniques involved in gene therapy.

Genetic engineering: Isolating **genes**, replicating them outside their own cells, and altering their structures and their relationships to the rest of the genetic material in a directed way. The means include **cloning** (isolation of specific genes [e.g., for insulin] and replicating them in bacteria or other vectors), directed **mutation**, and transfection (transfer of a particular gene from its own cell line to another — either within or between species). These techniques have led to an understanding of how genes act and are regulated, and to introduction of economically valuable traits into domestic animals and plants. They are now being used to introduce genes that produce a therapeutic product (e.g., that kills cancer cells, or produces a compound lacking in a genetic disorder) into cells that will transport the product to genetically defective tissues lacking the product.

Genetic marker: A genetically determined difference, which is useful for gene mapping and for **genetic testing** by linkage analysis. Where there are two or more forms of such a trait, none of which is rare, the trait is termed a *polymorphism*. Genetic markers may result from changes within a **gene** or in the **DNA** between the genes. The latter is more appropriately termed a *DNA marker*.

Genetic screening: Use of tests in population groups to acquire genetic information about individuals who are at increased risk for having an inherited trait or disease. Contrast with **genetic testing**, which applies to individuals rather than groups.

Genetic testing: Identifying an abnormal **gene** (e.g., **phenylketonuria**), abnormal protein (e.g., **sickle-cell anaemia**), chromosomal change (e.g., **Down syndrome**), or a **genetic DNA marker** near or within the gene (e.g., **Huntington disease**).

Genetics: Study of the structure, regulation, expression, transmission, and frequency of **genes**.

Genome: The total genetic material contained in the **chromosomes** of an individual's cells. The human genome contains about 100 000 **genes**.

Genotype: The genetic make-up of an organism with respect to a particular **gene** locus or the entire complement of genes, as contrasted to the outward appearance.

Germ cell or line: The cell or cell line that produces **gametes** (**sperm** or egg) for reproduction. Any changes to the germ line (**mutation**) may be passed on to the next generation.

Gestation: The period of fetal development in the **uterus** from conception to birth, usually considered to be 40 weeks in humans.

Gonadotropins: **Hormones** that stimulate the **testes** or **ovaries**. Examples are **follicle-stimulating hormone, human chorionic gonadotropin, human menopausal gonadotropin**, and **luteinizing**

hormone.   These can be administered to women with ovulatory dysfunction to stimulate the ovary.   See **ovulatory stimulants**.

Gonadotropin-releasing hormone: See **Gn-RH**.

Gonorrhoea: A sexually transmitted bacterial disease.   If not treated, in women it can spread to the **uterus** and the **fallopian tubes**, causing **pelvic inflammatory disease**; in men, it can cause inflammation of the **testes** and can affect **semen** quality.

H

hCG: Human chorionic gonadotropin. The **hormone** produced early in pregnancy (detected in one of the pregnancy tests) that keeps the **corpus luteum** producing **progesterone**, which prevents menstruation from occurring.   It can be extracted from the urine of pregnant women and used in conjunction with other substances as a treatment for **infertility** by triggering **ovulation**.   See **ovulatory stimulants**.

HIV: Human immunodeficiency virus. The **virus** that causes **AIDS**.   It produces a defect in the body's immune system by invading and then multiplying within white blood cells.

hMG: Human menopausal gonadotropin. A **hormone** preparation that can be extracted from the urine of newly menopausal women and injected to stimulate **ovaries** and **testes**.   It contains two hormones: **follicle-stimulating hormone** and **luteinizing hormone**.

Herpes, genital: An infection caused by the herpes simplex virus transmitted by vaginal, anal, or oral sex and sometimes through linens and towels.   Men may have sores on their penis, scrotum, perineum, buttock, anus, and thighs and women on their **vagina** and **cervix**.   The outbreaks recur and there is no medical cure.

Hormone: A chemical substance, synthesized in one organ of the body, that stimulates functional activity in cells of other tissues and organs.   See **endocrine system**.

Human chorionic gonadotropin: See **hCG**.

Human immunodeficiency virus: See **HIV**.

Human menopausal gonadotropin: See **hMG**.

Huntington disease: A disorder of movement, intellectual deterioration, and personality change, which usually manifests itself between the ages of 30 and 50 and which leads to death.   The disorder is inherited as an autosomal **dominant** and, thus, a person with the **gene** has a 50 percent chance of passing it on to each of his or her offspring.   As a result of the late onset, affected individuals may have children before they know they are carrying the gene.   The gene is situated near the end of chromosome 4, and the condition is detectable by family studies of linkage to a **DNA genetic marker** in most cases. The gene has now been identified.

Hydatidiform mole: An abnormal "pregnancy" or development of a growth resulting from a pathologic egg.

Hyperstimulation: A syndrome that may include ovarian enlargement, gastrointestinal symptoms (nausea, vomiting, diarrhea), abdominal distension, and weight gain. Severe cases may be further complicated with cardiovascular, pulmonary, and electrolyte disturbances, requiring hospitalization. See **ovulatory stimulants**.

Hypothalamus: A structure at the base of the brain that controls (among other things) the action of the **pituitary** hormones. By secreting and releasing **hormones**, the hypothalamus orchestrates the body's reproductive function in both men and women.

Hysterectomy: Surgical removal of the **uterus**, which results in inability to implant an **embryo**.

Hysterosalpingogram (HSG): An X-ray of the female reproductive tract after injecting a dye into the **uterus** that travels into the **fallopian tubes**. Since the dye is dense to X-rays, the outline of the uterine cavity and the degree of openness of the fallopian tubes can be seen.

Hysteroscopy: Direct visualization of the interior of the **uterus** to evaluate the presence of abnormalities. It is done by inserting a hysteroscope (a long, narrow, illuminated tube) through the **cervix** into the uterus. The uterus is inflated by injecting either a gas (carbon dioxide) or a solution of sugar in water through the **vagina**. This test, which is performed under a local anaesthetic, may reveal a septate uterus (a uterus divided into compartments), polyps, fibroids (benign tumours), or **adhesions**. Minor surgery, such as removal of fine adhesions, can be done using tiny forceps placed through special "channels" in the hysteroscope.

I

IUD: Intrauterine device. Contraceptive device, usually a loop made of plastic or metal that is inserted through the **cervix** into the uterine cavity in order to prevent pregnancy. It works by preventing the **zygote** from implanting. Use of IUDs has been associated with infections leading to **pelvic inflammatory disease** and to **infertility**.

IUI: See **Intrauterine insemination**.

IVF: *In vitro* fertilization. A technique used in **assisted reproduction**. Mature eggs are removed from a woman's **ovary**, usually after administration of an **ovulatory stimulant**, and fertilized with **sperm** in the laboratory. After **fertilization** and incubation, the fertilized egg is placed in the woman's **uterus**; it may also be transferred to another woman (see **embryo donation**). For a variation of IVF, see **ZIFT**.

Iatrogenic: Refers to conditions caused by medical intervention, including surgical, drug, or other procedures (e.g., **infertility** caused by **adhesion** following post-surgical infection, or **miscarriage** following a **prenatal diagnosis** procedure).

Idiopathic infertility: Infertility for which no organic problem has been identified in either partner.

Implantation: The process by which the **zygote** becomes embedded in the wall of the **uterus**, usually starting by the sixth and ending by the fourteenth day after **fertilization**.

Impotence: Inability to achieve or maintain sufficiently a penile erection.

Incidence: Proportion of instances of illness commencing, or of persons falling ill, during a given period in a specific population. More generally, the proportion of new events (e.g., new cases of a disease in a defined population) within a specified period.

Infertility: Diminished ability to bring about a live birth in spite of repeated attempts. It may include infecundity as well as pregnancy loss after conception (**miscarriage** and stillbirth). Infertility is said to be *primary* where a woman has never carried a pregnancy to live birth or a man has never caused conception, and *secondary* where the individual has had one or more biological children. The latter is sometimes called *one-child sterility*.

Informed choice: A decision about a particular course of action made after receipt of sufficient information about the non-medical and medical options. For example, in counselling of people who are infertile, the options might include adoption or remaining childless, as well as the medical means of overcoming **infertility**.

Informed consent: An agreement to proceed with a particular medical treatment, given after receipt of information about the risks and benefits of that procedure. In Canada, to avoid a negligence action, physicians are required to divulge a "material" risk or a "special risk with serious consequences" according to the needs of the particular patient. Whether a patient with this information would have consented is, however, evaluated from the objective of what a "reasonable patient" would have decided.

Insemination: Placement of **semen** within the **vagina** or **cervix**. See **donor insemination**.

Intracytoplasmic sperm injection: The **sperm** is washed and is put into a glass needle and injected into the **ovum**.

Intrauterine device: See **IUD**.

Intrauterine insemination: A form of **donor insemination** in which **sperm** are deposited directly into the uterine cavity. It may be used to overcome barriers to natural **insemination**, such as incompatibility between the sperm and **cervical mucus**, **impotence**, or **vaginismus**. See **sperm preparation**.

In vitro: Literally, *in glass*; pertaining to manipulations carried out on biological systems outside the body, usually in a culture dish or other laboratory vessel. Contrast *in vivo*.

In vitro **fertilization:** See **IVF**.

In vivo: Literally, *in life*. A term used to describe biological processes in their natural environment within the living organism. Contrast *in vitro*.

In vivo **fertilization:** **Fertilization** of the egg in the woman's body. This may occur by natural means or by **assisted insemination**. See **DOST**; **donor insemination**; **GIFT**.

J, K, L

Kallman syndrome: A congenital abnormality where a dysfunction of the **hypothalamus** causes problems, including failure to reach puberty.

Laparoscope: A narrow, light-transmitting instrument used to visualize organs within the abdominal cavity through a small incision in the abdominal wall.

Laparoscopy: A procedure, requiring a general anaesthetic, in which the reproductive (or other) organs are viewed through a **laparoscope** inserted near the navel after the abdomen has been inflated with carbon dioxide. It is used in investigation of **adhesions**, **endometriosis**, and **pelvic inflammatory disease**. A dye may be run through the **fallopian tubes** to show whether they are blocked. Surgical procedures such as removal of small cysts, adhesions, or endometrial tissue may also be performed with the instrument. It is used in **gamete intrafallopian transfer**, but its use in *in vitro* **fertilization** has been replaced by transvaginal **ultrasound** techniques.

Lavage: See **uterine lavage**.

Luteal phase defect (LPD): Failure of the endometrial lining of the **uterus** to develop properly after **ovulation** because of inadequate production of **progesterone** by the **corpus luteum** (cells left in the **follicle** after the egg leaves). This may prevent a fertilized egg from implanting in the uterus or may lead to early pregnancy loss. LPD is detectable by graphing morning body temperature, by measuring the blood level of **progesterone**, or by **endometrial biopsy**.

Luteinizing hormone (LH): The **pituitary** hormone that causes the **testes** in men and **ovaries** in women to make sex **hormones**. In women, when the egg is ripe, the pituitary releases a large amount of LH. As a result, within 24 to 36 hours, the egg finishes maturing and leaves the ovary. The remaining cells in the follicle (**corpus luteum**) start producing the sex hormone, **progesterone**. In men, the two pituitary hormones, LH and **FSH (follicle-stimulating hormone)**, are released together. LH, called *interstitial cell stimulating hormone*, stimulates **testosterone** production in the testes.

Luteinizing hormone releasing hormone (LH-RH): See **Gn-RH**.

M

MSAFP: Maternal serum alpha-fetoprotein. A test for the protein produced by the fetal liver that can be measured in a blood sample of a pregnant woman or in the amniotic fluid, which surrounds the **fetus**. The test on maternal blood — MSAFP — can be carried out around 16 weeks of pregnancy. An increased level of MSAFP may indicate that the fetus has a **neural tube defect** or certain other fetal anomalies, while a decreased level in the pregnant woman's blood may indicate a fetal chromosomal abnormality.

Medicalization: The process by which behaviours or conditions are defined in terms of health and illness.

Mendelian trait or disorder: A disorder controlled by a single **gene**, and therefore showing a simple pattern of inheritance (autosomal **dominant**, autosomal **recessive**, or **X-linked**).

Menopause: Cessation of the **menstrual cycle** when the **ovaries** are virtually depleted of eggs.

Menstrual cycle: A cycle of approximately one month in the female, during which the egg is released from an **ovary**, the lining of the **uterus** (endometrium) is prepared to receive the fertilized egg, and blood and endometrial tissue are lost via the **vagina** if pregnancy does not occur.

Meta-analysis: Pooling the results from studies with similar methodologies when each study on its own may not include sufficiently large sample sizes to provide reliable results.

Micromanipulation: Performance of surgery, injections, dissections with attachments to a microscope, which allows magnified visualization.

Microsurgery: Delicate surgery performed with the aid of a microscope or other magnifying apparatus. In cases of **infertility**, it is used to repair the **fallopian tubes** in women and blockage of the **vas deferens** in men.

Miscarriage (spontaneous abortion): The spontaneous shedding of the **fetus** or **embryo** from the **uterus** at any stage before viability, usually before the twentieth week after conception. The terms *habitual* or *repeated miscarriage* are applied where this occurs in three or more pregnancies. Causes include **chromosomal disorders** in one of the couple, uterine malformation, hormonal imbalance (see **luteal phase defect**), infection (see **mycoplasma**), and rejection of the **fetus** as a foreign tissue.

Morphology: The form and structure of living things, such as the shape of **sperm** during **semen analysis**. Abnormal morphology of sperm may affect movement (see **sperm motility**) and, thus, ability of the sperm to fertilize the egg.

Morula: A fertilized egg after a few days' growth, when the collection of cells resembles a mulberry in shape (Latin, *morula*) and is smaller than the period at the end of this sentence. This is the stage before the **blastocyst**.

Mosaic: An individual or tissue with two or more genetically different cell lines arising from a single cell line. Contrast **chimera**.

Multifactorial disorder: A disorder that is attributable to a complex interaction of environmental and genetic factors. See **polygenic**.

Multiple pregnancy: A pregnancy in which there is more than one **embryo** or **fetus**. The probability of occurrence is increased with use of **ovulatory stimulants**. In *in vitro* **fertilization**, more than one **zygote** may be deliberately transferred, to increase the chance that at least one will survive.

Mutation: A permanent change in the genetic material. When mutation occurs in a **germ cell** or its precursor, it can be passed on to subsequent generations. A **gene** altered by a mutation, and an individual bearing such a gene, is called *mutant*. A substance capable of inducing a mutation is called a *mutagen*.

Mycoplasma: A sexually transmitted micro-organism, which may be transmitted alone or with **chlamydia**. Women are often asymptomatic; men often have painful urination and discharge. This organism has been implicated in some studies as a cause of female **infertility, ectopic pregnancy, miscarriage**, and premature birth.

N

Neural tube defects: The neural tube gives rise to the central nervous system at about five weeks in the human **fetus**. Neural tube defects, which occur when the neural tube fails to close, include **anencephaly** and **spina bifida**. There is a higher frequency in some population groups. See **MSAFP** for prenatal detection.

O

Oligomenorrhea: See **amenorrhea**.

Oligospermia: Scarcity of **sperm** in the **semen**. If severe, it may result in **infertility**.

Oocyte: An egg cell produced in the **ovaries**. Its process of formation is termed *oogenesis*.

Oral contraceptive: A pill containing a combination of progestin (**progesterone**-like **hormone**) and **estrogen**. It stops **ovulation** by suppressing the **pituitary**, which then does not send out the usual signals to ripen and release an egg. After use of the pill is discontinued, normal ovulatory cycles and menstruation generally resume within three to six months. However, menstruation may not resume if the contraceptives were taken before the reproductive system matured or if they were repeatedly started and stopped. This may result in **infertility**.

Ovaries: Paired female sex glands in which egg cells are developed and stored and the **hormones estrogen** and **progesterone** are produced.

Ovulation: Release of an egg from a woman's **ovary**, generally around the midpoint of the **menstrual cycle**. Methods of timing ovulation include systematic measuring of morning body temperature, observing changes in the quantity and quality of **cervical mucus**, analysis of **luteinizing hormone** in the blood or urine, and high-resolution **ultrasound** scans of the ovarian **follicles**.

Ovulation induction: Treatment of ovulatory dysfunction using drugs that induce **ovulation** (see **ovulatory stimulants**) and as a part of **donor insemination**, **GIFT**, **IVF**, and their variants.

Ovulatory stimulants: These so-called fertility drugs include **bromocriptine, clomiphene citrate, gonadotropins**, and **gonadotropin-releasing hormone**, used in treatment of an ovulatory disorder; in *in vitro* **fertilization**, to produce eggs for retrieval (superovulation); and sometimes in **donor insemination**, to regulate timing of **ovulation**.

As a **fertility** treatment, ovulatory stimulants increase the risk of **multiple pregnancy** and may cause a serious condition — **hyperstimulation** syndrome.

Ovum (pl. *ova*): The female egg or **oocyte**, formed in an **ovary**.

P, Q

PID: Pelvic inflammatory disease. An inflammation of the upper reproductive tract involving the **uterus**, **fallopian tubes**, and **ovaries**, generally caused by **sexually transmitted diseases** or other infections. Organisms that cause **gonorrhoea**, **chlamydia**, or other infections can ascend from the lower genital tract through the lining of the uterus (causing **endometritis**), to the peritoneal (abdominal) cavity (causing peritonitis and **adhesions**), to the fallopian tubes (causing **salpingitis**), and possibly to the ovaries (causing their inflammation). The organisms may be transmitted by intercourse, by an abortion or childbirth, or by insertion of an **IUD**.

PKU: Phenylketonuria. An autosomal **recessive** inborn error of metabolism (a genetically determined biochemical imbalance in which a specific enzyme defect produces a metabolic abnormality), in which the enzyme phenylalanine hydroxylase is deficient. This results in a buildup of products that cause mental impairment. The condition is diagnosable at birth by a simple blood test and can be treated with a special diet during infancy and childhood to prevent mental impairment. If females with the disorder become pregnant, dietary treatment must be reinstated in order to prevent mental impairment and congenital defects in their heterozygous (having two different forms of a gene at a particular locus) offspring (i.e., the maternal disease acts as a **teratogen**). The **gene** has been mapped and can be detected prenatally.

PND: Prenatal diagnosis. Testing before birth with the aim of determining whether a **fetus** has a specific trait, usually a malformation or disorder for which the fetus is known to be at increased risk because of maternal age or family history; sex of fetus can also be detected.

PROST: Pronuclear oocyte salpingo transfer: See **ZIFT**.

Parkinson disease: A gradual loss of motor function with akinesia, rigidity, trembling, gait disturbance, and loss of postural reflexes.

Parthenogenesis: Development of the egg into a complete organism without **fertilization** with a **sperm**. It occurs naturally in some less complex species, but not in human beings.

Pelvic inflammatory disease: See **PID**.

Perinatal: Occurring near the end of pregnancy, during delivery, or soon after birth.

Phenylketonuria: See **PKU**.

Pituitary: The small organ at the base of the brain that produces **gonadotropins**, **luteinizing hormone (LH)**, and **follicle-stimulating hormone (FSH)**, which stimulate the gonads (**ovaries** and **testes**) to produce **gametes** and **hormones**.

Placenta: A tissue formed after the **zygote** becomes implanted in the **uterus**, through which the blood of the developing **embryo** proper and later the **fetus** and the gestating woman circulate in separate but closely apposed vessels; and through which the developing fetus receives nourishment. A part of the placenta, the trophoblast, lines the chorion (outer membrane surrounding the embryo and fetus) and secretes **human chorionic gonadotropin**.

Polar body: A small cell that buds off from the egg during meiosis and that contains one set of 23 **chromosomes**. Meiosis is a special type of cell division that occurs only in the germ cells (egg and **sperm**) during their formation.   As a result, the number of chromosome sets is reduced from two to one. See **preimplantation diagnosis**.

Polycystic ovary disease (POD): Also called *Stein-Leventhal syndrome* or *sclerocystic ovarian disease*. A disease of the **ovaries** caused by malfunction of the hormonal system.   Excess male **hormone** is converted into **estrogen** in fatty tissue. The high estrogen levels cause the **pituitary** to send a "confused" signal to the ovaries. This causes the eggs to start to ripen, but they never mature.   The trapped **follicles** build up, the ovaries become cystic, and **ovulation** and menstruation fail to occur. Women with this condition tend to be obese and have a male pattern of hair growth. Surgical removal of a portion of the polycystic ovary may result in ovulation.

Polygenic: A trait that is determined by many **genes**, each with a small effect, acting in concert. When environmental factors are involved as well, the trait is said to be **multifactorial**.   Some multifactorial disorders are relatively common (e.g., **neural tube defects**).

Preconception arrangement or contract: An agreement, commonly known as *surrogacy*, by which a woman agrees to gestate a child and then give up her parental rights to the commissioning party or parties. The woman may be artificially inseminated with **sperm** from the commissioning male or have a **zygote**, to which she did not contribute the egg, transplanted into her **uterus**. If the contract is for profit, it may be termed a *commercial contract*.

Predictive testing: Identifying an abnormal **gene**, protein, chromosomal change, or **DNA marker**. See **genetic testing**.

Pre-eclampsia: See **toxaemia**.

Pre-embryo: See **embryo**; **zygote**.

Preimplantation diagnosis: Diagnosis of genetic disorders or sex before **fertilization** or before the **zygote** is transferred to the **uterus**. One type involves analysis of the **polar body** of an egg that is heterozygous (having two different forms of a **gene** at a particular gene locus) for a known genetic disorder. If the polar body has the normal form of the gene, it may be inferred that the egg has the abnormal form and vice versa. Another type involves analysis of the **DNA** of one of a few cells of a zygote (e.g., following **IVF**). The **zygote** may continue to develop and, if the disorder is absent, can be placed or replaced in a woman's **uterus**.

Prenatal diagnosis: See **PND**.

Prevalence: Frequency of a condition in a population. Prevalence may be greater or less than **incidence**, depending on how long individuals with the condition live.

Progesterone: A steroid **hormone** produced by the **ovary** after **ovulation**, and by the **placenta**. It promotes development of the endometrium (uterine lining) essential for implantation of the **embryo** and continuation of the pregnancy. Progesterone may be used to treat a **luteal phase defect**. Its effectiveness in preventing **miscarriage** in such cases has not been adequately proven.

Prolactin: A **hormone** secreted by the **pituitary** that stimulates breast milk production in nursing mothers and supports gonadal function. Women with abnormally elevated levels of prolactin (hyperprolactinaemia) may not ovulate and may have either irregular or absent menstrual periods. Hyperprolactinaemia can be treated with **bromocriptine**.

Pronuclear oocyte salpingo transfer (PROST): See **ZIFT**.

Pronucleus: The precursor of a nucleus. The fully mature **ovum** loses its nuclear envelope and liberates its **chromosomes** to meet with those similarly derived from the male pronucleus. Together they comprise the genetic make-up of the **zygote**.

Prostate gland: A chestnut-size gland in males that surrounds the **urethra**, near the bladder, and produces a portion of the fluid that transports **sperm** into the **ejaculate**.

R

RU-486 pill: A pill available in France, but not yet in North America, containing a **progesterone** antagonist. When taken early in pregnancy, it reduces the progesterone level necessary to maintain a pregnancy, resulting in termination without surgical intervention.

Recessive: Refers to a form of a **gene** that will be expressed only if it is present in two copies (i.e., on both **chromosomes**). Compare with **dominant**: a person with a recessive condition will have inherited one abnormal form of the gene from each parent. When the parent has only one copy, he or she will not show the condition and is said to be a *carrier*. Two such parents have one chance in four of having a child affected with the condition.

S

SHIFT: Synchronized hysteroscopic insemination of the fallopian tubes. Passage of a catheter (small tube) through the **cervix** into the **fallopian tubes** under the guidance of a small scope. **Sperm** is injected via the catheter into the fallopian tubes.

STD: Sexually transmitted disease. Also called *venereal disease*. Infectious disease transmitted primarily by sexual contact, including **chlamydia**, **gonorrhoea**, **herpes**, **HIV**, **mycoplasma**, and **syphilis**. STDs are linked to **infertility**. See **PID**.

Salpingitis: Inflammation of the **fallopian tubes**, sometimes caused by **sexually transmitted disease** or other infections. In salpingitis isthmica nodosa, the end of the fallopian tube near the **uterus** is thickened with irregularly shaped nodules, which can block the fallopian tubes, causing **infertility**.

Self-insemination: Term for **donor insemination** when it is performed, without medical assistance, by the woman, her partner, or other non-medical support. Also known as *alternative insemination*. See **DI**.

Semen: Fluid secretion containing **sperm** that is emitted during ejaculation. Also called the *seminal fluid*, more than half of which is produced in the seminal vesicles, the paired glands at the base of the bladder.

Semen analysis: A diagnostic tool in evaluating male **infertility** that includes evaluation of the physical characteristics and presence of **antisperm antibodies** and micro-organisms in the semen, the shape and concentration of **sperm**, and **sperm motility**.

Sex chromosome: The X- and the Y-chromosome, which are responsible for sex determination. XY individuals are male; XX individuals are female.

Sex selection: Methods used to enhance the likelihood that **sperm** are X- or Y-bearing (sex-selective insemination); to produce a pregnancy of the desired sex by transferring only **zygotes** of one sex (sex-selective zygote transfer); or to eliminate **fetuses** of the undesired sex (sex-selective abortion). See also **preimplantation diagnosis**.

Sexually transmitted disease: See **STD**.

Sickle-cell anaemia: An often-fatal autosomal **recessive** haemoglobino-pathy (hereditary anaemia involving disorders of haemoglobin, the oxygen carrier in blood), which occurs most often in blacks. The **gene** defect renders the haemoglobin liable to crystallize and the red blood cells to form a sickle shape, to lodge in the small blood vessels, and to cause serious health problems. People who are "heterozygotes" have the abnormal gene on only one of the two chromosomes, are usually healthy, and are said to have the sickle-cell trait. The condition can be detected by biochemical technology, and the gene by molecular technology.

Somatic cell: Any cell in the body that does not become a **germ cell** (egg or **sperm**).

Sperm: The free-swimming male reproductive cell produced by the **testes** that interacts with the egg, resulting in **fertilization**.

Sperm bank: A place in which **sperm** are stored by **cryopreservation** for future use in **assisted insemination**.

Sperm count: The number of **sperm** in the **ejaculate**. The total effective sperm count is the estimated number of sperm in an ejaculate capable of **fertilization**, calculated from the proportion of sperm with forward progressive **motility** and normal **morphology**. When expressed as the number of sperm per millilitre, it is called the *sperm concentration* or *density*.

Sperm motility: Movement of **sperm**, the measurement of which is used as one indication of **fertility** in men. Forward progression is the quality of movement demonstrated by the majority of motile sperm.

Sperm-mucus cross test: A test to determine whether it is the **sperm** or the **cervical mucus** that is affecting sperm movement. The male partner's sperm is tested against the female partner's mucus and that of a woman known to be fertile, and the female partner's mucus is tested against the male partner's sperm and that of a male known to be fertile.

Sperm preparation: Methods of preparing **sperm** to increase the success rate of **assisted insemination**. These include: chemical or drug treatment with caffeine, the amino acid arginine, or the protein kinin to improve **sperm motility** or with antibiotics to eliminate bacterial infection; concentration, by high-speed spinning; swim-up, in which a layer of protein is placed over the **semen** through which the most motile sperm will swim up, leaving behind most of the abnormal and non-motile sperm; and washing, in which a semen sample is diluted with compounds to separate viable sperm from the other components of semen, such as prostaglandins (**hormone**-like substances), **antibodies**, and micro-organisms.

Spermatogenesis: The process of formation of spermatozoa (**sperm**).

Spina bifida: A defect caused when the neural tube fails to close, resulting in protuberance of some spinal cord tissue. See **neural tube defects**.

Sterility: Inability to reproduce. Surgical sterility results from a sterilizing operation, whether for contraceptive reasons or not (in men **vasectomy** and in women **hysterectomy**, oophorectomy [removal of one or both of the **ovaries**], and **tubal ligation**). In the latter, since the woman's eggs are left intact, they could be fertilized *in vitro*. Non-surgical sterility results from causes other than a sterilizing operation (e.g., accident, birth defect, illness).

Sterilization reversal: Surgery, called **reanastomosis**, to restore **fertility** by reconnecting tubes that have been severed in a **tubal ligation** (severing of the **fallopian tubes** or **vas deferens** for contraceptive purpose). The former is also called *salpingostomy* and the latter *vasectomy reversal*.

Streptococcal infection: Infections of the genital tract, which are not usually sexually transmitted. However, they sometimes travel through the lymphatic or blood vessels, causing **adhesions** to form around the outside of the **fallopian tubes**, thereby affecting **fertility**. The source can be an induced abortion, **miscarriage**, childbirth, or biopsy.

Syngamy: The process through which the 23 **chromosomes** of an egg cell and the 23 chromosomes of a **sperm** cell combine so that the new cell has 46 chromosomes.

Syphilis: A bacterial disease caused by a spiral-shaped bacterium, a spirochete. In infectious stages, it is transmitted through sex or intimate contact and may affect **fertility**. An infected pregnant woman can pass it on to the **fetus**, possibly resulting in stillbirth or congenital problems in an infant so affected.

T

TEST: Tubal embryo stage transfer. See **ZIFT**.

Tay-Sachs disease: A severe and fatal disorder that occurs predominantly in Ashkenazi Jewish populations. The affected baby appears normal at birth, but by six months of age has begun to lag developmentally. Progressive neurological deterioration occurs, with loss of muscle function throughout the body. Swallowing difficulties require eventual tube feeding; loss of respiratory muscles causes repeated pneumonias.

These children usually die within two to four years. An effective carrier test can be done on a small blood sample in Ashkenazi Jewish couples who wish to avoid the birth of an affected child.

Teratogen: An agent that causes a **congenital anomaly** by adversely affecting development of the **embryo**. The process by which this occurs is called *teratogenesis*. Contrast **mutation**.

Testes: The paired male sex glands in which **sperm** and the steroid hormone **testosterone** are produced.

Testicular biopsy: The excision of a small sample of testicular tissue through a small incision in the scrotum for microscopic pathologic evaluation to determine whether **sperm** are being produced.

Testosterone: A steroid produced in the **testes** that affects **sperm** production and male sex characteristics.

Thalassaemia: Chronic anaemia caused by a genetically determined reduction in the synthesis of globin (the protein of haemoglobin), which in some types is severe enough to lead to death. One type has a high frequency in persons of Mediterranean and African origin and another in persons of Far Eastern origin.

Thyroid gland: A gland, situated in the neck, that secretes the **hormone** thyroxin and controls many bodily functions. A low thyroid level, hypothyroidism, may affect **fertility** by raising the levels of **prolactin**, which, in turn, affects **ovulation** in women and decreases **sperm** number and **motility** in men. See **prolactin**.

Toxaemia: Often referred to as **pre-eclampsia,** an abnormal condition of late pregnancy characterized by swelling, high blood pressure, and protein in the urine. The condition can lead to convulsions.

Toxoplasma: A protozoan (unicellular animal organism) that may infect women during pregnancy and may cause **miscarriage** or nervous system damage to a surviving **fetus**.

Tubal ligation: Sterilization of a woman by surgical excision of a small section of each **fallopian tube**.

Turner syndrome: A natural process results in most of the immature eggs with which the female is born slowly degenerating during her childhood and reproductive years. Turner syndrome is a condition in which this process is accelerated, resulting in **infertility**. In this condition, women have one instead of two sex **chromosomes**. Those with the syndrome are usually infertile, since the gonads become streaks containing no eggs, and they lack normal ovarian **hormones**, do not go through puberty, and do not develop secondary sex characteristics unless hormonally treated.

U

Ultrasound: High-frequency sound waves focussed on the body and reflected to provide a video image of internal tissues, organs, and structures. Ultrasound scanning is particularly useful for *in utero* examinations of a developing **fetus**, for guidance of the needle in **amniocentesis** and **chorionic villus sampling**, for evaluation of the development of ovarian **follicles**, and for guided retrieval of eggs for *in vitro* **fertilization** and its variants.

Urethra: The canal that carries the urine from the bladder and, in the male, serves also as a genital duct that delivers **sperm**.

Uterine lavage: A flushing of the **uterus** to recover an egg or **zygote**. Not the method of choice because of risks to the woman, and not recommended.

Uterus: The womb; the female reproductive organ that holds and allows nourishment of the **fetus** until birth.

V, W

Vagina: The female organ between the **cervix** and vulva; the organ of sexual intercourse; the birth canal.

Vaginismus: Involuntary contraction of the muscles around the outer third of the **vagina**, which prohibits penile entry.

Vas deferens: The convoluted duct that carries **sperm** from the **testis** to the ejaculatory duct of the penis.

Vasectomy: Sterilization of a man by interrupting the **vas deferens**, usually by surgical excision.

Virus: A microscopic infectious organism without a nucleus or cell wall that reproduces inside living cells.

X, Y, Z

X-linked: Refers to any **gene** on the X-**chromosome** or traits determined by such genes.

ZIFT: A form of **assisted reproduction** in which a **zygote** obtained by *in vitro* **fertilization** is transferred to the **fallopian tube** usually by a catheter (small tube) through the **uterus** under **ultrasound** guidance.

This technique has also been called **PROST (pronuclear oocyte salpingo transfer)**; and **TEST (tubal embryo stage transfer)**.

Zona cutting or drilling: An experimental procedure in **in vitro fertilization**, whereby the **zona pellucida** is opened to make it easier for the **sperm** to fertilize the egg. There is a risk that the egg may be fertilized by more than one sperm (polyspermia).

Zona pellucida: Outer layer of the egg that interacts with the **sperm** at **fertilization**.

Zygote: The fertilized egg until approximately 14 days of development; from two weeks to eight weeks of development the developing entity is termed an **embryo**; from eight weeks to birth it is termed a **fetus**.

Zygote intrafallopian transfer: See **ZIFT**.

Mandate

◆

(approved by Her Excellency the Governor General
on the 25th day of October, 1989)

The Committee of the Privy Council, on the recommendation of the Prime Minister, advise that a Commission do issue under Part I of the Inquiries Act and under the Great Seal of Canada appointing The Royal Commission on New Reproductive Technologies to inquire into and report on current and potential medical and scientific developments related to new reproductive technologies, considering in particular their social, ethical, health, research, legal and economic implications and the public interest, recommending what policies and safeguards should be applied and examining in particular,

(a)   implications of new reproductive technologies for women's reproductive health and well-being;

(b)   the causes, treatment and prevention of male and female infertility;

(c)   reversals of sterilization procedures, artificial insemination, *in vitro* fertilization, embryo transfers, prenatal screening and diagnostic techniques, genetic manipulation and therapeutic interventions to correct genetic anomalies, sex selection techniques, embryo experimentation and fetal tissue transplants;

(d)   social and legal arrangements, such as surrogate childbearing, judicial interventions during gestation and birth, and "ownership" of ova, sperm, embryos and fetal tissue;

(e)   the status and rights of people using or contributing to reproductive services, such as access to procedures, "rights" to parenthood, informed consent, status of gamete donors and confidentiality, and the impact of these services on all concerned parties, particularly the children; and,

(f)   the economic ramifications of these technologies, such as the commercial marketing of ova, sperm and embryos, the application of patent law, and the funding of research and procedures including infertility treatment.

Participants in Public Hearings, 1990

Whitehorse, Yukon **September 11, 1990**	
Margaret Joe	Minister Responsible for the Status of Women Yukon Government
Jessica Simon	Victoria Faulkner Women's Centre
Linda McDonald, Pearl Keenen	Yukon Indian Women's Association
Valerie Fromme	Right to Life, Yukon
Paul Eagan	Yukon Medical Association
Yellowknife, Northwest Territories **September 12, 1990**	
Carol Roberts	Yellowknife Association of Women and the Law
Anne Lynagh, Brenda Percy	Yellowknife Women's Society
Linda Hudson	Tawow Society, Fort Smith
Wendy Colpitts	
Lynn Brooks	N.W.T. Status of Women Council
Jack Bromley	Fort Smith Pro-Life Group

Edmonton, Alberta **September 13, 1990**	
Noela Inions	Northern Chapter of Health Law Alberta Branch Canadian Bar Association
Elva Mertick	Alberta Advisory Council on Women's Issues
Ronald Gregg, Bernice Capusten, Robert Burns	Alberta Medical Association
Stephen Genuis	
Corry Morcos, Chuck Smith, Fawzy Morcos	Edmonton Pro-Life Society
Jackie Specken, Peggy Kemp	Fertility Management Services
David Cumming	Department of Obstetrics and Gynaecology Faculty of Medicine University of Alberta
Cynthia Boodram	Canadian Federation of University Women — Edmonton
Ris Grover	
Gwen Anderson	
Edwina Podemski, Denyse King	Abortion by Choice
Diana Andriasheik	Family Health Core Committee Alberta Public Health Association
Patricia Marck, John Dossetor	Bioethics Interest Group in Reproductive Ethics Joint Faculties Bioethics Project University of Alberta
Calgary, Alberta **September 14, 1990**	
Linda Smith, Brent Friesen, Sheila McDonagh-Firth	Calgary Health Services Calgary Board of Health
Janet Hutchinson, Elaine Rose, Pam Corbett	Social Issues Committee YWCA, Calgary

Chris Whittington	
Elizabeth Olsen	Women of UNIFARM
Barbara Johnson, Joanne Lewicky	Alberta Federation of Women United for Families
Michael Phair, Edwin Webking, Anne Jayne, Susan Radkey	Alberta Civil Liberties Research Centre
Peggy Webb, Judith Sloan, Melanie McLachlan, Roxanne LeBlanc	Planned Parenthood Alberta
Debra Morris, Carolynne Bouey Shank	The United Church of Canada Alberta and Northwest Conference
Richard Bickley, Connie Barlow	Personal and Family Planning Institute of Calgary
Patricia Blocksom, Sheilah Martin, Barbara Jantzen	Calgary Association of Women and the Law
Michael Malley	Calgary Humanae Vitae Centre
Ottawa, Ontario September 18-20, 1990	
Judith Allanson, Marie Geoffroy, Jean-Paul Woods, Diane Thompson	Division of Genetics Children's Hospital of Eastern Ontario
Hubert Doucet	Faculté de Théologie Université Saint-Paul
Patricia Gervaize	
Arthur Leader, David Mortimer	Ontario Medical Association
André Lafrance	Ottawa and District Physicians for Life
Leonard Borer	
Rose Mary Murphy, Anne Wright, Carla Marcelis	Women's Health Interaction
Lucien Saumur	

Marie Morrisey	Infertility Awareness Association of Canada
Paul Claman	GOAL Program Ottawa Civic Hospital
Norman Barwin, Bonnie Johnson	Planned Parenthood Federation of Canada
Nancy Jackson, Jennifer Smart	
T. Brettel Dawson	
Kirsten Kozolanka	
Les McAfee, Cecilia McWilliams	EGALE — Equality for Gays and Lesbians Everywhere
Cynthia Manson, Holly MacKay	Planned Parenthood Ottawa
Joanne Hurens, Louise Hall, Louise Marion	Public Service Alliance of Canada
Alice Baumgart, Judith Oulton, Heather Caloren	Canadian Nurses Association
Madeleine Dion Stout, Marg Lanigan	Indian and Inuit Nurses of Canada
Jane McDonald, Alan Park	Kingston Infertility Network
Monique Bégin, Christine St. Peter	Canadian Research Institute for the Advancement of Women
Carl Nimrod	Ultrasound Committee Society of Obstetricians and Gynaecologists of Canada
Quebec, Quebec September 26, 1990	
Ann Robinson, Colette Gendron	Groupe de recherche multidisciplinaire féministe
Claude Bouchard	Campagne Québec-Vie
Maria De Koninck, Marie-Hélène Parizeau	Étude sur la condition des femmes Université Laval

Edith Deleury	Faculté de droit Université Laval
Guy Bouchard	
Ninon Ricard	
Marcelle Dolment, Lily Audet	Réseau d'action et d'information pour les femmes

St. John's, Newfoundland
October 15, 1990

Robert Walley	Canadian Physicians for Life
Michael Langford	
Barbara Neis, Joanne Prindiville	Canadian Research Institute for the Advancement of Women, Newfoundland
Nancy Stokes, Joan Dawson	Planned Parenthood Newfoundland/Labrador
Wendy Williams, Martha Muzychka	The Provincial Advisory Council on the Status of Women, Newfoundland and Labrador
Bonnie James, Colleen O'Toole	Women's Caucus of the Newfoundland and Labrador New Democratic Party
Christine Anstey, Geraldine Druggett	

Charlottetown, Prince Edward Island
October 16, 1990

Linda Gallant, Lisa Murphy	Prince Edward Island Advisory Council on the Status of Women
Anne Lie-Nielsen	PEI Council of the Disabled
Lorna MacDonald, Allan MacDonald, Helen Turner	Catholic Women's League of the Diocese of Charlottetown
Cathy Pharo, Joan Terra	Prince Edward Island Association for Community Living
Barb Van't Slot, Gene Ginn, Edith Perry	Women's Network, Prince Edward Island
Lyle Brehaut	Prince Edward Island Rape and Sexual Assault Crisis Centre

Paul Chandler, Mona Doiron, George O'Connor	Prince Edward Island Right to Life Association
Christie Beck, Catherine MacDonald	Canadian Youth Pro-Life Organization of Prince Edward Island
Rita Ryan Sabada, Louise Polland	Prince Edward Island Union of Public Sector Employees
Doreen Beagan, Margaret Hickox, Genevieve MacDonald, Malcolm MacBeck, Claude Parent	Friends of the Family
Halifax, Nova Scotia October 17-18, 1990	
Lynn McIntyre	Canadian Public Health Association
Alexa McDonough, Muriel Maybee	Nova Scotia New Democrats
Janis Wood Catano, Heidi Atkins	Women's Health Education Network
Ann Marie Tomlins, Diana Smith	Council for Life — Nova Scotia
Carolyn Wallace	Women's Action Coalition of Nova Scotia
Pauline d'Entremont, Dian Day	Nova Scotia Advisory Council on the Status of Women
Linda Christiansen-Ruffman	
David Cole	Atlantic Research Centre for Mental Retardation
Sandra Lanz	The Halifax Morgentaler Clinic
Marie Patrell, Brenda Beagan	The Halifax Lesbian Committee on New Reproductive Technologies
Kit Holmwood, Kathy Coffin	Canadian Abortion Rights Action League
Jean Curran, Katherine Anderson	Metro Area Family Planning Association

B.A. Armson	Genetics Committee Society of Obstetricians and Gynaecologists of Canada
William Deagle	Campaign Life Coalition and Canadian Physicians for Life

Moncton, New Brunswick
October 19, 1990

Jeanne d'Arc Gaudet, Bernadette Landry	New Brunswick Advisory Council on the Status of Women
Thomas Barry	
Linda Hawes, Wendy Sweet	Business & Professional Women's Clubs of New Brunswick
Anna Girouard	
Herman Koops	
George Gilmore, Carole Gilmore	New Brunswick Right to Life Association
Bette Lee, Luanne Leonard	National Organization of Immigrant and Visible Minority Women of Canada

Winnipeg, Manitoba
October 23-24, 1990

Jennifer Cooper, Wendy Smith, Carol Scurfield	Women's Health Clinic
John Hamerton	Canadian College of Medical Geneticists
Marilyn Gault, Betty Nordrum	Manitoba Advisory Council on the Status of Women
Lynn McClure, Laurienne Ring, Chris Ansons	Klinic Community Health Centre
Paul Adams	
Penni Mitchell, Amanda LeRougetel	Manitoba Coalition for Reproductive Choice
Jeraldine Bjornson, Bev Suek	Charter of Rights Coalition (Manitoba)

Cécile Bahuaud, France Foubert, Alice Lambert	La ligue féminine catholique du diocèse de Saint-Boniface
Charlotte Johnson, Marion McNabb	Federated Women's Institutes of Canada
Joanne Peters, Elizabeth Arychuck	Winnipeg Infertility Support Group
Ardythe Basham, Linda Urich	Manitoba Association for Childbirth & Family Education Incorporated
Mona Brown, Louise Lamb, Kim Riddell	Manitoba Association of Women and the Law
Lois Neable, Laurie Potovsky-Beachell	Manitoba Women's Institute
Laurie Thompson, Janet Fontaine, Sue Hicks	Women's Health Directorate, Department of Health, and Women's Directorate, Status of Women Department, Province of Manitoba
Rachael Murray, Pat Soanan	Prairie Prolife of Portage la Prairie
Nerina Robson, Anne Zebrowski	Association for Community Living, Manitoba
Miriam Baron, Judith Hoeppner, Madeleine Boscoe	Planned Parenthood Manitoba
Jenny Robinson	Manitoba Action Committee on the Status of Women
Cheryl Greenberg	Section of Clinical Genetics Children's Hospital and Health Sciences Centre
Saskatoon, Saskatchewan October 25, 1990	
Leslie Biggs, R. Roy	Community Health Services Association Saskatoon
Nayyar Javed, Anne Marie Dilella, Bonnie Loewen	Immigrant Women of Saskatchewan
Chris Axworthy	Member of Parliament Saskatoon-Clark's Crossing Health Critic, New Democratic Party of Canada

Pat Beck, Linda Newson	National Council of Women of Canada
Dorma Guedo, Mavis Moore	Canadian Federation of University Women Saskatoon
Nayyar Javed, Sherri Moisiuk	Saskatchewan Action Committee, Status of Women
Cecilia Forsyth	Saskatoon Pro-Life, Inc. and R.E.A.L. Women of Saskatchewan
James Penna, Steven Penna, James Mahoney	Roman Catholic Diocese of Saskatoon
Charles Simpson	Infertility Clinic, Royal University Hospital
Françoise Sigur-Cloutier, Maria Lepage	Fédération provinciale des Fransaskoises
Jean Mahoney, Evelyn Wyrzykowski	National Council of the Catholic Women's League of Canada
Jeanne Martinson	Saskatchewan Business and Professional Women's Clubs
Karen Rongve	Saskatchewan Association for Community Living
Toronto, Ontario **October 29, 31, 1990**	
Judy Rebick, Pat Israel, Varda Burstyn	National Action Committee on the Status of Women
Ann Andrews	
John Lamont, Lorna Grant, Diana Ingram	Sexual and Social Issues Committee Society of Obstetricians and Gynaecologists of Canada
Christiane Bergauer-Free	
Kathleen Lahey, Sandra Kerr, Susan McDonald, Elaine Ceifets	Ontario Advisory Council on Women's Issues
Janet Atwood, Craig Carter, Robert Duncan	Canadian Baptist Federation

Gerald Vandezande, Carla Cassidy, James Olthuis, Diane Marshall	Citizens for Public Justice
Jamie Cameron	
Dormer Ellis, Doris Guyatt	Canadian Federation of Business and Professional Women's Clubs
Roy von Kutzleben, Jacqueline von Kutzleben	
Diane Allen, Bill Ross	
Stephen Lye, Libby Burnham, Ted Morgan	Genesis Research Foundation Department of Obstetrics and Gynaecology University of Toronto
John Hartley, Anne Leavitt	Human Life Research Institute
Patrick Hewlett	
Sharon Labow, Stephen Labow	
Denise Wiche, Loriann Webster, Jeff Atkins	Christians for Life, Toronto
Vicki Delany, Jenny Ami	Women of Halton Action Movement
Tiina Soomet Maltby, Michael Maltby	
Harold Reiter	National Tay-Sachs and Allied Diseases Association of Ontario
Philip Wyatt	
Nancy Riche, Penni Richmond	Canadian Labour Congress
Judy Armstrong, Brian Armstrong	
Pat Israel	DisAbled Women's Network Canada
Merrilyn Currie	Natural Family Planning Association
John Luik	

C. Jean MacLeod, Margaret McGovern	Women's Issues Group Canadian Federation of University Women North York
John Kraulis	Christian Medical Dental Society of Canada
John Collins	Genetics Committee, Society of Obstetricians and Gynaecologists of Canada
Carmelo Scime	Hamilton Physicians for Life
Lisa Leger, Maggie MacDonald, Michele Evans	Fertility Management Services
Thomas Baxter	Westfort Baptist Church, Thunder Bay
Thomas Palantzas	
John Tyson, Irene Orav, John McCoshen	Clinical Associates in Reproductive Endocrinology & Medicine
London, Ontario November 1-2, 1990	
Kim Perrota, Carol Ann Sceviour	Ontario Federation of Labour
Linda Burville, Susan Ward, Edward Hughes	2F Fertility Clinic at Chedoke-McMaster Hospitals
Catherine Young	Friends of Breastfeeding Society
Karen Sandercock	Vancouver Women's Reproductive Technologies Coalition
Stanley Brown, Arthur Leader, Jeffrey Nisker, M. Hearn	Reproductive Endocrinology and Infertility Committee, Society of Obstetricians and Gynaecologists of Canada
Michael Rieder	
Ann and Shawn Smith	
Jakki Jeffs, Regina Weidinger	Alliance for Life, Ontario
Sheila Howard, Michael Quinn	World Organization of the Ovulation Method Billings Canada

Eike Kluge, Judy Kazimirski, Douglas Geekie, Elaine Jolly, May Cohen, Noel Doig	Canadian Medical Association
Diana Majury	
Donna Launslager, Rosemarie Ashworth, Sue Picard	Parents of Multiple Births Association of Canada
Lorraine Greaves, Constance Backhouse	Women's Education and Research Foundation of Ontario
Margaret Buist	London Status of Women Action Group
Jack Jung, Alan Bocking, Jeffrey Nisker	Regional Medical Genetics Centre; Fetal Development Clinic; Reproductive Endocrinology Committee, University of Western Ontario
Gerald Kidder, Tom Kennedy, David Armstrong, Ann Rouleau	Reproductive Biology Research Laboratories University of Western Ontario
Lynne Scime	Family Forum
Kathy Tomanec	
Albert Yuzpe, Jeffrey Nisker, Heather Erskine	Department of Obstetrics and Gynaecology University of Western Ontario
Toronto, Ontario **November 19-20, 1990**	
Harriet Simand, Carol Allen	D.E.S. Action Canada
Linda Williams, Mary Saunders, Susan Mohamdee	Canadian Federation of University Women
John Harrington	Thomas More Centre for the Family
Phyllis Creighton	

Phil Wall, Cathleen Morrison, Manuel Buchwald, Sue McKellar	Canadian Cystic Fibrosis Foundation
Vicki Van Wagner, Cherie MacDonald	Ontario Coalition for Abortion Clinics
Anne McGlone-Rankin	
Nancy Stone, Diane Richler, Dulcie McCallum	Canadian Association for Community Living
Winnifride Prestwick, Margaret Purcill, John Kiernan	Campaign Life Coalition
Carol Aird, Ruth Sanderson	Peterborough Women's Health Care Centre
Joanne Johnson, Patrick Mohide	Genetics Committee Society of Obstetricians and Gynaecologists of Canada
Perry Phillips	Life Program and IVF Canada
Judy Anderson, Gwendolyn Landolt, Teresa McKenna	R.E.A.L. Women of Canada
Julie Tolentino, Karen Hunter, Jacklynn Rogers	
Terry Fallis, Donna Morrison-Reed, Evelyn Kent, Marion Powell	Planned Parenthood of Toronto
Sara Rowden, Denise Galszechy	The Turner's Syndrome Society
Elizabeth Stimpson, Sharon Wood	DisAbled Women's Network Toronto
Murray Kroach	Life Program and IVF Canada
Heather Marshall, Deirdre Flanagan, Ray Stringer, Guenther Zuern	

Laura Sky, Margrit Eichler	Feminist Alliance on New Reproductive Technologies
Sally Ballangall, Jean Emond, Rita Karakas	YWCA of Canada
Fran Bazos	
Jeff Rose, Dorothy Wigmore	Canadian Union of Public Employees
Vicki Lehouck, Claudette Pisa	Réseau des femmes du sud de l'Ontario
Robin Kilpatrick, Vicki Van Wagner, Edith Johnson	Association of Ontario Midwives
Brian Macdonald, Holly Kramer	Canadian Adoption Reunion Register
Henry Morgentaler	
Gus Gianello	Christians for Life National
Robert Casper, Monica Morris, Carol Cowell, Jocelyn Smith	Division of Reproductive Sciences Department of Obstetrics and Gynaecology University of Toronto
Donald DeMarco	
Katherine Arnup	
Brian Stiller, Eileen Van Ginkel, Paul Marshall, Denise O'Leary	The Evangelical Fellowship of Canada
Hudson Hilsden, Dan Cooper	The Pentecostal Assemblies of Canada
Laura McArthur, Eugene Pivato, Phillip Landolt	Right to Life Association of Toronto and Area
Colette Somerville	
Maureen Gibson, Sharon Cunningham, Bonnie Charbonneau	Spina Bifida and Hydrocephalus Association of Ontario

Montreal, Quebec November 21-22, 1990	
Cécile Coderre, Louise Marquis	Fédération des femmes du Québec
Yvette Grenier	
Gilles Létourneau, François Handfield, Derek Jones, Anne Marcoux	Commission de réforme du droit du Canada
Anne Kiss, Marilyn Bergeron, Larry Reynolds	Alliance pour la vie
Alain Klotz	
Claude Duchesne, Robert Sullivan, John Wright, Diane Brodeur	Section de reproduction du département d'obstétrique-gynécologie Hôpital Saint-Luc, Montréal
Marsha Hewitt, Phyllis Creighton, Joy Kennedy, John Baycroft, Don Thompson	Anglican Church of Canada
Geneviève Delaisi de Parseval	
Sonia LeBris	
Charles R. Scriver	
Gilles Grondin, N.M. Newman	Campagne Québec-Vie
Denis Perreault, Carmen Saint-Laurent	Confédération des organismes familiaux du Québec
France Tardif, Anne St-Cerny, Marie-Thérèse Forest	Fédération du Québec pour le planning des naissances
Donald Jansen, John Whyte	Cosmas and Damian Society of Ottawa-Hull

Annette Burfoot, Laurel Claus-Johnson, Barbara Mayo, Jill Smith, Andrea Calver	
Cécile Labrecque, Louise D. Fortin	Les Cercles de Fermières du Québec
Sylvie Poirier, Christiane Garcia, Marirrosa Lopez, Violaine Fortin	Association québécoise pour la fertilité inc.
Bernard Daly, Louise Simard, Réjean Plamondon, Benjamin Simard	Action Famille
Upendra K. Banik	BIOSCAN Continental Inc.
Jean Desjardins, Nuala Kenny, Gordon Crelinsten, Allan Bocking	Royal College of Physicians and Surgeons of Canada
Serge Bélisle, Robert Reid, Renée Martin	Society of Obstetricians and Gynaecologists of Canada and Canadian Fertility and Andrology Society
Monique Simard, Pauline Gauthier, Danielle Hébert	Confédération des syndicats nationaux
Del Hushley	
Christine Marion, Jacqueline Martin, Claire Levasseur	Association Féminine d'Éducation et d'Action Sociale
Gilles Bleau, Guy Beauregard	Centre de recherche en reproduction humaine de l'Université de Montréal
Chantal St-Pierre	Le Réseau National d'Action Éducation Femmes
Faustin Chouinard	
Vancouver, British Columbia November 26-28, 1990	
Barbara Romanowski	Expert Interdisciplinary Advisory Committee on Sexually Transmitted Diseases Health and Welfare Canada

Judith Daniluk	
Dawn Black	Member of Parliament New Westminster-Burnaby
Dorothy Shaw, Barbara Hestrin, Marcena Levine	Planned Parenthood Association of B.C.
Bonnie Waterstone	Vancouver Status of Women
Christo Zouves	IVF Program University Hospital
David Tkachuk	
John Stephens	
Sunera Thobani, Gulzar Samji, Betty Lough	Immigrant and Visible Minority Women of British Columbia
Sue Cox, Catherine Martell, Patricia Lee	Vancouver Women's Reproductive Technologies Coalition
Barb Sihota	
Timothy Rowe	Infertility Clinic, St. Paul's Hospital
Donna Doerksen, Glen Vockeroth	
Pamela Better	
Sue Cox	
Debbie Young, Jennifer Hillman	Vancouver Infertility Peer Support Group
Margo Fluker	
Tracey Jung	
Wendy McNeely	
Mary Anne McWaters	
Ted Gerk	Kelowna Right to Life

Will Johnston, Susan Allan, Iain Benson, Wendy Barta, Sukhder Singh Gill	British Columbia Chapter Canadian Physicians for Life
Janice Dillon, J.J. Camp, Terrence Wade	Canadian Bar Association
Lise Moreau, Arthur Specken	Office of Marriage and Family Formation Archdiocese of Vancouver
Jan Friedman, Barbara McGillivray	Department of Medical Genetics University of British Columbia
Barbara Chambers	Canadian PID Society
William Bowie	Sexually Transmitted Diseases Subcommittee, Canadian Infectious Diseases Society
Douglas Wilson, Lynn Simpson	Genetics Committee Society of Obstetricians and Gynaecologists of Canada
Kelly Maier, Gloria Wolfson, Stewart Alcock	British Columbia Association of Social Workers
Kristin Schoonover	
Christine Micklewright, Mary Rowles	B.C. Federation of Labour
Laura Jones, Elaine Davidson	Dalkon Shield Survivors Group
Mary Donlevy, Peggy Ross	The Federation of Medical Women of Canada
Laurie Brant	Maternal Health Society
Nancy Newman	IVF Program University of British Columbia
Frances Rosenberg, Lila Quastel, Shirley Hyman	Vancouver Section The National Council of Jewish Women of Canada
Yvonne Peters, Shelagh Day, Gwen Brodsky	Canadian Disability Rights Council

David R. Popkin, Dorothy Shaw	Society of Obstetricians and Gynaecologists of Canada
William Bowie	
Susan Kram, Halina Struser	South Surrey/White Rock Women's Place
Victoria, British Columbia November 29, 1990	
Elizabeth Cull	Member of the Legislative Assembly, on behalf of Lynn Hunter, Member of Parliament, Saanich-Gulf Islands
Maryanne Alto	Victoria Status of Women Action Group
Ann Livingston	Maternal Health Society
Shirley Pratten	New Reproductive Alternatives Society
Kathleen Toth, Moira Garneau	Canadian Organization of Catholic Women for Life, Faith and Family
John Jarrell	Society of Obstetricians and Gynaecologists of Canada

Participants in Symposia, Colloquia, and Other Commission Activities

Commission Colloquium on New Reproductive Technologies Ottawa, Ontario, March 21, 1990	
David Roy	Director Center for Bioethics Clinical Research Institute of Montreal Montreal, Quebec
Marsden Wagner	Director of Maternal and Child Health Regional Office for Europe World Health Organization Copenhagen, Denmark
Commission Colloquium on Ethical and Moral Aspects of New Reproductive Technologies Ottawa, Ontario, April 26-27, 1990	
Gordon Dunstan	Emeritus Professor of Theology The University of London and Member of the Interim Licensing Authority London, U.K.
Michael Prieur	Consultant to Bioethics Committee St. Joseph's Health Centre London, Ontario
Patricia Spallone	Honorary Visiting Scholar Centre for Women's Issues University of York, U.K.

Commission Colloquium on New Reproductive Technologies
Ottawa, Ontario, May 23, 1990

Edward Keyserlingk	McGill Centre for Medicine, Ethics and the Law Montreal, Quebec
Christine Overall	Associate Professor Department of Philosophy Queen's University Kingston, Ontario
Caroline Whitbeck	Senior Research Scholar Center for Technology and Policy Massachusetts Institute of Technology Cambridge, Massachusetts U.S.A.

Search Conference on New Reproductive Technologies
Wolfville, Nova Scotia, June 18-20, 1990

Louise Bouchard	Groupe de recherche sur les aspects sociaux de la prévention (GRASP) Université de Montréal Montréal (Québec)
Anne Bunting	Legal Researcher and Staff Lawyer Chair, Sub-committee on New Reproductive Technologies Women's Legal Education and Action Fund Toronto, Ontario
Heather Caloren	Nursing Consultant, Health Issues Canadian Nurses Association Ottawa, Ontario
John Collins	Professor and Chairman Department of Obstetrics and Gynaecology Faculty of Health Sciences McMaster University Hamilton, Ontario
Dian Day	Researcher and Statistical Officer Nova Scotia Advisory Council on the Status of Women Halifax, Nova Scotia
Edith Deleury	Vice-doyenne à la recherche Faculté de droit Université Laval Québec (Québec)

Bernard M. Dickens	Professor Faculty of Law and Faculty of Medicine University of Toronto Toronto, Ontario
Patricia A. Gervaize	Clinical Research Psychologist Department of Obstetrics and Gynaecology School of Medicine/Ottawa Civic Hospital University of Ottawa Ottawa, Ontario
Pat Israel	Chairperson DisAbled Women's Network Canada Toronto, Ontario
Nancy Jackson	Representative Infertility Awareness Association of Canada Ottawa, Ontario
John Jarrell	Professor and Head Department of Obstetrics and Gynaecology University of Calgary and Foothills Hospital Calgary, Alberta
André Jean	Bioéthicien Ministère de la Santé et des Services sociaux Québec (Québec)
Sandra Kerr	President Ontario Advisory Council on Women's Issues Toronto, Ontario
Eike-Henner Kluge	Director of Ethics and Legal Affairs Canadian Medical Association Ottawa, Ontario
Freya Kristjanson	Chairperson Health and Reproductive Issues Committee National Association of Women and the Law Toronto, Ontario
Raymond Lambert	Unité de Recherches en Ontogénie et Reproduction Le Centre Hospitalier de l'Université Laval Québec (Québec)
Anne Mason	Assistant to Programs Vanier Institute of the Family Ottawa, Ontario

Barbara C. McGillivray	Associate Professor Department of Medical Genetics Co-Director of Prenatal Diagnosis Program University Hospital Vancouver, British Columbia
Anne Mullens	Author Vancouver, British Columbia
Christine Overall	Associate Professor Department of Philosophy Queen's University Kingston, Ontario
Noreen L. Rudd	Professor Departments of Pediatrics, Obstetrics and Gynaecology University of Calgary, and Associate Staff Department of Pediatrics Alberta Children's Hospital Child Health Centre Calgary, Alberta
Mary Scott	Medical Consultant New Brunswick Department of Health and Community Services Fredericton, New Brunswick
Susan Sherwin	Professor Faculty of Arts and Social Sciences Dalhousie University Halifax, Nova Scotia
Janet Silverman	Co-Founder, "Infertility — Facts & Feelings" Toronto, Ontario
Jennifer M. Sturgess	Vice-President, Scientific Affairs Warner-Lambert (Canada) Inc. Scarborough, Ontario
Judith K. Sutton	Medical Advisor CIBA-GEIGY Canada Limited Mississauga, Ontario
Marie Vallée	Responsable du dossier des nouvelles technologies de reproduction Fédération des femmes du Québec Montréal (Québec)
Janis Wood Catano	Health Education Consultant Halifax, Nova Scotia

Katherine Young	Associate Professor Faculty of Religious Studies McGill University; Member, McGill Centre for Medicine, Ethics and Law Montreal, Quebec
Albert Yuzpe	Chief, Department of Gynaecology and Reproductive Medicine University Hospital London, Ontario

Symposium on the Impact of New Reproductive Technologies on Women's Reproductive Health and Well-Being
Vancouver, British Columbia, July 31, 1990

Heather Bryant	Professor Department of Community Health Faculty of Medicine University of Calgary Calgary, Alberta
Heather Caloren	Nursing Consultant, Health Issues Canadian Nurses Association Ottawa, Ontario
John Collins	Professor and Head Department of Obstetrics and Gynaecology Faculty of Health Sciences McMaster University Hamilton, Ontario
Jennifer Cooper	Executive Director Manitoba Women's Health Clinic Winnipeg, Manitoba
Mary Donlevy	President Federation of Medical Women of Canada
Marie-Thérèse Forest	Administratrice Fédération du Québec pour le planning des naissances
Hedy Fry	President Canadian Medical Association B.C. Division
Madonna Larbi	Executive Director National Organization of Immigrant and Visible Minority Women of Canada

Betty Lee	President National Organization of Immigrant and Visible Minority Women of Canada
Joan Meister	Past Chairperson DisAbled Women's Network
Diane Robert	President L'R des centres de femmes du Québec
Douglas Wilson	Assistant Professor University of British Columbia, representing the Canadian College of Physicians and Surgeons
Janis Wood Catano	Health Consultant, representing the National Action Committee on the Status of Women

Commission Roundtable Discussion on New Reproductive Technologies
Yellowknife, NWT, September 12, 1990

Jane Bishop	Family Practitioner
Lynn Brooks	NWT Status of Women Council
Debbie Dechief	Social Services
Reanna Erasmus	NWT Representative National Action Committee on the Status of Women
Alice Hill	Native Women's Association
Kate Irving	Women's Directorate
Ethel Liske	Dene Nation
Katherine Peterson	Lawyer Past President Status of Women Council
Jan Stirling	Community Health Nurse

Commission Consultation on New Reproductive Technologies
Ottawa, Ontario, September 26, 1990

Christian Byk	Conseil de l'Europe Conseiller spécial auprès du Secrétaire Général chargé de la bioéthique Strasbourg, France

Commission Colloquium on Meta-Analysis **Ottawa, Ontario, October 9, 1990**	
Andy Oxman	Department of Clinical Epidemiology and Biostatistics McMaster University Hamilton, Ontario

Commission Roundtable Discussion on *In Vitro* Fertilization **Newfoundland Hotel** **St. John's, Newfoundland, October 15, 1990**		
Mary Dawe Judy Gillis Mary-Martha Hale Joyce Hancock	Lois Hoegg Luanne Leamon Cindy Mills Dorothy Robbins	Antoinette Stafford Barbara Wood

Commission Colloquium on Infertility and Involuntary Childlessness **Study** **Ottawa, Ontario, November 15, 1990**	
Ralph Matthews	Associate Dean School of Graduate Studies McMaster University Hamilton, Ontario

Commission Roundtable Discussion **New Reproductive Alternatives Society** **Vancouver, British Columbia, November 28, 1990**		
Rona Achilles	Facilitator	
Participants	Faye Holly Judy Kim	Linda Ron Shirley Wayne

Commission Colloquium on New Reproductive Technologies **Ottawa, Ontario, January 23, 1991**	
Ursula Franklin	Consultant Toronto, Ontario

Commission Colloquium on Training, Education and Preparation **of Professionals Involved in New Reproductive Technologies** **Ottawa, Ontario, January 30, 1991**	
Orvill Adams	Consultant, specializing in health issues Curry Adams and Associates Ottawa, Ontario

Lynn Curry	Principal Curry Adams and Associates Ottawa, Ontario

Commission Colloquium on Constitutional Law
Ottawa, Ontario, February 27, 1991

Bill Black	Director, Human Rights Centre University of Ottawa Ottawa, Ontario
Sheilah Martin	Associate Professor Faculty of Law University of Calgary Calgary, Alberta
Patrick Molinari	Vice-Dean, Faculty of Law University of Montreal Montreal, Quebec

Commission Colloquium on Infertility Treatment and Outcomes
Ottawa, Ontario, March 15, 1991

Richard Lilford	Professor and Head Academic Department of Obstetrics and Gynaecology St. James's University Hospital Leeds, U.K.

Commission Colloquium on Decision-Making Analysis
Ottawa, Ontario, March 15, 1991

Richard Lilford	Professor and Head Academic Department of Obstetrics and Gynaecology St. James's University Hospital Leeds, U.K.

Commission Colloquium on Costs and Outcomes of *In Vitro* Fertilization
Ottawa, Ontario, April 16, 1991

Roberta Labelle	Department of Clinical Epidemiology and Biostatistics McMaster University Health Sciences Centre Hamilton, Ontario

Commission Colloquium on Surrogacy Issues **Ottawa, Ontario, April 23, 1991**	
Juliet R. Guichon	Teaching Assistant University of Toronto Toronto, Ontario
Commission Colloquium on Economic Issues Related to New **Reproductive Technologies** **Vancouver, British Columbia, April 25, 1991**	
Robert Evans	Health Economist; Director Population Health Programs Canadian Institute for Advanced Research University of British Columbia Vancouver, B.C.
Michael Rachlis	Health policy consultant Toronto, Ontario
Alistair Thomson	President Alistair K. Thomson Policy Inc. Ottawa, Ontario
Commission Consultation **College of Physicians and Surgeons of Ontario** **Toronto, Ontario, May 8, 1991**	
Anthony Shardt	Associate Registrar, Research and Policy Development, CPSO
Commission Colloquium on Costs and Outcomes of *In Vitro* Fertilization **Chedoke-McMaster Hospitals** **Hamilton, Ontario, May 9, 1991**	
John Collins	Professor and Head Department of Obstetrics and Gynaecology Faculty of Health Sciences McMaster University Hamilton, Ontario
Peter Dent	Vice-President, Medicine Chedoke-McMaster Hospitals Hamilton, Ontario
John Jarrell	Professor and Head Department of Obstetrics and Gynaecology University of Calgary and Foothills Hospital Calgary, Alberta

Roberta Labelle	Department of Clinical Epidemiology and Biostatistics McMaster University Health Sciences Centre Hamilton, Ontario
Susan Ward	Manager 2F Fertility Clinic Chedoke-McMaster Hospitals Hamilton, Ontario

Commission Colloquium on Framework for Health Technology Policy Decisions: A Case Study in British Columbia
Ottawa, Ontario, May 14, 1991

Arminee Kazanjian	Assistant Professor Department of Health Care and Epidemiology; Associate Director Centre for Health Services/Policy Research University of British Columbia Vancouver, B.C.

Commission Colloquium on Personal Decision-Making Models and Risk Assessment
Ottawa, Ontario, May 29, 1991

Raisa B. Deber	Professor Department of Health Administration University of Toronto Toronto, Ontario

"Addressing the Issues": Panel Discussion on the Social, Ethical, and Legal Aspects of New Reproductive Technologies
Halifax, Nova Scotia, June 19, 1991

David Cole	Geneticist Atlantic Research Centre for Mental Retardation, and Staff Member Izaak Walton Killam Children's Hospital
Jutta Dayle	Professor of Sociology and Anthropology St. Mary's University
Nuala Kenny	Chief of Paediatrics Dalhousie University and the Izaak Walton Killam Children's Hospital
Mary Miller	Chairperson, Adopted Parents Association

Commission Liaison with Community Leaders and Organizations Halifax, Nova Scotia, June 19, 1991	
Katherine Anderson	Education Coordinator Metro Area Family Planning Association
Sherry Bernard	President, Nova Scotia Chapter Women's Legal Education and Action Fund (LEAF)
Fiona Chin-Yee	Board Member Women's Health Education Network
Linda Christiansen-Ruffman	Representative Women's Caucus of Sociologists and Anthropologists (Atlantic)
Dian Day	Researcher Nova Scotia Advisory Council on the Status of Women
Pauline D'Entremont	Member Nova Scotia Advisory Council on the Status of Women
D.H. Dickson	Associate Dean, Research Faculty of Medicine Dalhousie University
Robert Elgie	Executive Director Institute of Health Law Dalhousie University
Judy Gabriel	President, Halifax Chapter Congress of Black Women of Canada
Gillian Graves	Obstetrics and Gynaecology Grace Maternity Hospital
Richard Hubley	Chairperson Criminal Law Section Uniform Law Conference of Canada
Joan Jones	President Congress of Black Women of Canada
Judith Kazimirski	Chairman of the Board Canadian Medical Association
Stella Lord	Chairperson Canadian Research Institute for the Advancement of Women

Mike McDonaugh	Representative The Canadian Association for Community Living (N.S. Division)
Martha McGinn	Research Assistant Mount St. Vincent University
Andrea McIntyre	Research Assistant The Institute for the Study of Women Mount St. Vincent University
Mary Miller	President Adopted Parents Association
Pauline Raven	Executive Director Planned Parenthood Nova Scotia
Joyce Robart	Association of Immigrant and Visible Minority Women of Nova Scotia
Denise Sommerfeld	School of Nursing Dalhousie University
Basil Stapleton	President Uniform Law Conference of Canada
John Philip Welch	Atlantic Research Centre for Mental Retardation Dalhousie University
Commission Consultation **Uniform Law Conference of Canada** **Halifax, Nova Scotia, June 19, 1991**	
Richard Hubley	Chairperson Criminal Law Section Uniform Law Conference of Canada
Basil Stapleton	President Uniform Law Conference of Canada
Commission Consultation **Fetal Tissue Transplantation Program** **Dalhousie University** **Halifax, Nova Scotia, June 20, 1991**	
Bernard Badley	President and Chief Executive Officer Victoria General Hospital
D.H. Dickson	Associate Dean, Research Faculty of Medicine Dalhousie University

Alan Fine	Associate Professor Faculty of Medicine Dalhousie University
T.J. Murray	Dean Faculty of Medicine Dalhousie University
Peter Weedon	Chair Hospital Board of Commissioners' Subcommittee on Ethical Review Victoria General Hospital

Commission Colloquium on New Reproductive Technologies and Women
Ottawa, Ontario, July 17, 1991

Jalna Hanmer	Reader in Women's Studies Department of Applied Social Studies University of Bradford Bradford, U.K.

Commission Colloquium on Child Health and Assisted Human
Reproduction
Ottawa, Ontario, July 29, 1991

Owen Adams	Chief Health Planning and Physician Human Resources Department of Health Policy and Economics The Canadian Medical Association Ottawa, Ontario
Tye Arbuckle	Bureau of Chronic Disease Epidemiology Laboratory Centre for Disease Control Ottawa, Ontario
Denise Avard	Executive Director Canadian Institute of Child Health Ottawa, Ontario
Corinne Dulberg	Senior Research Consultant Faculty of Health Sciences and School of Nursing University of Ottawa Ottawa, Ontario
Donna Launslager	Director for Multiple Services Parents of Multiple Births Association of Canada Waterloo, Ontario

Carl Nimrod	Director Division of Perinatology, and Acting Chief Department of Obstetrics and Gynaecology Ottawa General Hospital Ottawa, Ontario
Thomas Stephens	Consultant Social Epidemiology and Survey Research Manotick, Ontario

Commission Colloquium on New Reproductive Technologies, the Third World and the Pharmaceutical Industry Ottawa, Ontario, July 30, 1991

Pran Manga	Professor Faculty of Administration University of Ottawa Ottawa, Ontario

Commission Colloquium on U.S. National Survey on Family Growth Ottawa, Ontario, August 1, 1991

William Mosher	Demographic Statistician U.S. Department of Health and Human Services National Center for Health Statistics Hyattsville, Maryland U.S.A.
William Pratt	Chief, Family Growth Survey Branch U.S. Department of Health and Human Services National Center for Health Statistics Hyattsville, Maryland U.S.A.

Commission Consultation Canadian Bar Association Calgary, Alberta, September 10, 1991

Veronica Dalla-Longa	Chairperson National Health Law Section
Janice Dillon	Vice-Chair National Health Law Section, and Chair Special Task Force Committee on Reproductive Technology of the British Columbia Branch
Emile Kruzick	Past Chair National Family Law Section

Lynn Smith	Special Task Force Committee on Reproductive Technology of the British Columbia Branch
Terrence Wade	Senior Director Legal and Governmental Affairs

Commission Consultation
Alta Genetics Inc.
Calgary, Alberta, September 11, 1991

Robert Church	Faculty of Medicine, University of Calgary
Ted Mitenko	Vice-President
Steen Willadsen	Research Director

"Addressing the Issues": Panel Discussion on the Social, Ethical, and
Legal Aspects of New Reproductive Technologies
Calgary, Alberta, September 11, 1991

Carolynne Bouey Shank	Conference Division Church in Society United Church of Canada
Michael Burgess	Associate Professor Faculty of Medicine and Humanities Institute University of Calgary
Brent Friesen	Medical Officer of Health Calgary Health Services
Sheilah Martin	Associate Professor Faculty of Law University of Calgary

Commission Liaison with Community Leaders and Organizations
Calgary, Alberta, September 11, 1991

Viola Akitt	
Brenda Aries	Independent Living Resource Centre of Calgary
Eileen Ashmore	Calgary Women's Network
John Bracco	Court of Appeal of Alberta
Robert Church	Professor Departments of Medical Biochemistry and Biological Sciences Faculty of Medicine University of Calgary
Luigi Cusano	Barrister and Solicitor

Toby Eines	Research Assistant Faculty of Law University of Calgary
Michael Francon	Board Member Calgary Action Group of the Disabled
Arthur Frank	Department of Sociology University of Calgary
Beverly Frizzel	Calgary Birth Control Association
Kathryn Grand	Director of Community Services Women's Health Resource Unit Grace Hospital Women's Health Centre
R.E. Hatfield	
M.D. Hollenberg	Professor and Head Department of Pharmacology and Therapeutics University of Calgary
Janet Hutchinson	Chair Social Issues Committee Young Women's Christian Association, Calgary
Jo Hutchinson	Representative Women's Institutes of Alberta
Maureen Hutton	Planned Parenthood Alberta
Barbara Janzen	National Association of Women and the Law
Brian Lowry	Director Medical Genetics Clinic Alberta Children's Hospital
Blair Mason	Court of Queen's Bench of Alberta
Laura McKinnon	Calgary Status of Women Action Committee
Melanie McLaughlin	Alberta Status of Women Action Committee
Fiona Nelson	Department of Sociology University of Calgary
H.A. Pattinson	Infertility Clinic Foothills Hospital
Kathleen Payne	Vice-President Congress of Black Women of Canada Calgary Chapter
Diana Rach	Alberta Association of Midwives

Guadelupe Salguero	Vice-Chairperson Calgary Immigrant Women's Centre
Elly Silverman	Department of Women's Studies University of Calgary
Glenda Simms	President Canadian Advisory Council on the Status of Women
Colleen Stainton	Faculty of Nursing University of Calgary
J.L. Storch	Dean Faculty of Nursing University of Calgary
Linda Taylor	Women's Legal Education and Action Fund (LEAF)
Glen Willman	Executive Director Canadian Bar Association
Janet Yee	Women of Colour Collective
Kathleen Zang	Christ Church

Commission Colloquium on the Canadian Fertility Survey, 1984
Ottawa, Ontario, September 24, 1991

T.R. Balakrishnan	Professor and Chair Department of Sociology University of Western Ontario London, Ontario
Corinne Dulberg	Senior Research Consultant Faculty of Health Sciences and School of Nursing University of Ottawa Ottawa, Ontario
Evelyne LaPierre-Adamcyk	Department of Demography Faculty of Arts and Science University of Montreal Montreal, Quebec
Nicole Marcel-Gratton	Professor Department of Demography University of Montreal
Thomas Stephens	Consultant Social Epidemiology and Survey Research Manotick, Ontario

Commission Colloquium on Donor Insemination Issues **Ottawa, Ontario, September 25, 1991**	
Rona Achilles	Coordinator Family Planning Services Department of Health City of Toronto Toronto, Ontario
Fiona Nelson	Department of Sociology University of Calgary Calgary, Alberta
Daniel Wikler	Professor Program in Medical Ethics School of Medicine University of Wisconsin Madison, Wisconsin U.S.A.
Commission Colloquium on Prevention of Infertility **Ottawa, Ontario, October 22, 1991**	
Gerald Bonham	Medical Officer of Health East York Health Unit, and Professor Department of Preventive Medicine and Biostatistics University of Toronto Toronto, Ontario
William Bowie	Professor Faculty of Medicine Division of Infectious Diseases University of British Columbia Vancouver, British Columbia
Karen Messing	Directrice Centre pour l'étude des interactions biologiques entre la santé et l'environnement Université du Québec Montréal (Québec)
"Addressing the Issues": Panel Discussion on the Social, Ethical, and **Legal Aspects of New Reproductive Technologies** **Ottawa, Ontario, October 23, 1991**	
Paula Fedeski-Koundakjian	Board Member Infertility Awareness Association of Canada

Martha Jackman	Professor Faculty of Common Law University of Ottawa
Arthur Leader	Director GOAL Program for Assisted Reproductive Technologies; Associate Professor Obstetrics and Gynaecology University of Ottawa
Jennifer Leddy	Canadian Conference of Catholic Bishops
Paula Stewart	Associate Medical Officer of Health Regional Municipality of Ottawa-Carleton Health Department

Commission Liaison with Community Leaders and Organizations
Ottawa, Ontario, October 23, 1991

Denise Alcock	Associate Dean School of Nursing University of Ottawa
Hilliard Aronovitch	Acting Chairman Department of Philosophy University of Ottawa
Norman Barwin	Planned Parenthood Federation of Canada
Mathilde Bazinet	Faculty of Common Law University of Ottawa
Vicki Bennett	Canadian Centre for Research on Women and Religion
Heather Caloren	Nursing Consultant, Health Issues Canadian Nurses Association
Cathy Cameron	Women's Health Interaction
Anna Chiappa	Acting Executive Director, Women's Committee Canadian Ethnocultural Council
Linda Clippingdale	Canadian Research Institute for the Advancement of Women
Phyllis Colvin	Health and Welfare Canada
Hubert Doucet	Dean Faculty of Theology Saint Paul University

Bruce Halliday	Member of Parliament; Chairman Human Rights and the Status of Disabled Persons Committee
Tina Head	Canadian Advisory Council on the Status of Women
Greta Hoffmann-Nemiroff	Joint Chair in Women's Studies Carleton University/University of Ottawa
Gilles Hurteau	Executive Director Royal College of Physicians and Surgeons
Bonnie Johnson	Executive Director Planned Parenthood Federation of Canada
Agnes Klein	National Council on Bioethics in Human Research
Carole Lucock	Canadian Medical Association
Carla Marcelis	Women's Health Interaction
Trish Maynard	National Coordinator Infertility Awareness Association of Canada
Marnie McCall	Faculty of Law Carleton University
Heather Menzies	Institute for Women's Studies
Shelagh M'Gonigle	Women's Legal Education and Action Fund
May Morpaw	Women's Bureau Labour Canada
Betty Morris	Canadian Institute of Child Health
Eugene Oscapella	Office of the Privacy Commissioner
Freda Paltiel	Senior Advisor on the Status of Women National Health and Welfare
Diane Parkins	Midwives of Ottawa-Hull
Glenn Rivard	Ministry of Justice
Marge Robertson	School of Health Sciences Algonquin College
Michelle Simms	President, Ottawa Chapter Congress of Black Women of Canada

Edgar Simpson	President of the Board of Directors Planned Parenthood Ottawa (Inc.)
Kay Stanley	Coordinator Status of Women Canada
Chantale St-Pierre	Module des sciences de la santé Université du Québec à Hull
Paula Timmons	National Coordinator Infertility Awareness Association of Canada
T. Walker	Technology Policy Branch Industry, Science and Technology
Linda Williams	Canadian Federation of University Women
Ali Wooding	Planned Parenthood Ottawa (Inc.)
Susan Zimmerman	Law Reform Commission of Canada

Commission Consultation
Pharmaceutical Manufacturers Association of Canada
Ottawa, Ontario, October 24, 1991

Paul Bilodeau	President and General Manager Wyeth Ltd.
Don Brown	President Hoffmann-LaRoche
Don Buxton	President Roussel Canada Inc.
Peter Croden	President and General Manager The Upjohn Company
Judy Erola	President PMAC
Bernard Leduc	Regional Director Canadian Centre for Clinical Research and Development Wyeth-Ayerst Research
Pierre Major	Vice-President Scientific Affairs Syntex Inc.
Ariel Mouttet	International Marketing Responsible for Hormones International Marketing Division of Roussel (France)

Miklos Nadaski	Medical Director Wyeth Ltd.
Anthony Rebuck	Director Medical and Scientific Affairs Searle
Marvin Skripitsky	Vice-President Professional Health Services Parke Davis
Percy Skuy	President Ortho Pharmaceutical
Judith Sutton	Manager Clinical Investigation CNS/OTA Ciba-Geigy Canada Ltd.
Commission Consultation Roussel-Uclaf Ottawa, Ontario, October 24, 1991	
Don Buxton	President Roussel Canada Inc.
Ariel Mouttet	International Marketing Responsible for Hormones Roussel (France)
Louise Sylvestre	Responsible for Clinical Development of Hormones Roussel (France)
Commission Colloquium on Psychosocial Aspects of Infertility Treatment Ottawa, Ontario, November 6, 1991	
Antonia Abbey	Assistant Professor of Community Medicine Wayne State University School of Medicine, and Adjunct Assistant Research Scientist Institute for Social Research University of Michigan Ann Arbor, Michigan U.S.A.
Frank Andrews	Program Director Institute for Social Research, and Professor of Public Health and Psychology University of Michigan Ann Arbor, Michigan U.S.A.

Jill Halman	Research Investigator Institute for Social Research University of Michigan Ann Arbor, Michigan U.S.A.

"Whither Prenatal Diagnosis?"
Commission Colloquium on Prenatal Diagnosis
Ottawa, Ontario, November 13, 1991

Shelin Adam	Genetics Counsellor Predictive Testing Program for Huntington Disease Department of Medical Genetics University of British Columbia Vancouver, British Columbia
Judith Allanson	Associate Professor University of Ottawa, and Clinical Geneticist Children's Hospital of Eastern Ontario Ottawa, Ontario
Denis Cournoyer	Departments of Medicine and Oncology McGill University, and Division of Hematology Montreal General Hospital Montreal, Quebec
Neil Holtzman	Department of Pediatrics Johns Hopkins University School of Medicine, and Departments of Epidemiology and Health Policy and Management, Johns Hopkins University School of Hygiene and Public Health, Baltimore, Maryland, U.S.A.
Judith Miller	Director National Council on Bioethics in Human Research Ottawa, Ontario
Kate O'Connor	Health Care Evaluation Branch Department of Epidemiology University of Western Ontario London, Ontario
Tabitha Powledge	Consulting Science Editor and Writer Hollywood, Maryland U.S.A.

Susan Sherwin	Professor, Department of Philosophy Dalhousie University Halifax, Nova Scotia
Robert D. Wilson	Department of Medical Genetics University Hospital University of British Columbia Vancouver, British Columbia

Commission Consultation
Medical Research Council
Ottawa, Ontario, November 14, 1991

Robert F. Casper	Member, MRC Ad Hoc Committee; Associate Professor and Head Division of Reproductive Sciences Departments of Obstetrics and Gynaecology University of Toronto
William Fraser	Member, MRC Ad Hoc Committee; Département d'obstétrique et gynécologie Hôpital Saint-François d'Assise Québec (Québec)
Judith Kazimirski	Member, MRC Ad Hoc Committee; Chair Board of Directors Canadian Medical Association
T.D. Marshall	Member, MRC Ad Hoc Committee
Francis Rolleston	Chairman MRC Ad Hoc Committee; Director Scientific Evaluation, MRC
Denis Saint-Jean	Director of Communications, MRC

"Addressing the Issues": Panel Discussion on the Social, Ethical, and
Legal Aspects of New Reproductive Technologies
Winnipeg, Manitoba, December 3, 1991

Elizabeth Arychuk	Member Winnipeg Infertility Support Group
Madeleine Boscoe	Staff, Women's Health Clinic, Winnipeg; Member, Board of Directors Planned Parenthood Manitoba and Planned Parenthood Federation of Canada

Cheryl Greenberg	Associate Professor Department of Paediatrics and Child Health and Department of Human Genetics at the Health Sciences Centre Children's Centre Winnipeg, Manitoba
Dawne McCance	Associate Professor Faculty of Arts University of Manitoba
Kim Riddell	Member Manitoba Association of Women and the Law

Commission Liaison with Community Leaders and Organizations
Winnipeg, Manitoba, December 3, 1991

J.M. Badertscher	Chair Department of Religious Studies University of Winnipeg
Cécile Bahuaud	Représentante La Ligue féminine catholique
Jacques Belik	Canadian Medical Association (Manitoba Division)
Donna Blight	University Women's Club of Winnipeg
Madeleine Boscoe	Women's Health Clinic
Norma Buchan	President Women's Health Research Foundation of Canada Inc.
Blake Carter	Clerk of Presbytery Presbyterian Church in Canada
Robert Chartrand	Manitoba Métis Federation Inc.
Bernard Chodirker	Clinical Geneticist Faculty of Medicine University of Manitoba
Albert Chudley	Professor Department of Paediatrics and Child Health University of Manitoba
Ken Clarke	Manitoba Health Services Commission
Jennifer Cooper	Executive Director Women's Health Clinic

Heather Corbett	Manitoba Women's Institute
Irene Crowe	Manitoba Health Organizations Inc.
Jim Derksen	President The Canadian Disability Rights Council
George Desnomie	Executive Director Manitoba Indian Education Association Inc.
Shirley Forsyth	Provincial Coordinator Manitoba Action Committee on the Status of Women
Dianne Glass	National Council of Jewish Women of Canada
Pat Glen	Adoption Options Manitoba
Sylvia Guertin	President Manitoba Bar Association
John L. Hamerton	Professor and Head Canadian College of Medical Genetics Department of Human Genetics University of Manitoba
Robert P. Hamlin	Representative of the Winnipeg Presbytery United Church of Canada
Theresa Harvey	A/Assistant Deputy Minister Responsible for the Status of Women
Evelyn Hecht	Winnipeg Jewish Community Council
Michael Helewa	Department of Obstetrics, Gynaecology and Reproductive Science St. Boniface General Hospital
Verna Holgate	Executive Director Manitoba Association of Licensed Practical Nurses
Grace Ivey	Charter of Rights Coalition
Angie Kirkilionis	Head of the Cytogenetics Laboratory Faculty of Medicine Department of Human Genetics University of Manitoba
Jeremy Kredentser	Faculty of Medicine University of Manitoba

Jenniece Larsen	Director School of Nursing University of Manitoba
Karen Linde	Director Adoption Options Manitoba
Brenda Maxwell	President, Winnipeg Branch Federation of Medical Women of Canada
Peter Miller	Chair, Department of Philosophy University of Winnipeg
Anita Moore	Health Department, City of Winnipeg
Betty Nordrum	Policy Advisor Manitoba Action Committee on the Status of Women
Clara Orallo	Immigrant Women's Association of Manitoba
Laurie Potovsky-Beachell	The Manitoba Women's Institute
Kim Riddell	Manitoba Association of Women and the Law
Alan Ronald	Professor, University of Manitoba
Leonore Saunders	Chair Status of Women Group University Women's Club of Winnipeg
Margaret and Sinj Saxton	Baha'is of Winnipeg Spiritual Assemblies
Jim Schnoor	Executive Director Manitoba Law Reform Commission
Hilde Schurhoff	Executive Director Immigrant Women's Association of Manitoba
Bette Singer	Vice-President B'Nai Brith Women
Lea Smith	Reproductive Health Coordinator
John Stackhouse	Department of Religion University of Manitoba
Deborah Stienstra	Department of Political Science University of Winnipeg
Paddy St. Loe	Manitoba Human Rights Commission

Ken Stupak	Social Concerns Coordinator for the Pentecostal Assemblies of Canada
Bev Suek	Charter of Rights Coalition
Pat Swainson	Health Department City of Winnipeg
Sari Tudiver	Canadian Women's Health Network
Linda Uhrich	Manitoba Association for Childbirth and Family Education Inc.
Norma Walker	Congress of Black Women
Sherry Wiebe	Past National Vice-Chair Health Law Section Canadian Bar Association
Shari Wolfson	B'Nai Brith Women

Commission Colloquium on Survey of Canadian Fertility Clinics and Programs
Ottawa, Ontario, December 12, 1991

Rona Achilles	Coordinator Family Planning Services Department of Health City of Toronto Toronto, Ontario
Arthur Leader	Associate Professor of Obstetrics and Gynaecology University of Ottawa; Director, *In Vitro* Fertilization Program Ottawa Civic Hospital; Coordinator, Canadian *In Vitro* Fertilization Registry
Michelle Ann Mullen	Researcher Toronto, Ontario
Christopher Newton	Clinical Psychologist Department of Psychological Services University Hospital University of Western Ontario London, Ontario
Linda Williams	Researcher Ottawa, Ontario

Commission Consultation
The Vanier Institute of the Family
Ottawa, Ontario, January 30, 1992

Robert Glossop	Director of Programs and Research
Anne Mason	Assistant to Program

Commission Colloquium on Ethical Aspects and Guiding Principles
Surrounding New Reproductive Technologies
Ottawa, Ontario, January 30, 1992

Elizabeth Boetzkes	Assistant Professor Department of Philosophy McMaster University Hamilton, Ontario
Harold Coward	Institute for the Humanities University of Calgary Calgary, Alberta
Bernard M. Dickens	Professor Faculty of Law and Faculty of Medicine University of Toronto Toronto, Ontario
Will Kymlicka	Adjunct Professor Department of Philosophy University of Ottawa Ottawa, Ontario
Christine Overall	Associate Professor Department of Philosophy Queen's University Kingston, Ontario

Commission Consultation
Ares-Serono Group and Serono Canada Inc.
Ottawa, Ontario, February 19, 1992

Martin Barkin	National Practice Leader and Partner Peat Marwick Stevenson and Kellogg
Marlene Booth	Director Regulatory Affairs Serono Canada Group
Peter Brinsden	Medical Director Bourn Hall Clinic Cambridge, U.K.

Gina Cella	Manager Public Relations Ares-Serono Group
Aliza Eshkol	Chief Scientist and Director Scientific Communications Ares-Serono Group
Jason Nestor	General Manager Serono Canada Inc.
James Posillico	Scientific Director International Business Operations Ares-Serono Group

Commission Consultation
Canadian Public Health Association
Ottawa, Ontario, February 19, 1992

Ronald de Burger	Director AIDS Education and Awareness Program
Ian Gemmill	Chair Sexual Health Division
Janet MacLachlan	Assistant Executive Director National Programs
Margaret E. Millson	Member, CPHA; Assistant Professor Department of Preventive Medicine and Biostatistics Faculty of Medicine University of Toronto; and Director Community Medicine Residency Program University of Toronto

Commission Consultation
Royal College of Physicians and Surgeons of Canada
Ottawa, Ontario, March 19, 1992

Gordon L. Crelinsten	Member, Biomedical Ethics Committee; Associate Professor of Medicine, McGill University; Member of the Centre for Medicine, Ethics and Law, McGill University; and Chairman, Clinical Ethics Committee, Royal Victoria Hospital, Montreal
Pierre-Paul Demers	Director Office of Fellowship Affairs

Nuala Kenny	Member, Biomedical Ethics Committee, RCPSC
John L. Watts	Member, Biomedical Ethics Committee, RCPSC; Professor of Paediatrics, McMaster University; and Chief, Division of Neonatology, Chedoke-McMaster Hospitals

Commission Consultation
Canadian Advisory Council on the Status of Women
Ottawa, Ontario, March 20, 1992

Tina Head	Legal Analyst
Glenda P. Simms	President

Commission Colloquium on Research Findings Related to New Reproductive Technologies
Ottawa, Ontario, June 8-9, 1992

John Collins	Professor and Chairman Department of Obstetrics and Gynaecology Faculty of Health Sciences McMaster University, Hamilton "Effectiveness of Infertility Treatment"
Jane Evans	Associate Professor Department of Human Genetics Faculty of Medicine University of Manitoba
John Hamerton	Professor and Head Canadian College of Medical Genetics Department of Human Genetics University of Manitoba "Assessment of Canadian PND Services"
Ted Harvey	President, SPR Associates Inc. "Fertility Clinic Patient Survey" "Research on Human Reproductive Tissues"
Marc Renaud	Professor, Department of Sociology University of Montreal; Vice-President, Canadian Institute for Advanced Research; Director, Groupe de recherche sur les aspects sociaux de la prévention "Attitudes of Physicians Toward Prenatal Diagnosis"

Tom Stephens	Consultant Social Epidemiology and Survey Research Manotick, Ontario "Fertility Clinic Survey: Research Results" "Findings with Regard to Prevalence of Infertility"
Commission Consultation **Canadian Medical Association** **Ottawa, Ontario, June 11, 1992**	
Judith Kazimirski	Chairman of the Board
Paul Landry	Secretary General
Carole Lucock	Analyst Department of Ethics and Legal Affairs

Written Submissions and Opinions*

◆

Action Famille/Family Action

P. Adams

Adoptive Parents Association of Halton

Alberta Association of Registered Nurses

Alberta Health and Alberta Women's Secretariat

Alberta Public Health Association

Alberta Women's Institutes

C. Alexander

N. Allen

Alliance for Life, Saskatoon

S. Amrud

G. Anderson

L. Anderson, J. Hall, S. Lenon, K. Patrick

M. Anderson

---

* A further 500 individuals and couples wrote to the Commission about their personal experiences or participated in private sessions held across the country. The report "Personal Experiences with New Reproductive Technologies" is found in Research Volumes of the Royal Commission on New Reproductive Technologies, 1993.

G. Andreiuk

S. Andrews

Antigonish Women's Resource Centre

W. Arnott

K. Arnup

M. Artt

J. and R. Ashworth

Association des Acadiennes de la Nouvelle-Écosse

Association feminine d'éducation et d'action sociale

Association of Registered Nurses of Newfoundland

Atlantic Research Centre for Mental Retardation

F. and J. Ayers, M. and K. Morash

M. Bach

R. Baergen

E. Baine

L. Banwell

B. Barfoot

M. Bartlett

N. Bartolac

S. Beath and W. Rostas

G. Beauregard

J. Bellamy

Belmont Secondary School, P.A.C.E. Students

E. Bennett

C. Bernier

S. Bhimzh

E. Bickley

E. Bieri

Mrs. Bingley

N. Birss

D. Black, M.P.

J. Blanchard

S. Bobey, D. Fuhrer, C. Mitchell, J. Munday, A. Rodgers

J. Boivin

S. Borwein

J. Bouvier

J. Boyd

P. Boyer, M.P.

The Brethren

Bridge Research Foundation

British Columbia Association of Social Workers

British Columbia Council for the Family

British Columbia Provincial Council of Women

S. Brooks

B. Brown

C. Brown

K. Brown, J. Hogan, V. Klassen, P. Middleton, D. Vescarelli

L. Brown

D. Buckle

S. Bugdin

E. Bujold

A. Burfoot

M. Burgess and S. Harvey

K. Burke

K. Bush

N. Bush and P. Turner

Business and Professional Women's Clubs of British Columbia and Yukon

Calgary Association of Women and the Law

Calgary Board of Health

Calgary Infertility Clinic, Nursing Staff, Foothills Hospital/University of Calgary

G. Cameron

T. Cameron

D. Campbell

R. Campbell

Canadian Adoption Reunion Register

Canadian Advisory Council on the Status of Women

Canadian Association for Community Living

Canadian Association for Women in Science

Canadian Association of University Teachers

Canadian Bar Association/Alberta Branch

Canadian Child Welfare Association

Canadian College of Medical Geneticists

Canadian Conference of Catholic Bishops

Canadian Disability Rights Council

Canadian Ethnocultural Council

Canadian Federation of University Women, Edmonton

Canadian Fertility and Andrology Society

Canadian Medical Association

Canadian Obstetric, Gynecologic and Neonatal Nurses

Canadian Pelvic Inflammatory Disease Society

Canadian Physicians for Life

Canadian Public Health Association

Canadian Rehabilitation Centre

Canadian Research Institute for the Advancement of Women

M. Carriere

S. Carter

A. Casson

Catholic Health Association of Canada

Catholic Social Services, Edmonton

Catholic Women's League of Canada, Alberta McKenzie Branch

Catholic Women's League of Canada, St. Philip Neri

M. Champagne

J. Chappelle

J. Chauhan

Childbirth Nurses Interest Group, Registered Nurses' Association of Ontario

Children's Aid Society of the County of Kent

B. Chisholm

Christians Concerned for Life, Calgary

P. Cipro

Citizens for Public Justice

B. Clark

D. Clark

M. and T. Clarke

M. Coccamo

P. and G. Colquhoun, A. and T. Denstedt, R. and T. Furanna

Comité de la condition féminine, Centre de services sociaux du Montréal métropolitain

Comité "Vieillir au féminin" de l'Université du troisième âge, Université de Moncton

V. Commisso

Confédération des Organismes Familiaux du Québec

Conseil d'intervention pour l'accès des femmes au travail du Québec, Inc.

Conseil du statut de la femme

Consumers' Association of Canada

S. Conte

A. Continelli

D. Corbani

S. Corbani

D. Cornell Card

A. Côté

Council for Life — Nova Scotia

Council of Christian Reformed Churches in Canada

G. Couture

J. Cox

R. Craig

D. Cumming

K. Daly

T. Daly

D. and M. Davidson

U. Dawe

K. Dawson, J. Leeton, A. Trounson, C. Wood

J. Dayle

J. DeGoey

M. de Konick and H. Parizeau

C. de Laat

D. DeMarco

M. Demorest

Department of Public Health, City of Toronto

D.E.S. Action Canada

T. Digby

A. Di Muccio

R. Di Paola

P. Di Tillio

M. Doherty

J. Doodeman

M. Doucette

S. Drepaul

M. Dube

S. Dulong

L'Echo des femmes de la petite Patrie

Edmonton Genetics Clinic, University of Alberta Hospitals

L. Edouard

N. Efford, R. Keillor, M. Moghaddam, D. Newman

D. Egan

H. Emson

C. Endacott

H. Erskine

Evangelical Lutheran Church in Canada

K. Evans, J. Fenwich, J. May, W. Paslawski

Expert Interdisciplinary Committee on Sexually Transmitted Diseases

Faculty Association of the University of British Columbia

Family and Children's Services of the Waterloo Region

R. Fedele

Fédération des Associations des Familles Monoparentales du Québec

A. Feldshteyn

A. Ferenczy

Fertility Management Services

J. Finch

M. Fitzgerald

F. Fracassi

M. Francek

S. Franklin, M. Strathern

M. Frazer

G. Friesen, A. Poitras

L. Frost

G. Fry

S. Fryer

R. Garnett

Gay and Lesbian Parents Coalition International

S. Genuis

P. Geraghty

P. Gibson

C. Gilson

D. Giovannone

A. Girouard

I. Glavac

S. Glickman

J. Gloor

J. Goebel

Groupe de recherche multidisciplinaire féministe

A. Gunter

D. and J. Gwilliam

K. Habberfield

L. Hacock, J. Kozak, D. Peddle

M. Haflidson

Halifax Monthly Meeting

L. Hall

P. Hall

C. Halliday, S. Petricevic, C. Radke, J. Trosch

B. Hammond

J. Hanigsberg

P. Hansen

T. Harte

H. Hartin-Avon and L. MacLeay

J. Hasenpflug

T. Hay

Health Action Centre, Winnipeg

Health Action Coalition, Halifax

J. and D. Heard

F. Henderson

A. Hills, C. Powell, M. West

V. Hirko

B. Ho Lum

M. Holditch

D. Holtzhauer

M. Hoogstad

J. Houle Platt

V. Howard

M. Hucko

Humanist Association of Canada

S. Hunter

D. Huskey

H. Hutchinson

L. Huttram

K. Iannarelli

Immigrant Women of Saskatchewan

Infertility Awareness Association of Canada

S. Iodice

R. Jacob

A. Jacobs

M. Janes

I. Johnston

Joint Faculties Bioethics Project, University of Alberta

A. Jones

C. Jones

D. Jones

H. Jones

M. Kaczer

M. Kalabis

M. Katalinich

P. Kaufert

M. Keene, B. McVeigh, V. Norton

E. Kelly

Kelowna and District Pro-Choice Action Society

H. Kenny

P. Kent

J. Kiernan

K. Kimbell

M. King

W. Klein

J. Klentos

L. Knowles

H. Koops

S. Kopeechuk

J. Kosul

J. Kredentser

W. Kropf

M. Kurpis

KW Parents of Multiple Births Association

Laboratory Centre for Disease Control

J. Lafond and J. Levy

M. and N. Lahn

J. Lamarche Schmalz

D. Lametti

R. Lammers

I. Lane

T. Langstroth

S. Lapensee

M. Lasica

J. Lavery

L. Lavigne

L.E.A.F. West Coast Association

Lethbridge and District Pro-Life Association

C. Liberty

Lifeline

Lifesavers Moncton

la Ligue des droits et libertés

P. Linton

T. Loik

London and Area Council of Women, Child and Family

E. Lougheed

J. Lowell

S. Lundahl

Lutheran Church of Canada

C. MacDonald

P. Mackenzie

K. Mackie

P. Macmasters

A. MacNeil

C. Maddalena

L. Magaro

D. Magnusson

S. Malara

C. Manansala

Manitoba Association of Registered Nurses

Manitoba Coalition for Reproductive Choice

Manitoba Council for International Cooperation

Manitoba Physicians for Life

Manitoba Provincial Organization of Business and Professional Women's Clubs

Manitoba Public Health Association

L. Marchionda

S. Marker

K. and S. Marks

R. Marusyk and M. Swain

F. Mason Smith

J. Maxwell

P. Maxwell

P. McCann

G. and L. McCreath

E. McDermott

I. McDiarmid

L. McKay-Panos

F. McLaughlin

C. McManes

J. McMellon

C. McMillan

B. McNeil

K. McPhee

Medical Research Council of Canada

Medicine Hat Pro-Life Group

Mennonite Central Committee Canada

E. Merrin

Metropolitan Community Church of Toronto

Mrs. Mezish

MFL Occupational Health Centre Inc.

C. Miall

Midwifery Coalition of Nova Scotia

R. Miketic

R. Milano

J. Miller

S. Mintz

P. Miron

Monash Medical Centre, Centre for Early Development

Montreal Pro-Life

C. Moore

S. Morales

Muslim Women's Auxiliary

Naissance-Renaissance

J. Nash

National Association of Women and the Law

National Council of Jewish Women

National Council of Women

National Tay Sachs and Allied Diseases of Ontario

Natural Family Planning Billings Centre

G. Neff Bell

L. Nerman

New Brunswick Advisory Council on the Status of Women

New Brunswick Business and Professional Women's Clubs

New Brunswick Human Rights Association

Newfoundland and Labrador Federation of Labour

D. Newman

N. Newman

New Reproductive Alternatives Society

C. Newton

T. Ngotzamanis

T. Nibogie

L. Nixon

J. Noren

J. Norman

North Shuswap Women's Institute

Nova Scotia Medical Society Reproductive Endocrine Centre

B. Novak

L. O'Dea

F. Ogundele

D. Oleskiw

T. Oleskiw

D. Oliver-Cook

L. Olson

Ontario Association of Children's Aid Society

Ontario Coalition for Abortion Clinics

Ordre des infirmières et infirmiers du Québec

Organon Canada Ltd.

J. Orliffe

Ovulation Method Research and Reference Centre of Australia (W.O.O.M.B.)

J. Padova

R. Pagtakhan

W. Paslawski

N. Passarello

L. Patasius

L. Payne

D. Peddle

B. Pepper

D. Peters

J. Peters and M. Bowick

D. Pierre

V. Piscitelli

Planned Parenthood Alberta

Planned Parenthood Federation of Canada

Planned Parenthood Nova Scotia

Planned Parenthood Regina

Planned Parenthood Saskatchewan

Planned Parenthood Toronto

A. Plitt

P. Pomes

C. Powell, A. and W. West

C. Prailx Sem

C. Pree

Prepared Childbirth Association of Nova Scotia

Presbyterian Church in Canada

Prince Edward Island Committee on the Status of Women

Prince Edward Island New Democratic Party Women's Committee

Prince Edward Island Right to Life Association

Prince Edward Island Union of Public Sector Employees

Pro-Vie Clare

Provincial Council of Women of British Columbia

Provincial Council of Women of Ontario

Public Service Alliance of Canada

L'R des centres de femmes du Québec

C. Ramm

K. Ray

Registered Nurses Association of Nova Scotia

Regroupement provincial des maisons d'hébergement et de transition pour femmes victimes de violence

Regroupement québécois des centres d'aide et de lutte contre les aggressions à caractère sexuel

M. Reilly

Réseau des centres de femmes du Québec

J. Rhéaume

M. Ricci

Richmond Women's Resource Centre Association

M. Rieder

Right to Life Association of Mississauga and Area

Right to Life Association of Toronto and Area

L. Robertson

W. Rodger

D. Rodriguez

S. Rosenberg

H. Ross

W. Rostas

M. Royer

T. Sagloski

Salvation Army

Saskatchewan Christian Feminist Network

Saskatchewan Institute on Prevention of Handicaps

Saskatchewan Registered Nurses' Association

Saskatchewan Women's Institutes

Saskatoon Community Health Unit

C. Saunders

M. Saunders

E. Schneider

C. Scrives

E. Sejer Larsen

L. Sela

K. Selick

L. Seniuk

J. Seto

J. Shea

T. Shewchuck

K. Shields

M. Shinyei

V. Simms

P. Simonds

C. Simpson

The Sir Mortimer B. Davis-Jewish General Hospital

R. Skelly, M.P.

G. and P. Slade

J. Sliwinski

G. Smith

M. Smith

N. Smith

Society of Obstetricians and Gynaecologists of Canada

Spina Bifida Association of Canada

S. Stanford

A. Steden

W. Steeves

H. Stephens

St. Joseph's College, Centre for Ethics in Health Care

N. Street

E. Sumodobila

E. Sundstrom

Support for Parents Adopting Romanian Kids

Surrey-Delta Pro-Life Society

I. Switzer

C. Symonds

Mrs. Taite

G. Tanne

D. Taylor

D. Tennant

A. Tesan

D. Tesan

M. Thorne

L. Tittler

Z. Toor

Toronto Birth Centre

Toronto Fertility/Sterility Institute

Toronto Women's Health Network

S. Toth

D. Tripodi

J. Trosch

E. Truijen

W. Tucker

L. Tuckwell

I. Tummon

21st Century Media Communications
  Frank Ogden

United Church of Canada, Alberta and Northwest Conference

United Church of Canada, Division of Mission in Canada

University Women's Club of Calgary

University Women's Club of Vancouver

L. Van Asperen

Vancouver Health Department

Vancouver Infertility Peer Support Group

Vancouver Women's Health Collective

Vancouver Y.W.C.A. Board of Directors

W. Van Delft

S. Van den Spiegel

Vanier Institute of the Family

L. Van Straten

R. Velicevic

S. Vep

S. Verwolf

The Victoria Business and Professional Women's Club

Victoria Council of Women

Victoria Federal NDP Riding Association

Victoria Pro-Life Society

D. Villeneuve-Morinville

J. Wagner

P. Wakil

C. West

M. and R. White

L. Whitley

J. Wiener

L. Wilcox

J. Williams

C. Wilson

D. Wilson

V. Witherspoon

J. Witkin

J. Woiceshyn

Women for Life, Faith and Family, Ottawa Chapter

Women's Action Council of Nova Scotia

Women's Action Council of Peel

Women's Centre of Montreal

Women's Health Care Centre, Peterborough Civic Hospital

Women's Institute, New Brunswick

Women's Inter-Church Council of Canada

M. Wood

W.O.O.M.B. Canada (World Organization of the Ovulation Method Billings)

A. Wright

S. Wright

D. and H. Wulfman

L. Yorke

Young Women's Christian Association of Calgary

Young Women's Christian Association of Yellowknife

P. Zachariassen

Research Studies

◆

M. de Groh	Key Findings from a National Survey Conducted by the Angus Reid Group: Infertility, Surrogacy, Fetal Tissue Research, and Reproductive Technologies
Angus Reid Group Inc.	Reproductive Technologies — Qualitative Research: Summary of Observations
M. de Groh	Reproductive Technologies, Adoption, and Issues on the Cost of Health Care: Summary of Canada Health Monitor Results
S. Dutt	Survey of Ethnocultural Communities on New Reproductive Technologies
H. Coward	World Religions and New Reproductive Technologies
RCNRT Staff	Personal Experiences with New Reproductive Technologies: Report from Private Sessions

Volume 3
Overview of Legal Issues in New Reproductive Technologies

M. Jackman	The Constitution and the Regulation of New Reproductive Technologies
S.L. Martin	An Overview of the Legal System in Canada
E.L. Oscapella	Overview of Canadian Laws Relating to Privacy and Confidentiality in the Medical Context
M.M. Litman, G.B. Robertson	Reproductive Technology: Is a Property Law Regime Appropriate?
K.M. Cherniawsky, P.J.M. Lown	New Reproductive Technologies: Commercial Protection
M. Martin, A. Lawson, P. Lewis, M. Trebilcock	The Limits of Freedom of Contract: The Commercialization of Reproductive Materials and Services
J. Goulet	Appropriating the Human Being: An Essay on the Appropriation of the Human Body and of Its Parts
M. Ouellette	The Civil Code of Québec and New Reproductive Technologies
R.J. Cook	New Reproductive Technologies: International Legal Issues and Instruments

Volume 6 The Prevalence of Infertility in Canada	
W.L. Mitchinson	Historical Overview of Medical Perceptions of Infertility in Canada, 1850-1950
C.S. Dulberg, T. Stephens	The Prevalence of Infertility in Canada, 1991-1992: Analysis of Three National Surveys
T.R. Balakrishnan, R. Fernando	Infertility Among Canadians: An Analysis of Data from the Canadian Fertility Survey (1984) and General Social Survey (1990)
T.R. Balakrishnan, P. Maxim	Infertility, Sterilization, and Contraceptive Use in Ontario
K.J. Daly, M.P. Sobol	Adoption as an Alternative for Infertile Couples: Prospects and Trends
M. de la Roche	Annotated Bibliography on the Prevalence of Infertility
Volume 7 Understanding Infertility: Risk Factors Affecting Fertility	
A.R. Ronald, R.W. Peeling	Sexually Transmitted Infections: Their Manifestations and Links to Infertility and Reproductive Illness
J. Jantz-Lee	The Physiological Effects of Aging on Fertility Decline: A Literature Review
H. Boyer	Effects of Licit and Illicit Drugs, Alcohol, Caffeine, and Nicotine on Infertility
S.E. Maddocks	A Literature Review of the Physiological Manifestations Related to Infertility Linked to Weight, Eating Behaviours, and Exercise
B.N. Barwin, W. Fisher	Contraception: An Evaluation of Its Role in Relation to Infertility — Can It Protect?
A. Ponchuk	The Physiological Links Between Endometriosis and Infertility: Review of the Medical Literature and Annotated Bibliography (1985-1990)
S. Dumas, É. Guilbert, J-É. Rioux	The Impact of Medical Procedures on Fertility

P.K. Abeytunga, M. Tennassee	Occupational and Environmental Exposure Data: Information Sources and Linkage Potential to Adverse Reproductive Outcomes Data in Canada
J.F. Jarrell, J. Seidel, P. Bigelow	Evaluation of an Environmental Contaminant: Development of a Method for Chemical Review and a Case Study of Hexachlorobenzene (HCB) as a Reproductive Toxicant
P. Millson, K. Maznyk	Pilot Study on Determining the Relative Importance of Risk Factors for Infertility in Canada

Volume 8
Prevention of Infertility

A. Thomson	Prevention of Infertility: Overcoming the Obstacles
L. McIntyre	The Effectiveness of Sexually Transmitted Disease Infertility-Related Prevention Programs
R. Goeree, P. Gully	The Burden of Chlamydial and Gonococcal Infection in Canada
L. Hanvey, D. Kinnon	Social Factors Relevant to Sexually Transmitted Diseases and to Strategies for Their Prevention: A Literature Review
R. Goeree	Feasibility of Economic Evaluations of Sexually Transmitted Disease Prevention Programs in Canada
A. Yassi	Issues in Evaluating Programs to Prevent Infertility Related to Occupational Hazards
B. Hyndman, A. Libstug, I. Rootman, N. Giesbrecht, R. Osborn	The Integration of Theoretical Approaches to Prevention: A Proposed Framework for Reducing the Incidence of Infertility

Volume 9
Treatment of Infertility: Assisted Reproductive Technologies

Part 1: Overview of Assisted Reproductive Technologies

M.A. Mullen	Medically Assisted Reproductive Technologies: A Review

A. Rochon Ford	A Socio-Historical Examination of the Development of *In Vitro* Fertilization and Related Assisted Reproductive Techniques
L. Curry	The Professions Involved in New Reproductive Technologies: Their Present and Future Numbers, Training, and Improvement in Competence
L.S. Williams	Legislation, Inquiries, and Guidelines on Infertility Treatment and Surrogacy/Preconception Contracts: A Review of Policies in Seven Countries
Part 2: Assisted Insemination	
R. Achilles	Donor Insemination: An Overview
D. Wikler, N. Wikler	Issues and Responses: Artificial Insemination
R. Achilles	The Social Meanings of Donor Insemination
F.A.L. Nelson	Lesbian Women and Donor Insemination: An Alberta Case Study
R. Achilles	Self-Insemination in Canada
D. Wikler	The Conceptual Framework of Donor Insemination
M. Musgrove	Artificial Insemination: Bibliography
Volume 10 **Treatment of Infertility: Current Practices and Psychosocial Implications**	
T. Stephens, J. McLean, with the collaboration of R. Achilles, L. Brunet, J. Wood Catano	Survey of Canadian Fertility Programs
SPR Associates Inc.	An Evaluation of Canadian Fertility Clinics: The Patient's Perspective
J. Collins, E. Burrows, A. Willan	Infertile Couples and Their Treatment in Canadian Academic Infertility Clinics

R. Goeree, R. Labelle, J. Jarrell	Public Preferences Toward an *In Vitro* Fertilization Program and the Effect of the Program on Patients' Quality of Life
L. Hayward, D.E. Flett, C. Davis	The Child Health Study: Record Linkage Feasibility of Selected Data Bases: A Catalogue
C. D'Arcy, N.S.B. Rawson, L. Edouard	Infertility Treatment — Epidemiology, Efficacy, Outcomes, and Direct Costs: A Feasibility Study, Saskatchewan 1978-1990

Volume 12
Prenatal Diagnosis: Background and Impact on Individuals

I.F. MacKay, F.C. Fraser	The History and Evolution of Prenatal Diagnosis
RCNRT Staff	Risk Assessment of Prenatal Diagnostic Techniques
J. Beck	A Survey of Research on Post-Natal Medical and Psychological Effects of Prenatal Diagnosis on Offspring
P.M. MacLeod, M.W. Rosenberg, M.H. Butler, S.J. Koval	A Demographic and Geographic Analysis of the Users of Prenatal Diagnostic Services in Canada
K.R. Grant	Perceptions, Attitudes, and Experiences of Prenatal Diagnosis: A Winnipeg Study of Women Over 35
S. Tudiver	Manitoba Voices: A Qualitative Study of Women's Experiences with Technology in Pregnancy
J. Milner	A Review of Views Critical of Prenatal Diagnosis and Its Impact on Attitudes Toward Persons with Disabilities
L. Dallaire, G. Lortie	Parental Reaction and Adaptability to the Prenatal Diagnosis of Genetic Disease Leading to Pregnancy Termination

Volume 13
Current Practice of Prenatal Diagnosis in Canada

J.L. Hamerton, J.A. Evans, L. Stranc	Prenatal Diagnosis in Canada — 1990: A Review of Genetics Centres

J. Wood Catano	An Assessment of the Readability of Patient Education Materials Used by Genetic Screening Clinics
M. Renaud, L. Bouchard, J. Bisson, J.-F. Labadie, L. Dallaire, N. Kishchuk	Canadian Physicians and Prenatal Diagnosis: Prudence and Ambivalence
G.M. Anderson	An Analysis of Temporal and Regional Trends in the Use of Prenatal Ultrasonography
B.N. Chodirker, J.A. Evans	Maternal Serum AFP Screening Programs: The Manitoba Experience

Volume 14
Prenatal Diagnosis: New and Future Developments

M. Cooke	Ethical Issues of Prenatal Diagnosis for Predictive Testing for Genetic Disorders of Late Onset
S. Adam, M.R. Hayden	Prenatal Testing for Huntington Disease: Psychosocial Aspects
L. Prior	Screening for Genetic Susceptibilities to Common Diseases
M. Thomas	Preference for the Sex of One's Children and the Prospective Use of Sex Selection
Z.G. Miller, F.C. Fraser	Attitudes of Genetic Counsellors with Respect to Prenatal Diagnosis of Sex for Non-Medical Reasons
F.C. Fraser	Preimplantation Diagnosis
L. Prior	Somatic and Germ Line Gene Therapy: Current Status and Prospects

Volume 15
Background and Current Practice of Fetal Tissue and Embryo Research in Canada

M.A. Mullen	The Use of Human Embryos and Fetal Tissues: A Research Architecture
B.M. Dickens	Legal Issues in Embryo and Fetal Tissue Research and Therapy

A. Fine	Human Fetal Tissue Research: Origins, State of the Art, Future Applications, and Implications
SPR Associates Inc.	Report on a Survey of Use and Handling of Human Reproductive Tissues in Canadian Health Care Facilities
SPR Associates Inc.	Report on a Follow-Up Survey of Use and Handling of Human Reproductive Tissues (Survey of Medical Laboratories and Medical Waste Disposal Firms)
K.J. Betteridge, D. Rieger	Embryo Transfer and Related Technologies in Domestic Animals: Their History, Current Status, and Future Direction, with Special Reference to Implications for Human Medicine
A. McLaren	Human Embryo Research: Past, Present, and Future
Additional background papers prepared for the Commission	
K. Capen	"The Medical, Social, and Ethical Implications of Prenatal Diagnosis Using Fetal Cells Extracted from Maternal Blood"
L. Edmonds/ M. de Groh	"Demographic Trends in Delaying Childbearing"
D. Flett	"Inventory of Provincial Data Bases"
J. Gunning	"Assisted Reproduction: Bibliography"
L. Holt	"Review of Federal and Provincial Health Expenditures on Health Promotion and Disease Prevention"
J. LaPierre	"Historical Perceptions of Infertility: 1870-1970"
R. Lambert and M.-J. Dufour	"History and Current Status of Research on the Human Embryo"
H. Laplante	"Psychogenic Factors Related to Infertility: A Survey of the Literature"
M. Lavoie	"Inventory of Canadian Federal Statutes and Regulations Pertinent to the Prevention of Male and Female Infertility"
J. Loten	"Inventory of Federal Programs and Services Associated with the Prevention of Infertility"

J. MacKenzie	"Judicial Intervention in Human Reproductive Processes: Background Paper"
R. Matthews	"Social Psychological Responses to Infertility Treatment Evaluation Study: Preliminary Analysis"
B. McGillivray	"Prenatal Diagnosis and Women's Autonomy"
J. Nedelsky	"Choosing Legal Frameworks for Potential Life"
J.P. Nicholson	"Socio-Demographic Trends in Canada"
J. Payne	"Review of Reproductive Technology: A Property Law Analysis"
M. Preus	"Terms Associated with New Reproductive Technologies"
J. Hatcher Roberts	"Feasibility of Establishing Canadian Infertility and *In Vitro* Fertilization Outcome Registries in Canada"
T. Schrecker	"Political Economic Approach to New Reproductive Technologies"
S. Tudiver	"The Global Context of the New Reproductive Technologies: Some Implications for Canada and Proposals for Further Research"

Others who contributed to the Commission's data-gathering, reviewing or analytic activities

Mona Acker	Associate Professor of Social Work University of Regina Saskatchewan
Carol Lyn Aird	Nurse practitioner Women's Health Care Centre Peterborough Civic Hospital
Judith Allanson	Associate Professor University of Ottawa; Clinical Geneticist Children's Hospital of Eastern Ontario Ottawa
Bruce Anderson	Anderson Strategic Research, Ottawa
Robert Armstrong	Assistant Professor Department of Paediatrics University of British Columbia Vancouver

Brenda Baker	Chair and Professor Philosophy of Law, Ethics, Ethical Theory and Biomedical Ethics Department of Philosophy Calgary
Monique Bégin	Dean Faculty of Health Sciences University of Ottawa
Thomas R. Berger	Berger and Nelson Barristers and Solicitors Vancouver
Patricia Birch	Research Assistant Department of Medical Genetics University of British Columbia Vancouver
Elizabeth Boetzkes	Assistant Professor Department of Philosophy McMaster University, Hamilton
Gerald Bonham	Medical Officer of Health Toronto, Ontario; Professor, Preventive Medicine and Biostatistics University of Toronto
Guy Bourgeault	Faculty of Educational Science University of Montreal
William Bowie	Professor Faculty of Medicine Division of Infectious Diseases GF Strong Research Laboratory University of British Columbia Vancouver
Mary Breen	Researcher, social issues Peterborough
Heather Bryant	Director Program for the Early Detection of Breast Cancer Alberta Cancer Board Calgary; Professor Department of Community Health Faculty of Medicine University of Calgary

Robert Church	Professor Departments of Medical Biochemistry and Biological Sciences Faculty of Medicine University of Calgary
John Collins	Professor and Chairman Department of Obstetrics and Gynaecology Faculty of Health Sciences McMaster University, Hamilton
Janice Dillon	Former Chair Canadian Bar Association; Lawyer, specializing in health law, civil litigation, and family law, Vancouver
John B. Dossetor	Professor of Medicine; Director, Division of Biomedical Ethics Faculty of Medicine University of Alberta
Hubert Doucet	Dean and Professor Faculty of Theology Saint Paul University Ottawa
Robert Elgie	Executive Director Institute of Health Law Dalhousie University
Robert Evans	Health Economist and Director Population Health Programs Canadian Institute for Advanced Research University of British Columbia Vancouver; former member British Columbia Royal Commission on Health Care and Costs
David Feeny	Professor Department of Economics and Department of Epidemiology and Biostatistics McMaster University
Alan Fine	Department of Physiology and Biophysics Faculty of Medicine Dalhousie University Halifax

John Frank	Director of Research/Senior Scientist Ontario Workers' Compensation Institute; Assistant Professor Department of Preventive Medicine and Biostatistics Division of Community Health Faculty of Medicine University of Toronto
Jan Friedman	Professor and Head Department of Medical Genetics University of British Columbia
Hedy Fry	Chair Negotiating Team British Columbia Medical Association; Past President British Columbia Federation of Medical Women Vancouver
Joan Marie Gilmour	Candidate for doctorate of laws degree; Assistant Professor Osgoode Hall Law School York University Toronto
Barton Gledhill	Division of Biomedical Sciences Lawrence Livermore National Laboratory University of California, U.S.A.
Jonathan Glover	Professor of Philosophy New College Oxford, U.K.; Chair, Working Group on New Reproductive Technologies Council of Europe
Elyse M. Goldstein	Rabbi Reformed Church of Judaism Toronto, Ontario
Clyde Hertzman	Associate Professor Department of Health Care and Epidemiology Faculty of Medicine University of British Columbia
Barry Hoffmaster	Director Westminster Institute for Ethics and Human Values — London; Professor of Philosophy University of Western Ontario

Martin Hollenberg	Dean Faculty of Medicine University of British Columbia
Neil Holtzman	Professor of Paediatrics University School of Medicine Johns Hopkins University, and Departments of Epidemiology and Health Policy and Management Baltimore, Maryland, U.S.A.
Alastair Hunter	University of Ottawa Ottawa Civic Hospital
Martha Jackman	Professor Faculty of Law University of Ottawa
Dagmar Kalousek	Program Head Cytogenetics/Embryopathology Laboratory British Columbia's Children's Hospital
Will Kymlicka	Adjunct Professor Department of Philosophy University of Ottawa Ottawa, Ontario
Arthur Leader	Associate Professor, Obstetrics and Gynaecology University of Ottawa; Director, *In Vitro* Fertilization Program Ottawa Civic Hospital; Coordinator, Canadian *In Vitro* Fertilization Registry
David Lichtman	Rabbi Orthodox Judaism Calgary, Alberta
Richard J. Lilford	Professor and Head Academic Department of Obstetrics and Gynaecology St. James's University Hospital Leeds, U.K.
Sheilah Martin	Dean Faculty of Law University of Calgary

Davis McCaughey	Associate Professor Department of History University of Melbourne; Former Member Medical Research Ethics Committee National Health and Medical Research Council of Australia Australia
Thelma McCormack	Professor, Sociology; Director, Institute for Social Research; Director, Graduate Program in Women's Studies York University Toronto
Angus McLaren	Professor Department of History University of Victoria
Anne McLaren	Medical Research Centre Mammalian Development Unit London, U.K.
Heather Menzies	Researcher/Writer, Ottawa
David Mortimer	Health Sciences Centre University of Calgary
Mike Murphy	Secretary Demography Project Demographic Review Secretariat Statistics Canada, Ottawa
Fraser Mustard	President Canadian Institute for Advanced Research Toronto; Professor Emeritus McMaster University Hamilton
Vasudha Narayanan	Researcher Hindu Religion University of Florida Miami, U.S.A.
Harjot Oberoi	Researcher Sikh Religion University of British Columbia Vancouver

Kate O'Connor	Researcher Health Care Evaluation Branch Department of Epidemiology University of Western Ontario London
Christine Overall	Associate Professor Department of Philosophy Queen's University Kingston
Leslie Pal	Professor Department of Public Administration Carleton University
Duncan Pedersen	Associate Director Health and Community Health Sciences Division International Development Research Centre Ottawa
Tabitha Powledge	Consultant (science editor and writer) Maryland, U.S.A.
Marilyn Preus	Researcher Law and Human Genetics, Montreal
Philip Reilly	Executive Director Shriver Centre for Mental Retardation Walthane, Maryland, U.S.A.
Barbara Romanowski	Director Sexually Transmitted Disease Control Alberta Health Calgary
David Sackett	Head Division of General Internal Medicine Faculty of Medicine McMaster University Hamilton
Peter D. Seaton	Former Member, British Columbia Royal Commission on Health Care and Costs Vancouver, British Columbia
Eliane Silverman	Associate Professor Faculty of General Studies University of Calgary

Louis Siminovitch	Director Samuel Lunenfeld Research Institute of Mt. Sinai Hospital Toronto; Professor Emeritus University of Toronto
Lynn Smith	Dean Faculty of Law University of British Columbia
Fiona Stanley	Director The Western Australia Research Institute for Child Health; Professor Department of Paediatrics The University of Western Australia Perth, Australia
Winona Stevenson	Researcher Religion (Native American) University of California at Berkeley
Greg Stoddard	Centre for Health Economics and Policy Analysis Department of Clinical Epidemiology and Biostatistics McMaster University Hamilton, Ontario
Janet Storch	Professor and Dean Faculty of Nursing University of Calgary
Wayne Sumner	Professor Department of Philosophy and Faculty of Law University of Toronto
Shoyo Taniguchi	Student in Religion (Buddhism) University of California at Berkeley
John Tkachuk	Researcher Eastern Orthodox religion Christian Church Montreal
Peter Tugwell	Physician in Chief Department of Medicine Ottawa General Hospital

Veronica Vertinsky	Dean and Professor Faculty of Education University of British Columbia Vancouver
Stephen Walter	Professor Ministry of Community and Social Services Government of Ontario Toronto; Department of Clinical Epidemiology and Biostatistics McMaster University Hamilton, Ontario
Sandra Webb	Coordinator of Reproductive Technology Health Services Statistics and Epidemiology Branch Health Department of Western Australia Perth, Australia
Joan Webber	Adoption Officer Ministry of Community and Social Services Government of Ontario Toronto, Ontario
William Webber	Associate Vice President, Academic University of British Columbia; Former Member British Columbia Royal Commission on Health Care and Costs Vancouver, B.C.
Caroline Whitbeck	Senior Research Scholar Center for Technology and Policy Massachusetts Institute of Technology Cambridge, Massachusetts U.S.A.

Staff of the Commission

◆

The following people served the Royal Commission at some period during our inquiry.

John Sinclair, Executive Director
Mimsie Rodrigue, Executive Director (from July 1993)

Research and Evaluation Program

Sylvia Gold, Director
Nancy Miller Chenier, Deputy Director
Janet Hatcher Roberts, Deputy Director
F. Clarke Fraser, Deputy Director
Burleigh Trevor Deutsch, Deputy Director

Consultations and Coordination Program

Dann M. Michols, Director
Mimsie Rodrigue, Deputy Director
Judith Nolté, Deputy Director
Anne Marie Smart, Deputy Director
Denise Cole, Deputy Director

Administration and Security

Mary Ann Allen, Director
Gary Paradis, Deputy Director

Alphabetical Listing of Personnel

Jill Abramczyk
Sylvie Allard
Dolores Backman
Zelia Barbosa
Louise Barnard

Julie Beck
Denis Bédard
Carmen Bélanger
Jo-Anne Bélanger
Millie Bilsky

Sharon Blakeney
Heather Blumenthal
Lynn Bouchard
Susan Bour
Yvonne Boytel
Gérald Brazeau
Diane Brousseau
Claire Brunet
Linda Cameron
Filomena Clemente
Nicole Cundell
Rosalind Currie
Louise Dagenais
Ginette Danis
Lynda Davies
Margaret de Groh
Thérèse de la Bourdonnaye
Suzannah Denholm
Michelle Dennis
Matthew Dionne
Bonnie Donaldson
Tracey Donaldson
Penny Douville
Elizabeth Driscoll
Madeleine Dugas
Hélène Dwyer-Renaud
Louise Edmonds
Deirdre Follett
Denise Fournier
Kate Frohlich
Rita Gaetano
Berdj Garabedian
Beverly Gifford
Gail Godbout
Annie Hall
Carol Hearty
Linda Hegmann
Margaret Hodgson
Kate Holmes
Louise Holt
Lorrie Hubbert
Stephanie Jackson
Teresa Jennissen
Gisèle Jones
Duy-Ai Kien
Jennifer Kitts
Karen Kozak
Dave Kyambadde
Will Kymlicka
Isobel La Bonté

Mireille Lacelle
Sylvie Lacroix
Lucie Lamontagne
Paula Jo Lapierre
Michelle Lavoie
Terrence Léger
Mario Lemire
Judith Lewis
Carol Ann Love
Anne MacDonald
Ian MacKay
Karen Madden
Marnee Manson
Jean Mathieu
Christine Mattson
Shelagh McInnis
Jessica McNally
Françoise McNamee
Michael Mears
Gail Miller
Claudia Mills
Maimuna Mohamed
Margaret Moyston-Cumming
Roxanne Mykitiuk
Kim Nash
Diane O'Grady
Melinda Piecki
Marcel Perkins
Josée Perrier
Carole Philippe
Susan Pollonetsky
Lori Pratt
Martine Renaud
Vicky Richardson
Annie Roberge
Silvana Rossi
Linda Russell
Lorraine Saulnier
Michelle Simoneau
Paul Sobering
Christiane Spencer
Danielle St-Jean
Nancy Ann Sutton
Nancy Swainson
Jeannine Taschereau-Haley
Neil Tremblay
Patricia Tremblay
Crista Williams

Summer Students

Anna Braeken
Michael Dupuis
Michele Musgrove
Rupa Patel
Karen Radford

Contractors for Specialized Services

Karine Asselin
Carmen Ayotte
Jeannette Bertrand
Tamara Blenkhorn
Pierre Chagnon
Jacqueline Cusson
Michelle Deshaies
David Eadie
Anne Hooper
Ann McCoomb
Janice McLean
Tessa McWatt
Mary Murphy
Ghyslaine Ouellet
Kathryn Parsonage
Jacqueline Perrault
Jennifer Rae-Brown
Kathryn Randle
Patricia Rutt
Janet Shorten
Violette Talbot
Michelle Toupin
Jennifer Wilson
Gwen Woyzbun